Imagining for Real

What does imagination do for our perception of the world? Why should reality be broken off from our imagining of it? It was not always thus, and in these essays, Tim Ingold sets out to heal the break between reality and imagination at the heart of modern thought and science. *Imagining for Real* joins with a lifeworld ever in creation, attending to its formative processes, corresponding with the lives of its human and nonhuman inhabitants. Building on his two previous essay collections, *The Perception of the Environment* and *Being Alive*, this book rounds off the extraordinary intellectual project of one of the world's most renowned anthropologists.

Offering hope in troubled times, these essays speak to coming generations in a language that surpasses disciplinary divisions. They will be essential reading not only for anthropologists but also for students in fields ranging from art, aesthetics, architecture and archaeology to philosophy, psychology, human geography, comparative literature and theology.

Tim Ingold is Emeritus Professor of Social Anthropology at the University of Aberdeen, UK. He is the author of many books, including *Lines*, *Making*, *The Life of Lines*, *Anthropology and/as Education* and *Correspondences*.

'*Imagining for Real* demonstrates beyond doubt why Tim Ingold is one of the most original thinkers of our time.'

Arturo Escobar, University of Carolina, Chapel Hill, USA

'With the publication of *Imagining for Real*, Tim Ingold completes the landmark trilogy that secures his standing among a very select group of writers that have the power to transform our thinking about life's most basic questions. To read these lucid, insightful, and compelling essays is to discover oneself stitched into a dynamic world overflowing with possibilities. It is to know and feel oneself more fully alive. I can't recommend this work highly enough.'

Norman Wirzba, Duke Divinity School, USA

'An inspiring, profound, theoretically scintillating, yet refreshingly down-to-earth account of human imagination, *Imagining for Real* is the book we need to navigate reality in the 21st century.'

Jill Bennett, University of New South Wales, Australia

'Tim Ingold offers a compelling and original treatise on humans and their relations with the world. Addressing a variety of classic and emerging issues in plain language, this book is *a tour de force*, acutely relevant for our times.'

Gísli Pálsson, University of Iceland

'Ingold's distinctive sense of direction and wayfinding allows him to travel into unmapped territories. *Imagining for Real* takes us on such a journey along previously unknown paths that connect imagination and reality. Along the way we get to know "creation from the inside" and to "imagine for real" using anthropology's transformational capacity. Never before has a book made this journey possible.'

Lambros Malafouris, University of Oxford, UK

'*Imagining for Real* is genuine Ingold, featuring the author's unique ability for concrete-abstract thinking.'

Ton Otto, Aarhus University, Denmark

Imagining for Real

Essays on Creation, Attention and Correspondence

Tim Ingold

LONDON AND NEW YORK

First published 2022
by Routledge
2 Park Square, Milton Park, Abingdon, Oxon OX14 4RN

and by Routledge
605 Third Avenue, New York, NY 10158

Routledge is an imprint of the Taylor & Francis Group, an informa business

British Library Cataloguing-in-Publication Data
A catalogue record for this book is available from the British Library

Library of Congress Cataloging-in-Publication Data
Names: Ingold, Tim, 1948– author.
Title: Imagining for real: essays on creation, attention
and correspondence / Tim Ingold.
Description: Abingdon, Oxon; New York, NY: Routledge, 2022. |
Includes bibliographical references and index.
Identifiers: LCCN 2021019999 |
Subjects: LCSH: Anthropology–Philosophy. | Human ecology–Philosophy. |
Imagination (Philosophy) | Reality. |
Creation (Literary, artistic, etc.) | Perception (Philosophy)
Classification: LCC GN33 .I47 2022 | DDC 301.01–dc23
LC record available at https://lccn.loc.gov/2021019999

ISBN: 978-0-367-77510-0 (hbk)
ISBN: 978-0-367-77511-7 (pbk)
ISBN: 978-1-003-17171-3 (ebk)

DOI: 10.4324/9781003171713

Typeset in Sabon
by Newgen Publishing UK

For Anna

Contents

Figures

Preface and acknowledgements

This book is a collection of essays written over the past ten years or so. Along with my two previous essay collections, *The Perception of the Environment* (2000) and *Being Alive* (2011), it is intended to form a trilogy of which this is the third and final volume, and in so doing to round off three decades of study. In *Perception* I had brought together work produced during the 1990s, on the themes of livelihood, dwelling and skill, and in *Being Alive* I followed this up with a series of essays, written in the 2000s, in which I developed the themes of movement, knowledge and description. This new volume charts the development of my thinking since then, and up to the present. Its core themes are creation, attention and correspondence.

I could not have known, when I embarked on this intellectual voyage three decades ago, where it would lead. But in retrospect, it describes a kind of arc that carries on without limit yet nevertheless revolves around a centre. That centre is the inescapable condition of human existence in a world. The essays assembled in *Perception* are centred, accordingly, on a conception of the human being as a singular nexus of creative growth, or ontogenesis, within a continually unfolding field of relationships. My aim was to bring to bear on this process of growth a synthesis of relational thinking in anthropology, developmental systems thinking in biology and ecological thinking in psychology. Ontogenesis, as I came to regard it, is a movement along a way of life. By 'way of life' I meant a path to be followed, rather than a body of tradition – or a culture – to be handed down. Along such paths, I argued, and not from within the confines of bounded places, lives are lived, skills are developed, and understandings grown. Human beings, in short, are wayfarers.

In *Being Alive* I went on to explore the dynamics of wayfaring, leading me to introduce the critical idea of the meshwork, as a texture woven by multiple lives as they carry on their lives together – in their movements and perceptions, in the stories they tell, in the knowledge they grow, and in the traces they leave. One crucial element, however, was still missing from these explorations. While I had set forth a comprehensive theory of movement and perception, there appeared to be no room in the theory for imagination. The problem was how to make allowance for imagination without reopening a gap between humanity and nature that, in my work on perception, I had gone to great lengths to close. At the root of the problem, I believe, lies a peculiarly modern severing of imaginary worlds from the world of real life. All the essays in the present book, in one way or another, seek to heal this rupture between imagination and reality. They do so by enriching the domain of reality itself. Imagining for real, I argue, is not about adding layers of fiction over a substrate of fact, nor of conjuring a past or a future set over against the present. It is rather an opening into the fullness of the real, in both its temporal incipience and experiential depth.

This, I believe, is as good a definition as any of what it means to study. It is a way of honouring the world, and of offering something in return for the gift of existence. Yet over the years I have felt increasingly outraged by protocols of academic research that demand precisely the opposite. These protocols define our relation to the world on the basis of taking rather than giving, extraction rather than reverence. Researchers are expected to mine the world for data, and then to process these data by means of theory into so-called 'knowledge products' for human consumption. I was determined to prove that things can be done differently – to develop a way of study, or a method, that would join *with* the people and things with whom and which we share a world, allowing knowledge to grow from our correspondences with them. In 2012 I submitted an application to the European Research Council (ERC) for a project along these lines, entitled 'Knowing From the Inside', or KFI for short. In brief, the project comprised a series of experiments in imagining for real, across the fields of anthropology, art, architecture and design. I had the good fortune to be awarded an Advanced Grant, which funded the project for a full five years, from 2013 to 2018 (project no. 323677–KFI). The majority of essays assembled here were first composed either while the project was going on or soon afterwards, building on what I had learned from it.

I owe a massive debt of gratitude to the ERC for supporting such a risky and subversive project. Without the Council's support, this book could not have been written. Above all, however, I am hugely grateful to everyone involved in the project for having worked together to create such a collaborative and inspirational environment. There are too many of you to list individually, but I extend my heartfelt appreciation to all. Perhaps my greatest inspiration, however, has come from the doctoral students – many now launched on academic careers of their own – with whom I have worked over the past decade. I would like to take this opportunity to thank you by name: Annemiek Prins, Caroline Gatt, Cesar Giraldo Herrera, Christine Moderbacher, Cristián Simonetti, Deborah Pinniger, Elishka Stirton, Elizabeth Hodson, Enrico Marcore, Ester Gisbert Alemany, Francesca Marin, Franz Krause, Germain Meulemans, Graeme Wilson, Gyorgy Henyei

Neto, Jennifer Clarke, João Francisco Canto Loguercio, Judith Winter, Marc Higgin, Maria Nakhshina, Mike Anusas, Montse Pijoan Vives, Paolo Gruppuso, Paolo Maccagno, Pelle Tejsner, Peter Loovers, Rachel Harkness, Robert Pontsioen, Sara Schroer. Shomik Mukherjee, Simon Peres, Sophie Elixhauser. I am indebted to you all!

Once the KFI project was officially concluded, in 2018, it was time to take my next big step: to retire. This step turned out to be more precipitous than I had imagined. No one could ask for a more brilliant group of departmental colleagues, and I feel as much a part of it as ever before. So far as the university was concerned, however, I might as well have stepped over the edge of a cliff. Once having conferred upon me the grandiose title of Professor Emeritus, the university promptly wiped its hands of my existence. Yet it was not long before I discovered the considerable advantage, for my part, of being able to wipe my hands of the university. Over the years preceding my retirement, the place had been through troubled times. While I had completed my three-year sentence as Head of the School of Social Science back in 2011, and since then – thanks to funding from the Leverhulme Trust and subsequently the ERC – had been on continuous research leave, these troubles posed a real threat to my department, and had sometimes seemed all-consuming. With a change of management at the top, however, they are largely resolved. Meanwhile I am now finding, in retirement, the best kind of research leave of all: fully funded, open-ended, and with no reporting requirements!

Retirement also meant that by the start of 2020, I had grown quite accustomed to working from home. Thus the sudden onset of the coronavirus pandemic, in March of that year, had little impact on my daily life. Indeed with all travels cancelled, and engagements moved online, I was at last able to catch up on a massive backlog of writing commitments. All the essays in this book, however, had already been written – at least in their original versions – before the pandemic struck. This existential crisis, though it has rocked the world, is not even mentioned in the chapters to follow. I wonder whether I would have written them differently had I been composing them during the twelve months past. My guess is that I would not. The truth is that the pandemic has left me feeling as confused and anxious as everyone else. I expect it to take some years for the experience to settle, and until then I have no words of wisdom to offer. I do, however, recoil at the unedifying spectacle of legions of academics, primarily from the humanities and social sciences, having discovered overnight that they are experts on the subject of pandemic disease, competing to profit from the world's discomforts with instant analyses of the situation, laced with haughty, told-you-so cynicism. I want no part in that!

The fact remains, however, that the period of three months during which I was putting these essays together, between December 2020 and March 2021, was a time of immense national and indeed worldwide distress. Though the distress is not reflected in these pages, it needs to be acknowledged. The feeling of having had the rug pulled out from under our feet is, I think, shared by everyone. We had been sleepwalking, thinking that life can be taken for granted. Now we know better, as indeed our forebears did, that the world does not exist at the behest of humans but is, for the most part, utterly indifferent to their suffering. Living, like walking a tightrope, is a perpetual balancing act. But it takes two to balance, to sustain an equilibrium. And I know that without the loving company of my wife, I would have lost mine long ago. It is not only a matter of balance, however. Being cooped up together in virtual isolation for the best part of a year, with ever-lengthening hair, has also given a whole new meaning to the idea of entanglement. It is therefore with the greatest pleasure that I dedicate this book to my long-time companion in entanglement, Anna Ingold.

Most of the essays contained herein have been previously published. They have however been extensively revised for the present volume, largely in order to remove overlap or duplication of material. Some have been virtually rewritten.

Chapter 1 began life as the revision of a previously published paper, 'The creativity of undergoing' (*Pragmatics & Cognition* volume 22(1), 2014, pp. 124–39). It eventually grew, however, into something quite different, which I offered as a contribution to the papers of the 11th International Process Symposium (PROS), held in Chania, Crete, in June 2019. It is included in the symposium volume, *Organizing in the Digital Age: Understanding the Dynamics of Work, Innovation, and Collective Action*, edited by Michael Barrett, Emmanuelle Vaast, Ann Langley and Haridimos Tsoukas. The volume is one of series from the PROS Symposia, *Perspectives on Process Organization Studies*, published by Oxford University Press.

Chapter 2 was originally written as the J. B. Willans Lecture, presented at the University of Aberystwyth in February 2012. I subsequently expanded it into my single-authored 'Introduction' for the volume *Imagining Landscapes: Past, Present and Future*, which I co-edited with Monica Janowski. The volume was first published by Ashgate in 2012 (pp. 1–18). In revising it for the present book, I have cut out material specific to the volume. Figure 2.1 is reproduced courtesy of the National Gallery of Washington and DACS, and Figure 2.2 courtesy of Artimage/DACS.

Chapter 3 was written for a volume entitled *Veer Ecology: A Companion for Environmental Thinking*, edited by Jeffrey Jerome Cohen and Lowell Duckert, and published by the University of Minnesota Press in 2017 (pp. 421–33). It has been considerably revised for this book. I am especially grateful to Jeffrey Jerome Cohen for helpful feedback on the original version, and to Tracy Hudson for her inspirational teaching in the art of spinning. Figure 3.1 is reproduced courtesy of the Tate Gallery.

Chapter 4 began as my contribution to the conference 'Human distinctiveness: wisdom's deep evolution', held at the Notre Dame London Global Gateway in July 2017. It was published in the following year by the Center for Theology, Science, and Human Flourishing, University of Notre Dame, in the online conference volume, *Evolution of Wisdom: Major and Minor Keys*, edited by Agustin Fuentes and Celia Deane-Drummond. See https://ctshf.pressbooks.com.

Chapter 5 has a long history. It was first sketched out in May 2011, in a presentation to the Third Biennial Conference of the European Forum for the Study of Religion and the Environment, at the University of Chester, on 'Animals as religious subjects'. I later wrote it up, under the title 'Walking with dragons: an anthropological excursion on the wild side', for presentation as the Firth Lecture, on the occasion of the conference of the Association of Social Anthropologists Conference at the University of Wales Trinity St. David at Lampeter, in September of the same year. In subsequent revisions I have been advised by numerous colleagues, and special thanks are due to Nat Barrett, Maan Barua, Brian Brock, Lieve Orye, Koen Stroeken and Matthew Engelke. I also want to thank Jan Peter Loovers, on whose remarkable doctoral dissertation I draw for the final section of the essay. It was my privilege to supervise Peter's work at the University of Aberdeen, alongside my colleague David Anderson, and it was my experience of helping him pull together the sections of his thesis on literacy and living on the land that first planted the idea for the essay in my mind. It was first published in its present form in *Journal of the Royal Anthropological Institute* (volume 19, 2013, pp. 734–52).

Chapter 6, which has not been previously published, is based on a lecture presented in December 2018 at the Royal Netherlands Academy of Arts and Sciences, Amsterdam. In writing the lecture, I drew on ideas first developed in the course of preparing a concluding commentary for *The Oxford Handbook of Light in Archaeology*, edited by Costas Papadopoulos and Holley Moyes, published online by Oxford University Press in June 2017. Figure 6.1 is reproduced courtesy of the Museum of Cultural History, University of Oslo, and Figure 6.3 courtesy of the Museum of Modern Art (MoMA), New York, and Scala, Florence.

Chapter 7 was originally written for the volume *Navigating Noise*, edited by Nathanja van Dijk, Kerstin Ergenzinger, Christian Kassung and Sebastian Schwesinger (Köln: Walther König, 2017, pp. 38–57). I subsequently revised it for a volume of the Orpheus Institute, Ghent, entitled *Sensorial Aesthetics in Music Practices*, edited by Kathleen Coessens. The volume was published in 2019 by Leuven University Press (pp. 47–60). My essay is reproduced here, with some further revisions, by kind permission of the Press. I am very grateful to Fabrizio Manco for discussions on acoustic ecology which have considerably influenced the text.

Chapter 8 was first presented in 2016 as the Elizabeth and Todd Warnock Lecture at the Department of Art History, Northwestern University, Chicago, under the title 'Beauty from the North: six propositions'. It was subsequently published in the volume *Anthropology and Beauty: From Aesthetics to Creativity*, edited by Stephanie Bunn (Routledge, 2018, pp. 449–64). It is reproduced here with some revision.

Chapter 9 was provoked by my participation in the international workshop 'The symbolic animal: evolution and neuroethology of aesthetics', held at the Ettore Majorana Foundation and Centre for Scientific Culture, Erice, Sicily, in October 2016. I am grateful to the Foundation, to the Centre, and to the organisers of the workshop – Leonida Fusani, Vittorio Gallese and Stefano Parmigiani – for the invitation to participate, without which this essay would never have been written. It was first published in *Practical Aesthetics*, edited by Bernd Herzogenrath (Bloomsbury, 2021, pp. 45–62), and is reproduced here by permission. Figure 9.1 is reproduced courtesy of the Tate Gallery and DACS, and Figure 9.2 courtesy of the British Psychological Society and John Wiley & Sons.

Chapter 10 was first drafted as a keynote address to the conference 'Home, hearth and household in the circumpolar north', held in Tromsø, Norway, in October 2008. It was subsequently published in the conference volume, *About the Hearth: Perspectives on Home, Hearth and Household in the Circumpolar North*, edited by David G. Anderson, Robert P. Wishart and Virginia Vaté, and published by Berghahn Books in 2013 (pp. 11–28). The essay has been substantially rewritten for this volume. Figure 10.1 is reproduced by courtesy of Hilde Jåstad.

Chapter 11 was first sketched out in a presentation to the colloquium 'La fin des cartes', held at École Nationale Supérieure d'architecture de Paris-Belleville in November 2015. It was subsequently presented as a lecture to the 'Living Maps Network' at Birkbeck College, University of London, in January 2016. Since then the text has undergone numerous further revisions, which I have presented at venues including the University of Graz, Austria, in 2017, and the ZODIAK Pavilion of Architecture, Warsaw, in 2019. It has been completely rewritten for the present volume. I am grateful to David Lemm for the original inspiration and for permission to use the image reproduced here as Figure 11.1, and to Germain Meulemans and Ester Gisbert Alemany for conversations that have greatly influenced the text.

Chapter 12 was initially drafted as a contribution to the symposium on 'Earth-writing: literature and geography', hosted by the University of

Düsseldorf in April 2016. I am most grateful to Philipp Erchinger for the invitation to participate. I presented a revised version, in 2018, at the Royal Academy of Fine Arts, Brussels. The text was subsequently published, in the same year, under the title 'Surface textures: the ground and the page', in a special issue of the journal *Philological Quarterly* devoted to papers from the Düsseldorf symposium (volume 97, 2018, pages 137–54). I am grateful to the journal's editor, Eric Gidal, for permission to reproduce it here.

Chapter 13 has its origin in a panel of the 17th Congress of the International Union of Anthropological and Ethnological Sciences (IUAES), held in Manchester in August 2013, entitled 'Surfaces: contesting boundaries between materials, mind and body'. An invitation to contribute to the opening symposium of the International Print Biennale at the Hatton Gallery, Newcastle, in June 2014, gave me the opportunity to develop my ideas, which were further inspired by discussions at the 2015 Rencontres Internationale de Lure, held in the Haute-Provence village of Lurs, France. I eventually drafted this essay, in summer 2017, for the conference 'Art and presence', at the University of Southern Denmark and Faaborg Museum, Odense, in September of that year. The essay was submitted in its present form for a volume of papers from the original IUAES Congress panel, *Surfaces: Transformations of Body, Materials and Earth*, edited by Mike Anusas and Cristián Simonetti, and published by Routledge in 2020 (pp. 14–28). It is included here with minor revision.

Chapter 14 began as a contribution to the Ravenstein Seminar on 'Memory studies and materiality' at the University of Utrecht, in January 2019, and was subsequently inspired by the opportunity to present my ideas, later that year, at the symposium 'Monsoon [+ other grounds]', at the University of Westminster, and in a lecture presented at the University of the Arts London, Central St Martins. It later formed the basis for my keynote address to the 14th Congress of the International Society for Ethnology and Folklore (SIEF), held in Santiago de Compostela, Spain, in April 2019. This version appears in a special issue of the journal *Disparidades* (volume 76(1), 2021), dedicated to papers from the Congress. It has been extensively rewritten for the present volume.

Chapter 15 was originally written as the annual William Fagg Lecture, delivered at the British Museum, London, in November 2017. I would like to thank the Museum for inviting me to present the lecture, and particularly Amber Lincoln and Jago Cooper for reading it out, after I had lost my voice. Versions of the essay have been presented on a number of further occasions, but it has up to now remained unpublished.

Chapter 16 was first sketched out for a presentation at the 'Festival bricologique', held at the Villa Arson, Nice, France in 2016, and was presented again in the same year at the Van Eyck Academy, Maastricht, the

Netherlands. An earlier version was published in the volume *Thinking in the World: A Reader*, edited by Jill Bennett and Mary Zournazi (Bloomsbury, 2020, pp. 202–222). It has been extensively revised for this volume. I am particularly grateful to Christopher Williams for inspiring discussions on musical notation, and to Malcolm Goldstein for permission to reproduce excerpts from his work *Sounding the Full Circle.*

Chapter 17 would not have been written had it not been for the opportunity to participate in the conference 'Connecting materialities / material connectivities [mat~con]' at the Center for Advanced Studies, Ludwig Maximilian University of Munich, in February 2017. I am grateful to Philipp Schorch and Martin Saxer for inviting me, and for their patience in waiting so long for a written version that turned out very differently from the sketch I originally presented. This version was first presented as the Dean's Lecture, Faculty of Archaeology, University of Leiden, in 2018. It was published in the volume *Exploring Materiality and Connectivity in Anthropology and Beyond*, edited by Philipp Schorch, Martin Saxer and Marlen Elders (UCL Press, 2020, pp. 17–35). I thank Simon Peres for his perspicacious comments on an earlier draft.

Chapter 18 has been expanded from my essay 'Afterword: to basket the world', originally published in The *Material Culture of Basketry: Practice, Skill and Embodied Knowledge*, edited by Stephanie Bunn and Victoria Mitchell (Bloomsbury, 2021, pp. 265–9). This volume was, in part, an outcome of the 'Woven Communities' project, directed by Stephanie Bunn at the University of St Andrews, in which I was privileged to participate. In expanding the essay, I drew on ideas developed in my presentation to the 2nd Riga International Biennal of Contemporary Art (RIBOCA 2), August–September 2020.

Chapter 19 was originally presented as the Edward Westermarck Memorial Lecture, in May 2013, at the University of Helsinki, Finland, and was first published in the same year, in *Suomen Antropologi / Journal of the Finnish Anthropological Society* (volume 38, pp. 5–23). Figure 19.1 is reproduced by courtesy of Sage Publications.

Chapter 20 was first presented as the Georg Foster Lecture, at the Gutenberg University of Mainz, in September 2019. I thank the University's Research Center of Social and Cultural Studies (SOCUM), especially the members of its Junior Research Group, for the invitation, and for facilitating the event, which formed part of the Center's 4th Symposium, 'Posthuman? New perspectives on nature/culture'. The text of the lecture is published in a special issue of the journal *Nature + Culture* devoted to papers from the symposium (volume 6(1), 2021, pp. 83–103).

Chapter 21 began life in 2016 as a talk to Deveron Arts, Huntly, Aberdeenshire, at the invitation of its Director, Claudia Zeiske. Later in the same year I presented it at the Centre for Human Ecology, Govan Folk University, Glasgow. After further revision, it was delivered at the Department of Anthropology, University of Pennsylvania, in 2018, and at the Irish Museum of Modern Art, Dublin, in 2019. Parts of the text were incorporated into my keynote address to the Royal Anthropological Institute Conference on 'Art, materiality and representation', held at the British Museum, London, in June 2018, and subsequently published in the *Journal of the Royal Anthropological Institute* under the title 'Art and anthropology for a sustainable world' (volume 25, 2019, pp. 659–75). The essay has been substantially rewritten for this volume.

Chapter 22 was written for a volume of papers in honour of the anthropologist Philippe Descola. Published by Tautem in 2019, the volume is entitled *Au seuil de la forêt: hommage à Philippe Descola, l'anthropologue de la nature*, and edited by Geremia Cometti, Pierre Le Roux, Tiziana Manicone and Nastassja Martin. My contribution is on pp. 471–84. It is reproduced here in a revised form, by courtesy of the editors.

Chapter 23 was first sketched out at the conference 'The human condition: reinventing philosophical anthropology' at the Institute of Advanced Studies, University of Aarhus, in June 2015. The first written version was presented as a seminar at the Department of Anthropology, McGill University, in the following October. I went on to present it to the Creation of Reality Group conference at the University of Edinburgh in December 2015, as the J. J. Bachofen Lecture at the University of Basel in March 2016, as the inaugural lecture for the Anthropology Programme at the Catholic University of Chile, Santiago, in April 2016, and at the 2nd AIBR International Conference of Anthropology, in Barcelona, in September 2016. It was thoroughly revised on each occasion, before being eventually published in a special section of the journal *HAU: Journal of Ethnographic Theory*, devoted to papers from the original Aarhus conference (volume 8, 2018, pp. 158–71). I have revised it once again for this volume.

Tim Ingold
Aberdeen
March 2021

General introduction

The perception of the environment

Why do people perceive their environments in different ways? This has long seemed to me to be the central question of anthropology. For much of the history of the discipline, answers have revolved around the concept of culture. And for those anthropologists who took on the study of culture as their primary vocation, it was something of an article of faith that despite the prodigious variability of cultural forms around the world, all are manifestations of an underlying capacity that is not only universal to human beings but also marks them out from the rest of creation. Equipped with this capacity, it was supposed, humans are uniquely able to forge the chaos of stimuli that assail their senses into patterns of meaning, which in turn guide their actions. Thanks to culture, in short, the world opens out and becomes intelligible to humans in a way that lies beyond the wit of any other creature. The forms that lend meaning to experience, however, are to be found not in the world but in the mind. To study culture was therefore to study the human mind, with regard not so much to its mechanisms – that was a task for psychologists – but to its content, variously understood as ideas, concepts, representations or schemas. On the other side lies the world in its raw, unprocessed and unintelligible nativity. Culture, in human being and knowing, comes face to face with nature.

I myself had imbibed this way of thinking through my anthropological training, and for many years it remained unquestioned at the back of my mind. My research interests, however, commencing with fieldwork in Lapland, would draw me into the study of human–animal relations, from which they subsequently broadened out, in both research and teaching, into the wider domain of ecological anthropology. Mentored in the field by people whose livelihood depended, in part, on herds of reindeer, I had observed that these animals are highly sentient, intelligent, possessed of considerable powers of memory and socially organised. They might have lacked the powers of speech, rational thought and symbolic imagination, but why should these faculties be singled out, above all else, as keys to humanity? My

DOI: 10.4324/9781003171713-1

Sámi hosts would not have presumed to do so, nor – for that reason – was the exceptional standing of humans vis-à-vis the natural world, for them, a foregone conclusion. Yet the ecological anthropology of the time, in the 1970s and 80s, was largely convinced that the lives of nonhuman beings are wholly confined within the bounds of organic nature, and that they can participate in human cultural worlds only as figures of myth or belief, or as objects of ritual attitude. In effect, nonhumans were supposed to double up, as living organisms in the world of objective biophysical fact, and as vehicles of signification in the world of culturally constructed meaning. Ecological anthropology was preoccupied with understanding the relation between the two. Much of it was devoted to showing how cultural models fulfil an adaptive function, in so far as they motivate actions conducive to maintaining the balance of ecosystemic relations.

For some years I connived in this double act, but with every passing year it grew harder to sustain. I could reconcile myself neither to the reduction of nonhuman life to the reactivity of organisms, bound by their separate natures, to the physical conditions of their environments, nor to the elevation of humanity to a level that transcends these conditions. Eventually, the tensions became too great, and I realised that I would have to begin again, starting this time from the premise that humans and nonhumans, just like Sámi people and their reindeer, are fellow inhabitants of a lifeworld – a world that is continually coming into being in and around them, even as it is shaped by their actions. For this I would need an alternative theory of perception. Instead of regarding perception as the mind's way of fitting sensory data into the received categories of culture, I would have to be able to show how the world opens up to perception from within the very current of animate life. It was this that attracted me, initially, to the ecological psychology of James Gibson (1979) and his followers, who were proposing just such an approach. Perception, for them, does not lie in the operation of mind upon the deliverances of the senses, but is rather an achievement of the whole organism, moving around in and actively exploring its environment. The perceiver could be human, but could equally be any other animal, for this kind of sensory exploration, while it calls for finely tuned powers of attention, does not rely on such capacities of representation or conceptualisation with which human beings might be uniquely endowed.

Here, then, was a way of rebuilding ecological anthropology that would allow us to account for differences of perception without having to put human beings on a pedestal, over and above the world in which they and other organisms live. If creatures perceive differently, it is because they are differentially attuned, by virtue of past experience, to attend and respond to what the environment affords for the activities on which they are presently embarked. This is not of course the only approach to perception to start from the inescapable condition of the perceiver's existence in a more-than-human world. Alternative approaches have been offered by advocates of biosemiotics on the one hand, and of ecophenomenology on the other. Biosemioticians take their bearings from the visionary writings of naturalist Jakob von Uexküll (2010), mostly dating from the 1930s, who had proposed that every living being inhabits a meaning-world, or *Umwelt*, of its own creation. Ecophenomenologists tend to go back to philosopher Maurice Merleau-Ponty's magisterial *Phenomenology of Perception* (2002), first published in 1945, with its premise that perception is founded in an awareness, at once pre-objective and pre-conscious, of bodily immersion in an environment. Notwithstanding their manifold differences, to which I shall have occasion to return throughout this book, all these approaches have been inspirational for me. Yet they leave an unresolved problem in their wake. So long as we had been content to toe the classical line – taking perception to be an operation in the theatre of mind, resulting in images that may or may not represent what is 'out there' in the world – there is not much to distinguish it from the work of imagination. But if, as we now assert, perception is part and parcel of the activity of a being in its immediate, real-world environment, what happens to imagination then?

Imagining for real

Critics of my earlier work have often put this question to me, and I have never been able to provide a satisfactory answer. Indeed I have had to admit to avoiding the question, for fear of reinstating the very division between human and nonhuman conditions that I had been at such pains to eliminate. How can we even talk about imagination without reviving the spectre of human exceptionalism? Must we conclude that in their capacity not just to inhabit the world as it is but to configure worlds as they might be, and even to create the actual in the figure of the possible, humans are truly without parallel in the animal kingdom? A concern to reframe the question so as to get around its seemingly inevitable conclusion lurks, in one way or another, behind most if not all of the essays making up this book. That is to say, they all struggle with the limits of an approach to perception that is so tied to proximate presence that it is unable to accommodate what I call the *stretch* of human life. I cannot claim to have arrived at a single answer, let alone to have applied it consistently. Readers looking for what I *really* mean by imagination will be disappointed, since I am far from settled in my understanding of it. I'm not even sure that a final answer would be desirable, for it could act as a roadblock to further inquiry. The great virtue of inconsistency is that it provides an opening through which to move on. The one thing I am sure of, however, is that the stretch I am after is *not* a power of mental representation. It has nothing to do with the construction of images. And for that reason, the word 'imagination' is singularly ill-suited to capture it.

As scholars who work with words, however, we have no alternative but to make do with the hand that language has dealt us. If there is no word to express precisely what we mean, then we can only assemble elements of the existing pack into a phrase that somehow points in the direction we want to go. This is what I intend with the title of this book, *Imagining for Real*. The very last thing I mean by this, however, is what might first come to the minds of readers accustomed to anthropological debates on these matters, which continue to recycle the idea of the 'imaginary' as a modish alternative to the more traditional notions of culture or worldview: a system of meanings deeply embedded in the consciousness of a people, delineating the texture and contours and of what, for them, is the reality of their social world (Stankiewicz 2016). The presumption that what others take for reality is no more than a figment of their collective imagination – that it exists only as an insubstantial veil of ideas and sentiments – has long served social analysts as a ploy by which to bolster their claims to be able to see through it. They alone profess to discern the real, or 'etic' reality behind its more or less phantasmagorical, or 'emic' representations. Analysis, for them, is tantamount to demystification. But it is also a way of preserving what *they* take for reality from any risk of contamination from understandings that may grate against it. For so far as analysts are concerned, vernacular truth is mere belief, leaving their own truth untouched.

My aim, with *Imagining for Real*, is quite different. It is to find a way that would take us *beyond* both imagination and reality, in so far as each term limits the other by dint of their opposition. It is thanks to this opposition, so often assumed in our secular era, that reality comes to be identified with objective fact, and imagination with fiction or fantasy. A more generous understanding of reality would admit to a world that is not already precipitated out, into fixed and final objects, but launched in ever-flowing currents of formation; a more generous understanding of imagination would allow it continually to overspill the limits of conceptualisation and representation, into unmapped realms of conscience and feeling. By imagining for real, then, I don't mean the suspension of disbelief, an excursion into the land of 'what if', or the artifice of taking an interior mental model or world-picture for a putative exterior world that may or may not exist in fact. I refer, rather, to a way of entering from the inside into the generative currents of the world itself, by balancing one's very being on the cusp of its emergence.

This is not something a mind can do from within the safety and security of its corporeal housing. On the contrary, imagining for real, in the sense implied here, means setting existence loose amidst the flux of creation. It is a release from confinement which repudiates any separation of mind from body, or of self from world. Here, imagining joins with the real instead of playing off against it. Simultaneously at large in the cosmos and at the core of being, both everywhere and somewhere, it is the way life has of ever surpassing itself, even as it is enfolded into the experiences and memories – or in a word, into the *souls* – of the living. As such, imagining for real has three defining properties. First, it harbours the promise, and the potential, of *creation*. Second, its creative dynamic is marked by a quality of *attention*. And third, this attention is also responsive; that is, it sets up relations of *correspondence* among co-inhabiting beings. These are the terms of my subtitle. Since each entails the others, they cannot be addressed separately or sequentially, and in this book, I will not attempt to do so. By way of introduction, however, I shall say a few words about each in turn, beginning with creation.

Creation, attention and correspondence

I choose 'creation' advisedly, in preference to the currently more fashionable 'creativity'. For my aim is to get to know creation from the inside, rather than to seek the exterior conditions of its production. The temptation, in our commodity-obsessed age, is to start with end-products, and to read back to the concepts of which they are taken to be the realisation. The all-consuming logic of commodity capitalism configures the imagination as an incubator for ideas, the creativity of which is defined as the measure of their novelty. It sometimes seems, indeed, that a concept has to be new, to exceed what others might be thinking already, for it to be valorised as an idea at all. That is why creativity is so commonly identified with innovation, an identification that, for many, appears so obvious that it is barely questioned. Its effect, however, is to drain the realisation of ideas, in practice, of any creative impulse, by offloading it onto an imaginative faculty – namely, of creativity – that is alleged to precede and underwrite it. Under this logic, creativity drives creation much as productivity drives production, in an input-output relation that binds ideas to objects with a mechanical necessity which only serves to highlight, by way contrast, the very spontaneity of their initial conception. My purpose is to subvert this relation. It is to think of creation not as the realisation of an image but as a way of imagining for real, that is generative at once of things and of the ideas by which we come to know them. Creation, then, is not an outward expression of creativity but harbours its own impulse of growth and renewal. In a word, it is *crescent*. Imagining thus has its source in the habitation of a world that, in its very mode of existence, is crescent rather than created.

A crescent world, however, demands continued attention, and this is the second term of my inquiry. Attention is another word for what I referred to earlier as the *stretch* of human life. This, indeed, is implied in its very derivation, from the Latin compound of *ad-* ('towards') plus *tendere* ('to stretch'). My argument is that in attention, human life is stretched not between mind and body, or between knowing and being, reason and emotion, intelligence and instinct, or any of the other antinomies bequeathed by modern thought, but between sedentism and flight. On the one hand, it is unceasingly fugitive, running ahead of itself as if swept up in the wave of creation. But on the other hand, the need to keep a grip in a world heavy with materials, with their own inertia, forever holds it back. We all experience this tension, even as we walk, tumbling forward with every step, only to prevent ourselves from falling by settling the next foot on solid ground. As this example shows, there are two sides to the coin of attention. One side connotes the perceptual attunement that allows the skilled or masterful practitioner to pick up information specifying salient features of the environment – such as firm ground for the walker – and to adjust his movement to them. But the other side connotes a stance not of mastery but submission, of exposure to a world that is not yet settled in its dispositions. Here, to attend means to wait (in French, *attendre*). It is to submit to the befalling of things (Ingold 2015: 138). Thus if, in one sense, the world is ready and waiting for the practitioner, in the other the practitioner is obliged to wait upon the world. In both senses, however, attention opens a way for an imagination that does not oppose but reaches into, and joins with, the real.

This joining is what I mean by correspondence. The term first came to mind as I was looking for a way to express how anthropological observation, founded in participatory dialogue, answers to the experience of habitation. This dialogue, I explained, is a way of corresponding with oneself, with others and with the world (Ingold 2011a: 241). What began, however, as an expedient has since wormed its way into my thinking to the point that it is now an anchor around which it largely revolves. It is central to my understanding not just of anthropological ways of knowing but of the general conduct of social and material life (Ingold 2017b). The key to correspondence lies in the twin principles that life is not confined to fixed points or locations but lived along lines, and that as they go along together these lines – rather like melodies in musical counterpoint – continually differentiate themselves from within the texture of their polyphony. I call this 'interstitial differentiation', and it is an idea that crops up repeatedly throughout this book. Correspondence, in short, is about *living together in difference*. As such, it contrasts with the more usual view of social life as interaction, involving a back-and-forth exchange between parties confronting each other face-to-face. Admittedly, others – following philosopher of science Karen Barad (2007) – have framed much the same contrast in terms of an alternative concept, namely 'intra-action'. This concept, however, doesn't quite work for me, for two reasons. First, it fails to convey the essential feature of mutual responsiveness, of answering and being answered to. And second, reversing the between of *inter-* to the within of *intra-* cancels what is critical to relations of correspondence, that they are neither between nor within but along, not lateral but longitudinal. Correspondence, strictly speaking, is not the inverse of interaction, but orthogonal to it. That's why for me, imagining is about not intra-acting with the real but corresponding with it.

Anthropology, philosophy and other delights

In prefacing my last collection of essays, *Being Alive*, my opening words were 'I am an anthropologist' (Ingold 2011a: xi). At the time, I was in no doubt about my disciplinary identity. Now, a decade later, I am no longer so sure. I am not even sure that this is an anthropological book. The topics I address, and the works I have consulted in doing so, range over many fields of inquiry, from biology and psychology to theology, art, architecture, aesthetics, archaeology, human geography, comparative literature, semiotics, music, material culture studies, visual studies, design studies, and more. Somewhere in the midst of all these lies the study of anthropology. But philosophy is in there too. Have I strayed, then, from anthropology into philosophy? Am I a philosopher now?

Literally, philosophy means 'love of learning', and I am happy to sign up to that! The question is: with whom, and from whom, are we prepared to learn? It is here that academic disciplines tend to close in on themselves. In every field, students learn, first and foremost, with and from scholars of their own profession, whether directly or through the influence of their writings. As a scholarly discipline, philosophy is no exception, and nor is anthropology. Each, in its establishment and consolidation, has inexorably wound up as the study of the conditions of its own inquiry. My love of learning, however, strains against this academic involution. Nor do I have much faith in the much-touted alternatives of inter-, multi-, or trans-disciplinarity. For these merely reproduce the territorialisation of each discipline as its own dominion, calling for the equivalent of treaty negotiations between them. I believe the solution lies, rather, in releasing the imagination from its confinement within the concepts and idioms of one or several disciplines, and setting it loose amidst the befalling of the crescent world. It lies, in short, in imagining for real.

The essays in this book, then, are not just *about* imagining for real. They are practical ways of *doing* it. When it comes to *how* to do it, there is no better advice than that which the philosopher Gilles Deleuze (2006: 363) offered in a letter to his colleague Jean-Clet Martin: 'I have only one thing to tell you: stick to the concrete, and always return to it.' By sticking to the concrete, of course, the last thing Deleuze means is that our deliberations should be restricted to an analysis of the facts. For this would merely precipitate its opposite, in forms of theoretical thinking that rattle around inside cages of our own construction without touching the world at all. We would be back to the old opposition between imagination and reality, now mapped onto one between theory and data. What Deleuze recommends is something quite different. It is not that we should go to the world for the materials we need to answer questions we have asked from within the echo-chambers of our own thought; we should go there, rather, to find the questions that the world itself both presses upon our attention and binds us to follow in our thinking, keeping our noses to the ground as we go. They are questions like: What does it take for light to shine? Or for sound to be heard? What happens when the earth meets the sky? How are things formed? Why do they last? What does it mean to join things? What is human and what is animal? What is everything? What is a world? How can it keep going?

These are just a few examples of the questions I ask in this book. And in answering them, we answer to the world – or in a word, we *correspond* with it. As Deleuze writes in another context, with his collaborator Félix Guattari, all our thinking, our imagining, should amount in this sense to 'an experimentation in contact with the real' (Deleuze and Guattari 2004: 13). In the experiments to follow I have been guided by much the same advice that Deleuze offers for philosophy, only in my case it has always been a starting point for the study of anthropology. For me, to study anthropologically means allowing ourselves to be taught by the world itself, and all the beings – human and nonhuman – that inhabit it, rather than only by those, styling themselves as 'knowledge producers', who profess to have come away with its secrets. Perhaps, then, it is in the trials of imagining for real, tossed in the mêlée of a worlding world, that anthropology and philosophy truly run together. But this will not be the anthropology of the anthropologists, nor the philosophy of the philosophers, caught as they are within the respective circuits of their own self-referentiality. Maybe that's why, in practising a philosophical anthropology, or anthropological philosophy, I find myself not so much bridging the two disciplines as in a no-man's land, on the one hand estranged from anthropology, and on the other a stranger to philosophy. Yet there is nowhere else I would rather be. Indeed I have relished the freedom to go where the wind blows, without having to be registered under any disciplinary flag, living the life of a buccaneer on the high seas of scholarship.

The book

Buccaneering, however, does not mix well with the regimentation of the book, which imposes its own order on the record of my voyages, requiring them to be organised into a chapter-by-chapter sequence. For ease of navigation I have grouped the 23 chapters making up this book into five parts, of four or five essays per part, each with a short introduction of its own in which I set out its principal themes. This division into parts, while it lends the volume greater internal coherence, is largely a matter of expository convenience. The parts are by no means watertight, and although there are more connections within each part than between them, there are also multiple points of contact at which ideas raised in one chapter are picked up in another, maybe far removed in the sequence of the book. I have indicated these points with cross-references.

In the first part, 'Creating the world', I elaborate on the idea that to create is to participate from within in the continuous coming-into-being of the universe of relations of which we are intrinsically a part. In 'Light, sound and experience', the second part, I show how a phenomenological approach to light and sound, understood not as vectors of energetic transmission but as varieties of sensory experience, bears on the work of perception and the exercise of aesthetic judgement. In the third part, 'Surface tensions', I distinguish the idea of surface as a layer, dividing off what lies on one side from what lies on the other, from that of the 'deep surface' as a zone of penetration which brings them together. Surfaces of the latter kind cover, but do not cover *up*; we do not therefore need to look for meaning behind or beneath the surface, but by the same token, meaning can only be lost through erasure, not deletion. In the fourth part, 'Material thinking', I challenge the assumption that puts materials on one side, and thought on the other, of a division between matter and mind. As we think with materials, thought itself can be 'hands-on', messy and noisy. Finally, in 'Life as a whole', I develop the idea of life not as an internal property of individual beings but as a perpetual movement from within which beings emerge and are held in place, each for their allotted span. Thus wholeness is not the same as totalisation. Life as a whole is never complete, but always overtaking itself. The same, of course, is true of scholarship. Long may it continue!

Part I

Creating the world

We humans owe our existence to a world. But is there a world – or are there worlds – that owe their existence to us? If so, what is the relation between creaturely humans and their creations? For the past two millennia, controversies surrounding this conundrum have turned on the question of whether it is possible to create something from nothing, or whether creation necessarily involves the recombination of elements already to hand. It is a question that has divided theologians and philosophers from classical through medieval times. Following the Renaissance, however, and in the subsequent rise of modern science, creation came to be strongly associated with the recombinant power of intelligent design. In Chapter 1, I show how, since the mid-twentieth century, this association went on to drive creativity research in psychology, leading to an exclusive focus on the novelty of ideas and products which left no room for the creativeness of life itself, in its intrinsic potential for renewal. How might we bring it back? For help in this, I turn to the ideas of John Dewey, Henri Bergson and Alfred North Whitehead, on questions of philosophy, religion and art. It is one thing, I argue, to associate creativity with novelty; quite another to see in creation the ceaseless emergence of the absolutely new. One gives us a cornucopia of ends, the other promises perpetual beginning. For the sake of coming generations, this promise needs to be restored.

How might this restoration, then, affect the way we think about imagination? What if the power of imagination lies not in the projection of ends but in the very origination of things? I begin Chapter 2 with a painting. It is by René Magritte, who intended it as a statement of the human condition. It is a fact about this condition, Magritte believed, that what we take for exterior reality is really just an interior mental representation of the same. This division between the worlds of reality and of the imagination, or of fact and fantasy, has haunted the discourses of modernity for generations. Alternative approaches to the psychology of perception, respectively cognitive and ecological, have only reinforced the division: the former by treating the perceived world as a product of the imagination, vis-à-vis an objectively given reality; the latter by aligning perception with

DOI: 10.4324/9781003171713-2

the disclosure of a real-world environment, vis-à-vis a free-wheeling imagination. Both approaches, however, assume a world already laid out, awaiting the attention of the perceiver. In this chapter I argue, instead, for a mode of attention that waits upon the world, joining with the processes of its formation. To imagine, then, is not to dwell in appearances rather than reality, but to participate from within, through perception and action, in the very appearing of things. It is, in this sense, to move upstream, to inhabit the cusp upon which, at every moment, the world is on the verge of disclosure.

Yet amid the restless churn of imagination, in the ferment of world creation, we nevertheless find ourselves surrounded by forms that show every sign of permanence. How can that be? How can the forms of things withstand the currents that threaten dissolution as much as they hold the promise of generation? Perhaps we should follow Bergson in comparing living forms to eddies whipped up by the wind. Every lifecycle, then, would be a kind of whirl. This is my theme in Chapter 3. I begin by contrasting the revolution of the whirl with mechanical rotation, as of a clock. The rotating hands of the clock describe a circle. But whereas the circle presupposes a centre, the whirl gives rise to it, not as a point around which it turns but as a place of stillness at its heart. The countermovement to the whirl, in that sense, is the hurl: the one gathers up, in an acceleration; the other throws out, as a spin-off. In the practice of spinning, we can see how the winding movement of revolution goes against the grain of time. While the spindle revolves, the thread evolves. But as with breathing in and breathing out (or *whirl* and *hurl*), revolution and evolution – though continuous with one another – are nevertheless countervailing movements. As the whirl gives way to the hurl, so eventually the cycle of life, all energy spent, melts back into the onward current of vitality. In death, beings are overwhelmed by life.

What, then, does all this mean for science, and for the scientific imagination? A possible answer comes from the philosopher Gilles Deleuze, in collaboration with psychoanalyst Félix Guattari. They draw a distinction between major and minor science. The former imagines a world formed of a limited set of discrete, elementary particles, which nevertheless combine into ever more complex and variable configurations. The latter, by contrast, starts from a material plenum, in which forms are produced by the folding and crumpling of surfaces and volumes. Though neither science is possible without the other, the mainstream theory of evolution, by variation under natural selection, is written unequivocally in the major key. In Chapter 4, inspired as much by the philosophy of Whitehead as by that of Deleuze and Guattari, I set out its complement in the minor key. This is an evolution of mind as it is of life. In the major, the mind is described as an intelligence, configured as a facultative property of the individual self. But in the minor, it is a process, an infolding and unfolding of affective relations. The mind infolded is what we call the soul, and the soul unfolds in wisdom. Thus as intelligence is to wisdom, so the self is to the soul. In this chapter I propose to bring wisdom back into our thinking about evolution through a focus – inspired by anthropological studies of animism – on the life of the soul.

Where does this parsing of intelligence and wisdom leave the imagination? In Chapter 5, I return to the rift between the real world and our imagination of it, which underpins the official procedures of majoritarian science. Although such science is not averse to dreams of the imagination as potential sources of novel insight, they are banished from the reality it seeks to uncover. Ever since Francis Bacon and Galileo Galilei, the science of the major has likened nature to a book that will not willingly give up its secrets to human readers. Far from having been an invention of modernity, however, this idea of the book of nature goes back to medieval times. In the monastic traditions of medieval Europe it was common to compare reading to a practice of wayfaring, in which travellers would listen to and take counsel from the creatures they encounter, or from their stories, in a manner strikingly akin to the ways in which the indigenous inhabitants of northern lands would 'read' the world around them, listening to its creatures, its terrain, and its winds and storms. Could studies of medieval monasticism and of northern indigenous ontologies show us how the rupture between reality and imagination might be healed? By acknowledging our imaginative participation in a more-than-human world, and the commitments this entails, we might at last be able to reconcile scientific inquiry with religious sensibility, as openings to knowing-in-being. Herein, finally, lies the way of imagination.

Chapter 1

Creation beyond creativity

Creation holds the promise of a world to come, of the renewal of life. Yet at some point in its two-thousand-year history, the promise of creation took a wrong turn. What would it take to bring it back?

Theology

The word 'creation' comes from the Greek *κτίσις* and Latin *creatio*, referring fundamentally to the act of bringing forth or begetting – as parents, for example, beget their children. It was used in just this sense, and often, by the Roman author Titus Lucretius Carus, in his prose-poem *De Rerum Natura*, dating from the first century BCE. Addressing Nature, pointedly in the feminine, as 'the creatress of things' (*rerum natura creatrix*), Lucretius implicitly compared her generative capacity to that of giving birth. However when, five centuries later, St Jerome chose to import *creatio* into his translation of the old testament from Hebrew into Latin, in what became known as the Vulgate Bible, the term took on an entirely new significance. For the testament's opening words, 'in the beginning, God created heaven and earth' (*in principio creavit Deus caelum et terram*), implied the creation of something out of nothing. Following this precedent, the doctrine of *creatio ex nihilo* went on to become foundational to the Christian theology of the time. It was a doctrine, however, that flew in the face of the long-accepted philosophical principle, as Lucretius had put it, that 'nothing's made of nothing' (*ex nihilo nihil fit*). Already in the fifth century BCE the Greek philosopher Empedocles – whose poem *On Nature* Lucretius would later adopt as the model for his own work – was insisting that everything there is arises from the 'mixture and exchange of what was mixed'. Though subsequently expressed in many different ways, not least by Aristotle – for whom all coming-into-being involves the unification of form and matter – the idea that in substance, the world is eternal, admitting only to processes of composition and corruption, was widely accepted.[1]

DOI: 10.4324/9781003171713-3

For many centuries, scholars grappled with the problem of how to reconcile theological and philosophical principle, and all sorts of distinctions were drawn. For example Peter Lombard, Bishop of Paris in the twelfth century, distinguished 'to make' (*facere*) from 'to create' (*creare*) on the grounds that whereas the former means to fashion something out of present material, the latter is to produce something from nothing. Mortal beings can make, but God alone can create. Not long after, Boethius of Dacia went on to suggest that there is one kind of truth pertaining to nature, wherein everything comes from the rearrangement of materials already to hand, and another kind of truth pertaining to faith, according to which the world was indeed created *ex nihilo* – only to be condemned by the official Church for trafficking in 'double truth'. It was left to Thomas Aquinas, in the thirteenth century, to resolve the problem by giving the doctrine of *creatio ex nihilo* a firm foundation in philosophy. His masterstroke was to acknowledge that what is created out of nothing is not a universe of things, of one sort and another, but existence itself. With existence comes everything else: forms, materials, even time. It is thus absurd, argued Aquinas, to suppose that the Creator temporally preceded his Creation, with His plan for the world preformed and ready to roll. Rather – and this is the critical point – the Creator and the work of Creation *are one and the same*. Or to put it another way, for Aquinas, God the Creator is immanent as the generative power of His creation, and is revealed in every part of it – in ant, tree and stone, mountain and cloud, and of course in human beings.

It makes no more sense, then, to put God on one side, and the world on the other, of a division between creator and created, than it does to attribute the world's coming into being to a capacity such as we might attribute to a subject. The world according to Aquinas came into existence in an act of creation, not as the result of any plan, or through the exercise of any faculty, that paved the way for it. For who would be so foolish as to say: 'God must have been very creative to come up with all that'? In the fourteenth century William of Ockham – Franciscan friar, theologian and philosopher – warned explicitly against mistaking an abstract, conceptual generalisation, drawn from our retrospective evaluation of acts of creation, for a pre-installed capacity deemed responsible for bringing them about in the first place. To put creatures down to the 'creativity' of their maker, Ockham argued, is no less absurd than putting laughter down to a faculty of 'risibility', with which the jester is allegedly pre-endowed. Creation, like laughter, exists only in the act.[2] And if it has its reasons, they are reasons that think themselves out in the creative process itself, rather than preceding it. Creation is not so much the product of reason as reason at work.

However, the onset of the Renaissance, in the fifteenth century, heralded a shift in attitudes towards creation that would prove to be decisive. For while medieval commentators would often compare God to a painter, sculptor or architect – yet one so masterly as to will his creatures into existence not just in part but in the entirety of their being – Renaissance artists would appeal to divine creation as the measure of their own genius, expressed not just in the excellence of their workmanship but in the perfection of their design.[3] While claiming godlike powers for themselves, they would also see in their work the realisation of a mental capacity to conceive of forms in advance of their realisation in the material. With that, creation 'jumped the fence', as it were, from world to mind. It came to be identified with a faculty of intelligence. And the will of God, by the same token, was transformed into a capacity for intelligent design. He really had thought it all up in advance. The world itself, by contrast – the world He created – was left on the other side of the fence. Godless and mechanical, it revealed nothing of the will of the Creator, offering but silent evidence of His virtuosity. Yet by the same token, it presented a suitable field of inquiry for the natural sciences, whose flourishing marked the onset of what we now call modernity (Chapter 5, pages 71, 76). For as Newton would go on to show, the universe – having once been created – can be left to run by itself, with the precision of clockwork.

It is no wonder, then, that the theologian William Paley, writing at the turn of the nineteenth century, would point to the intricacy of design of living creatures, by comparison to the far more rudimentary mechanism of a man-made watch, as proof of the existence of an intelligence of infinitely greater power than anything to which a mortal mind could aspire.[4] Nor does it come as any surprise that the science of evolution, after Darwin, would claim an equivalent power for natural selection. Indeed only a fine line divides advocates of intelligent design, nowadays branded by their scientific opponents as 'creationists', from neo-Darwinian fundamentalists for whom natural selection offers a necessary and sufficient explanation for the phenomena of life. For both, the design – whether written by God or natural selection – precedes its material instantiation, and for both it is in the design, not in the instantiation, that the creativity is to be found. This, however, is to understand creativity, as a faculty preceding and underwriting acts of creation, in a sense dismissed by Ockham as absurd, and that would have been unrecognisable to Aquinas and indeed to the theologians and philosophers of earlier centuries. Yet following its migration from theology by way of philosophy, this was the sense in which the concept of creativity finally fetched up in what was then – in the early decades of the twentieth century – the relatively young discipline of psychology.

Psychology

Though the term cropped up from time to time in earlier writings, the minting of 'creativity' as a key concept in psychology owes much to the efforts of one individual, Joy Paul Guilford. A pioneer in the study and measurement of human intelligence, Guilford first introduced his idea of creativity in a chapter on 'Invention', included in his comprehensive survey of the field, *General Psychology*, published in 1939. He began the chapter with a parable of what the world would be like, were it not for the inventive capacity of human beings:

> There would disappear from the world all cities, towns, and country homes, and even the crudest dwellings of primitive man. All means of transportation, including the ships of the air and the seas, trains and motor cars, railroads and highways would vanish. All these things, and many more, are creations of the human brain. *They were present in thought before they appeared in tangible form.*
>
> (Guilford 1939: 461, emphasis added)

In short, without invention there would have been no history, no arts or culture, no civilisation worthy of the name. Humankind would have remained at the level of the brutes, stuck where they have always been, doing what they have always done, confined to the slow lane of biological evolution. In Guilford's worldview, nature, left to her own devices, brings forth nothing without precedent, only more of the same. And God isn't even in the picture. Instead, all the creative work is left to humankind. More specifically, it is left to the human brain, the seat of intelligence, and is fully accomplished before a hand is even lifted in its physical execution. Moreover, short of the intercession of divine agency, there can be no creation *ex nihilo*. Echoing the philosophy of the ancients, if not their humility when it comes to human powers of creation, Guilford assumed that nothing could come from nothing, and therefore that new ideas or patterns of thought could only come from breaking down old ones and remixing them in novel combinations.[5] There could be no composition without disintegration.

Following the intervention of the second world war, Guilford returned to the theme of creativity in a presidential address delivered in 1950 to the American Psychological Association. In a grotesquely obsequious account of the occasion, psychologist Robert Keith Sawyer sets the scene:

> As the applause swelled, Dr. Guilford took a deep breath, smoothed his tie and jacket, and began to walk to the podium. It was Sept. 5, 1950, and Dr. Guilford was at the peak of his long and industrious career. He had dedicated his life to psychological research. He's played a key leadership role during World War II, helping the U.S. military carry out the most massive testing program in history. And now, he had attained the highest honor that the discipline of psychology can give – he had been elected president of the American Psychological Association. … As Dr. Guilford began to talk, the hundreds of assembled psychologists in the room were shocked when they realised the topic he had chosen: the APA president had chosen to talk about creativity.
>
> (Sawyer 2012: 15)

So what did Guilford say? Not much. His concern was principally to bring to the fore what he saw as a neglected and unresearched topic of inquiry. Today, now that the concept of creativity has spilled over from psychology into a host of other disciplines from arts education to management and business studies, when the sheer number of research publications on the subject is so great that they can only be reviewed through a sampling procedure,[6] and when the c-word has been so thoroughly absorbed into the fast-talking, shallow-thinking patter of legions of advertisers, market consultants and business analysts that it has ceased to raise any eyebrows, it is hard to believe that only seventy years ago, the topic was so novel as to surprise the audience at Guilford's presidential address. Any listeners hoping for a clear definition of creativity, however, would have been disappointed. Instead, they were treated to such tautologies as the following: 'creativity refers to the abilities that are most characteristic of creative people'; 'creative behavior ... includes such activities as inventing, designing, contriving, composing, and planning'; 'people who exhibit these types of behavior to a marked degree are recognized as being creative'. The search is on, then, for some X-factor – or more likely, as Guilford admits, a suite of factors combined in ways that would probably be unique to each individual – capable of magnifying an intelligence common to all to this higher degree. Not many make it. Of all the people who have ever lived in historical times, Guilford (1950: 444) estimates, only about two in a million have any claim to genius.

Whatever Guilford may or may not have said, his presentation certainly had an impact, for in the following two decades, of the 1950s and 60s, creativity research took off to the point that it soon became an unstoppable bandwagon. Looking back on developments since then, Sawyer (2012: 4) is confident that 'after decades of research, we're closer than ever to an explanation of creativity'. Complete explanation will come, however, only when creativity is finally reduced to what Sawyer defines it to be, namely a capacity to combine 'two or more thoughts or concepts that have never been combined before' (2012: 7). In this view, as in that of most cognitive psychologists, thought can never surpass itself. It can only recombine its elements in endless sequences of novel permutations and combinations. All ideas and concepts, Sawyer assures us, are formed thus, from the dissection of old thoughts and the reassembly of their fragments into new ones. It follows that to explain creativity, all you have to do is to show how the human mind is equipped with mechanisms capable of effecting this kind of cognitive bricolage.

Yet if thought-combinations are deemed creative only when they are new, then how are we to tell them apart from combinations that merely repeat what has gone before? After all, what is new to me may be old hat to everyone else. Philosopher and cognitive scientist Margaret Boden (1990: 32) deals with the problem by introducing a distinction between two kinds of creative ideas: psychological and historical, P-creative and H-creative. An idea is P-creative, she says, when it is novel with respect to the individual who had it. But if it is novel with respect to the *whole of human history*, then it is H-creative. Others have expressed the same contrast in terms of a distinction between 'little-c' and 'big-C' creativity: on the one hand those solutions to everyday problems that represent a 'first' for each of us, but which thousands if not millions of people have come up with before; on the other hand those flashes of eminent genius, unique to the history of the world, that 'drive civilisation forward' (Hennessey and Amabile 2010: 570, 572; Sawyer 2012: 8–9).[7] Every C- or H-creative event, to recite the mantra of lunar exploration, is 'one small step for man, one giant leap for mankind'. These events, as they happen, are the steps of history, forged by prodigal masterminds, while all the individual c- or P- creative events allow the rest of us to catch up by recapitulating the same steps for ourselves. Thus does genius, poised at the cutting edge of historical advance, pull the rest of humanity in its wake.

History

What, then, can history be? It can only be a record of world-leading innovations. Yet if this is what history is, then it can play no part in the formation of creative ideas themselves. For a cognitive scientist like Boden, or a psychologist of innovation like Sawyer, minds are completely outside of history, as are the fundamental materials of thought. New thought-combinations, we are led to believe, simply pop up, with apparent spontaneity, in the mind of the creative individual. Paradoxically, the ideas that Boden calls historical, or H-creative, are distinguished by the fact that they arise *de novo*, independently of any historical influence whatsoever. By the same token, history itself has nothing to do with the origination of ideas, only with their recognition and dissemination. It is history that determines whether an idea, having come to the mind of an individual, will be judged by society to be appropriate, useful or valuable, such that it enters into wider circulation. Ideas that fail to find any purchase in society merely fall by the wayside, and are lost to history. But in coming up with creative ideas in the first place, every mind is on its own, cut off from the world of persons, things and relations in which it necessarily subsists. As Boden (1990: 29) states, quite categorically, 'the mind's creations must be produced with the mind's resources'. Only *after* they have been created do ideas enter history.

But if we are to regard history as a record of innovations, then how are we to tell whether something is new or not? Perhaps it might be possible to determine if an idea is new in the life of some particular individual: indeed creativity researchers, according to Sawyer (2012: 8), have devised all sorts of clever experiments to do exactly that. But determining whether the idea is new *in the history of the world* is another matter altogether. Suppose that an idea has occurred to me and I want to know whether it is truly historical, in Boden's terms. The only way to find out would be by doing a search to see whether anyone has had it previously. The probability is a million to one that someone has. So then: no history; just a bit more of the same, another turn of the wheel of perpetual reinvention. I thought for a moment that it might have been a historical idea, that it was genuinely without precedent, but no, it was merely psychological. But suppose that I found, in my researches, that actually no one had had it before, then indeed, history was made with my idea – or at least potentially made, since the idea has no chance of actually *entering* into history unless it is communicated to others, and thereby added to the pool of ideas already in circulation.

Events, in this view – and it is one that is widely held, albeit more implicitly than explicitly – can only be historical if they are truly unprecedented. A thing is novel, it is historical, only when it makes its first appearance. With every subsequent iteration its quotient of creativity, so to speak, wears thinner until the normality of its repetition comes to mark nothing more than the passage of time. As the art historian George Kubler argued, in an essay on history and time penned almost sixty years ago, time is beaten out in the repetition of events, against which history stands out as the incidence of the unique. Here's what he wrote:

> Our actual perception of time depends on regularly recurrent events, unlike the awareness of history, which depends on unforeseeable change and variety. Without change there is no history; without regularity there is no time. Time and history are related as rule and variation: time is the regular setting for the vagaries of history.
>
> (Kubler 1962: 71–2)

This is why art historians typically get so exercised over the question of whether a work is an original or a copy. Originals belong to history, but copies do not: they sink back into time. In this sense, Kubler (1962: 39) suggests, historical events are analogous to prime numbers: they cannot be factored as multiples of what has already happened. Yet if the analogy holds, then more must be at stake in the creative process than the mere combination and recombination of pre-existing elements. It suggests, rather, a creation whose primacy lies precisely in a coming-into-existence that surpasses any compound of what had gone before. Something, it seems, is missing from the account of creativity as recombination: something wherein time, creativity and history come together as one.

To get at what this is, we will need to retrace our steps from where it all began, with the idea of creation as a bringing forth, epitomised in the birth of a child to its parents. Can there be any more creative process than that by which a baby – as the Biblical psalm has it – is 'knit together' in its mother's womb?[8] On greeting the baby when it first comes into the world, would we say: 'that is indeed novel, we have never seen the like before?', or, conversely, 'Oh, just another one: babies, they are all the same'. In truth the latter remark, which one might imagine coming from the lips of a fatigued and disgruntled midwife, was set down in writing as a statement of scientific fact by the evolutionary psychologists John Tooby and Leda Cosmides (1992: 33). 'Infants', they say, 'are everywhere the same', in that they all come into the world already equipped with a universal cognitive architecture primed for the acquisition of culture. But supposing that unlike these scientists, we admit that this baby, at least, was creatively fashioned, rather than a mere replica run off from a universal human genotype in advance of its encounter with a cultural environment, would we then credit the happy parents with having brought about an unprecedented creative event at the moment when they conceived the child, whose blessed realisation is now cradled before them? Does the creativity of conception lie wholly in accidents of genetic recombination?

For the child herself, after all, this is only a start. Her life begins in the womb, and proceeds, after birth, through infancy, childhood, youth and maturity, and eventually into old age. Is this not a creative process in itself? There is surely more to it than the mere expression, over time, of a design laid down at the outset. For in both growing and being grown, human beings undergo histories of development and maturation within fields of relationships, established through the presence and activities of others. And critically, this growth is not just in strength and stature but also in knowledge, in the work of the imagination and the formation of ideas. For the latter is just as much a full-bodied knitting together of materials and experience as is the former. Ideas, after all, don't just pop up, ready-formed, from nowhere. They too have lives. Every idea is like a place you visit. You can return to it over and over again, but each time it is a little different, enriched by the memories of your previous stay, and by what has transpired since. Or to echo the aphorism of the philosopher Heraclitus, you cannot step twice into exactly the same idea, which is why the notion of checking through the record of the past to see whether anyone has had it before – and thereby to determine whether it is of truly historic significance, rather than a mere milestone in the life of the individual – is not just impracticable but ludicrous.

Philosophy

What is omitted from the equation of creativity with recombination, then, is growth, becoming, the actual forming or making of persons and ideas, or in a word, *ontogenesis*. Many years ago, in the course of writing a book on the meaning of evolution,[9] I came across a succinct statement of this absent dimension in the work of the American theologian Henry Nelson Wieman (1961). For me, it was a seminal discovery. There are two senses of creativity, Wieman argued, and it is important to distinguish them. In one sense, he says, creativity is a characteristic doing of the human person. A human being is creative in this sense 'when he constructs something according to a new design that has already come within reach of his imagination' (1961: 65). This is a sense already familiar to us from our discussion of the power of intelligent design, and is most commonly invoked whenever creativity is identified with innovation. It is found by looking back from a final product – what Wieman calls a 'created good' – to an unprecedented idea in the mind of an agent, in whose doing or making it was actualised. The origination of the idea is extraordinary, but the product follows from the idea, in its realisation, with an ordinary, even mechanical inevitability.

But in the second sense, according to Wieman (1961: 65–6), creativity is *what a person undergoes but cannot do*. His argument is that behind the contingencies of what people do, and the miscellany of products or created goods to which these doings give rise, is the 'creative good' that is intrinsic to human life itself, in its capacity to generate persons in relationships. This is the kind of creativity that does not begin here, with an idea in mind, and end there, with a completed object. Rather, it *carries on through*, without beginning or end. It is, for Wieman, 'what progressively creates personality in community' (1961: 66). Consider again the example of the infant, progressing through childhood and adolescence within the nurturing matrix of family and kinship relations. To be sure, he or she may create many things in the course of growing up, and many more in later life: things imagined, and subsequently made or done. But there is surely more to the creativity of a life than the sum total of a lifetime's achievements. For every act carries its own burden of suffering: every doing is also an undergoing. And it is precisely in Wieman's second sense, in the undergoing rather than the doing, that the creativity of the life process itself is to be found. This is a sense, however, that has been largely banished from the discourses not only of contemporary psychology, but also of other human sciences that have drawn on them. The question is: how can we bring it back?

Three philosophers of the early twentieth century can help us in this enterprise: Henri Bergson, Alfred North Whitehead and John Dewey, and it comes as no surprise to find that Wieman had been strongly influenced by all three. It was almost certainly from Dewey that Wieman took the key distinction between doing and undergoing, for Dewey himself had placed it at the centre of his reflections on *Art as Experience*, published in 1934. Every experience, Dewey (1987: 50) had argued, entails its quotients of doing and of undergoing, and the key problem for him was to figure out the relation between them. They cannot simply alternate, he thought, for otherwise there could be no continuity from one doing to the next, and life would fragment into a scatter of disconnected episodes. What happens in reality, to the contrary, is that undergoing always overflows doing, to the extent that whatever you do next takes into itself something of the experience of what you did before.[10] Thus, while in our doings we fashion a world, in our undergoings we are the creatures of our own self-fashioning. Or as Bergson had written in his *Creative Evolution* of 1911 (1922: 7): 'It is ... right to say that what we do depends on what we are; but it is necessary to add also that we are, to a certain extent, what we do, and that we are creating ourselves continually.' This endless creation of ourselves – this becoming – corresponds precisely to Wieman's idea of a creativity undergone rather than done.

Now to understand creativity in this sense is to read it forwards, in the unfolding of the relations and processes that actually give rise to worldly beings, rather than back, in the retrospective attribution of final products to initial designs. It is to recognise, with Bergson, that ontogenesis not only takes time but is also irreversible. Its time is duration: not a succession of instants but the prolonging of the past into the actual. 'Duration', Bergson wrote (1922: 4–5), 'is the continuous progress of the past which gnaws into the future and which swells as it advances.' This, in his terms, distinguishes creation from mere fabrication. For fabrication, Bergson argued, 'even when it invents, it proceeds, or imagines itself to proceed, by a new arrangement of elements already known'. In the combination and recombination of pre-existing materials, nothing comes into existence that was not there before: in the endless production of novelties, nothing ever truly begins. Creation, however, is the wellspring of existence itself, bringing forth new life and time. 'If everything is in time', Bergson (1922: 48) continued, 'everything changes inwardly, and the same concrete reality never recurs.' There is no going back. What follows, then, cannot be factored into any multiple or combination of that which preceded it: before and after are truly incommensurable. It is as if in every breath, we open our eyes on the world for the first time.

Like Bergson, Whitehead was also keen to emphasise the difference in perspective that comes from relinquishing our view of the world from the outside, as a fait accompli, for a position from the inside of its coming-into-being. From the outside you see creatures, each the living embodiment of a design, and each set apart from all the others and the environment to which it is adapted. But from the inside the creature turns out to be none other than the process of its own self-creation, a process that, at each and every moment, enfolds an entire universe into a singular nexus. Already in his Lowell lectures of 1925, *Science and the Modern World*, Whitehead (1925: 140) had been at pains to distinguish these outside and inside perspectives, reserving what he called 'creativeness' for the latter (Chapter 4, pages 53–4). A year later he returned to the same theme in a second series of lectures, *Religion in the Making*, in which he attempted to apply the same ideas to religion that he had previously applied to science. Again, he distinguishes the two sides, or perspectives, positing the creature on the one side as an 'emergent fact', and on the other 'as the cause of itself, its own creative act' (Whitehead 1926: 101–2).

Yet in truth, Whitehead concludes (1926: 102), there are not two things, the creativity and the creature: 'There is only one entity which is the self-creating creature'. This is a key move which, with one stroke, demolishes the wall between creator and created that, as we have already seen, had had the effect of reducing creativity to a faculty of intelligent design. Indeed in his insistence that creator and creation are one and the same, Whitehead is of the same mind as Aquinas, and indeed as Ockham. For Aquinas, as Maryniarczyk puts it (2016: 257), 'the Creator is existence'. For Ockham, too, 'neither God nor his creating represents anything caused by the intellect'; rather, creation signifies God himself, 'as divine essence, really creating' (Leff 1975: 463–4). What is coming into being with creation, then, is nothing less than existence, life itself, refracted in the proliferation of its worldly creatures. To bear witness to this becoming is to join in a moment of creation that, apperceived from the inside, stretches to eternity. And for Whitehead, a man of deep religious conviction, this is what it meant to enter into the presence of God.

Art

Let me take a step back. It was in the Renaissance, as we have seen, that the idea took root of the artist, and also the architect, as a mortal second only to God in powers of intellect and skills of execution. Ever since, at least in the Western world, this idea has formed a central plank in art's rhetoric of self-promotion. An entire mythology has grown up around the figure of the artist as a creative genius. Even today, now that art has been incorporated within the ambit of so-called 'creative industries', artists are regarded as prime innovators, celebrated for their capacity to come up with designs that are unprecedented in their imaginative reach. A key motif in the myth of genius is that artists are ahead of their time. Always in the vanguard, they are the premier exemplars of H- or C-creativity. Yet while artists themselves, in the interests of patronage and promotion, have often and willingly connived in the myth, they have also had to wrestle with a pervasive tension between the public persona they present to the world, and their actual experience of artistic creation. For whereas the art world, in thrall to the market in high-end, luxury commodities, is looking for completed works ripe for both monetary and aesthetic evaluation by dealers and critics alike, in the experience of the artist no work is ever finished. 'The work of art', wrote the painter Paul Klee (1961: 78) in his notebooks, 'is first of all genesis; it is never experienced purely as a result'. For the artist the *work* goes on, even as life does; what the market eagerly gobbles up are but the cast-offs of the daily struggle to begin afresh. And it is in this struggle, in the undergoing, that true artistic creation lies.[11]

Once again, we can turn to Bergson for inspiration. He invites us to picture an artist, whom he presumes to be male, positioned before a canvas, his colours already on the palette, his model seated before him. Do we not know already what will appear? Perhaps in a vague way we do, as we can expect a portrait that will bear some resemblance to the model. For the artist the presence of the model is a problem, to which the portrait will eventually fall out as a provisional solution. Yet this solution, writes Bergson (1922: 360), 'brings with it that unforeseeable nothing which is everything in a work of art'. And this nothing that is everything *takes time*. It has a duration that is unshrinkable.[12] It is this, he argues, that makes the difference between the work of art and, say, a jigsaw puzzle. Let's suppose that the original portrait, having subsequently achieved iconic status, is reproduced as a puzzle, available for sale in the gallery shop. Having bought it for yourself, you set to work to assemble the pieces. With the completion of the portrait the puzzle is solved. Yet comparing your completion of the reproduction and the painter's completion of the original, the relation between problem and solution in the two scenarios could not be more different. For with the puzzle the solution is already at hand before the work begins. With practice, you can speed up the assembly; in principle it takes no time at all. Not so, however, for the painter of the original work. For him the creation would have evolved even as he worked on it. 'The time taken up by the invention', as Bergson (1922: 359) puts it, 'is one with the invention itself'. Enfolded into it, as we shall see further in Chapter 9 (pages 144–6), is the duration of the artist's very life and soul.

For the artist, in short, the solution overflows the problem. And it is precisely in the overflow that its creative quotient lies. Like a prime number, it is a quotient that is in no wise reducible to any function of its original conditions. The artist does not live to execute thoughts that think themselves in him, as rearrangements of the fragments of earlier ones. For the thinking of artistic invention always surpasses thought, precisely as undergoing – as we have already seen – surpasses doing. Thinking as undergoing, as Dewey (1987: 59) realised, surrenders to existence, yet this is not a passive surrendering but an active 'taking in', akin to inhalation, which readies the thinker for further release into activity, just as breathing in prepares a body for breathing out. Every breath is new, of course, *but it is not a novelty*. Though it might sound like splitting hairs, there is a fundamental distinction to be made here between newness and novelty, just as there is between creation and creativity. There is a newness to artistic invention that goes beyond the recombination of thought, in its ever-shifting patterns. For whereas the latter delivers only endings, the former ushers in perpetual beginning. Newness, again to borrow Bergson's (1922: 49) words, is a 'ceaseless upspringing'. To apprehend newness is to inhabit the cusp, the moment of incipience in which the world is on the point of revelation. In novelty, however, that moment is already past, congealed into objects that present themselves to our attention, retrospectively, as candidates for appropriation.

The composer Manuel de Falla once observed that to write a piece of music is to give birth to a new life. In the throes of creation, the composer allows himself to be taken over by the work, to have it inhabit his very being as it swells within him. Eventually, after a period of gestation, the composition bodies forth, and goes on to live a life of its own in the world. It is not as though the work was finished, at the moment when the composer laid down his pen. Its life, unless cut short by the calamity of stillbirth, is only just beginning. It is a life lived in its performances. In this sense the musical work is crescent, not created, continually coming into being for as long as it lives. It is a thing that carries on, or *perdures* (Ingold 2014d: 129). While you can return to the same piece over and over again, just as you can to an idea, it is different with every performance. You can never step twice into the same work, any more than you can into the same idea. What is true of music, moreover, applies equally to visual art, even if it is shown rather than performed. For showing, too, is a modality of presence, and the present never repeats. Even the work of art, then, is not fixed, despite the interventions of conservationists, armed with sophisticated technology, to preserve for eternity an imagined state of completion. The work of art, like music, is always crescent. And to compose or respond to any work of art, visual or musical, means participating in the creative process that Bergson (1922: 11) called *invention*: 'the continual elaboration of the absolutely new'.

This is to understand invention, however, in a sense that could not be more different from that invoked by the psychologist Guilford, for whom – as you will recall – it denotes a capacity of the human brain to preconfigure, in thought, 'what never existed before'. By and large, the scientific study of creativity, following Guilford's lead, remains locked into a consumerist logic, driven by the imperatives of problem-solving, product innovation and marketing, which offers only a superabundance of ends (Hennessey and Amabile 2010: 572). With this logic every new thing, every novelty, is over even before it is begun. The creative idea is already configured in thought in advance of the product, the solution in advance of the problem to which it is to be applied. To follow Bergson's lead means turning this around, putting things before ends rather than ends before things. It means setting newness before novelty, creation before creativity. We can no longer be content, then, to regard invention as a power of mental representation, or intelligent design. Invention does not set things up, in thought, in advance of their realisation in the world. It does not even belong to individual human beings, let alone to their brains. It belongs to the world, to existence, perchance to God. To invent, after Bergson, is not to create a world but actively to participate from the inside in the world's ceaseless creation of itself – and, since we belong to the world, of ourselves as well. It is once again to reunite creator and created in one act. And at a time of present crisis, with the world on a knife-edge, this step has never been more needed. For only by restoring faith and hope in the perpetuity of beginning – or, in a word, in *creation* – can we open a real future to coming generations.

Perhaps then, after its two-thousand-year odyssey, the promise of creation can at last come home.

Chapter 2

Landscapes of perception, landscapes of imagination

The human condition

In 1933, the Belgian surrealist artist René Magritte composed a painting which he entitled *La Condition humaine* (Figure 2.1). The painting depicts a window, curtained on either side, as seen from the inside of a room. In front of the window, and taking up about half of its area, is placed an easel upon which is mounted a completed painting. The painting (within the painting) is of a landscape including a tree, verdant hills, and a blue sky with scattered clouds. Through the remainder of the window aperture not obscured by the painting, one sees what appears to be a continuation of the same scene. The viewer is consequently led to believe that the painting represents, with canny realism, precisely what would be seen through the area of the windowpane that it occludes, were it to be removed. The tree in the painting, for example, hides a tree that – if the painting were not standing in the way – could actually be seen through the window, and which would look exactly the same. Thus the tree is at once inside the room, in the painting, and outside it, in the actual landscape. Five years later, Magritte referred to this picture, in a lecture entitled 'Lifeline' (*La ligne de vie*), presented at the Museum of Fine Art in Antwerp. Its purpose, he explained, was to reveal something fundamental about the way in which human beings see the world. 'We see it', he said, 'as being outside ourselves, even though it is only a mental representation of what we experience on the inside.'[1]

The human condition, in Magritte's hands, is that of a being who can know the world, recognise its forms and appreciate their beauty only in so far as they are already cast as interior images from the materials of sensory experience. We think we see an outside world with our eyes, but that – for Magritte – is an illusion. In fact we see an inner world with our mind's eye. Since what this mind's eye sees is a picture of the world, the world as seen and its pictorial representation are continuous with one another, and only the faintest rectangular outline of the canvas (indicated by a clip at the top, an edge on the right, and a slight occlusion of the curtain on the left), along with the presence of the easel, allow us to tell where one ends and the other

DOI: 10.4324/9781003171713-4

Figure 2.1 René Magritte, *La Condition humaine* (1933).
Courtesy of the National Gallery of Washington, © ADAGP, Paris and DACS, London, 2021.

begins. Percept and image are all but indistinguishable. Do we seek the real tree behind its painterly representation? It too, as it turns out, would be part of a picture – one that Magritte might have painted of the same room, had he first removed the easel, with its canvas, from its position before the window. And the tree in this second picture would be identical to that in the first. Right now I am writing at a table in front of a window, not unlike the one that Magritte depicts. Outside the window I see the lawn of my garden, bushes and trees, the outer walls and roofs of houses on the street next to ours, and a generally cloudy sky which is just beginning to clear after yesterday's rain. I do not think I am imagining these things – they truly exist for me. Yet if I were Magritte, I would have to admit that what I claim to see is really but a picture that my mind has painted for me.

All seeing, in this view, is imagining. To perceive a landscape is therefore to imagine it. This is the premise on which the historian Simon Schama bases his magnum opus, *Landscape and Memory* (1995). 'Before it can ever be a repose for the senses', Schama (1995: 6–7) contends, 'landscape is the work of the mind. Its scenery is built up as much from strata of memory as from layers of rock.' Literally, landscape means 'land shaped', and the unification of land and shape for Schama is one of physical substance and ideal form. The world as it exists beyond the pale of human sensibility is formless and inchoate, comprised of matter in the raw – layers of rock deposited though geological processes. It is our 'shaping perception', Schama (1995: 10) asserts, that converts this raw material into the kind of vista that we recognise as a landscape. And it does so by imposing a design whose source lies in the sedimentations of memory, ratified by convention and transmitted in culture, upon the otherwise chaotic flux of bodily sensation. 'What lies beyond the windowpane of our apprehension', writes Schama (1995: 12), referring back to Magritte's depiction of the human condition, 'needs a design before we can properly discern its form, let alone derive pleasure from its perception. And it is culture, convention and cognition that makes that design; that invests a retinal impression with the quality we experience as beauty.'

For the psychologist of perception James Gibson, however, this conclusion could not be more wrong. It is simply fallacious, Gibson argues, to suppose that vision entails the mental enhancement of impressions stamped upon the surface of the retina. For the retina is not an eye: it may be in receipt of sensory stimuli, but it is not an organ of perception. The eye is a perceptual organ, or rather part of the dual organ comprised of our two eyes, set in a head that can turn, in a body that moves from place to place. When we see, Gibson (1979: 53) insists, this entire eyes–head–body system is at work. Thus visual perception is the achievement of the whole organism as it moves around in its environment; not that of a mind confined within the interiority of a body and bound to the interpretation of patterns projected onto the back of the retina. As we move around, the array of light reaching our eyes, reflected from surfaces in our surroundings, undergoes continuous modulation. Underlying these modulations, however, are parametric constants, or so-called 'invariants', that specify the properties and qualities of the things we encounter. To see these things is to extract their invariants from modulations of the optic array. Thus it is not the mind that gives shape to what we perceive. It does not shape the land, or its features. For these shapes are already there in the world, awaiting discovery by any creature, human or nonhuman, whose perceptual system is so attuned as to attend to them – or more precisely, to pick up the invariants by which they are specified.

It follows that the real word and the perceived world do not lie on opposite sides of an impermeable division between 'outside' and 'inside'. For Gibson the perceived world *is* the real world, as it is given in relation to a being with certain capabilities of action and perceptual attunements – or in short, as an *environment*. In this perceived reality, however, there is no place for the imagination. Perceiving and imagining, far from being more or less the same, are poles apart. Gibson (1979: 256–8) proposes a series of tests that enable us to distinguish the reality of the perceived world from its imagistic representation. They boil down to the point that no more can be gleaned from an image than what has already been put there in making it. Suppose that you have before you, either on canvas or in your mind's eye, an image of a tree, painted with the exquisite realism of a Magritte. Taking a magnifying glass to the leaves will not reveal the intricacies of their veins, nor will microscopic examination reveal their cellular structure. But with a real tree, there is always more to be discovered. The key test, in Gibson's (1979: 257) words, 'is whether you can discover new features and details by the act of scrutiny'. The real world is inexhaustible; the image contains only such information as the mind has already contributed to it. No amount of scrutiny will reveal what is not there.[2] True, one might find meanings in an image of which one had not at first been aware, but this is to add to it by way of interpretation, not to discover more of what there is. Perceiving is to imagining, then, as is discovery to interpretation.

It seems, in short, that Gibson's ecological approach to perception has contrived to close the gap between the reality of the world and our perception of it, only by opening up a chasm between perception and imagination. But are we forced to choose between these alternatives? Must we side either with those who would attribute a decisive role to the imagination in giving shape to the landscapes of our perception, or with those for whom it plays no more than an ancillary or retrospective role, in the interpretation of landscapes already perceived? My aim in this chapter is to find a way beyond these alternatives: a way that would reunite perception and imagination while yet acknowledging the human condition, *contra* both Magritte and Schama, to be that of a being whose knowledge of the world, far from being shaped by the operations of mind upon the deliverances of the senses, grows from the very soil of an existential involvement *in* the sensible world. To achieve this aim, we will need to reconsider the significance of imagination: to think of it not just as a capacity to construct images, or as the power of mental representation, but more fundamentally as a way of living creatively in a world that is itself crescent, always in formation. To imagine, we suggest, is not so much to conjure up images of a reality 'out there', whether virtual or actual, true or false, as to participate from within, through perception and action, in the very becoming of things. What follows is an amplification of this suggestion.

Truth and illusion

According to one commonly accepted meaning of the term, 'to imagine' means to conjure up, in the mind, or perhaps in words and images, things or happenings that are not actually present to the senses. One definition, gleaned from several in the *Oxford English Dictionary*, may serve as an example: 'that faculty of mind by which we conceive the absent as if it were present'. Thus the archaeologist or environmental historian might imagine how a landscape could have looked in the past, and a landscape architect or designer might imagine how it could look in the future. The novelist might imagine a landscape that could conceivably have existed, but which is nevertheless of his own invention; the surrealist painter might imagine one that could not conceivably exist at all. We could, if we were so inclined, distinguish landscapes of memory, of design, of fiction and of fantasy. But we could, just as well, adduce all sorts of reasons why these distinctions cannot be watertight. What work of fiction, for example, is not informed by its author's memories and anticipations? And when have these memories and anticipations not been infused by – and in turn infused – our dreams and fantasies? It is not my intention to address these questions here. However a more general problem has to be tackled. How is it possible to square the ontological division between domains of reality and the imagination with the division between presence and absence? Despite their radical differences, this is a problem that both the approaches introduced above have had to confront.

Let us consider first the view that in the shaping of landscape, the mind brings its own conceptions, culturally acquired and sedimented in memory, to the interpretation of retinal impressions. If what we believe we see 'out there' is, as Magritte would have it, but the projection of an internal image, then must we conclude that some images are imaginary and others real? Picture yourself in the room of Magritte's *La Condition humaine*. The painted landscape includes a tree. You want to know whether a tree really stands outside, beyond the window. So you remove the painting from the easel and take a look. No tree. Did the painter, then, just imagine it? Did he paint an imaginary reality, so as to produce an image of the imaginary? Or alternatively: the tree is indeed there. So did the painter paint a real reality, so as to produce an image of the real? An image of the imaginary is, of course, what is more commonly known as an *illusion*, and it comes as no surprise that among both historians of art and psychologists of vision who have adopted this approach to perception, the study of illusions and of what gives rise to them has become something of an obsession. The problem, in essence, is this: if we can have no direct access to the world – if it cannot reveal to us what is there and what is not – and if, to the contrary, we can know the world only by bringing our own mental representations, bequeathed by culture and convention, to bear on the evidence of the senses, then how can we possibly distinguish truth from illusion?

The answer is that we cannot. The most we can do is to regard perception as a kind of guesswork. 'There seems to be no sudden break between *perceiving* an object and *guessing* an object', writes visual psychologist Richard Gregory (1973: 61–2), weighing his words with emphasis. 'If all perceiving of objects requires some guessing, we may think of sensory stimulation as providing *data* for *hypotheses* concerning the state of the external world.' Thus every perception is a hypothesis, or a conjecture about what might be there. Illusions, then, are failed hypotheses (1973: 74). But we can never know, a priori, whether a perception is illusory or not. A hypothesis thought to be false may, on further testing against the data of experience, turn out to be true, and vice versa. For Gregory, the creative power of the human imagination lies precisely in its capacity to come up with hunches, conjectures, even visions of other worlds, which deviate from accepted truth. Though most will fail the test of experience, some may not, and in an ever-changing world it is the latter that open the way to invention and discovery (1973: 94).

In this, Gregory appeals to the model of progress in the history of science originally proposed by the philosopher Karl Popper (1950). Scientific knowledge, Popper had argued, advances through a perpetual process of conjecture and refutation. But an identical case can be made for the history of art, as Ernst Gombrich showed in his celebrated work, *Art and Illusion* (1960). As science proceeds by hypothesis, test and revision, so in art, according to Gombrich (1960: 272), there is an endless process of 'making, matching and remaking'. At any moment in this process, however, the artist can only paint – that is, project onto canvas – what is in his mind. He cannot copy what is in the world. So too, according to Gregory (1973: 89), it is on the basis of our conjectures of the world, not of the data of experience, that we act. The direction of formal projection is univocally from mind to world, not from world to mind.

Turning now to the alternative, ecological approach to perception, the problem of presence and absence appears in quite another guise. It is no longer a question of separating truth from illusion. Most people, most of the time, are not fooled by what they see, precisely because what they see is *not* a picture of the world. Take yourself back for a moment to the room of Magritte's painting. Would you really be tricked into confusing the painting on the easel with the view through the window? Of course not, for one simple reason that Gibson is at pains to stress. The painting on the easel is two things at once: it is a representation of a scene, and it is an artefact with a textured surface and edges. 'A picture', as Gibson (1979: 281) explains, 'is always a treated surface, and it is always seen in a context of other, non-pictorial surfaces.' In this sense, the picture has just the same artefactual status as, say, the curtains flanking the windowpane. The treated canvas of the painting is just as real – just as present – as the woven fabric of the curtains, and indeed as the bark or foliage of the tree you see outside. All may be subjected to the same test for reality: they can be inexhaustibly scrutinised by the moving observer. That is why the conceit of the *trompe l'oeil* painters, to have fooled us into mistaking their depictions for reality, rings hollow (Gombrich 1960: 172–3; Gibson 1979: 281). The eye of the observer is fooled only if artificial constraints are placed on the viewing situation that prevent him from being able to pick up the invariants that specify what he is looking at. Such constraints, often built into the design of experiments on vision informed by retinal image optics, have no counterpart in the world outside the laboratory.

But if we can access, by direct perception, what is really there, what are we to make of our awareness of things that do not currently exist, or that cannot be discovered through the processes of information pickup that Gibson describes? This awareness, as Gibson acknowledges, can take many forms, including reminiscence, expectation, imagination, fantasy, and dreaming. Yet he is convinced that they have no essential role to play in perception itself: rather, 'they are kinds of visual awareness other than perceptual' (1979: 254–5). How, then, are we to account for these kinds of 'non-perceptual awareness'? How is it possible, for example, to imagine a landscape other than that in which we find ourselves? Gibson's answer is tentative and far from clear. Of one thing, however, he is certain, namely that imagining cannot be understood purely as an operation of the mind, nor should it be supposed to result in the production of mental imagery. Perceiving and imagining may be quite different, but they have in common that they do not begin with a stimulus input and end with an image. Rather, they *carry on*.

Starting from this premise, Gibson's best guess is that imagining is the activity of a perceptual system, but one that is temporarily relieved of its routine business of information pickup. It is what happens when a system already attuned to the extraction of particular invariants from the stimulus flux is disengaged from that flux and enters what we might call a 'free-wheeling' or auto-generative mode. In this sense, imagination is as much an achievement of the whole organism in its environment as is perception. It is, in Gibson's (1979: 256) words, 'an activity of the system, not an appearance in the theatre of consciousness'. But it is an activity of a system decoupled from its usual engagement with the world, and that has, as it were, turned in upon itself. Yet here, I think Gibson is profoundly mistaken. For all the evidence at our disposal – ethnographic and otherwise – inclines to the view that in acts of imagination the perceptual systems of the observer, far from being decoupled from immediate involvement with the environment, are more closely engaged than ever.

My contention is that perceiving *is* imagining – not, however, because the percept is an image, but because the world that is perceived is continually brought forth, or called into being, in the very act of imagination. Gibson's mistake, it appears, was to assume that while perception is always going on, always casting about, the world as perceived is pre-cast in fixed and final forms, as a structure of invariants. But what if the world, too, carries on? What if it is always in the casting? We could take our cue here from the celebrated *Creative Credo* of Paul Klee. 'Art', Klee declared, 'does not reproduce the visible but makes visible.'[3] Thus the painter does not project onto canvas forms that already exist as representations inside his head, but rather brings these forms into existence – or 'grows' them, as the gardener might grow a plant from its seed – in his very activity of mark-making, so that they are there to be seen. Perception is imaginative, then, in so far as it is enrolled in the generation of a world that is continually coming into being with and around the perceiver, in and through his or her own practices of movement, gesture and inscription.

Imagining is being alive

It has long been the conceit of planners and policy-makers, or of those entrusted with projects of 'development', to suppose that to imagine the future is to predict: that is, to conjecture a novel state of affairs, as yet unrealised, and to specify in advance the steps that need to be taken in order to get there. Governments and other agencies demand what they call scenarios: images of what the world will look like, say, twenty, fifty or a hundred years from now. What we have learned from the foregoing, however, is that the work of imagination lies not, as Gregory (1973: 94) for example would have it, in 'continually inventing a fictional future', but rather – to follow dance philosopher Erin Manning (2009: 69) – in so flying ahead of things as to disclose the present, in every moment of its emergence, as the future's past. To imagine is to live upon the cusp of this moment. As we say colloquially, the imagination is wont to 'roam', and in so doing, it opens up paths in and through the world, rather than fixing endpoints in advance. It consists, then, not in the power of prediction but in the gift of prophecy or foresight (Ingold 2013a: 69). Seeking not to speculate *about* the future but to see *into* it, to exercise this gift is to improvise a passage, rather than to innovate with representations of the unprecedented. It is to tell how things will go, in a world where everything is 'not preordained but incipient, forever on the verge of the actual' (Ingold 2011a: 69). In this world, indeed, there are no objects to represent, only materials; no fixed and final forms, only potentials for things to grow and transform. To foresee means joining forces *with* materials in the anticipation of what might emerge, bearing witness, as the philosopher Maurice Merleau-Ponty (1964: 181) put it, to how 'things become things, how the world becomes a world'.

An imagined landscape, then, is a landscape not of being but of becoming: a composition not of objects and surfaces but of movements and stillness, not there to be surveyed but unfolding in the current of time. It is, in this regard, closer to music than painting. In an essay first published in 1940, Jakob von Uexküll (2010: 185–90) – Estonian-born naturalist and pioneer in the study of the perceived worlds of animals and humans – compared the landscape of our imagination to polyphonic music. In similar vein, philosopher Gilles Deleuze and his collaborator, psychoanalyst Félix Guattari (2004: 351), speak of *melodic landscapes*. The melodic landscape, they explain, is not a landscape associated with a melody: it is not as though the melody stands for the landscape, like a placard or poster, or – as a music-lover might remark of the compositions of Jean Sibelius – that they depict the lakes, forests and birdlife of his native Finland. Rather, say Deleuze and Guattari, 'the melody itself is a sonorous landscape'. This is not at all the same as what many have taken to calling the soundscape, in which the sonic medley is fed back into our own ears, in its audible record (Ingold 2011a: 136–7). The melodic landscape sounds itself into existence. Consider the songbird, an inhabitant of this landscape. Does it sing simply to announce the boundaries of its territory, in a world already laid out? Or does it sing in counterpoint to the currents of life that flow around it? The latter is the mark of what Deleuze and Guattari call the 'musician bird'. To describe the bird as a musician is to indulge not in anthropomorphism but in geomorphism. It is to say that the bird, in its singing, resonates with the song of the earth.

So too, does the human, in such practices of singing as the Sámi *joik*, in which the singer lends his or her own voice to the earth's chorus, participating from within in the perpetual self-making of the world (Aubinet 2020). This is to join with a world in which things do not so much *exist* as *occur*, each along its own trajectory of becoming. In the life of the imagination, the landscape is a bundle of such trajectories, forever ravelling here and unravelling there. One could, with geographer Doreen Massey (2005: 12), think of every trajectory as a story and of the totality of the landscape at any particular moment as the 'simultaneity of stories-so-far'. Human beings have their stories, of course, but so do animals, trees, mountains, mud and water, in so far as in their growth, movements and displacements they continually and mutually respond to each other's presence – or in a word, they *correspond*. Life, I contend, is lived in correspondence (Ingold 2017b). To imagine the landscape, then, is to enter into correspondence with it, or as anthropologist Stuart McLean (2009: 231) puts it, 'to respond creatively to the creativity of the world's ceaseless self-transformation'. This is to intuit an essential continuity, McLean (2009: 232) argues, between 'human acts of imagining and fabulation' and 'the processes shaping and transforming the material universe'. Such intuition, which flows like an undercurrent through myth and folklore, art and literature, philosophy and science, presents a fundamental ontological challenge to any division we might attempt to force between the reality of the world and its representation.

To appreciate the distance we have come from where our inquiry began, let me reprise Magritte's characterisation of the human condition, as that of a being who can only know what is 'out there', on the far side of the eyes or beyond the skin, through recasting its forms as images in the mind. The human, for Magritte, is caught between the worlds of imagination and reality, or fantasy and fact, fated ever to wager one against the other in recurrent tournaments of conjecture and refutation. My conclusion, to the contrary, is that humans are not divided between two worlds but are inhabitants of one – a world between, a middle place, or literally a *milieu* – an ambience of immanence or becoming that has yet to bifurcate into the counter-facing terrains of the real and the imagined.

With this conclusion in mind we can return to Gibson, and to his failure, on which I have already remarked, to marry perception and imagination. I have already hinted at the reason for this failure, which lies in a fundamental asymmetry in Gibson's approach. For the very movement and activity that he ascribes to the perceiver, he denies to objects of perception, which appear fixed and stable by comparison. The task for the perceiver is accordingly to pick up or extract information from an invariant world, not to venture into the turmoil of a world *in formation*. Extraction, not adventure, is the name of the game. But for inhabitants of the milieu, it is precisely the other way around. They are primarily adventurers, and only secondarily extractors. Literally, adventure implies 'an exposure to that which is about to happen' (Savransky 2016: 40), a risky endeavour at the best of times. And it is surely in this – in placing one's very being at risk – that we find the crux of what it means to be alive, in a world that also seethes with vitality.

Could imagination, then, lie in this sense of adventure, in the impulse of a life that continually risks exposure by running ahead of itself (Ingold 2015: 140–41)? Humans, of course, are not alone in living. But are they alone in imagining? Is there, after all, something about the way of imagination that is peculiar to the human condition? Perhaps other animals imagine too, but short of metamorphosing into nonhuman kinds, as shamans are alleged to do, it is hard to ascertain what it might mean to imagine like a bear, a whale or an eagle. We can however ascertain from observation how other creatures move, and notice that of all creatures, human beings move in a manifestly peculiar way, namely, by walking on two feet. Could the mundane act of taking a step hold the key to the relation, at least in human experience, between perception and imagination? Leaning into the step while lifting one foot, you place yourself at imminent risk of falling forward into the void, only to restore your postural equilibrium as the foot comes temporarily to rest in adjusting to the surface of the ground, preparing you, in the next step, to repeat the same movement with the other foot. Imagination, here, sets you free to fall, while perception restores your balance so you can go on. The first signals an adventure, the second offers confirmation, and it is in their alternation that pedestrian life is lived (Ingold 2015: 138–41).

This understanding of perception and imagination, however, could hardly be more different from that from which we began. To highlight the difference, let me introduce the work of another artist, Richard Long, for whom walking is central to his practice. Long walks lines into the landscape, whether it be a grassy meadow, a wood, desert sands, a snowfield or a mountain plateau. He is a direction-maker. His lines tend to be straight, and they make their mark precisely because of the direction they impart. It is in this very casting forward – of his whole being in the world, on the ground, along a line of movement – that the imaginative work of art consists. It is not in this form, however, that Long's works are generally rendered accessible to others. Instead, what we get to see, as his public, are mainly photographs, conforming in every respect to the romantic ideal of the scenic panorama, each showing an already completed line stretching from the foreground into the middle distance (Figure 2.2). These photographs are assembled into sumptuously illustrated books (Fuchs 1986; Long 2002) which adorn the occasional tables of many a discerning, art-loving household, as an index of good taste. Such books, and countless others like them, are designed to appeal to an aesthetic sensibility that perceives beauty in finished forms, and not in the processes that give rise to them. They are, indeed, very attractive. Yet paradoxically, the very medium of photographic representation, while it affirms the work of art in the sight of others, wipes out the artistic intention that motivated its original production.

Figure 2.2 Richard Long, *Walking a Line in Peru* (1972).

Is the point of the photographs, then, to release or slough off the burden of representational aesthetics so as to leave intact the artistic integrity of the real work, the walk itself? Can they be seen, as philosopher and critic Herman Rapaport (1997: 91) suggests, as epitomising 'the very aesthetics that the walks have dropped by the side of the road'? Are they the cast-offs of artistic production? During a symposium in the Scottish Highlands in 2014, in which we both participated, I put these questions to Long himself.[4] His reply was to insist that the photographs were no less important to him than were his walks. He had his reasons, of course, since as a public artist, he was as committed to the accessibility of his work as to its integrity. I was nevertheless astonished by his response, since it seemed to me, much as it did to Rapoport, that the scenic picture-book deliberately conceals the real purpose of the art by affirming, almost to the point of caricature, the very premise that the art sets out to refute. This is the premise upon which Schama builds his account of landscape and memory, according to which it is the mind, in its recollections of things past, that contributes design to the raw material of sensory experience, allowing us to discern forms and derive pleasure from their perception (Schama 1995: 10, 12).

Perhaps we can leave this view, along with the picture-book images it yields, at the roadside, as bait to feed the market in fine art. For in walking the line, Long demonstrably performs an apprehension of landscape that lies not in the unification of memory and rock, image and object, appearance and substance, or mind and matter, but in the never-ending, contrapuntal interweaving of material flows and sensory awareness. The walk of life advances in an alternating movement of casting forward and drawing up, of imagination and material practice. But these are movements of the entire being in its world, not alternately of cognition and locomotion. Perceiving the landscape is, in short, tantamount to imagining the landscape, in so far as we do not just live *in* the world but are simultaneously alive *to* it.

Chapter 3

Life in a whirl

Herein wonder not
How 'tis that, while the seeds of things are all
Moving forever, the sum yet seems to stand
Supremely still.

(Titus Lucretius Carus, *De Rerum Natura* ['On the Nature of Things'], 50 BCE)

The nature of infinity is this: That every *thing* has its
Own Vortex; and when once a traveller thro' Eternity
Has passed that Vortex, he perceives it roll backward behind
His path, into a globe itself infolding; like the sun:
Or like a moon, or like a universe of starry majesty,
While he keeps onwards in his wondrous journey on the earth.

(William Blake, *Milton*, 1804)

Life in general is mobility itself; particular manifestations of life accept this mobility reluctantly, and constantly lag behind. It is always going ahead; they want to mark time. Evolution in general would fain go in a straight line; each special evolution is a kind of circle. Like eddies of dust raised by the wind as it passes, the living turn upon themselves, borne up by the great blast of life. They are therefore relatively stable, and counterfeit immobility so well that we treat each of them as a thing rather than as a progress, forgetting that the very permanence of their form is only the outline of a movement.

(Henri Bergson, *Creative Evolution*, 1911)

The generative turn

Life begins in whirling. By 'life', I do not mean an interior property that distinguishes some things we call 'animate' from everything else we call

DOI: 10.4324/9781003171713-5

'inanimate'. It is not to be found in the behaviour of some magic molecule such as DNA that, in the right circumstances, can turn out replicas of itself. I mean, rather, the potential of a world given in movement to generate the forms of things, to hold them fast, and in turn to portend their dissolution. In a world of life, things are formed as eddies in the flow, that is as centres of stillness or dynamic stability which, far from having been fortified against the currents that would otherwise sweep them asunder, are constituted in these very currents. In this sense the whirling nebulae are phenomena of life; so too are the atmospheric storms or the oceanic maelstroms of our own earth, along with creatures of every kind that inhabit its lands and waters. It was in this vein that the Roman author Lucretius, in his essay-poem *De Rerum Natura*, described all things as having been formed in the never-ceasing flows of atomic particles which, falling rectilinearly through the void, swerve ever so slightly from their downward path so as to cause a cascade of collisions and combinations. Out of this commotion a world is formed, of things that, in our eyes, stand still. We see the forms and not the flow, and think of them not as movements but as objects in themselves. It is no wonder, then, that we look to some inner principle, some harbinger of agency or vitality, that would bring them back to life.[1]

In *Milton*, composed in 1804, the visionary poet William Blake was onto much the same theme. In the infinitude of space and the eternity of time, everything is formed as its own vortex in the currents of the cosmos. Blake imagines himself riding with the flow, a cosmic traveller adrift on its tides, sailing into the vortices of things. But only once he has passed through each, looking back, does he see them closing in or imploding, so as to give the appearance of bounded bodies that fall ever behind as he carries relentlessly on.[2] So too Henri Bergson, in his equally visionary *Creative Evolution* of 1911, compares every living thing to an eddy or whirlwind in the 'great blast of life' (Bergson 1922: 134). In thinking that life in general is given in movement, Bergson is with Lucretius, save for one thing: instead of raining downwards, Bergson's 'great blast' erupts upwards. Perhaps he's thinking of balloon flight, which at the time was in its heyday! Be that as it may, Bergson is as convinced as Lucretius that for there to be particular living things it is necessary for this movement to veer from a course that would otherwise be absolutely straight – that is, for it to *turn aside*. It is as if the living were to accept the movement of life with a degree of reluctance: as if they were to turn in upon themselves, lagging behind – or marking time – while life itself moves on. But whereas Blake, riding the cosmos, looks back to see the things that once had sucked him in closing up and receding into the distance, for Bergson this closure is an illusion of the intellect in whose eyes, cast ever rearward, the 'whirl of organism' reappears as an immobile figure set off by an outline against the ground of a ready-made world.[3]

Whirling, of course, is a movement, but as Bergson realised, it is not just *any* movement. It is, specifically, a movement that moves: one that, at every moment, veers off course. That is to say, it perpetually inflects or *turns*.[4] But nor is it just *any* turning. Of the mechanical clock, we may observe that its hands turn, or rotate, about a fixed and predetermined centre. The turning of the whirl, however, does not so much presuppose a centre as give rise to it, as a place of relative stillness, as a form. In the mechanism of the clock, the working parts – cogs, ratchets, hands – have all been manufactured in advance, and their movements are prescribed in their axial displacement from point to point. But in the whirl of organism, movement and form co-constitute one another: movement turns into form, and form into movement. Thus where Bergson distinguishes between the evolution of life in general and the special evolution of a particular life – the one straight, the other describing a 'kind of circle' (1922: 134) – we would do better, I think, to distinguish the *evolution* of the former from the *revolution* of the latter. By 'revolution' I mean a turning that is also a turning *into*; revolving as becoming, becoming as revolving.

As such, the *revolution* of the whirl is quite different from the *rotation* of the clock. The whirl's revolution is generative, it is a movement of growth; the clock's rotation is mechanical, amounting to the spatial relocation of pre-existing parts. Yet on second thoughts, this may not do justice to the clock. Suppose that it is of the pre-digital, pre-electronic spring-loaded variety. In order for it to go we have had to wind it up. The very act of winding – performed, of course, by a living being – charges the material of the spring with incipient movement; as it is wound, the spring itself becomes a whirl. The cogs and hands of the clock might rotate, but at its heart is the revolution of the spring. And as Bergson said of the living organism, the spring – in turning in on itself – contrives to hold out against the passage of time. Yet eventually, it marks time in its unwinding: in a cumulative sequence of escapements that punctate the evolution of life in its onward progress. As we shall see shortly, this has its precise parallel in the winding and reeling of thread.

On describing a circle

To better understand the circularity of life, let me set an exercise that will no doubt be familiar to anyone who has undergone lessons in school geometry. The task is to draw circles, using only a pencil and a compass (Ingold 2008b: 1796–7). Try as you might, you will never be able to produce a perfect circle. This is because the human body, like the bodies of most living creatures, is not designed for rotational motion. In the history of technology, the introduction of the crank marked a key step in converting the reciprocal back-and-forth movement of the limbs to a rotary one (White 1962: 103–17). With the compass, we attempt to achieve the same effect by gripping a shaft mounted at the apex between thumb and forefinger, and rubbing back and forth in a gesture known as 'twirling'. As I show below, twirling is whirling on a point, and the line that appears under your hand is the trace of this gesture, a form generated in its revolutionary movement. As such, it inevitably betrays the conditions of its production. For the velocity of the turn is never constant; moreover the uneven pressure of the pencil tip on paper inevitably leads to a line that varies in width and density. You have to start the line somewhere, and it is virtually impossible to conceal this starting point as it is always a little darker where the pencil point first makes contact with the paper, or where – in your effort to close the circle – the ending of your line overlaps its beginning.

Now we are taught, in school, to disregard these imperfections. Unavoidable they may be, but they are considered irrelevant to understanding the circle as a perfect geometrical form. The perfect form of the circle, however, is not a form of life. For in nature, as philosopher Michel Serres (2000: 58) points out, there are no perfect circles, only vortices. Where things are generated in the turning, and turn themselves, there can be 'no exact rounding off, no pure circumference ... The circle winds down in a conical helix'.[5] The perfect circle, to the contrary, neither turns nor is produced by turning. In its closure and finality – in masquerading as the outline of a figure rather than the trace of a movement or gesture – it is the very opposite of the helical whirl. No doubt this is what Blake had in mind when, in a polychrome print dating from 1795, he depicted the figure of Isaac Newton, the most celebrated mathematician of the age, submerged underwater, peering down at a geometric figure comprising the arc of a perfect circle within a triangle (Figure 3.1). Compass in hand, he measures the arc. For Blake, Newton's eye and compass epitomised the reduction of a spirit that, in its single-minded quest for geometric perfection, had turned its back on the vibrant and multicoloured profusion of the living world and sunk into the inky, stone-cold and lifeless depths of rational insensibility. Note, however, that Blake's Newton is measuring the arc with his compass rather than actually drawing it. The fingers of one hand hold the compass; with the index finger of the other hand, he points to a line. But the figure is already drawn, calling for no inscriptive movement on his part. How different things might have been, had he been called upon, like a schoolchild, to draw it himself!

Nowadays, of course, the compass has been all but banished from the classroom, to make way for computers that can instantly project or print out, to order, perfect circles of any desired diameter. Whether substituting the computer for the compass has actually enhanced mathematical thinking, however, is debatable. Many mathematicians argue to the contrary, and rail against the insistence, in conventional teaching, on logical closure and final proof (Lockhart 2009). They would say – and I agree – that real mathematical understanding can develop only when it is released from the dead hand of intellectual perfection. In drawing circles with compass and pencil, and never quite succeeding, the student can achieve a feel for the phenomenon of circularity that repudiates any distinction between the operations of the

Figure 3.1 William Blake, *Newton* (1795), print with pen and ink, and watercolour. Courtesy of the Tate Gallery.

intellect and skilled bodily practice. Such understanding is both open-ended and in touch with life, as intuitive as it is cognitive. In this sense, geometry is akin to music. With music, the more you practise a piece – the more you inhabit it – the more your understanding grows. This growth is inexhaustible, not convergent upon a limit. So too, by inhabiting the circle and entering into the whirl of its inscription, you can begin to know it from the inside, not as some timeless geometrical abstraction but as the temporal revolution of the ever-turning wheel of life.

Questioning words

Etymologically, 'whirl' is derived from Old Norse *hvirfla*, 'to turn' or 'to spin', and is one of a host of similarly sounding words, including 'twirl', 'swirl' and 'hurl'.[6] The precise derivation of these words is anyone's guess. Did 'twirl', perhaps, come from a compound of 'twist' and 'whirl'? Or did it come from Old English *þwirl* (meaning 'pot-stirrer')? Is 'swirl' just a variant of 'whirl', perhaps with its roots in the Dutch *zwirrelen* rather than the Norse *hvirfla*? Did 'hurl' have a quite different origin, in Low German *hurreln* (to throw, to dash), from which we also get the word 'hurry'? Perhaps then the resemblance of 'hurl' to 'whirl' is fortuitous. But if it is, why does 'hurl' have, as one of its meanings 'to drive a wheeled vehicle', a meaning it has in common with 'whirl', whence comes the Scots term *hurlbarrow* for what we more commonly call the wheelbarrow? Is there a connection, after all, between 'whirl' and 'wheel'? No one knows the answer to any of these questions. Yet what the words I have listed all share is a strong component of phonological iconicity (Gell 1995; Kohn 2013: 27–33). We can learn more of their meaning from simply pronouncing them, and from the feeling this induces. With twirl, as we have already seen in the exercise of drawing a circle with a compass and pencil, the revolution is centred on a point, vividly expressed by the hard, consonantal 't-' before the '-wirl'. It could be the compass point, or the pointed shoe of the ballerina performing pirouettes on stage, or the finger-point of the gentleman twirling his moustache. With swirl, by contrast, what counts is the fluidity of liquid motion, with the hissing of the fricative 's' conveying a sense of escape rather than punctuality.

But perhaps the comparison with 'hurl' is the most interesting. Say the word out loud and you feel the air being let out from the chest without obstruction. Say 'whirl' and it feels quite different. It is as though the air were partially bottled prior to release: an incipient rather than an actual exhalation, a preparation for letting go. Indeed the difference between mouthing the two words, 'whirl' and 'hurl', is a bit like what happens in athletics, when the discus-thrower first whirls with his body, round and round, gaining angular momentum while the discus remains in his hand, only to release it, hurling the object as far as he can where it hits the ground, all energy spent. For the athlete the whirl is a gathering up, an acceleration: in the idiom of Gilles Deleuze and Félix Guattari (2004: 28), it is 'where things pick up speed'. The hurl, to the contrary, is a spin-off. So it is too with breathing in and breathing out. Breathing in is a gathering, a rewinding; breathing out a propulsive release. One sweeps around, the other launches forth through an opening at the centre thus formed (Ingold 2015: 66–8). Of course one cannot literally speak on the inhalation; nevertheless one can deflect the flow of air to create an eddy, so as momentarily to hold it back, like a bubble that has still to burst. Why should the onomatopoetic variant of 'whirl', by which we imitate what we commonly take to be its sound, end with a rolled 'r' that can be continued for as long as one has breath left to pronounce it? *Whirrrrr* ... It could be the sound of a flying insect, or of the helicopter's rotor as it lands or takes to the air, or of the ship's propeller in water, or of the bullroarer. Unlike the continuous hum or murmur, the roll of 'whirr' suggests a movement that goes against the grain, a ratcheting, an infolding. This, in turn, sets up the aerial or aquatic vibrations that make it such a noisy affair. In the rolled 'r', you can almost feel the revolutions of the whirl, right there in your mouth.

Most remarkable, however, is the fact that 'whirl' begins with the very same sound that, in the English language, prefixes all interrogatives. As noted above, the whirl is not a resultant but a becoming, a turning *into* that which remains unknown, a ceaseless questioning from which any answer continually recedes. With the whirl, the thing is not yet settled; neither in its present nor in its future form. It is a problem, for which the steps towards a solution are not already given. Whither is it going? When will it arrive? What will it be? Why? We don't know. Whirl is a question, *where*? Hurl delivers the answer, *here*! The scribes of medieval Europe must have known this when they converted what used to be prosodic markers to help the orator in the declamation of a text into what we now know as punctuation. The form of the question mark, with which we are so familiar today, is no less than a miniature whirl.

?

Moreover since every question solicits a response, it is addressed to the ear of the listener. The iconic resemblance of the question mark to the involute form of the human ear, with the curl above as the helix and the dot below as the lobe, is surely not fortuitous. What the early architects of punctuation probably did not know, however, is that as sonic vibrations penetrate deep within the ear, they are funnelled into the spiralling tube of the cochlea. It turns out that every one of us carries a miniature whirl in each ear! And when you place one cochlear form over another, by covering the ear with a spiral shell, the combination spontaneously generates its own sound, at once reminding us of the maelstrom of the ocean, itself a whirl with an oasis of stillness at its eye. In book IV of *The Excursion*, William Wordsworth pictured a curious child holding a seashell to his ear, astonished by the sound that seems to issue from it. 'Even in such a shell', he mused, 'the Universe itself / Is to the ear of Faith', imparting tidings of 'central peace, subsisting at the heart / Of endless agitation'.[7]

Spinning threads

Tracked along another path, the chain of word associations leads into the language of spinning, in which *whirl*, taken as a noun rather than as a verb, is simply a variant of *whorl*. The whorl is a small, doughnut-shaped disc, of some three or four centimetres in diameter, commonly carved from stone, bone or hardwood (Ingold 2015: 56–7). Topologically, the whorl takes the form of the torus,[8] but mounted on a shaft or spindle it bears comparison with the spinning top. Standing upright only for so long as it whirls around, the top – as Serres (2000: 29) remarks – is literally a *circum-stance* which, thanks to its properties of dynamic, rotational stability, 'may serve as a little model of the world'. Just such a model, indeed, was proposed by Plato, in

Book X of the *The Republic*, in which a nested series of eight whorls, of a form just like those used on earth, and mounted on a cosmic spindle, were supposed to hold the planets in their orbits. Back on earth, scaled down to ordinary size and in the hands of the spinster, the whorl is fitted to the lower shaft of the hand-held drop-spindle in order to give weight and angular momentum to the spindle when spinning a fleece from a distaff. Due to its relatively imperishable material, the whorl is often the best evidence we have of the practice of spinning in deep prehistory, where nothing remains of the threads or the fabrics woven from them.

Nowadays, when most thread is industrially produced, much of it from synthetic material, spinning has all but disappeared and is sustained – at least in Western societies – only by a select band of hobbyists and craftspeople. But for the greater part of human history, among peoples from around the world, it was a ubiquitous activity carried on day after day, for hours on end, in some societies only by women, in others only by men, and in yet others by both men and women. Considering its ubiquity, however, spinning has attracted remarkably little attention from historians and ethnologists. For most historians, it only comes into the picture with the onset of industrialisation; for ethnologists the focus has always been more on weaving than on spinning. It is all too easy to forget that there can be no weaving without thread, and no thread that has not first been spun (Mitchell 2006).

Indeed I am as guilty of this neglect as anyone. In a work on the history and anthropology of the line (Ingold 2007a: 39–71) I had distinguished two major classes of line, threads and traces, and had shown how threads transform into traces in the formation of surfaces, as in weaving, and traces into threads in their dissolution, as when a woven textile is unravelled. It had seemed to me that weaving could be taken as a model for both making and thinking. To treat making as a modality weaving is to emphasise process over product, to see form and pattern as emergent within the process rather than pre-conceived and imposed on raw material. To treat thinking as a modality of weaving is to adumbrate an alternative mathematics, rooted in the routines of everyday life, which permits an open-ended exploration of the multiple possibilities of permutation and recombination, and of the patterns and symmetries that result. Making and thinking, thus conceived, could both be understood as ways of working with lines.

Yet in all this, I had given no thought to how these lines are generated in the first place. Whatever happened to spinning? What if we were to regard making and thinking as modalities of spinning rather than weaving? Does not the turner spin his wood on the lathe, and the potter his clay on the wheel? Do we not turn over ideas in our minds, and get our heads into a spin? And do we not spin our narratives before weaving them into text? Might the whirl be as generative as the weave? Or yet more so? I have scarcely begun to address these questions, and can offer no more than a few speculations on the topic, partly provoked by my first lessons in how to spin from a distaff, using a drop-spindle, under the guidance of one of the few specialists in the comparative ethnography of spinning, Tracy Hudson.[9]

What took me most by surprise, in my initial attempts, was just how discontinuous an operation it is. Naively, I had imagined that with the revolution of the spindle, the thread would just come spooling out. Of course it did not, for one very interesting reason. This is that the twist travels upstream, and not downstream, from the revolving spindle up towards the distaff. Periodically, then, you have to interrupt the spin, reel the thread you have spun onto the shaft of the spindle (starting from above the whorl), and commence the spin again. The mistake I often found myself making was to reel on in a way that simply reversed the spin, thus undoing what I had just done. Though I have yet to think through the implications of this discovery for our understanding of thinking and making, it does lead me to question what I have certainly assumed up to now, namely that making and thinking entail an ongoing forward movement. What if every act of making and thinking took you *back* to the source from which your materials were derived, rather than further from them, such that the actual growth of the work would be an accumulation or ratcheting up of these successive backward movements? Is it only by the accumulation of successive gatherings or recollections, of memories, that we can advance? Is the future a succession of vortices in each of which we must necessarily find ourselves spinning into the past, only to reel on to the next?

Evidently the whorl winds up, not down; drawing tension into the thread, not releasing it. It is here that we can return to the parallel with the clock. For winding the thread, just like winding the clock, is a return towards the source, a revolution that goes against the grain, in which the materials – whether the metals of the spring or the fibres of the fleece – turn in on themselves, straining against the inexorable march of time. And just as with the rotations of clock, or indeed with the rolled 'r' of 'whir', it is through the accumulation of escapements, reeled upon the spindle, that the line of thread is advanced. What, then, is the relation between the whirl of the spindle and the line of thread? This is what I had missed, in my earlier comparison of the thread and the trace. With the trace, as when I draw circles with pencil and compass, the line issues directly from the movement of the tool and from the gesture of the hand that holds it. But with the thread, the line does not record the revolutions of the whorl, even though it is formed by them. Earlier, I observed that in the whirl, the turning movement continually gives rise to a centre of relative rest – an 'eye', if you will. And the thread-line, far from moving *around* the eye, issues *from* the eye itself as it moves. This observation brings me to my final theme, which concerns the meanings of wind.

The whirling wind?

Bergson, it will be recalled, compared living things to eddies of dust raised by the passing wind. It seems that the atmospheric wind is itself inclined to *wind*, turning upon itself into a whirl. Wind and *wind* are of course the same word, nowadays distinguished only in pronunciation, which is why I have had to resort here to italics in order to distinguish the turn of the whirl, as when we *wind* a clock, from the current of air, as in a windstorm. But if the gyre of the *wind* gives rise to things, that of the wind can rip them asunder. The very same vortex which grows the bodies of the living, as Serres (2000: 29) notes, can also destroy ships at sea: it is 'order and disorder at once'. When the gyre is of moderate acceleration we call it a whirlwind, but if the acceleration grows to be of destructive force, it becomes a tornado, or on a greatly expanded scale, a cyclone. At its heart is the eye. We can track the movement of a storm in the path of its eye, and in the trail of dust or destruction it leaves in its wake. That is, we can track its evolution. That the storm evolves is not in doubt, since its movement is not like the transport of a solid body from one location to another across the sky. The storm does not move like an aeroplane! To the contrary, it moves by perpetually winding up on its advancing front while unwinding at the rear (Ingold 2015: 54). Indeed we might say of the storm that it is continually losing the thread, much as happened to me in my first attempts at spinning when, every time I would reel my thread onto the spindle, I would undo what I had just spun. That is why the storm leaves no trace of its evolution in the air, but only on the ground. Nevertheless, we must distinguish – as we have done before with regard to life in general and its specific cycles – between the evolution of the storm and its revolution.

Let's get back to Bergson. Here he is, once again insisting on the same distinction:

> The act by which life goes forward to the creation of a new form, and the act by which this form is shaped, are two different and often antagonistic movements. The first is continuous with the second, but cannot continue in it without being drawn aside from its direction.
>
> (Bergson 1922: 129)

So it is, too, with the storm. Yesterday, a powerful storm struck the coast of eastern Scotland, where I live. I went walking along the shore, and had to struggle against the wind coming from the south. Later, the strength dropped, only to be replaced by a northerly. The storm itself, however, was tracking from west to east. Walking below as the storm passed overhead, my experience was of an airflow that had been 'drawn aside', as Bergson would say, from its prevailing westerly direction and put into an anti-clockwise spin. First the leading edge arrived, as the wind direction swung from west to south, then came the eye, and finally the trailing edge as the wind got up again from the north. And now, in the aftermath, only a gentle westerly remains. Could this image of the passing storm, I wonder, provide the key to solving a problem by which I had long been perplexed? Expressed in its most general terms, the problem is of how to understand the environment we inhabit.

I had come up with two possible answers. One was to think of the environment as a *meshwork*, woven by the myriad lines of living beings as they thread their ways through the world. The other was to think of it as an *atmosphere*, an aerial domain suffused with light, sound and feeling. Is the environment, then, a meshwork or an atmosphere, or is it both? And if both, what is the relation between them (Ingold 2015: 87–8)? Perhaps the answer lies in respiration – in the alternation, common to all forms of animate life, between breathing in and breathing out. With every intake of breath, we draw the wind into a bodily circulation that deviates from, or even reverses, our direction of travel. But with every outbreath we release it once again into the prevailing current. Thus the body, according to cultural theorist Astrid Neimanis (2012: 85), is 'a singular, dynamic whorl dissolving in a complex, fluid circulation'. Serres (2000: 37), likewise, compares himself to 'a vortex ... that comes undone', unwinding as fast as it is formed. Recall the discus thrower: the whirl prepares, the hurl delivers. *Whirl – hurl; whirl – hurl.* With every whirl, we draw in the atmosphere; with every hurl we weave a path in the meshwork. The same principle is at work, whether with the organism, the clockwork spring, the spindle-whorl or the wind. In every case, linearity issues from circularity, and circularity from linearity, in a rhythmic oscillation that is foundational to the whirl of life.

Chapter 4

Evolution in the minor key; or, the soul of wisdom

The major and the minor

There are two kinds of science. One of these has long been ascendant in the Western canon. It imagines a world of elementary constituents, particles of matter that interact and combine in ever more complex and diverse configurations to compose the world we know from experience. In this world, solidity is primordial, fluidity derivative, identity and constancy come before difference and variation, movement can be described as the displacement of a body from point to point across the void of space, and complexity can be factored out by way of the quantitative computation of its elements. But the world imagined by the other kind of science is opposite in every way. It is matter-full, not full of matter; its elements are given not as discrete particles but in the plenum of materials. Here the properties of things emerge not as the compound effects of punctual and punctuated interactions but as variation or irregularity in the material flux. The slightest deviation, amplified in its effects, can spin out a cascade of more or less ephemeral forms. Differentiation and heterogeneity, then, are not so much statistical as topological, produced in the folding and crumpling of surfaces and volumes rather than the aggregation and dispersal of particulate substance. Things in this world are not naturally solid; they have to be kept that way and, like eddies in a stream, they will do so only for as long as the flow carries on.

Following Gilles Deleuze and Félix Guattari (2004: 398), I shall call the first kind of science – the one with which we are most familiar – the science of the major. And I shall call the second the science of the minor. I shall insist that we cannot have one without the other, that the major always trails the minor like a thing and its shadow, even though the latter is routinely suppressed. This is as true of the sciences of life as it is of physics and chemistry, and as true of the sciences of mind as of those of life. It is with life and mind that I am principally concerned here. I want to show that the theory of evolution by variation under natural selection, while almost universally accepted today, is written unequivocally in the major key. As such, it is fundamentally incomplete, shorn of the minor variations that are of the essence

DOI: 10.4324/9781003171713-6

of life itself. I draw inspiration, here, from the philosophy of Alfred North Whitehead, on which I already touched briefly in Chapter 1. Living things, for Whitehead, can be apprehended in two ways, either from the outside, as the embodiments of evolved design, or from the inside, by joining with the generative movement of their growth and formation. To follow the second course is to enter into an evolution in the minor key. But this is as much an evolution of mind as it is of life, if indeed the two can be distinguished at all. And that's where wisdom comes into the picture.

In the major, the mind figures as a suite of cognitive capacities – or more comprehensively as an intelligence – fashioned like the body by the cumulative effects of natural selection. Intelligence, we suppose, is a property of the self. It belongs to the individual, and underwrites its ability to interact with others in a way that is both intentional in its objectives and cognisant of the intentions of others. But in the minor, mind is not a property but a process, the infolding and unfolding of a continuum of affective relations. The mind infolded is what I shall call the soul. And wisdom, I shall argue, lies in its unfolding. If intelligence underwrites the power of intentionality, wisdom is about attending to things, both opening up and responding to their presence. Where the self is the seat of intention, the soul is the wellspring of attention. As the self is to the soul, so intelligence is to wisdom, the major to the minor. Wisdom, in short, is not an evolved capacity of mind but mind evolving, in the minor key. To bring wisdom back into our thinking about evolution, then, is not to speculate on the nature and origins of intelligent design. It is rather to recognise that there is another side to the evolutionary process that is about neither intelligence nor design, but about the ongoing generation of being, or in a word, *ontogenesis*.

The evolution of life

To begin to unpack this rather condensed formulation, let me return to Whitehead. In his *Science and the Modern World*, Whitehead (1925) argued that there are two sides to what he called 'the machinery involved in the development of nature'. The first, generally going under the rubric of natural selection and associated with the name of Darwin, has 'a given environment with organisms adapting themselves to it'. But the second, 'the other side of the evolutionary machinery, the neglected side, is expressed by the word *creativeness*' (Whitehead 1925: 140). So what is this creativeness – the emphasis is Whitehead's own – to which mainstream science has allegedly turned a blind eye? Many biologists, architects of the so-called modern synthesis of Darwinian theory and population genetics, were convinced that variation under natural selection is a force of creation in itself, and that nothing further needs be added. One of them was Theodosius Dobzhansky, according to whom selection is the 'antichance factor' that would test the genetic variations produced by chance mutation, in countless permutations and combinations, so as to arrive at adaptively coherent patterns. For Dobzhansky, selection is creative precisely because of its capacity not just to weed out deleterious mutations, but to construct such patterns from the building blocks of heredity. This creativity, Dobzhansky (1974: 329) thought, bore comparison with the arts of invention, having all the qualities of intelligent design but with the selective figure of antichance substituting for any transcendent or mortal design agent. Indeed we can regard every new pattern, he declared, 'as an artistic embodiment of a new conception of living'.[1]

A conception of living is one thing, however, life itself is another; and to have constructed a design for a new form of life is not enough to fashion a living being. In an evolution that consisted only in the phylogenetic succession of designs, and their modification, ontogenesis could be no more than a spin-off, expended within each generation in bringing about the replication of design elements in the next. Life, it seems, falls through the cracks of hereditary variation and recombination. And it was specifically the creativeness of the life process itself that Whitehead was after. His inspiration owed much to the philosophy of his contemporary, Henri Bergson (1922). In Bergson's understanding, as we already saw in Chapter 1 (page 24), there is nothing creative in the rearrangements of elements already known. It would be like shaking a kaleidoscope: every shake reveals a new pattern, but there is nothing in the new not already present in the old. Similarly, the recombination of hereditary elements – that is, of elements that, *by definition*, are already present at the inauguration of every new lifecycle – is bereft of creative potential. However, there is more to life and growth, Bergson insisted, than the reconfiguration of the known, and it was in this excess that he found the source of creative evolution. It is as if life were ever surpassing itself, giving rise to further life as growth gives rise to further growth. This is the life of *natura naturans*, of nature's becoming, rather than *natura naturata*, the infinite diversity of ready-created forms which so impressed Dobzhansky.

To refer to this process of nature's surpassing itself, Whitehead (1929: 410) coined the term 'concrescence'. *Crescent* means always undergoing creation – growing and developing – rather than that which is already created; the prefix *con-* means 'together with, or alongside'. Literally, then, concrescence is the condition of *things or beings undergoing creation together with or alongside one another*. This is the condition of living beings, ontogenetically and relationally co-evolving. In order to grasp this evolution, however, it is necessary to imagine the world in a way very different from what is commonly assumed in the science of the major. The majority assumption is that a living organism is an object, albeit of great complexity, constructed from simpler elements by means of templates that have themselves been assembled from a basic biochemical vocabulary. This assumption, however, both depends on and in turn reproduces the imagination of a world composed of primordially discrete and enumerable entities. As nature 'builds up' from the elementary to the complex, we suppose that it is the mission of science to 'drill down', to engineer in reverse what nature has first assembled in order to reveal what are often dubbed the building blocks of life, and to fathom the principles of their construction. Indeed the very idea of complexity precipitates its opposite, namely simplicity, with its connotations of singularity of form and homogeneity of substance. Merely to say of an organism that it is complex is to take it for a whole that can, in principle, be reduced by analysis into its simpler parts.

But there are things, in our experience, that defy such analysis. Is a crumpled piece of paper more complex than its plane equivalent? Do we simplify our clothes by ironing them? Is the tree simplified on shedding its leaves in autumn, or the meadow simplified under a winter blanket of snow? Is a river in spate, a stormy sea or a cloud-ridden sky more complex than the gentle flow, flat calm or ethereal blue of river, sea or sky in fair weather? Questions of simplicity and complexity do not arise here because in every case, we start not with a vacuum filled with matter but with a matter-full plenum, rendered heterogeneous through differential infolding and unfolding. The crumples of paper and crease-lines in fabric emerge as the material is first folded up and then unfolded; likewise, tree leaves and meadow-grass unfold from buds and seeds. The river's eddies and ripples are the folds of its running waters, the foaming waves folds of the sea and clouds folds in the crumpled air-mass of the atmosphere. In every case, the fold is intrinsic to the material: difference; in other words, it is brought about from within. It is interstitial. I refer to the process of folding, accordingly, as one of *interstitial differentiation* (Ingold 2015: 23). What if we were to think of life, too, as such a process? It would be the task of life, then, not to assemble parts into wholes, distinguished by the diverse configurations of their elements, but to draw things out from the primordially undifferentiated flux of potential and hold them there, albeit only for a while, until they dissolve once more. It would be a task, in short, of differentiation, not of construction.[2]

This is precisely how Bergson thought of it. Life in general, in his view, is movement or flow; it is the very substance of time or duration, and of our own existence as temporal beings. We cannot go against it, or resist it entirely, but we can temporarily draw it aside. For Bergson, as we saw in the last chapter, every living organism comes into being through such a deviation in the flow. You could compare it, as he did, to a whirlwind or to an eddy in the stream. Something – some irregularity of bank or bed – causes the otherwise evenly running waters to swerve. Amplified and accelerated under its own momentum, the swerve turns in on itself to become a vortex, holding back the waters caught up in it until they are released once again into the mainstream. Thus while life in general continually advances, along a line that would be perfectly straight were it not for the irregularities in its course, particular manifestations of life lag behind, never stopping the flow but deflecting it into circuits, each of which is a lifecycle. And though we might imagine the lifeform to be a relatively stable, self-contained object, with an inside and an outside, Bergson (1922: 125) shows us that the appearance is deceptive, for in truth the permanence of the form is but the envelope of a movement. Like the eddy in the stream, the living organism is not a container and it has no content. Its topologically convoluted surfaces, which defy any opposition between interior and exterior, are really but folds in the plenary fabric of the ever-worlding world.

The self and the soul

Let us now turn from life and the organism to wisdom and the soul. For it is my contention that a parallel argument applies. I aim to show that just as the organism is a vortex in the flow of life, so the soul is a vortex in the flow of awareness or consciousness. And in this regard, the soul's enfoldment of wisdom stands in stark contrast to the intelligence of the self.[3] As wisdom shadows intelligence, so the soul shadows the self. To grasp the contrast, however, we first need to address a confusion that afflicts much anthropological writing on the soul. This concerns the question of what it means to say of the soul that it is an interior property of being, in essence spiritual rather than material or physical. While there has been a tendency throughout the history of Judaeo-Christian thought to narrow the soul to human beings, on the grounds that humankind alone was created in the image of divinity, people of other faiths – or whose practices appear to rest on alternative ontological foundations – have long been more generous in crediting some form of inner life to nonhuman kinds.[4] Most generous of all are people known to anthropology as subscribing to various forms of 'animism', including many indigenous folk around the world in regions as diverse as Amazonia, Southeast Asia and the circumpolar North. For them, not only are animals and plants of every kind potentially and often multiply endowed with souls, but so also are manifold phenomena that we might think of as inanimate, from hills and mountains to rivers and pools, stones, and even artefacts.

If there is one characteristic of animism that we can all accept, writes anthropologist Philippe Descola (2013: 129) in his magisterial survey of the diverse ways human beings have sought to organise their relations with the world they inhabit, and to render this world intelligible, it is 'the attribution by humans to nonhumans of an interiority identical to their own'.[5] In this plethora of souls, common to all, beings and things of different kinds are distinguished, according to Descola, by their physical properties. Animals, for example, are distinguished by their bodies, which enable them to operate in the particular ways they do: the fish to swim, the bird to fly, the human to walk, and so on. Everything has a soul, but everything also has its distinctive way of manifesting its physical presence in the world. Indeed, for Descola, this division between what he calls 'interiority' and 'physicality' is by no means unique to animism but underwrites all human efforts, whether practical or linguistic, to come to terms with being. For those of us raised in Western societies, and who consider ourselves to be 'modern', the same division appears in the form of the familiar dichotomy between mind and nature. What is peculiar to animism, however – distinguishing it, *inter alia*, from the naturalism of the West – is that the attribution of interiority is generalised across the board rather than being confined to humans. But conversely, manifest differences on the plane of physicality are not assimilated in animism, as they are in modernity, to a universalising concept of nature.

The concept of interiority, however, inevitably begs the question 'interior to what?' This, I think, is where Descola goes astray. For in opposing it to physicality, he contrives to set up the interior as a bounded domain, set over against an exterior world. As the occupant of this domain, the soul appears contained. From the point of view of its possessor, it is 'in here'; the physical world 'out there'. Locked up inside its bodily or earthly container, the soul is immobilised. It cannot then be animate in itself; it cannot live or breathe. It can exist only as an immaterial principle, of which life is no more than an exterior emanation. This is not unlike the way in which modern thought construes the intelligence of the self: as a hidden design agent that resides inside its hard, bodily shell and pulls the strings of action. The self thinks, reflects, forms its own theories of what might be out there, or of the thinking of selves equally hidden from direct perception, considers its options, delivers its intentions. But it is left to the body to engage in lively intercourse with the world. The mistake that Descola makes, along with legions of anthropological predecessors, is to suppose that the soul of animism is similarly enclosed within its physical housing, and thereby insulated from the turbulence of worldly existence. For everything that people credited with an ontology of animism have been telling us points to the contrary.[6]

What they tell us is that the soul is itself the breath of life, that souls are not agencies but movements, that they are sites not of intention but of affectation, that they are not closed but radically open to the world and therefore vulnerable to attack or loss, that they are concentrations of energy and vitality that must ever remain in circulation if life is to carry on. How, then, should we think of the interiority of the soul? The answer, I suggest, is to shift into the minor key. It is to enter into a plenary world of concrescence, where things – to adopt an apt expression from Erin Manning (2016: 112) – are not yet settled but ever 'edging into form'. Interiority, in such a world, conveys a quality not of containment but of *immanence* (Deleuze 2001). Immanent life, far from taking refuge within the bounds of final forms, unfolds in the very relations and processes that continually give rise to them. It abides in the interstices wherein, as with the singular surface of a Möbius strip, its twin faces – of interiority and physicality – become one. Far from being *opposed* to physicality, as is the interiority of containment, the interiority of immanence runs into physicality, and physicality into interiority, with no breach of continuity (Ingold 2016a: 311). Apprehended topologically, in the minor key, the world has only one surface, and every soul is borne along in its folds.

Let us return to Bergson's image of the living organism as a vortex, brought about by a swerve or deviation in the current of life. We have noted that the vortex is not a container, and it is not contained; it is rather the ever-emerging form of turbulence. The soul, likewise, can be envisaged as vortex in the stream of consciousness, continually winding and unwinding, infolding and unfolding, in an unceasing circulatory movement. Here's Michel Serres (2000: 37), baring his own soul: 'I am myself a deviation, and my soul declines, my global body is open, adrift. It slips, irreversibly, on the slope. Who am I? A vortex.' Serres's soul is not inside his body; on the contrary, it seems that his body is like a ship in a maelstrom, adrift in the vertiginous tumult of his own soul. Only at the eye of the vortex does stillness reign. Like the vortex, the soul arises in a deviation, a transient 'falling out of step' with life, as fellow philosopher Gilbert Simondon (1993: 300) describes the process of ontogenesis – or what he calls individuation – wherein the metastable forms of being emerge from the generative flux of becoming.[7] But in this falling out of step also lies the work of memory. Indeed, in a certain sense, the soul *is* memory, understood not as a faculty of cognition but as a winding up of the generative forces of life which – like the winding of a spring-loaded clock, to recall a parallel from the last chapter – both holds out against the passage of time and charges the body with incipient movement. In this charge lies the potential for future transformation.

Wisdom is ecological

This brings me, finally, to wisdom. For my thesis is that wisdom lies in the transformative potential of the soul. I have four points to make in support of this thesis. The first is that wisdom is quite different from knowledge; indeed they may operate at cross-purposes. The self, in carving out a place for itself in the world, seeks the safety and security of established positions. Every increment of knowledge adds another stone to the walls with which it shores itself up against the onslaught of physical externality. Thus knowledge breeds inattention, as the self is driven ever further within a citadel of its own making. The soul, by contrast, is defenceless, and therein lies its wisdom. Whereas knowledge treats the world as its object, for wisdom the world is its milieu. Knowing is about fixing things within the concepts and categories of thought; wisdom unfixes and unsettles. To know is to have things accounted for, explained away or embedded in context so they no longer trouble us; to be wise is to bring things back into the fullness of presence, to pay attention, and to care. Knowing is rational and intellectual; wisdom relational and affective. Knowledge has its challenges, wisdom has its ways; but where the challenges of knowledge close in on their solutions, the ways of wisdom open out to a process of life. Where knowledge protects, wisdom exposes; where knowledge makes us safe, wisdom makes us vulnerable. Knowledge empowers, wisdom does not. But what wisdom loses in power it gains in existential strength. For while knowledge may hold the world to account, it is wisdom that brings it to life. Knowledge is in the major key, wisdom in the minor.

My second point is that wisdom is fundamentally attentional. It continually draws our awareness out into the world, rather than referring it back to an originating intention in the mind of the subject. For an act to be intentional, according to the psychology of cognition, it must be founded in an evolved capacity to grasp what is 'out there' within the frame of received concepts and categories. You first have to know what or whom you are dealing with; only then can you interact with them. In the case of other persons, this means speculating on their mental states, or on what their intentions might be, on the evidence of observed behaviour. In short, you have to be in possession of what psychologists call a 'theory of mind'.[8] Closure, here, is the default position, from which we are supposed to attribute intentions, motives and standpoints to others. But the soul, as we have seen, is not a sanctuary. It does not aim to theorise about the world, or about other minds, from within the space of its own reflections. Rather, it already mingles with the ebbs and flows of the phenomenal world, even before there can be subjects with intentions, or objects towards which these intentions are directed. The soul is there in the very incipience of the world, in its moment-to-moment coming-into-being. In its wisdom it cuts through the transverse connections between intentions and their objects as a river between its banks. This flow has neither beginning not end, neither origin nor destination. For as life generates further life, wisdom perpetually surpasses itself.

Thirdly, while wisdom is different from knowledge, it is very close in its meaning to skill. For skill lies not in the imposition of form from without, upon homogeneous matter, but in the division, from within, of materials that have their own vitality and inclinations. The wise practitioner knows to respect these inclinations and to work with them rather than against them. In effect, wisdom – just like life itself – is a process of interstitial differentiation. It draws out form from within the flux of materials. The judgement of wisdom, therefore, does not sit in sovereignty over the world, but enters into it, always *in medias res*, going along with things and splitting them this way and that. It is not transversal, delivering a final verdict for execution on the basis of information received, but longitudinal, following the grain of the world's becoming and bending it to an ever-evolving purpose (Ingold 2011a: 211). The very etymology of the word 'skill' points to judgement of this kind. With its roots in the Middle Low German *schillen*, 'to make a difference', and in the Old Norse *skilja*, 'to divide, separate, distinguish, decide', it also shares an etymological affinity with the word 'shell', a casing that is opened up by splitting or cleaving along the grain (Ingold 2018a: 42). Thus wisdom is not a faculty, not a supplement that might be added to a being, which some perhaps possess, and others lack. It is not possessive at all, but existential. Wisdom is not what you have but what you are. It is a way of going along in the world, and it has paths rather than endpoints.

Wisdom, in short, evolves in the minor key. It is alive with transformative potential, but this is not a potential that is ever actualised. For wisdom does not transform the world, it is rather the world's never-ceasing transformation of itself – that is, its worlding. This is my final point, and once again it distinguishes the minor from the major. In an evolution in the major key, as we have seen, every life begins with a novel conception and ends with its material realisation. In the same vein – and referring specifically human life – we speak of education as enabling the immature human being to fulfil his or her potential. Once fulfilled, the potential is exhausted, used up. But wisdom's potential, like that of life itself, is both inexhaustible and undestined.[9] One can never say of life, or of wisdom, that it is ever closer to its realisation or further from it. For it is a movement not of closure but of opening: an opening to experience, to becoming, to difference. Like a spring from its source, wisdom continually wells up from within the continuum of affective relations that animates the soul. To borrow another phrase from Manning (2016: 6), wisdom is the 'potential for a collectivity alive with difference'. But this is not collectivity as it would be understood in the science of the major, as a plurality of discrete individuals. It is rather an ecology of relations, unfolding from the inside in a continual movement of interstitial differentiation. This unfolding is an evolution in the minor key. And wisdom, as its dynamic, is not cognitive but ecological.

Chapter 5

Dreaming of dragons

Facing the facts

In the year 1620, the English philosopher-statesman Francis Bacon set out a plan for what was to be a massive work of science, entitled *The Great Instauration*. Dedicated to King James I, who had recently appointed Bacon as his Lord Chancellor, the work was never completed. In his prolegomenon, however, Bacon railed against traditional ways of knowing that continually mixed up the reality of the world with its configurations in the minds of men. If only the mind were as clear and even as a perfect mirror, then – said Bacon – it would 'reflect the genuine rays of things'. But it is not. Cracked and deformed by flaws both innate and acquired, by instinct and indoctrination, the mind distorts the images that are cast upon its surface, by way of the senses, and cannot – if left to its own devices – be relied upon to deliver a true account of things as they are. There is but one way out of this predicament, Bacon argued, and that is by appeal to the facts. 'Those', he wrote, 'who aspire not to guess and divine, but to discover and know, who propose not to devise mimic and fabulous worlds of their own, but to examine and dissect the nature of this very world itself, must go to the facts themselves for everything' (Bacon 1858: 27–8).[1]

Bacon's words have an unmistakeable contemporary ring. Today's science continues to found its legitimacy upon its recourse to the data, which are repeatedly checked and rechecked in a never-ending search for truth through the elimination of error. And for the most part the sciences of mind and culture, psychology and anthropology, have ridden on the back of the same enterprise. That is to say, they have colluded in the division between what Bacon called the 'world itself', the reality of nature that can be discovered only through systematic scientific investigation, and the various imaginary worlds that people in different times and places have conjured up and which – in their ignorance of science and its methods – they have oftentimes taken for reality. Where anthropologists busy themselves with the comparative analysis of these imaginary worlds, psychologists purport to study the mechanisms, presumed to be universal, that govern their construction. All

DOI: 10.4324/9781003171713-7

agree that the realms of reality and the imagination should on no account be confused. For the very authority of science rests upon its claim to disclose, behind the home-made 'figments' that the imagination paints before our eyes, the facts of what is really there. One can of course study figment as well as fact, so as to deliver what many anthropologists still call 'emic' rather than 'etic' accounts, but to mix the two is to allow our judgement to be clouded by error and illusion. 'For God forbid', as Bacon (1858: 32–3) put it, 'that we should give out a dream of our imagination for a pattern of the world.'

My contention in this chapter is that Bacon's injunction, which modern science has taken to its heart, has had fateful consequences for human life and habitation, cutting the imagination adrift from its earthly moorings and leaving it to float like a mirage above the road we tread in our material life (Ingold 1997: 238). With our hopes and dreams suffused in the ether of illusion, life itself appears diminished. Shorn of its creative impulse, it no longer gives cause for wonder or astonishment. Indeed, among those of us educated into the values of a society in which the authority of scientific knowledge reigns supreme, the division of real life and the imagination into the two mutually exclusive realms of fact and fable has become so engrained as to be self-evident. The problem, in our estimation, has been one of how to reach some kind of accommodation between the two. How can we make a space for art and literature, for religion, or for the beliefs and practices of indigenous peoples, in an economy of knowledge in which the search for the true nature of things has become the exclusive prerogative of rational science? Do we suffer the imagination to persist in our midst, or tolerate its penchant for fantasy, out of a compensatory wish for enchantment in a world that has otherwise ceased to enthral? Do we keep it as a sign of creativity, as a badge of civilisation, out of respect for cultural diversity, or merely for our own entertainment? Such questions are endemic, yet the one thing we forget in posing them is how hard it is, in our experience, to split the reality of our life in the world, and of the world in which we live, from the meditative currents of our imagination. Indeed the problem is the very opposite of what we take it to be: not of how to reconcile the dreams of our imagination with patterns in the world, but of how to separate them in the first place.

Historically, this separation was but slowly and painfully achieved, in the religious upheavals of the Reformation and the turbulent beginnings of early modern science, in which Bacon – along with his exact contemporary, Galileo – played a pivotal part. But the historical process is recapitulated today in the education of every schoolchild who is taught, on pain of failure in his or her examinations, to distrust the sensuous, to prize intellect over intuition, and to regard the imagination as an escape from real life rather than its impulse. Almost by definition, it seems, the imaginary is unreal: it is our word for what does *not* exist. As every modern parent knows, for example, *there's no such thing as a dragon.*[2] We grown-ups are convinced that dragons are creatures of the imagination. Having seen them pictured in the books we read when we were children, and that we in turn read to our own offspring, we are familiar with their general appearance: scaly bodies, long forked tails, flared nostrils, sabre-like teeth and flaming mouths. These monsters roam the virtual terrain of children's literature alongside a host of other creatures of similarly fictive provenance. Some, of course, have real zoological counterparts. While the ever-popular tyrannosaurus rex is conveniently extinct, other animals – from cobras to crocodiles and from bears to lions – are still around and occasionally claim human lives.[3] On encountering such creatures in the flesh, we would do well to fear them.

Their fictive cousins, however, give no cause for alarm, for the only people they can eat are as imaginary as themselves. Along with the stuff of nightmares, these creatures are sequestered in a zone of apparitions and illusions that is rigorously partitioned from the domain of real life. We calm the sleeper who wakes in terror, at the point of being consumed by a monster, with the reassuring words, 'don't worry, it was only a dream'. Thus the boundary between fact and phantasm, which had seemed momentarily in doubt at the point of waking, is immediately restored. What, then, are we to make of the following story, which comes from the *Life of St Benedict of Nursia*, composed by Gregory the Great in 594 CE? The story tells of a monk who encountered a dragon. This monk was restless: his mind was given to wandering and he was itching to escape from the cloistered confines of monastic life. Eventually the venerable father Benedict, having had enough of the monk's whingeing, ordered him to leave. No sooner had he stepped outside the precincts of the monastery, however, than the monk found his path blocked by a dragon with gaping jaws. Convinced that the dragon was about to eat him up, and trembling with fear, he shouted to his brothers for help. They came running. Not one of them, however, could see any dragon. They nevertheless led their renegade colleague – still shaking from his experience – back inside the monastery. And from that day on he never again went astray, or even thought of doing so. It was thanks to Benedict's prayers, the story concludes, that the monk 'had seen, standing in his path, the dragon that previously he had followed without seeing it' (Carruthers 1998: 185).

The shape of fear

Perhaps the monk of this cautionary tale was merely suffering from nightmares. Medieval people, however, would not have been so readily reassured as their modern counterparts by the realisation that in their encounters with dragons and other monsters, what they had seen was but a dream. They were not so gullible as to suppose that dragons *exist*, in the specific sense of existence invoked by modern people when they assert, to the contrary, that dragons do *not* exist. It is not as though the monk, in our story, came face to face with some other creature that, with the benefit of scientifically informed hindsight, we moderns might recognise as a species of reptile. Remember that the brothers who came to his rescue saw no dragon. What they did see however, was that the monk was trembling. No doubt they saw the look of terror etched in his face. And yet when the monk cried out to be saved from the jaws of the dragon, the brothers understood his predicament at once. They did not react to his outburst – as the modern psychiatrist might react to the ravings of a lunatic escaped from the asylum – as the idiosyncratic, possibly drug-induced hallucinations of a fevered and unsettled mind. Rather, they immediately recognised, in the vision of the dragon, the form of the monk's otherwise inarticulable agitation, and imperilled themselves in responding, affectively and effectively, to his distress. The monk was on the point of being consumed by fear, and already felt the symptoms of personal disintegration. The dragon was not the objective cause of fear; it was the shape of fear itself.

For the brethren of monastic communities, this shape would have been well-known to all, drummed in through rigorous discipline of mind and body. In this training, stories and pictures of dragons and of other, equally terrifying monsters were used not as we would today, to create a comfort zone of safety and security by consigning everything that might be frightening to the realms of make-believe, but to instil fear in novices, so that they might experience it, recognise its manifestations and – through a stern regime of mental and bodily exercise – overcome it. As the manifest form of a fundamental human feeling, the dragon was the palpable incarnation of what it meant to 'know' fear. Thus in medieval ontology, the dragon existed as fear exists, not as an exterior threat but as an affliction instilled at the core of the sufferer's very being. As such, it was as real as his facial expression and the urgency in his voice. But unlike the latter, it could be neither seen nor heard save by the one who was himself afeared. That is why the monk's rescuers saw no dragon themselves. They were most likely motivated by a feeling of compassion, which may for them – in the idiom of the time – have called to mind the image of a saintly figure, radiating light. Both saints and dragons, in the monastic imagination, were concocted from fragments of text and pictures shown to novices in the course of their instruction. In that sense, to adopt the apt term of historian Mary Carruthers (1998: 187), they were 'figmented'. But these figments of the imagination, far from being cordoned off in a domain separate from that of 'real life', were for medieval thinkers the outward forms of visceral human experience, lived in the space of rupture between heaven and hell.[4]

The monk of the story was torn between the two. Expelled from the monastery by the saintly Benedict, he was confronted by the devil – in the shape of the dragon – waiting for him outside. Rescued in the nick of time, he was led back in. Thus the story unfolds along a path of movement, from inside to outside and then back inside again. From the very beginning, we are told, the mind of the monk was prone to wandering. Indeed in a puzzling twist at the end of his tale, Gregory recounts that for all that time, the monk was following the dragon *without actually seeing it*. It is as though he was sleepwalking. What happened when he stepped outside was a loss of bearings, of the kind that occurs when one is thrust into an unknown environment. It was a rude awakening. He panicked, and at that moment the dragon reared up before his eyes, blocking his path. So in truth, the story concludes, Benedict did the monk a good turn by throwing him out, since it led him to see – and thus to know – the dragon that he had otherwise blindly followed. For writers in the monastic tradition, as the narrative brings out so clearly, knowing depended on seeing, and both proceeded along trajectories of movement. To understand what they meant we have to think of cognition, as Carruthers (1998: 70) explains, 'in terms of paths or "ways"'. The medieval thinker was a wayfarer, who would travel in his mind from place to place, composing his thoughts as he went along (Ingold 2007a: 15–16, 95).

Dreams and reality

I shall return in due course to the question of wayfaring. In the meantime, let me introduce another example. Among the Ojibwa, indigenous hunters and trappers of the Canadian North, there is said to be a bird whose sound, as it swoops across the sky, is a peal of thunder. Few have seen it, and those who have are credited with exceptional powers of revelatory vision. One such, according to the ethnographer A. Irving Hallowell, was a boy of about twelve years. During a severe thunderstorm, Hallowell recounts, the boy ran out of his tent and saw a strange bird lying on the rocks. He ran back to call his parents, but by the time they arrived the bird had disappeared. The boy was sure it was *pinési*, the thunder bird, but his elders were unconvinced. The matter was clinched, and the boy's account accepted, only when a man who had *dreamed* of the bird verified the boy's description (Hallowell 1960: 32). Clearly, *pinési* is no ordinary bird, just as the dragon is no ordinary reptile. Like the sound of thunder itself, the thunder bird makes its presence felt not as an object of the natural world but, more fundamentally, as a phenomenon of experience (Ingold 2000: 278–9). It is the incarnate form of a sound that reverberates through the atmosphere and overwhelms the consciousness of all who hear it. Just as the monk's brethren, as they rushed outside, saw no dragon, so the boy's parents did not themselves witness *pinési*. But as the conventional shape of a powerful auditory sensation, it would have been entirely familiar to them. The thunder bird may be a figment of the imagination, but it is an imagination that has saturated the fullness of phenomenal experience.

The philosopher Gaston Bachelard (1988: 65–89) has written eloquently of how the bird of our dreams and that inhabits the realms of the poetic imagination is not a thing of flesh and feathers but a composition of air and movement in which the dreamer himself is borne aloft and carried along. The bird, Bachelard (1988: 77) says, 'is the dynamic eye of the storm': its body the wind, its breath the tempest and its wings the sky. For it to appear in its customary avian form the dreamer must 'climb back up towards the day' (1988: 73), yet the apparition can only be momentary since the very climb causes it to be eclipsed as the quotidian boundary between seeing and dreaming is restored. Though Bachelard's sources are from Western literature – notably the visionary writings of William Blake – Ojibwa people would have immediately understood the point, along with its corollary, namely that the flesh-and-feathers bird is but a manifestation of the real bird of the dream-storm, rather than the other way round, and could not exist without it. Likewise, the fearsome dragon of Gregory's account was the form of incandescent terror enveloping the subject at the moment of awakening self-awareness. It should come as no surprise, then, that in the incident related above, the boy's observation was verified by a dream. The direction of filiation, as Bachelard (1988: 71) puts it, is 'from spirit down to corporeal beings', allowing the latter to be brought to life by the former. Bacon, had he known about the case, would have been appalled. For us moderns the direction of filiation is precisely the reverse, from the reality of living beings to their more or less fantastical apparitions. Thus it is more usual, and certainly more acceptable, to require that dreams be verified by observation than vice versa.

A well-known instance is the story of how the chemist Friedrich August Kekulé discovered the structure of the benzene molecule, comprised of a ring of six carbon atoms. According to Kekulé's own, admittedly retrospective and possibly embellished account, it happened one night in 1865 while he was staying in the Belgian city of Ghent. He had been up late in his study, at work on a textbook. Making little progress, he had turned his chair towards the fire and dozed off. In his reverie, atoms gambolled before his eyes, twining and twisting in snake-like motion.

> But look! What was that? One of the snakes had seized hold of its own tail, and the form whirled mockingly before my eyes. As if by a flash of lightning I awoke; ... I spent the rest of the night in working out the consequences of the hypothesis.
>
> (In Benfey 1958: 22)[5]

Whatever Kekulé might have felt at the moment of waking, we can be sure that once the flash that shook him from his slumber was extinguished, the gyrating serpent of his dream was no longer an affectation of vision and had become instead an abstract figure of thought – a snake 'good to think with' – that was peculiarly apt for deciphering the structure of a given reality. Thus the serpent and the benzene ring fall unequivocally on either side of an impermeable ontological division between imagination and reality. It is this that allows the one to stand metaphorically for the other. The congruity between serpent and ring reinforces the division rather than breaking it down.

The dream-induced conjecture, however, is but a chimera until subjected to empirical test. It was in this vein that Kekulé went on to advise his audience. 'Let us learn to dream, gentlemen, then perhaps we shall find the truth… But let us beware of publishing our dreams till they have been tested by waking understanding' (in Benfey 1958: 22). Indeed, subsequent experimental work in the laboratory proved Kekulé's hypothesis to be substantially correct, and it went on to become a cornerstone of the emerging field of organic chemistry. The dream itself, however, did not. In the light of day, the dream vanished into oblivion. Thus science concedes to the imagination the power of conjecture – to think 'outside the box' – but only by banishing imagination from the very reality to which it affords insight. For the Ojibwa, by contrast, it would have been quite the other way around. For them, the truth of things is not only found but also tested by personal oneiric experience, which is why the boy's sighting of *pinési* could be corroborated by his elder's dream. In this quest for knowledge through experience, the powerful more-than-human beings that inhabit the Ojibwa cosmos, including thunder birds, are not analogical resources but vital interlocutors. This cosmos is polyglot, a medley of voices by which different beings, in their several tongues, announce their presence, make themselves felt, and have effects. To carry on your life as an Ojibwa person you have to tune into these voices, and to listen and respond to what they are telling you.

Another thunder bird story from Hallowell – admittedly told him by an informant – perfectly illustrates the point. Hallowell's informant was sitting in a tent, one stormy afternoon, with an old man and his wife. The thunder rolled and clapped. At once, the old man turned to his wife. 'Did you hear what was said?', he asked. 'No,' came the reply, 'I didn't quite catch it.' Commenting on the exchange, Hallowell (1960: 34) remarks that the old man 'was reacting to this sound in the same way as he would respond to a human being whose words he did not understand'. This was not a simple failure of translation. It was not as though the thunder bird had a message for the old man that he failed to grasp because of his imperfect command of bird language (Hymes 1964: 16). 'By and large', Hallowell observes, 'the Ojibwa do not attune themselves to receiving messages every time a thunderstorm occurs'. It transpires that this particular man had, in his youth, become acquainted with the thunder bird through the dreams of his puberty fast, and had gone on to develop a close relationship of tutelage with *pinési* (Hallowell 1976: 459). In the context of this relationship, listening and responding to thunder was a matter not of translation but of empathy, of establishing a communion of feeling and affect or, in short, of opening oneself up to the being of another.[6] And it is above all in dreaming, where the boundaries that surround the self in waking life are dissolved, that this opening up occurs.

Such exposure was not something that a sober scientist like Kekulé could even contemplate. For him, the path to true knowledge lay not in opening a dialogue with beings of the more-than-human world, but in an exact and literal reading of the facts already deposited there. The investigator who would 'follow the paths of the Pathfinders', Kekulé advised, 'must note every footprint, every bent twig, every fallen leaf. Then, standing at the extreme point reached by his predecessors, it will be easy for him to perceive where the foot of a further pioneer may find solid ground' (in Benfey 1958: 23). The object, as Bacon had put it (1858: 33), was to write a 'true vision of the footsteps of the Creator', inscribed in the works of His creation. It was a matter of unlocking the secrets of nature. But these secrets were not to be discovered through immediate sensory perception or affective involvement, nor would nature yield them willingly. Rather than letting other-than-human creatures speak for themselves, and listening to what they had to say, the natural philosopher was obliged to penetrate their hidden operations by means verging on torture: to 'twist the lion's tail' until she would cry out (Eamon 1994: 285). As Bacon wrote in his *The New Organon* (the second part of the uncompleted *The Great Instauration*), 'the secrets of nature reveal themselves more readily under the vexations of art than when they go their own way' (Bacon 1858: 95).

Galileo, for his part, was of the same mind. Nature, he opined, cares not 'a whit whether her abstruse reasons and methods of operation are understandable to men' (in Galilei 1957: 183). To all intents and purposes, she had turned her back on humanity. In a now celebrated passage of his book *The Assayer*, dating from 1623, Galileo had compared the natural universe to a 'grand book' which, though accessible to all, was nevertheless unreadable without a knowledge of the language and the characters in which it is written. That language, Galileo argued, is mathematics, and the characters are 'the triangles, circles, and other geometrical figures without which it is humanly impossible to understand a single word' (in Galilei 1957: 237). And what triangles and circles were for Galileo, the serpentine ring became for Kekulé – a character of rational thought.

Word of God, works of God

The idea of the book of the universe, or of nature, is of considerable antiquity, and was as current among medieval scholars as it was subsequently to become in the rise of modern science. Historian of religion Peter Harrison traces it to a number of contemporaneous ecclesiastical sources from the twelfth century, among them the Parisian philosopher-theologian Hugh of St Victor who, in his *De tribus diebus*, declared that 'the whole sensible world is like a kind of book written by the finger of God' (in Harrison 1998: 44). The idea rested, at root, on a homology between the *word* of God (*verbum Dei*), in the composition of the scriptures, and the *works* of God, in the creation of the world and its creatures (Bono 1995: 11). The question was: 'how could humans read those twin books?'

With this, we can return to the monks of the medieval era, for whom – as I have already observed – the meditative practice of reading liturgical texts was a process of wayfaring. Again and again, they would compare their texts to a terrain through which they would make their way like hunters on the trail, drawing on, or 'pulling in', the things they encountered, or the events to which they bore witness, along the paths they travelled. The word in Latin for this drawing or pulling in was *tractare*, from which is derived the English 'treatise' in the sense of a written composition. As they proceeded, the personages whom they would meet on the way, and whose stories were inscribed on the pages, would speak to them, with words of wisdom and guidance, to which they would listen and from which they would learn. These were known as the *voces paginarum*, 'voices of the pages' (Leclercq 1961: 19–20, Olson 1994: 184–5). Indeed, reading was itself a vocal practice: typically, monastic libraries were abuzz with the sounds of reading as the monks, murmuring the voices of the pages, would engage with them as though they were present and audible (Cavallo and Chartier 1999: 17–18).[7] To read, in its original medieval sense, was to be advised by these voices, or to take counsel (Howe 1992), much as the old Ojibwa man would have been advised by the voice of his mentor the thunder bird – if only he had caught what it said!

Surrounded by the voices of the pages as the hunter is surrounded by the voices of the land, the medieval reader was a follower of tradition (*traditio*). Derived from the Latin *tradere*, 'to hand over', tradition meant something rather different from what it is commonly taken for today. It was absolutely *not* a corpus of teachings, or codified knowledge, to be passed from generation to generation. The word was rather used to signify an activity or performance, thanks to which it was possible – relay fashion – to *carry on*. The scriptures, far from giving content to tradition, laid down the paths along which this movement could proceed. Each path – each story – would take the reader so far before handing over to the next. The resemblance of the Latin *tradere* to Old English *trade*, whence is derived 'track', is accidental; however as theologian Peter Candler (2006: 120–21) suggests in a commentary on the writings of Thomas Aquinas, the monks' calling was as much a trade as a craft. In his encyclopaedic survey of animals in myth, legend and literature, Boria Sax (2001: x) writes that 'to study a tradition is to track a creature, as though one were a hunter, back through time'. Each creature *is* its story, its tradition, and to follow it is at once to perform an act of remembrance and to move on, in continuity with the values of the past.

Often, the name of the creature is itself a condensed story, so that in its very utterance, the story is carried on. But it is carried on, too, in the calls or vocalisations of the creatures themselves – if they have a voice – as well as in their manifest, visible presence and activity (Ingold 2011a: 165–75). As a node or knot in a skein of depictions, stories, calls, sightings and observations, none more 'real' than any other, every creature is not so much a living thing as the instantiation of a certain way of being alive, each of which, to the medieval mind, would open up a pathway to the experience of God. So it was, too, with the letters and figures of the manuscript which, according to Isidore of Seville, writing in the seventh century, enable readers to hear again and retain in memory the voices of those not actually present (Carruthers 1990: 106). Thus was the book of nature, written by the finger of God, mirrored in the nature of the book, read with the finger of man – a second nature comprised not of works but of words (Clingerman 2009).

For Isidore, reading should be done quietly, but could not be altogether silent since it depended on gestures of the throat and mouth (Saenger 1982: 384). The manuscripts of the time were normally copied in *scriptio continua*, that is, with no spaces between words. The only way to read, then, was to read *out*, following the line of letters with the fingers while murmuring with the lips, much as one would follow a line of musical notation, and allowing the words to emerge or 'fall out' from the performance itself (Cavallo 1999: 73; Ingold 2007a: 12–18). In the twelfth and early thirteenth centuries, however, there was a gradual shift towards reading with the eyes alone, unaccompanied by voice or gesture. What made this possible was the division of the line of text into word-length segments, each of which could be taken in at a glance, with spaces in between (Illich 1991: 169–71). This removed the need to mouth the letter-line, or to retrace it with the fingers. Medievalist and palaeographer Paul Saenger has shown how, with such visual reading, the voices of the pages were silenced (Saenger 1982: 378, 397; 1999: 136). As long as everyone in a monastic library was reading aloud, the sound of one's own voice would have screened out the voices of others. But when one is trying to read silently, the slightest sound can be a distraction. So it was that silence came to reign within the cloistered confines of the monastery. In the world outside the monastery, however, in lay society, oral reading continued to predominate well into the fourteenth and fifteenth centuries. As historian of cognition David Olson (1994: 143–4) has pointed out, it was the Reformation that heralded the key transition in ways of reading, from reading *between* the lines to reading what was *on* them, or from the search for revelations or 'epiphanies' to the discovery of the one true meaning lodged in the text, and available to anyone with the necessary key to extract it.

Reading the new book of nature

In the early sixteenth century, Martin Luther urged readers to abandon the dreams and fantasies that their predecessors had found in their attunements to voices which they felt were speaking to them through the pages of the manuscript, and to draw a line in the sand between the given meanings of words and their subsequent interpretations (Olson 1994: 153–4). Scripture for the reformers was to be read not figuratively or allegorically but as an authoritative record of historical truth (Harrison 1998: 92–3). Nor should this record be tampered with. The book that had lain open in the medieval scholar's hands or on his desk, affording endless re-readings and retellings, and ever receptive to the insertion of glosses between the lines or in the margins, was now packaged as a complete object, bound between front and back covers and lying closed upon the shelf (Candler 2006: 12, 32). So too, nature was to be regarded as a closed book: a book already written from beginning to end, whose secrets could be prised out only through rigorous investigation in which every discovery represented not so much a revelation as a breakthrough.

It was in this spirit that Bacon insisted on an absolute distinction between dreams of the imagination and patterns of the world. Nature, too, was to be read literally, by appeal to nothing but the facts. While it was assumed that the intricate patterns and mechanisms to be found there had been authored by God and were an index of His omnipotence, there was never any suggestion that they could open up to an experience of divine revelation. No image of God was to be seen in the face of Nature, only mute testimony to His intelligence and handiwork (Bono 1995: 193). For Bacon and his contemporaries, as Harrison puts it:

> Nature is no longer an autobiographical text, in which direct references to the author may be found. It is more like a mathematical treatise, which has no meaning as such, and does not speak directly of its author, but from which we can make inferences about certain of the qualities of the person who produced it.
>
> (Harrison 1998: 203)

I wish to draw attention, in particular, to two corollaries of this transition in ways of reading the natural world. The first concerns performance. I have shown how for medieval readers, meaning was generated in the vocal-gestural activity of reading *out* (Cavallo 1999: 74). Doing and knowing, here, were as clearly coupled as chewing and digestion – an analogy explicitly drawn in the ancient characterisation of thinking as rumination. To ruminate, we still say, is to chew things over – as cattle chew the cud – and to digest their meanings (Carruthers 1990: 164–5; Hamesse 1999: 104; Ingold 2007a: 17). Moreover, medieval people, as we have seen, would have read the book of nature in the same manner, through their practices of wayfaring. Reading the voices of nature, of the more-than-human world, people were advised by them and would follow this advice, in parallel with their own experience, in laying down a path. With a sensibility attuned by an intimate perceptual engagement with their surroundings, they could *tell*, not only of what has been, but also of what will come to pass. Thus, knowledge of nature was forged in movement, in the course of going about in it. This knowledge was performative in the strict sense that it was *formed through* the comings and goings of inhabitants. Reading as performance, in short, was both word-forming and world-forming. As the case of the Ojibwa and the thunder bird clearly demonstrates, in a way of knowing that is performative – that *goes along* – any boundaries between self and other or between mind and world, far from being set in stone, are provisional and fundamentally insecure.

In a science constructed in the spirit of Bacon, by contrast, to know is no longer to join *with* the world in performance but to be informed *by* what is already set down there. Significantly, the analogy with hunting persisted from reading the old book of nature to reading the new. Indeed one of the most detailed elaborations of the hunting metaphor came from Bacon himself, who compared his experimental method to the way a hunter tracks his prey, guided by footsteps and signs (Eamon 1994: 283). The reappearance of the metaphor over two centuries later, in Kekulé's advice to the aspiring scientist to 'note every footprint, every bent twig, every fallen leaf', is a measure of its resilience. However, the image of the hunter had subtly changed: no longer a follower of traditional tracks and trails, he had become an explorer of wild and uncharted territories, a civiliser, who would bring these domains – and the creatures they contained – under his control.

In short, rather than making his way through a familiar terrain that is continually unfolding, in which neither words nor works are ever the same twice, the scientist sets out to map a *terra incognita* that is ready made – that is to discover, through some process of decoding or deciphering, what exists already in fact and *in toto*. The book of nature having been *in*-scribed by the Creator in the language of things, the task of the scientist – for Bacon, as indeed for Galileo – was to *de*-in-scribe, or in a word, to 'describe' what was written there.[8] This is to obtain knowledge not by reading *out* but by reading *off*. It entails a shift, as Candler (2006: 10) puts it, 'from a story told and performed (with the whole of its body) to a text seen and interpreted'. And from the moment when the former gave way to the latter, the world ceased to offer counsel or advice and became instead a repository of data that, in themselves, afforded no guidance on what should be done with them. The facts are one thing, values quite another, and the latter had their source not in nature but in human society. Thenceforth, wisdom took second place to information.

The second corollary takes us back to the idea that animals and other beings of the more-than-human world were known in medieval times by their traditions, as skeins of stories, depictions and observations. To track an animal in the book of nature was like following a line of text. But just as the introduction of word-spacing broke the line into segments, so also – in the book of nature – creatures began to appear as discrete, bounded entities rather than as ever-extending lines of becoming. Nature thus became amenable to the project not of trail-following but of classification. The lines were broken, but the resulting objects could be ordered and arranged, on the basis of perceived likeness or difference, into the compartments of a taxonomy. One could speak, for the first time, of the building blocks of nature, rather than its weave, and of its architectonics. Nature, in short, was perceived to be built up from constituent parts rather than woven from entangled lines. And the creatures of this natural world were known no longer as traditions but as taxa.

Those creatures, however, that were known *only* by their traditions, and for which no corroborating evidence could be found in the facts of nature, fell through the cracks. There are no dragons or thunder birds in scientific taxonomies. It is not just that they *do not* exist in the new book of nature; they *cannot*, since their story-bound constitution is fundamentally at odds with the project of classification. Dragons, along with other beings that rear up or make their presence felt along the ways of the world, can be told but they cannot be categorised. Nor can they be precisely located, as on a cartographic map. Just as they fell through the cracks of taxonomy, so also – in the words of Michel de Certeau (1984: 120–21), Jesuit scholar and philosopher of everyday life – were they 'pushed into the wings' of a scientific cartography that had no place for the movements and itineraries of life. The same is true of experiences of fear, and of the sounds of thunder. They, too, can be neither classified nor mapped. But this does not make them any less real or true for a person who is frightened or caught in the eye of a storm.

Science and silence

It seems, then, that as the pages lost their voice with the onset of the modern era, so the book of nature was also silenced. No longer does it speak to us, or tell us things. And yet this allegedly silent nature can be, and often is, a deafeningly noisy place. As philosopher Stephen Vogel (2006) observes, the world of nature abounds in movement and gesture, much of which is manifested as sound: think of the clap of thunder and the howling of the wind, the cracking of ice and the roar of the waterfall, the rustling of trees and the calls of birds. We may furthermore admit that at one level, human talk may also be understood as vocal gesture, and that – as we will go on to explore in Chapter 15 (page 232) – the voice manifests human presence just as the call manifests the presence of the bird and the clap the presence of thunder. On this level, voice, call and thunder are ontologically equivalent: as the voice *is* human being in its sonic manifestation, so the call *is* the bird and the clap *is* thunder. Yet none of this, Vogel maintains, warrants the conclusion that natural entities actually *converse* with human beings, let alone with one another. This is for two principal reasons. Firstly, conversation requires participants to attend and respond, in turn, to one another. Humans do indeed attend and respond to the sounds of nature: they listen out for birdcalls and are moved, even terrified, by thunder. But does nature, Vogel asks, respond to us? 'Do the self-speaking entities we attend and respond to in nature ever give us their full attention ..., engage us, respond to our claims?' The answer, he is convinced, is 'no' (Vogel 2006: 148). The sounds of nature, he suggests, are more like the commands of a monarch who is deaf to his subjects but compels their obedience. Secondly, a conversation is necessarily *about* something (2006: 151–2). It enables participants to compare each other's perceptions of the world in the common task of figuring out how it actually *is*. Human interlocutors do this, but birds, trees, rivers, thunder and the winds do not. It is not that they are irresponsible interlocutors; rather, they are not interlocutors at all (2006: 157).

For Vogel, then, the silence of nature means that however much noise it makes, it takes no part in the conversations we hold about it. It might sound to us *as if* nature is speaking, but that is a delusion. 'I have listened carefully', writes Vogel (2006: 167), 'and I hear nothing.' Recall the old Ojibwa man and the thunder bird. He thought the thunder was speaking to him, but could not comprehend what it said. Was this a failure of translation, as Hallowell seems to suggest? I have argued that it was a failure of empathy. For Vogel, however, had the old man comprehended thunder's speech, he would have succeeded neither in translating it nor in empathising with it. He would rather have performed an act of ventriloquism. For whereas the translator speaks for another but in his own tongue, the ventriloquist projects his own words onto a mute object while creating the illusion that it is the object speaking for itself (Vogel 2006: 162). This charge of ventriloquism is the foundation for the scientific abhorrence of anthropomorphism, where those who claim empathy with nonhuman creatures, or to know what they are feeling, stand accused of projecting their own thoughts and sentiments onto their unwitting subjects.

The accusation, however, has not gone unchallenged. In a debate conducted in the pages of the journal *Environmental Values*, Nicole Klenk (2008) has entered on the other side. Writing as a critic of the environmental sciences, she replies that nonhumans *can and do* respond to human voice, gesture and presence in ways that are meaningful both to them and to us. It is true that nonhumans may not compare their perceptions of the environment with humans in a collaborative effort to establish the truth of what is actually 'out there'. But to insist that conversations can only take this form, Klenk argues, is to take such a narrow view of conversation that it would end up excluding most of what we commonly call conversation in the human world. For most people, most of the time, conversation is a matter of understanding what others are telling us – of 'getting the story right', not of verifying the rightness of the story (Klenk 2008: 333). Thus human beings who take it upon themselves to render in words what nature is saying are indeed translators and not ventriloquists. For Klenk, this is precisely what happens in scientific work. Were this not the case, she concludes, scientific interpretations would be mere fictions created through dialogue among humans, rather than the results of careful interaction with – and observation of – components of the natural world.

But in this, I believe Klenk is mistaken. Or more to the point, she is mistaken so long as we remain bound by the methodological protocols of normal science. For the claim of science is that as a specialised knowledge practice, it *does* seek to verify the rightness of the story, rather than merely getting the story right. Ever since Bacon, science has insisted on discovering the truth of what is there, and thus on the strict separation of fact and interpretation. Reading what is *on* the lines of the book of nature, rather than between them, the one thing that scientists insist they do *not* do is what Klenk takes to be their number one priority: 'to listen to the voices of those beings they interact with' (2008: 334).[9] Arguably, indeed, scientists do all they can to *avoid* listening, for fear that it would interfere with or compromise the objectivity of their results.

So there is, I contend, a real parallel in the modern constitution between the book of nature and the nature of the book, each understood as a completed work whose contents can be deciphered by those with the keys to do so. The parallel lies in the idea that both are to be read in silence: not in the course of an ongoing conversation whose manifold participants open up to one another and whose stories intertwine, but as a record of results that – rendered inert and impassive, in objective and objectified forms – have turned their back on us, presenting to our inspection only what geneticist Mae-Wan Ho (1991: 348) has called an 'opaque, flat, frozen surface of literalness'. To science, the facts are given; they comprise the 'data'. But the world does not ostensibly give of itself to science as part of any offering or commitment. What is 'given', in science, is that which has fallen out of circulation and has settled as a kind of residue, cast off from the give and take of life. It is this residue – dredged, sampled and purified – that is then subjected to a process of analysis, the end-results of which appear on the written page in the forms of words, figures and diagrams. Thus the knowledge so constituted is created as an overlay or wrap-around, on the outside of being. Having silenced the world, we find knowledge in the silence of the book.

Knowing in being

The very concept of the human in its modern incarnation, as we shall see further in Chapter 20 (pages 313–14), expresses the dilemma of a creature that can know the world of which it is existentially a part only by taking leave of it. Yet in our experience as inhabitants, moving through the world rather than roaming its outer surface, our knowledge is not built up as an external accretion but grows and unfolds from the very inside of our earthly being. We grow into the world, as the world grows in us (Ingold 2011a: 6). Perhaps this grounding of knowing in being lies at the heart of the kind of sensibility we are apt to call 'religious'. It is all the more ironic, then, that leaders of the Reformation should have campaigned *in the name of religion* to turn the relation between knowing and being inside out. In so doing, they assisted materially in the birth of empirical science. As Harrison observes (1998: 268), the reformists' stress on the ostensive truth of words and works, while proceeding from the purest of religious motives, inadvertently set in train a process that would eventually undermine the biblical authority they were so keen to promote. Inevitably, the religion of the reformists was trumped by the very science it unloosed. For in any contest over the facts, science is bound to win, and religion to lose, leaving the puzzle of why people – including many scientists – tenaciously adhere to representations of reality that are demonstrably false.

Yet questions about which can better *represent* the world, religion or science, are wrongly posed, for the real contest lies elsewhere. It turns on whether our ways of knowing and imagining are enshrined within an existential commitment to the world in which we find ourselves. It is a contest, in Candler's (2006: 30–40) terms, between the 'grammar of representation', which disowns such commitment, and the 'grammar of participation', which depends on it. Michel Serres (1995b: 47) draws our attention to the derivation of 'religion' – according to an interpretation attributed to Cicero – from the Latin *re-legere*, 'to re-read', in that sense of reading which we have already identified as taking counsel, and of being receptive to what one's textual interlocutors have to offer. What, then, is its opposite? It is *neg-legere*: 'to not-read'. It is to fail to take heed, to neglect or cast aside those offerings, to refuse the commitments that their acceptance would entail. 'Whoever has no religion', Serres concludes (1995b: 48), 'should not be called an atheist or unbeliever, but negligent.'[10] *The opposite of religion, then, is negligence.* But if re-readings or re-tellings, cast in the performative grammar of participation, are refracted through the distorting lens of a cognitive grammar of representation that neglects or denies, *a priori*, the very commitments on which participation depends, then they are bound to be thrown up as a spectrum of apparently irrational beliefs in entities such as 'spirits' – and, of course, dragons – which, if they existed in fact, would violate obvious principles of physical or biological causation.[11]

Just such a fate was suffered by one of the more celebrated dragons of anthropological literature – the one that Filate, an old man among the Dorze of southern Ethiopia, challenged anthropologist Dan Sperber to kill (Sperber 1985: 35, 60–63). It was reputedly gold all over, had a heart of gold and one horn on the nape of its neck, and lived not far away. For the rational anthropologist – a stranger to participation, commitment and the passion that infuses it, or, in a word, to *faith* – Filate's challenge evidenced 'a certain representational belief of semi-propositional content' (meaning that the content itself was but partially understood and open to multiple interpretations). Yet as John Morton has shown in a critical review, to dismiss Filate's 'heartfelt conviction' concerning the dragon's existence in these terms 'is clearly to do some violence to that conviction, disposing in particular with its affective qualities'. For like the dragon encountered by the monk in the story of St Benedict, Filate's vision was, in Morton's reappraisal, the outward form of his 'inner emotional state' (Morton 1986: 74–7). The dragon was a *topos* in the field of participation, not a half-baked proposition in the field of representation.

As this example shows, comparisons of religion and science in terms of the tenacity of apparently irrational beliefs build a stance of denial into their founding axioms – a denial, amongst their adherents, that in their conscious deliberations, whether scientific or spiritual, the world owes anything to them, or they to the world. In other words, negligence has become the foundation for a debate concerning the rationality of beliefs *about* the world. But if, to the contrary, it is acknowledged that we owe our very existence to the world, and if the world, at least in some measure, owes its existence to us, then we need to ask instead: what is the nature of these owings, these commitments? 'What do we give back', asks Serres (1995b: 38), 'to the objects of our science, from which we take knowledge?' Or to put the same question in another way, how can our ways of knowing and of imagining let us, and the creatures around us, *be*? For it is surely in this discharge into being, of ourselves and others, that the common ground between religion and science is to be found.

This is where Klenk might be right after all. All science depends on observation, and observation depends in turn on an intimate coupling, in perception and action, of the observer with those aspects of the world that are the focus of attention (Ingold 2011a: 75). Perhaps the most striking characteristic of modern science lies in the lengths to which it has gone to deny or cover up the practical, observational commitments on which it depends. To highlight these commitments – to attend to the practices of science rather than its formal prescriptions – means recovering those very experiential and performative engagements which, unwritten and unsung, have fallen through the cracks or been pushed into the wings of scientific conceptualisations. Let us not forget the advice of August Kekulé, to follow every footprint, twig and fallen leaf. In practice, scientists are as much wayfarers as are people of faith, and must perforce tread where others have gone before, ever attentive and responsive to the rustlings and whisperings of their surroundings. Joining with things in the processes of their formation, rather than merely being informed by what has already precipitated out, practising scientists do not just *collect* but *accept* what the world has to offer them. They may, in deference to official protocols, feign not to listen to the voices of beings around them, but listen they must, if they are to advance beyond the bare pick-up of information towards real understanding. Like it or not, they too are beholden to the world. And it is in this more modest profession, rather than in arrogating to itself the exclusive authority to represent a given reality, that scientific inquiry converges with religious sensibility as a way of knowing-in-being. This is the way of imagination.

Let me be clear: to follow this way is not to reach an accommodation between science and religion, nor is it to create a space where religion can flourish alongside science in easy accord, with their labours neatly divided between the spiritual and the material sides of things. In contemporary debates on religion and science, at least in Western societies, declarations to this effect have become commonplace, whether from practising scientists who claim to have embraced religious faith or from reasonable churchmen anxious to appear friendly to science. Such declarations, however, invariably take as their point of departure the very separation I have sought to repair, of the life of the spirit from its material matrix, or of imagination from reality. My contention is precisely the reverse, namely that if it is to be conducted ethically – with care, attentiveness and commitment, and with due acknowledgement of our debt to the world for what it has to teach us – then science *is* religion in action. And conversely, as a disciplined, systematic but open-ended way of knowing in being, religion *must* at heart be a practice of science.

Where science and religion converge, moreover, so too do anthropology and theology. This conclusion points to a certain realignment between the two disciplines. Up to now, as Joel Robbins (2006: 286–7) observes, anthropologists have for the most part approached theology in one or other of two ways. Either they have found in theology an aid to disciplinary self-reflection and critique, in revealing how key concepts such as 'culture', 'nature', 'agency' and even 'religion' have their roots in the Judaeo-Christian tradition. Or they have treated theologians as informants and their writings as just another source of ethnographic data, on the very Christian culture that informs them. Neither approach has dented the division between ethnographic data and social theory with which contemporary anthropology, in keeping with the protocols of normal science, remains largely compliant. This division, Robbins suggests (after Milbank 1990), is the breakdown product of a decayed theology. There is however a third way. It is to turn to others for what they have to teach us of knowing-in-the-world as a form of commitment, of being and letting be, and to find in the ontological and ethical force of this commitment a foundation for hope. It is in this spirit that I turn from the teachings of medieval monasticism to one final example from the circumpolar North.

The Bible and the land

The example comes from a recent study by Peter Loovers (2010), carried out among Teetl'it Gwich'in people living in and around Fort McPherson, in the Canadian Northwest Territories. The study is exceptional in combining a sensitive account of the ways in which people relate to their environment as they hunt, trap and move around on land and water, with a detailed history of Gwich'in engagements with the written word – above all in the translation and reception of the Christian Bible. The immense work of translation was undertaken by Archdeacon Robert McDonald. Born in 1829 of a Scottish father – an employee of the Hudson's Bay Company – and an Ojibwa mother, McDonald was educated at the Anglican mission school at the Red River settlement and spent a decade serving with the Ojibwa people before embarking, in 1862, on a mission to bring the Anglican faith to the people of the Mackenzie River district. Over the ensuing years, McDonald worked tirelessly to introduce Christian teachings to native Gwich'in communities, and many of the men and women he encountered on his travels became key advisers in helping him to transcribe liturgical texts into their own language, known at the time as Tadukh. For McDonald, the translation of the entire Bible into Tadukh was a lifelong endeavour, and the work was not completed until 1898.

Though the Tadukh Bible was warmly received by the Gwich'in, this reception was not quite as McDonald intended. Unlike his rivals from the Catholic mission, who took a rather more relaxed attitude, McDonald was steeped in the traditions of the reformed church, and believed that the text of the Bible was to be read literally, as the unalterable record of a singular truth that is not open to negotiation. Much to his discomfort, however, many Gwich'in people, including several of McDonald's own pupils, began to experience dreams and visions in which, it seemed, the pages of the Bible were talking to them, issuing instructions and revealing prophecies. These pages spoke with the voices of their elders, the people with whom McDonald had been working in transcribing the text (and whose particular dialectal idiosyncrasies had become incorporated into it), and even with the voice of McDonald himself. Thus for the Gwich'in, to read the Bible was to open up a conversation with these elders, to listen to their voices, to be taught by them, and to learn. For his part, McDonald was mightily displeased, and felt compelled to denounce the 'false prophecies' that were being mouthed by the people (Loovers 2010: 117). The mismatch between these ways of reading was not, however, confined to the Bible. It has continued to surface in other contexts, notably in the interpretation of treaties and land claims agreements drawn up with officials of the Canadian government. In these cases the dismay was on the side of the Gwich'in, who were surprised to discover that documents which they had thought to open up to ongoing dialogue with those whose voices were incorporated therein, were treated by officialdom as set in stone, silent and unyielding (Loovers 2010: 138).

Exactly the same mismatch, as Loovers shows, can be found in ways of reading the land. For colonisers, explorers, scientists and others who have come to the land from outside, whether on a mission to civilise it, to develop it, to research it or to appreciate its natural beauty, there is no disputing that what is there is already fixed, awaiting discovery, explanation and possibly transformation at the hands and by the minds of men. For the Gwich'in, however, it is quite different. To read the land, for them, is to attend to the multiple clues that reveal the activities and intentions of its manifold human and more-than-human inhabitants. These clues, Loovers (2010: 300) tells us, 'include animal movements, trails, old and new camps and cabins, marks on the land, wood, snow and ice conditions in winter, river-banks in summer, and places where events have unfolded'. Wherever they go, Gwich'in are listening, remembering, learning, *taking counsel* from the land. It is their teacher, not just a repository from which can be extracted materials for the construction of propositional knowledge. Thus the land speaks to people with many voices, just as the Bible does.

Should we then go along with Archdeacon McDonald and conclude that such a way of reading the land is equally false, or that it rests on the kinds of delusions to which, in Western colonial eyes, allegedly primitive, native peoples have always been supposed to be prone? Even McDonald, with his Ojibwa upbringing, would have known that there is more to indigenous understandings than this. And so, in light of what I have argued in this chapter, do we. I have shown how studies of medieval monasticism and of indigenous ontologies point to alternative ways of reading, and of writing, which might allow us once again to take counsel from both the voices of the pages and the world around us, to listen and be advised by what they are telling us, and thereby to heal the rupture between the world and our imagination of it. This healing, I contend, must be a first step towards establishing a more open-ended and sustainable way to live.

Part II

Light, sound and experience

The world we inhabit, the world of our experience, is suffused with light and sound. This luminous and sonorous ambience is the stream in which imagination swims and soars. It animates the body and nourishes the soul. The experience of light and sound, moreover, is no illusion. It is entirely real. But its reality is not that of the physical world described by science. Nor, conversely, does the experience register only as a state of mind, as described by psychology. It is neither 'out there' nor 'in here'. The chapters in Part II are all about coming to terms with sensory awareness, of the kind commonly characterised as aesthetic, in a way that escapes the complementary reductions of psychology and physics which, having divided mind from matter, have in combination bridged the gap only to allow all of experience to drain away with the waters flowing beneath. There is, of course, more to this experience than light and sound. Neither can exist without feeling. But feeling is above all about going along and corresponding with materials, which is my theme for Part IV. Indeed it is a thread that runs through all the chapters of this part. That's why, for now, I shall stay primarily with light and sound. While neither can be truly understood without the other, I shall focus on light in Chapter 6, and on sound in Chapter 7.

Beginning, then, with light, we immediately face the problem of what we mean by it. Does light consist of energetic radiation, of which the experience of illumination is an effect, or does it consist in that very experience, in the luminosity for which radiation is but a condition? Both definitions can be right, but only because they set out from opposite poles, respectively physical and phenomenological. The light that travels from source to recipient, conventionally depicted as rectilinear rays, cannot shine, glow or flicker. Conversely, sunshine, the glow of burning embers and the flickering flame of the candle do not travel in straight lines. Yet sun, fire and candle not only illuminate our world; they warm us too. Their lines are of combustion rather than radiation; they are not straight but curl in response to atmospheric conditions. As beams rather than rays, they belong to the phenomenal and not the physical order of reality. I will show how this distinction plays out in theories of colour, associated respectively with Isaac Newton

DOI: 10.4324/9781003171713-8

and Johann Wolfgang von Goethe, and conclude with some reflections on the meaning of shadow, whether as the linear projection of an object form, or as the spectral double of a material presence.

In the shadow of complete darkness, of course, we cannot see. Everything appears black. Yet we can be equally blinded by intense light, as in the whiteout of a snowstorm. Both the blackout and the whiteout yield experiences of seeing next to nothing. It is precisely the same, however, with sound. In complete silence I hear nothing. But I also hear nothing if I am overwhelmed by noise. The question, then, is how can we tell white from black, sound from silence? Just as with light, this is a question that takes us to the heart of the problem of what we mean by sound, which is my focus in Chapter 7. Building on the distinction between ray and beam – the first a line of emission, the second a line of combustion – I find the sonic equivalent of the beam in the idea of pitch. In the physics of sound, however, pitch, like colour, has been spectralised, with the result that another concept, timbre, is needed to comprehend the quality of sound that overflows its measured representations. To grasp the full experience of sound, I argue, pitch and timbre must be rejoined, just as it is necessary to reunify colour with lustre if we are to grasp the experience of light.

In the remaining two chapters of this part I return to the subject of aesthetics. It is a subject that I had previously shunned, as it always seemed to me to mask the study of perception under another name, one moreover freighted with largely unwarranted evaluative overtones. Yet opening perception to imagination, I now realise, means opening to aesthetics as well. I could no longer avoid the subject. In Western philosophy, of course, the study of aesthetics has classically been bound up with judgements of beauty. Scholars have offered a variety of explanations for why some things are deemed beautiful and others ugly. They share the assumption, however, that these things are to be beheld as final, complete works. In Chapter 8 I question this assumption. My ambition is to frame an alternative aesthetics that would attend, first and foremost, to the doing of things, to skills of performance and the captivation of attention in the spell of unfolding events. Here, judgement does not follow on from presentation, but inheres the fine-tuning of perception by way of environmental experience. I draw on two sources – my experience of anthropological fieldwork among Sámi reindeer herders, and my attempts to master the violoncello – to elaborate on five propositions: that beauty is attentional, that it lies in the unity of affects, that it is enchanting, that it is experienced in both hearing and seeing, and that it is sensed along a path of presence.

Finally, in Chapter 9 I address the field of science that studies human responses to art. Known as empirical aesthetics, its roots lie in the psychophysics of Gustav Fechner, who was the first to turn aesthetics from a way of studying objects – as proposed by Immanuel Kant – into an object of study in its own right. This move, however, effectively discounts the lived reality of aesthetic experience. Drawing on recent work in the field, I offer a critical review of the way empirical aesthetics models what it calls the 'aesthetic episode'. This begins when a viewer stands before a work of art, and ends with a judgement of the work, on a scale of preference, and an emotional response to the viewing experience. Empirical aesthetics sees every encounter with art as a problem-solving exercise, and it is the satisfaction of solving the problem, rather than the work itself, that underpins the response. The idea of problem-solving, however, implies that a solution is already at hand, merely waiting to be found. Yet surely what distinguishes the work of art from a puzzle is precisely that it is a problem without a ready solution. I am with the pragmatism of John Dewey, in supposing that to encounter an artwork means reviving the temporal process of its creation. In place of an empirical focus on discrete episodes, this calls for a praxis that would release the work from its psychophysical reduction, back into the fullness of lived experience.

Chapter 6

What in the world is light?

Physics and phenomenology

Light is among the fundamental constituents of our universe; but it also lies at the heart of human experience. It is both so near that it invades our being, and yet so far that beside it our human presence pales into insignificance. We know a great deal about it, and yet we do not know what it is. It could be an energetic ray, a beam, the illumination of surfaces, an atmosphere. It could be the shining of the sun, the moon and the stars. It could be a flickering flame, a lamp or torch, the glowing embers of a fire. It could be whiteness, or a spectrum of colour. It could be a release from darkness, an enlivening of the spirit, divine presence, the power of reason. Indeed, light could be all of these things, but only because – as we pass from one thing to another – we continually shift the grounds of definition. Light has no stable ontological foundation, not because in the present state of knowledge we are still some way from a definitive explanation, but because what light is depends on where we are coming from. There is no right way that would enable us to pronounce with confidence on what light *actually* is, as if all other expressions were illusory or metaphorical.

My argument in this chapter is that since light is in and of the world, what light is depends on what we take this world to be. This, in itself, is not a problem. It only becomes a problem when things get mixed up – that is, when the properties attributed to light when the world is taken in one way are assumed still to apply when it is taken in another. And in the study of visual phenomena, such confusions are endemic. To take a very simple example, to which I shall return later: if light is the flame of a fire, then it doesn't travel in straight lines. And conversely, if light is a rectilinear ray, then it doesn't flicker like a flame. You cannot have it both ways at once.

Now if I were a physicist or an astronomer, I might be inclined to insist that, fundamentally, light is a form of electromagnetic radiation, on a scale from ultraviolet to infrared, perhaps limited to the range of frequencies to which photoreceptors in the eyes of human beings or other animals are able to respond. I would say that light emanates from a source, at a speed that is

DOI: 10.4324/9781003171713-9

constant in a vacuum but reduced in passing through a transparent medium, whence it may eventually be picked up by receptors, whether these be eyes or instruments like cameras or telescopes. But light, thus understood, has no need of eyes, cameras or telescopes to exist. Nor, moreover, is it something we ever see. We may see things by means of light, thanks to rays reflected from their surfaces and reaching the eyes, but we do not see light itself. 'Of all the things that can be seen', asked James Gibson (1979: 54) in his pioneering work on the ecology of visual perception, 'is light one of them?' He answered categorically in the negative, only to tie himself in knots trying to explain why sunlight and moonlight, candlelight and firelight, which we do manifestly see, are not species of light 'as such'.

But if I were a painter, seeking to capture the play of light and shadow on, say, a landscape or a human face, then for me these sources of manifest light, along with the shifting illumination of the surfaces on which they fall, would be of the essence. I would insist not only that I see their light, but also that the light is no less than me, seeing. No seeing; no light. This, broadly, was the position of Maurice Merleau-Ponty (1964), in an essay on the phenomenology of light, entitled *Eye and Mind*, directly inspired by the painting of Paul Cézanne. For Cézanne, as Merleau-Ponty shows, light is there before us only in the echo it awakens from within. And it was this restless and flickering echo that the artist sought to capture in his paintings.

There is nothing to gain, and much to lose, by insisting upon a single definition of light that would exclude all others, or cast their manifestations as merely ancillary or epiphenomenal. If we do not see light as such, but only objects in the light, then what should we make of the history of painting? Is it nothing more than a record of hallucination, caused by the overstimulation of hypersensitive minds? Or again, what should we make of the experience of people with visual impairments which prevent them from being able to make out the shapes or contours of objects, but who can still tell light from dark? If light cannot really be seen, is the experience an illusion? For a physicist or psychologist to argue along these lines would indeed be absurd, but no more so than for the historian or anthropologist to dismiss scientific advance in the study of electromagnetic radiation, on the grounds that it has nothing to say about human affective experience. The experience of light is real; the physical fact of radiation is also real; but physical and experiential realities are not the same.

To appreciate the difference, consider the flickering flame of the candle that you hold in your hands as you walk the corridors at night. Is candlelight the flame, rising from the wick, or is it the rays emitted therefrom? In your experience, the light you see, and see with, is indeed the flame. It flickers because of atmospheric currents set up, in part, by your own movements and by the flame's heating of the surrounding air. As you pass, the flame casts shifting patterns of illumination and shadow on the walls of the corridor. Ask a physicist, however, and he would explain that these patterns are not compositions of light and shade, but differential effects of light caused by the parallactic displacement of the source relative to reflecting surfaces. In the physics of light, flickering describes the behaviour of the source; it is not a property of the radiation it emits. Light itself does not flicker. Nor, in this account, does the light travel – as you do, candle in hand – at walking pace. On the contrary, as physics assures us, it travels, at least through space, at a staggering 186,000 miles a second! Even in atmospheric air, it slows only by a factor of three in ten thousand.

Yet much of what passes for the study of light, above all in fields of the humanities from fine art and art history to architecture and theatre studies, is an investigation of the very phenomena that physics would regard as light's effects. Is it wrong, then, to refer to the effects themselves, along with their production or staging, as 'light'? Surely not. For there is nothing hallucinatory about our experience of an illuminated world, of sunbeams and moonshine, of the blaze of the fire or the gleam of torches, lamps, candles or electric bulbs. Were it not for emissions of radiant energy, photoreceptors in the eyes, and associated neural pathways, we could not have this experience. But the experience should not be confounded with its conditions. To the physicist who states that light is radiation and the experience of illumination but an effect, the phenomenologist could respond, with equal assurance, that light is the experience of illumination for which radiation is but a condition. Both can be right, but only because they set out from opposite poles, respectively physical and experiential.

The opposition, however, has profound implications. For it affects not only what we mean by light, but also our very conception of the material world. The question is whether light is a vector of transmission or a constitutive element of the things we see around us. Does light intercede between a world 'out there' and the eye of the beholder, so as to render the constituents of this world to perception in their objective forms, ready at a glance? Or does it enter materially into the incessant formation of the world – and of ourselves as well, given that we exist as beings within it?

What it takes for light to shine

We can ask these questions both of landscapes and of artworks or artefacts. Is a landscape, for example, the same, whether seen by day or night, or under variable weather conditions? Or does it vary continually as conditions change, unfolding over time like a musical composition (Ingold 2011a: 129–30)? Do landscapes flicker with the light? Do they change as the sun goes in and out, or as it makes its way across the sky? Painters, seeking to capture not things in themselves but the very experience of opening one's eyes to them, would surely allow that light is among the materials they use, and colour too. Of course, painters work with a palette of colours, but colours – for them – are not just variations along a spectrum but material ingredients, squeezed from a tube, which can be mixed to form the distinctive lustre of the composition. This lustre is the light of the painting.

Turning from artworks to artefacts, we can likewise ask whether artisans incorporate light as a material ingredient into their manufactures. Certainly, for the makers of stained glass, their compositions would literally be lacklustre without it. When sunlight streams through the window, it is transformed from dull to brilliant (Morphy 1992). Similarly, the gold-encrusted icon, an object of ritual devotion, would lose its lustre without the light that causes it to glitter. For the maker as for the devotee, the glitter of gold is not incidental, a mere by-product of its physical irradiation. It is immanent in the thing itself, and a manifestation of its power. The way the material responds to illumination – its glittering – announces gold for what it is. Light, in short, is constitutive of the material itself. Another celebrated example is traditional Japanese lacquerware, which was made to be seen in dim candlelight, its burnished surfaces glowing in the shadows. Placed in a museum case, under the glare of spotlights, it would lose its allure (Tanizaki 2001: 21–5). Is the 'real thing', then, the ware by candlelight or under the illumination of the display?

No condition of illumination, of course, is innocent. The painting, the stained-glass window, the icon and the lacquerware will look quite different under different conditions. The question is whether these appearances offer partial views of a given reality, or demonstrate that the reality itself is fluid and fickle, ever changing with the light. Most languages have a wealth of verbs to describe the varieties of luminous experience, and English is no exception: besides glitter, we have shine, gleam, glow, blaze, flash, flicker, sparkle, shimmer, and more. Common to all, however, is that *they cannot take radiant energy as their subject*. The light that shines, that casts shifting patterns of brilliance and shade on the walls of a cave, that glows red in the furnace, that sparkles in the rippling waters of a lake, is not the electromagnetic impulse that travels from source to recipient, and that we conventionally depict as rectilinear rays. For shining is not a moment of transmission but an affectation of being that carries on, in real time, along an axis orthogonal to the straight line connecting the seer to the seen. This is the time of sentient awareness as it meets and mingles with the movement of things in their ongoing generation. In it lies the continual birth of vision.

To establish the point, it might help to draw a comparison with sound. We have as many words for the varieties of sonic experience as for their luminous counterparts, among them bang and rumble. One is sudden, brief and intense; the other diffuse and sustained. Yet with both, the sound is registered not as a series of discrete auditory inputs, transmitted from the source by way of vibrations in the medium, but as the modulation of the input over time. The bang and the rumble, if you will, have distinctive modular curves. To listen is to align one's attention to the curve as it unfolds.

Now the luminous equivalents of the bang and the rumble are the flash and the glow. We might witness the flash as a sudden streak, such as a fork of lightning, and the glow in the dying embers of a fire. But like the flame of the candle, they are manifestations of combustion, not vectors of transmission. And to witness the flash, or to bask in the glow, is to join with the process of combustion for as long as it carries on.

Let's suppose that far off, a storm is raging. We see the flash of lightning before we hear its thunder, and we know why: it is, we say, because light travels very much faster than sound. But the 'light' that travels is not the light that shines in our eyes; nor is the 'sound' that travels the sound that resonates in our ears. For the durations of lightning's flash and thunder's rumble are in no wise dependent upon the velocities with which their signals, respectively electromagnetic and vibratory, are propagated. They belong to entirely distinct temporal registers. The light of lightning and the sound of thunder, as they erupt in our visual and auditory experience, are not physical emissions but the reverberations of a consciousness that, far from having closed itself off from a world 'out there', has opened up to the boundless expanse of sky. To prove the point, take yourself out on a clear night to observe the stars. What do you see? Astronomers, of course, inform us that we see the stars thanks to radiant energy that has reached us only after the lapse of hundreds or thousands of years. This light, they say, having traversed billions of miles of space, delivers the stars to us as objects of perception. That may be *why* you see the star, but it isn't *how* you see it. For to you it appears as a pinprick of light in the night sky. It seems to you to shine, even to twinkle. And this shining, this twinkling, goes on, for as long as it follows the arc of your attention.

The stars we see, in short, are not distant astronomical objects. They *are* their lights, not sources of light, and they are right here, in our eyes, even as we – seeing – are at large in the visible cosmos. We and the stars, for a while at least, carry on our lives together, *and therein lies their shining*. It is as though our eyes and the stars were interchangeable, a point that William Shakespeare already grasped when he put these words into the mouth of Romeo, serenading beneath the window of his beloved Juliet:

> Two of the fairest stars in all the heaven,
> Having some business, do entreat her eyes
> To twinkle in their spheres till they return.
> What if her eyes were there, they in her head?[1]

Romeo is, of course, the personification of the star-struck lover. Were we to think of eyes anatomically, as spherical organs of the body, and of stars astronomically, as the globular fragments of an exploding universe, then the idea of swapping stars for eyes would indeed be fanciful. For they would stand at opposite ends of a line, extending through space-time, of almost unimaginable length. But as we join Romeo beneath the canopy of the night sky, and open our eyes to the stars, our experience is not that we are looking out upon the distant heavens through holes in the head that afford optical access to a beyond. Rather, the head itself appears to vanish as we merge, in our awareness, with that very beyond. And yet we remain where we are, rooted to the spot, at home in our bodies. Indeed, exactly as Shakespeare has Romeo proclaim, even as our eyes – no longer confined within their sockets – are with the stars, the stars – distant beyond measure – are so close as to touch the soul. That is what it means for stars to shine, and for the eyes to experience their light.

The ray and the flame

What, then, of our very own star, the sun? What must the sun be, for it to shine? Astronomers, once again, are quick to remind us that solar radiation reaches the earth only after having crossed some 93 million miles of space. Without it we would be plunged into darkness, as indeed we are every night due to the earth's rotation. But this radiation is not the light that shines, nor does the shining light connect me, by a long straight line of transmission, to its source in a distant cosmic object. For sunlight, in our experience, does not arrive from afar but erupts in the consciousness of the seer who sees *with* it, with eyes bathed in its luminosity. As with the blaze of the woodfire or the flicker of the candle, the sun's shining, rather than spanning an interval of transmission, endures in the glare of combustion. Corresponding in its duration with our sentient awareness, in the midst of a world forever on the burn, it spins out the diurnal cycle under which we and the sun measure out our days together.

'If the eye were not sun-like', pondered the poet-scientist Johann Wolfgang von Goethe, 'the sun's light it would never see.'[2] Note that Goethe is wondering how the eyes see the sun's *light*, not the sun as an object *by way of* its light. The sun, of course, is a star, and a telescope can detect the stars by their lights. But it does not see the light of the stars. And it is to the sun itself, and not to a telescope, that Goethe wants us to compare the eye. Its function is not to pick up energetic signals conveying information about distant objects, and to refer them on to an interior mental device, or mind-brain, for processing. Our sun-like eyes, for Goethe, are not the organs of a body, nor does the comparison rest upon the spherical form of both the eyeballs and the solar orb. He sees in the eye, rather, the affective disposition of a body that, in opening itself to the heavens, becomes a creature of the light. It is as though the body, bathed in light, were to become all eye – as though we were eye-bodies, not bodies with eyes. And it is to understand the sun likewise, not as a celestial body – an *object* of vision to be seen, at best, through a glass, darkly – but as that which lights our existence and the world from within, on the hither side of vision. As the sun *is* its shining, so it shines in our own eyes. Like the sky itself, sunshine belongs to the phenomenal rather than the physical order of reality.

For us humans, of course, sunlight not only illuminates our world; it warms us too. So, on an infinitely lesser scale, do the flames of the fire. In the eyes of medieval people, for whom the naked flame was far more central to both warmth and nocturnal illumination than for most of us today, light and combustion were inseparable. Wherever there was light, something was burning. The rising flames of a fire twist and curl in response to atmospheric conditions, much as do the trunks of trees, rising from the earth. The metaphor of the beam of light has its source in this comparison. The word referred originally to a living tree, a usage preserved in the names of such common arboreal species as whitebeam, hornbeam and quickbeam. The archetypal incendiary analogue of the tree-trunk was the biblical *columna lucis*, the fiery 'pillar of light' by which, in the Book of Exodus, the Israelites were guided on their way at night. We have it on the authority of the Venerable Bede, writing in the eighth century, that the beam was the light or fire ascending from the body of a saint. Light beams from the saintly body, according to Bede, as the tree trunk grows from the earth.[3]

Here, the beam was a flame. So, too, the thirteenth century painters who decorated the wooden ceiling of the stave-church of Ål, in central Norway, depicted sunbeams as flames, spewing out in all directions from a blazing solar fireball (Figure 6.1). Only later was the beam straightened. Eventually, it would refer to straight-cut timber, not the living tree; to the rectilinear ray and not the flame.[4] The timber was felled, the flames extinguished, light dematerialised. The world was straightened out, geometricised. Yet the geometry of rays, and

Figure 6.1 The sun and the moon. Detail from a painting from the wooden ceiling of the stave-church of Ål, in central Norway, dating from the thirteenth century.

Courtesy of the Museum of Cultural History, University of Oslo.

with it the idea of radiation, of straight lines issuing from a central point, did not have to await the birth of modern physics, let alone the discovery of electromagnetism. It was already there, in Ancient Greece, in the set-up by which a stake in the ground, rising erect like the *gnomon* of the sundial, would cast its shadow by the sun's rays, allowing measurement by proportion. In this set-up, as Michel Serres (2017: 139) remarks, 'there is no place for the eye, nor site that can be called a point of view'. The sun alone disposes, leaving mortal eyes to pick out the forms of things from patterns in the light, while blind to the light itself. Whereas the beam is as much in the eye as it is in the sun, the ray of light is in neither, but connects the two.

In short, the ray is as distinct from the flame as emission from combustion. They rest, fundamentally, on wholly different ontologies of the sun and its light. As an emitter of rays, the sun is transcendental, master of the cosmos, invisibly disposing its visible objects according to geometric laws. But as a beaming fireball, it is elemental, shining in the eyes and warming the hearts of all who are dazzled by its splendour. It is no wonder that throughout human history, those with aspirations to absolute power have sought to enlist the sun in their enterprise, or even to model their rule upon that of the sun itself. Nor is it any accident that 'royal' and 'radial' are derived from the same root, or that the 'ruler' is both a sovereign and an instrument for making straight lines (Ingold 2007a: 160). Yet no ruler has managed to resolve the duality between the two suns, of geometry and of fire. The monarch who would order his kingdom politically, according to principles of geometry, but would also dazzle his subjects spiritually, with the brilliance of his light, must command both.

Perhaps that is why the sun-god Inti, worshipped by the rulers of the Inca people, is depicted as a golden disk radiating arms that are alternately wavy and straight (Figure 6.2). These are the arms of different suns, with different lights. The straight arms are rays, they ordain the political order of the Inca state, with its straight roads radiating out from the capital, Cusco. With their sharp points, they pin the people to the land, each community in its appointed place. But the wavy arms are flames; they are sources of heat and vitality, of divine power. With them, the sun-god wraps his devotees in the warmth of his embrace. And as we go around the sun's disk, first the ray, and then the flame, is invoked. In late medieval Europe, heraldic depictions of the 'sun in splendour' adopted a similar solar imagery, again with an alternation of wavy and straight arms, to signify the unity of Church and State. In a synthesis of Amerindian and European traditions, we even find the same iconography reproduced today, in the national flags of Uruguay and Argentina.[5] In the Uruguayan version the sun has 16 arms, in the Argentinian it has 32, but on both flags, rays take turns with flames. The straight, radial lines order the universe, but it takes the wavy lines for the sun itself to shine. And it is in its shining, in our very own eyes, that the sun arises in its full splendour.

Figure 6.2 Pachacuti, the ninth ruler of the Inca state, worshipping the sun-god Inti, at the temple of Coricancha. From the seventeenth-century chronicles of Martín de Murúa.

Observing the stars

Which of these is light: flame or rays? Physics would answer with the latter. Light consists in the rays we cannot see but which afford the sight of things, and radiate in straight lines from a source. But phenomenal experience tells us otherwise: that light can be seen as plainly as the flame of a candle; that it does *not* travel in straight lines but curls up and around, much like the smoke of a fire, but along a path orthogonal to the radii that connect the centre of the flame to all points on the periphery. Perhaps that is why Vincent van Gogh, in his celebrated painting The *Starry Night*, drew swirls of light, spiralling around the stars and moon, rather than lines radiating out from them (Ingold 2015: 96).[6] In a letter to a friend, dating from 1888, van Gogh had signalled his intention to paint the night sky in a way that would go beyond the 'single brief glance at reality' offered by the visual snapshot (Soth 1986: 301). He wanted his stars to shine, and this meant painting them in a way that would correspond with the duration of a gaze that, wandering among the stars, is not instantaneous but indefinitely prolonged. His first attempt, in a painting entitled *Starry Night Over the Rhone*, had not been entirely successful since, bowing to convention, he had depicted each star as a yellow point from which short yellow streaks radiated into a chunky, deep-blue sky. But in *The Starry Night* (Figure 6.3), the radial streaks gave way to concentric halos, and every star became a vortex in the sky's swirling current. And look at the tree in the foreground. Though dark, it rises and curls exactly like a flame!

How does the painter's observation of the stars, then, compare with that of the astronomer? One difference is that whereas the painter observes with the naked eye, the astronomer typically has resort to a telescope. Any diagram of the workings of the telescope will depict light as rectilinear rays. It is supposed that stellar rays, after a millennia-spanning traverse through outer space, eventually enter the aperture of the telescope, only to be refracted or reflected to a focal point by a convex lens or concave mirror,

Figure 6.3 Vincent van Gogh, *The Starry Night (De sterrennacht)*, June 1889. Courtesy of the Museum of Modern Art (MoMA). © Scala, Florence.

before passing through the eye-piece and into the eye of the observer. For the astronomer, these rays, captured and brought to a focus by the telescope, serve as vectors of projection, delivering information in their array that specifies the layout and distribution of these distant and mysterious cosmic bodies, at a magnification that allows for their optical resolution. But the stars themselves, in the astronomer's understanding, are not light; they are emitters of light. And however much they might have appeared to glow or shine in the eye of the observer, in the paper record their lustre is extinguished. On a map of the night sky, every star appears as a mere dot, each in its exact and proper location. But the dots don't shine. It is as though, in rendering the stars not as light but as objects seen *by means of* light, their fires have been put out.

Remember Romeo? His soul is on fire, and he would enlist the stars in the heavens to light the eyes of his beloved. Van Gogh is equally star-struck, but in his ecstasy the eyes the stars ignite are his own. As his gaze roams the vault of the heavens, he recovers the core of his own being (Ingold 2015: 95–6). Herein, as Merleau-Ponty (1964: 186) put it, in an essay to which I have already referred, lies the essence of vision. It is, he wrote, 'the means given me for being absent from myself, for being present at the fission of Being from the inside – the fission at whose termination, and not before, I come back to myself'. Whatever does he mean? We are familiar enough with the idea, bequeathed to us by René Descartes in his *Optics* of 1637, that the inner self, unitary and indivisible, is divided off from the cosmos, which it sees only thanks to the operation of the *cogito* on the input of visual information conveyed in rays of light, and passed by the way of the retina and optic nerves to the brain. 'It is the soul which sees', wrote Descartes (1988: 68), 'and not the eye; and it does not see directly, but only by means of the brain.' Yet Merleau-Ponty seems to be saying precisely the opposite, namely that in vision we are at once united with the cosmos and yet divided from ourselves. How, then, can the fission of my being from the inside terminate in its fusion? How can my very absence amount to a restoration? To resolve the paradox, we will need nothing less than an alternative topology of the self.

The Cartesian topology, to which we are accustomed, installs the self within a bodily container, bounded by the skin. We imagine the skin as an interface, dividing a mind, confined to the inside, from an outside world, with apertures that allow the passage of information from one side to the other. From this point of view the telescope, in its basic design, magnifies the capacity of the eye without fundamentally altering the nature of vision. Descartes, indeed, was an enthusiast. Since sight is the noblest of the senses, he opined, there can be no more useful inventions than those, such as the telescope, which increase its power (Descartes 1988: 57). Looking through a telescope, it is as if one were peering not just through an aperture in the head, but through a tube, the other end of which opens to the sky. In use, the telescope certainly tends to induce this sense of tunnel vision, of being on the inside looking out. Yet you have only to put the instrument aside and open your eyes to an illuminated world, for your experience to be is transformed. For far from peering through one aperture or two, you will find yourself cast into the open, free from bodily confinement. Yet you still have eyes to see, along with ears to listen, a nose to smell and a mouth to speak. You still have a face. So the topological question is: what kind of surface is this? How does the face relate to the head, and to the body of which the head is a part? How can you inhabit it?

The head is part of the body. It has the shape of a semi-enclosed cavity, of measurable volume. It is thus constituted anatomically within what Gilles Deleuze and Félix Guattari (2004: 186–93) call the 'volume-cavity system'. Like all bodies of this type it has an inside and an outside. But the face, claim Deleuze and Guattari, is not part of the body at all, nor even of the head. It is rather a surface of a quite different order, of the 'black hole/white wall system', constituted by the play of illumination and shadow that brings out its bulges and orifices, lines and wrinkles.[7] Perhaps it could be compared to a landscape of glistening rocks and dark pools, in which the recesses of the earth meet and mingle with the brilliance of the sky. As earth and sky are fused in the ground surface, so are self and world fused in the surface of the face. The head may be a container that divides self from world, but the face is more comparable to a veil that brings them together. The veil, in this sense, is not a material that covers the face or hides it from prying eyes. Nor can one look *through* it, from one side to the other. As with the sky, whether by day or by night, so too with the veil, one can only look *into* it. A tear in the fabric, far from opening it up to reveal something of substance on the other side, would rather give way to nothingness: not the liquid nothingness of an empty sky or even interstellar space, from which everything comes, but an absolute nothingness that holds no potential whatever for becoming.

As a surface, then, the face does not divide inner from outer worlds. It rather separates existence from non-existence. This, in turn, offers a clue to the solution of Merleau-Ponty's paradox. For we can now see that eyes that shine, that brighten our world like the sun, belong to the black hole/white wall system of the face and not to the volume-cavity system of the head. And in their shining, the infinitely far merges with the infinitely close. For in our experience, what is closest to us and what is furthest away, the self and the star – far from lying at opposite ends of a continuous line of immeasurable length, that would pierce the heavens like a ray of light – fuse, on approach to infinity, into a singular experience of Being. In Merleau-Ponty's phenomenology of visual perception, closeness can only be reached through distance, and distance through closeness. There is no halfway-between. And in the veil, as in the face, the two infinites – of distance and proximity – come together.

Colouring in the darkness

To observe the stars, we must go out at night. For only then do they show up as pinpricks of light adrift in the liquid darkness of the night sky. But if it is hard enough to fathom what light is, how much more unfathomable is darkness! Nominally, dark is the absence of light. The meaning of darkness, then, must depend on what we take light to be. Thus if light is defined as radiation, darkness would be the point of zero-emission. Without light, in this sense, we would see nothing. Yet in our experience, complete darkness seems well-nigh impossible to attain. Even in the confines of the photographer's darkroom, one is assailed by flashes and streaks of light, an experience presumably shared by those who, in Palaeolithic times, ventured into the deepest caves to leave marks of their presence. The motifs they left there, including dots, zigzags and grids, resemble those familiar to anyone who has suffered the aura presaging an attack of migraine (Lewis-Williams and Dowson 1988). However, simply closing one's eyes is enough to produce a darkness peppered with scintillations. Where does this light come from?

Even with our eyes open, radiant light, entering the pupils, gets no further than the back of the retina. From where, then, comes the light we see, that saturates our awareness? How can we experience daylight, if inside our heads it is dark? And how can we tell the difference between different shades of darkness? The liquid darkness that we experience on a moonless night is quite unlike the dense and claustrophobic darkness of the cave, and both, again, are unlike the darkness that comes from closing one's eyes in readiness for sleep. The absence of optical stimulation no more explains these variations in the experience of darkness than does its presence explain differences in the experience of light. To resolve these issues, we will need to return to a theme that I have so far only touched upon, in raising the question of whether light can be understood as a constituent of the material world, or whether it merely intercedes between our eyes and the objects of visual perception. This is the theme of colour. Darkness, we say, is black – pitch black. Light, at its most intense, is white. But white and black are not colours; or are they? What about grey? There are many shades of grey, as there are of white and black. Are they, then, in between? And if so, where do we put the colours of the rainbow?

At the root of the problem of colour is the elision of the beam with the ray. At the turn of the eighteenth century, it caused Goethe – in his *Theory of Colours* of 1810 – to launch a blistering attack on the optics of Isaac Newton (Goethe 1840). For Newton, mathematician and physicist to the core, light meant rays. And rays, when differentially refracted by means of a prism, would yield up all the colours of the rainbow, from red to violet. Recombined, they would merge into 'colourless' white. Colour, then, was strictly a property of rays, and as such, given quite independently of our experience of it. But Goethe would have none of this. For him, light was a phenomenon of experience – an affective intermingling of our own awareness with the turbulence and pulsations of the medium. It was the flame of the candle, not its rays, and it illuminated the world, as do the flames of a fire, in the combustion of materials. As with the blaze of a wood fire, light at its most intense is white, grading off through yellow, red and blue to the black of cold charcoal or of the pitch that oozes from charred roots.[8] Thus light acts on matter as fire on wood, generating all the colours in the process, on a scale not from red to violet but from white to black. This is a scale not of quantitative variation, as would nowadays be measured in terms of wavelength, but a qualitative scale of affective intensity. And only on such a scale can we register the contrast between black and white, or distinguish darker colours from lighter ones. Indeed for Goethe, as the physicist and philosopher Henri Bortoft (2019: 13) explains, 'colours arise from light and dark alone', whether in lightening the dark or in darkening the light.

I began this chapter by recalling how Gibson (1979), in his ecological approach to visual perception, gets himself into difficulties on account of his refusal to accept that light can be seen. We only see the objects in our environment, he asserts, *by means* of light; we do not see light itself. He is then forced to go to some lengths to explain away the experiences of firelight and lamplight, sunlight and moonlight, that are so familiar to everyone. They are all 'manifestations of light', he insists, 'not light as such'. Thus 'a fire with coals or flames, a lamp with a wick or filament, a sun or a moon – all these are quite specific objects and so specified; no one sees merely light'. Even the star we see as a point of light in the heavens is not really 'light', but a distant source that is specified by it (Gibson 1979: 54–5). Now these specifications, given in the optic array, can include differences of hue. Ecologically speaking, Gibson argues, these differences, caused by variations in the capacity of surfaces to reflect light of different wavelengths, can convey important information, for example about whether a fruit is ripe for eating. You can see why this would have been a matter of great interest to ancestral humans, dependent on the fruits of the earth for subsistence. But these differences are ranged along the spectrum, as they were for Newton, not on a scale from light to dark, as for Goethe. Spectral differences, according to Gibson (1979: 31), are 'chromatic', whereas differences of lightness or darkness are 'achromatic'. And the question, then, is: how do we perceive variations on the achromatic scale, from black to white?

This brings us back to grey. Is it a colour at all? It is certainly not on any colour spectrum. 'Grey', argues artist David Batchelor (2014: 78), 'is the colour not just of not-colour but of anti-colour, in theory.' But as Batchelor admits, it is only anti-colour 'in theory' because whenever you compare different greys, they always turn out to be chromatically inflected: this grey here is bluish, that grey there reddish, and so on. In other words, it is not possible in practice to hive off strictly chromatic from strictly achromatic variation, or spectral hue from luminosity. Indeed Gibson admits as much, for in a discussion of the changes of texture that a surface can undergo – such as in the greening of plants, the blackening of burned wood, or the reddening of rusty iron – he admits that chromatic and achromatic variations are practically indistinguishable. Perhaps his most interesting and problematic observations concern the colour of fire. 'A fire with flames', Gibson (1979: 98) assures us, 'consists of complex motions and deformations, fluctuating luminous surfaces, reddening and blackening of the opaque surfaces, billowing smoke, and finally a disappearance of solid surfaces.' Now that may be accurate enough as a description of modulations in the texture of burning materials, as they are gradually reduced to ash. In their fiery transformation, the materials do indeed change colour, and this is ecologically relevant. Something, however, is missing.

The missing element is the flames themselves. No blazing timbers dazzle with their yellow light, nor do the red-hot coals to which they are eventually reduced actively glow. What Gibson presents to us, in fact, is not a fire but the simulacrum of a fire, an assemblage of surfaces made to look like one, as for example on a stage set. His flames might as well be crumpled cellophane, in various shades of yellow and red; his coals could be made of plastic coated to make them look as though they glow. And this returns us to the nub of the problem with which we began: can light itself be seen, or do we only see objects in the world by means of it? If, with Gibson, we were to agree that the one thing we never see is light itself, then the fire could only be an object whose textured surfaces are revealed in the light; it cannot be the actual, incandescent event of burning, with flames that leap as much in the atmosphere as, coextensively, in our own eyes. Can there be a more compelling demonstration of the cul-de-sac into which we would be led, were we to limit the definition of light to radiant energy? For to repeat, in our experience, light *is* the fire. It is a process of combustion, manifested in the reactive transformation of materials. We may only see it thanks to the radiation it emits, but what we see is the light – the flame – not an object in the light. So, too, we see the lustre of the gilded icon, of stained glass bathed in the light of the sun, of the painting whose colours literally glow. In our experience, indeed, colour and lustre are inseparable.

In the shadows

After all this talk of flame and sunshine, of brilliance and lustre, I should like to conclude this chapter on a more sombre note, by entering into the world of shadows. We may agree that shadow is the negative of illumination. But what difference does it make, whether we think of light as rays or as beams? If light has no truck with the material world but serves merely as a vector, delivering its objects to our eyes, then the shadow can be no more than the form of absence, of invisibility. Shadowed things cannot be clearly seen since whatever casts the shadows blocks out incident light that would otherwise be reflected from their outward-facing surfaces. Everything under the sun casts its shadow, upon itself, on other things, and on the earth. Yet unlike things, these shadows have no substance, and they come and go. Out of doors they flicker with the breeze, as it brushes the surfaces of leaves and makes them tremble; indoors they flicker with the light-source, whether it be candle-flame or fire. They come and go, too, with the passage of clouds in the sky. Whenever the sun disappears behind a cloud, the shadow also vanishes. This is not – as is often thought – because the cloud blocks out the sun's rays, for were that so, every passing cloud would pitch us into black night! What happens in fact is that these rays are dispersed in all directions by atmospheric vapour, with the result that the illumination of surfaces is evened out. Thus, areas that were in shadow when the sun is out actually brighten up when the sun goes in. What fades is the contrast.

This, indeed, comes close to an ideal condition of illumination. For the default assumption, under a regime of modernity, is that shadows obscure rather than reveal. To see things as they really are, we insist, they must be brought out from the shadows. That is why we invest so heavily in the all-around, static illumination afforded by electric light, along with perfectly transparent glass and white walls. Yet whether shadows actually conceal or reveal depends, to an extent, on whether our interest is in the objective forms of things or in the textures of their self-shadowing surfaces. Texture shows up much better in a light that rakes the surface, coming at a shallow angle. Art historian Michael Baxandall (1995: 125) makes precisely this point. In an ordinary illuminated environment, he writes, one is 'aware of being in an indescribably intricate ambience of micro-shadow. It may usually be called texture, a word that somehow invokes the sense of touch, but it consists visually of almost pure shadow – very small self-shadows, derived shadows, and slant/tilt shadings.' Every crease or bump shows up in the contrast between the relative illumination of its light-facing facets and the relative darkness of facets in their shade. The weave of cloth, ripples of water, inscriptions in stone, blades of grass, a human face: all are picked out in these shadowy variations.

Critically, to attend to surface as texture, rather than as the envelope of a form, entails a quite different understanding of the surface itself. It is one that we have already encountered in our earlier discussion of the face and the ground. As we have seen, far from separating inside from outside, or above from below, the texture is an intermingling. Just as earth and sky intermingle in the ground, so self and world intermingle in the face. Neither face nor ground, however, can be taken in at a glance. We have rather to follow its variations of illumination and shade by joining in its temporal unfolding, almost as one would listen to an orchestral composition. The world that is revealed to us by doing so, far from being laid out in fixed and final forms, is launched in unceasing movement. That this should come as a surprise is an index of the extent to which light has been co-opted in the service of the modern project of objectification, and lighting technologies to its architectural and artefactual realisation. It is this, in turn, that has led to light's abstraction from materials and its reduction, in scientific discourses, to radiant energy.

However to people of pre-modern times – that is, for the greater part of human history – light meant something altogether different. Theirs was a light that, far from travelling in straight lines from source to recipient, shone, flickered and glowed, flashed in lightning and curled in the flames of a fire. It was the light of combustion, unfolding in experience, and it was perfectly real. This was abundantly evident to medieval church-builders, whose priorities were quite unlike those of their contemporary counterparts, the architects of museums and galleries. They were masters of shadow, of surface convolutions and dark corners, hiding things in alcoves and vaults in such a way that they would appear to emerge only with the shining of the light, through windows or from lamps, only to fade back into the woodwork or masonry once the light has passed (Bille and Sørensen 2017).

But if the shining light enters materially into the constitution of the world, then surely so also does shadow. It is not so much an objective absence as an affective presence. Like darkness, it can be sensed, experienced, and feared. Where light warms us, we feel the shade in its cool. Perhaps it makes us shiver. And as it passes, it can leave a material residue: the ash of the fire, the scorched earth of a lightning strike, the black pitch oozing from the burning tree-trunk, the mound of wax from an exhausted candle. These shadows have substance: they are not projections of rigid form but the residues of material flows, admixtures and mutations. Moreover they are as closely bound to the beings or things that cast them as is the carpet of leaves, for example, cast on the ground by a tree in autumn, bound to the tree itself, or as the ghost – if you have ever experienced such things – is bound to the person. The shadow, here, is the spectral double of the fire that both animates every living being and assures its eventual destruction. And my claim, in finale, is that to take the fire of combustion rather than electromagnetic radiation as a point of departure could open up an entirely new – but also old and long forgotten – chapter in thinking about the phenomena of light.

Chapter 7

Between noise and silence

On the meaning of sound

Black and white

Who can define what noise is? It is a word that points to the sheer impossibility of definition. If anything is something, it is not noise; if it is somewhere, it is not noise; if it is intelligible, it is not noise. In all these ways, noise appears to be the sensory equivalent of dirt. Where dirt, as anthropologists say, is matter out of place, noise is sense out of place – or in a word, nonsense.[1] It is a manifestation of the disorder of the world, of its entropic tendencies. And since noise is undefinable, it cannot define. It pays no respect to categorical boundaries. It makes concentration hard, focus impossible. It rocks the foundations of existence, condemning us to ride the ocean of sensation like landlubbers on the deck of a ship, heaving every which way in the swell. Indeed it is from the Latin *nausea*, with its reference to seasickness, that our word 'noise' is derived (Home-Cook 2015: 28). Yet precisely because of its formlessness, noise harbours an unlimited creative potential. Every cycle of life starts in noise, even if it ends in silence: between life and death, noise and silence, lies everything of form and significance. In his *Principles of Psychology*, William James (1890: 488) famously wrote that 'the baby, assailed by eyes, ears, nose, skin, and entrails at once, feels it all as one great blooming, buzzing confusion'. If that is noise, then it is not limited to the auditory realm but covers every possible way in which the world is present to the senses. In what follows, however, I am principally concerned with the 'buzz' of auditory sensation, though I will also draw comparison with the 'bloom' of the visual.

My question is this: if we begin in noise and end in silence, then how can they be distinguished? Or are they just the same? Do we end, in life, where we began? The paradox of noise is that it can be deafening. When noise is at its most intense, it is impossible to hear anything. Yet where nothing is audible, is that not silence? Both noise and silence, it seems, are experiences of hearing *nothing*. But hearing *something* – that, surely, is an experience of sound. Are noise and silence, then, two extremes of a continuum between which lie every shade and intensity of sound? If so, how are we to tell them

DOI: 10.4324/9781003171713-10

apart? It does not help to observe that noise is ... well, noisy! Or that silence is silent. Posed thus, in the field of aural perception, the conundrum has its counterpart in the field of visual perception in the question of how to tell day from night. Absolute silence is often compared to the blackness of the night. When it is pitch dark, and with neither moon and stars nor any artificial light for illumination, you cannot see anything. All around and in your head is black. But light can be blinding, just as noise can be deafening. The more blinding the light, or the more deafening the noise, the more it inclines to white. The counterpart of white noise is the whiteout of a snowstorm, or a thick fog, in which daylight visibility is reduced virtually to zero. Both the black of the blackout and the white of the whiteout are experiences of seeing nothing. In between, every shade and intensity of light affords an experience of seeing something. What is the difference, then, between black and white?

Resolving the conundrum takes us to the heart of the problem of what we mean by light and sound. Picking up from the last chapter, let me begin with light, by returning once again to James Gibson's (1979) ecology of visual perception. Recall that for Gibson, light is no more and no less than what physics says it is, namely 'photons or waves or radiant energy' (1979: 55). If that is so, then despite the name 'optics' having been assigned to the physics of light, there can be light even without eyes to see. Nothing more is needed than a source of emission. Even if eyes are present, they see not light itself, but objects revealed to vision by means of it. What matters for vision, according to Gibson, is the patterning that comes from the way rays of light are reflected or refracted by surfaces in the world. The continuous modulation of these patterns, as they are picked up by the moving observer, is sufficient to specify the features of the environment that we actually see (Chapter 2, page 31). When, in our experience, we see nothing, it is because for one reason or another, the patterning has been eradicated. This could be because the light source has been occluded, as the sun is at night, or because rays of light have been diffracted at random by particles of moisture in the atmosphere, as in a fog, with the result that any differentiation in ambient light that may have specified environmental information has been dissolved. In this respect, as Gibson himself observes, there is nothing to distinguish ambient light from ambient darkness. Either way, we see not something but nothing – pure emptiness (Gibson 1979: 52).

It is just the same with sound. Physicists explain that sound is a mechanical vibration in the medium, set off by some initial disturbance – be it the impact of one object on another or the friction of materials in movement – and emitted in all directions from the source. In this sense, sound has no more need of ears to exist than light has need of eyes, and acoustics is as much a misnomer for the physics of sound as optics is a misnomer for the physics of light. What then do we hear? If we apply the same logic to aural perception as Gibson applies to vision, then we arrive at a conclusion that is both surprising and counterintuitive. It is that the last thing we hear is sound itself. What we actually hear, and commonly mistake for sound, are patterns or invariants in the sonic milieu whose modulations allow us to identify events or properties of the environment.[2] When asked to report on what we hear, we tell not of the sounds themselves but of the objects and events they bring to our attention: a dog barking, a door slamming, a car passing. And when we report that we hear nothing – not even the dog, the door or the car – it is because there is no discernible pattern in the acoustic signal. This may be because the signal has faded out or been occluded by a barrier, or because it has been completely scrambled by interference. 'White noise', as cultural historian Hillel Schwartz (2011: 834) tells us, 'is patternless sound ... rather than an olla [concoction] of all sounds'. In their effects, black silence and white noise are no different. Either way, nothing is heard. With hearing as with vision, it seems there is no telling black from white.

Outside or inside?

Yet manifestly, we *can* tell the difference. The contrast between being blinded by light and cast into darkness is palpable, even though in neither case can we see anything. And so is the contrast between being deafened by noise and cocooned in hermetic silence, even though – again – in neither case can anything be heard. What, then, is the light that blinds, and the noise that deafens? They cannot be the energetic impulses to which physicists refer, for the ray penetrates only as far as the retina, and the sonic vibration as far as the eardrum. Might their sources rather lie within? Could the eyes and ears be sites not for the reception, respectively, of light and noise, but for their generation? If the senses are like keyboards, might the player actually be inside the piano? Much attention has been paid to the study of entoptic phenomena, such as the zigzag streaks of light auguring a migraine attack, or the 'floaters' that dart about in the eye, invading the field of vision.[3] That the eyes have their own lights can be confirmed merely by closing them for a moment and concentrating on the darkness of a field lit up by specks as innumerable as stars in the night sky. They have their counterparts in the repertoire of buzzing, hissing and clicking noises that torment sufferers from tinnitus. All of us experience these noises to a degree, even if – for most of the time – they remain in the background. And as the composer John Cage (2011: 10) observed, total silence is impossible as long as the blood of the body keeps circulating and nerves remain on edge.[4]

Now clearly, closing one's eyes on a summer's day will not stop the sun from emitting radiation; nor will stopping one's ears quell the vibrations set off by an explosion. Light and sound, in their physical definitions, remain real and present even if you shut yourself off from their sensory impact. In these terms the dazzle you experience behind closed eyes even in the absence of external light, and the buzz of nerves inside your head even in the absence of external sound, can be no more than visual or auditory hallucinations. Perhaps they mimic the sensory effects of exposure to external, luminary or sonic stimuli, but they are not light and sound in themselves. If, however, we allow that our dazzled eyes and buzzing ears do indeed fill our heads with light and sound, and that there is no escaping either – even in a darkroom or anechoic chamber – then evidently, the physics will not help us. Could psychology offer an alternative? Are light and sound 'inside the head', rather than 'out there' in the world? Are they affectations of the mind, sparked off by neural impulses that are either triggered in response to external stimulation or set off of their own accord? If that is so, then light is light, and sound is sound, whether or not it can be attributed to an external source. The bang that I hear, then, is a 'bang in the head', regardless of any explosion that may have taken place – if at all – in the world (Porath 2008: 647–9).

Classical psychology imagines that an interface separates mind and world and mediates all exchanges between them. That interface is the body, including its sensory organs such as eyes and ears as well as the touch-sensitive envelope of skin. On the outside, the body is energetically buffeted by photoelectric radiation and by vibrations in the medium. On the inside, it registers light and sound. This is a separation, however, that is belied by experience. We are inhabitants not of our bodies, but of a world. The body, with its organs of sense, affords an opening to this world, not a means of separation: it offers exposure, not immunity. Light and sound, then, are neither 'in here' nor 'out there', neither mental nor physical. On the contrary, the very experience of light, or of sound, is one in which the interface is dissolved – in which mind and world, the sensing and the sensible, fuse together and, in so doing, constitute a field of perception. As Maurice Merleau-Ponty (2002: 370) put it, light and sound present themselves as 'kinds of symbiosis, certain ways the outside has of invading us and certain ways we have of meeting this invasion'. The symbiosis, if you will, is of the affective and the cosmic. Wherever the two collide – where our attention is let loose upon the world – there is ignited a kind of spark. Herein, says Merleau-Ponty (1964: 163–4), lies the continual birth of our visual awareness, that is, of light itself. But he could have said just the same of sound (Ingold 2015: 96, 107–8).

Let me return to William James and the new-born baby, assailed as he says by blooming, buzzing confusion. Opening its eyes upon the world for the first time, the baby recognises nothing. 'The first time we see *light*', wrote James (1892: 14), 'we *are* it rather than see it'.[5] Struck blind from that moment, the baby nevertheless knows something that its elders, recognising everything they see around them, have long forgotten: a sense of what light really is, in its first incarnation. Not until we find ourselves lost in a whiteout, rekindling the experience of that 'first opening', does the memory return. Could it be the same with sound? The baby is immersed in sound long before being exposed to light, for its auditory awareness has already developed in the bubbling, thumping and gurgling environment of the womb. Perhaps, in the experience of the unborn child, sound is not what she hears but what she is, until that moment of birth when she becomes a being of the light as well. Of course we were all there once. And while we can only speculate as to what it must have been like, it seems that the primordial memory of sound has not been eradicated, in the minds of modern people, to the extent that we have lost the memory of light. The difference shows up in the radical distinction that is commonly drawn in so-called western societies between vision and hearing. We see *things*, it is said, but hear *sounds* (Ingold 2000: 244). Why is that? Why should the objects of vision appear broken off from the light that renders them to us, whereas the things we hear seem to be sculpted from the very stuff of sound itself?

Making things out

According to a widely held view, vision sets things at a distance, in their proper places. And looking is a targeted act of perception. In their verb *skopein*, 'to look', the ancient Greeks compared it to shooting an arrow. But hearing, we are told, is immersive: it lets sound in, gathering it from every direction, and concentrating it at the very core of our awareness. We find ourselves not set apart but at the centre of our auditory world.[6] Now to this, one could object on two counts. On the one hand, listening to things can be just as targeted as looking at them: indeed the one assists the other, since in swivelling the head to balance the auditory input from the source, our eyes are precisely oriented in its direction, helping us to pick it out. On the other hand, the luminous experience of a whiteout can be just as immersive as that of all-around noise, just as constitutive of our existence as sentient beings. In their eagerness to contrast vision and hearing, scholars seem inadvertently to have chosen to foreground targeted perception in the former case and immersive experience in the latter. This is hardly to compare like with like. It appears, in effect, that the alleged contrast between hearing and vision has been introduced as a surrogate for a distinction of more fundamental ontological consequence, between the nascent experience of a world in constant becoming, in which things are ever on the point of emerging from the fluxes of their generation, and the retrospective review of a world of being, in which everything has already precipitated out and has fallen where it will, in this position or that.

Thus, each time I identify a thing I hear as its sound, I am reminded of the work it takes to differentiate both myself as hearer and the thing heard from the continuum in which we were both primordially immersed. The thing has to be 'made out', and in so doing I make myself out as well, fashioning a self in the very act of hearing. Wrapped up in the sound of the thing is the memory of its once having been dissolved in an ocean of vibrant materials, and – wrapped in my hearing of it – is the memory of having been flooded by noise, even before I was born. In hearing, my auditory awareness remains saturated with the medium whence it emerged, as is the thing heard. The puzzle is why we, modern people, should have come to think so differently about vision: why it is that when we use our eyes rather than our ears, we should think of ourselves as already completed beings, and of the world as one in which everything has fallen finally into place. It seems that as vision has been co-opted to serve the ends of the modern project of objectification, we have forgotten how things are not just there to be seen but have themselves to be made out from mist or darkness as sculptures of light and shadow. And so we say of a thing or matter that 'it appears', as though the 'it' were already there and waiting to be revealed to our prying eyes, while oblivious to the 'appearing' that must be done to bring it forth. To say 'appears it', as Henri Bortoft (2012: 95–6) remarks, may be grammatically aberrant, 'but it is better philosophically'.

Perhaps the co-option of vision has something to do with the translucence of glass, the ubiquity of mirrors and the conquest of the dark by electric light. As a material, glass is not naturally translucent, and it has taken a massive technological effort to develop procedures to make it so. This effort has been driven by an ideal of perfection according to which the truth of things is to be seen objectively, as through a window, yet without distortion. Perfectly translucent glass both separates us from the object of perception, while yet affording a correct and complete picture. And if glass completes the world as its picture, the mirror completes the self in its own image. We do not need others in whose eyes we can fashion ourselves, when the mirror, as philosopher Peter Sloterdijk (2011: 205) has it, already provides 'technical means of self-completion'.[7] Finally, with electric light, things emerge from the shadows, as fully formed objects in their own right, given independently of their illumination. But throughout the greater part of human history, illumination through the long hours of darkness came only from the light of the lamp or the fire, glass – if used at all – was uneven and partially opaque, while only the waters of a clear pool could offer reflection. Things looked differently then. In the previous chapter (page 88), we already encountered the example of traditional Japanese lacquerware. Finished in dusky shades of black, brown or red but decorated with flecks of silver and gold, the ware would come into its own in a room lit not by the sun or electricity but by a single lantern or candle. The novelist Junichiro Tanizaki, in his classic essay *In Praise of Shadows*, first published in 1933, describes how ware that looks dull and garish by day, would glow in the lamplight of an evening. It was meant to be seen in the dark (Tanizaki 2001: 21–5).

When we make out sounds from silence, then, are we not doing something similar to Tanizaki, when he admires lacquerware by candlelight? In the flickering flame, the ware emerges from the shadows. It is appeared, made out. Perhaps we should compare sound, then, to a flame. Now there are two ways of describing a flame, and in drawings these are often combined.

The flame itself is conventionally drawn with curvy lines that rise up from the wick but in no determinate direction. The convention conveys a sense of the liveliness of an apparition that exists only in the process of combustion. Fanning in all directions from a point at the centre of the flame, however, we draw another set of lines. These are straight and oriented. In the world the drawing depicts, although we can see the flame, no such lines can be seen.[8] But they are meant to indicate the rays that, invisible in themselves, illuminate the surfaces on which they fall. The simple drawing of a candle thus reveals two quite different ways of thinking about lines of light (Figure 7.1). There are lines of emission; these are *rays*. But there are also lines of combustion; I call them *beams*. Nowadays, of course, we tend to identify beams with rays, thinking of both – like the beams of milled timber that give structural support to buildings – as essentially rectilinear. Sunbeams break through clouds like the spokes of a wheel; a projector is otherwise known as a 'beamer'; spotlights and lasers cast beams that strake the sky with intersecting lines. Yet originally, as we saw in the last chapter, the beam was the trunk of the living tree, rising from the earth. And by analogy, the beam of light was the flame rising from the woodfire. It was a line, in short, not of emission but combustion, and it is in this original sense that I adopt the term here.

Pitch-line and earline

What, then, would be the sonic counterpart of the beam? I would nominate the word 'pitch', which coincidentally refers to the black, oozy substance released from the roots of the pine tree after it is fired (Ingold 2015: 108). But it is in another of the word's multiple senses that I adopt it here. 'To pitch', among other things, is to cast, toss or throw. As the tree grows, and as flames rise from the pyre, so – in the ongoing collision of cosmos and affect – sound erupts into the atmosphere formed of their unison. Once again, a clear distinction has to be made between the line of emission, connecting a source and a recipient, by which 'sound' is generally known to physics, and the line of eruption which describes the trajectory of sound as it unfolds in experience. The latter is its pitch. Imagine for example the sound of a siren, of the kind that in times of war, warns of an impending air-raid. It is produced by blowing air, with a fan, through an apparatus comprising a rapidly rotating disk within a static cylinder. Both disk and cylinder are punctured with holes that, as they come in and out of alignment, alternately block and release the air flow so as to generate vibrations of greater or lesser frequency, depending on the speed of rotation. These vibrations, conducted through the medium of air, eventually impinge on your ears – maybe some seconds or even minutes later, depending on the distance. On a diagram, you could draw a straight line from generator to ears, measure the distance, and calculate the time it takes for the auditory signal to traverse it.

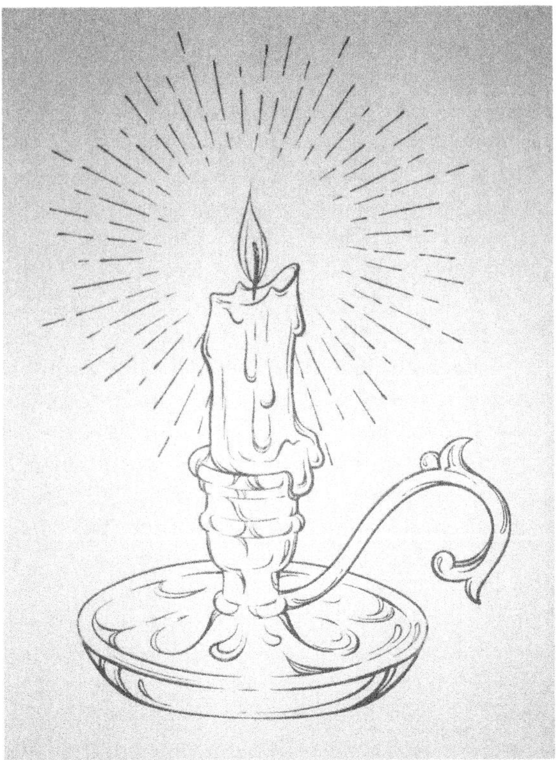

Figure 7.1 Conventional depiction of a candle, with flame and rays.

The line you have drawn is not however the same as the pitch-line of the sound itself, as you experience it. For the latter is a line that corresponds with the stretch of your own aural attention as it opens up upon the world. You would likely describe it as having no determinate start or end point, but as rising and swelling, holding for a while at a peak level, and then falling and trailing away. This line describes the trajectory of experienced sound. And the time it takes is the real-time duration of the siren's wail. We make no mistake, then, in identifying the wail as a sound rather than as a pattern *in* the sound. The generator, after all, produces nothing except aerial vibrations. The mistake is rather to confuse the *experience* of sound – that is, its pitch – with the mechanical signals that, along with a well-functioning auditory system, are among the conditions for the experience to occur. This would be the precise equivalent, in the field of aural perception, of confusing beam and ray in the field of vision. The wail of the siren is the analogue of the flame of the candle. As the flame is a beam of light, the wail is a pitch of sound. Both, in our experience, are entirely real. Yet here's the catch: neither the flame nor the siren is truly an *object* of perception. To observe the candle is to see by candlelight; to listen to the siren is to hear by its wail. With both vision and hearing, as Merleau-Ponty (1968: 140) pointed out in posthumously published notes, what captures our attention has a way of 'coiling over' so as to inflect the very process of attending.

It follows that light and sound are at once on the far side and on the hither side of vision and hearing respectively. What I see conditions my own way of seeing, what I hear my own way of hearing. Recall that for Merleau-Ponty, light and sound are neither 'in here in the head' nor 'out there in the world', neither mental nor physical, but experiential and atmospheric. It is at the very moment when the somatic boundaries between inside and outside dissolve, allowing the space of affect to fill the cosmos – and reciprocally, to be filled by it – that light ignites, and sound erupts, into our awareness. What happens, then, to eyes and ears? Anatomically speaking, they are organs firmly cemented in place at the front and sides of the head, primed to receive and respond to photoelectric and vibratory stimuli. But when I open my eyes and ears to the world – when I look, listen and attend – it seems to me that my head has disappeared. However my eyes and ears have not, they have rather expanded to pervade the entirety of visual and acoustic space, into which my whole existence is now poured. I am, as we say colloquially, 'all eyes' and 'all ears'. Sure, I can tap with my fingers, and confirm that a head is still there. But in the experience of light and sound, where my head is, there's a world! From being a body with eyes it seems that I am becoming eye-body; from being a body with ears I am becoming ear-body. 'An ear body', as sound-performance artist Fabrizio Manco (2016: 89) puts it, 'is an inclination to untie and to realise this radical openness, not only through the anatomical hearing ear, but also by becoming one'. How, then, is it possible to become ear?

For the body to become ear it has first to be decomposed anatomically, in order that it can then be reconstructed as something like a tissue of affects (Chapter 16, pages 252–3). This is not a surgical operation, of course, but a switch of perspective from acoustics to the phenomenology of auditory perception, or in other words, from objectification to experience. The ears – and for that matter the eyes as well – are thenceforth no longer the *organs* of a body but the affective dispositions of what Gilles Deleuze and Félix Guattari (2004: 165–84) call a 'body without organs'. According to Manco (2010: 102), the ear-body listens by tracing what he calls 'earlines'. If the cast of sound is its pitch, the earline is the stretch of attention that follows it like an elastic thread. The line can be inscribed on paper by drawing, or on the ground by walking, but the stretch itself is aerial. To get a sense of it, take a sheet of paper and crumple it up into a tight ball; then spread it out again. It will reveal a dense and irregular mesh of folds and creases, not unlike the surface of the ocean ruffled by the wind. It is a characteristic of folds and creases that they emerge from the surfaces in which they are formed, but never part from them. Where the paper or the ocean is crumpled on the surface, the air is crumpled in its volume. Noise is equivalent to the volume's 'crumpledness'. And while the overall impression may be one of chaos, every crease or fold potentially affords a line that can be followed. Just like the crease in the paper or the ruffle in the sea-surface, however, the line is *in* the noise, and never parts from it.

The colour of sound

This has an important corollary, namely that tracing an earline is an effort of continuous differentiation.[9] Theatre scholar George Home-Cook (2015: 24) describes thus his efforts to 'hear himself think', against the background noise of children playing next door: 'it is to listen out intently for my thoughts as they momentarily and haphazardly pop into view within this sonic barrage'. What is this listening out? It is not about search and retrieval. To hear something, rather than nothing, is not to come away with some material substance or object found. But nor should this imply that sound is immaterial. It is rather *in*-material, just as grain, for example, is *in*-wood, crease *in*-sheet, and path *in*-ground. Earlines are traced in the grains, creases and pathways of crumpled noise. They are no more and no less than lines of difference. To hear something is always to cut a fine line between the indifference of silence and of noise – or of what Deleuze (1994: 28) has called 'black nothingness' and 'white nothingness'. I have referred to this process of cutting from within, quite generally, as one of *interstitial differentiation* (Ingold 2017b: 13). By this I mean to oppose it to the external accretion by which assemblies are formed from initially discrete and self-contained elements.[10] It may be that the energetic sources of sound can be added one to another, as were the voices of neighbouring children for Home-Cook. But to attend to any particular sound or voice is not to set it apart by subtraction but to cut along its line, as the carpenter cuts along the grain, the seamstress along the crease or the walker along the path.

With black and white nothingness – silence and noise – we return at length to the question with which I began. How can we tell noise from silence, white from black? With a clearer understanding of what sound is, we have some hope of answering the question. We can do so by returning to the comparison with light, but this time with regard to the aspect of colour. Many people, gifted with a synaesthetic sensibility, will readily associate colour with the quality of experienced sound, generally known as its timbre. Indeed the association is so well established that in the German language, for example, the word for timbre, *Klangfarbe*, literally means 'sound-colour'. The philosopher Jean-Luc Nancy (2007: 39–40) has observed that there is 'no pitch ... without timbre (just as there is no line or surface without colour)'. How come, then, not only that pitch is specified in the notational conventions of classical music, on the stave score, quite independently of timbre, but also that the surface which – more than any other – is iconic of modernity, namely the transparent pane, mirror or screen, is perfectly colourless? Pitch, it seems, has been abstracted from the cast of sound, and colour from the luminosity of surface, only to be aligned on a scale of quantitative variation which allows the properties of energetic emissions to be objectively specified without regard to the qualities or intensities of sonorous or luminous experience induced in those with ears to hear or eyes to see. In effect, both pitch and colour have been spectralised: the one laid out on a spectrum of vibrational frequencies; the other on a spectrum of wavelengths (Ingold 2015: 111).

Analysts have struggled to find terms, including 'brightness', 'saturation' and 'value', to capture the ordinal qualities of light that are left once colour has been siphoned off. None, however, exhausts the inherent lustre, say, of Japanese lacquerware. Nor can their equivalents in the analysis of sound, such as 'amplitude' or 'tone', exhaust the qualities of timbre. In the case of light, as we saw in the last chapter, the problem has its source in the collapse of the beam into the ray, so as to elide the difference between them. Once beaming is reduced to radiant emission, light can no longer shine in our eyes. It remains for us to show that in the case of sound the problem lies, correspondingly, in the collapse of pitch into measured variations in frequency of the auditory input. With that, sound no longer erupts in our ears. Recall the difficulty we found in separating 'chromatic' variations, ranged along the colour spectrum, from 'non-chromatic' variations on a scale from white to black. Though the separation could be posited in theory, it proved impossible to achieve in practice. Exactly the same problem would arise, were we to attempt to separate out variations of pitch from 'non-pitch' variations. It is no accident that in musical theory the sequence of twelve adjacent and equidistant pitches, each separated by a semi-tone and together making up an octave, is called a *chromatic scale*. In an explicit parallel to spectral hue, pitch appears to vary from high to low, depending on the vibrational frequency of the signal, as colour varies with wavelength.[11] What, then, becomes of the non-pitch residue? Between white noise and black silence, is there a sonic equivalent of pure grey?

The answer in practice is no, since it is no more possible to separate out pitch from non-pitch variation, in the field of sound, than it is to separate chromatic from achromatic variation in the field of light. Were the colours of the fire confined to spectral variations in its radiant emissions, we would lose the flame, which could just as well be simulated artificially. So too, were we to limit variations of pitch to the different wavelengths of auditory emissions, we would lose the sonic cast of the siren that wails in our ears. This cast is what we conventionally call timbre. An acoustics limited to the detection of invariance in pitch patterns has no place for the experience of timbre. Not just the wail of the siren, but the clang of the bell, the honk of the horn, the buzz of the insect, the whoosh of the wind, the thump of the beating heart – all these sounds, which have inspired such a rich vein of onomatopoeia – would be lost to perception. Each would be the sonic equivalent of the vanishing flame. And the solution? It is to restore timbre to the pitch of sound, bringing them as one into the fullness of phenomenal experience. This is the precise equivalent, in the field of sound, of restoring lustre to colour in the field of light. As colour regains its lustre, the flame is rekindled; likewise as the pitch of sound regains its timbre, it once again erupts in our ears, as in the atmosphere. Only then can we finally understand how, starting from the blooming, buzzing confusion of the womb, and following with our earlines along the ways of the world, we end with the silence from which, like the number zero, everything comes.

Chapter 8

The cello and the lasso

Five propositions on beauty

From forms to relations

What makes some things beautiful and others ugly? In the tradition of Western philosophy, aesthetics has been the area of study that seeks answers to such questions. Although different approaches to aesthetics yield varied and contentious answers, they rest on the common premise that beauty is to be apprehended as a quality of finished things. To speak of the beauty of these things is, then, to understand each as an object of regard that stands, fully formed, before the beholder. In art, this is to seek beauty in the gallery, where work is on display, and not in the artist's studio or workshop. In architecture it is to contemplate the completed building rather than to witness the commotion of the construction site. For a landscape to be treated as an object of aesthetic appreciation it has likewise to be distilled from both the elemental forces and the activities of inhabitants that have shaped it, and imagined as a ready composed scene. Even the body, in order to be judged a thing of beauty, must be divorced from the practices of quotidian domesticity through which every human being is raised and sustained. Aesthetics, in short, does not look for beauty behind the scenes, in the workshops of life, but in the products that are turned out from them.[1]

In addressing the theme of beauty, orthodox approaches in the anthropology of art do not depart significantly from the Western philosophy of aesthetics, insofar as they set out from a division between the viscerality of immediate sensation and the rationality of its judgement and interpretation, attributing the former to innate psychic universals and the latter to the conceptual or cognitive models of an acquired culture.[2] They differ from the mainstream only in rejecting the ethnocentrism of much academic art history, emphasising that judgements of style and form in non-Western societies may be based on criteria other than those familiar to Western analysts. With both the anthropology and the history of art, however, things are there to be sensed before they are judged – the one can follow from the other only because the thing itself is complete at the point of apprehension. In what follows I aim to establish an alternative to this aesthetics of final forms. Its

DOI: 10.4324/9781003171713-11

guiding ambition is to resituate the generation and apprehension of beauty within a relational ontology that accords primacy to processes of growth and emergence rather than to the things to which they finally give rise. Sensing the world, in this approach, is not prior to the exercise of judgement but inseparable from it, and both sensibility and judgement depend on skills of perception and action nurtured in the course of ontogenetic development.

The inspiration for the approach comes from two sources. The first lies in the experience of anthropological fieldwork in regions of the circumpolar North – which, in my case, was among Sámi people in northeast Finland. The second lies in my attempts, over the past several decades, to master the violoncello. These may seem, at first glance, oddly unmatched, yet by the end of this chapter I hope to have shown that learning from the Sámi and learning with the cello correspond in ways beyond the happenstance of my involvement in both. The approach I draw from these sources, I believe, offers a way of understanding the perception of beauty that applies quite generally, even to people in nominally 'Western' societies – and not only to the musically inclined among them. Rather than appealing to the duality of human nature and its cultural inflections, we begin by acknowledging the positioning of every human being as an undivided centre of attention and awareness within a continually unfolding field of relationships. It is this positioning within a universe of relations, I suggest, and not the superimposition of cultural rules and representations upon a bedrock of universal dispositions, that gives rise to differences in the ways in which beauty is generated and apprehended in the course of everyday social life. Taking this suggestion as a starting point, I aim to establish five propositions concerning beauty, and to exemplify each of them with reference to the experience of peoples of the North, and of cello-playing. I begin, however, with a separate introduction to each.

High latitudes

In the Western imagination the North has long figured as a region profoundly hostile to human habitation, inducing in visitors a feeling of isolation and fragility in the face of the immensity of nature. Throughout the history of contact, visitors to the North – barring those few who got to know its inhabitants well – have commented on the rudeness of its aboriginal peoples, on their unkempt appearance and ramshackle dwellings, their primitive arts and uncouth speech. Supposedly condemned to live on the margins of survival, their harsh living conditions were thought to leave virtually no scope for the refinement of aesthetic tastes. The sublime beauty of northern landscapes, which inspired such awe in travellers, had – according to their accounts – left no apparent impression on native minds. Even collectors, folklorists and ethnologists who, by training and profession, were more ready to acknowledge the artistry of native productions, have been inclined to suppose that it takes their own eyes and ears to recognise beauty that is not apparent to the producers themselves. For the latter, it seemed, only the imperatives of survival mattered, and the value of everything was measured by that end.

My own experience, however, which is shared by the majority of ethnographers who have spent time living with indigenous peoples of the far North, is that these peoples are no less concerned with beauty than are those of us schooled in occidental aesthetics. Their concern, however, is one that does not alienate things from processes, or achievements from persons and relationships. Whereas in the 'eye' of the West, beauty lies in the distanced contemplation of final forms, beauty from the North – if we can call it that – is to be found in the close interweaving of material flows and sensory awareness wherein persons and things mutually bring each other into being.

There is beauty, for example, in the close, almost myopic concentration of the seamstress as she stitches pieces of prepared hide into a garment or decorates it with beadwork, thinking all the while on the person for whom the garment is intended; this beauty is appreciated by the animals that the wearer will subsequently herd or hunt – it draws them to him.[3] The hunter or herdsman, in turn, senses the beauty of the animals not in the perfection or majesty of their appearance but in the affection of their regard, or in the way the animals are disposed towards him (Ingold 2000: 61–76). There is beauty, too, in the lay of the land, apprehended not as picturesque scenery but as a mesh of paths which afford opportunities for productive activity or for the creation of kinship. The familiar, well-trodden path has a beauty of its own, as does an old fireplace or tent-ring that betokens the presence of ancestors, and the things left lying around that make it possible for stories to be told. The stories themselves are beautiful, not just because of their form or construction but because of the memories they evoke and the persons they restore to life (Nelson 1983). Finally, there is beauty in a dwelling: in the care of its construction and in the gathering, at its hearth, of the lives of inhabitants and of the materials for their subsistence (Anderson, Wishart and Vaté 2013; see also Chapter 10). In short, beauty from the North inheres in the movements, cadences and attunements of skilled practitioners whose conduct responds fluently, and with sensitivity and precision, to the nuances of their relationships with both human and nonhuman others.

Low notes

Over the years I have also been trying to achieve beauty in my cello playing. Of course, we might observe that the instrument itself is an artefact of great beauty, a product of consummate craftsmanship. For the player, however, the beauty of the instrument does not lie in the perfection of its appearance; indeed most well-played instruments look pretty beaten-up, full of scratches and cracks, multiply repaired, which tell of a rich and eventful life. Mine, for example, still bears the scars of having been once left behind on a train when I was a boy. Protected only by a soft canvas case, it was returned to me with a six-inch crack at the bottom (Figure 8.1). Nor did it take kindly to the extremes of temperature, or the dry air of a stove-heated cabin, during my subsequent sojourn in Lapland. Of the cello of the greatest player ever, Pablo Casals, it is said that it looked the worse for wear, that it was full of matches which had fallen into the sound holes when Casals had paused to light his pipe, and that it had a piece of paper wedged under the bridge for support and a broken matchstick stuck under a string in the pegbox to keep it taut (Siblin 2009: 158–9).

But this imperfect, patched-up thing of wood and strings begs to be played. The cellist is not content to look *at* the instrument, like a visitor to a museum. He or she longs to be *with* it. Like everyone and everything else, however, the cello has its on-days and off-days. Almost as soon as I set my bow to the strings, I know what kind of day it is. On some days it sings,

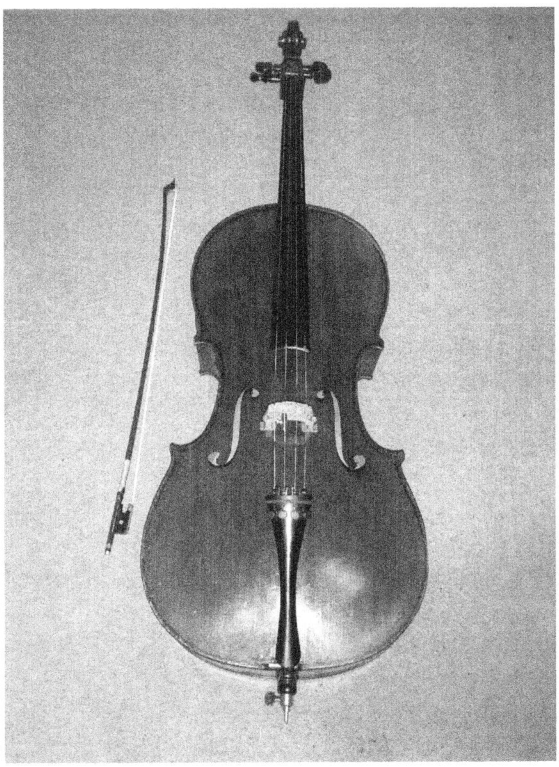

Figure 8.1 My cello.
Photo by the author.

apparently requiring almost no effort from myself. On other days it grinds and grumps, or responds to my coaxing with a sharp-edged whine or sand-papery scratch, as though it were suffering from a sore throat. I have never been able to understand the causes of this moodiness; all I know for sure is that the fluctuations of the cello's moods are quite unrelated to mine, so that the occasions when we are *both* in a good mood, at the same time, are relatively rare. But these are beautiful moments, of pure exhilaration, when I and my cello and the world seem in perfect accord. At such times, it seems, anything is possible.

Beauty, then, lies in the act of playing itself. That, at least, is how it is for me. Most often I practise by myself, and there is no one else within earshot. The sudden awareness of another's presence can intrude into the intimacy of the conversation between sound and feeling in which I am otherwise immersed, breaking the spell and throwing the performance off course.[4] But I often wonder how it might be for listeners. One of the frustrations of playing an instrument like this is that you never know. Everyone who has ever heard a recording of their own voice realises that it sounds quite different, to others, from hearing oneself speak. It is the same with the cello. Because you are so close to it, and because its harmonic resonances course through your own body, it is impossible to hear with the ear of a distanced listener. I can therefore only respond to the question of how it sounds to listeners in terms of my own experience of hearing the cello played, in concert, by another performer. And my experience is that the sound draws me in. I think this is not unlike the way in which the beautiful clothing of the hunter attracts his prey. It is, I suppose, a kind of enchantment. Precisely what this means is a question to which I will return.

Beauty is attentional

One essential item of equipment that Sámi reindeer herdsmen always carry with them, slung in a coil across the shoulder when not in use, is a lasso (Ingold 1993b). It consists of a length of rope, half a centimetre thick and some twenty metres in length, tied at one end to a sliding toggle through which the other is looped. I carried one too, whenever I attended roundups, though more for show than anything else since I never became a competent user (Figure 8.2). Casting the lasso in the roundup enclosure, so as to catch a chosen animal by the antler or back-leg when it is running at full tilt in the throng, is a skill that takes years to acquire. This is not just a matter of mastering a particular movement, involving a throw of the arm, a flick of the wrist, a tug on the rope and digging in with the feet to take the strain. Above all, it involves fine judgement: of pitch, velocity and direction; and of just the right moment to throw so as to ensure that the trajectory of the rope with its evolving loop is perfectly timed to answer to the running of the animal. This timing is exemplary of what in ancient Greece was called

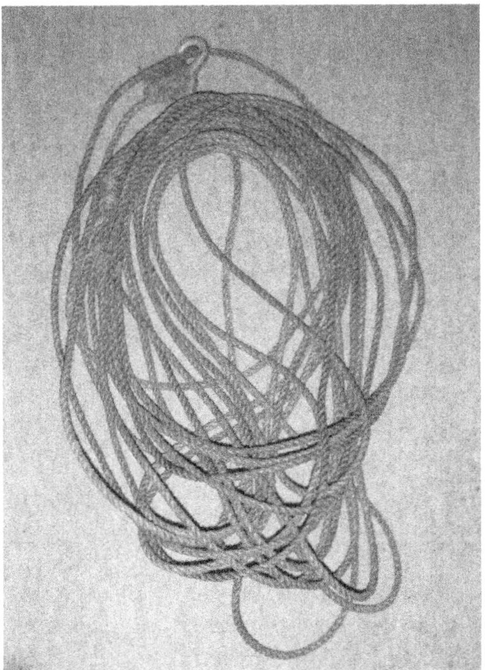

Figure 8.2 My lasso.
Photo by the author.

kairos: the moment that must be seized in any process of skilled work, when 'human action meets a natural process developing according to its own rhythm' (Vernant 1983: 291; see also Chapter 15, page 234). Nurtured in practice, timing is intrinsic to the action itself, and is what marks it out as fundamentally concentrative. To concentrate is to gather concurrent movements into a focus, and to seize the moment of their convergence. It is to be ever-alert to a world that is continually incipient – where nothing is given, and everything just on the cusp of presence.

Among Sámi people – even among those not actively involved in herding – skill with the lasso is greatly appreciated, so much so that lasso-throwing competitions are popular fixtures on festive occasions. An impressive throw is greeted with acclaim. The beauty of it lies in the way in which a simple manual gesture, expertly performed, is converted into the lively form of a flying noose. Perhaps this is one instance in which the cliché 'poetry in motion' genuinely applies. For the form is literally made in movement. It is not given at the outset, nor does it outlast the throw, as a final outcome. It exists only in the moment, or on the fly. But when I play the cello it is just the same. To play is to pull a pitch from the instrument and to cast a line in sound (Ingold 2015: 109). Like the form of the flying noose, the musical phrase is shaped in a movement which it does not outlast. It shares with speech, and with the cast of the lasso, the property of ephemerality that linguists call 'rapid fading'. As Walter Ong (1982: 91) wrote of the sounds of speech, musical sound 'exists only as it is going out of existence'.

And again, the ability to play the cello, like the ability to throw the lasso, is not just a matter of mastering the right movements. Judgement is everything, and this calls for constant attention. The beauty of the performance lies not in the compositional form of the music as such, as if the job of the instrumentalist were only to deliver the form, ready-made, to a receptive audience. Nor does it lie in the manual dexterity of the player, in its technical execution. It lies rather in what might be called 'feeling'. By this I mean a quality of attention by which, as the line is cast, the performer's gestures – felt, for example, in the pressure of the bow against the string and the vibrato of the left hand – are ever responsive to the perceived tonality of the resulting sound (Ingold 2000: 413). Feeling means simply that I listen as I play, just as with the lasso, I watch as I throw.

Now as varieties of action, both playing and throwing may be intentional, in so far as they are tasks which I set out to perform, and for which I am prepared. But in the actual performance, what stands out is not the intentionality which precedes and informs them, but their intrinsic *attentionality*. As George Home-Cook (2015: 2) emphasises, '"attention" is inherently associated with the notion of *stretching*'. Etymologically, the word comes from the Latin *ad-tendere*, meaning 'to stretch towards'. Playing the cello and throwing the lasso are evidently ways of stretching, implying an element not only of effortful movement but also of elasticity. This elasticity means that in stretching towards we also hold back, thus building tension into the line, be it of rope or sound. In casting the lasso, I dig in my heels, even as the force of the ensnared animal tugs at the noose; in pulling a pitch from my cello, I hold my nerve even as the swell of sound threatens to tear me away (Ingold 2011a: 139). This is how forms are held in the suspense of performance: not through the *im*-position of prior conceptual design on passive substance, but through the *contra*-position of equal and opposed forces, of stretching and holding, attention and retention.

Beauty is in the unity of affects

Even for the most adept of practitioners – the most skilled herdsman, the most accomplished cellist – the stretch of attention is fraught with risk (Ingold 2015: 138). Reaching out beyond what is already to hand towards that which is not yet present or even conceivable, it forsakes the security of the fragile centre that we may have drawn around ourselves for an uncertain and unknown future. 'One ventures from home', write Gilles Deleuze and Félix Guattari (2004: 344), 'on the thread of a tune'. Thus to attend is not to take up a position but to be pulled out of it. 'It is about exposition', as philosopher of education Jan Masschelein explains; 'about being out-of-position'. Or in the most literal sense, attention is a practice of *exposure* (Masschelein 2010: 278). Masschelein is describing the act of walking, but what he says is equally true of throwing a lasso or playing the cello. The beauty of exposure lies not in the finessed display of forms from which all evidence of their production has been assiduously erased or covered up, so as to make it look as though they had magically appeared *ex nihilo*, but in an opening up of the inner workings of things which turns the lives of practitioners inside out. Abandoning the realms of studied perfection in which everything is complete but nothing what it seems, we cast off into the aleatoric indeterminacy of a world-in-formation whose very imperfections afford possibilities for continuation. This casting off – this opening up of the self, from the inside – amounts to an offering. And it can be erotically charged.

Among indigenous peoples around the circumpolar North, the most powerfully erotic sentiments arise in connection with activities of hunting.[5] The hunt often begins with a dream, in which the animal is revealed to the hunter as a beautiful woman. She beckons him on. Enchanted, he follows. On waking, roused by a desire for this fugitive vision, the hunter resolves to head off in pursuit. Successful hunting demands an intimate knowledge of the ways of the animal. You have to know how it perceives and how it acts, what it seeks and what it avoids, the things that make it nervous or frightened and the things that will calm it down. With this knowledge you can anticipate the animal's every move, and steal a march on its progress. But hunting also involves an element of deception. Dressed from head to foot in garments made from hides of the very same creature, and imitating its characteristic gestures and vocalisations, the hunter comes close to passing as one of its kind. In the moment of encounter, deceived into thinking of the hunter as a lover, the animal offers itself up to him and meets its death. For the hunter, however, this lure is replete with existential ambivalence. For in taking on so much of the animal's character and behaviour, he is at risk of actually *becoming* the animal, and of losing his human bearings. Indeed the episode could equally end with his own death, rather than that of the animal. Many stories are told of how the hunter, seduced by his voluptuous prey, eventually drifts into the prey's world, in which the animals appear to him as human. There he carries on his life while lost, presumed dead, to his own people.

Just like in hunting, to play the cello means putting one's existence on the line, albeit not with the same potentially life-threatening consequences. And just as the hunter needs to understand the dispositions of prey animals, so the cellist needs an intimate knowledge of the temperament of the instrument, and to respond to its moods as best he or she can. Although rumours of an erotic relationship with my cello are greatly exaggerated, historically such relationships have been reported often enough. In the embrace of both male and female performers, the cello has been credited alternately with feminine and masculine attributes. Cellist and musicologist George Kennaway cites an extraordinary review, in the magazine *Country Life*, of a performance by the former pupil and one-time partner of Casals, Guilhermina Suggia, in 1927, in which she is portrayed as a sexual dominatrix seeking fulfilment from the 'tortoise between her knees', and emerging enraptured from the experience. But it could work the other way too, as in the case of a devout cellist from the Isle of Man, Tom Taggart, known for playing hymn-tunes in his local church, who was said to have stroked the brown wood of his instrument while remarking apologetically: 'Herself here has never what you could really call sinned to – but I'm admitting she likes a lively tune!' (Kennaway 2014: 201–3).

Old Tom had a point. I don't know whether the cello ever appeared in his dreams, but from time to time it does appear in mine. A persistent theme of these dreams is that the instrument has fallen apart, along with what I experience in the dream as a dissolution of my own self. The cello is in pieces and so am I. So when I sit down to play, I have to pull myself and the instrument together again. This pulling together, however, is not a matter of bolting my body to the instrument so as to produce the equivalent of a centaur, with human arms and head, a trunk of wood and strings, and an endpin for a leg. On the contrary, in the moment I begin to play the instrument seems to explode into its constituent materials – of wood, varnish, metallic strings, rosin, bow-hair and resonant air – just as it did in my dream (Ingold 2015: 108–9). In the playing these materials respond to one another, and to my touch and gesture, in particular ways. That is to say, they *correspond*. And what comes out from this correspondence is musical sound. There is certainly a sense, here, of me and the cello having become one. But this unity is not anatomical or organic. It is a unity of *affects* (Chapter 16, pages 252–3). Or in a word, it is an enchantment. When it works it is beautiful, and I become an enchanted being.

Beauty is enchanting

In the unity of affects, respectively with the instrument and with the animal, both the cellist and the hunter are at risk of enchantment. This is to take the word 'enchantment', however, in a rather literal sense. The chant, after all, is a song, and to become enchanted in this sense is to enter with the singer into the song, to join *with* it in its temporal unfolding. The victim of enchantment, as we say, becomes spellbound, hooked like a fish on the pitch-line of vocal intonation. Thus it was, in classical Greek and Roman mythology, that the fabled Sirens could draw sailors to their deaths on rocky shores. It was the song of the Sirens that lured them: once caught, they could not tear their attention away from it. So too the northern hunter would lure his prey, or the prey the hunter, depending on a balance of affects that could tip either way. And likewise when I play, my gestures, my touch and my awareness are comprehensively caught in the resonances and reverberations of the instrument. When, alternatively, I listen to the performance of another player, my auditory attention is coupled with that of the performer, and even though I scarcely move, I nevertheless feel the performer's movements in my limbs. I am drawn into them, even snared by them, as is a beast of prey by the movements of the hunter.

I should stress that this allure has nothing to do with technical virtuosity, as anthropologist Alfred Gell would have it in his notion of the 'enchantment of technology'. By this, Gell (1999: 163) means 'the power that technical processes have of casting a spell over us so that we see the real world in an enchanted form'. Gell's approach to aesthetics is thoroughly conventional, in so far as it apprehends beauty as a value attributed to the *objects* of our regard, be they sunsets, horses, human bodies or artworks. Moreover, despite his appeal to the idea of enchantment, for him it is the sight of these things, not their sound, that captivates. Among the plethora of eye-catching objects, Gell singles out artworks for special treatment, since unlike the phenomena of nature, they are the products of artifice, of skilled making. If sunsets attract by virtue of their sensational colours, horses by the strength and majesty of their bearing, and human bodies by their poise and perfection, for artworks, according to Gell, it is the skill invested in them that gives them their particular aura.

With respect, I think Gell has got the wrong end of the stick. He is misled by the very conventions of art history he claims to flout. For enchantment lies in the affective correspondence of movements, not in the gravitational pull of any objects in which – were we to look back upon a path already travelled – we might see these movements resolved. Indeed the chant, whether sung with the voice or played on an instrument, is not really an object of perception at all. It is a way of perceiving. It offers a path for my attention which I can follow, or even one to which I am compelled to submit. In precisely the same way, the animal offers a path for the attention of the hunter. This is, in effect, to move the apprehension of beauty upstream, from the contemplation of finished things to a kind of dwelling in the moment, at which beings are on the verge of appearance and sounds on the verge of release. The enchanted traveller is one who, at every such moment, opens his or her senses to the world as if for the first time.

It could be argued, of course, that whether beauty is apprehended 'upstream' or 'downstream' depends on the properties of the sensory register on which we choose to focus. According to this argument, it is no accident that we follow with our ears but look back with our eyes, for it is in the nature of hearing that we join with occurrences as they unfold, whereas the nature of vision is to behold the totality of what lies before us in a single glance, as if complete and fully formed. It is no wonder, then, that a predominant focus on visual aesthetics sees only objects while remaining blind to the processes that give rise to them. Nor is it any surprise that an aesthetics modelled on musical perception would incline to the other extreme. For example the phenomenologist Alfred Schutz (1951: 90), in a classic paper, describes how a listener, on hearing a work that may have been composed centuries ago, 'participates with quasi simultaneity in the [composer's] stream of consciousness by performing with him step by step the ongoing articulation of his musical thought'. It is as if they were together in real time, sharing the same 'vivid present'.

Schutz is not alone in drawing attention to the intrinsic temporality of listening, and to the requirement that music or song makes of its audience to enter into the currents of its production. Many other scholars have argued along the same lines. What is disclosed over time, as philosopher Hans Jonas (1966: 137) insists, is also apprehended over time: thus in listening, 'the duration of the sound heard is just the duration of the hearing itself'. With vision, by contrast, you have only to open your eyes and the world is already there for you to see, in all its range and depth. Vision reveals the manifold, as Jonas (1966: 136) puts it, 'in a flash'. It is as though in hearing, rather as in the game of grandmother's footsteps, everyone and everything creeps up behind your back, only to freeze in the instant you turn around to look. Paradoxically, the power of vision to take in the world at a glance is bought at the expense of its always arriving a moment too late.

Beauty is in hearing and seeing

But is it really in the nature of vision that its properties should be so distinct from those of hearing? Northern circumpolar scholarship seems initially to confirm the distinction. In a study of the Inuit people of Southampton Island, in the Canadian Arctic, anthropologist Edmund Carpenter (1973) argued that in the Inuit world, nothing is ever complete or ready-made. To inhabit this world is not to look out upon a space of objects, arrayed in their proper locations, but to participate from the inside in the perpetual movement of their generation. Everything there is – people, animals, tools and implements, materials, winds and weather – establish and reveal their presence by way of what they do, in their ongoing behaviour. This was enough to convince Carpenter (1973: 33) that for Inuit people the world is defined, above all, by sound rather than sight. There is a direct parallel, for example, between singing and hunting, in that both are practices of enchantment in which lines of song mingle with the ways of animals. Among the Sámi people with whom I worked, the same commingling is evident in the form of singing known as the *joik*, in which the voice of the singer travels through the terrain, resonating as it goes with diverse animals, with the paths of the land and with the spirits of ancestral persons who continue to inhabit it (Aubinet 2020; see also Chapter 2, page 37).

Yet while sound and hearing are evidently important for northern circumpolar people, Inuit and Sámi alike, the inference that vision is correspondingly downplayed in their sensory register is ethnographically unfounded. Even Carpenter (1973: 36) admitted to having been amazed by the visual acuity of his Inuit companions. That there is a close association between seeing and hunting is confirmed by another seasoned ethnographer of the Inuit, Jarich Oosten. It is through his clear and penetrating vision, Oosten (1992: 130) shows, that the hunter initiates an encounter with the prey, which is in turn consummated with the latter's self-surrender to the hunter. Working with Sámi reindeer herdsmen, I was similarly impressed by the importance of vision to their herding operations, and by their skills of observation, whether in scouring the distant horizon for signs of movement or in identifying particular animals from their earmarks in the dense mêlée of the roundup – something that requires years of practice and that I could never learn to do. And while this kind of 'skilled vision' (Grasseni 2007) is generally at some remove from its target, albeit mitigated through the use of binoculars, there are other kinds, such as in the close-up work of stitching and beading normally undertaken by women, in which attention binds myopically with the weft of materials. Is vision, then, really so different from hearing, or watching so different from listening? Is not to watch, also, to enter into the movements of things, into their growth and formation? And if there is beauty in hearing, can there not be beauty in seeing just as well?

To answer this question, let me return to music. In learning to play the cello, as indeed any musical instrument, it is common for the novice to be accompanied by the teacher. To accompany is to join with another in the activity of performance. In a recent study of learning to play jazz trumpet, anthropologist Eitan Wilf (2012) describes how trainees are required to copy from audio-recordings of solos by the great jazz masters of the past. Attending to all the nuances of rhythm, tone and timbre, they are instructed to tailor their performances to the model as closely as they can. Ideally, they should be able to achieve such perfect correspondence that the recording effectively 'disappears' into the student's performance. In these moments the student does not just join with the masterwork but *inhabits* it, experiencing from within the ever-advancing swell of incipient sound on the verge of release. For the student, this is an experience of almost mystical fusion with the master whose work he is copying. He is indeed enchanted! But it is an enchantment, according to Wilf (2012: 37–8), that is uniquely afforded by the aural modality. It could not happen, for example, in learning to paint.

Suppose that the novice, in the painting studio, is likewise instructed to copy the works of past masters. It would be impossible, Wilf argues, for him to inhabit the painted masterwork in the real-time dimension of its production, in the way the novice trumpeter inhabits the musical one, since in this case the model, rather than unfolding over time, is given all at once, in its totality. Now this may be so, with painting. But in the art of calligraphy, which also employs the visual rather than the aural register, what happens is precisely akin to instrumental learning in music. Like trainee instrumentalists, novice calligraphers are also instructed to copy past masters. And with calligraphy the source text, too, unfolds in time, as does the manual gesture that produced it. In a study of the power of calligraphy in contemporary Chinese society, anthropologist Yuehping Yen (2005) shows that no work of calligraphy can be observed, let alone understood, merely by looking at it. One has to inhabit it, and to reunite one's vision with that of the calligrapher in the production of her 'inked traces' (Yen 2005: 89–90). The calligraphic mark, in short, is not an *object* of vision at all. It is rather a way of seeing, and offers a line of beauty for the reader's visual attention to follow. In so doing it reignites, in her limbs, the sensation of the gestural movements that give rise to it.

Beauty is sensed along the path of presence

Exactly the same occurs in listening to the sound of the cello. This too, as we have seen, offers a path for the listener's aural attention, and reanimates his or her limbs with the gestures of its production. In effect, *the listener is a silent accompanist*. Listening with music, just as much as seeing with calligraphy, is a mode of correspondence, not of objectification. It is not then the prioritisation of vision, ostensibly characteristic of Western modernity, which leads us to see beauty in finished things or in a world of completed being. It is rather the enrolment of vision in the modern project of objectification – a project that turns the movements of life, and the traces they leave, into bounded continents of experience.

For precisely this reason I take issue with much recent writing in what has come to be known as 'the anthropology of the senses', which starts from the premise that the worlds people inhabit, depending on their cultural provenance, are themselves marked by sensory qualities (Howes 2003). Thus there are said to be 'visual worlds', 'auditory worlds', 'haptic worlds' and so on. In this conversion, the senses are effectively turned from open-ended modalities of exploratory perception, or ways of *sensing the world*, into self-contained experiential domains or *worlds of sense* (Howes and Pink 2010; Ingold 2011b). And by the same token, the eyes, ears and skin cease to figure as organs of a body that, as it makes its way in an environment, attentively looks, listens and feels where it is going, and come to be regarded, instead, as instruments of playback that aim to capture a world in its totality and render it *back* to the self-consciously reflexive subject. In vision, for example, it is as though the eyes opened not upon the real, but upon a simulacrum whose objects already bear witness to the experience of sight and return that experience to us in our gaze. These objects, as art historian James Elkins (1996) alleges, 'stare back'. They are images.

This is why, for so many students of visual culture, seeing apparently has nothing to do with the observational accompaniment of real life and everything to do with the interpretation of images. For them, as indeed for most art historians, without images there is nothing to be seen. All viewing, then, is *re*-viewing. But if all one can ever see is itself a reflex of vision, how can one ever see the world itself? Are we so blind to what is going on around us? A principal claim of the anthropology of the senses, of course, is to have dethroned vision from the sovereign position it is supposed to have held in the intellectual pantheon of the Western world, and to highlight the contributions of other, non-visual sensory modalities, above all to the sensory formations of non-Western peoples (Howes 1991). It is therefore ironic that in 'rediscovering' these modalities – of hearing, touch, smell and so on – anthropologists of this persuasion have implemented exactly the same manoeuvre as students of visual culture. To the world of images conjured up by the latter, they have simply added worlds of sounds, of feelings and of smells. So if the eyes return the world to us in its visual image, conceived in art-historical terms as a landscape, then likewise the ears reveal a soundscape, the skin a touchscape, the nose a smellscape and so on. These multiple 'scapes', however, refer not to the practically and productively inhabited world but to the virtual worlds conjured up when experiences of habitation – captured for posterity – are rendered back, in artificially purified forms, for interpretation and consumption. Expelled from the temporal movement of perception and action, aesthetics re-enters here on the rebound.

Yet in reality, the northern hunter or herdsman, as he makes his way through tundra or forest, is alive to the surroundings through all his senses. His environment is no more sliced up along the lines of the sensory pathways by which he ventures within it than is the environment of the cellist, who likewise listens and feels as he or she plays. For both hunter and cellist, to look, to listen and to feel are ways of paying attention to one undivided and indivisible world, rather than to inhabit multiple scapes in parallel. There is beauty in the 'worlding' of this world, by which it becomes vividly and vitally *present* to us, and not only in the postcards we send ourselves back from the places that we have visited along the way. The sliced-up world, by contrast, is a recreation of the retrospective, post-performance multi-media animation or slideshow. I fully concur, therefore, with literary theorist Hans Gumbrecht (2004: xv) in pleading against the systematic bracketing of presence, along with the uncontested centrality of interpretation, in contemporary discourses of aesthetics, above all in the academic disciplines of the arts and humanities. It is perhaps the great illusion of our age to have mistaken the slideshow for reality, and to have consequently abandoned presence for interpretation, and the judgements of perception for the mediations of semiosis.

Five propositions

Let me conclude by rounding up my five propositions.

- *Beauty is attentional.* Brought forth in time along a path of movement, beauty is manifested in the fluency of this movement and in the concentration and judgement through which it is attuned to the variable conditions of the task at hand. It is suspended in the tension between opposed forces of stretching forth and holding back.
- *Beauty is in the unity of affects.* It lies not in outward appearances but in an opening up towards others, on the inside, that puts one's very existence on the line. Every such line establishes a relational pathway for the flow of affect. Beauty arises when these lines correspond in unison.
- *Beauty is enchanting.* Enchantment comes not from the gravitational pull of objects invested with magical charm through the artfulness of their production but from the correspondence of movements of attention. To be spellbound is to be caught in a mesh of affective relations.
- *Beauty is in hearing and seeing.* Enchantment literally refers to the singer's joining with the song, in its temporal unfolding. It would therefore seem to be specific to the aural register. However, to look is also to enter into the movements of things in their formation. Enchanting beauty may therefore be experienced in vision as in hearing.
- *Beauty is sensed along the path of presence.* The apprehension of beauty is not about the reflexive interpretation of worlds already endowed with sensory (visual, aural, or tactile) attributes. It is about sensing the world through active looking, listening, or feeling. It is therefore judged in perception rather than evaluated in retrospection.

These five propositions contain all the clues to why, at least in my experience, what I have learned from Sámi people and from my attempts to master the cello have so much in common. First, both have taught me of the importance of attentionality. I have come to understand that paying attention is not about shining a spotlight on this or that object in the world, but about going along with things, opening up to them and doing their bidding. Intention is premised upon attentionality, not attention on intentionality (Ingold 2017b: 19). Second, I have learned what it means to inhabit a world in which all things – animals, people, music – exist only in so far as they go along, following paths that answer to one another, or correspond. This is a world not of objects but of affects. Indeed, only because objects fall apart can affects be pulled together. Third, I have understood what it means to be enchanted: not to stand in awe before the congealed monuments of either nature or art, but to join with things, or accompany them, in the movements of their formation. It means working our way upstream from a world of appearances to the very appearing of things, their incipience.

To be enchanted is never to be awestruck, but it is perpetually to be filled with wonder. Fourth, the experience of playing the cello might have led me to think that enchantment is exclusively aural. But working with the Sámi made me realise that it is visual as well, and that seeing and hearing are not as different as they are commonly made out to be. Fifth, and finally, I have learned that the only way to grow in skill and wisdom is through an education of perception and judgement that better enables us to attend to what is going on, and to respond with sensitivity and precision. It is a matter of finding things out for ourselves, not by holding a mirror to the world and seeing it only in its reflections, but through a direct, practical and experimental exposure to the vagaries of real.

Chapter 9

Episode zero

The reduction and revival of aesthetic experience

I recently attended an interdisciplinary conference, including evolutionary biologists, ethologists, sociocultural anthropologists, evolutionary psychologists, neuropsychologists and philosophers, tasked with investigating 'the biological mechanisms that underlie symbol making and the perception and appreciation of beauty'.[1] At the conference, I was introduced to some of the cutting-edge research now underway in the field known as empirical aesthetics. Lavishly funded, and founded on the principles of cognitive science, this research claims to unpack the mechanisms by which the mind, operating by way of various regions of the brain, is alleged to convert the inputs of sensation emanating, say, from a work of art into outputs such as emotional reactions and aesthetic judgements. Every such input–output conversion, we were told, amounts to an 'aesthetic episode'.

I was appalled by what I heard. It was as if I had entered a dystopic world wherein living, breathing human beings had been cloned by disembodied mind-brains, their eyes and ears having been co-opted as sensory ports into which objects of art can be plugged and their information downloaded, for processing and conversion into products calculated to provide immediate gratification for the mind-brains' witless hosts. This struck me as not just bizarre, but a wilful and perverse corruption of the aesthetic imperative at the heart of art and experience. In the heat of my outrage, however, I was unable to articulate my objections with any coherence. My uncontrolled outburst not only caused offence at the conference; it also left me feeling deeply unsatisfied with myself. To make up for it, I resolved – at some future opportunity – to undertake a more careful study and critique of empirical aesthetics in order that I could explain, to myself and others, why art and experience, if they are to be taken seriously, call for an approach to aesthetics that is practical rather than empirical. This chapter is the result.

As I was going to St Ives

I begin with a brief reminiscence that will help to set the scene. Not long ago, during a trip to the southwestern tip of the British Isles, in the county

DOI: 10.4324/9781003171713-12

of Cornwall, my wife and I had the opportunity to visit the seaside town of St Ives, which has been a magnet for artists ever since the sculptor Barbara Hepworth made her home there in the 1950s. In 1993 a branch of the Tate Gallery was established in the town to celebrate its artistic heritage, and we were keen to visit it. Our visit was memorable in many ways: for getting soaked in torrential rain on the way there; for the loveliness of the new building; for way the light streamed in through the windows of the café, opening to a view over the sea, when the sun eventually burst through; for the struggle I had with reading the captions for the works on display, having forgotten my spectacles in the pocket of my raincoat now confined to a baggage locker; and for our subsequent walk on the sandy beach between the gallery and the sea, in brilliant sunshine that had suddenly and miraculously replaced the thunderous clouds of only a couple of hours before.

Then there were the works themselves, which we had ostensibly come to see. More, of course, caught our attention than I could possibly list, but I would like to mention one that, for me especially, remained a highlight of the visit. It was the painting *Thermal* (1960), by Peter Lanyon (Figure 9.1). A native of Cornwall, Lanyon was one of a group of painters active in St Ives in the post-war years. He had started with landscapes, but later developed a passion for gliding. This soon came to dominate his painting as well, in which he began to cover the canvas with swathes of paint much as the skies in which he would fly are filled with swirling expanses of air. These expanses are moved by powerful forces of convection, which can not only afford lift to the glider but also obstruct its movements, almost as if it were hitting a brick wall. A sky that looks empty and featureless to a spectator on the ground becomes, in the experience of the glider pilot, something more like the roaring ocean for the mariner. And this is what Lanyon had painted in *Thermal*, one of the most powerful of his glider compositions. Perhaps it was a premonition. Only four years later, Lanyon died from injuries sustained in a gliding accident.

Why was this work, above all others, the highlight of my excursion to the gallery? The immediate reason is that I had seen it before, a few years previously, on a visit to the Courtauld Institute in London. It happened that the Institute was staging a temporary exhibition devoted to Lanyon's work.[2] Knowing nothing about it, I decided to take a look, and was intrigued by what I saw. I thought no more of it, however, until three months later, during a flight from London to Chicago. I was writing an essay to accompany a major installation by the artist Tomás Saraceno, who has pioneered solar-powered balloon flight as part of an ambitious vision for a future epoch envisaged as the Aerocene.[3] Balloons and gliders have in common that they ride the air currents, as birds also do, rather than forcefully drilling through them like missiles powered by an external energy source. It occurred to me, as a passenger on board a transatlantic airliner, that the plane was

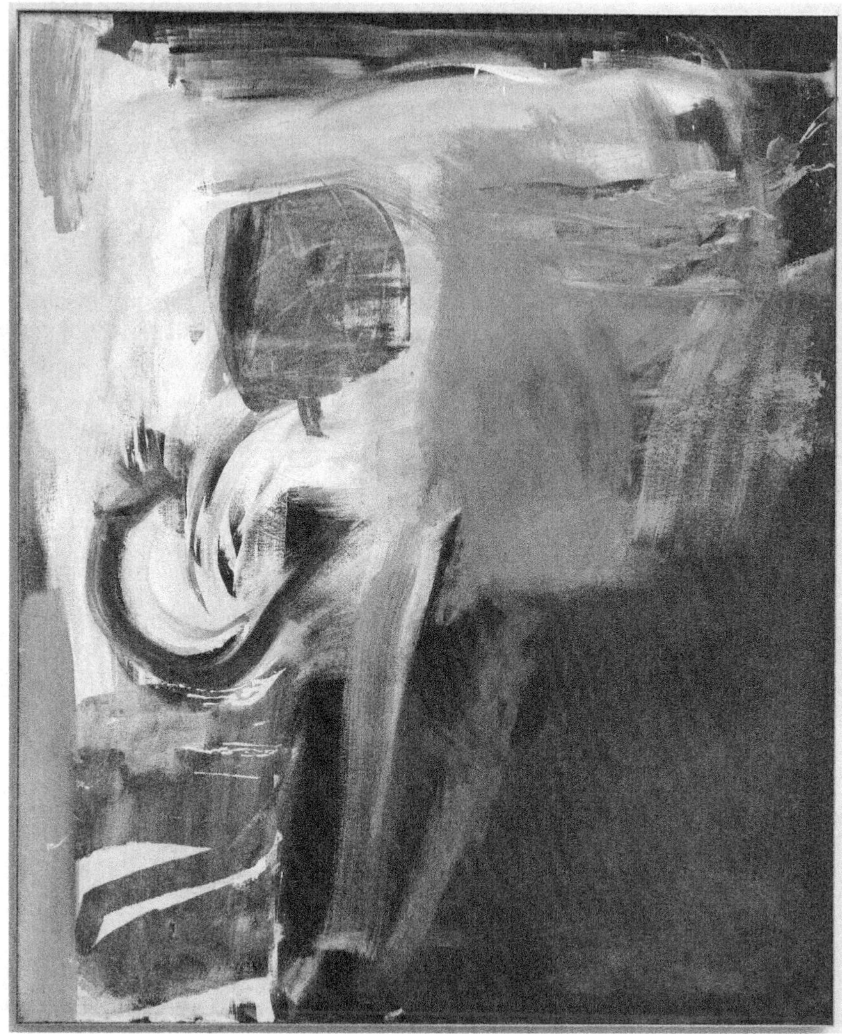

Figure 9.1 *Thermal*, 1960, by Peter Lanyon (1918–64).
Courtesy of the Tate Gallery, © Estate of Peter Lanyon. All Rights Reserved, DACS 2021.

more analogous to a missile than a bird, and that sat inside the fuselage, strapped to my seat, the one thing I definitely was *not* doing was flying (Ingold 2017a). And it was at this moment that Lanyon's glider paintings came back to mind. Of these paintings, *Thermal* was the most powerful, and I brought it into my essay to show how the air, in Lanyon's own words, 'is a very definite world of activity as complex and demanding as the sea'.[4]

That's why, when I came across it again some three years later, in the gallery at St Ives, it felt like greeting an old friend. 'So nice to see you again', I wanted to say, 'and what a coincidence! I had been thinking about you. Let me introduce my wife, I don't think you have met'. So it was that this meeting, along with the soaking in the rain, the sunlit café, the mislaid spectacles and the walk on the beach, became part of the story of our trip to St Ives. What is more, neither in my memory nor in the way I tell them do these incidents stand apart from one another. Each, rather, lends a certain colour to all the others. With this in mind, let me now revert to the matter at hand. Suppose that I were an aficionado of empirical aesthetics, what would I make of it all? Before arriving at an answer, I will need first to sketch in some of the background to the history of aesthetics, as a *subject* of study, and then to show how it was subsequently converted into its empirical *object*. This, in turn, will lay the foundations for my critique. Empirical aesthetics, I argue, by zeroing in on the aesthetic *episode*, effectively discounts aesthetic *experience*. I conclude with a practical way to bring it back.

An art of thinking beautifully

The notion of *aesthesis*, referring to the nature and quality of sensory perception, has been around since classical Greece. But its co-option to denote the field of inquiry now known as aesthetics is generally attributed to the eighteenth-century philosopher Alexander Baumgarten.[5] In the very first sentence of his *Aesthetica*, published in 1750, Baumgarten defined his subject as 'the science of sensitive cognition'. That there was a need for such a science stemmed from his conviction that there is more to thinking than the work of intellect. It is not that Baumgarten was against intellection; on the contrary it was for him the highest faculty of cognition. Yet it has, as its complement, a lower faculty that operates not with concepts but with sensations. Both faculties strive for perfection, but for the one it is the perfection of logic, for the other the perfection of beauty. If logic is the art of thinking intellectually, by means of concepts, aesthetics – according to Baumgarten – is the art of thinking beautifully (*ars pulchre cogitandi*), by means of the senses (Beiser 2009: 132).

Aesthetica was a somewhat fragmentary work. Although a second volume was published in 1758, with Baumgarten's premature death in 1762 his overall philosophical project lay largely unfinished. There is no knowing how he might have developed it. The subsequent reception of the work owed much to both the advocacy and the criticism directed from the pen of Immanuel Kant. Key to Kant's view, advanced in his *Critique of Judgement* of 1790, was that no properly aesthetic judgement can be made that is not from a position of pure disinterest. Can beauty be so judged? It may give us pleasure, but if pleasure is to be combined with disinterest, then it cannot be laced with desire, or with any will to possess. Pleasure without desire, for

Kant, is the basis for judgements of taste, or at least for those judgements deemed to be 'pure'. Beauty, then, is a matter of taste. And since taste falls outside the realms of cognition, an aesthetics that strives for beauty cannot find a place within the science of cognition. In essence, this was the point on which Kant took issue with Baumgarten who, as an avowed rationalist, believed that it could (Beiser 2009: 133–4).

It is hardly necessary to venture into the dense thickets of eighteenth-century German philosophy to realise that there is a difference between the art of thinking beautifully, and judging the beauty of art. Thinking beautifully, for Baumgarten, was an art of skilful composition, working with the materials of feeling. But it was also an art of attention, in so far as there can be no feeling without a kind of sensory coupling, in perception and action, between the thinker and those aspects of the world with which he or she is preoccupied. In this conjoining of composition with attention lies the work of imagination. Beauty lay primarily in the imagining, rather than in any products to which it might yield. Baumgarten was particularly interested in poetry, for which the materials are words whose very sounds evoke their own resonances. Indeed, much of his *Aesthetica* is a kind of manual for poets, laying down rules for beautiful writing. But he could just as well have been talking about music or painting. With Kant, however, there is a shift of emphasis from process to product. The imaginative work is over and done; its object already present: the question is, how to judge it? This shift had fateful consequences from which the philosophy of aesthetics has yet to recover.

For reasons that will become apparent as we proceed, I am more with Baumgarten than with Kant. I am for process over product, more for feeling than its objects. Yet the idea of 'sensible cognition' – of thinking with feeling – at the heart of Baumgarten's program, still leaves us with a conundrum. For how can a mind feel if it knows only by way of the deliverances of the senses, of what they yield to thought? Or to put the question in reverse: how can feelings, born of sensory commerce with the world, be enrolled into the cognitive operations of a mind confined to the interior space of its own deliberations? How can they register as anything other than abstractions, mere husks of sentience, appearances without substance, or – in a word – as representations? A mind that is free to mingle with the world can hardly be expected, at one and the same time, to remain dispassionately on the sidelines. Is aesthetics asking the impossible, for the mind to do both things at once: both to stir in the fluxes of sensory experience and to offer its considered assessments like judge and jury at a beauty contest?

The birth of empirical aesthetics

One way to set about answering questions such as these is to treat the mind itself as an object of investigation. In the 1870s, principally in Germany and the United States, a new science of experimental psychology was proposed to do just that. And one of the first fields of mental activity to attract its attention was aesthetics. What had begun as an artful way of thinking – and had subsequently morphed into a way of thinking about art – became, in the hands of scientific psychology, an object of empirical study in its own right. With this, empirical aesthetics was born, not as the study of art, but as the study of how minds *respond* to art. The acknowledged founder of the field, Gustav Theodor Fechner, had started out as a physicist but was driven by his conviction of the unity of the physical and spiritual worlds to inquire into the relation between physical stimuli and the sensory responses they induced. Having coined the term 'psychophysics' to describe his approach, Fechner went on to apply it to the domain of aesthetic sensation, notably in his *Introduction to Aesthetics*, published in 1876.[6]

There are two kinds of response, Fechner surmised, to objects of art. One kind is direct, the other associative. The direct response is immediate and is triggered by properties intrinsic to the object such as its colour, or its symmetry. The associative response depends on the way the observer might place it among other things, or ideas, that occupy his or her attention. A work that is overtly representational is bound to call to mind a host of other images linked to the memory of what is represented. Such associations, grounded in the specificity of experience, are liable to override and obscure the more direct, visceral response evoked by the object itself. For this reason, Fechner advised the student of empirical aesthetics to concentrate on the perception of objects stripped of any representational content or functional significance, namely those that could be regarded as purely ornamental. The study of responses to ornament, he thought, could take us closer to an appreciation of the universal in aesthetic responsiveness (Westphal-Fitch and Fitch 2015: 388–9).

As we shall see, this duality between the visceral, working from the 'bottom up', and the contextual, working from the 'top down' – the one opening to universals of mental functioning, the other to their cultural and historical inflections – still reverberates in contemporary studies. Its persistence suggests that more is at stake than matters of research strategy. At stake, indeed, is the very possibility of a science of aesthetics. As happened in so many other areas of empirically based, experimental science – among them, technology and biology – so too in the foundation of empirical aesthetics, the principles integral to a field of study, its concepts and theory, were transferred onto the object of study itself, whence they were supposed to generate observable results.[7] Thus technology, once the study of technique, came to denote the operational principles already embedded in technical objects; biology, once the study of living organisms, was reconfigured as an interior program directing their morphology and behaviour. And in psychology the same inversion happened. The mind, once a congress of thinking and feeling, was turned into a mechanism that neither knows nor feels, but of which thoughts and feelings are the terminal products. As a branch of psychology, empirical aesthetics is concerned with the workings of this mechanism, in so far as it responds to stimuli of exceptional intensity – above all, those triggered by encounters with objects classified as 'art'.

In short, the 'aesthetics' in empirical aesthetics has nothing to do with the artfulness of thinking of its practitioners, or with the beauty of what they study. It is entirely to do with the measurement of observable responses to sensory stimuli. Indeed, any empirical science that pretends to have converted aesthetics from a study of objects into an object of study, has necessarily to be purified of all aesthetic elements, lest its claim to objectivity be compromised. Thinking with feeling, or sensible cognition, can play no part whatever in its modus operandi. The things that science observes, and seeks to explain, should stay on their side of the fence, and not start telling scientists how to observe, let alone participate in their own explanation! A by-product of this purification, however, is that aesthetic experience, no longer buoyed up in the imaginative movements of attention and composition, is deposited as a kind of precipitate. Ways of knowing and feeling are reduced to repositories of inarticulate thoughts and raw emotions. In effect, the logic of empirical science drives a filtration process by which conceptually explicit propositions rise to the top, and inchoate feelings sink to the bottom, of an imaginary column of consciousness which is often – especially in the language of neuroscience – mapped to a stratified conception of the brain, with its cortical and sub-cortical regions.

It is no wonder, then, that a psychology looking for primal aesthetic drives, common to all humans, should gravitate in its interests towards the lower end of the scale (Westphal-Fitch and Fitch 2015). Nor does it come as any surprise that critics of scientific reductionism should seek its complement in a humanistic approach that attends to matters of interpretation – to the decipherment of aspects of style and meaning sensitive to variations of historical and cultural context (Currie 2003). Its interests rise to the top. Advocates of the so-called 'psycho-historical' approach never cease to remind us of the need to bridge the gap between the 'two cultures', of the sciences and the humanities, here represented by empirical and neuro-aesthetics on the one hand, and art history and criticism on the other (Bullot and Reber 2013). Each drives the other's cause. What use is there, however, in bridging academic cultures if all the water flows underneath? On the bridge, with one foot on each bank, the human mind is pictured as a compound of two parts: one part brain; one part art critic. But streaming between the two banks, respectively of mechanism and interpretation, is precisely what we are after, namely, human aesthetic experience.

To begin with the input

Returning to the conference from which my story began: among those who spoke for empirical aesthetics was one of its leading advocates, the psychologist Helmut Leder. I began my inquiries, therefore, by reading an authoritative outline of the approach, co-authored by Leder and his colleagues Benno Belke, Andries Oeberst and Dorothee Augustin. Their aim, they say, is quite simply 'to explain why people are attracted by art' (Leder et al. 2004: 489). To do this, they construct a model of what they call an 'aesthetic experience'. In a reassessment of the model, which Leder published a decade later with co-author Marcos Nadal (Leder and Nadal 2014), the aesthetic experience is rebranded as an 'aesthetic episode', and it was in these terms that Leder referred to it in his conference address. The episode begins with a viewer, such as myself, standing before an object of aesthetic interest, such as an artwork. It ends with two things: an evaluative judgement and an emotional reaction. Between beginning and end, or input and output, a great deal of processing is supposed to go on in the viewer's head, some of it automatic, some of it under deliberate or conscious control. Diagrammatically, the aesthetic episode is depicted in the form of a box, with inputs to the left and outputs to the right. Inside the box are a number of smaller boxes, each depicting a particular cognitive operation, and sequentially linked by way of arrows (Figure 9.2). Some arrows point only one way, others point both ways, but with various possibilities for feedback (Leder et al. 2004: 492).[8]

Let us, then, begin at the beginning, with the input. For Leder and his team, the input for their model is a work of art. Certain questions immediately arise. For surely, aesthetic experience – whatever it may be – does not come only from encounters with things that happen, for sundry curatorial and institutional reasons, to be classified as artworks. Light streaming through windows is not an artwork, nor is the sun bursting through clouds, yet both can be profoundly moving. Conversely, artworks can have countless other-than-aesthetic resonances: they may, for example, carry an explicit political message, or appeal to environmental concerns. Acknowledging the problem, Leder and Nadal (2014: 445) narrow down their interest to 'the aesthetic appreciation of art', as distinct both from non-aesthetic kinds of art appreciation, and from the aesthetic appreciation of non-art. It lies, in other words, at the area of intersection of art and aesthetics. Even with this qualification, however, all manner of contextual factors can affect the way an object already classified as art is experienced. For example, viewers accustomed to the idea that an object of art should be unique, bearing the hallmark of individual genius, are predisposed to respond more positively to an original than to a copy. They want to see the real thing, and a copy – even if perfectly executed – is not the same, as it upsets their understanding of the work's causal history (Bullot and Reber 2013: 132). The same goes if the original is seen not directly but remotely, by way of its projection on a screen. Either way, whatever feelings are evoked by the work itself, taken on its own merits, will probably be tinged with disappointment (Leder and Nadal 2014: 453–4).

How, then, can the aesthetic responses specifically attributable to a work of art be separated out from the effects of all this contextual noise?

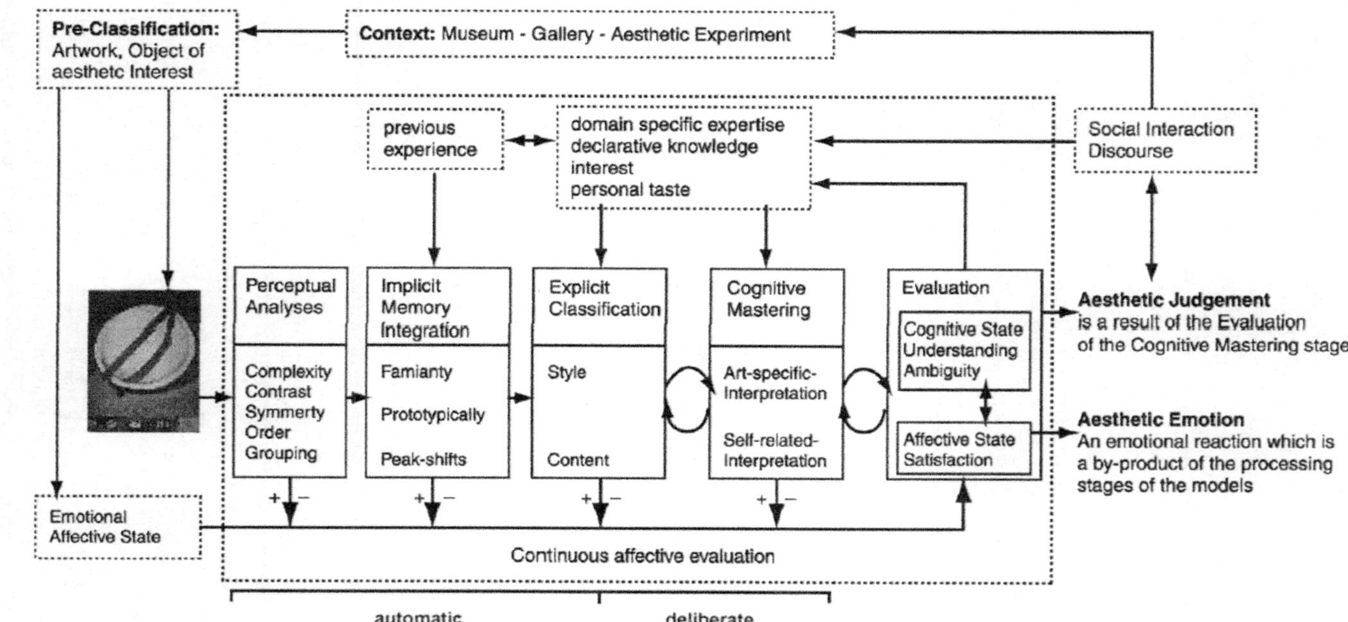

Figure 9.2 The aesthetic episode.

Reproduced from Leder et al. (2004: 492), courtesy of the British Psychological Society. © John Wiley & Sons.

Experimental science typically proceeds by removing the site of investigation from real-world settings, such as the street or the gallery, to the simulated environment of the laboratory. Artificially isolated from extraneous influences, so far as is practicably possible, the work can be viewed under strictly controlled conditions. Indeed, one reason for the recent advances in empirical aesthetics reported by Leder and Nadal (2014: 444) is technological, for it is now possible, under laboratory conditions, 'to present and to manipulate high-quality stimuli on computer screens for well-controlled durations'. You can even put your subjects inside an fMRI scanner and get them to look at reproductions of artworks, while having their brains examined (Kirk et al. 2009)! Yet laboratory controls are not neutral, and they can have their own effects on the viewing experience. It is not only that people prefer the real thing to screen images; they also much prefer the gallery to the laboratory as a place for viewing art.

Studies have indeed confirmed that viewers tend to spend more time before artworks in the gallery than in the lab, as well as showing greater interest in them (Brieber et al. 2014). As Leder and Nadal (2014: 454) are forced to admit, the laboratory context, in which most research in empirical aesthetics is carried out, can attenuate the experience of art. No one wants to spend longer in the laboratory than they have to, least of all cocooned inside a brain-scanning machine. Then there's the question of mood, or what psychologists call 'affective state'. If you are otherwise in a bad mood – that is, in a 'negative affective state' – then this might depress what might otherwise be a positive experience of art. In one study, by psychologists Vladimir J. Konečni and Dianne Sargent-Pollock (1977), subjects were deliberately subjected to 'treatments' that made them either angry or happy. Anger was induced by an unpleasant sound they could not control; happiness by the reward of a small sum of money. Their state of arousal, whether positive or negative, as measured by skin conductance, was then correlated with their responses to Renaissance and twentieth-century paintings. If they were angry, they preferred Renaissance art; but if they were happy, they preferred the art of the twentieth century. But if they were neither positively nor negatively aroused, they were quite indifferent to both!

As these results suggest, what counts as input to the aesthetic episode, and what count as contextual factors qualifying that input, depend on the model, not on the actual situation as it is encountered by the subjects of experiments. An experiment designed to test reactions to artworks under laboratory conditions could just as well turn out to test reactions to laboratory treatments under conditions ameliorated by the presence of artworks. For the moment, however, let us pass over this indeterminacy and move on to the next phase. This is the part of the model inside the box and consists of what Leder and his colleagues call 'processing mechanisms' (Pelowski et al. 2016: 2), which act on the informational input from the artwork so as eventually to deliver certain attitudinal and behavioural outputs. On its way, the received information passes through a sequence of stages. These are: perceptual analysis, implicit memory recognition, explicit classification, cognitive mastering and evaluation (Figure 9.2). In what follows, I shall briefly review each of these in turn. First, however, a few words are needed on the general approach of cognitive science to vision.

Inside the box: from brain to critic

There is a common belief, writes Semir Zeki (1998: 77), a leading figure in visual neurobiology, 'that one sees with the eye rather than with the cerebral cortex'. But this belief, he insists, is erroneous. The eyes see nothing, they are but passive receptors stimulated by the continually changing flux of incident radiation. It is the brain that actively sees, and it does so by first distilling from the flux only what is necessary to identify the constant properties of the objects seen, extracting such features as line, contour, symmetry and colour, and then matching these properties against a record, stored in memory, of all the objects it has seen before. In this way the brain manages to create the illusion that what we see is actually present, as such, in the physical world, when in fact it is but an image that the brain has constructed for us by fitting together the raw material of sensation, reduced to its bare essentials, with the knowledge it already possesses, based on past experience.[9] In the stratified language of neuroscience, this involves a combination of 'bottom-up' and 'top-down' processing, the first deploying hard-wired mechanisms, built into the brain at birth, the second bringing to bear higher cognitive faculties, of attention, association and imagery, by which the brain makes an informed guess of what might be 'out there'. Every percept, then, is in the nature of a hypothesis, and in visual perception the brain continually tests these hypotheses against the data of experience without, however, ever reaching complete certainty about what it sees (Gregory 1973: 61–2).[10]

Broadly speaking, this is the approach that Leder and his team bring to the question of what happens when we observe a work of art. It begins with the 'bottom-up' stage of perceptual analysis (Figure 9.2). This occurs in the instant that the image of an artwork is flashed before the viewer's eyes. At this moment the brain extracts salient features from the visual stimulus, including contrast, pattern complexity, colour, symmetry, grouping and order. The process is extremely rapid, automatic and apparently effortless, and it quickly leads on to the next stage, of implicit memory recognition. This is the first step in matching identifiable features with the record of things previously encountered. It is implicit because its results can affect subsequent stages of aesthetic processing without ever reaching the level of consciousness. Recognition may rest on familiarity, prototypicality or 'peak-shift'. Familiarity comes from simple repetition of the stimulus, as when the same image is flashed up over and over again. With prototypicality, the object or image is recognised as a representative of a class. With peak shift, object recognition is enhanced through the artificial magnification of core features (Leder et al. 2004: 494–7).

The apparent parallel between what the brain does, in perceptual analysis and memory recognition, and what art is alleged to do, in extracting the essence of things and bringing out their most salient characteristics, has not gone unnoticed. For Zeki (1998: 76–8), the artist is the very personification of a brain: whatever the artist does, the brain does also, not because the artist *has* a brain but because he, or she, *is* one. Could the appeal of art, Zeki asks, lie precisely in the way it mimics or extends the operations of the visual brain? Could part of the pleasure in viewing, say, a painting stem from its gratification and reinforcement of the brain's natural drive to get to the bottom of what the painting represents? One might even say, with neuroscientist Vilayanur Ramachandran and philosopher William Hirstein, that the very purpose of representational art is to 'titillate the visual areas of the brain', playing above all on their susceptibility to peak shift, by exaggerating the essential characteristics of the things represented in order to activate more powerfully the neural mechanisms that would otherwise be triggered in the presence of the things themselves. 'All art', they say, 'is caricature' (Ramachandran and Hirstein 1999: 17–18).

After implicit memory recognition, the next stage is explicit classification (Figure 9.2). With this, we begin to cross the Rubicon from neuroscience to art history, for classification is about identifying a work in terms of content and style. This does not, in itself, require any prior knowledge or expertise on the part of the viewer: even so-called 'naïve' observers can tell the difference between one style of painting and another – between, say, baroque and rococo – and may perhaps derive some satisfaction from being able to do so (Hasenfus et al. 1983; Leder et al. 2004: 497). Nor need the identification be put into words. Indeed, the ability to discriminate between styles appears to be common to a range of animal species that lack anything approaching human verbal competence. In one of the strangest experiments to be reported in the literature, a team of behavioural scientists in Japan trained pigeons to discriminate between the styles of Monet and Picasso. Correct answers were rewarded with access to a feeder containing hemp seeds. Once trained, the pigeons could even distinguish between paintings by the two artists they had never seen before (Watanabe, Sakamoto and Wakita 1995). We can safely assume that the birds were motivated by a desire for the reward they received on picking the right answer, rather than by any feeling for the art itself. The question is whether it should be any different for a human brain turned critic.

Acknowledging that not all discrimination need be put into words, Leder and his team (2004: 497–8) nevertheless place stylistic processing in the box of explicit classification, on the grounds that it is, in principle, verbally explicable. And with explication, they argue, comes expertise. With the growth of expertise, knowledge about the artist, the technique employed, the historical significance of the work and the context in which it was made all become part of the content. They confer an added value. Thus, Monet's celebrated painting *La Gare Saint-Lazare* is not just a picture of a railway station with steam engines. It is a Monet, and an exemplar of Impressionism! Art criticism trades in values such as this. And it is in the final stages, of cognitive mastering and evaluation, that the balance between the two parts of the human mind – the brain and the critic – finally pivots towards the latter. Top-down interpretation, based on prior knowledge, semantic association and personal taste, trumps the neural machinery of bottom-up processing. Rather than following one another sequentially, however, evaluation and cognitive mastery are supposed to proceed in tandem, the one guiding the other by continually measuring its success (Leder et al. 2004: 499–500; see Figure 9.2).

From the perspective of empirical aesthetics, the encounter with a work of art is fundamentally an exercise in problem-solving. Modern art is said to present problems of exceptional difficulty, due to the plethora of its styles and the obscurity of its meanings (Leder et al. 2004: 499). It is nevertheless assumed that every problem already contains its solution, hidden inside the work. Perhaps the artist deliberately put it there; perhaps it crept in of its own accord. Regardless of how it got there, the task of the viewer is to find it – to ascertain what the work means, what it represents, and to what school or movement it owes its conception. Following the cognitive model of visual processing outlined at the start of this section, the answers are supposed to be found through the successive construction of hypotheses and their testing against the data of experience. Getting them right undoubtedly brings a sense of satisfaction. In the language of neuroscience, it activates rewarding centres in the brain. According to Ramachandran and Hirstein (1999: 33), it is nothing less than a 'law of aesthetic experience' that solving perceptual problems is self-rewarding. Perhaps, as Leder and his team (2004: 500) suggest, 'the self-rewarding character of art processing … explains why perceivers continue to perceive art'. They are like contestants in a quiz show, competing for the title of mastermind. Once hooked, they become addicted. It is doubtful, however, whether the rewards of winning the competition have anything more to do with the feeling for art than did hemp seeds for the pigeons which managed to tell a Monet from a Picasso.

The end of the episode

Finding the solution brings closure to the aesthetic episode. The work is now understood, cognitively mastered, leaving a glow of satisfaction induced by the feeling, not for the work itself, but of having cracked it and decoded its contents. With that, viewers can put the work behind them and move on to the next. Introducing his essay of 1912, 'On the spiritual in art', the painter Wassily Kandinsky wrote despairingly of visitors to the gallery who – catalogue in hand – would parade from picture to picture, identifying each one as by this artist, of that school, painted in such-and-such a year, and representing this or that person, landscape or object. 'And then they leave', Kandinsky (1982: 130) observes, 'just as rich or poor as when they came in, immediately absorbed once again by their own interests, which have nothing whatever to do with art. Why ever did they go?' They went, of course, to see the pictures, and so that they could say they had seen them, and could pronounce with authority on their provenance and meaning. But the *life* in each work – with its torments and doubts, its moments of ecstasy and insight, the life that cries out to be heard – completely passes them by (Ingold 2011a: 205).

The aesthetic episode is entirely congruent with Kandinsky's caricature of the visitor experience. It begins with its inputs and ends with its outputs. Every episode begins, as we have seen, at the point when the viewer sets eyes upon the work – eyes which relay its visual input to the brain. The outputs, according to Leder and his team, are twofold: aesthetic judgements and aesthetic emotions (Figure 9.2). The judgement is no more of the work itself, however, than is the emotion triggered by it. The claim, rather, is that both judgement and emotion depend on the relative ease of processing through the immediately preceding stages of cognitive mastery and evaluation (Leder et al. 2004: 503). One can be happy or pleased with the result, when it is felt to have gone well, or annoyed and frustrated when it has not – when, for example, efforts to solve the work have led nowhere, so that the episode cannot be satisfactorily closed. The aesthetic judgement, in short, is in the nature of a self-assessment, a rating of the mind's success in critically evaluating the work at hand. And the aesthetic emotion is kindled not by the work but by the rewards of successful processing, or conversely by the penalty of failure. Judgement and emotion, however, do not necessarily go hand in hand. One can solve a problem without enjoying it: indeed, the Leder team suggests that the superiority of experts over naïve perceivers lies precisely in their being better able to distance the work of critical evaluation from feelings of pleasure or displeasure (Leder et al. 2004: 502). They are ruled, as we might say colloquially, by their heads rather than their hearts.

At what point, then, does the episode end? It ends, presumably, when the problem posed by the work has been solved. In terms of the model, this is the point at which the processing of visual information yields up to its outputs. But how can we tell when, or whether, this point has been reached? A study from the Metropolitan Museum of Art in New York, conducted by Jeffrey and Lisa Smith (2001), found that the mean time for perceiving artworks was 27.2 seconds. Another, from a temporary exhibition of paintings by the artist Gerhard Richter, found averages per picture of between 25.7 and 41.0 seconds (Carbon 2017). But measurements of this kind tell us little. Viewers who have successfully identified a picture, and already classified its style and content, might choose to linger in its presence, perhaps even to breathe its atmosphere. Or to the contrary, they might give up on their attempts at mastery and evaluation, and move on to another work, perhaps in frustration, before reaching any kind of conclusion.

In laboratory studies, viewers have been artificially exposed to images of artworks for controlled durations, of 3 seconds or less, much shorter than what would be usual in the gallery. The idea is that by incrementally reducing presentation times, it might be possible to isolate early processing stages and estimate their durations. In an experiment conducted by Leder and his colleagues (Augustin et al. 2008), subjects were tasked with spotting differences of style and content between images flashed up for periods of between 10 and 3000 milliseconds. The experimenters were careful to exclude anyone who reported having been educated in the arts or art history, who might perhaps have had an unfair advantage, knowing the answers in advance! Even for those who did not, however, the experiment showed that content differences could be identified with astonishing speed, even within the minimal 10 ms margin, but that stylistic identification needed up to 50 ms. Other studies have suggested processing times of between 300 and 600 ms.

This temporal attenuation, though in itself remarkable, is possible only because the work of art is understood as a problem that contains its solution. It is, in this sense, a puzzle. As we know from virtuosi with the Rubik's cube, or with the crossword, the time it takes to solve a puzzle can be progressively reduced to the point of virtual instantaneity. It is an approach to zero. In theory, since the result is already given, finding it requires no time at all. The work of art, however, is not a puzzle. In making it the artist has joined in his or her own thinking and feeling, for an indefinite period, with the materials of the work, which gradually takes shape or form in the process of their going along together. This is the work of time, and the time of work. 'To the artist who creates a picture by drawing it from the depths of his soul', as Henri Bergson (1922: 359) observed long ago, 'time is no longer an accessory; it is not an interval that may be lengthened or shortened without the content being altered. The duration … is part and parcel of his work.'[11] Without time, the work would be empty.

But if time is not accessory to the artist, no more is it accessory to the viewer. In his essay of 1934, *Art as Experience*, John Dewey (1987: 60) insisted that to perceive a work of art, 'a beholder must create his own experience'. Moreover, 'this creation must include relations comparable to those which the original producer underwent'.[12] In Dewey's pragmatic philosophy, an experience undergone is also actively done. The beholder surrenders to the work, as the artist to the materials of which it is made, not passively but actively: 'we must summon energy and pitch it at a responsive key in order to take in' (1987: 59). Thus understood, experience is not – and cannot be – episodic. Neither can it be contained within a temporal interval, however long or short; nor can one interval follow the next like beads on a string, each separate from those preceding and following. For experience actively undergone always takes in what is past, even as it gives out into that which is to come. It does not begin here, and end there, but continually turns endings into beginnings, digesting the former as it extrudes into the latter. Dewey (1987: 62) compared it to breathing in and out, and like breathing, it is essential to the continuity of life.

The work goes on

Shifting the register from inputs and outputs to breathing in and out involves more than a change of idiom. For it entails a quite different sense of process. For empirical aesthetics, as we have seen, it is axiomatic that encounters with art involve processing of information by the mind-brain. The verb 'to process' is here understood in a transitive sense, commonly employed in the field of computing, where it means to operate on a corpus of data by way of a programme. Neuroscientists disposed to model the brain as a massively complex computer have adopted the idea of processing in much the same vein. Breathing, however, is part of a life process, and key to this process is that far from effecting a conversion from input to output, it keeps on going, continually overtaking itself. Or to return to an earlier analogy, it does not, like a bridge, afford transport from one riverbank to another, but rather flows with the water between. Life processes in an intransitive sense, not carrying *across* from one state to another, but carrying *along*. This is to regard processing, as I have stated elsewhere (Ingold 2000: 18), 'not ... as a step-by-step refinement or repackaging of sensory data already received, but rather as the unfolding of the whole system of relations constituted by the multi-sensory involvement of the perceiver in his or her environment'.

In this intransitive sense of processing lie the foundations of an approach to aesthetics that, following the lead of Dewey, is practical rather than empirical. It starts from the premise that art, in its making as in its experience, is a process of life. It carries on. Neither the making of a work, nor the experience of it, is ever truly finished. This does not mean that it is half-finished, as if the process had been interrupted and prevented from reaching a final conclusion. With art as with life, the process is not heading to a conclusion but always issuing into fresh beginning. In it lies the 'continued birth' of vision (Merleau-Ponty 1964: 168). Even if the work appears complete as it is hung in the gallery, and is carefully curated to keep it so, it nevertheless lives on in the imaginations of those who come to see it. Just as a piece of music lives on in its performances, or a story in its tellings, so the work of art has an afterlife in the manifold ways in which viewers create for themselves an experience comparable to that of its original making. Even Leder and Nadal (2014: 449), in their retrospective review, admit that 'long extension in time' may be precisely what makes an experience aesthetic – meaning that it is in the very nature of the aesthetic episode that an extended period needs to be devoted to 'perception-cognition-emotion interactions'. Whole episodes, they say, may take place over different time scales and interact in complex ways. Nevertheless, the transitive sense of processing, and its episodic character, imply a movement towards closure. For practical aesthetics, to the contrary, what is fundamental to the experience of art is that it affords an opening.

The work of art is a problem. But unlike the puzzle, it does not already contain its own solution. Problems of this kind, like the life to which they belong, do not close in on their solutions but open to further generation, variation and metamorphosis.[13] They are less cognitive than affective; they call on us not to be the masters of art but to submit to it – not to put art in its place but to go along with it, and to attend. For art, if it is to carry on – if it is to undergo the continued birth on which its vitality and renewal depend – must ever escape the clutches of identification, classification and evaluation that continually threaten to pin it down. With art we cannot put the work behind us, or close the episode, thinking that once understood and interpreted, it need trouble us no further. The work carries on as life does; it stays with us, as we stay with it. To borrow a phrase from cultural theorist Donna Haraway (2016), we *stay with the trouble*. And together we move on, never further from a beginning or closer to an end, feeling our way as we go and improvising a passage. On the journey, works of art are our travel companions, not the contents of our baggage.

A practical aesthetics, then, that attends to living art and thinks by way of it, cannot align with the episodic but rather cuts a way through, in real time, like the river between its banks.[14] It is the work of a mind that, far from projecting fantasies of its own making from its prison within the head, reaches along the lines of its sensory participation into an ever-forming world. While visual neuroscience adheres doggedly to the view that the mind completes a world-picture by adding its own share, dredged from the sediments of memory, to the deliverances of the senses (Kandel 2016: 20–21), experience teaches us otherwise, namely, that perception is the achievement, not of a mind in a body, but of a whole being in a world, moving around in, and exploring, what it affords. This being has eyes to see, ears to hear and skin to feel – eyes, ears and skin that are not just passive receptors for sensory data to be sent to the brain for processing, but organs of a perceptual system tuned to respond to variations of light, sound and pressure in its surroundings. As James Gibson (1979: 64) put it in his pioneering work on the ecology of visual perception, 'there is no sender outside the head and no receiver inside the head'. There is a being, alive and present to a world.

Lanyon's revenge

Many years ago, the anthropologist Claude Lévi-Strauss reminded the delegates at a conference that seated among them was an 'uninvited guest' who – unbeknown to them – had all along been quietly directing their deliberations. That guest, he said, was the *human mind* (Lévi-Strauss 1968: 71). Could it be that I, too, had brought with me an uninvited guest to the Tate Gallery at St Ives? Invisibly stowed inside my head, like a homunculus, it would have had no ticket and paid no fee for admission. Yet what a useful guest it would have been! Once in the gallery, it could have done all the work for me. For painting after painting, I would have only had to stand there, placing my eyes squarely before each canvas to ensure an adequate scan. The mind could then get to work on the visual input, starting from the bottom with basic brain functions and then working up to the top with more complex cognitive operations, until, perhaps only a fraction of a second later, it would issue a receipt that would have not only told me what I had seen but also provided it with a neurally certified preference rating.

This scenario might sound fanciful, but it is not far removed from what, according to empirical aesthetics, happens in reality. Picture the scene. After having viewed many other works in the gallery, I eventually find myself standing before Peter Lanyon's *Thermal*. My mind, quickly recognising that I have seen it once before, calls up the relevant contextual data – it was in the exhibition at the Courtauld. This feeds directly into implicit memory integration, adding a level of domain-specific expertise that piques interest levels. Out comes an evaluation that is highly positive. It puts words into my mouth. Turning to my wife, I explain: 'You see, this is a painting by Peter Lanyon, one of the school of artists working in post-war St Ives. Lanyon was a keen glider pilot, and in *Thermal* he depicts the pilot's feeling for air.' To be able to pronounce on the matter with such authority gives me a warm glow inside, a sense that even though other works have proved hard to comprehend, I am at least the master of this one. And the glow colours my appreciation of the work. I'll definitely give it a high preference score, maybe I should even purchase a reproduction in the gallery shop!

But wait. As I linger before the picture, a shadow falls across my eyes. Doubt creeps in, unsettling my composure. The air around stirs, tingling the skin with its cool draught. Suddenly, there's a great blast and I am swirling in the elements. It is as though the walls of the gallery had tumbled, and the turbulent weather outside had permeated the space. At the same moment, the picture dissolves. Canvas melts into air. I cannot see it clearly: I am, as you will recall, without my spectacles, and things are out of focus. Yet it seems to me that a figure emerges from the mist. Could it be the shade of Lanyon himself? For hark, it speaks, with tones of admonishment and despair: '*Why are you here?* Were my life and death for nothing? Can you not feel for yourself the air, the violence, the sheer force of the elements? This is what it means to be alive, this is what I died for. I cannot explain it; I cannot describe it. But this *is* it.' As I cast my eyes again towards the painting, I find that I am already there inside it – inside the movement of its generation. I feel the wind blowing through, the rush of air that had once both swept the hand of the painter in the throes of composition and borne him aloft in his craft. This, I realise, is not painting of or about the wind; it is wind-painting, and I am flying in it, my mind churning in the very same currents that animate the artist's immortal soul. It is churning still, as I write these lines.

Then I remember the art of Saraceno, an art that literally transports us into an aerial milieu, carried along on a balloon. Is this not an aesthetic experience, every bit as powerful as being bathed in sunlight streaming through the windows, or watching the sparkling breakers on the shore and listening to the roar and hiss of their surge and ebb? In a commentary on Saraceno's work, literary theorist Eva Horn urges us to recover the phenomenological dimension of inhabiting the air, of breathing it and feeling it. It is a matter, she emphasises, of developing an *aesthesis of air*, of exploring 'new and different forms of *being in the air together*' (Horn 2017: 26). This is not about understanding or judging works of art, let alone about transforming them into objects. Nor is it a matter of putting work on show, or turning aesthetic performance into a spectacle, designed to elicit a response from among those who pay to see it. Were the aim of art to stage a life, to re-present it as drama, then the work itself would be devoid of feeling – it would be but a vehicle for its evocation, calculated to produce an effect. Art would be reduced to advertisement.

This kind of aestheticisation of the real, as philosopher Gernot Böhme (2017: 20) has observed, is an endemic feature of societies in the advanced phases of capitalism. Under such an economic regime, experience becomes the acquisition of 'experiences'. Ways of being and going along together, in which the viewer is enrolled as co-producer in the ongoing life of the work, become objects of consumption, or commodities, appealing to individual wants. Ways of seeing become sights, ways of hearing sounds, ways of feeling impressions. Sights, sounds and impressions, plugged readymade into the mind-brain, are strategically targeted to convey subliminal messages and to elicit specific behavioural and attitudinal responses in an audience who are now no longer co-producers but consumers. This is the logic of advertising. What the advertising industry needs, and what empirical aesthetics offers, is a theory of consumer behaviour underpinned by the economic logic of neoliberalism. Dressed up in the apparel of science is a highly sophisticated and slightly sinister form of market research. Far from affording a window into aesthetic experience, empirical aesthetics effectively reduces it to zero.

Part III

Surface tensions

Scholars have long held surfaces in disdain. Whether for want of confidence or for an excess of it, surfaces are either deemed to cloak the true significance of things behind a veneer of superficiality, or to furnish no more than a featureless background or underlay for the matters that truly command our interest. We either distrust them or take them for granted. Distrust motivates us to seek real meaning behind or beneath surface appearances; overconfidence leads us to focus on the figures and ignore the ground. Either way, attention is drawn away from the surfaces themselves. But what if it were otherwise? Could it be that surfaces cover nothing but themselves? Unravelling a ball of wool leaves only more wool; digging into a mound of earth reveals only more earth. Everything of interest is going on at the surface, where the wool meets the knitter's fingers, allowing a garment to take shape, and where earth comes into contact with humid air and sunlight, allowing plants to grow. These surfaces neither hide what lies within or behind, nor do they serve as a base or back for what is set above or in front. They rather comprise a zone for the admixture or interpenetration of materials, which in turn affords a matrix for life and growth. The chapters making up this Part are all concerned with ways in which things can be reanimated by way of a return to the surface.

We begin, in Chapters 10 and 11, from the foundations. A building, small or large, must have a solid base to stand on, must it not? Here, I question this assumption. In Chapter 10 we are in the forests of the circumpolar North, visiting the ostensibly slight and ephemeral dwellings of their indigenous peoples; in Chapter 11 we are at the other extreme, on the city streets, surrounded on all sides by towering apartment blocks. But whether in the boreal forest or the windy city, I find myself wondering whether I am on solid ground at all. Could the conical lodge of northern forest-dwellers, fashioned from wooden poles covered with the hides of reindeer or caribou, be compared to a boat, the covering of which is likewise stretched over a wooden frame? Could the lodge float in the earth like a boat in water, under the same, overarching sky? And could the hulking buildings of the city be compared to ships at sea? Rather than standing on a rigid platform,

DOI: 10.4324/9781003171713-13

perhaps they are submerged below in the semi-fluid medium of the earth whilst contending above with the aerial fluxes of wind and weather. Does the formal integrity of the building have continually to be won against the forces of the elements?

Questions such as these cast doubt on the very fundaments of architecture: that it should be formed of structures built to the specifications of prior design, and sited in a solid landscape. In Chapter 10 I show that the conical lodge is a thing woven rather than made, and as such, not so much an object in a landscape as a nexus of growth in a world of earth and sky. Here, in the lodge, earth and sky are not divided at the horizon, as they might seem to be when viewed through a window set in the wall of a modern house. They are rather unified at the centre, where the smoke from the hearth rises to meet the sky whose light streams through the smoke-hole at the apex. Returning in Chapter 11 from the forest to the city, I reflect upon how we might think differently of buildings, were we to imagine the ground to heave like the ocean with the swell of the elements. For the mariner, the ship is a point of stillness in a turbulent world of sea and sky, and his attention is directed not so much to the surface as to currents below and winds above. Is it likewise above and below, rather than at ground level, that the city has to contend with the forces of disintegration? And with rising sea-levels, could this offer a glimpse into a future world of pervasive wetness?

From the ground surface, we move in Chapter 12 to the surface of the page, following the career of the very word 'page', itself derived from the Latin *pagus*, meaning a stretch of inhabited country. In medieval Europe, reading was likened to wayfaring through the terrain, the *paysage*, and the lines inscribed on parchment to paths trodden on the ground. Based on this analogy, the ground resembles a severally reused parchment, otherwise known as a palimpsest. The analogy has been especially influential in the field of archaeology, in which the palimpsest is typically understood in terms of material deposition. Yet in truth, the palimpsest results not from the successive deposition of layers but from repeatedly stripping them away. Its formation is thus governed by what I call an anti-stratigraphic principle. Why, then, do modern people commonly understand both ground and page in stratigraphic terms? I find the answers in technologies of paving and printing. Both separate the space of imagination from our habitation of the earth. Is it possible, then, to bring imagining and inhabiting back together? I believe this can be done, and adduce a couple of literary examples. At the end, however, it all comes down to how we think of mind and memory: as archive or palimpsest?

From the page, then, we proceed to the book. On the shelf, the book appears to be a measurable volume of rectangular pages. And so long as the book remains closed, each page remains in intimate, surface-to-surface contact with its neighbour on either side. What happens to these surfaces, then, when the book is opened? In Chapter 13 I show how, in the history of the book, the surface of the page has borne comparison, successively, to that of a veil, pane, sheet, face and screen. The medieval scribe, inscribing the parchment page with pen and ink, would weave his lines much as cloth might be woven on the loom, to form a veil-like texture. With the Renaissance discovery of perspective, however, the page took on a different aspect, comparable to a windowpane. To read was to look through the pane, to recover the meanings behind. Yet this same period, in Europe, saw the introduction of the press, which works by imprinting a precomposed typographic assembly upon a sheet, to be subsequently folded into pages. To read the printed page is not to become absorbed into its surface texture, as with the veil, nor to look through the surface, as with the pane, but to confront it face on. The page becomes a face, meeting the face of the reader much as in society, people meet face-to-face with one another. For many nowadays, however, most reading is done on-screen. And with that the reciprocity of face-to-face relations is yielding to an atomised world in which every other is a projection of the self.

In Chapter 14, finally, we ask what goes on when surfaces are effaced, or when the marks they carry are redacted. In editing text by hand, lines may be struck out, in acts of deletion, or rubbed out, in acts of erasure. But far from being equivalent, as is often supposed, deletion and erasure are utterly distinct, both operationally and in their surface effects. While the strikethrough physically crosses words out, ontologically it makes no more contact with the surface on which they are written than does a line inscribed on a mirror with that which is reflected in the glass. It is as if the stroke were drawn across another plane, layered over the page of writing. Rubbing or scratching out, however, erodes the surface itself. We thus arrive at a distinction between two sorts of surfaces. Those of one sort spread as layers of determinate thickness, which cover over what has gone before and will in turn be covered. But surfaces of the other sort cover nothing. From above, they extend indefinitely in depth, and from below indefinitely in reach. Camouflage works by tricking us into taking one sort for the other. In burial, however, both principles can combine. Yet burying the past will not make it go away. Only when it finally rises to the surface can the past be wiped out once and for all.

Chapter 10

The conical lodge at the centre of the earth-sky world

Entering the lodge

It is October 2008, and I am attending an anthropological conference in the Norwegian city of Tromsø, convened as part of a comparative project on 'Home, Hearth and Household in the Circumpolar North' (Anderson, Wishart and Vaté 2013).[1] We are in the University Museum, and on a lawn outside the main entrance a conical tent or lodge has been erected, of a kind once widely used among indigenous peoples throughout the circumpolar region. These are peoples whose livelihood was traditionally based on hunting and trapping, in northern North America, supplemented or replaced across northern Eurasia by a form of pastoral nomadism centred around large herds of semi-domestic reindeer. The frame of the lodge is made of long, stout wooden poles that converge at the apex but splay out at ground level around the perimeter of a circle. This is covered with laboriously prepared caribou skins, carefully sewn together. Though extending all the way to the base of the frame, they reach not quite to the apex but to a level just short of it, leaving the apex itself uncovered.[2]

Entering through the door-flap, I find myself in a remarkably capacious, interior space, at the centre of which is a place for the fire. I kneel on the ground. It is still daytime and the light streams in through the apex, which remains open to the sky. Looking up, it makes me blink (Figure 10.1). At the same time, through my knees, I feel the clammy depth of the earth which gives me support. In a moment of revelation, I understand what it means to inhabit a world of earth and sky. It is to be at once bathed in light and rapt in feeling. But it also dawns on me how closely the idea of landscape to which I am accustomed from my own upbringing is linked to a particular architecture: to the habitation of rooms with hard floors below, ceilings above, and windows set in vertical walls. Imagine yourself as the resident of a modern suburban apartment, with large picture windows that afford a commanding, panoramic view of the surrounding countryside. When you look out from the windows you see the land stretching out into the distance, where it seems to meet the sky along the line of the far horizon. Inside the

DOI: 10.4324/9781003171713-14

Figure 10.1 Looking up through the apex of the conical lodge, the linear poles interweave to form a complex knot, from which each nevertheless continues, reaching up into the open sky.

Photo by Hilde Jåstad.

lodge, however, there are no horizons to be seen. Earth and sky, far from being divided at the horizon, seem rather to be unified at the very centre of my emplaced being. Enwrapped within the lodge I nevertheless feel open to a world. But this world is not a landscape so much as what I shall henceforth call the *earth-sky*.

Further reflection leads me to think that what is at issue here is not just a particular architecture but the very idea of architecture itself. For more than five centuries, it has been both the claim and the conceit of the architectural profession that every building is a monument to the genius of its creator, standing as the enduring realisation of an original design concept. But it is not only the building that answers to a design; so too does the landscape in which it is set. Indeed it is in this idea of architecture that the roots of the modern landscape aesthetic are to be found. Serving as both stage and scenery, the landscape is taken to furnish not only the solid platform upon which the architectural monument is erected but also the backdrop against which it is displayed to best advantage. Together, the monument and its landscape are understood to comprise a totality, complete and fully formed.

If the bedrock of the physical world provides the matter, then the human mind contributes the form. Land is to scape, then, as material substance to ideal form, and the land is shaped by their unification (Ingold 2013a: 83; see also Chapter 2, page 31).

With these reflections on the meanings of architecture and landscape in mind, let me return to the conical lodge. I contend that we misunderstand the lodge by imagining it as an instance of architecture: that is, as a structure built to the prior specifications of a formal design, and set upon the stage and amid the scenery of a landscape. Admittedly, those who hold such a view – and they include many in the fields of ethnology, cultural anthropology and material culture studies – would hesitate to attribute the design to an individual creator. Rather, as an example of what they call 'vernacular architecture', it would be credited to the genius of cultural tradition. The builders of such traditional structures, according to architectural theorist Christopher Alexander, do not knowingly implement designs of their own making but rather submit to the reproduction of forms carried unknowingly in their minds and passed from generation to generation through force of custom. Their building is, in this sense, 'unselfconscious' (Alexander 1964: 36). Here, while nature supplies the raw materials, it is culture that adds the form. And every time the unselfconscious builder puts up a lodge, this form is projected upon the substrate of the material world.

In what follows I want to propose an alternative view of building: not as the projection of form onto matter but as a binding together of materials in movement. The lodge, in this view, far from being erected upon rigid and impervious foundations, is stitched into the very fabric of the earth. Instead of positing the lodge as a material artefact set in a landscape, I argue that it would be better conceived as a nexus of materials in a world of earth and sky. The argument is set out in five steps. In the first, I consider the mutuality of earth and sky, and what it means to say of the lodge that it is both of the earth and of the sky. In the second step I connect the idea of the earth-sky to that of smooth space, and show how this connection is manifested in the covering materials of the lodge. In step three, I contrast the accord of earth and sky, in the conical lodge, with their discord in the life and dwelling of the peasant farmer, by drawing a comparison with the mariner's relation to the ocean. In the fourth step I show how the idea of landscape, in its modern guise, entails a transition from the gathering of experiences to their projection, or from a haptic to an optical mode of perception. Finally, I explain the conical form of the lodge as an upended vortex, the envelope of a vital spiral of growth and regeneration.

Earth and sky

In a treatise published in 1851, the Hamburg-born architect Gottfried Semper (1989) proposed a division of architecture into four 'elements': the earthwork, the framework, the enclosing membrane and the hearth. To the construction of each, he assigned a particular trade. Building the earthwork, from solid materials such as stone or brick, weighed down by gravity, was the task of the mason. The framework, elevated from its foundations in the earthwork, would be intended to provide support for a covering. The construction of the framework, typically made of wood, was a job for the carpenter. The membrane, of relatively lightweight material draped over the framework, called for the arts of weaving. With the membrane finally in place, the building would be clad or covered so as to form an enclosure. Finally the hearth, at its centre, was the place of fire, and of the crafts that depend on it, including ceramics and metallurgy. Though Semper concerned himself with all four elements, he was particularly interested in the relation between the earthwork and the framework. For the principles of construction involved in each are quite different, and in many ways opposed.

The masonry of the earthwork rests on principles of *stereotomics*. Derived from the classical Greek *stereo* ('solid') and *tomia* ('to cut'), stereotomics is the art of cutting solid blocks into shapes that fit snugly to form a robust assembly. The carpentry of the framework, by contrast, rests on principles of *tectonics*. This term, too, has its roots in classical Greece: it comes from *tekton*, originally referring to the work of the carpenter, though subsequently extended to many other areas of artisanal activity. The key difference, however, is this: stereotomic structures are held in place by the weight of every block on those beneath and ultimately on foundations; in tectonics, linear constituents are fitted into a frame held together into a tensile structure by joints or bindings. Where the mason is above all a *layer* of bricks or blocks, the carpenter is, first and foremost, a *joiner* of beams. Architectural historian Kenneth Frampton (1995: 7) has shown how these 'dialogically opposed modes of construction' strain in reverse directions, with the stereotomic earthwork showing 'the propensity of mass form not only to gravitate towards the earth but also to dissolve into its substance', and the tectonic framework, contrarily, reaching 'for the immateriality of the sky'.

In these cosmic associations, the building is revealed as a marriage not of form and matter but of earth and sky, and as the consummation of their union. That's what it means to situate the building in an earth-sky world. And it is in these terms that I propose to consider the conical lodge: not as an artefact in the landscape but as a particular synthesis of earth and sky that allows human life to take root and grow, nourished by the earth even as it breathes the air. Yet – returning to Semper's four elements – while the lodge clearly has a framework of wooden poles, a membrane of skins stitched together, and a hearth at the centre, it apparently has no earthwork. There are no solid walls, not even foundation stones. How, then, to recapitulate Frampton's words, can it 'gravitate towards the earth'?

To answer this question, we'll need to take a closer look at the earth itself, and more particularly at its surface, namely the ground. In his manifesto for an ecological psychology, James Gibson (1979: 10, 33) compares the ground to the floor of a room. It is the 'the underlying surface of support', he says, on which all else rests. Yet just as the room must be furnished if we are to carry on our everyday activities in it, so the ground, likewise, can harbour life only because it, too, is furnished with objects of one kind and another. 'The *furniture* of the earth', Gibson (1979: 78) insists, 'is what makes it liveable'. Like the room, the earth is cluttered with all manner of stuff which affords the diverse activities of its innumerable inhabitants. Among this stuff would be such things as trees, stones ... and buildings. But do trees, stones and buildings really stand on the ground like furniture on the floor? Gibson certainly thought so. The inhabitant – placed according to Gibson at the centre of a world comprising the earth below, the sky above and the ground between – sees a world strewn with objects. He sees 'objects on the earth and in the sky, ... mountains and clouds, fires and sunsets, pebbles and stars' (1979: 66).

Is the conical lodge, then, an object *on* the earth? Is it part of the furniture? Or is it, alternatively, an object *in* the sky? I contend that it is neither. For the sake of comparison, let us ask the same questions of a tree. Surely, the tree does not stand upon the earth, since its roots penetrate deep into it. Nor does it hang in the sky, although its branches reach skyward, providing a framework of support for the canopy of leaves vaulting overhead. These principles of rooting and branching, however, are not opposed like the principles of layering and joining, or stereotomics and tectonics, in the construction of the building. The tree, after all, began life as a seed that had once fallen to the ground from its parent body. At that moment, as Paul Klee (1973: 29) wrote in his notebooks, 'A certain impetus from without, the relation to earth and atmosphere, begets the capacity to grow ... The seed strikes root, initially the line is directed earthwards, though not to dwell there, only to draw energy thence for reaching up into the air.' The growing seedling is not mounted *upon* the ground surface so much as rooted *in* it. For that very reason it is simultaneously earthly and celestial. It is so, as Klee pointed out, since the commingling of sky and earth is itself a condition for life and growth. It is because the plant is *of* (and not *on*) the earth that it is also *of* the sky (Ingold 2015: 44–5).

The same, I argue, is true of the conical lodge. It, too, is at once of earth and sky: a place where earth and sky are brought together in the growth and experience of its inhabitants. Evidently, then, the ground of the lodge is no mere platform. It is rather an enveloping matrix that both anchors and nourishes the lives of its inhabitants, just as the ground beyond its circumference nurtures the vegetation that grows there and the animal life that feeds on it. Thus, the ground outside the lodge does not resemble the ground inside because it is similarly furnished with objects. To the contrary, it is the ground inside the lodge that resembles the ground outside, since it provides a place of nourishment for its residents. It is not on but *in* this earth, as the philosopher Martin Heidegger (1971: 42) put it – in this zone of growth and transformation – that 'man bases his dwelling'. Yet the earth, Heidegger insisted, is unthinkable without also thinking of the sky, and vice versa. Earth and sky are not, then, separate hemispheres which, put together, add up to a unity. Rather, each binds the other into its own becoming. The earth, 'rising up into plant and animal' (Heidegger 1971: 149), binds the sky in the growth of living tissue; the sky binds the earth as it sweeps the surface in currents of wind and submerses it in falls of rain and snow. And at the centre of this world, where the earth's arising meets and mingles with the sky's befalling, lies the conical lodge.

The smooth and the striated

Even if this argument is accepted, however, we have still to account for the *specific* way in which earth and sky are brought together in the conical lodge. How, for example, does the lodge compare in this regard with the traditional dwellings of people who lived by farming rather than by pastoral herding?[3] To begin to answer this question we will first need to revert to the third of Semper's elements of architecture, namely, the membrane. Recall that for Semper, the membrane is in in the nature of a textile, stretched over the framework to form an enclosure, and that as such, it calls for the arts of the weaver. Writing in the final decades of the twentieth century, the eccentric philosopher of design, Vilém Flusser, advanced a rather similar view. Just as Semper had distinguished the earthwork from the membrane, so Flusser (1999: 56) distinguishes the *solid wall*, hewn from rock or built up from heavy components, from the *screen wall*, such as that of a tent. Like the wing of a glider or the sail of a ship, the purpose of the screen wall is not to raise the earth into a defensive fortification, but to deflect the skyborne currents of wind and weather in ways that harmonise with human dwelling.

Now the screen wall of the tent, according to Flusser (1999: 57), is typically a woven fabric that gathers, holds and disseminates the lives of those who dwell within. It is, he suggests, 'open to experiences', and draws people in. But does it really? Semper (1989: 254–5), after all, had assumed to the contrary that the function of the membrane was, first and foremost, to enclose, that is to keep some things in and shut others out. Writing more than a century later, albeit without reference to Semper, Gilles Deleuze and Félix Guattari (2004: 524–5) seem to agree. For them the fabric weave, comprised of two kinds of parallel elements that intersect perpendicularly – one fixed, the other mobile, passing above and beneath the fixed – is exemplary of what they call *striated space*. And fabric, they say, specifically in its use among sedentary peoples, encloses the body, both proximally, in the clothes it wears, and distally, within the interior of the house. Yet with Flusser, Deleuze and Guattari also maintain that the nomads' tent is open to experience in a way that the house of sedentary people is not. This is possible, in their view, because the material covering of the tent is not fabric at all, but *felt*.

Felt, Deleuze and Guattari (2004: 525) contend, is the very opposite of fabric: it is an 'anti-fabric'. For whereas the weaving of fabric entails the intertwining of separate threads, running in parallel, with felt there is 'no separation of threads, no intertwining, only an entanglement of fibres', which go every which way to form a kind of mélange. That's why felt, for them, is exemplary of a space that is not striated but *smooth*. In striated space, the hallmark of an agrarian regime, the land is streaked with rigs and furrows, just as is cloth with its intersecting threads of warp and weft. This, in times gone by, was how farmers and woodsmen, working with plough and axe, would shape the land in the original, medieval sense of 'landscape' (Olwig 2019: 130; Ingold 2011a: 133). Smooth space, by contrast, is the open space of nomadic herdsmen: a heterogeneous field of continuous variation, extending without limit and in all directions. As felt is made up of entangled fibres, so the ground of smooth space is comprised of the entangled trajectories of people and animals as they wend their ways, following no predetermined direction but responding at every moment to locally prevailing conditions and the possibilities they afford to carry on.

Now this idea of comparing the difference between sedentary agriculture and nomadic pastoralism to that between fabric and felt is certainly appealing. The trouble is, however, that while felt is indeed the predominant tent material of herding communities throughout Inner Asia, it is by no means common to pastoral peoples everywhere. The nomadic pastoralists of North Africa, for example, know nothing of felting. Rather, they use wool to weave their tent-cloth. How can we take woven fabric to be a hallmark of agrarian life, when it is found equally among pastoral nomads? Deleuze and Guattari, admittedly, are quick to acknowledge the problem. To get around it, they displace their initial distinction between felt and fabric onto one between two kinds, or conceptions, of fabric, corresponding respectively to the striated and the smooth, and to agrarian and pastoral regimes. Whereas, they argue, the fabric weaves of sedentary farmers tend to annex space to the closure of the immobile house; the weaving of the pastoral nomad indexes 'the house itself to the space of the outside, to the open smooth space in which the body moves' (Deleuze and Guattari 2004: 525). Fabric, it turns out, can be either striated or smooth, depending on whether it is tied to the fixity of sedentary enclosure or oriented to the open horizons of nomadic life. But with no independent criterion by which to distinguish one kind of weave from the other, this attempt to evade the problem is mired in tautology.

No such problem arises, however, with the conical lodge, which is draped neither with felt nor with fabric but with a stitched patchwork of prepared animal hides. For just like felt, the patchwork has no consistent direction, or lines of striation, and can be extended without limit. With their characterisation of the patchwork as 'an amorphous collection of juxtaposed pieces that can be joined together in an infinite number of ways', Deleuze and Guattari (2004: 526) have no difficulty in assimilating it to their idea of smooth space. The covering of the lodge is thus of a kind with the lifeways of its inhabitants, albeit calling for the skills of the seamstress, already used to stitching skin garments, rather than those of the weaver or felter. With the reassurance that this is so, we are perhaps better placed to resolve our earlier question. How, exactly, does the perception of nomadic pastoralists, the archetypal denizens of smooth space, differ from that of sedentary farmers in their activities of shaping the land? How do the gatherings and stitchings, and the sensory engagements, of smooth space differ from those of the striated? Only when we have answered this question can we specify precisely how earth and sky come together in the conical lodge.

The peasant, the mariner and the nomad

All life is lived under the sun, and in this, the farmer is no exception. People who wrest a living from the land have to contend with the vagaries of wind and weather, whatever their mode of subsistence. 'It is evident', write Deleuze and Guattari (2004: 531), that 'even the sedentary peasant participates fully in the space of the wind, the space of tactile and sonorous qualities.' But while nomad and peasant may live under the same sky, and imbibe the same atmosphere, their respective relations to the earth are fundamentally different. For in the peasant's labour of shaping the land, the earth presents itself as a field not of forces to be harnessed but of resistances to be overcome. Here, earth and sky meet not in unison but in discord. Straining respectively downward and upwards, they endlessly battle it out over the surface of the ground. In the construction of the dwelling, as we have seen, this discord is played out in the opposition between stereotomics and tectonics. Whereas in the tent of the nomad, earth and sky meet at the hearth, in the house of the peasant they are divided between the stereotomic mass of the walls and foundations, which gravitate towards the earth, and the tectonic frame and the covering of the roof, which reach for the sky. In the division between roof and walls, the peasant dwelling is divided against itself. The world of the peasant, we might say, is not so much an *earth-sky* as an *earth/sky*.

To highlight the contrast, let me introduce another comparison, this time between the farmer's life on land and the mariner's at sea. The ocean is surely smooth space *par excellence* (Deleuze and Guattari 2004: 529). The mariner ensconced in his vessel, feeling the waves as they lap the hull and catching the wind in his sails, all the while scanning the sky for the movements of birds by day and of the stars and other celestial bodies by night, is a point of rest in a world in which all around is in movement (Gladwin 1964: 171–2). In striving to rein in the forces of the elements he is the precise opposite of the farmer who bends muscle and sinew to counteract the friction of an immobile and often unyielding earth, dragging himself and his equipment over the hard ground and inscribing furrows and tracks in the process. For precisely this reason I believe it is a mistake to describe the mariner's surroundings, by comparison to those of the farmer, as a *seascape* (Cooney 2003). For waves and troughs, or becalmed or turbulent waters, have nothing of the permanence and solidity that allows the farmer to give lasting shape the land (Ingold 2011a: 132). It is why the Vikings, who knew a thing or two about both farming and sailing, would readily compare their oceangoing long-ships to horses, but only rarely to ploughs. They could ride the waves, but could not carve their furrows (Jesch 2016: 321).

Thus the mariner, on setting sail, does not simply relinquish one set of surfaces, of the land, for another, of the sea. Rather he enters a world in which surfaces take second place to the circulations of the media in which they are formed. Here the grounded fixities of landscape give way to the aerial fluxes of wind and weather above, and the aquatic fluxes of tide and current below. These fluxes, and not the surface of the sea, absorb the mariner's effort and attention. The world he inhabits is not, then, a seascape but an *ocean-sky*. Could the same not be said, then, of the nomadic pastoralist? As mariners ride the waves, nomads ride the pastures, roaming the windswept expanses of steppe, sand and snow, and responding in their movements to both celestial and subterranean forces (Ingold 2011a: 133). Likewise, at home in the lodge, the nomad feels the earth with his body as his gaze mingles with the sky. Indeed, as a centre of stillness and a calming of the winds, the conical lodge is comparable to a vessel at sea, and not just in the fact that the cladding of both boat and lodge is stretched over a tectonic frame. Micronesian mariners, when travelling far out of sight of land, reportedly lie on their backs on the bottoms of their canoes, gazing directly heavenwards while sensing with their bodies 'the rise and fall, yawing, and slapping of sea against the hull' (Davenport 1960: 21). If for the mariner in his boat, the world is a blend of sky and ocean, then for the nomadic pastoralist in the lodge, it is likewise a blend of sky and earth.

This is to think of the land as smooth rather than of the sea as striated. There are surfaces in the nomads' earth-sky world, of course, just as they are in the earth/sky world of the peasant. But they are surfaces of a different kind. For the farmer the surface of the land is marked, in its carving and striation, by the slash that rips the earth from its atmosphere, turning the one against the other. This surface, as Deleuze and Guattari (2004: 530) would say, is closed off and apportioned. But in smooth space the slash is replaced by a hyphen. Here in the earth-sky, the surfaces of the land – like those of the sea – open up to the sky and embrace it. In their ever-changing colours, and patterns of illumination and shade, they reflect its light; they resonate in their sounds to the passing winds, and in their feel underfoot or under-hoof they respond to the dryness or humidity of the air, depending on heat or rainfall. In smooth space, to continue with Deleuze and Guattari (2004: 421), 'there is no line separating earth and sky'. Each enfolds the other into its own element.

From gathering to projection

With this conclusion in mind, let me return to the screen wall of the tent – a wall that, to recall Flusser's (1999: 57) words – is 'open to the wind, open to the spirit'. The screen, he continues, 'assembles experience, processes it and disseminates it, and is to be thanked for the fact that the tent is a creative nest'. It could be a patchwork of hides; it could be of felt – it could even be a 'piece of cloth', as Flusser himself supposes. Whatever it is made of, in its openness to experience, to wind and to spirit, it is manifestly a surface of the sort that Deleuze and Guattari would regard as smooth rather than striated. What, then, happens to the screen when its setting shifts from the tent to the house, with its surrounding earthwork of solid, enclosing walls? Typically, it goes up on the walls as a hanging covering or tapestry. Indeed exactly the same happened with the carpet, another invention of tent-dwellers, as Flusser goes on to show. The carpet, he writes (1999: 95), is 'to the culture of the tent what architecture is to the culture of the house'. Initially, when carpets entered the house, they went up on the walls. Even Semper referred to carpets as wall-hangings and to carpet weavers as among the first wall-fitters, or *Wandbereiter* (Semper 1989: 103–4).

Nowadays, however, we would hardly expect to find a carpet on the walls. For modern urban dwellers, the proper place for a carpet is the floor! In any metropolitan house or apartment, the floor is expected to provide a level and rigid base upon which can be mounted the furniture of everyday life. Strip all these things away and it is left barren and lifeless. It cries out to be covered. We are even inclined to extend this idea metaphorically to the ground outside, which we say is 'carpeted' with vegetation, as though – instead of growing from the ground – it was rolled out over it.[4] With this idea of the ground as a solid floor, covered with a carpet and cluttered with objects as the interior room of the house is cluttered with furniture, the agrarian landscape of medieval times gives way to the stage and scenery of the landscape in its modern incarnation: as a space not of gathering but of projection. As such, it calls for a radically different mode of perception, one that is *optical* rather that *haptic*.

The space of gathering is haptic. It is a space of close-up, hands-on engagement, for example of the weaver with her threads, the ploughman with the soil, or the carpenter or mason with wood or stone. Deleuze and Guattari (2004: 543–4) distinguish between this haptic space and the optical space of distance and detachment, wherein the forms of the architectural imagination, conceived off-site, are projected onto material substance. They are right to point out that this distinction crosscuts that between eye and hand: thus one can see close up (as in weaving) and touch at a distance (such as on a keyboard). They are wrong, however, to equate the opposition between the haptic and the optical with that between the smooth and the striated. It would be closer to the mark to recognise that the optical and the haptic correspond to two, quite different ways of striating space. And this, indeed, is what distinguishes the modern sense of the landscape from its medieval precursor (Ingold 2011a: 134).

The landscapes of modernity are striated, but not by the warp of the loom, the furrows of the plough or the marks and cuts of masons and carpenters, whether etched in stone or following the grain of timber. Rather, they are striated by the abstract lines, ratios and proportions of projective geometry. These striations, then, are of an entirely different order. To appreciate the difference, we only have to compare the woven fabric of the tent wall with the opaque surfaces of projection – such as in the cinema or conference room – upon which are cast images of one kind and another. For most contemporary readers, the word 'screen' is more likely to bring to mind surfaces of the latter kind (see Chapter 13, pp. 210–11). Curiously, Flusser (1999: 57) believes that they, too, assemble and store experience, in just the same way as the fabric walls of the tent. This, however, is precisely what they do *not* do. In the cinema, the movements of life are projected onto the screen, not drawn into its fabric. The screen itself remains blankly impervious to the images that play upon its surface. Light, sound and feeling, the fundamental currents of sensory experience for the tent-dweller, are reduced in the world of cinematic representation to vectors of projection in the conversion of objects into images (Ingold 2015: 102).

Indeed the difference between the screen as a woven fabric and as a surface of projection precisely parallels the contrast in ways of thinking about building – between the gathering together of materials in movement and the projection of ideal form onto material substance – that I have sought to establish. As Frampton (1995: 2) writes, 'the unavoidably earthbound nature of building is as tectonic and tactile in character as it is scenographic and visual'. But only building that is tectonic and tactile can enter into the weave of experience, and carry it forward. In the scenographic and the visual, by contrast, the building is already complete. We can only look back on it, as it retreats into the distance.

The hearth of renewal

In his *Tristes Tropiques*, Claude Lévi-Strauss (1955: 299) linked the birth of architecture to the invention of writing, and both to the creation of cities and empires with their attendant structures of power and exploitation. Both writing and architecture strive for hierarchy, monumentality and permanence. Their forms are stereotomic, assembled from blocks and made to last. In the tectonic world of the earth-sky, however, nothing lasts. There are no indelible records, enduring monuments or rigid hierarchies. From an architectural point of view, the built forms of the earth-sky world appear ephemeral – as ephemeral, even, as spoken words. It would seem, indeed, that the monument is to the lodge, and the landscape to the earth-sky, precisely as writing is to speech. Just as the words of oral narrative dissolve in the very act of their production, so the binding of materials in smooth space is always accompanied by their unbinding. Yet it is in this binding and unbinding that forms are sustained. To inhabit the lodge, then, is to join with the material flows and circulations of vital force of which its form is the ever-emergent outcome. Whereas the monument was built, once and for all, the lodge is always building and rebuilding. Thus for the inhabitant, it is the architectural monument that seems ephemeral, buried in the sands of time while life goes on. As writing eventually fades, so also – in time – the monument, though designed to last in perpetuity, cracks and crumbles (Ingold 2013a: 78–80).

The lodge, however, *perdures*, in a constant process of renewal, just as do the narratives that inhabitants tell in it. I have accordingly sought to understand the conical lodge as a locus of growth and regeneration in an earth-sky world, where materials welling up from under the ground mix and mingle with air and moisture from the atmosphere in the ongoing production of life. As a gathering place of forces and materials, the lodge is not closed over. It does not turn its back on us. It is open: a confluence of persons and materials, drawn together in the movements of its formation. This brings me, finally, to the last of Semper's elements of architecture – after the earthwork, the framework and the membrane – namely the hearth with its fire. Last, maybe, but certainly not least. On the contrary, among indigenous peoples of the circumpolar North, the fire of the hearth is universally venerated, not just as a source of light and heat – though these are of obvious practical importance – but as the generative source of life itself. The fire, indeed, is a being in its own right, and is clothed as are animals and humans. Where living animals are clothed in their own skins, and humans in the skins of animals, the fire-being is clothed with the whole patchwork of skins comprising the covering of the lodge (Anderson 2013: 272–4). Yet within each lies a beating heart on which the entire circulation of life depends. The hearth is the heart of the lodge.

Where life binds, in the growth of living things, fire unbinds, in their cooking and combustion (Ingold 2011a: 122). In the smoke of the fire, materials nourished by the earth, and bound together in life, are released once more to the sky, whence they will fuel further growth. I conclude with the suggestion that we can best understand the conical form of the lodge in relation to this perpetual cycle of binding and unbinding. Instead of thinking of this form in terms of pure geometry, as a cone set upon a plane, we should perhaps regard it as the envelope of an upward spiral – that is, as an upended vortex with the hearth as its eye and the knotted tent-poles at its tip. The spiral is a movement that goes around and up, rather than a surface that divides inside from outside. It thus signifies growth and regeneration rather than enclosure. In short, as a vortex in the currents of earth and air, where the smoke from the hearth rises to meet the sky, the conical lodge brings to a focus the generative fluxes of a world that is for ever worlding.

Chapter 11

What if the city were an ocean, and its buildings ships?

Landmarks

The inspiration for this chapter comes from an exhibition of work by the artist David Lemm, at the Edinburgh Printmakers' Gallery, in the spring of 2015.[1] Entitled *Debris and Phenomena*, the work consisted of a number of pieces in which iconic marks were superimposed upon old nautical charts. What had intrigued Lemm was that these charts, which he had found by chance amid piles of discarded papers, had once been vital tools for navigators in shaping their perception of the maritime world. How, then, did they end up being thrown away? Does discarding the maps mean relinquishing a perception that we could not have had without them? Can such perception really rest on such a fragile foundation that it can disappear with a few scraps of wastepaper? If, to the contrary, it does not depend on them, why were the maps so important in the first place?

Intrigued by these questions, Lemm had saved the charts. They showed very little. Here and there were numbers, recording depth, with occasional contour lines, and on every sheet, a graded semicircle indicating all the degree points of the compass. On each sheet, Lemm had overprinted a schematic map of a small neighbourhood of the city of Edinburgh, in the faintest of colour, which did no more than separate the spaces of open ground from blocks of buildings. This then provided the almost blank surface upon which were stamped fragmentary icons, in bold black ink. There were zigzags, hatched circles, crosses, a squiggle, an icon that looked a bit like a ladder, another that looked like a satellite aerial and yet another that resembled the outline of half a mushroom with dots (Figure 11.1).

On a very windy Edinburgh day in March 2015 I attended an event entitled *Landmarks*, in which the artist challenged us – his audience – to recreate a version of one of these prints by walking a route in the neighbourhood. Each of us was provided with a sheet of paper mounted on a clipboard. The sheet was blank apart from the shapes of the spaces in which we could wander, blocked out in faint pink on a white background. We were to proceed along a route marked out with a number of waystations, where

DOI: 10.4324/9781003171713-15

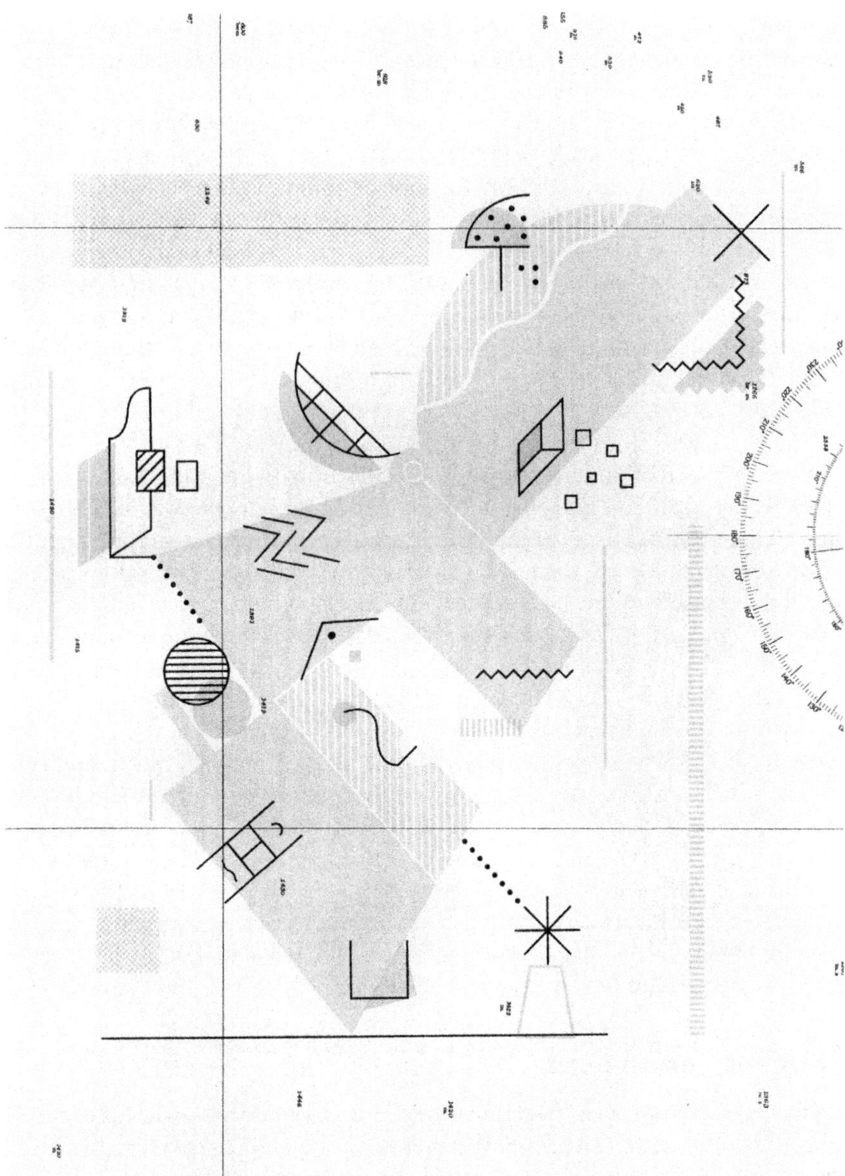

Figure 11.1 *Landmarks*, 2015, by David Lemm. Screen print on found admiralty chart. Courtesy of the artist.

Lemm had placed balloons and posted volunteers to guide us on. At every station he had also placed a rubber stamp and an inkpad. Each stamp was cut with a particular icon, selected from the repertoire of icons that Lemm had used for his prints. The icon stood for a particular detail of the urban fabric visible from that point: perhaps a flight of steps, or some railings, or the lintel of a door – little details that could take some time to locate, but which held your attention once you spotted them. To discover them was at the same time to realise just how much passes us by, unheeded and unremarked: how much we simply fail to notice, which is almost everything. But to certify that we had been there and seen the detail in question, we were to stamp our paper at the appropriate place on the pink layout. Thus, after wandering for an hour or so, we returned with our sheets stamped with some ten different icons. Each of us had, in our modest way, recreated one of Lemm's pieces, save that ours were on plain paper rather than nautical charts.

For Lemm, all of this was meant as a meditation on the fragmentary nature of experience, and on the tension between the bird's eye view of urban space and the street-level view of the built environment and its features. He also wanted us to reflect on the idiosyncratic construction of narrative meaning, and on how this influences our perception of place. For me, however, the exercise brought to mind another set of concerns, which were perhaps highlighted by the fact that it was such a windy day. As I walked the streets, I felt almost as if I could have been sailing. And having already viewed the exhibition, and seen how Lemm had reused the old charts, I began to imagine that I was myself at sea, that my ample raincoat was a sail, and that the balloons that marked the waystations through which I had to pass were buoys. Suddenly, the features that I was to seek out began to seem like bric-a-brac afloat in oceanic waves. Holding my coat before the wind, was I sailing a flooded city? In reality, of course, I was on dry land, and the features were all firmly fixed in place. I was not sailing but walking, and the pavement remained firm beneath my feet. But what if it were otherwise? What if the ground of the city were an ocean, and its buildings ships?[2]

Humans and the sea

Oceans cover more than two-thirds of the surface of our earth. Beneath the planet's outer crust, in the mantle, there may be enough water to fill all of its oceans combined, twice or even three times over. Every time a volcano erupts, some of this water gushes out as steam and, on cooling and condensing, rains down on the earth. Perhaps that is how the oceans formed in the first place, some four billion years ago. Be that as it may, it was in these waters that life first evolved, eventually finding its way onto land only once organisms had developed ways to hold on to the aqueous fluids that still formed the greater part of their bodily substance. In this sense, human beings – among the most recent of species to have inhabited the earth – are still creatures of the ocean even though they undoubtedly evolved on land, probably far from any shore, with bodies adapted to conditions of life in relatively open, terrestrial environments. Moreover, notwithstanding some rather fanciful theories[3] that, among other things, have attributed the orientation of masculine chest hair to the prowess of ancestral swimmers, or the origins of language to the breath control required of them, humans have only a very limited capacity to endure beyond reach of land. Even the most athletic of them can swim unaided over only a relatively short distance, and hold their breath underwater for no more than a few minutes. To go further, or to spend a longer time at sea, our ancestors needed some kind of watercraft.

It is hard to know when they first took to the waves, for things that float tend not to last, being necessarily fashioned from lightweight and perishable materials. Most likely, the first voyages were accidental, when storm or tide took craft designed for inshore waters far out to sea. But the subsequent development of ocean-going vessels, along with the ways of life that have surrounded them, has been among the most remarkable chapters of human technical evolution. In many ways and for several millennia, it turned the world inside out, as the great expanses of the sea offered the best opportunities for long-distance travel and trade. The land, by contrast, became a barrier, with its fast-flowing rivers, treacherous marshes, deserts and mountain ranges presenting formidable obstacles to movement. Islands, once remote and cut off, became centres of human commerce, while inland tracts, unreachable by water, became *terra incognita* – a situation that persisted until the transport revolutions of modern times brought road, rail and latterly air travel to the fore, relegating many islands once again to the periphery. As the geographer Kenneth Olwig (2019: 93) remarks, history itself could be characterised in terms of such changes in the relative predominance of waterborne and landborne infrastructure.

There are signs, however, that humanity's relation to the ocean is about to be redefined once again. This time, much of the responsibility lies with human beings themselves, first in the development of an industrial economy, the exponential growth of which has been fuelled by the combustion of fossil fuels, and second in the clearing of the land to make way for the prodigious numbers of domestic animals that allow more and more of the earth's ever-growing human population to enjoy a diet rich in meat. The consequent release into the atmosphere of massive quantities of carbon dioxide and methane gases is causing temperatures to rise, around the globe, at a rate not seen since the yet more rapid global warming that heralded the end of the last ice age some twelve millennia ago. The melting of the huge ice sheets of the Arctic and Antarctic regions, expected over coming decades, looks set to finish off what remains of the last glaciation. Not only will this raise sea levels to a point that will threaten many low-lying coastal conurbations around the world; it could also redirect the ocean currents that control much of the earth's climate. As a result, global warming could push some regions accustomed to balmy temperatures into a much chillier regime, while yet leaving other regions overheated and desiccated. With the encroachment of oceans upon the land, submerging once populous regions, fresh water will be the next scarce resource over which nations will compete, or even go to war.

All this is well known. Indeed, some sort of collapse seems inevitable. Prognostications for the future vary from apocalyptic visions of species extinction to utopian fantasies of a once-and-for-all geotechnical fix that will secure humanity's tenure of the planet for eternity. Just as the initial glacial melt that marked the onset of the Holocene epoch is popularly supposed to have set the stage for human history, so its final melt, at the onset of what is billed as our new epoch – which scientists have been quick to name the Anthropocene – is predicted to bring down the curtains. Whatever the merits of the designation, which are much debated, neither the apocalyptic nor the utopian version of Anthropocene destiny seems remotely plausible. More likely, chroniclers of a thousand years from now, if there are such, will look back on an 'event', roughly spanning the four centuries 1700–2100, marked by a seemingly unstoppable surge, followed by an equally calamitous crash, after which it was back to business as usual for the human species, albeit in a world that could take millennia to recover from the event's impact. Come what may, the oceans will continue to eat away at terrestrial shores, presenting an unceasing existential danger for their inhabitants, to whose fate they are utterly indifferent.

The sea is not level

There is nothing new, however, in the oceans' threats to overwhelm inhabited lands. They have done so often enough before, most notably at the end of the last glacial period. We are, after all, but the survivors of previous inundations, stranded on what can only be described, from an oceanic perspective, as the high ground of the continental crust – its plateaus and mountain ranges – still poking out above the waters. From Doggerland in the North Sea to much of the Recherche Archipelago of Western Australia, many lands previously home to flourishing human communities now lie undersea, silent and mysterious. Occasionally, tools and weapons once used for life on land turn up in the nets of fishing vessels. It was a massive landslide along the edge of Norway's continental shelf, dated to around 6200 BCE, and the resulting tsunami, that is thought to have engulfed much of Doggerland, leaving only a few residual islands. In other cases, the immediate causes of flooding were seismic. The ancient city of Pavlopetri, in the Peloponnese, was submerged as a result of an earthquake some three thousand years ago. In the year 365 CE another earthquake sank an island off the coast of Egypt that that had formed part of the ancient port of Alexandria. Yet another violent quake, in 1692, left two-thirds of the city of Port Royal, in Jamaica, underwater. But it was more gradual if relentless bombardment from the waves that, in 1929, caused the cliffside neighbourhood of San Pedro, in Los Angeles, to slide gracefully but inexorably into the Pacific, as the clay foundations on which its desirable homes were built eventually crumbled.

What these and many other comparable events show, is that the sea has not risen imperceptibly, creeping over the land so gradually that no one in their lifetimes would have noticed. Rather, rising seas were witnessed then, as they are now, in the more frequent incidence of catastrophic events. In living memory, tidal floods, storm surges and typhoons, along with earthquake-induced tsunamis, have torn at coastlines and brought massive destruction and loss of life to people in many parts of the world. Each time catastrophe strikes, it reminds us of the fact that the surface of the sea *is not level*. It rather sloshes about: one huge, continuous mass that is stretched, crumpled and swirled by forces of earthly and lunar gravity, by the rotation of the planet, by the differential heating of the sun, by the friction of the irregular sea-bed below and the convulsions of the atmosphere above. Along the coasts this sloshing is visible in the cycle of the tides, and in the formation of sand or shingle beaches, alternately exposed and submerged as the tides go in and out. But for mariners at sea it is experienced as currents and gradients. If you are operating a fishing boat from the shore, you can save fuel by leaving at high tide, 'free-wheeling' down the slope of the sea, and then returning once the gradient is reversed.

'Sea level', in short, is a cartographic abstraction, and a strange one at that. Look at a map of the world, and it is as if the sea itself had solidified into a single, isotropic and featureless plane. It has no waves, no currents, nothing lies above nor is there anything underneath. You cannot sink into it, let alone drown in it, though you could lose your bearings. Indeed, in the eyes of cartographers and the landlubber authorities they serve, sailing is fundamentally a problem of navigation, not of handling ships at sea. Perhaps it was the peculiarity of this navigational perspective that Lewis Carroll aimed to satirise when, in *The Hunting of the Snark*, he had the ship's Bellman bring on board 'a large map representing the sea, without the least vestige of land'. It was a map, cried the crew, 'they could all understand ... A perfect and absolute blank!'[4] Upon this blank surface are then mounted irregular shapes, both great and small, of curious and convoluted outline. These represent land masses, which may be further built up upon the maritime base-level, contour by contour, by adding further layers of progressively diminishing extent. Lands of all shapes and sizes, then, appear contained within their outlines. That is why we call the most extensive of them continents. The ocean, on the contrary, is perceived to be incontinent. It has no boundaries, no outlines of its own. We often speak of crossing the ocean to get from one land to another, but rarely of crossing the land to get from one ocean to another. On our maps, straits are commonplace, but the isthmus is an anomaly.

What appears on the map as an outline, however, is – in the world it represents – but a shifting and indistinct line of transition, indicated on rocky shores by differential staining or in the distribution of barnacles, on flats by saltwater vegetation, and on sands by the wash of the tide. Beyond it the land carries on, undersea as its elevation falls, oversea as it rises. In truth the land is no more enclosed within its shores than is the sea kept out by them. Fishers know their offshore grounds as intimately as farmers their soils: they can be worked, dredged, even cultivated, just as surely as farmers work the land onshore (Howard 2019). But if the land extends into the ocean, so also the ocean extends into the land in the precipitation, borne of evaporation from ocean surfaces, that feeds the land's freshwater basins and subterranean aquafers. Geographers Kimberley Peters and Philip Steinberg (2019) go so far as to suggest that the ocean should be understood better as *extension* than as entity, as a material excess that always overflows whatever barriers we might put up against it. As such, they say (2019: 295), 'the ocean exists far inshore, above ground, underground, in our senses, and as part of fantasy'. The relation of land to sea, then, is one of over-and-under, not of side-to-side, requiring us to think in terms of the relativities of shallowness and depth rather than the absolute, bilateral switch of onshore and off (Bremner 2016: 291). Like the land, the ocean is everywhere, in us and around us. We need not visit the coast or go to sea to meet it.

Lands and ships as containers

Yet the division between land and ocean, however indistinct it may be in real life, has long been foundational to the very idea of the polity, at least as this has come down to us in the canons of Western thought. The many city-states of Ancient Greece dotted around the islands and peninsulas of the Aegean archipelago, while dependent on the sea for travel and trade, took pains to protect their political order from its transgressive influence (Olwig 2019: 88). The polis had continually to defend itself against attack from the sea and its waterborne forces; never the other way around. In Book IV of his dialogue *Laws* (Bury 1926: 257), Plato had the Athenian, a stranger to the isle of Crete, declare that the sea, while pleasant enough as a daily companion, can be a 'right briny and bitter neighbour',[5] which brings to its shores all manner of raiders, rogues and tricksters. For safety and security, he insisted, the city should be located well inland. Even Aristotle, while stressing the importance of access to the sea for commerce, acknowledged – in Book VII of his *Politics* (Jowett 1885: 216) – that the influx of strangers caused by the sea's proximity can corrode good government. Every polis, then, figures as an island of order, anchored in the ocean of disorder that threatens ever to unravel it. It is an idea that continues to resonate today in the trope of the urban archipelago, consisting of islands of formal architectural regularity set amid a sprawling ocean of deregulation and decay (Bremner 2016).

The containment of the polity, as a node in a network of trading relations, has its counterpart in the containment of the ship, conceived as a vessel which should ideally keep its cargo intact as it plies from port to port across the incontinent expanse of the ocean. In this sense the ship is an example of what philosopher Bruno Latour (1986) would call an 'immutable mobile', an object that can undergo displacement through otherwise empty space while maintaining its properties as it goes. The object, in his terms, is 'Galilean'; the space 'Euclidean' (November, Camacho-Hübner and Latour 2010: 590). Depending on the nature and packaging of its cargo, the ocean-going vessel of today is envisaged as a colossal container, or a container for containers, designed to span the distance between continents without discharging any of its content to the sea. As the continent is supposed to contain its immoveable territory within its shores, so the ship should contain its moveable cargo within its hold. Each implies the other. But real lands are not like that, nor are real ships. Neither do they contain, nor are they contained. And it is by considering how real lands and ships differ from the ideal that we can begin to see how the classical opposition between the city and the ocean might be dissolved.

The real ship is a rusting hulk that, as it goes, pumps quantities of greenhouse gases into the atmosphere even as it leaks fuel into the sea, along with the effluent of life lived on board and the inevitable spillages of cargo that occur in rough weather. According to one estimate, some 1,500 containers are lost at sea every year, or the equivalent of roughly four per day (Peters and Steinberg 2019: 303). Thus the ship is not so much a vessel as a floating centre of concentration and discharge sunk within a turbulent but semi-supporting medium. Real lands, too, are not sealed within their borders but carry on a perpetual dialogue with the sea: in the hydrological cycle, in the harvesting of maritime and undersea resources by terrestrial populations, and in the atmospheric effects of industrial emissions as they are absorbed by ocean currents. Indeed, lands discharge no less than ships into the sea, which is gradually filling up with such quantities of waste as to form floating islands, which may eventually become home to terrestrial life-forms, possibly including humans. Already, landfill is being used for reclamation projects to create airport runways, marinas and resorts in shallow waters. And finally, the real ocean, intrinsically incontinent, is not merely an empty space to be traversed but a dynamic element which requires of the mariner detailed knowledge and constant attention if he is to handle his ship without mishap. In short, the ship, the continent and the ocean all challenge the logic of container and content, with its neat apportionments of the materials of life to the categorical compartments of law and politics.

Nothing but waves

During the war years of the early 1940s, Carl Schmitt – political theorist, jurist and prominent Nazi – was at work on a book subsequently published as *The Nomos of the Earth*. In it, he made much of the division between land and sea. Only on land, Schmitt (2003: 42–3) insisted, can the earthling, 'man', make his mark. He can make no mark in the sea, for 'on the waves there is nothing but waves'.[6] The surfer, of course, might retort indignantly that on land, where Schmitt's 'man' would fight his wars, there is nothing but trenches. In the trench, the body sticks and its senses clog, but the surfer in the wave is hyper-alert, his entire existence borne along on this one, overwhelming but self-annihilating movement (Anderson 2012: 578). Where the trench is a place of death, to ride the breaking wave is to feel truly alive. But if the surfer lies at one extreme in his relation to the waves, at the other lie the passengers on board a cruise liner. Provided with everything they could desire for a life of luxury in what is, in effect, a giant floating hotel, they might witness the sea as a blue expanse, and enjoy the uninterrupted skies. But the last thing of which they would have any direct experience would be the waves. To all intents and purposes, the ocean looks to them entirely flat, save only for the curvature of the earth that causes distant ships to appear to drop below the horizon rather than to contract into a vanishing point (Higman 2017: 9).

In short, if the surfer on his board cannot see the ocean for the waves, then the passenger on board the liner cannot see the waves for the ocean. One lives for the moment, inside the breaking event, the other hankers for an eventless eternity. Perhaps, as historian Barry Higman argues, it is all a question of perspective. Depending on the scale of observation, whether close-up or from on high, we witness either 'the local chaos of crashing waves or the great curve of the Earth' (Higman 2017: 66). We are faced, it seems, with a choice between one and the other: the more our attention is captured by the waves, the less we see of the ocean; the more our vision pans out over the ocean, the less we see of waves. The ocean, in this scenario, has no waves. Flat and monotonous, it is like the Bellman's map, 'a perfect and absolute blank'. Conversely, as locally situated events, waves have no ocean; they could just as well be made by a machine.[7] And so, while the passengers in the cruise-liner glide serenely over the vacant surface of the ocean, the surfer occupies a wave-bubble that will burst on the instant it breaks upon the shore. Here, both the surfboard and the liner afford means not to inhabit a world but to escape from it, whether through instant gratification or timeless reverie.

Indeed, for the real world to intrude, from either end, would spell disaster. Passengers on board the liner, like their ill-fated predecessors on the *Titanic*, only experience the waves as the ship goes down; surfers experience the ocean only when the wave becomes a tsunami and engulfs them all. We discover, in these catastrophes, that the waves and the ocean can be held apart only by artifice, by feats of engineering on an ever-greater scale – involving bigger and bigger ships on the one hand, and ever more impressive marine defences on the other – and that all such attempts are bound ultimately to fail. The mariners of old, however, would never have imagined the ocean as a blank sheet. Nor could they separate the ocean from its waves. They rather found themselves in the midst of an elementary struggle between waters below and airs above, caught in the wind-driven crumple and churn of the roiling brine. Here, out at sea, waves don't break but alternately swell and subside in an unceasing movement of formation and dissolution. That's what the ocean is for the mariner: not so much a body of water as the condition of a world in flux. And waves, in his experience, are the ocean's way of making its presence felt, above all in the pitch, yaw and roll of his vessel.

Moreover the mariner's ship, as we have already seen, is not a Galilean object in a Euclidean sea, nor does it bore through ocean waters, indifferent to their flux and variation. If this is true even of the massive ships and liners of today, how much more so it would have been in the days of sail! The ship of those times was a place of gathering, of wind into sails, currents into timbers, and above all, crew into a community wherein life depends on the seaworthiness of the craft. For it is here perhaps that we find the most fundamental difference between life at sea and on land. People on land depend on others for many things, but one thing they can normally be sure of is that the ground will support them even without others to hold them up. Social life on land rests on this confidence that whatever else may be at stake, the ground lies firm underfoot. But at sea, there can be no such confidence. What lies beneath is not a cushion of support but an abyss. And people must hold to one another, and maintain their craft, if they are not to sink. Not for nothing does the word *ship*, used alternately as noun and suffix, connote both the vessel and – as in 'fellowship' – a community of sorts. Yet in this sense the ship – as much as its converse, *terra firma* – is as much a state of mind as a physical condition. For there are times, even on land, when we lose confidence in the ground's support and fall back on others for assistance. At such times, as we say, we are all at sea.

Underground, overground

In just such a moment of uncertainty, I wake from my dreams of oceans and ships, and – still swaying in my senses as sailors do, on first setting foot on dry land after months at sea – find myself back on the windy streets of Edinburgh. I am surrounded by buildings, laid out on a grid. Do these buildings, I wonder, rest upon the ground like solid blocks on an underlying platform of support? Or do they float like ships in the ocean? The conventional discourse of infrastructure and superstructure, of course, inclines us to the former view. But as I sail the windy streets, holding in my mind Lemm's nautical charts, I wonder whether it might be otherwise. What if we were to think of buildings not as raised upon rigid foundations but as suspended in a world of flux, with the swirl of the winds above and the churn of the earth below, and the ground between as the more or less turbulent medium of their altercation? For my dream of the sea had caused me to doubt what once I had taken for granted, namely that the ground is originally *there*, as a foundation for everything else that might occupy my attention.

To be sure, the paved street seems solid enough. But its surface was not given from the outset: it had, at some time in the past, to be engineered. First, the soft earth would have been drained, wresting islands of solidity from the originally waterlogged substrate, while confining the liquid residue to run along pipes and conduits, or between embankments. This created the urban equivalent of an archipelago. Then the earth, now dried and hardened, would have been surfaced, by coating with a rigid layer of water-resistant material such as concrete or asphalt. Only by these means is the ground fashioned as an infrastructure, upon which the superstructure of the city can be erected. Yet even the most heavily engineered of grounds cannot withstand the elemental forces of the sky and earth that erode it from above and subvert it from below. Eventually, it cracks and crumbles, exposing the soils beneath to light, moisture and currents of the air. With that, it bursts into life, overwhelming human attempts to cover it up (Ingold 2011a: 120–25). Even as I walk the Edinburgh streets, I have to watch my step for tree roots that have lifted paving stones, for weeds that have grown through the cracks, and for water-filled potholes in the tarmac. The hard surface, it turns out, is but the thinnest of crusts, beneath which the earth, slowly but surely, continues its heave and swell.

What, then, becomes of buildings? The architect might like to think that the ground is no part of the building as such, but merely a placeholder, a reference surface, a plot for it to stand on, or a purely horizontal platform for his constructions. Perhaps he prefers not to dwell on the fact that there can be no building without excavating – without, that is, both digging foundations on site and drawing or quarrying from the earth the materials from which the building is made, and to which, ultimately, they will return. For there to be building, excavation is as necessary as construction. And whenever material is taken out by excavation, pressures from the surrounding earth – which may behave very like a fluid and have a high liquid content – can cause the walls of the new-formed crater to cave in. To prevent this from happening, foundation walls have often to be propped up with temporary reinforcements. Architects' plans and elevations, however, show nothing of what is going on underground. The bulb of earth that absorbs the pressure of the building bearing down upon it remains invisible to them, as do the seismic shifts that occur when pressure bulbs collide. Beneath the ground, the foundations of buildings converse with soil and tree roots, with burrowing animals and subterranean waters. It is there, down below, and not at the ground surface, that the city has to contend with the forces of disintegration.

I know no better example of this than the story of the hillside church of Saint-Germain de Charonne, on the outskirts of Paris, as told by anthropologist Germain Meulemans (2021). Originally built in the twelfth century, the church had stood soundly for eight hundred years, although the nineteenth-century addition of flying buttresses on the down-facing side indicated that some stability issues had been encountered in the past. These were hugely exacerbated, however, in the years following the Second World War, as intensive urbanisation led to the demolition of the small workers' dwellings that had once neighboured the church, and the construction of large apartment blocks higher up the hillside. By the early 2000s, cracks were beginning to appear in the church, which eventually became so dangerous that it had to be closed. The engineers called in to investigate the problem discovered that the weight of the new buildings was causing the layers of clayey soil to slide down the hill and beneath the church. The solution they adopted was to drill holes beneath the floor of the church to the depth of solid bedrock, and to fill the holes with concrete. In effect, the church is now standing on piles, supported by the bedrock, while the soil continues to flow beneath. In this regard, as Meulemans (2021: 2) suggests, it resembles the pile dwellings traditional to many swampy or riverine environments, except that in this case, the fluid element is 'a slowly sliding layer of soil'.

Not only below ground, however, do buildings have to contend with the forces of the elements. Above, they are lashed by wind and weather. These are elements the modern architect would rather not have to deal with, unwelcome guests in the studio of design. Confounding reason, refusing containment, eroding structure and caring nothing for progress, weather has long figured in the modern imagination as architecture's nemesis (Ingold 2015: 71). Yet there is no avoiding it in practice. Weather, moreover, is also weathering, and weathering – as architects Mohsen Mostafavi and David Leatherbarrow (1993: 16) argue – is a process of not only deterioration but also renewal, a 'continuous metamorphosis' that lends the building an ever-changing finish. Here, amid the swirling atmosphere above and the shifting soil below, we begin to see how the building, just like a ship at sea, serves as a nexus for the concentration and discharge of materials, and for the gathering of its inhabitants, sunk in a semi-supporting medium and placed at the centre of a world of earth and sky. By the same token, the ground becomes a surface not so much of support as of transition, subject to its own variations and instabilities. Like the ocean, it is everywhere, and our buildings float in it.

Debris and phenomena

At a time of climatic warming, with rising seas and an increasing frequency of flooding events, whether from storms and cyclones or marine inundation, we can ask – with landscape architects Anuradha Mathur and Dilip da

Cunha – whether the world we live in 'is better served by being thought of as an ocean of rain rather than a landscape of rivers, and what this might mean for spatial design' (in Bremner 2019: 12). The riverine perspective favoured by most governments presents the landscape as a mosaic of dry, solid grounds suitable for settlement, dissected by channels for draining away surplus water. Flood, then, is perceived as a problem of inadequate drainage. The alternative, which Mathur and da Cunha (2019: 116) advocate, is to see the land itself as an ocean, a ubiquitous 'wealth of wetness' that is everywhere before it is somewhere, that rises and falls with the rains, soaks before it flows, seeps before it runs, spreads before it gathers, blurs before it clarifies (Mathur and da Cunha 2014). This wetness, they insist, is not a problem so much as an invitation – an inducement to build *differently*, with the ocean as our milieu. With the efforts of engineers to barricade the land from watery invasion already close to breaking point, and sustainable only at prohibitive cost not just to society but to the environment, this alternative is to be welcomed. What might it mean, then, to re-engineer the city in a post-terrestrial world?

In a discussion of this question, Steinberg (2011: 2114) wonders what would happen, were we to put aside the assumptions on which civil engineering has largely proceeded up to now – namely, that society occurs on land, and that protecting society means defending it from the sea – and seek instead to incorporate the sea into the very foundations of the city, thus 'joining the city and the sea together'? Or to return to my opening question: what if the city were an ocean, and its buildings ships? My answer is that the idea of buildings floating in a fluid medium is not just a speculative vision for the city of the future, nor a radical innovation in the present.[8] It is rather a realistic depiction of urban infrastructure, as it has existed from times past until today. Rather than conniving in the archipelagic illusion that the city is erected upon islands of solidity, set against the surrounding seas, this is to substitute an image of what island scholar Philip Hayward (2012: 2) calls the *aquapelago*, an 'integrated land and aquatic space' which opens equally to the air above, to the weather that occurs in it, to the windblown seeds born by it, and to the birds that are as much in their element in the air as they are in the sea or on land. Whereas the archipelago divides the land from the sea, and both from the sky, in the aquapelago, land, sea and sky are all rolled up together. The virtue of this aquapelagic perspective, for architectural theorist Lindsay Bremner (2016: 287), is that it acknowledges the essential fluidity of the earth in which we found our buildings, and of the atmosphere with which they are destined to contend. Adopting such a perspective, I argue, allows us to draw on architectural experience from both the past and the present in designing the sustainable cities of the future.

As we observed in Chapter 10 (page 161), the attention of the mariner is directed not primarily to the surface of the ocean, but to what is going on below, in the watery depths, and above, in the sky. Starting with David Lemm's nautical charts, I have suggested that the ground of the city may not, after all, be so different from the surface of the ocean, and that buildings – like ships – are not so much raised upon the ground as sunk into it. As the ground heaves with the swell of the elements, so buildings buoyed up by the earth set sail under the heavens, corresponding not with the striations of the urban grid at ground level, but with soil and air in the smooth space of the earth-sky world. Imagine a map of the city that would document such a world or help us navigate in it. On this map the outlines of buildings, as seen from above, would appear as mere shadows. The ground surface itself would not be represented since, like the surface of the ocean, it is unmappable. Indeed it is not really a surface at all but a zone of transition and transformation, where earth meets sky in the ongoing generation of life. But the map would record the depths of foundations, corresponding to points on the seabed. A compass rose would enable us to plot the variable directions of the wind, which we feel on our cheeks and in the folds of our clothing. And a range of icons would be placed on the map at points corresponding to the locations of marker buoys. We would have arrived back to where we began, with *Debris and Phenomena*.

Chapter 12

Palimpsest

Ground and page

Prologue

The last several years have seen a remarkable revival of interest in surfaces, not only in my own discipline of social anthropology but also in human geography, architecture and design, and in studies of literary, visual and material culture.[1] What has unlocked this interest is also a certain unlocking of both the body and the earth – an ontological inversion, or a turning inside out – that has undone the modernist assumption that the true essence of things and persons is to be found deep inside them, in an inner core that can be reached only by breaking open the external appearance behind which it hides. It is this assumption that so often leads us to equate the surface with what is 'superficial'.[2] It is why we distrust surfaces and the meanings they convey: why we think we have to break through them or peel them aside, if ever we are to arrive at real significance. Psychologists aim to penetrate behind the machinations of the body to discover the inner sanctum of mind; archaeologists dig deep into the earth in the hope of finding treasure-filled chambers; literary scholars plumb the depths of their texts to recover historically repressed meanings. But what if there is nothing underneath? What if surfaces are the real sites for the generation of meaning? Then by mining them, excavating them, or clearing them away, we may be destroying precisely what we seek to find, and that lies under our very noses, convinced as we are that the truth can never be on the surface but somewhere deeper down.

In this chapter I am concerned with two kinds of surface with which we deal at every moment of our quotidian lives. They are the page and the ground. We encounter the page most often as the leaf of a book, or perhaps of an unbound manuscript or document, which is either blank or more or less covered in writing. We encounter the ground as a surface of support for our activities, a terrain either cleared for cultivation or building or inscribed with the traces of our passing such as footprints, paths and tracks. My purpose is to compare the two. Is a blank page like cleared ground? Is there an analogy, even an equivalence, between walking the ground and writing the page, or between following a trail and reading a text? I shall argue that

DOI: 10.4324/9781003171713-16

for modern writers and readers, accustomed to a technology of print, the page is not what it was for the scribes of medieval times who wrote with quill on parchment, or for the readers of their hand-copied works. But nor, I suggest, is the ground, for modern people, what it once was for medieval husbandmen who drew their living from the earth. My claim is that as surfaces, ground and page have analogous properties today, as they did in the past, but only because each has undergone a parallel historical metamorphosis. It is this metamorphosis that I attempt to capture here.

But I have a further aim. It is to find a way to restore the literate imagination to our experience of inhabiting the earth. Just as the ground, in modernity, appears to set up a barrier between the material or earthly conditions of existence and the forms and meanings that the human mind projects upon them, so it seems that the page divides the literary expression of these forms and meanings from the world of which they tell. Are we fated, then, ever to read and write *about* a world whose substance hides from us, on the far side of the page? Does the very opacity of the page stand for the world's impenetrability? Or could we find a way of writing, and of reading, that enters into the very weave of the world, in the ongoing formation of its surfaces and textures? Could the page, like the ground, become a zone of habitation – a zone in which experience and imagination fuse? In this endeavour, I believe, we would come close to the most literal sense of geography as *earth-writing* – a writing that is not *about* the earth, that does not seek to describe, copy or represent the earth by means of words, but rather that writes *on*, *with* or *through* the earth, driven by forces analogous to those that move its living inhabitants. The inspiration behind this idea comes from the monastic traditions of medieval Europe, to which I have already referred in Chapter 5 (pages 68–70). It is from these that I begin.

Land, tree and book

One day in the eighth or early ninth century CE, a Christian monk from Verona, writing with pen and ink on parchment, set down a riddle, as follows:

> *Se pareba boves*
> *alba pratalia araba*
> *albo versorio teneba*
> *negro semen seminaba*
>
> Driving oxen before him
> Tilling the white fields
> Holding a white plough
> Sowing black seed.[3]

The riddler's plough is, of course, a quill pen, probably made from the white feather of a goose or swan. His fields are blank sheets of parchment, and the seeds he is sowing are letters, inscribed in black ink. It is a riddle of writing. Notice however that the monk is comparing writing with the pen to the work of the husbandman, not the other way around. In his day, the labour of tilling the soil would have been familiar to all, whereas writing was largely the specialism of monastic scribes. Today, the tables have been turned. We all learn to read and write, but how many know how to drive an ox or handle the plough? It is no wonder that for us, reading and writing refer in the first place to the verbal arts; even the book is assumed to be a volume of words, set out on its pages. So when we speak of the book of nature, and of its interpretation, the assumption is that we are drawing an analogy from the world of letters, in which we are inclined to bury our heads, to the physical world in which we find our feet. The direction of analogical extension is from page to ground. But in the riddle, it is precisely the reverse: from ground to page.

A short excursion into etymology confirms the point. Let us begin with the page itself. It comes from the Latin *pagus*, originally referring, in the gloss of the theologian-philosopher Ivan Illich (1991: 189), to 'a cultured expanse of fields and buildings that invite one for a walk'. It was a region of the countryside with its habitations. The inhabitants of the *pagus* were, of course, peasants – a word that comes from the same source.[4] As they tilled the soil around their hamlets, peasant farmers would write the page. For the verb 'to write', from Old Saxon *writan*, originally meant to scratch, tear or score (Howe 1992). So wherever on earth things were incised, scratched, cut or torn – things like animal tracks, split wood and ploughed furrows – there was writing (Figure 12.1). Only by extension did the word come to refer

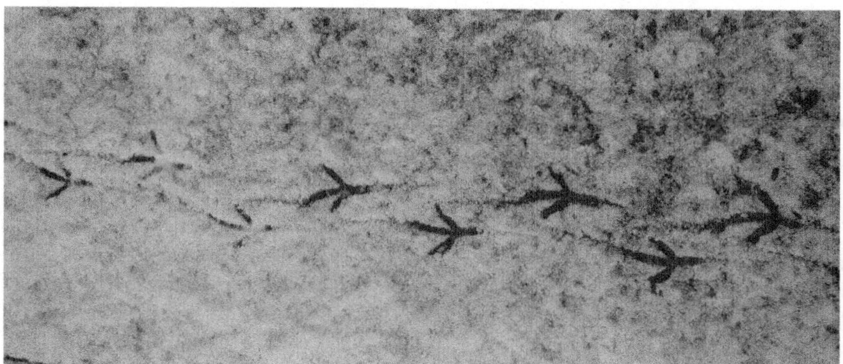

Figure 12.1 Bird writing, a track in the snow.
Photo by the author.

to the human act of incising marks in stone, and thence to the inscription of other kinds of surfaces, from parchment to paper. And only then did its meaning narrow from inscriptions of any kind to those that took the particular forms of letters. Thus it came about that the hand that had once held the axe, the hoe and the plough now held the pen. Such was the hand of our Veronese monk, in whose vision the lines the husbandman draws in the earth had morphed into lines of writing, and the field into a manuscript page.

Reading, too, began off-script. Derived from Old Saxon *ræd* and its Germanic equivalents, 'to read' literally meant to listen to others and be advised by what they are telling you, to observe and follow the ways of the world. Someone who is 'unread' has failed to pay proper attention; someone who is 'ready' is well prepared for challenges to come from having done so. The object of reading, then, becomes a riddle, a term derived likewise from the same root. To the wayfarer, nature presents itself as a compendium of riddles, each of which must be solved if the journey is to continue. Thus the hunter reads the tracks, the woodsman the grain, the ploughman the furrow. Words, too, are riddles, and like the phenomena of nature, their meanings are often obscure. So it was that when the monks of medieval times applied the term 'reading' to their practice of poring over manuscripts, they meant that the pages were as full of riddles as the inhabited world, and that you could only carry on, and get closer to the truth of things, by paying attention to them, and to what they might reveal. Even trees spoke in riddles, pronouncing prophecies in the rustling of their leaves, none more so than the mighty oak and its relative the beech (in Old English, *boc*), from which the book takes its name (Bucklow 2014: 43–4). And every page of the book was a leaf. To read the book was to listen to the voices of the pages as one would listen to the rustling of leaves in the woods.

The tree and the book, then, were of a kind, and not just because of their whispering leaves. Before paper came into general use the wood from trees – especially the beech – was commonly used for writing tablets.[5] And it was from trees, also, that writers obtained their ink. It came from the galls of the oak, crushed and boiled with a rusty nail. If the oak's prophecies were pronounced through its leaves, it is perhaps no wonder that they were written in the dissolution of its galls, or that this writing should be fixed with nails as the carpenter fixes planks and beams. But besides ink, of course, medieval scribes needed pen and parchment. The parchment began life on the backs of grazing animals – usually sheep, goats or calves – and required intensive preparation prior to use. The pen came from a feather that had once graced a bird in flight. Thus to bring pen to parchment was already to unite the elemental domains of sky and earth. Where sky meets earth lies the surface of the ground, a surface seasonally inscribed by the feet of the wayfarer or husbandman, or by the hooves of his flocks and herds, only to be wiped clean by wind, rain and snowmelt before being inscribed once again, in the next season. It is the same with pen and parchment, and this brings me to the crux of the analogy between the ground and the page.

Anti-stratigraphy

Due to its expense and the labour of preparation, it was common for one parchment to be reused many times. Between each writing, it had to be cleaned of previous inky traces by scraping the surface with a penknife otherwise used for cutting the quill and scoring guidelines. The alternation of writing and scraping, writing and scraping, would continue until the material was so reduced as to be no longer usable. A parchment that bears the traces of successive reuse is known technically as a *palimpsest* (Figure 12.2). In what follows I aim to show that the cycle of inscription and erasure through which the palimpsest is formed precisely parallels that which sculpts the surface of the ground, and that this gives to both a quite distinctive character. The parallel has indeed been seized upon by archaeologists who have adopted the palimpsest as a term by which to refer to a ground that, like a parchment, has borne the brunt of successive workings. In the early 1950s one of the originators of the analogy, Osbert Crawford, expressed it thus:

> The surface of England is like a palimpsest, a document that has been written on and erased over and over again; and it is the business of the field of archaeology to decipher it. The features concerned are of course the roads and field boundaries, the woods, the farms and other habitations, and the other products of human labour; these are the letters and words inscribed on the land.
>
> (Crawford 1953: 51)

All of England, for Crawford, is a work of earth-writing. Setting aside the nationalist tenor of his remarks, I would like to draw attention to the paradox they embody, namely that it sets archaeologists to work in deciphering traces of a past that, by rights, should have already been erased by the present. That there is something left for them to work on is an index of the fact that the erasure is never complete, that something always remains. Once again, it is the same with the serially reused parchment. However hard you scrape with the knife it is difficult to eliminate all vestiges of previous markings. But this reveals the palimpsest to be a surface of a very peculiar kind. I shall call it *anti-stratigraphic*. For it is formed not by adding layer upon layer but by taking layers away. In it, traces of the past rise to the surface even as those of the present sink into the depths. Thus if archaeologists really want to read from the palimpsest the marks of earlier earth-writings,

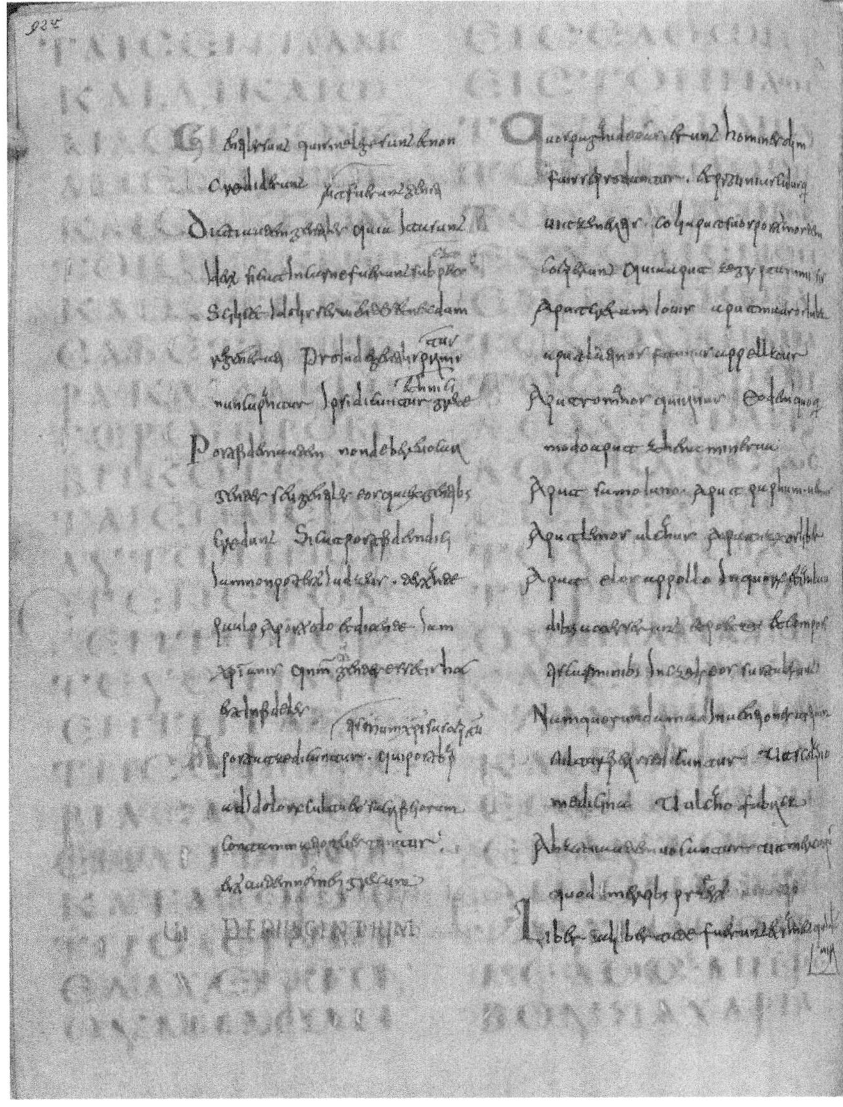

Figure 12.2 Example of a palimpsest. Inscribed in the thirteenth century with a text from the *Origines* of Isidore of Seville, this palimpsest still bears the traces of an earlier Greek text from the sixth century, of verses from the Gospel of St Luke (Codex Guelferbytanus 64 Weissenburgensis, folio 92 verso).

then the last thing they should do is strip it of its uppermost layers. For the result would be to eliminate what faint traces of past inscription still remain.

Suppose, for example, that you are surveying a landscape for evidence of ancient trackways. The more ephemeral paths will have long since disappeared, wiped away by wind and weather, and by the effects of subsequent land use. But of the most heavily used tracks, which would once have cut deep grooves in the landscape worn by feet, hooves and cartwheels, visible traces still remain. They appear as the shallowest of impressions, which it might take a trained eye to see. Yet all around you are the much more visible marks of recent and present activity, seared deep into the earth. Centuries from now, the deepest of these marks might still be visible on the surface, until they are eventually dissolved by atmospheric erosion. Once again, it is the same with the page as with the ground. It is because the writer's ink sinks deep into the parchment – becoming absorbed into its very substance – that the traces it leaves are so persistent. The deeper the absorption, the harder they are to erase. Palaeographers call the vestiges of earlier inscriptions preserved in parchment the *scripto inferior*, or 'underwriting', and what is overwritten the *scripto secunda*. But it would be closer to the mark to say that the present underwrites what, of the past, is left over. It is not that the past shows up from below, through the semi-translucent surface of the present, but rather that the present penetrates the depths even as the past rises to the surface. Present and past, in short, are upside down. Such is the topsy-turvy, anti-stratigraphic character of the palimpsest.

Deposition is not inscription

This inversion is hard for the modern mind to grasp. We are so used to thinking that the present stands to the past as activity to deposit, such that every successive present lays its own past over the pasts of its predecessors, with older layers sinking as newer ones are added on top. Archaeology itself owes its foundation, as an antiquarian pursuit, to this idea of the past as a depository for the ever-accumulating discards of history (Chapter 20, pages 310–11). It comes as no surprise, then, that archaeologists are inclined to think of the formation of what they call 'the record' in terms of processes of deposition whereby, over a period of time, fragments fall or are dropped to earth, like coins down a well, such that later pieces come to rest over earlier ones. For example in deep prehistory, in coastal zones where the staple diet was shellfish, the discard from daily shell-gathering episodes, each negligible in itself, could pile up over millennia to form substantial features in the landscape. And on cave floors where people would have knapped stone to make tools, the debris would likewise have accumulated into heaps (Bailey 2007: 204). In these as in countless other examples, at issue is the extent to which earlier deposits are preserved, disturbed or removed by subsequent activity.

At one extreme, we can picture the floor of a Neolithic house, kept meticulously clean by its erstwhile residents. Before every round of activity, they would have swept away the debris of the previous round, leaving nothing more for the archaeologist to recover than the loose bristles of their brooms. At the other extreme are their untidy neighbours who, never bothering to clean their floors, would allow everything to stack up, layer upon layer, much to the subsequent delight of archaeologists for whom these layers reveal a readily discernible sequence of depositional episodes. Between these two extremes are assemblages in which much remains of earlier deposits, but in which these remains have been so disturbed by subsequent activity, or so compressed by the weight of materials bearing down from above, that it is no longer possible to detect the original order of deposition. Such is typically the case in the examples of the shell middens and knapping floors adduced above. According to Geoff Bailey (2007), a leading proponent of the palimpsest concept in contemporary archaeology, this is the kind of situation most commonly encountered in the field. He calls it the 'cumulative palimpsest'.

Now this may be accurate enough as a description of the messy reality that archaeologists often have to contend with in their investigations. Strictly speaking, however, there is no comparison between the manuscript page that still bears the residues of past writing, and the ground of the archaeological dig, littered with the residues of past activity. Indeed, extending the idea of the palimpsest from the former context to the latter reveals a double confusion: on the one hand of inscription with deposition; on the other of erasure with cleaning. Compare, for example, the house floor that is repeatedly swept with the parchment repeatedly scraped. The surface has been tainted in the one case by deposits, in the other case by inscriptions. Deposits are dropped onto it; inscriptions are cut into it. Sweeping the floor brushes away the deposit without significantly eroding the surface. But scraping the parchment to remove the inscriptions strips the surface itself. And it is these surface scrapings that are brushed away afterwards. That's why erasure, which effaces a surface and obliterates its inscriptions, albeit partially, differs so fundamentally from cleaning which merely removes the deposit.

The characterisation of the palimpsest by another leading archaeological theorist, Gavin Lucas, illustrates what happens when the two are confused. According to Lucas (2012: 115), the palimpsest 'preserves the marks or traces of earlier acts of writing beneath the visible, uppermost marks of the last act of inscription'. Yet how can earlier rounds of inscription remain *beneath* later ones, as Lucas maintains, if the latter are separated from the former by an intervening round of erasure? Perhaps, at the back of his mind, Lucas is thinking of the chalkboard, familiar to anyone used to working in the classroom. It offers an obvious case for comparison. How often have we had to draw on a board that has not been properly cleaned, only to find that the remaining traces of earlier drawings, left by previous users, compromise the legibility of our own? On the chalkboard, new marks do indeed override old ones. The key difference, however, is that chalk marks are not inscribed. Rather than sinking into the surface, as ink into parchment, the chalk is deposited. And cleaning the board, like sweeping the house floor, partially removes the deposit while leaving the surface intact.

Closer to the genuine palimpsest is the situation often confronting students of ancient rock art, in which stone slabs have been repeatedly engraved, often with the figurative silhouettes of animals or other beings, leading to what appears on the surface as a virtually unintelligible jumble of criss-crossing lines (Bailey 2007: 205). Did the engravers, in reusing the slabs, simply ignore the lines already incised? More probably, they would have attempted to remove them by grinding or polishing the stone surface. Or perhaps it was worn anyway, through natural erosion. Regardless of whether the surface is ground down or eroded between episodes of inscription, the fact remains that later marks will cut deeper than what is left of earlier ones, giving rise to a palimpsest in the strict sense of the term. Thus the palimpsest is not, as Lucas (2012: 117) would have it, 'a "flattened" stratigraphy', formed when sediments from different pasts are squashed, under the weight of the present, into the same horizon.[6] It is rather an anti-stratigraphy, wherein the past turns up over the present. In the palimpsest, in short, the past is not so much deposited as *unearthed*.

What is the ground?

Rock art excepted, nothing in archaeology comes closer to the formation of a palimpsest than the investigations of archaeologists themselves, which, in digging deep, bring the evidence of the past to the presently exposed surface. Where the earth is thought to be formed of superimposed strata, theirs is literally an anti-stratigraphic practice of unearthing, of turning things up. In this, however, they are joined by scholars of many other disciplines, ranging from geology to history (Simonetti 2015), which have in common what could be called a depositional approach to the past. For the archaeologist the section, for the geologist the core and for the historian the archive – all, in their accumulated depositions, are supposed to hold a record of a past conceived to accrue in layers or strata, even though present activities can mix them up to the point that their order is difficult if not impossible to discern. And the aim of research is to bring them up. The more fundamental the research, the deeper it goes, the more it lifts into the light.

Architects, too, while their objective is to construct the future rather than unearth the past, are equally prone to this kind of thinking. For them, one can only build the new by clearing away or burying the residues of the old. Even if they have nothing yet lined up to build, renewal depends on 'rolling out', to adopt an expression much in vogue in corporate media, as if to lay an immaculate ground for projects to come. The reflections of architectural theorist Francesco Careri (2002) on the aesthetic practice of walking offer a case in point. Here Careri refers, inter alia, to the work of artist and sculptor Richard Long, which we have already encountered in Chapter 2 (pages 39–40). Long is famed for walking straight lines in the landscape, following lines which he has first ruled on a map. Long inscribes the earth with his feet, which leave their mark in the trodden grass of a meadow or the stony ground of a desert plateau. This is not, in practice, about laying out a two-dimensional surface on which to walk; indeed Long insists that what distinguishes his art is that it lies in the act of walking itself. Nevertheless, in commenting on Long's work, Careri (2002: 150) does not hesitate to compare the ground surface to a vast canvas, 'an immense aesthetic territory ... on which to draw by walking'. Each walk, he says, adds 'one more layer'.

But how can a walk add a layer? The stratigraphic imperative of modern thought, it seems, has led Careri to recast the act of inscribing a line in a surface already laid bare by the elements as the rolling out of a surface already inscribed by line! It is as though, preparatory to every round of inscription – in a cycle of seasons, years or ages – a fresh carpet were unfurled over the entire terrain, only to be buried by the next (see Chapter 10, page 162). Each round, then, belongs to its own time, and comes with its own inscriptions. And with every additional stratum the past, far from rising to the surface, sinks further down; you would have to peel away more recent accretions to find it. But if we admit, to the contrary, that the ground does not exactly cover the earth like a carpet, then what kind of surface *is* it? How many sides does it have? Does it divide or unify? Does it cover or cover up? Must it be penetrated if we are to find what lies beneath? In a nutshell, what on earth *is* the ground?

One of the few to tackle these kinds of questions head-on was James Gibson, whose pioneering work on the psychology of visual perception we have already touched on in previous chapters. For Gibson, surfaces are one of three components of the terrestrial environment; the other two are *medium* and *substances*. It is in the separation of medium from substances, Gibson (1979: 16–32) surmised, that surfaces are formed. For us humans, the medium is the atmosphere: it allows freedom of movement, and as a conductor of light, pressure waves and olfactory molecules, it affords the possibility of vision, hearing, touch and smell. Substances are of or pertain to the earth; being more or less solid they limit movement and perception but nevertheless afford support and nutrition for living creatures. All terrestrial objects, resting on the earth and surrounded by the atmosphere, have their surfaces, but all, too, bear upon the ground. As the fundamental surface on which all else rests, the ground figures in Gibson's account as 'the reference surface for all other surfaces' (1979: 33). It is the primary interface between medium and substances, making it so that earth and atmosphere keep to their proper domains and do not mix.

With the palimpsest, however, this principle of separation is subverted. For far from dividing earth from atmosphere, the palimpsest emerges as a surface in their very fusion. It is where tracks, grains and furrows in the earth, welling up from the depths, are laid bare by atmospheric forces of weathering and erosion that bear down from above. The ground as palimpsest is a blend of earth and atmosphere. One thinker who came close to picturing the ground in these terms was the Victorian critic and connoisseur John Ruskin. Introducing the fifth and final volume of his *Modern Painters*, published in 1860, Ruskin (1905: 14–15) described the ground as a 'veil of strange intermediate being'. At bottom, he argued, the earth is dead and cold, but at its surface – in the textures of its meadows and forests, rocky outcrops, moor and heath – it ministers to its inhabitants through this veil: 'which breathes, but has no voice; moves, but cannot leave its appointed place; passes through life without consciousness'. Perhaps, then, we could follow Ruskin in thinking of the ground as a veil of intermediacy rather than a plane of separation. Ruskin (1905: 13) himself began with the injunction: 'To dress it and keep it'. Dressing here, is an act of care, of looking after. The veil covers, but does not cover up; it is a revelation, not a disguise. Imagined as a veil, the ground does not hide the earth's depth *beneath* its surface but allows us to feel the depth *in* its surface.

Two sides or one?

What if the same could be said of the page? Thus understood, both ground and page exemplify what architectural design theorist Lars Spuybroek (2016: 57–8), inspired by the writings of Ruskin, calls a 'deep surface', formed of forces that operate, constitutively, from the inside out, and erosively, from the outside in. Such surfaces are both of inestimable depth and limitless in their atmospheric reach. To venture upon such a surface, as the wayfarer does, or the medieval reader of liturgical texts, is to inhabit an entire milieu. Might this account for what otherwise seems like a curious incongruity in the meaning of the verb, 'to wear'? It can refer to adornment, as in 'wearing clothes', and to erosion as in 'wearing away'. In a stratified world, these meanings would be contradictory. It is one thing to add a layer, another to strip it off. But with the anti-stratigraphic principle of the palimpsest, epitomised by the Ruskinian veil, adornment and erosion become one and the same. Here, worn earth and worn parchment wear the veil of their wearing away. It is in the very erosion of substance, whether of earth or parchment, that the veil rises to the surface. It is 'pressed out' of the material, as Spuybroek (2016: 57) puts it, extruded from the interior rather than impressed from the exterior.

The sculptors of classical times and their Renaissance emulators, who turned rough-hewn blocks of marble into human figures draped in velvet robes, would have known this. They did not dress up their stone, but through chiselling, grinding and polishing, allowed the dress to emerge from it. But it is no different when we say of the worn face, wrinkled and ruddied by long exposure to sun and wind, that it wears its expression, of worn hands that they wear the folds and calluses from years of working with materials, or of ancient stone steps that they wear the patina of countless passing feet. And so too, it is the erasure of the palimpsest that reveals its text, and its texture. One important consequence follows. As an anti-stratigraphic surface, the veil has only one side. There is no far side, beyond which lies naked flesh or bare earth. One can look *into* the veiled surface, but not *through* it. No nude figure lies behind the drapery of the marble statue to titillate the desire of the voyeur. But nor does the surface present an absolute barrier to vision. It is not the case, as literary scholars Stephen Best and Sharon Marcus (2009: 9) maintain, that the only alternative to seeing *through* a surface is to look *at* it, as if it had length and breadth but no depth. We are not, in other words, forced to choose between a world draped in meaning and one stripped down to its bare materiality, or – as the language of modernity has it – between culture and nature.

The veil, in short, is not an *interface*. By definition, according to cultural theorist Branden Hookway (2014: 4), the interface has two sides, interior and exterior, or upper and lower, and serves both to separate what is on one side from what is on the other, and as a conduit for the transmission of information across the threshold between them. For Gibson, as we have seen, the ground was an interface in this sense, separating the substance of the earth from the medium of the atmosphere. But with the ground as veil or palimpsest, earth and atmosphere are folded into one another. The earth is not hidden beneath the ground; rather the ground *is* the earth's arising, its welling into life. By way of the ground, to recall the words of Martin Heidegger (1971: 149), the earth 'spreads out' into rock and water, 'rises up' into plant and animal. Or to return to Ruskin, it is at the surface that the earth 'ministers' to its inhabitants. So too, in medieval times, the page would minister to its readers. Its text, welling to the surface, would reveal the words of God much as the textures of the ground – its rocks, vegetation and trees – would reveal His works. Herein lies the equivalence of words and works that grounds the idea of the book of nature.

But if the page is akin to the ground, then it, too, can have only one side. Of a book, bound and closed on the shelf, this might seem an odd thing to say. Is the book not physically comprised of pages piled one over another to form a stack? If every page is a stratum, then the book itself would be tantamount to a stratigraphic assemblage. For medieval readers, however, the book was never closed but always lay open, in the scholar's hands or on his desk (Candler 2006: 12; see Chapter 5, page 71). In an open book, you pass from page to page not by working your way down but by turning. To turn a page is like the wayfarer's turning a corner, or surmounting a pass, at which point a new vista opens up ahead. Where in a stack, every page has a front and back, or top and bottom, in the open book it has two faces, one of which is the reverse of the other, as verso to recto. Every page of the book, then, is not so much a layer as a fold. In reading a book and turning its pages, one passes from fold to fold, opening each in turn only to close its predecessor behind you. In turning, not deposition, lies the passage of history.[7]

The origins of stratigraphy

How come, then, that we – self-styled 'moderns' – are so inclined to think of both the ground and the page in stratigraphic terms? The answer, I believe, lies in two technologies that did much to establish the particular character of the modern era, namely paving and printing. Both served to place life and letters on a hard and featureless foundation. Paving, for a start, was designed to cover the substantive earth with a layer of rigid and impenetrable material that would keep it where it belongs, below ground, and prevent it from having any intercourse with the air. For architects and planners of the modern city the rationale for paving was partly one of public health, since the mixture of earth and air was commonly thought to give rise to noxious vapours, and partly one of improving the conditions of transport, allowing movement across the surface unimpeded by the perils of mud and swamp, scrub and forest, rocks and stones, that would formerly have encumbered the wayfarer.[8] Paving places a lid on the rising of the earth from below, at the same time as it resists the erosive forces of the atmosphere, of wind and weather, from above. Unlike unpaved ground, paving did indeed establish an interface, with topside and underside, both keeping earth and air apart and allowing regulated transmission from one domain to the other, for example through drainage and sewage systems. And with the ground assumed by default to be paved, everything else – rather than rising from it – was supposed to rest upon it, as furniture rests upon the floor of an apartment, scenery on the boards of the stage, buildings on concrete foundations or industrial plant on a production platform (Ingold 2015: 37–40).

It was the same with printing. In the very principle of its operation, the press is stratigraphic, in that it works by overlaying one surface upon another. It is a meeting of pre-formed surfaces, not a constitution of surface in the meeting of substance and medium. Thus the press put an end to writing, understood as an act of scribing the page. In writing by hand on parchment, the pen would leave its mark in the material as the enduring trace of a manual gesture, much as a path is left in the ground in the wake of passing feet. The letterline of writing, like the trodden path, would continually emerge as a differential within the surface texture, while nevertheless remaining fully *of* that texture. It is not as if the line had lifted off onto a plane of its own, allowing the page or ground to sink back into blank homogeneity. That is why, to recall our earlier example, the feet of artist Richard Long do not, in fact, roll out a new layer over the terrain, as you might roll out a cartographic map, every time he takes a walk! The line of his walking is traced in the deep surface of ground, not layered over it. Or as Gilles Deleuze (1994: 29) puts it, in his treatise on difference and repetition, the line distinguishes itself from the ground 'without the ground distinguishing itself from the line'. Difference, in other words, is unilateral.

But with letterpress printing it is quite otherwise. For far from emerging from within the matrix of the surface, as text in texture, individual letters are pre-engraved in miniature blocks of metal, or 'sorts', which have first to be assembled in the galley before being inked and placed in the press. Here the labour of the scribe is pre-empted by that of the engraver and typesetter. Only after having been laid out in its entirety (albeit in mirror reversal) on the plane of the galley, is the composition then levered down from above upon the initially flat and featureless surface of the signature sheet. Thus whereas handwritten letters are 'pressed out' from the material of the page, printed letters are impressed upon it. 'Typography', as literary scholar Anna Reynolds (2017) puts it, 'is now a digital process, with ink sitting on top of, rather than within, the surface of the page.' Each letter is, in itself, a discrete fragment or particle, broken off from those preceding and following in the string of letters making up a line.

The line, then, is not the trace of a movement or gesture but a connected sequence of verbal particles, or what linguists call a syntagm. And being *on* the surface rather than *of* it, the lettering is no more intrinsic to the page than the page to the lettering. Instead of the one unilaterally registering a difference within the other, they are bilaterally indifferent. Following Deleuze, we could speak of the 'black indifference' of the letters to the page, and the 'white indifference' of the page to the letters. In Deleuze's (1994: 28) vivid metaphor, letters are strewn across the page like scattered members, 'a head without a neck, an arm without a shoulder, eyes without brows'. But less anatomical comparisons could be drawn, as with the arrangement of furniture on a floor, of props on the stage, or of houses on an estate. Such is the character of the hard-surfaced world (Ingold 2015: 45).

The transition, then, from manuscript culture to printing, and from earth-walking to hard surfacing, was essentially one from the anti-stratigraphic to stratigraphy, of from turning to deposition. Once again, we can take our cue from Deleuze, writing this time with his collaborator Félix Guattari, for whom the distinction between the principles of stratigraphy and anti-stratigraphy, as I have set them out here, comes down to that between the *tracing* and the *map* (Deleuze and Guattari 2004: 13). Unfortunately, however, Deleuze and Guattari confuse everyone, themselves included, by using these terms back to front. In a nutshell: what they mean by mapping is actually the formation of a trace, as in walking a path or handwriting a line; while what they mean by tracing is actually the vertical superposition of layers, as when a map is rolled out over the terrain. Nevertheless, even though they have the terms the wrong way around, the distinction holds. The logic of stratigraphy (mapping for us, 'tracing' for Deleuze and Guattari) articulates and hierarchises successive states of affairs, each of which comes ready-made, piling one upon the other like printed sheets in a stack, or like the successive levels of a tree- diagram that mediate between a deep structure below and a surface structure above. Anti-stratigraphic logic, by contrast, is rhizomatic: here the roots, like those of a real tree growing in the ground, rise up from the depths into the surface. To make a trace ('mapping' for Deleuze and Guattari) is then to join with, and to follow, the textures of the surface, as when walking a path or inscribing a line. It is 'an experimentation in contact with the real' (Deleuze and Guattari 2004: 13). And meaning falls out of it.

Re-entering the page

Is it any longer possible, then, for us to re-enter the page as we once walked the ground, to restore our literate imagination to our habitation of the earth? Or are we forever excluded from it? Can there be an earth-writing in which stratigraphic and anti-stratigraphic principles are combined? 'We will never have understood writing', protests literary theorist Juliet Fleming (2016: 141), 'if we continue to think in layers, for "on" is only a special case of being "in" the world.' The ink of the printed page may be on top of, rather than within, the surface of the page, but the page nevertheless remains within, not on top of, the world itself. How then, might we simultaneously be *on* the page and *in* the world? I would like to conclude with two very different experiments to show how this might be done; there are doubtless many others. They proceed, however, in very different ways. In one example, words printed on the pages of a book serve, in effect, as notation for a performance, of reading aloud, in which the speaking body itself relives the experience of ground-habitation. In the other example, both writing and reading blow apart the syntactic structures of the text, as wind and weather invade the structures of being, in such ways as to open up to a domain of affective resonance.

One of the finest pieces of contemporary earth-writing I know is a popular children's book, immortalised by the author Michael Rosen, with illustrations by Helen Oxenbury (1989). It is called *We're Going on a Bear Hunt*, and every page carries the same refrain:

> We can't go over it,
> We can't go under it.
> Oh no!
> We've got to go through it!

Four children, their father and the family dog are off to find the bear. On their way, they walk through long grass that goes '*swishy-swashy*' as they pass, through a deep river that goes '*splish, splosh*', through wet, oozy mud that goes '*squelch, squerch*', a dark forest where they go '*stumble trip*', and a whirling snowstorm that howls '*hooo wooo*'. When the family does eventually come across the bear, everyone is so terrified that they run back home as fast as they can, bolt the door, and tuck themselves safely up in bed. The bear, once again starved of the company he craves, is left outside, lonely and forlorn, treading wearily back to his cave. It is an achingly sad story.

What makes it so poignant, however, is the way it is performed. As you read it, preferably aloud – as you mouth the words *splish, splosh*, *stumble trip* or *hooo wooo* – the earth and its weather reverberate in sound and feeling. Say the word *squelch*, and you can almost feel the ooze of wet mud around your boots in the way your tongue scours the roof of your mouth, and hear the mud's suction in the sound it makes. This is not just a case of onomatopoeia. *Squelch* doesn't stand as a copy of the sound of mud-mired suction. The resemblance between the sounds is rather an outcome of their having been produced through analogous processes. *Squelch* is the sound of a voice that has absorbed the experience of wet mud into its very way of speaking. It is to speak *with* mud, not *about* it. And of course it is not just mud that you speak with, for wind, grass, running water and tree-roots also get into the sound of your voice. With every page, moreover, you remind your listeners that it *falls* to you to mouth these sounds. You are as bound, in reading, to the imperatives of the page as you are, in walking, to those of the ground; there is no short-cut. The ground of the story – a ground neither under nor over which you can go – is equivalent to the Ruskinian veil, a meeting of earth and atmosphere akin to the palimpsest, where the constitutive forces of the earth meet the erosive forces of weather.

Yet here's the paradox, for the book's pages are printed and its letters are of type. On the printed page, unlike the ground it describes, there is nothing to stop you from skipping from one place to the next. The text – now more resembling a map than a landscape, read optically, from a distance, rather than through a haptic or auditory pilgrimage through the country of the page – allows for multiple access points (Marin, Masschelein and Simons 2018: 53–4). Page and ground, then, are not equivalent after all; they rather seem to rest on opposite principles. How can that be?[9] The answer lies in the difference, and the relation, between reading a printed text and reading it *out*. We have seen that medieval monks, in their reading, would trace the letters on the page with their fingers while murmuring the corresponding sounds. For them, fingering and murmuring were inseparable aspects of one and the same performance. It was almost as if the digits and the vocal cords were synchronised with each other. And the words would fall out from the performance: they were both felt and heard, but not so easily seen – especially when the text was written in *scriptio continua*, without wordbreaks.

For modern readers of the printed word, by contrast, the text itself is neither felt nor heard. It is rather scanned by eye. But this scanning is not, in itself, part of the performance. Reading words is one thing; reading them *out* is another. And it is the separation of the latter from the former that establishes the script as a *notation*. Strictly speaking, you do not perform a notation; you perform *from* it. In classical music, for example, it is conventional to indicate a note to be played by means of a dot, positioned on or between the ruled lines of the stave. On the score, the dot is silent, inert and self-contained. But in performance, it is drawn out into a sustained and vibrant line of sound (Chapter 16, pages 248–9). So it is too with letters. Thus each individual 'o' in the phrase *hooo wooo* is punctual and inert, but in performance a string of o's translates into a prolonged aspirant sigh, resembling that of the wind. In short, and unlike the literate wayfaring of medieval readers, the ground of the *Bear Hunt* is not enacted in tactile contact with the page, but recreated 'off-page' as a phenomenon of haptic and auditory experience.

But what if there is no performance? Suppose that we read a text silently, as we usually do these days with printed books. We are just reading the words; nothing more. Can we nevertheless inhabit the book's pages as we inhabit the land? This brings me to my second example. In a recent study of writings and films from the Canadian Arctic, literary scholar Rebecca Fredrickson points to an ontological equivalence between land and page, and to the writing of both. She attributes the equivalence, however, to a specifically northern sensibility, rooted in the experience of inhabiting an environment characterised by marked seasonal variations in light and darkness, by extremes of warmth and cold, and by immense expanses of land, sea and sky that are not always clearly differentiated. Her claim is that this sensibility underwrites what she calls a 'northern textual ecology'. Let me cite one short passage from Fredrickson's study which, I think, puts the claim in a nutshell and, at the same time, introduces the idea of what she calls 'weather-writing':

> As a connected part of the flux of life, that is, the processes that *are* life, literature draws the forces of its physical environment – storms, sudden winds, rain, melting – into its compositions. All literature is a kind of weather-writing. It is not a mimetic reproduction of the weather, but a place of becomings where the material of language produces forces analogous to the weather.
>
> (Fredrickson 2015: 14)

Though Fredrickson's ostensive concern is with weather-writing and mine is with earth-writing, in truth I believe they come to much the same thing.

After all there can be no earth without weather, or weather without earth. Who can say where the blizzard ends and the snowfield begins, or draw the line between rainfall and mud, mist and mountain, wind and dune? In the ground-veil, as we have seen, earth and weather merge and blend. So too, earth-writing and weather-writing must necessarily fold into one another.

I do however want to stress the distinction that Fredrickson insists upon here, between *mimesis* and *analogy*. Her point is that the affective forces that move the hand of the writer in the process of composition, or that infuse the soul of the reader in silently reliving the experience on the page, are of a kind with those that bear upon and impel wayfarers as they plant their feet in the land. The book may appear to be a finished artefact, with all its letters and words syntactically joined up into well-formed sentences. But in the process of writing, and in the experience of reading, it is not like that at all. Fredrickson's point, if I understand her correctly, is that in the turbulence of writing and reading, the syntactic structure is blown apart, releasing both writer and reader – like the weather-beaten wayfarer of northern climes – into the ever-flowing currents of world-formation. As Fredrickson (2015: 31) puts it, 'there are blizzards blowing through syntax'. Our habitation of the page, as of the earth, is not so much performative as affective.

Epilogue

At stake, here, are ways of speaking of the mind. For these, too, have long drawn on parallels with both the ground and the page. Is the surface of the mind akin to a palimpsest, inscribed with memories, the deepest of which are the most recent, while those from further back in time rise to the surface, eventually to melt into air? Or is it composed of a series of strata, each of which covers over and buries its predecessor? There is no doubt that medieval people, for whom the purpose of both reading and writing was above all to commit texts to living memory, would have taken the former view, while modern people, for whom the text serves as a record that *substitutes* for living memory, destined for deposition in the stacks of an archive, would be predisposed to the latter.[10] It is surely no accident that contemporary neuropsychologists speak of the mind-brain as offering a neural *substrate* capable of supporting all manner of cultural accomplishments. For them, it is hard-surfaced like the earth. But what if we were to think of the ground of human culture as something more like the soft carpet of vegetation covering field and forest? In treading such a ground, writes philosopher Alphonso Lingis (1998: 14), 'we do not feel ourselves on a platform … but feel a reservoir of support extending infinitely in depth'. It is this depth of support, affording rootedness and growth, and not the hardness and rigidity of a surface which affords neither, that counts in this instance. Drawing an analogy with the carpeted ground, might we not liken the mind-brain – as do Deleuze and Guattari (2004: 17) – to a field of grass?

You can see why Deleuze and Guattari prefer grass to trees. It is because their trees are not living specimens rooted in the ground, but dendritic diagrams that articulate a hierarchy of levels of resolution, from deep to surface structure (Chapter 23, pages 350–1). But to close this chapter, I think we could well return to the ancient analogy between the tree and the book, to the oak and the beech, their tangled roots threading the earth, their emergent trunks rising to an equivalent tangle of branches and twigs in the canopy, their rustling and chattering leaves mingling with wind and weather. Perhaps the domain of mind could itself be compared to a dense patch of woodland. In writing and reading, then, we would not move *across* a hard, preformed surface, as boots on tarmac or on-road vehicles. We would rather find or push our way *through* the ground-page and, in so doing, contribute to its ever-emerging texture. This is the kind of movement I have called wayfaring – a movement that seeks not to connect pre-determined points or territories but rather, at every moment, to keep on going. It is not a form of being but a way of becoming. And it is along this way, perhaps, that we can find the real meaning of earth-writing.

Chapter 13

On opening the book of surfaces

A book – this book, which you now have open as you read these words – is a three-dimensional stack of rectangular pages, aligned and bound along one edge. Each page is of identical size, thickness and texture. The only variation lies in the covers, of a thicker material that wraps around the front, back and spine of the stack. The covers are coloured, and bear a design. But the pages, while uniformly white, are sprinkled all over with tiny black marks, neatly aligned in parallel rows, within margins equally offset from the outer edges. The marks are letters, combined into words, in turn strung end to end in sentences and paragraphs. Words sparkle like jewels on the page. Is the book, then, like a jewellery box? Imagine a box of exactly the same size and proportions as this book. We can lift the top like a lid to reveal thousands of tiny gems, perhaps arranged into compartments. We could list the compartments like the chapters of the book, and make an inventory of their contents. Both the book and the box are containers of a kind; the contents of both can be revealed by an act we call opening, and hidden away again by an act of closure. Inside the box are gems; inside the book are words. But to open the box and to open the book are operations of very different kinds.

There is only one way to open the box – that is, by lifting the lid – but having done so, all the precious stones therein are equally accessible, making it easy for a thief to rob the contents without having to take the box as well. All he has to do is empty the jewellery into a sack and make off with the haul. The book's contents, however, are not enclosed within its surfaces but indelibly imprinted on them, to the extent of partaking of their very substance. They are not easily stolen, then, without taking the whole book, or at least without ripping out some of its pages. Nor can they be accessed all at once. This is because the book affords as many different ways of opening as it has pages, and every way reveals a different array of words. Since every opening of a book is a possible unfolding, to unfold it at any one page means folding up all the others. The book as a whole, then, is the sum of all the different ways of opening it. It is a compendium of surfaces, and the

DOI: 10.4324/9781003171713-17

words are hidden in its folds. It follows that the book's interior surfaces do not enclose a volume – as do the surfaces of the box – rather, they *comprise* a volume. To open a book is not to lift the covers but to turn the volume inside out. It is at once to fold and to unfold.

My question is this: what is the relation, in a book, between the words and the pages on which they appear, and indeed between the pages themselves? Is the page a 'blank slate' on which anything could be written? Even if the page is indifferent to the words' semantic values, might the ways in which ink binds materially with surface contribute to meaning? Our predecessors of medieval times, it seems, approached these questions very differently from the way we do today; moreover in a world increasingly dominated by the paraphernalia of digital technology, our thinking on these matters appears to be changing yet again. In what follows I shall set out five ways of thinking about word and page in the history of the book, corresponding respectively to five kinds of surface, namely, veil, pane, sheet, face, and screen.

In the first, corresponding to medieval scribal culture, the surface of the page is comparable to a textured veil woven by the lines of handwriting. In the second, inaugurated with the Renaissance discovery of the principles of perspective, the surface came to be remodelled as a transparent window-pane, through which the reader looks to discover the meanings behind. The contemporaneous introduction of the printing press, however, cast the page in a completely different light. For in the practical operation of the press, letters and words bear down upon a sheet, of which every page is a fold, relating to others through surface-to-surface contact. Yet reading the printed page, rather than walking along with the handwritten line as our guide, means coming face to face with it. This is the fourth way of thinking about the page. However the face the modern reader sees, in facing the page, is not another's but his own, as if reflected in a mirror. And that brings us finally, in our hypermodern digital era, to the screen: a projective interface that, in every respect, is the opposite of the veil from which we began.

Veil

Writing, in medieval times, was a way of weaving. That's why the manuscript pages to which it gave rise were called texts, from the Latin *texere*, 'to weave'. Just as in weaving, the weft goes back and forth between the warp-lines stretched taut on the loom, so in the medieval art of writing, the letter-line, inscribed with pen and ink, would oscillate between ruled lines that had first to be scored in the parchment. Indeed the woven textile and the written text are produced by operations that are formally identical, barring the critical difference that they deal in alternative kinds of lines, respectively threads and traces. What kinds of surfaces, then, do they yield? If the woven fabric has a characteristic pattern and texture, so too does the page of writing. The resemblance of a page densely packed with Gothic script to a blanket weave is unmistakeable, and it lies behind the designation of one such hand, dating from the fifteenth century, as *textura*. Significantly, it was *textura* that Gutenberg adopted for his first printed type.[1] But it raises puzzling questions. How does writing change the way the surface of parchment is perceived? And what difference does it make to this perception when the lines that weave the texture are no longer inscribed on parchment but printed on paper? I begin with the first of these questions, before embarking on the second.

We might be tempted to answer that the weave of the text adds another layer to an otherwise bare surface, much as a naked body might be covered by clothes. Yet such a view is belied by all the scoring and scratching that is done to the surface itself in the course of its inscription – and of its scraping as well if old parchment is reused. However, taking up our comparison of the page to the ground, from the previous chapter, leads us towards an alternative answer. For the ground, too, has its textures, woven from the tracks and trails, roots and runners of its plant and animal inhabitants. There is no such thing as a bare ground over which the texture is draped. To the contrary, texture wells up from within and beneath, from the depths of the earth, only to be laid bare by atmospheric forces of weathering and erosion. Thus are seams of rock scoured by ice, swathes of vegetation levelled by wind, footprints washed away by rain. Far from imposing an impermeable barrier between sky and earth, the ground is an interstitial surface, where the constitutive writing of the earth, in its lines and wrinkles, rises from below to mingle with the erosive influences of the sky that bear down on it from above.

Let's return to John Ruskin's characterisation of the ground as a veil (Chapter 12, page 190). The ground-veil is worn, in both senses of the term: as outer coating and as material abrasion. The earth wears the ground, yet in that very ground is the earth's wearing away. And if the ground is a veil, in Ruskin's sense, so too is the manuscript page. Its texture, too, is woven in the tracing of its lines. Like an assiduous gardener, the scribe tends to his lines as they grow or issue forth from the soil of the parchment, without ever detaching themselves from its surface. In writing by hand, all the care and devotion that goes into the work translates directly, through manual gesture, into the traces it leaves. The ever-composing lines, as they divide, spread and multiply over the page, enter with it into a relation of sympathy. For while the scribe suffers through the labour of writing, he joins in his suffering with the parchment that is written upon. With Lars Spuybroek, one could say that the scribe *dresses* the parchment, or clothes it in a veil, 'in an everyday act of caretaking, calm and dutiful' (Spuybroek 2016: 98). Yet as Spuybroek insists, dressing is one thing, dressing-up quite another.[2] To dress up is to hide a plain reality behind an overlay of ostentation. But that is not what writing, even of the most ornate kind, does to parchment. As with the veil, the parchment is dressed in the tracery of written lines, but is not dressed up in it.

Once we turn from writing on parchment to printing on paper, however, it is quite otherwise. For while the *textura* that Gutenberg adopted for his printed type might have looked like a weave, the appearance was deceptive. It was indeed a cover-up. Far from having been woven into the surface of the page, the letter forms were externally imposed upon it. No longer did the script emerge, as in a handwritten work, from a performative engagement with the material; it was rather deposited, pre-assembled from discrete verbal fragments, onto the paper surface. Technically, printing severs the link between the manual gesture and its trace: while the *ductus* of the writing hand would flow without interruption into the inflections of the letter-line, the shapes of the graphic marks delivered by the press bear no relation to the movements of their production (Ingold 2007a: 26). And whereas the lines of the scribe would continue without beginning or end, carrying on from the completion of one copy to the commencement of the next, the printed work is an already completed composition, even before it is committed to paper. Not that the process was any less laborious: letters had to be engraved, and assembled in a galley, and this required at least as much care and devotion as the work of the scribe. But once done, multiple copies could be run off without too much effort. They were not however woven. To call these printed works texts is indeed an anachronism, motivated in large part by nostalgia for a lost tradition.

With the disappearance of the scribal letter-line, the page lost its voice (Ingold 2007a: 24–6). It was silenced. Recall that throughout the Middle Ages, it was usual for liturgical texts to be read aloud, with a murmuring sound often compared, by the monks of the time, with the buzzing of bees, while simultaneously tracing the letter-line with a finger. Thus the words could be heard and felt, but so long as they were written in *scriptio continua*, without breaks, they could not easily be seen.[3] Marks printed on the surface, to the contrary, could be seen, but neither felt nor heard. Where the ear and the finger of the medieval reader would follow the line of text, always remaining close to the surface, the reader of the printed page had no lines to follow, no emergent texture of sound or feeling. The reader's attention, now more cognitive than performative, more optical than auditory or haptic, was no longer guided on its way to meaning *along* the textual paths threading the page, but cut orthogonally *through* it, looking behind the printed words for their meaning. For an attention that cuts through, moreover, the graphic designs of the marks themselves, rather than affording paths to meaning, are perceived to distract from it. They are more likely to ensnare the gaze. A reader overly absorbed in their calligraphic formation risks becoming apotropaically stuck to the surface of the page, and never making it through to the meaning behind.[4]

In a world of print, in short, calligraphic virtuosity is a manifestation not of sympathy but of trickery and deceit, or of hyperbolic ostentation. As we've already found with Gutenberg's *textura*, it is a way of dressing up, of making it look *as if* the writing carried an affective charge, when in fact it does not. The scribal line emerges in feeling, from the haptic engagement of pen and parchment. But printed letterforms can only stand as surrogates for feeling. Nor is the substitution confined to the written word. A print-saturated culture such as our own enjoins us to take a similar approach to speech. We suppose that hearing the spoken word is equivalent to looking at the printed one, as if there were some sonic counterpart to the page which we have to pierce in order to reach the meanings that lie behind. That is why a philosopher of our times, steeped in its conventions, can write that language-as-word, 'even while sounding, does not draw attention to itself *as* sound' (Ihde 1976: 161). It rather draws attention *through* sound to the meaning it conveys. Thus the verbal chant that medieval readers would once have passionately followed has come to be recast as an enchantment that distracts. Listeners are warned not to be lured by the melodic inflections of the voice, as readers might be lured by inflections of the line, lest they fail to attend to the meaning of what is said.

Pane

The reader of the printed work, in short, no longer inhabits the page as a walker inhabits the terrain, betwixt sky and earth, making his way by finger rather than foot. He is rather set over and beyond it, transcendent rather than immanent, and holds it in his sights. Unlike the ground-veil, which covers but does not cover up, the page is perceived to have a near side and a far side. The reader is on the side of cognition; on the other side is a world of meaning to which he seeks access. With no line for the finger to follow, no surface on which it can find purchase and that might be compared to the ground underfoot for the walker, the depth and opacity of the textured veil, whether of ground or parchment, gives way in perception to a spatial surface that is now homogeneous, transparent and wafer-thin, measured out not with the pacing of feet or the oscillations of the pen, but with the calculated partitions of an abstract grid. Black and white, once absorbed and absorbent, appear to part company: the black lifts off as the white recedes.[5] It is as if the letters were sucked from the page, through the black holes of the eyes' pupils, into the inner sanctum of the *cogito*, at the same time that the whiteness of the paper withdraws into a background upon which the mind projects its meanings. Drained of both black and white, the page remains as no more than the ghost of its material presence: an invisible and insubstantial pane that one does not so much read as read *through*.

The resemblance of this ghostly page to the picture plane of perspective drawing is not accidental. It is usual, in treatises on the subject, to compare the latter to a windowpane, transparent and infinitely thin. Every drawn mark indicates a point of intersection where the line of sight, linking the eye with the thing seen, punctures the plane. Leon Battista Alberti, introducing the principles of perspective in his *De Pictura* of 1435, likened the line of sight to a thread so fine that it could not be split.[6] Many such lines, Alberti reasoned, would fan out into a surface akin to a veil. This veil, however, did not – like Ruskin's – cover the earth. It rather stretched from eye to world. The lines of the drawing are where the veil bisects the picture plane. Though the printed word is not bound by the same geometrical conventions or commitments to realism as the perspectival drawing – and indeed differs from the drawing rather as algebra differs from geometry – it could nevertheless be suggested that every graphic mark registers the intersection of a line of thought with what could be called the 'plane of letters'. As the line of sight connects the eye with the thing seen, so the line of thought connects cognition with its objects. A veil of threads, made up of such lines, intersects the plane of letters just as it does the picture plane.

Thus the overall effect of print was to convert the ever-ramifying lines of the medieval journeyman-scribe into a total verbal composition, visible at a glance, drawn not *along* but orthogonally *through* the surface of the page, turning the totality inside out – as Michel Serres (2017: 132) has it – 'like the finger of a glove or a simple optical diagram', and plunging it into the innermost, utopian recesses of the mind. 'This black hole', continues Serres, 'absorbs the world'. In short, with the transition from handwriting to print, and from parchment to paper, the generative principle of the line was subordinated to the projective principle of point and plane. Herein, according to Serres, lie the seeds of modernity. Yet only in our times have these seeds finally born fruit, with the development of a technology that has the digital point and the projective plane at its heart. The perspectival windowpane has become a computer screen, while the page, as a substantial surface, has vanished. To medieval people the idea that one could read writing without a page to read from would be as absurd as supposing that you could go for a walk without ground to walk on. The fact that we can dispense with this surface with equanimity – that we are not baffled by the thought of off-page reading – can be attributed to the separation of black from white inaugurated by printing. Yet with the press, this perceptual decomposition of the page did not amount to its material dissolution. Quite to the contrary, as I shall now show, the printing press is a technology of surfaces *par excellence*.

Sheet

Is there really no feeling in the printed word? Historians of language have adduced compelling evidence to show that as print media became more widely distributed, there was a veritable explosion in the coinage of new words to describe qualities of feeling, motivation and experience. These words were needed, as they had never been before, to compensate for the lost expressive power of the handwritten line.[7] And as we have seen, this lexical explosion was accompanied by a fundamental change in attitude towards the surface of the page. However to concentrate on the words alone, in their relation to the page, is to miss out on what is perhaps most fundamental to the printing process itself: that it entails a relation *between surfaces*. How, after all, can there be a press without pressure, and how can there be pressure without one material surface forcefully bearing on another? Indeed in retrospect I realised that in an earlier work on lines (Ingold 2007a) I had missed this obvious point myself. I had understood print only negatively, as the enemy of the scribal practice of handwriting, rather than positively, as a craft in its own right, with its own repertoire of tools and techniques for engraving, etching and pressing, as well as materials for inking and for taking the press itself. To gain a richer understanding of printing, I realised I would have to redirect my attention back from line to surface. What would happen, I wondered, if we were to think of printing as a way of working with surfaces rather than lines?

The point is that print is not just about making marks on surfaces. It is more fundamentally about bringing two surfaces together: the inked surface and the surface destined to receive it. The feeling that is lost, in breaking the link between the manual gesture and its trace, is at least partially recovered in the sympathy of surfaces for one another. Could this be a source of meaning in itself? There is a certain magic about the way ink takes to paper, in an engagement entirely hidden from the view of printmakers themselves. The attention of the scribe can join with the trace, and follow its evolution, but for the printmaker there is no knowing what is going on between surfaces under the press – not, at least, until it is opened up for inspection and the results revealed. No sooner are they revealed, moreover, than they are folded away again, concealed from sight like an old-fashioned letter in an envelope. Nowadays, paper is commonly cut to size by machine prior to printing, but in the past, what would end up as several pages would first be printed as one large signature sheet, which would then be folded to page-sized sections for binding. For example in octavo, the sheet would be folded three times, yielding a section of eight leaves or sixteen pages. In the folding, pages would be brought together that, on the original sheet, were positioned not only far apart but even upside down relative to one another. Only in the folding were the pages brought back into a concordance kept like a hidden secret.

Before anyone could read the book, however, the pages had first to be slit open along the folds, by means of a paperknife. Even after cutting, the rough edges and slight unevenness from page to page – as each would have to be slit separately, by hand, and along different axes – would give the book an unfinished look, drawing attention to a process of gestation that runs seamlessly from printing to folding to binding to slitting and finally to opening and turning the pages, whereupon the book's words are at last birthed into the world. On opening the book, words that had intimately touched one another, within the folds of the signature sheet, are once again parted on opposite sides of the centrefold, apparently denying that they ever had anything to do with one another! Concentrating on the words and their meanings, we are inclined to forget how central the act of page-turning is to reading (see Chapter 12, pages 191–2). Yet every turn is a moment of profound revelation, affording not an end but a new beginning. On the page as in the world, is it not in the intimacy of surface-to-surface contact – as it were, between the sheets – that all new life is generated? With this question in mind, let me return to my earlier point that printing is fundamentally about bringing two surfaces together, in an intimacy of contact that is itself generative of life and meaning. Can this tell us something more about the relations not just of page to page, but of page to face, and of face to face?

Face

To address this question, I begin with a story which at first glance might seem far from the history of the book, and yet which shows it up in an unaccustomed light. The story concerns Sangama, a man of the Piro people native to the Peruvian Amazon, and a reputed shaman.[8] Though formally illiterate, Sangama had observed that his white masters – Spanish landowners and colonial officials – would spend long hours reading their newspapers. They appeared absorbed in these complex patterns of black marks arrayed on a white background. Sangama, too, claimed to be able to read the newspaper. But what he saw in the sheet were not messages encoded in the marks printed on it. Rather, he saw a *face*. It was the face and lips of a beautiful woman, and she was speaking to him. He – Sangama – was lip-reading. Now in terms of Piro cosmology, this makes perfect sense. Piro suppose that their bodies are suffused with vibrating patterns that come to them with the shimmering light, and are transformed at the surface of the skin into sound. Piro bodies and artefacts are covered all over with these radiant patterns, through which they speak and sing. So it is no wonder that Sangama interpreted the patterns of newsprint in the same way. He was reading the woman's face.

The face is indeed a mystery. Remember that except in a culture such as ours, which has surrounded itself with mirrors, the face is one part of the body that its owner cannot normally see. Rather, where the face is, we see the world, including other persons who may or may not be looking at us. So is the face part of the body at all? Or more specifically, is it part of the head: seat of the brain, eyes, ears and the organs of speech? Gilles Deleuze and Félix Guattari (2004: 186–90), to recall our earlier discussion in Chapter 6 (page 96), argue that it is not. The body, they say, including the head, is constituted anatomically within the 'volume-cavity system'. Surrounded by the epidermis, it has an inside and an outside. But the face is not included in the body, nor is it confined to the head. With its lines, wrinkles and contours, its glow and pallor, the facial surface is of another order altogether.[9] And it is produced by a quite different system: the 'white wall/black hole system'. Black and white, here, are not the poles of an absolute dichotomy; they rather denote the way in which the face emerges from the play of affect and meaning. A face that speaks and sings, smiles and frowns, that wears its expressions on its surface, must have a surface on which to express them. And for these expressions to well up from the depths of feeling, sunk into the surface must be orifices from which these affectations spring. In the idiom of Deleuze and Guattari, the surface is the white wall, the orifices are the black holes, and together they furnish the conditions of emergence for what we perceive as a face, with its luminous surfaces and shadowy orifices.[10]

This, precisely, was what Sangama saw in the paper he was reading: a surface with holes, from which there appeared a lively face reading his. But it is not what modern readers see, accustomed as they are to the conventions of print media. For as we have already learned from Serres, the principle of projection that lies at the very genesis of modernity has pulled the black hole, like the inverted finger of a glove, into an apical point where the eye opens to the mind of the conscious subject, while the white wall has receded to a plane on which the subject projects its meanings. The hole is like the lens of a projector; the wall like a cinematic screen, indifferent to the images that play upon its surface. The modern subject, peering through the eye's pupil as through a lens, sees no other face than their own. It is their peculiar predicament that they can see without being seen, read without being read, save by themselves.

Historically, this predicament is the exception, not the rule. 'Looking at the entire early history of human faciality', notes philosopher Peter Sloterdijk (2011: 192–205), 'one can say that humans have faces not for themselves but for the others'. Throughout this history what each face offered the other was not so much a reflection or reproduction as what Sloterdijk calls an 'affective echo'. Faces, in short, did not exist independently, as though each adhered to its own body as a unique index of personal identity, but were necessarily constituted in relations of interfaciality, and therefore presupposed, at the very least, a bipolar configuration, like an ellipse with two focal points. It was the ubiquitous mirror, Sloterdijk (2011: 295) argues, that eventually cut the ellipse in two, setting up 'a pseudo-interfacial relation with another that is not another'. The face before the mirror, he continues, 'can relish the illusion of being in a closed field of vision, as it has expelled ... the others from its inner space and replaced them with technical means of self-completion – the media in their modern function'.

Is this, then, the function of the printed page: to furnish the reader with such means? When we look at the surface of the page, are we – like Sangama – observing the face of another, both beaming at and speaking to us? Or are we – like Sloterdijk's modern individual – gazing into the mirror, seeing in it the reflection of our own self? Could it be because the page has taken on a mirror function, in a system of projection, that reading has become the solitary, silent and self-absorbed activity that it is today? What if we were to restore the pages of the printed book to the primary relation of interfaciality, given not in the optics of the mirror but in the mechanics of the printing press? And finally, could such interfaciality, in which each renders the other not a reflection but an affective echo, give us a model for human social life itself? These are large questions, and I am not yet sure how to answer them. What I am sure, however, is that they require us to think of the 'interface' in a quite different way from that to which we are accustomed.

Classically, in the field of design, the interface is understood as a *face-between*. As such, it is one component of a triad that defines the closed form of an object. The other components are surface and infrastructure.[11] The surface, characteristically smooth and opaque, divides exterior from interior – or, from the perspective of a 'user' of the object, the near side from the far side. The infrastructure comprises the inner workings of the object that lend it its functionality. Hidden and protected by the surface, they cannot usually be touched or seen. The interface, then, is made up of one or several interruptions or perforations in the surface that afford some sort of exchange between exterior and interior, allowing the user to activate the infrastructure. They come in the familiar form of buttons and keys, switches and knobs, all of which puncture the surface. The configuration of interfaces has always been a dilemma for designers. Too few, and the user's ability to control the object is compromised; too many, and the integrity of the object itself is placed in jeopardy. For it would end up, in the striking image of Vilém Flusser (1999: 81–4), 'with as many holes as a Swiss cheese'.

Now at first glance, there is a striking parallel between this view of the object surface riddled with holes and what Deleuze and Guattari have to say about the surface of the face. Recall that for them too, the face is a 'holey surface' (Deleuze and Guattari 2004: 189). In truth, however, these are surfaces of entirely different kinds. For like the body with its head – including apertures that are also said to mediate material and sensory exchange between exterior and interior – the object is constituted by the volume-cavity system. But the face, as we have seen, is produced by the white wall/black hole system. And in the terms of this latter system, the interface is not a face-between but a *between-faces*. Where the face-between is single but has two sides, near and far, the between-faces is double, but neither of its twinned surfaces has a far side. An obvious example of the former, which we have already encountered, is the windowpane. A slightly

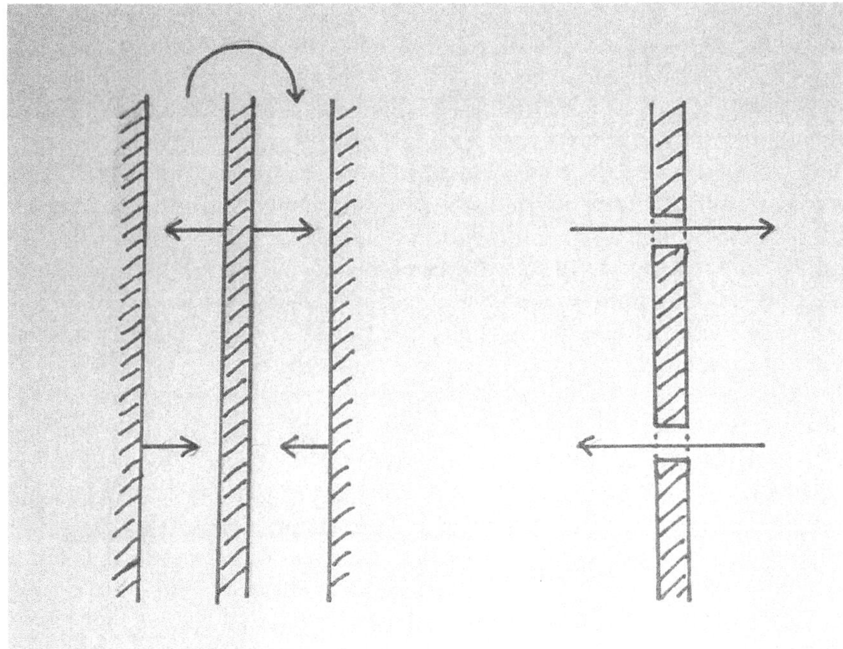

Figure 13.1 Two between-faces (left) and a face-between (right), in cross section. Whereas information can pass in either direction from one side of the face-between to the other, it is only possible to transition from one between-faces to another by turning.

less obvious example of the latter is in the meeting of surfaces under the press or, subsequently, in the surface-to-surface contact of pages in a printed book. This example is less obvious since ostensibly, a page is as two-sided as a pane. But it would be more correct to say of the page, printed front and back, that it has a reverse than that it has a far side. For like the two visages of the mythical Janus, god of transitions, back and front face in opposite directions; nothing passes through. To turn the page of a book is not to cross a face-between but to transition from one between-faces to another (Figure 13.1).[12]

Screen

Let me briefly double back to the comparison with which I began, of a printed book with a jewellery box. With its surface dividing inside from outside, its shiny contents, and the lid serving as an interface, the box is clearly constituted within the volume-cavity system. Perhaps the book, with its front and back covers and spine, could also be considered to be partially boxed. Raising the front cover lifts the lid on the book. But when it comes to turning the pages, the book no longer figures as a cavity with volume, accessed by way of a face-between, but as a volume in itself, comprising a gathering of between-faces. Ever since the birth of print, the materiality of the page, with its two faces pointing in contrary ways, each in surface-to-surface contact with the page preceding or following, has come increasingly into contradiction with a mode of perception that cuts directly through, as vision cuts through a pane. It is a contradiction between the two modes of interfaciality, respectively between-faces and face-between. Only in recent decades has the contradiction been resolved, decisively in favour of the latter, through the development of digital devices with flat-panel screens. On screen, there are no more pages to open or turn, only windows to look through. And with this, we come to the fifth and final chapter in our history of the relation between mark and surface. It is the story of the screen, and of how it has evolved to be the opposite, in every respect, of what it was originally.

Once upon a time, the screen was a woven fabric. From our earlier discussion in Chapter 10 (page 158), we may recall Gottfried Semper's idea of the membrane, draped over a tectonic frame, which dresses the rudimentary dwelling much as a body is dressed in clothes. In support of this idea, Semper (1989: 103–4) had drawn attention to the link between the German words for *Wand*, referring to a lightweight interior partition or exterior cladding,[13] and for dress or clothing, *Gewand*. Reworking the same idea, Flusser (1999: 57) would go on to describe the tent wall as a screen of woven fabric that gathers the experience of all who reside within its folds. The very word 'screen', for Flusser, brings to mind 'a piece of cloth that is open to experiences (open to the wind, open to the spirit) and that stores this experience'. He could equally well have been speaking, however, of the written or woven text. The screen could be a veil, a *Wand*, which – like *Gewand* – dresses a surface without dressing it up. Indeed Ruskin's earth-veil, Semper's *Wand* and Flusser's screen wall are of a kind with the hand-written manuscript. For as we have already seen, the text is also a surface that assembles, processes and disseminates experience in the very weave of its lines. Yet here I am, writing these lines on a laptop computer (to my regret and by force of circumstances, knowing that I would rather be putting pen to paper), staring at what everyone tells me is a screen. And it seems to have absolutely nothing in common with the textual surface. Indeed, so great are the differences that it might better be called an anti-screen. For the sake of clarity, however, I shall refer in what follows to the textual screen as *screen-T*, and to the computer screen as *screen-C*.[14]

The surface of screen-T is heterogeneous; on it, writing emerges as a continual differentiation within its veiled texture. But the surface of screen-C – the one I am staring at now – is perfectly homogeneous; it has no texture.

It is wholly unresponsive to the fragmentary letterforms that play on it, forms that seem to dance before my eyes. They are set off against a white background; however the background is not the same as the surface but lies somewhere behind, and shines through. Instead of a complex pattern of light and shade, screen-C sets up an invariant opposition of transparency and opacity. Moreover, while the lines of screen-T are woven with an attention that *goes along* – that is close-up, kinetic and haptic, infused with movement and feeling – screen-C demands an attention that *cuts through*, stopping movement and feeling in their tracks. This attention is optical, not haptic, and rests on a principle not of gathering but projection. As already noted (Chapter 10, pages 162–3), the distinction between the optical and the haptic overrides that between vision and touch: thus the medieval reader's vision is haptic as it accompanies the finger in tracing the letter-line; the touch of the computer operator is optical as the finger makes only punctual contact with the keyboard. Finally, if the epitome of screen-T is the fabric, the epitome of screen-C is the mirror. Writing on the laptop, nothing but my own words come back at me. There is no 'other'.

What we have in screen-C, in short, is something akin to the perspectival pane of optical projection, a perfectly transparent window that opens to a white wall, upon which the isolated and cogitating subject casts its thought. Indeed, the operating system I use, along with millions like me, is known as 'windows', and is branded with a design showing projected beams of light streaming through four rectangular panes of glass. Clearly, the manufacturers of the system are thinking along the same lines. They want us to compare the computer's screen to a windowpane, and it is not hard to do so. For them, moreover, it is an interface in the classical sense, coming between me and the hidden workings of the machine. With the apparent triumph of screen-C over the printed page, the material conditions for the production of the written word seem to have been cleared of any remaining vestiges of feeling. The fate of the book, in this clearance, surely gives a foretaste of what might become of our own social lives, which up to now have been lived for the most part like the book's pages – that is, between faces. What would social life be like in a world of face-betweens, a world in which every other is a projection of the self? Some would say that this is indeed the modern predicament. And where modernity goes, technology follows, bent on converting its imagined world into an experienced reality. Is it a world we really want? As you close the book of surfaces, and return it to your shelf, spare a thought for the future!

Chapter 14

Strikethrough and wipe-out

Tactics for editing the past

Under erasure

We are all familiar with 'track changes', as a function of word-processing. It allows us to insert deletions and additions into a text in such a way that these amendments remain visible to another party. But this is only a mechanical imitation of what we used to do in the past, when everyone wrote with a pen. Then, if you wanted to correct something, you would have to cross it out, maybe adding some substitute text between the lines or in a balloon. But what if you didn't want anyone else to see what you had done? With the word processor, erasure is all too easy: merely block the text, and with a touch of a button it is gone for good. How many of us, at one time or another, have erased text precipitately or by accident, only to regret it later? In a lecture delivered in 1990, Ivan Illich described the reactions of some of his associates in the early days of word processing, as they tried to get to grips with the new technology. Their first encounter with the 'delete' key left them upset, and in two cases physically sick. 'The disappearance of a blocked sentence', Illich (1991: 192–3) reports, 'and the closing of the gap by an onrush of words, were experienced by each of them as something offensive'.

Trying to cover your tracks on a handwritten manuscript, however, is another matter altogether. The older among us will surely recall the trials of removing pen-lines with a coarse ink-rubber. It was impossible to succeed without scuffing the paper itself. The challenge was to remove the line without rubbing off so much of the surface as to put it at risk of tearing. Marks made with a graphite pencil, of course, were easier to erase, yet the impressions made in the surface by the sharp pencil point would still remain. No paper, once written upon, could ever be restored to pristine purity. And if we go back even further in time, to the days when scribes wrote on parchment or vellum, the only way to erase previous writing was to scratch the surface with a knife. But since the inky stains could never be removed completely, new writing would always have to contend with interference from the traces of the old. In this, as we saw in Chapter 12, lies the genesis of the palimpsest.

DOI: 10.4324/9781003171713-18

While much has been written on the arts of verbal inscription, deletion and erasure have received less attention.[1] Rather more surprisingly, where they *have* been considered, there has been a tendency to confuse the two. Philosophers from Martin Heidegger to Jacques Derrida have described deletion as a matter of putting words 'under erasure' (*sous rature*).[2] My principal objective in this chapter, is to show, to the contrary, that deletion and erasure are operations of completely different kinds, with opposite effects not just on words but on the surfaces on which they are written. More generally, I shall show how this difference bears on the preservation, concealment and obliteration of traces of the past, whether on the page or in the ground, and thus on what it means to remember and forget. I shall show that what deletion strikes *down*, erasure brings *up*, and therefore that the idea of putting the past 'under erasure' is as oxymoronic as supposing that the way to bury a body is by exhuming it. Yet there is more, since passing off one as the other – deletion as erasure – is key to the illusion of camouflage. It has been used throughout history as a tactic to conceal acts of violence, and to contrive to eradicate the evidence of atrocity. Masking a deleted past under cover of erasure tricks us into thinking that it never happened.

To begin, however, I shall return to the operations themselves. What results when you cross words out or strike them through? How does the stroke of the pen, in the act of deletion, differ from the wiggling micromovements of the hand which produced the original text? How do both the stroke and the wiggle differ from the gesture or rubbing or scratching, in the act of erasure? And above all, what do these differences tell us about the relations between line and surface?

Crossing and wiping

In a world of life, lines grow from the tip. Roots and runners, feeling their way through the soil, twist and turn in response to ever-varying conditions. Shoots and saplings flex as they compete to find their place in the sun. On land, animals track erratically through the undergrowth, while birds flutter from branch to branch, or soar on winding currents of air. On a city street people weave in and out to avoid collision; in the countryside they walk irregular paths as they negotiate hedgerows, outcrops and puddles. And in the simple act of writing with a pen, fingertip gestures of the thinking hand leave a meandering trace in the form of the letter-line. This may proceed from left to right, as in most occidental writing systems, or from right to left or top to bottom. Yet whatever its orientation, the pen makes only slow progress from one margin of the page to the other. Much of the time it oscillates across the general direction of travel, or even loops back before issuing forth again. On a ruled page, as in an exercise book, the letter-line oscillates between the rules, much as on the loom, the weft oscillates between the warp threads. If the textual surface is woven, then to write on a page already written is not so much to write *over* it but to insert an additional thread *into* it. But with the stroke of deletion, as we shall see, it is quite otherwise.

The strikethrough is impetuous, violent and explosive. The axe, striking through timber, cleaves it in twain; the swords of warriors, striking through flesh, leave the battlefield strewn with severed limbs; heads roll from under the guillotine. And a canvas, slashed by the vandal's knife, is left with a gaping tear. In every case, the cutting edge is propelled like a projectile, under its own momentum. Striking through text with a pen, the gesture is no less forceful and impulsive. The hand swings into action, and proceeds without hesitation or deviation. While the letter-line, on its meandering course, gropes its way forward from the tip, never entirely sure where it is going, the line of the strikethrough flies like a projectile, under its own momentum, cutting through everything in its path. Unless guided by a rule, it leaves an arc-like trace in its wake.

Yet unlike axe, sword, guillotine or knife, the pen does not cleave the material but leaves it intact, its surface undamaged. An image such as on a picture postcard, crossed by a stroke, can still be seen; a text, as on the reverse of the card, can still be read. To be sure, the intruding line can get in the way, making both viewing and reading a little more difficult. But compared to slicing or shredding, which would tear the surface itself, splitting letters into fragments that would have to be reassembled to be read, the inscriptive strikethrough uniquely preserves its deletions, and may even enhance their significance. As the artist Jean-Michel Basquiat admits: '~~I cross out words so you will see them more; the fact that they are obscured makes you want to read them.~~'[3] Indeed it takes only a slight downward shift to convert the crossover into an underline, and deletion into emphasis. The question is: how is this possible?

Before proceeding to an answer, we need first to turn from deletion to erasure, and to consider what is involved in that other operation, of scratching or rubbing out. This calls for a back-and-forth oscillatory movement perhaps best described as a 'wipe' – a word derived from the Proto-Germanic *wipjan*, 'to move back and forth' (Ingold 2017c: 101).[4] To erase a parchment you would scratch the surface with a knife. This is to use the instrument in a manner contrary to its proper function. The knife is designed for cutting, but in erasure the sharp edge is drawn not longitudinally but laterally, so as to scrape material from the surface rather than incise a line through it. For erasing indelible lines on paper you would likely use a hard, abrasive rubber. Grasping the rubber firmly between the thumb and index finger, you drag it back and forth over the line you seek to erase, gradually shifting the axis of oscillation along its length. Both the paper surface and the rubber itself are progressively ground down by this operation, leaving a granular residue to be swept up afterwards.

Compared to both writing or drawing and crossing out, where the movement is brought to a focus at the point of pen or pencil, with erasure – whether with knife or rubber – it is distributed across a surface. The wipe is neither precisely measured out nor targeted; it covers a surface without delimiting it, and ever exceeds or overflows any delineations it seeks to remove. If the wandering of the pen, in writing, can be likened to the procession of roots through the soil, or of feet on a path, then scratching or rubbing out is akin to the way wind and rain work the surface of the ground, exposing roots, eroding footprints, and washing away tracks and trails. And it is precisely by this surface erosion that erasure is distinguished from deletion.[5]

Writing on the mirror

We can now return to the question I left hanging a moment ago: how can the strikethrough preserve, or even highlight, its deletions? Comparison with the cutting stroke of the axe, sword or knife offers a clue to the answer. For the woodcutter, for example, axe and tree belong to the same reality as he does, and the operation of felling timber sets up a circuit of perception and action in which all three – cutter, axe and tree – are conjoined. It is the same when you take a sword to flesh, or a knife to canvas. But with the stroke of the pen it is different. Physically, of course, the pen-nib is in contact with the very same surface, of paper or parchment, that already bears the inscriptions it sets out to delete. And the line it inscribes intersects the original lines of text. Ontologically, however, the text and its deletion belong to parallel but distinct planes of reality which are layered, one over the other, *without ever making contact.*

To explain how this is possible, let me revert to the example of the picture postcard. Suppose that the picture side bears a photo of an Alpine landscape, dominated by a famous peak. With a pen, you strike a line across the profile of the peak. Of course the mountain itself remains unscathed because your line has only effaced its image. But now, turn the card over, and do the same, striking your line across the handwritten message on the reverse. Is it any different? 'This is the Matterhorn', the message says, 'I am holidaying here and can see it with my own eyes'. Your correspondent is there, with the mountain, in the vastness of its presence. But you are not. You are at home, examining a small piece of card. And for you, as you read the words on the card, the experience they convey appears as inaccessible as a mirage. You can strike them out physically, but ontologically the words have a phantom presence that can be no more scarred by your pen than can the mountain.

We touch here on the same paradox as did René Magritte, in his celebrated painting of 1929, 'The Treachery of Images' (*La Trahison des images*). Beneath a cannily realistic depiction of a smoker's tobacco pipe, Magritte wrote the words *Ceci n'est pas une pipe*, 'this is not a pipe'. His point was that you cannot stuff a painting of a pipe with tobacco, however realistic it may be, let alone smoke it. Had he written 'this is a pipe' below the image, Magritte protested, he would have been lying. Yet despite his protestations of innocence, it is actually Magritte who is playing a trick on us, his viewers. The trick is to place both the image and the writing in the same picture plane. What we see, then, is an image not just of the pipe but of the writing. And the writing tells a lie, because in the reality the painting depicts, the pipe is indeed a genuine object, which you could stuff and smoke.

Likewise, your correspondent would have been lying had she written on the card, 'This is not the Matterhorn.' Of course a photograph of a mountain is not literally a peak that you can climb. Yet her actual words, 'this is the Matterhorn', framed as they are within the same edges of the card that frame the photo, tell the truth. What is real to her, however, is accessible to you only by way of its reflections. It is as if you were seeing it in a looking glass. Your deletions mark the glass, but they do not touch what is reflected therein. Your lines can no more tangle with the letter-lines of the text than they can penetrate behind the glass. Nor, conversely, can the letter-line emerge from behind the glass into the reality on the hither side. To be sure, the line can loop around itself and, as we have already seen, other lines can be woven into the same text. But the one thing the letter-line absolutely cannot do is cross itself out. Notwithstanding Magritte's claim to the contrary, *self-deletion is impossible*.

Thus while it might make no sense, as we shall see, to think of placing written words 'under erasure', the idea of placing them 'under deletion' – or better, perhaps, '*behind* deletion' – is not without merit. It would be equivalent to placing them behind bars or on the far side of a framed window. Just now, as I write indoors, at my desk, I can see through a picture window to the trees at the back of my garden. But the window is divided into panes, and the horizontal transom that divides the upper from the lower panes cuts straight across my view, obscuring a feature I want to see. I only have to raise my sights a little, however, and the transom line shifts, through parallax, from across the feature to directly beneath it, lending it a heightened prominence within the frame. Yet the transom, of course, belongs to the interior space of my study, not to the vista behind the glass.

So too with the strikethrough and the letter-line. All it takes to turn a strikethrough into an underline is to shift one's gaze a little. It is as if the two planes, respectively before and behind, or over and under, were not fixed in place but could slide relative to one another. But written lines exist in two dimensions, and cannot jump the planes to which they are confined. If self-deletion is impossible, so likewise, is self-underlining. And yet a certain kind of jump is possible; it is what we know as imagination. Thus while I cannot access the reality of my friend's Alpine holiday directly, I can fly there in thought. I can imagine it. Perhaps, then, the superimposition of the two planes epitomises the condition of the writer whose imagination roams heaven and earth while his hand, restricted to the interiority of the study, is locked into a myopic engagement with the page.

Rolling, folding and stacking

It is now time to return from the strikethrough of deletion to the wipe-out of erasure. I suggested earlier that erasure brings things up, rather than putting them below or behind. To explain this, we need only recapitulate our argument from Chapter 12. We saw there how repeated cycles of inscription and erasure, whether on the page or on the ground, lead to the formation of a palimpsest in which older inscriptions, far from being preserved beneath later ones, progressively rise to the surface. Here, the past comes up as the present goes down, in a movement of turning that I described as anti-stratigraphic, by contrast to the depositional layering of stratigraphy. To erase a surface is not to remove extraneous matter that may have been deposited onto it, but to rase the surface itself by stripping it down – whether by scraping, shaving, scratching, grinding, rasping or polishing. Common to all these operations is the removal of surface material. As with the erosion of a landscape through the prolonged impact of weather, erasure can expose to the elements features that were once deeply embedded, even as they are penetrated by the marks of present inscription.

Yet as I went on to show in Chapter 13, the surface of erasure or erosion *has only one side*. Whether it be the ground, the face or the page, we can see *into* it, but there is no going *through* it. Of course a mountain may be said to have more than one face, and every page has its reverse. But the only way to get from one to the other is by turning: by going around the base of the mountain or over the summit; or, as with the pages of a book, by lifting each page by its edge from the right, turning it over the spine, and then lowering it on the left. In this movement of lifting and lowering, such that one portion of a surface lies reversed over another, lies the meaning of the verb 'to fold'. The book itself, then, is a thing of folds. Originally, however, the written surface was not folded, in the manner of a concertina, but rolled up to form a scroll. To read, it had to be unrolled. This is where our word 'volume' comes from; it is derived from the Latin *volvere*, 'to roll'. Historically, the scroll gave way to the manuscript book, or codex, at the point when the parchment was gathered into sheets, folded and bound along one edge, and these gatherings, in turn, bound between hardwood covers (Boudalis 2018). With that, rolling and unrolling gave way to turning over. But the book was still called a volume. Open in the reader's hands, or on his desk, it would be seen not in its thickness but in the spread of its pages.

Not until the manuscript was replaced by the printed word was the book finally closed. For in the printed book, the pages are laid one over another to form a stack. Although you still have to turn the pages to read it, the book itself is now perceived as a thing of layered sheets to be worked *through*, top to bottom as beginning to end. Today, when you retrieve what you call a 'volume' from your shelf, it is to the layered stack that you refer. The book is now encased within its covers, giving it the character of a box. It has become a container, and the words its contents (Chapter 13, pages 199–200). By extension, then, the volume of any form, whether material like a wooden box or ideal like an abstract geometrical figure, becomes the measure of its capacity to contain. The voluminous gives way to the volumetric. What then becomes of the ground? Has it suffered the same fate, historically, as the book?

It is not, of course, possible literally to roll up the ground like a sheet of parchment. But it can be turned. Consider the medieval ploughman, who would turn the ground with every seasonal turn in the agricultural calendar: in April for spring crops, June for the late summer harvest, and October for winter wheat and rye. The purpose of ploughing was both to prepare the earth for future planting, by breaking up the surface residues of the previous crop, and to bring up nutrient-rich soil from deeper down. Unlike the scribe, working with parchment, who would have first had to scrape the surface before writing his lines, with the curved ploughshare the husbandman could combine erasure and inscription in a single act, at once cutting into the surface and raising soil from the depths. Thanks to this continual turnover, the ground would continue to yield, year after year. Following a cycle of rotation, fertility born of the past would bear fruit in present flourishing.

Indeed the ground, speaking to the husbandman with the bounty of previous harvests, was a surface not just of cultivation but of remembering. For with every turn, memories of persons who lived or events that happened long ago would be brought to the surface so that inhabitants could engage with them directly, as if present in the here and now. Again, this has its parallel with the pages of the book, which would speak to the reader with voices of the past, its letters and words springing to life in the present like seeds germinating in the soil. With the page as with the ground, the past would rise up, even as the present sinks down. And time, as it passed, would continue to turn.

In the modern imagination, however, enshrined in the political logic of the territorial state, the ground is not for turning. It is for conquest, colonisation and occupation. Far from inscribing its ways into the land as does the husbandman, or like the penman into parchment, the state imposes sovereignty from above, much as with the printing press, letters are imposed upon the sheet. Every new impression, then, calls for a new sheet, or a new ground. The ground, here, figures not as a surface to be actively restored and cultivated but as a passive substrate upon which to map out the strategic designs of the present. As such, it holds no potential for renewal. For the past is already over, sunk into its own stratum, overlain and deleted in the execution of present designs. And whatever their claims to perpetuity, these designs are destined, in their turn, to be deleted by those of the future. The earth's depth is now understood to be not so much enrolled in a cycle as layered in a stack, wherein every layer belongs to its own time, only to be superseded by the next. Renewal depends upon superimposition – on adding another layer to the stack, and then another, and another.

Time, then, no longer turns or folds the ground into a volume. It rather pierces through successive grounds like an arrow, pointing either upwards from past to present, or downwards from present to past. Here every ground, every layer, establishes its own plane of synchrony, while layer succeeds layer in a diachronic sequence.[6] To reach the past, as in archaeological excavation, you have to dig down. Memory has become an archive, deposited in a stack with the oldest records furthest down. And there they stay, sinking ever deeper as time moves on.

Camouflage and burial

Setting out from the distinction between deletion and erasure, or strikethrough and wipe-out, we have arrived at another, between two kinds of surface, whether of page or ground. One is the layered surface, which covers up what went before and is closed to what follows. The other is the deep surface, that covers nothing but itself yet nevertheless rises into the open. One is stratigraphic, the other anti-stratigraphic. I have presented these as alternatives, even to the extent of aligning them to a contrast between modernity and tradition. It is no accident that my examples of erasure have come from the practices of medieval scribes and ploughmen, whereas for deletion I have turned to the strategic machinations of the modern state.[7] Yet this contrast is surely artificial. Is it not more reasonable to suppose that these alternatives, far from standing on opposite sides of a great divide in the history of the world, have always existed, and have continually responded to one another?

In different periods, or regions, one side may have been ascendant, or weighted with greater ideological prominence, but the other would have ever been present in the background. It is, after all, in the nature of ideologies to be lop-sided. And they can deceive, by leading us to mistake one kind of surface for another. This is how camouflage works. It tricks the perceiver into supposing that what is actually a double-sided layer, covering up that which is hidden within or beneath, is really a face that is open to the world. Thus the military commander paints the tarpaulins under which he conceals his tanks in motley shades of green and brown, rendering them indistinguishable, to aerial reconnaissance, from the face of the earth. The face, as you will recall from the previous chapter, is a front without a back. And having no back – unlike a mask of disguise – it appears to have nothing to hide.

But the deceit can work the other way as well, though perhaps less intentionally. In many parts of the world, landscapes are dotted with mounds of various sizes, from the insignificant to the monumental. They have been around since time immemorial. Prehistorians call them *tumuli*. Just how and why tumuli were formed remains a matter of controversy, which need not detain us. Suffice it to note that any accumulation of waste material, whether from the construction of earthworks or from everyday domestic habitation, is liable to settle, more or less of its own accord, into the form of a mound (Ingold 2013a: 75–8). As such, the mound is no more than a swelling of the earth that covers nothing, and is open to the elements. This has not, however, deterred legions of prehistorians from excavating their *tumuli*, in the conviction that buried inside each must be a body, or perhaps a cache of treasure. Occasionally, they have struck lucky, to be rewarded with sensational finds. But more often than not, their excavations have yielded only quantities of earth and rubble. Their error has been to imagine the face of the earth as a twin-sided layer or enclosure which, consequently, must have *something* to hide. But could the practice of burial point to a different conclusion?

That many (though not all) humans are accustomed to burying their dead is irrefutable. In his *New Science* of 1725, the Enlightenment philosopher Giambattista Vico went so far as to speculate that the very word 'human' has its source in the Latin word for burying, *humando*, itself derived from *humus*, soil. Humans, then, would above all be people of the soil, who bury their dead (Chapter 20, pages 310, 318). They come from the earth, and will ever return to it. Might burial, then, establish a peculiarly human relation to the ground, and to the past, in which opening and closure, far from being mutually exclusive, may actually alternate?

Imagine the phases of a burial, as it might have been practised in antiquity. First, the earth is opened. Material is removed to form a pit, into which the body is laid. After the necessary ritual formalities, it is then covered with a slab of stone. In the grave, the slab forms a layer with two sides, upper and lower, concealing the body beneath. For the living, however, sealing the slab does nothing to extinguish the memory of the deceased; on the contrary, it remains deeply engraved in their hearts and minds. Yet with the passage of time and generations, memories gradually fade, even as vegetation encroaches over the slab, contributing to the formation of soil. Eventually, after many centuries or even millennia, the grave site is left indistinguishable from its surroundings, save perhaps for a small hump or a stone to mark its location. Once again, the ground of the site shows its face to the sky. With the grave long forgotten, people go about their lives completely unaware that anything lies below, until, perhaps, it is exposed by natural erosion or the ministrations of archaeologists.

As this story of burial shows, bringing closure to the past is one thing; erasing it quite another. Drawing a line over the past, or sealing it underground, will not make it go away. If anything, as with text under deletion, we strain harder to read it, bringing it even more insistently to our attention. Just as the insomniac's attempts to fall asleep make him all the more wakeful, so our efforts to forget the past have the opposite effect of bringing it more vividly to mind. Yet as surely as sleep eventually comes, so the past will be forgotten. In the mind, however, as in the landscape, it fades not by sinking deeper down but by rising to the surface.

And finally ...

What does all this mean for the way we think about memory? Our modern sensibilities, as we have seen, are profoundly conditioned by the idea that everything is formed of layers – that the ground, trees, buildings, books and even human minds are built up, layer upon layer, with each layer already marked up with its own striations. The past, then, is visible only by way of the translucence of the present. But the anti-stratigraphic logic of the palimpsest teaches us otherwise. It tells us that with the passage of time, material is not added but worn away, and that to mark it up means cutting deep. As in the palimpsest, our oldest memories are not the deepest, nor are the most recent the shallowest. On the contrary, what is furthest in the past is closest to the surface. In our minds as well as in the ground we tread, our recent deeds and words are most profoundly seared, while traces of the distant past are so shallow as to be on the point of disappearing altogether, erased by the winds of present suffering. Like old paths grown so faint as to be no longer recognisable, memories only truly fade as they surface into a present whose texture, like that of a veil, is opaque.

There is surely a lesson here for tyrants everywhere. For there is no denying that throughout history, deletion and erasure, which in the hands of the scribe or craftsman can be practices of curation or care, have also unleashed indescribable violence, visited by the powerful upon their victims. A defeated people may be ruthlessly incarcerated, struck from the record, or driven underground. Or they may be wiped out, and their lands and habitations destroyed. Total wipe-out, however, is no more possible than permanent deletion. On the one hand, the destruction of the wipe-out only brings more vestiges of the past to the surface; on the other hand, a past that has been covered up cannot be forever concealed from posterity. Deeds have their come-uppance, and will only be gone, once and for all, when they are finally obliterated by the ravages of time.

Part IV

Material thinking

Suppose you are a researcher, interested perhaps in construction, architecture, manufacture or handicraft. Coming across people at work – be it on a building site, in an architectural office, on the factory shopfloor or in a craft studio – you might ask them to explain what they are doing, or what they are making. And you might ask them about the thinking intrinsic to both doing and making. While I would not presume to anticipate the answers, I am pretty sure that the questions 'what are you doing?' and 'what are you making?' would evoke responses of very different kinds. The first would tell of the tasks that need to be carried out: on the building site, excavating foundations or bricklaying; in the office, drawing, modelling or consulting with clients; on the shop floor, tending to machinery, inspection and quality control; in the studio, maintaining tools and working with materials. But with the second, the focus would shift to final outcomes: the building, the architectural design, manufactured products, craftworks. And this difference between tasks and outcomes, in turn, would likely condition the sorts of answers you might receive to the question of thinking. The thinking that goes into tasks would involve attention, concentration and judgement, with decisions, for example, about when to begin or end any particular operation, or about the kinds, quantity and consistency of materials to use. But the thinking that goes into outcomes would be more representational. It would be about constructing an image of the end to be achieved, and keeping it in mind from start to finish of the fabrication process.

All of these responses would be of potential interest to your study. But in analysing the results you would face a problem. In a word, it is a problem of priority. Which comes first, making or doing? And depending on the answer, does representational imagining come before attentive concentration, or vice versa? A visitor from outside the working environment, such as a client or customer or an owner-manager, with little or no practical experience of what goes on in it, would likely recognise the end results, and judge them by comparison with initial expectations, while preferring not to dwell on all that happens in between. Researchers with backgrounds in cognitive psychology, trained to place the operations of the intellect before their

DOI: 10.4324/9781003171713-19

practical enactments, whether bodily or mechanical, tend to adopt a similar stance. Like business operatives, they would be inclined to attribute product innovation to the intelligence of a design process that lies in the novel recombination of ideas. For in the high tide of postmodern consumerism, novelty pre-empts the promise of renewal. Much of the hype that currently surrounds making feeds on the commercial imperative to innovate. From fab-labs to sandpits, places of making are turned into havens for self-styled 'creatives' to engage in tournaments of intellectual juggling, or bricolage, while the productive engagement with materials that actually gives birth to things is reduced to little more than the three-dimensional equivalent of a printout, calling for neither attention nor judgement. Doing, here, is hidden inside the box of making.

My aim in the chapters to follow is to reverse this prioritisation of making over doing. What if doing, instead, were to take precedence over making? And what if the thinking that informs it joins with materials as they are mixed, bent, shaped and transformed? For this is how it feels for practitioners engrossed in their tasks, in amongst the stuff and equipment of their respective trades. The builder, on site, is a protean earth-shifter; the office-bound architect a draughty pencil-pusher; the factory worker an artful mechanic and the craftsperson a deft handler of materials. All, in what they do, move stuff across a threshold from the virtual to the actual. The maker, then, is a demiurge who stands on the cusp, tasked not with bringing matters to a head, or designs to their conclusion, but with launching new beginning, giving birth to a world. This is what it means to place making within the fold of doing. Makers can still be conjurers, or bricoleurs. There is deviousness in their art, and a capacity for improvisation. But the improvisation of making-in-doing is antithetical to the innovation of doing-in-making; it is the wellspring of renewal rather than the brandmark of novelty. Real bricoleurs – unlike their fictional counterparts whose kaleidoscopic minds form new patterns with every shake of their fragmentary contents – have a feel for the heterogeneous materials with which they work, and breathe new life into them even in the course of their recomposition and reuse. The original meaning of *bricoler*, after all, is to tack or zigzag, to deviate. Thus with making-in-doing, the elements of a construction are not just added up but go along together. They don't only *ad*here; they also *co*here. Time enters constitutively into their production.

This, then, bears on how we think of thought. For the thinking that goes along with making-in-doing inhabits the fluidity of a world-in-formation, swirling in-between the fixed points that the logic of doing-in-making joins up. Thinking, in this sense, is not connective but contrapuntal, ever responsive to the material fluxes which occupy its field of attention. This is a far cry from the teachings of cognitive science, which has long presumed, as a matter of faith, that no new thought can arise save by reconfiguring the elements of old ones. In truth, a mind can only think the thoughts it does because of what the world lends to its continued functioning. Its thinking, then, is not inside-the-head but in-the-world; not cognitive but ecological. It is, as we say colloquially, an inspiration, a drawing in and holding of breath, wherein we take pause to recollect, to wonder and attend. 'Wait!', we say, 'hold on a moment, let's just think about this'. This sort of thinking is stressful, it winds up the thinker's mind with mounting tension, until finally, it is released back into action. Thinking-in-the-world thus disturbs thoughts-in-the-head, unravelling their connections and leaving loose ends for the wandering mind to follow. Without these loose ends, indeed, we'd be stuck. What would happen, then, if – instead of putting thought at the beginning, and the made object at the end, with the doing sandwiched in between – we were to situate both thinking and making within the life of doing? In these chapters, I venture some possible answers.

I begin this part, in Chapter 15, by taking aim at the much-vaunted concept of embodiment, with its implication that knowledge born of customary use is deposited as a silent or 'tacit' sediment, beyond the reach of conscious awareness and verbal expression, while words ascend to the heights of disembodied intellect. Focusing on the habits of craft, I argue that practitioners are anything but silent and unreflective. On the contrary, they think and speak as they work, with minds and voices enlivened by the sounds and feelings of the milieu. Both work and words, I insist, issue forth in practice as ways of telling. In Chapter 16 I draw on my own practice of cello playing to show how a thinking that opens up to life is marked by a quality of attention that brings things into presence, so that we can both feel and respond to them. Thinking that is 'response able', to adopt a term from composer John Cage, is also audible. But conversely, nothing more completely consigns thought to silence than closing it to feeling, or stopping it up like notes on a printed score. On the score, notes are joined *up*, or articulated, but in performance every note is a sustained line, which joins *with* other lines that differentiate themselves as they go along. That is, they correspond. In Chapter 17, I draw out the contrast between these two principles of joining, respectively of articulation and correspondence, to show how they are always found together, like a thing and its shadow. That is why the world we inhabit, though full of connections, is also one in which everything takes time to build and nothing lasts forever. Finally, in Chapter 18, I draw the craft of basketry into a reflection on what correspondence means for understanding the passage of overlapping generations and the continuity of life.

Chapter 15

Of work and words

Craft as a way of telling

Personal knowledge and the *habitus*

The greater part of what we know, we cannot explain. This is *savoir faire*, or know-how. The philosopher Michael Polanyi (1958) called it 'personal knowledge' – knowledge that adheres so closely to the person of the practitioner that it cannot be held up to scrutiny or posited as an object of reflection or analysis. Without it, Polanyi argued, nothing could be practicably accomplished. We could not tie our shoelaces, beat an egg, hold a pen, or ride a bicycle. But nor, for that matter, could we design a building, solve an equation, or compose a symphony. In these as in countless other tasks, we 'feel our way forward', as Polanyi (1958: 62) put it, following a trail and relaying it as we go instead of executing a predetermined and fully articulated programme of explicit rules or representations. It is not that there are no rules at all. But rather than furnishing the pegs that underpin the landscape of action, they more resemble signposts in the landscape itself, which point us in the direction we need to go. They are what we call rules of thumb, offering guidance without specification. In practice, they are more ostensive than prescriptive. Once set upon a course, we rely upon the reservoir of personal knowledge to carry on.

To uncover this reservoir, Polanyi believed, it is necessary to strip away the veneer of articulate representations, so as to 'lay bare the inarticulate manifestations of intelligence by which we know things in a purely personal manner'. What is revealed, then, is 'an immense mental domain, not only of knowledge but of manners, of laws and of the many different arts by which man knows how to use, comply with, enjoy or live by, without specifiably knowing their contents' (Polanyi 1958: 65–7). Here, as elsewhere, Polanyi could hardly have been more emphatic that his inquiries had disclosed a realm of *mind* – a 'mental domain' – the existence of which had been previously unacknowledged, or that until then, had not been accorded its due. Yet his discovery was destined to suffer an ignominious fate at the hands of subsequent social theory which had, albeit belatedly, realised that human beings are only present in the world because they

DOI: 10.4324/9781003171713-20

have, or rather *are*, their bodies. This realisation is commonly traced back to an influential essay on 'Techniques of the body', penned by the ethnologist Marcel Mauss in 1934.

Drawing attention to the sheer diversity of postures and gestures involved in such everyday tasks as walking, carrying loads, eating and sleeping, Mauss (1973: 73) realised that there is more to this than the kind of idiosyncratic variation that marks one individual from another and that in French would be called *habitude*. It is not just a matter of what you might happen to pick up or, conversely, of what you might improvise for yourself. Some children, Mauss noted, are more inclined than others to imitate the behaviour they observe around them, yet both weak and strong imitators, if they belong to the same society, are similarly educated by example and correction into forms of bodily comportment deemed proper to their age and status. To denote these forms, socially imposed rather than individually acquired, attributable to education rather than imitation, and thus enshrined in a tradition, Mauss (1973: 72–3) co-opted the Latin term *habitus*.

Mauss's prospectus for a comparative ethnology of techniques of the body was sketchy at best, and was soon forgotten by the anthropology of the time. With its fragmentary catalogue of apparently miscellaneous customs from around the world, the essay was so anachronistic in its formulation, and yet so far ahead of its time in terms of the questions it opened up, that it largely fell on deaf ears. Thus when, some forty years later, sociologist Pierre Bourdieu (1977) reintroduced the *habitus* as the cornerstone of a theory of practice centred upon the dispositions of the body, few recalled that he was following the precedent set by Mauss – nor did Bourdieu go out of his way to acknowledge the fact. Perhaps it was as well that he did not, since he took the term in a quite different sense. For by *habitus*, Bourdieu means a kind of practical mastery – a capacity to improvise conduct strategically attuned to the conditions of its production – that is neither picked up haphazardly, as one might pick up an infection, simply through personal contact, nor deliberately inculcated through precept and prescription. It is transmitted, rather, by what Bourdieu (1977: 88) highlights as the '*structural exercises*' which every society provides for its members.

These are exercises in which a body participates not as an instrumental means for the implementation or expression of a moral tradition but as a productive agent in its own right. Its postures and gestures, far from merely expressing thoughts and feelings already imparted through an education into societal values, are in themselves ways of thinking and feeling, through which these values are continually re-produced. Crucially, according to Bourdieu (1977: 87), the principles of mastery that are passed on by way of these exercises never rise to what he calls 'the level of discourse'. Psychologically, they remain underground, beyond the reach of consciousness. They cannot be articulated, or rendered explicit. Ineffable, incommunicable and therefore inimitable by any conscious effort, these principles are given body, made body, or literally *embodied*, as Bourdieu (1977: 94) puts it, 'by the hidden persuasion of an implicit pedagogy'. Now so far as I know, Bourdieu makes no reference to the work of Polanyi: he may not even have read it.[1] Yet with one hugely significant exception, the particular construction that Bourdieu places upon the *habitus* matches, point by point, what Polanyi claimed for personal knowledge: it cannot be articulated or specified; it is non-propositional and non-declarative; it is acquired and deployed without conscious awareness; yet it nevertheless subtends and makes possible everything we think and do.

It is no wonder, therefore, that for the generation of social scientists brought up on Bourdieu – and I am one of them – the temptation is to look back at Polanyi through Bourdieuvian spectacles, and to jump to the conclusion that by personal knowledge, he meant a knowledge whose proper domain is the body. Indeed Polanyi has even been criticised, in his insistence on the division between personal and articulate knowledge, for reproducing a Cartesian dualism of body and mind! Yet nothing could have been further from Polanyi's intention. As I have already noted, he was emphatic in his verdict that personal knowledge inhabits the mind, belonging to what he called the dimension of the *tacit*. In distinguishing the tacit from the explicit he makes it abundantly clear that his concern is to establish a division between two regions of the mind, not between mind and body. But this has not stopped many analysts, influenced by their reading of Bourdieu, from taking 'tacit' and 'embodied' to mean the same thing. The concept of embodied knowledge, as it has entered the received vocabulary of contemporary social science, rests fair and square on this conflation.

The silence of explication

In this chapter I want to take issue with the idea of the embodiment, by focusing on what I shall call *habit* – the habit of craftspeople, artisans, musicians, and scholars. My argument has two components. The first is to show that the habits that enable practitioners to move on in the accomplishment of their tasks are not so much sedimented in the body as generated and enacted in an attentive and kinaesthetic correspondence with tools, materials, and environment. And the second is to insist that this is as true of working with words as it is of working with non-verbal materials. To reach the domain of habitual practice, then, does not mean giving up on words, or probing beneath them. But it does mean giving up on the techniques of intellectual distillation that allow words to float to the top, and habits to sink to the bottom, of some imaginary column of consciousness (Figure 15.1). It is one thing, I contend, to argue that habits resist explication; quite another that they resist verbalisation. That the two have become confused owes much to ambiguities inherent in the notion of the tacit, and it is to these that I turn first of all.

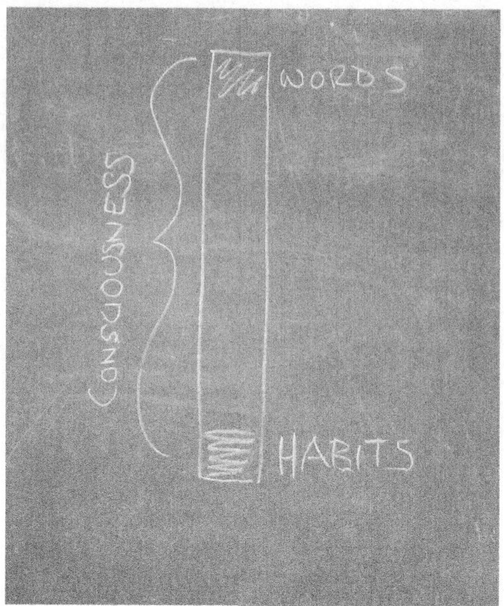

Figure 15.1 Words and habits in the column of consciousness.[a]

[a] This figure, like the others in this chapter (Figures 15.2 and 15.3), reproduces a blackboard sketch made during a lecture in which I first presented these ideas. I photographed this and the other sketches myself.

The philosopher Ludwig Wittgenstein concluded his celebrated *Tractatus Logico-Philosophicus* of 1922 with the most austere of pronouncements. 'Whereof one cannot speak', he intoned, 'thereof one must be silent' (Wittgenstein 1922: §6.54).[2] Taken literally, this injunction would consign to silence all ways of knowing and doing, all wisdom and experience, save that which can be expressed, linguistically or mathematically, in the form of logically interconnected propositions. Just because some things we know remain unspoken, however, does not mean we can do without them. It was Polanyi's great achievement to show that knowledge in its articulate expressions amounts to no more than the tip of an iceberg, the overwhelming mass of which lies submerged beneath the waves (Figure 15.2). His purpose was not to denigrate this submarine dimension but to highlight its contribution to thought and practice. As he put it, introducing a set of lectures entitled *The Tacit Dimension*, 'we can know more than we can tell' (Polanyi 1966: 4). But why did he choose the word 'tacit' to refer to this untold and untellable residue?

The word itself is tantalisingly vague. Derived from the Latin *tacere*, 'to be silent', it refers in the first place to that which remains unvoiced.

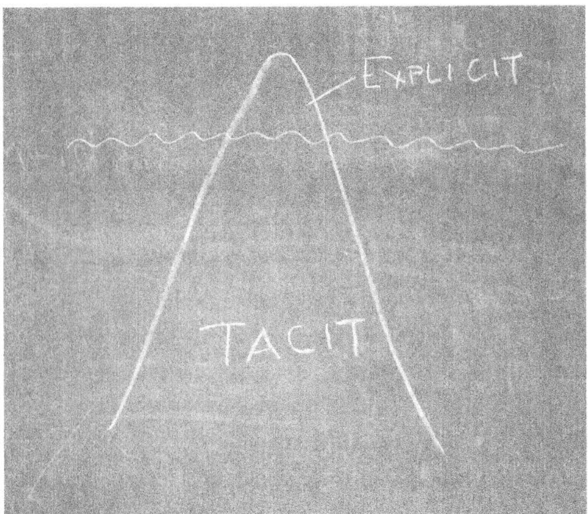

Figure 15.2 The explicit as the tip of an iceberg, with the tacit beneath the waves.

Yet voiced sounds need not be verbal, and verbal utterances need have no explicit propositional content. What are we to make, for example, of a song without words? And what of an utterance the force of which is illocutionary – such as an oath, a warning, a greeting, or a direction? Conversely, of many things that could be stated explicitly we may prefer to keep our mouths shut, for reasons of discretion or security. As philosopher of science Harry Collins (2010: 4) explains, in an extended commentary on the tacit/explicit distinction, whether a matter is voiced or even verbal is not really the issue for Polanyi. The tacit, for him is not so much the opposite of 'explicit' as of 'explicable'. It consists of things that cannot, by their very nature, be explicated.

So what does Polanyi mean by explication? Two terms keep cropping up in his account of what it entails, namely, 'specification' and 'articulation'.[3] To specify means to pin things down to fixed coordinates of reference; to articulate means to join them up into a complete structure. Thus we specify when we plot dots on a graph, enter values in an equation, or type words on a page; we articulate when we join them up: dots with lines, values with plus or minus signs, words with spaces. As these examples indicate, explication is not limited to verbal forms; it may also be algebraic or mathematical, or expressed in the peculiar language of symbolic logic. And it may also occur in the conventions of musical notation, where each note is specified by a dot, and where the dots are joined into phrases by ligatures. What do the graph, the mathematical equation, the written sentence, and the scored phrase have in common? They are all absolutely silent. Where everything is pinned down and joined up, nothing can move. And without movement there can be no sound. Specification and articulation, while they may be the keys to logical explication, lock the doors to movement, to sound and to feeling. They stop it up.

This brings us, however, to a rather surprising result. It is that nothing so effectively silences the world than rendering it in explicit, propositional terms. Strictly speaking, indeed, *it is the explicit that is tacit*, not the reservoir of habit or know-how for which Polanyi reserved the term. Habit, on the other hand, is turbulent and sometimes noisy. It swirls around in between the points that explicit knowledge joins up, like waters flowing around and between the islands of an archipelago (Ingold 2013a: 111). We have been persistently misled, I think, by the analogy of the iceberg, with the picture it presents of explicit knowledge at the tip and the mass of inexplicable know-how below. For far from having come to rest, frozen in submarine psycho-corporeal depths, know-how is restless, fluid, and dynamic. Above all, it is not deposited as a stable substrate, housed in lower levels of consciousness, but is fundamentally animate – immanent in the sensuousness of a body that is mobile, alive, and open to the world. Such a body – unified not anatomically but in its affective resonances – far from retreating into silence, dwells in sound.[4] Habits, in short, are not embodied; rather the body, in its habitation of a world, is ensounded.

Telling in the zone of hapticality

Evidently, tacit is a misnomer for the dimension of habitual practice. By what better term, then, should it be known? I would like to borrow for this purpose a concept from educational theorist Stefano Harney and literary scholar Fred Moten (2013: 98), namely *hapticality*. By this, they mean 'a feel for feeling others feeling you'. In effect, hapticality fills the void of the tacit. Where the tacit is silent, the haptic is noisy; where the tacit is embodied, the haptic is animate; where the tacit is sunk into the depths of being, the haptic is open and alive to others and to the world. With this concept in mind, we can return to Wittgenstein's injunction from the *Tractatus*. Is the world beyond the shutters of propositional language truly to be cocooned in silence? Try telling that to the birds, the wind, and the waterfall! They may have nothing to say – no facts to pronounce – yet how loudly they proclaim their presence in the world. And it behoves us to listen, for we can tell much from what we hear: whether the birds are calm or agitated, whether the wind is gentle or strong, whether the river is dry or in spate. And if we know the birds by their calls, the wind by the way it rustles the leaves, and the waterfall by the roar of its cascade, then likewise, it is by their voices that we know our fellow humans. The voice is the means we human beings have both of making our presence felt, and of feeling the presence of others. It is, for us, a medium of hapticality.

Does hapticality, then, lie beyond speaking, beyond telling? Is it beyond the shutters, while speaking and telling remain closeted within? This could only be true if we were to limit speaking, with Wittgenstein, to logical proposition or telling, with Polanyi, to articulate expression. Yet in practice, nothing can be proposed or expressed without feeling. There is thus another side to both speaking and telling, a side enacted in performance, in which points of specification take second place to the movements that swirl around and between them. My concern, at this stage of the argument, is with telling – I shall return to speaking in the final section of this chapter, when I move from work to words. For the present, then, let me return to Polanyi's premise, namely that we can know more than we can tell. Polanyi was interested, above all, in what it means to know. Right now, however, I am more interested in what it means to tell (Ingold 2013a: 109). Is there really no more to telling, I wonder, than explication? Might the capacity to tell, in truth, lie precisely in ways of knowing that *overflow* the fixity and logical closure of specification and articulation?

'To tell', of course, can mean many things. It is one of those ancient verbs that comes to us already thickly encrusted with the residues of previous use. Its origins, however, lie in the idea of reckoning or counting. In the past, a teller would be the one who would keep a tally, and whose place, even to this day, would be at the counter or the till. His modern representative, of course, is the accountant. Yet an account rendered in words rather than numbers is a narrative, a story. What, then is the difference between the accountant and the storyteller? The former assembles initially separate, point-specific entries into rows or columns. This, as we have seen, is the work of articulation. But the latter goes along, finding a way between and through the accountant's entry points. Storytellers are wayfarers (Ingold 2007a: 90–92). And like all wayfarers, they need to attend to things as they go, to recognise subtle cues in the environment and to respond to them with judgement and precision. They need to be able to tell, for example, where animals have been from their tracks, how the weather is about to change, how the river runs. This is the sense of telling I invoked a moment ago, in relation to the birds, the wind and the waterfall. It is about attention and response.

Now each of these two senses of telling – respectively the recounting of stories and the art of paying attention – entails the other. It is through having their stories told that novices learn to attend to things, and to what they afford, in the situations of their current practice. Contrariwise, it is because of the resulting feel for things – a kind of intimacy that comes from sharing a life together – that experienced practitioners can tell their stories. Moreover the capacity to tell, in these twinned senses, is critical to the practice of any craft. It is perhaps the principal criterion by which the expert can be distinguished from the novice. On the one hand, stories allow experts to tell of what they know *without* specifying it. The stories carry no information in themselves, no coded messages or representations. They rather offer guidance or directions which less experienced listeners, finding themselves in a situation similar to that related in the story, can both recognise and follow. On the other hand, by paying attention, experts can tune their movements to the ever-varying conditions of a task, as it unfolds in practice. They can tell precisely the right moment at which to make a move, when the forces that bear upon the success of an enterprise are in favourable alignment.[5] This, and not in the practised ability to execute standardised movements with greater speed or ergonomic efficiency, is where real skill resides.

In both senses, then, craft is a way of telling. It is a way that proceeds not by serial integration – not by adding or joining *up* what began as discrete, pre-specified entries in the book of accounts – but by joining *with* others, including the materials with which one works, along with other people and things in the environment. As such, the way of telling abhors explication. It sets down nothing in advance, nor does it project a future outcome in the present. What it does do is offer an itinerary, a path to follow, along which one can keep on going. This is about feeling forward, about anticipation rather than prediction, in a circuit of attention and response.[6] Along the way, of course, decisions have to be made, and every decision involves a kind of cut. The cut of telling, however, goes with rather than across the grain of action, not so much dividing it into segments as causing it to veer in one direction or another. Every veer is tantamount to what Erin Manning (2016: 118) calls an *inflection*: not a movement in itself, but a variation in the way movement moves. In effect, inflection establishes a differential from within the interstices of a field of practice, along which every practitioner lays down their own recognisable line, as distinct from the lines of others. In the zone of hapticality, in short, telling is a process of 'interstitial differentiation' (Chapter 4, pages 59–60).

Vortices of thinking and of sound

Now all this attention and response, all these decisions, are surely proof that craft practitioners are thinking. But have you ever wondered why we should think that thinking should be silent? Or that it should be invisible? Surely, if thinking is not tacit but as haptic as feeling is, if it is not buried in the body but overflows into the environment, if it unfolds in the telling, then it can be just as noisy. And we can watch it too. By what curious logic are we led to suppose that while we can watch the gestures of the potter as they caress the clay on the wheel, or hear the bowing of the cellist on the strings, the thought of both cellist and potter remains both invisible and inaudible? This logic is perhaps the legacy of a Cartesian division between cognition and action that continues to plague much theorising on these matters. For with this division, every deliberate action must be preceded by a thought which it serves to execute. Inevitably, then, thought breaks into action, interrupts it, gets in the way. It can even be said to paralyse action, as in the apocryphal story of the millipede which, when asked how it managed to co-ordinate the movement of its thousand legs, never moved again.

Yet manifestly, craftspeople are not paralysed by thought. For they are perfectly capable of thinking, even of reflecting on what they are doing and of assessing their work, *without ever breaking away from performance.* 'Reflection', as anthropologist Anna Portisch (2010: 69) writes, 'is a constitutive aspect of all levels of practice.' Portisch pitches her critique against many students of craft practice, myself included (Ingold 2000: 415), who have argued that the frequent need to reflect on progress, or to stop-and-check, is typical of novice practitioners, giving their work a jerky or stop–go character which gradually disappears with increasing mastery of the craft. In this view, the more fluent the practitioner, the less reflective the practice. But from her own study of women's crafts in Mongolia, Portisch (2010: 71–3) concludes, to the contrary, that reflection and assessment are integral to the practices of novices and accomplished craftswomen alike. Learning a craft, she argues, is at every level a process that is both dynamic and responsive, involving a continual dialogue with one's environment.

I am persuaded by her argument, but I still wonder whether reflection and assessment mean quite the same thing for the novice as for the old hand. It seems to me that the difference lies in the extent to which the practitioner has incorporated the tools and materials of her trade, as well as other salient constituents of the environment, into the dialogue itself. True, the old hand is as thoughtful – as meditative and reflective – as the novice, if not more so. But perhaps she is thinking *with* things more than she is thinking *about* them, letting them in as accessory to her own reflections. Perhaps her thinking is that of a mind that is not confined within the body but that extends outwards to include tools, materials and surrounding conditions, or what philosopher of cognition Andy Clark (1998) calls its 'wideware'. Could the measure of enskilment lie in the distal extension of the mind, radiating outwards from its seat in the body? The answer depends on how we choose to describe the mind.

For Clark, the mind is essentially a computational device that works to produce solutions to problems posed by the environment, on the basis of information received. But this device may include extra-somatic components. A mathematician, for example, may use pencil and notepad to perform a calculation, and a navigator takes up ruler and compass to plot a course. Thus pencil and paper in the one case, and ruler and compass in the other, are integral to the 'extended mind' of mathematician and navigator respectively. To explain what he means by the extended mind, and by way of analogy, Clark asks us to consider the prodigious talents of a fish, the bluefin tuna. Why, Clark asks, can the tuna swim so fast? The answer is that it couples its own bodily energies to the fluid dynamics of the water through which it swims, setting up eddies and vortices through the swishing of its tail and fins which themselves exert a propulsive momentum beyond any muscular force of which the fish alone is capable. Swimming, then, is an achievement not solely of the fish but of what Clark calls a swimming machine, comprised by 'the fish in its *proper context*: the fish plus the surrounding structures and vortices that it actively creates and then maximally exploits' (Clark 1998: 272). Thus it is not, strictly speaking, the fish that swims, but the fish-in-the-water.

It is just the same, Clark suggests, with the mathematician and the navigator. If the totality 'fish-plus-eddies-plus-vortices' comprises a mechanism for swimming, so the totality 'mathematician-plus-pencil-plus-notepad' or 'navigator-plus-ruler-plus-compass' comprises a mechanism for computation. The cognitive machine, in the human case, is extended in just the way that the swimming machine is for the fish. Or is it? I am not so sure that swimming can be understood in such mechanical terms. After all, eddies and vortices cannot exactly be connected up like the wheels, cranks, and pistons of an engine, in such a way as to deliver propulsion as a motor effect. They are energetic movements in themselves, as indeed is the fish. To recall our discussion in Chapter 3 (pages 42–3), the fish-in-the-water – like every other living being in its proper medium – is a *whirl* (Cavell 1969: 52). It is not an object that moves but the emergent form of a movement.

Might the fish, then, offer a better analogy for why the thinking that goes into craft practice *cannot* be understood in computational terms? Perhaps we could say of this thinking, too, that it is a churning of the mind, as it stirs up and is in turn stirred by the sounds and feelings of its milieu. The mind, then, is not so much a computational device as a vortex in the mix. How else can a potter armed only with a wheel turn clay into the myriad forms of jugs and vessels? How can the scribe, armed only with a pen, turn parchment into text? How can a player armed only with a cello make such an immense and variable sound? Not, surely, because the practitioner's brain, body and instrument, joined together, make up a machine, whether for potting, writing or playing. In practice the hands of the potter join *with* the clay, in the rotation of the wheel, in such a way as to give form to the contours of feeling. It is the same for the scribe, whose every gesture leaves its mark, by way of the pen, on the writing surface (see Chapter 12). And taking up my cello, as I bring my bow into contact with the string, I feel its vibrations under the finger of my left hand as I bow with my right, while the sound gushes out from the unison of breath and gesture with wood, hair and metal.[7]

In every case – be it the potter, scribe, or cellist – the anatomical unity of practitioner plus instrument gives way to a hapticality of sensory awareness and vital materials. It is for this reason that I believe we should resist the temptation to describe mind, body, and world as overlapping fields which, in their enlargement, are inclined to encroach upon or even encompass each other's domains. The mind is not 'taken into' the body, as conventional appeals to the concept of embodiment tend to imply, nor does it 'take up' the world, as implied by the theory of its extension. The fish-in-the-water gives us a better picture, in my view, of a whirligig world of spiralling movements that run into one another: of thinking spiralling into rounded vessels of clay, into the oscillations of the scribal letter-line, into vortices of sound, all of them dynamically sustained formations in the current of life (Figure 15.3).

The principle of habit

We have come a long way from Bourdieu, and from his understanding of the *habitus* as a set of dispositions that both generate the mastery of the skilled practitioner, and are in turn generated by it, all beneath the radar of conscious awareness. For what we have discovered, on the other side of explicit logical articulation, is not a lack of awareness but *an awareness of a different kind*. It is the awareness of feeling others feeling you – or in a word, it is hapticality. This explains why craftspeople, absorbed into their tasks, by their own report tend to experience their own presence and movement, and the presence and movement of the persons and things with whom and with which they engage, with heightened rather than diminished intensity. Colloquially, the word we use for this is *concentration*. By this, we don't

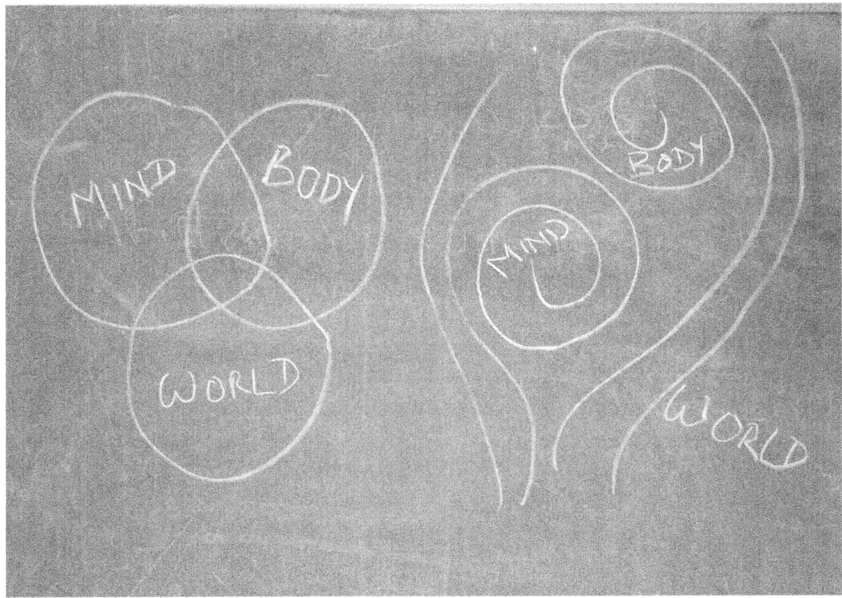

Figure 15.3 Mind, body and world, as overlapping fields (left), and as spiralling movements (right).

mean the kind of cognitive processing that delivers solutions for implementation. It is not the operation of a joined-up computational mechanism, whether inside the head or extending beyond it. Concentration lies rather in the affective unison of haptic and kinaesthetic awareness with the movement and vitality of materials.

The recognition of this other form of awareness, concentrative rather than cognitive, haptic rather than explicit, at last offers a way of resolving a question to which the answer has long eluded us. For there is no doubt that many things we routinely do involve no concentration at all. We are often scarcely aware we are doing them. With these operations, the more practised we are at them, the less thought and attention they demand of us. They are markedly unresponsive to surrounding conditions, to the extent that if conditions change, they can break down or lead us astray. They seem virtually automatic. In principle, automatic operations could just as well be done by machine, and indeed in the history of technology they have often been among the first to be mechanised. The question is: how are we to distinguish such automatisms from the practised mastery of a craft?

If no other awareness were possible save that which reflects and reports on practice from the outside, which intrudes into it and holds it to account, then we would risk reducing craft practice to the level of bodily automatism. It would be negatively characterised by the absence of conscious deliberation. And to an extent, this is precisely what has happened in social scientific writing on embodiment and the tacit dimension. You would think, from reading much of this literature, that there is not much difference between touch-typing and performing a Rachmaninov piano concerto. It may be that the latter is a lot more difficult, and takes a great deal of practice that none but the most dedicated musician would willingly endure. In both cases, however, we are led to believe that it is all a matter of leaving the fingers to take care of themselves, freeing the mind for higher things. But if the pianist is truly thinking with his fingers, if his thought flies with the sounds of the keys, if he feels the presence of listeners whose ears stretch to catch every passing sound, and if he and they are truly moved by the experience, then there is all the difference in the world between his performance and – say – that of a player-piano that has been mechanically programmed to reproduce the same piece. And the difference is simply this: the master-pianist's performance unfolds along a way of telling, the machine performance does not. All true craft, as I have endeavoured to show, is a way of telling.

The ossification of telling in the language of embodiment, its reduction to a kind of sediment, has its parallel in the way we tend to speak of habit. It has become common to treat as habits the things we do unthinkingly, and without consideration. They are often regarded as the unwanted detritus of ordinary activity, behaviours that have fallen out of active commerce with the world and become stuck in repetitive patterns or even addictions that may have meant something once but no longer have significance today. They do not require to be learned so much as unlearned. Usually they are judged to be bad. When did you last hear anyone talking about their 'good habits'? But I believe there is more to habit than this, for it is a word that speaks more affirmatively of custom, of use, of dress, of care, and even of virtue. Indeed this latter sense of habit, as inherently virtuous rather than addictive, has a long and distinguished pedigree in Western thought, going back to Aristotle, continued by Hegel, and culminating in Félix Ravaisson's famous essay of 1838, *Of Habit*. Yet according to philosopher Catherine Malabou (2014), in a recent preface to Ravaisson's work, his great achievement was to show how there cannot be one sense of habit without the other – how the very recognition of habit as rote repetition depends on habit in the other sense, as a 'power of beginning', thanks to which repetition comes to be perceived as difference (Malabou 2014: viii–ix).

The difficulty with the concept of habit has always been to decide where to place the doer (Carlisle 2014). Are we, so to speak, in front of our habits or behind them? Do we make our habits or do our habits make us? The problem arises so long as we are forced to choose between the active and the passive voice of the verb, that is, between what we do and what we undergo. But in his reflections on art as experience, John Dewey (1987) argued that we would do better to understand habit in terms of the relation between the two.[8] Neither in front of what we do nor behind it, we are in the midst: our doing is also our undergoing, what we do is also done in us. In our intercourse with the world, Dewey (1987: 109) explained, we also inhabit the world. Or in a word, we *dwell* in habit (Ingold 2018a: 21–2). This, perhaps, is as good a definition as any of what it means to practise a craft. A way of telling is also a way of dwelling, of inhabiting, which – far from remaining stuck in a groove of endless repetition – continually reopens to new possibilities of use. I would like to think of habit, like craft, as a way of telling.

With the principle of habit, moreover, telling is also using. To use something, after all, is to draw it into your habitual, or usual, pattern of activity. Both you and it work together as brothers-in-arms, to joint effect. And conversely, to be used to a thing is to accept it into your life as part of your custom. For philosopher Giorgio Agamben (2016: 64), habit is first and foremost 'use-of-oneself', in which the user puts their very existence at stake by allowing it to be affected, even constituted, by the thing used. Thus 'human being and world are, in use, in a relationship of absolute and reciprocal immanence' (Agamben 2016: 30). This is how habitual use differs from utilisation. For to utilise a thing is not to put one's existence at stake at all, but rather to repudiate any affective involvement, or common feeling. The protection of the self behind the triple lock of *-ise*, *-ate* and *-ion* ensures that the instrument and what it touches are held at arm's length, eliminating any possibility of cross-infection between human being and world. Utilisation, however, is the modus operandi of explication and articulation, not that of telling. Things become instruments of telling only in their use.

And when the things we use are words, our ways of telling become ways of speaking. With this, I come to the final part of my argument, in which I shift my focus from works to words.

Beyond verbalisation and embodiment

Words are the habit, the dress, of human life. For most of us, as we go about our business, they furnish our principal means of telling. With words we invite others to gather round, converse with them, join our own life-stories with theirs, attend and respond to what they say and do. Our words can be noisy or quiet, turbulent or serene. Enriched by the patina of everyday use, ever varying in texture, they can caress, startle, enchant, repel. In speech they well up on the breath, their sounds sculpted by movements of the tongue and lips. The words of signed language are no less animate, although formed by gestures of the arm, hand, and fingers rather than the voice. Nor do I only speak or sign. For my speaking speaks me into being, into life. So too, my signing signs me. Whether spoken or signed, my words bring me into the presence of others with ears to listen or eyes to observe, who know me by voice and gesture for the being I am. Even in writing, words spill out onto the page as the hand – now hesitating as it waits for coming thought, now racing to catch up with it – leaves a meandering trail in its wake. And while I might write unobserved, the traces that my hand leaves upon the page, when they eventually meet the eyes of the reader to whom they are addressed, can nevertheless rekindle the feeling that went into their formation.

In every case, whether spoken, signed or handwritten, words are performed in bodily practice, and birthed into the zone of hapticality. Why then, in the writings of social and cultural theorists, are words so often expelled from this zone, as if they had no business there? Why should they be consigned to the space of inanimate articulation? We are repeatedly told that words can never take the measure of feeling, that they can offer at best a stunted window on the reality of bodily experience, and that we have to go *behind* the words, or *beneath* them, if we are to plumb this experience to its depths. In the eyes and minds of theorists, words have been stripped of their power to move, to affect or to evoke. They have instead become tools of the intellect, utilised rather than used, wholly given over to projects of explication. Drained of feeling, removed from the tumult of performance, and barred from contact with the things of which they speak, words find themselves imprisoned in the silent seclusion of what they are supposed to stand for, namely concepts. But words cannot be held to blame for their own incarceration. The blame lies, rather, in the suppression – above all by an academic establishment anxious to defend its authority in matters of representation – of those very voices that inhabit the word, that breathe life into language and cause it to tremble (Manning 2016: 24).

Like all other organisms, human beings must breathe to stay alive. They breathe, alternately, in and out. The voice, however, is carried only on the outbreath. In a society such as our own, in which fluent, articulate speech is viewed as the supreme index of intelligence, the outbreath tends to be relatively prolonged, and the inbreath foreshortened, so as to reduce pauses to a minimum and not to interrupt the flow. Of course the pauses are there, but we are trained to conceal them, lest we should appear lazy, hesitant, or indecisive.[9] There is nothing universal, however, about this effort to conceal the pause. It is rather a historical consequence of the modelling of speech as literate articulation – that is, as an enchainment of letters and words into rigid syntactic structures. In this model, the pause is an unproductive gap that should ideally be closed. It is considered unproductive because all the thinking, which the words are meant to convey, is assumed to have already been done by a cognitive machine that sits atop the apparatus of speech, and delivers its outputs for execution. This assumption, as we have seen, is shared even by cognitive theorists, such as Clark, who would extend the mind beyond the compass of the brain to include the body in which it is housed, and the world in which both brain and body subsist.

The extended mind, in the view of these theorists, is a cognitive engine with the logical connectivity of a machine, the operation of which is undisturbed by the aerial currents that swirl around and in between its interlinked parts. It is the machine – now including somatic and extra-somatic components – that does the thinking, leaving the voice, on the outbreath, to manage the speaking, and the inbreath with nothing else to do than to reload with air. Thinking, then, is speechless, and speaking thoughtless. In our experience, however, thinking cannot be thus cut off from the life-sustaining process of respiration. Rather, we think even as we breathe. The pause on the inbreath is itself a pause for thought, where to think is to feel, to pay attention to things, to gather the forces and energies of one's surroundings, to recollect and prepare. It is, quite literally, to draw inspiration – to breathe in as one is breathed upon (Ingold 2015: 139). And on the outbreath, in turn, this pent-up feeling, modulated by the voice, vents into the zone of hapticality. Here, in inspiration and expiration, the muscular heave of the lungs merges with the cadences of the voice, with speech and song, and with thinking. All are together on the same plane of being, in the spiralling currents of mind, body and world (Figure 15.3).

That breathing is a bodily process goes, of course, without saying. It is another matter altogether, however, to say of the practice of breathing that it is embodied. Literally, the *em-* of embodiment signifies an implosion, deposition or incorporation, whereupon the body folds in on itself. And this is the very opposite of breathing. For on the outbreath, the body gives out to the world rather than taking it in. Were it prevented from doing so – were the intake of breath to settle inside – the body would suffocate! It is precisely in its suffocation at the hands of social theory, albeit not literally but figuratively, that words and muscles part company, appearing in separate registers of verbal cognition and behavioural sediment (Gatt 2020; Ingold 2020). As words are raised to a pinnacle of self-consciousness, so bodily practice sinks the silent depths of unconscious automatism. The result is the opposition between verbalisation and embodiment, the one allegedly explicit, the other tacit, that so much academic analysis has taken as its starting point. My objective, to the contrary, has been to restore both words and habits, ways of speaking and ways of telling, to hapticality. Habits are no more sedimented in the body than words liberated from it; rather, both words and habits are *animate*, carried forth on the breath of life.

Chapter 16

Thinking through the cello

Opening declaration

'I have nothing to say and I am saying it.' So began the composer John Cage (2011: 109), in his *Lecture on Nothing*, presented in New York in 1949. Behind the play on words, Cage was being deeply serious. In this chapter I want to explore what he was getting at, and to draw out its implications for the way we think, not just about the world we inhabit but about thought itself. In the spirit of Cage, I shall conduct my inquiry by way of an instrument. That instrument is a violoncello. In an ideal world, I would be present in person with my cello as you read this, so that you could both hear me speak and listen as I play. Instead, I will have to ask you to imagine my voice and my performance. I realise that this is a big ask, but it is critically important that you attempt it, since unlike Cage, I do have something to say, and it is to show why a thinking that opens up to hopes and dreams – that is, to life – must be one that is attentive to things, that brings them into presence so that we, in turn, can be present to them. For only in the presence of things can we feel them, and only through feeling them can we respond. My inquiry, in short, is into the conditions of what Cage (2011: 10) called 'response ability', though for reasons I shall explain below, I prefer the term 'correspondence'.[1] I want to establish the possibility of a form of scholarship that sets out neither to understand the world around us, nor to interpret what goes on there, but rather to correspond with its constituents.

Imagine, then, that I sit down to play. Let us suppose that I play the opening bars of the prelude to the third suite for unaccompanied cello by Johann Sebastian Bach (Figure 16.1). If you are familiar with the piece, or if you are a cellist yourself, you will know that these bars launch the suite with such pomp and certitude as if you were throwing open the ceremonial doors to a great banqueting hall, after which the guests start streaming in. Later, they will perform a series of courtly dances, making up the following movements of the suite. The first bars of the prelude are tantamount to a declaration: let the festivities begin! Yet, in playing them, I have nothing to declare. No coded information is smuggled in with the notes. It is not as

DOI: 10.4324/9781003171713-21

Figure 16.1 The first lines from my copy of the score of Bach's third suite for unaccompanied cello. The pencilled annotations are my own.

Photo by the author.

though I wrap some contraband into the sound which you unpack upon receipt, like the contents of a parcel. Nothing is sent or received. The bars stand only for themselves. Their force – to adopt a technical term from the philosophy of language – is *illocutionary*: it resides in the performance itself and what it achieves, not in some semantic content to which it refers.[2] To play is to create an auditory ambience in which anyone within earshot can participate. And to listen is to harness one's own awareness to this ambience, to join with it and respond to it. In this your entire body becomes an extended ear, alive to the sonorities of the environment (see Chapter 7, page 110). When I play those first bars of the prelude, I throw open the doors to the suite; as you listen, your ear-body sweeps through them into the gilded rooms that continue to unfold as the performance proceeds.

Letting sound be

This, precisely, was Cage's point. He wanted us to acknowledge that to listen is to be in the presence of sound, to lay ourselves open to it and attend, not to extract some meaning from the sound that has first been encoded into it and for which it serves as a vector of propagation. His aim, as he put it, was to 'set about discovering means to let sounds be themselves rather than vehicles for man-made theories or expressions of human sentiments' (Cage 2011: 10). To achieve this, he explains, the first step is to cease thinking of sound, in the first place, as music, and of hearing as what we do, specifically, when listening to music. For no sooner do we declare that what we hear is music than we impute to it an intention by which it is distinguished from the unintended sounds of nature, whether of the wind or rain, or a waterfall, or thunder, or even the nervous excitation or heartbeat of one's own body. If there were no sound not deemed to be musical, then these 'natural' sounds would be expunged from conscious awareness. We would be deaf to all sound that does not disclose a motivation and that leaves no expression in its wake. That is why we are inclined to speak of the 'silence of nature', despite all the noise it makes! Straining to discern the music from its background, we close our ears not only to the terrestrial and subterranean echoes of earthly existence but also to the celestial sonorities of wind and weather.

In effect, this is to split music from life. 'When we separate music from life', said Cage (2011: 44), 'what we get is art (a compendium of masterpieces).' The cello suites of Bach are commonly considered to be masterpieces. But that is because the arbiters of high culture have decreed that they be apprehended not as sound, but as formal compositions *rendered* in sound, much as the portraits hanging on the walls of the banqueting hall are rendered in paint. But colour is everywhere, not just in paintings. So too, sound is everywhere, not just in music. We do not only see, as art historians sometimes seem to think, when looking at paintings; nor do we only hear when listening to music. A sound does not project itself as the expression of a thought, nor does it depend on other sounds for its elucidation. It is *there*, becoming itself, in all its urgency and singularity, unimpeded and energetically broadcast, 'occupied', as Cage (2011: 14) put it, 'with the performance of its characteristics'. To attend to sound *as* sound (or likewise, to attend to colour *as* colour) is to feel these characteristics – of duration, pitch, amplitude and timbre – and to respond to them. Once we allow sounds to become themselves, once we attend to them as such – and not to anything that might be being conveyed by their means – we cannot remain unfeeling in their presence. The *feeling* of sound: that is what Cage (2011: 10) meant by 'response ability'. This feeling invests both my playing and your listening with a quality of attention.

The move, in Cage's thinking, from intention to attention is critical. For if intention separates subject from object, mind from nature, art from life, attention restores the player or listener to that which is real and present in the immediacy of lived experience. Etymologically, as noted in Chapter 8 (page 120), the word 'attention' comes from the Latin *ad-tendere*, meaning 'to stretch toward', and it well describes what happens when I begin to play the cello. Perhaps I intend to practice or perform. I take the instrument from its case, apply rosin to my bow, adjust the endpin, take my seat and tune up. But once under way, it seems that I and my playing are one and the same. I *become* my playing, and my playing plays me. I am there, not in front but in the midst of it, animated by its gesture and rhythm. I feel the pressure of the bow against the strings and the vibrato in the left hand, as I stretch the sounds from the resonant chamber of the instrument as if they were viscous or elastic filaments. Listening, you stretch your ears to join with them, as indeed I do myself, ever responsive to their perceived tonality. The thread of sound and the thread of feeling twist around one another, as each – in its ongoing movement – answers to the other, much as a stream, swollen by rain, answers to the earth through which it runs while at the same time continually reshaping it. In an essay on musical improvisation, violinist and composer Malcolm Goldstein draws precisely this analogy:

> I follow the line,
> am molded by it, yielding, as I mold it
> like a brook after rain pours through
> dirt, rocks, trees and grass, finding
> new subtle twists and turns as things move,
> are moved in the flow.
>
> (Goldstein 1988: 4)[3]

Like stream and earth, sound and feeling co-respond. That is what I mean by 'correspondence' (Ingold 2017b). And if I prefer the term to Cage's 'response ability', it is simply because of the emphasis, conveyed by the prefix, *co-*, on the mutuality of the response, of going along together.

What then is silence? In a world of life, according to Cage, absolute silence would be impossible. Silence could never be anything other than a quality of ambient sound, reliably if unpredictably present to those with ears to hear – ears not so preoccupied with their owners' intentions as to be inattentive to the world. 'Where these ears are in connection with a mind that has nothing to do', as Cage (2011: 23) put it, 'that mind is free to enter into the act of listening, hearing each sound as it is, not just as a phenomenon more or less approximating a preconception.' You were listening long before I began to play. You heard my chair-legs squeak on the floor as I took my seat; you heard me tune up; you heard the rustling crisp-packet of your neighbour and the cough from the back row. And now you hear sound pouring from my cello. What's the difference? That there is a difference is not in doubt, since with my playing I command your attention. 'Listen to me', I demand, 'and do not be distracted by coughs and crisp packets.'

I would not go so far as Cage, however, in attributing the difference to the existence in my mind of a preconception, which the sound from my instrument is purported to deliver to your receptive ears. As I play those opening bars of Bach's third suite, I am declaring but have nothing to declare. I am opening the doors to the banqueting hall, not providing an inventory of its contents. However certain the declaration, it does not give voice to a preconception. It has no propositional content. 'I have nothing to say', to repeat Cage's own declaration, 'and I am saying it.' The paradox is that if silence lies in having nothing to say, how come that it can be so overwhelmingly sonorous? Conversely, does saying something really make any sound at all?

To play is to feel

Let me return to my foray, in the last chapter, into the nature of telling by reiterating Ludwig Wittgenstein's notorious aphorism from the *Tractatus Logico-Philosophicus* (1922: §6.54): 'Whereof one cannot speak, thereof one must be silent.' Now I cannot deny that I would be hard pressed to explicate what happens when I sit down to play the cello, least of all in terms that would come close to satisfying Wittgenstein's conditions of logical consistency. I could neither specify its conditions with any precision nor articulate them in the form of instructions for action. And as we found from our discussion of Michael Polanyi's approach to personal knowledge (page 231), specification and articulation are the twin keys to explication. I might, however, like cellist and psychologist Dor Abrahamson (2020: 224), find other ways to register my experience in words. Abrahamson describes how he would jot down in a notebook the 'fragile, evanescent insights' from each day's practice, later to condense them into epigrams, 'idiosyncratic turns of poetic phrase', which he could then, on the following day, 'animate back into practice'. These were not articulated in the strict sense, nor did they specify exactly what to do. But they did help to restore a certain feeling, allowing each day to pick up from where the last left off.

But what of the music itself? Granted that there are ways of using words that are non-propositional, is it not also the case that there are ways of explicating propositions that are non-verbal, as for example in mathematics and symbolic logic? Could not music also be one of these ways? Did not Bach, for example, *specify* that I should open the third suite for unaccompanied cello by playing a middle C? And are this and the following notes, making up those first two bars of the prelude, not *articulated* to form an elegantly structured phrase? Might it not be argued, then, that a musical structure is indeed *explicated* in performance? Never mind that the music is composed of notes and phrases rather than letters and words, is the principle not the same in both cases? According to the visionary landscape architect Lawrence Halprin (1969: 12), the notation of Bach 'is as precise and controlling as he could make it, what was left for the performer was a matter of technique and interpretation'. Reaching out over the centuries, it is as if Bach had left us with no alternative but to follow his specifications to the letter. The performer, for Halprin, is a mere technician, his task to execute in every detail an immaculately conceived design. In principle, a machine – less fallible and untroubled by affect – could do a better job.

There are of course many ways in which this view can be faulted. It is historically inaccurate, in that Bach was writing long before the idea of the composer as the independent and sole author of complete musical works had even emerged.[4] And as anyone who has tried playing Bach's music knows all too well, so much is left unspecified in the notation that the same piece, in alternative hands, can sound altogether different. But that is not what presently concerns me. My point is rather that it is simply impossible for a living being to play without feeling – without the awareness we have of our own movement, and of its correspondences, otherwise known as *kinaesthesia* (Sheets-Johnstone 2011: 115–28). With the cello as any other musical instrument, playing and feeling, movement and attention, are two sides of the same coin. As I have argued elsewhere, 'to play is itself to feel, so that in playing, I put feeling *into* the music' (Ingold 2000: 43). To feel is not to pin things down but to join *with* them in their growth and movement. Wherever there is life there is feeling and, as Cage taught, wherever there is feeling there is sound. The note printed on paper has no feeling, and is therefore soundless. But as soon as I begin to play, the note erupts into sound, into life. Thus what is notated on the score as a point becomes, in my playing, a sustained and vibrant line.

To play even a single tone, such as middle C, is no simple matter. It is rather like drawing an absolutely straight line freehand. To draw the line, one's body must be finely balanced and tensed throughout, with an acute awareness of its immediate environs, while the elbow of the right arm, holding the pencil, describes a trajectory at once outward and backward as the angle of the joint varies from obtuse to acute and the wrist adjusts to compensate.[5] Bowing involves similarly controlled movements of the right arm, elbow and wrist, to ensure that the position where the bow remains in contact with the string, between bridge and fingerboard, remains more or less constant (Winold and Thelen 1994). In short, the singular tone arises from a complex choreography of highly attentive, mutually attuned movements, of arm, wrist and bow. Feeling lies in this kinaesthetic attunement. The ancient Greeks called it harmony (from *harmos*, meaning 'joint'), a word that originally had no musical reference at all. It could refer to the joining of beams and masonry, in the building of houses, temples or ships, but also to the joining of limbs in the body (Ilievski 1993). From the root syllable **ar*, common to both the noun *harmos* and the verb *ararisko* ('to join'), are derived a host of other words including the 'arms' of the body, the 'arts' of the builder and of course 'article' and 'articulate'.[6]

In modern usage, however, despite sharing the same root meaning of the join, 'harmony' and 'articulation' have parted company. Whereas harmony, now commonly applied to musical contexts, retains the sense of the joining *with* or correspondence of sympathetic movements, articulation has come to mean the connection of rigid and discrete parts. Such is the articulation of the bones of the skeleton which, in anatomical reconstruction, appear joined *up* rather than *with*. Divorced from life, the bones feature as the elements of an assembly. So too, with standard notational conventions, musical notes are set out the stave, joined by ligatures (Figure 16.1). The ligatures themselves do not index sounds but only the connections between them, and their temporal ratios. Here, articulation is an exterior connection, a coupling of pre-specified elements. With correspondence, to the contrary, every movement participates from the inside in the generation of every other, while at the same time distinguishing itself.

Am I, then, using my cello to assemble the notes as I transition from one note to the next in the musical score? Is my performance an articulation? Certainly not! A sustained tone, as we have seen, is a movement in itself. To shift from tone to tone is thus to bring about a movement in the movement, or in a word, an *inflection* (Manning 2016: 117–18). Through inflection, every tone – itself a line of movement – emerges with its potential directionality, differentiating itself from what came before. It follows that musical form arises not from the connection of points but from the inflection of lines. To play a phrase such as in the first two bars of the Bach suite is not to link predetermined tones into a chain but to split them from the inside through a series of inflections. Or to recall a concept that I have already introduced on several occasions, it is an exercise not in specification and articulation but in *interstitial differentiation*.

The silence of the score

This exercise of differentiation is anything but still and silent. On the contrary, it is alive with movement, and vitally sonorous. Yet pinned down and joined up as on the printed score, reduced to mere notes, sounds are rendered lifeless and inert. They have no room to move or breathe. If sound is what we want, or what we mean to hear, then we should cease our attempts at explication, remove or brush aside the stoppages that drive feeling underground, and allow things into sentient presence. Cage's declaration – 'I have nothing to say and I am saying it' – can thus be read as a direct rebuke to the author of the *Tractatus*. For Cage refuses to be silenced. His words may have no object, no referent, no matter to convey, yet he has a voice and will be heard. *Whereof one cannot speak, thereof let it resound*!

Consider again the difference between the melodic line that I stretch out from my cello and the sequence of connected notes printed as black dots on the stave. The line weaves its way through the field of ambient sound in rather the same way as a path through the variegated undergrowth of a forest or the grasses of a meadow. Made by walking and traced along the ground, the path marks a line of differentiation. It emerges from the interstices of the ground in the very course of walking it. But while the path-line thus differentiates itself from the ground, the reverse does not hold. In Chapter 12 (pages 192–3), I argued that this is also true of the letterline of handwriting, whether on parchment or paper. Here, the line distinguishes itself from the surface without the surface distinguishing itself from the line (Deleuze 1994: 29). And so too the melodic line, while it distinguishes itself from ambient sound, never parts from it. The line is rather woven into the texture of its ambience.

With the notes of the score, however, it is as if the line of sound were detached from the matrix of its generation and divided into measured segments. Each segment is then stopped up into a point, and each point staked out upon a flatly homogeneous surface. Every note is a stoppage, reconnected to other notes in sequence by means of ligatures which bear no more relation to the surface than does the surveyor's rope, tied between stakes, to the ground.[7] Where the path differentiates itself from the ground without ever parting from it, the rope stands high and dry above the ground across which it is stretched. The path is the trace of a movement, the rope a connection of stoppages. As with the stakes and the rope, the notes of the score and their connecting ligatures are indifferent to the surface on which they are printed, as indeed is the paper to the notation. In the case of the score, the surface is a sheet of white paper, while the notation is printed in black. The score is literally black-on-white. On the score, difference is bilateral: as the notes and ligatures distinguish themselves from the paper surface, so the paper is distinguished from the notation printed upon it. Like an exploded diagram, the score specifies the elements of a completed work and shows how they articulate. Moreover it is silent. Its silence is the empty, exoskeletal silence of a world already broken up and dismembered, all energy spent, eviscerated of any traces of affect.

There is however another kind of silence which is just the opposite. It is the silence of a world so compressed, so concentrated, so tightly knotted, that nothing can move (Ingold 2015: 111). This is not the silence of an already exploded world, but of a world on the verge of exploding. It is the silence of the predator, all eyes and ears, waiting to pounce, or of ice before break-up, or of the eye of the storm. Let us return to the score of the third prelude and to the very first note. It is middle C, and is marked by a solid black dot, crossed through by a ledger line one up from the five lines of the stave. Remember that in Bach's day, composition and performance were not clearly demarcated as they are today. One could almost think of the work of composition itself as a calligraphic performance, carried on not with instrument and sound but with pen and ink. We can imagine Johann Sebastian (or just as probably, his wife and copyist Anna Magdalena), pen in hand, hard at work on the score of the third suite. Think of how much mental energy is concentrated in the gesture by which he digs his pen (or she hers) into the manuscript to inscribe that first middle C. Think of the attention and expectancy that go into that black dot! Is the silence of the score, then, so empty after all? Perhaps it is so, in the mechanically printed reproduction, filed away in a drawer or on a shelf. But what of the handwritten original?

In his essay of 1926, *Point and Line to Plane*, the great pioneer of modern abstract painting, Wassily Kandinsky, considered the dot of musical notation as one exemplar of the elemental point (Kandinsky 1979: 43–5). Like any other element, Kandinsky argued, the point can be experienced either outwardly or inwardly. Outwardly, the point or dot is simply doing its job within the conventions of a notational system, just like a well-functioning tool in a toolbox. In a verbal text the full stop or *punctus* indicates the end of a sentence. A dot on the stave-score indicates a note. And so long as we remain on this outward level of the 'practical-useful', to which we are accustomed by force of convention, we remain indifferent to the stop or dot as a figure in its own right. Context is everything. But suppose instead that we wrench the element from its usual habitat and enlarge its mass. As we do so, Kandinsky (1979: 25–8) writes, 'as we gradually tear the point out of its restricted sphere of customary influence, its inner attributes ... come out of the depths of its being and radiate their energy ... In short, the dead point becomes a living thing.' Freed from the practical-useful, the point begins a new 'inner-purposeful' life as an *independent being*. To apprehend the point inwardly is to feel its explosive potential. With this the dot that marks middle C on the score appears no longer empty but full to bursting. It is like a seed on the point of germination.

Were Bach and his wife, then, methodical gardeners, planting their seeds in orderly rows such that they will burst forth in an ever-growing tangle of vegetation? Digging the pen into the manuscript, as the gardener would press seeds into the earth, they would have sown their notes not in a void of silence but in the field of ambient sound, whence – in performance – they would take root and grow. Thus, far from inheriting from Bach a comprehensive set of specifications for the execution of an already completed work, as Halprin would have it, we find ourselves tending the garden that he and Anna Magdalena planted together – a garden that will continue to grow for as long as their music is performed. Playing the music of Bach, I draw the threads of sound from the dark, resonant depths of my instrument, much as green shoots rise from their black, earthen matrix. In performance, the inner tension compacted in the dot of the score is transferred to the outward tension of the string. At the moment when I apply the bow and the string begins to vibrate, the potential energy of the dot is released, and it becomes a line. Neither will seeds grow, however, nor will written notes erupt into sound, if filed away in a drawer or on the shelf. To come to life they must be restored to the open air. I am reminded of the words of one of the great contemporary exponents of experimental music, Cornelius Cardew (1971: 108): 'A musical score is a logical construct inserted into the mess of potential sounds that permeate this planet and its atmosphere.'

Taking flight

What, then, are these sounds that permeate the atmosphere? They are not simply physical vibrations in the medium, nor are they sensations confined within the mind of the hearer, beyond the reach of any vibration. As we discovered in Chapter 7 (pages 104–5), drawing on the phenomenology of

Maurice Merleau-Ponty (1964), sound is neither in 'in the head' nor 'in the world', neither mental nor physical, but experiential and atmospheric. It is generated in the fusion of the affective and the cosmic, where what is heard turns out to be our own hearing. Yet in this fusion we are also blown apart such that – much as in a dream – we are simultaneously at home in our bodies and at large in the cosmos. This is true moreover of the experience not only of sound but also of light. The parallel is instructive, as we can observe from a simple experiment.

Go outside and cast your eyes skywards. Then bring your index finger to your forehead and give it a tap. Feel the hard, bony surface. Yes, you are definitely still there, at home in your body, and have not melted into the ether! But on second thoughts you are not so sure, for you are perplexed to find that in the visual field your finger strikes no surface but rather looms as a ghostly, intruding presence that casts its shadow in the void. It is, as you might say, 'in your face'. Now head and face, as we learned from our discussion in Chapter 6 (page 96), belong to different orders of reality, respectively anatomical and physiognomic, which rest on different topologies of the self. One puts you inside your body, as its interior inhabitant, but in the other the walls of the body dissolve and you find yourself at large in an atmospheric world that returns the body to you as a spectre. That's why we can have two such different experiences at once. Suppose, now, that I repeat the experiment with my cello. In the anatomy of the cello, the fingerboard is its forehead and the resonant chamber its chest. Bringing my finger down on the fingerboard, I feel the hardwood surface just as I felt the bony surface of my forehead.[8] Yes: I am here, and here is my cello; we are joined anatomically. Yet again, on second thoughts, the finger is but a phantom presence that touches nothing but has inveigled itself into the midst of the physiognomic field of audition.

With both iterations of the experiment, we find that the finger shows up simultaneously in two quite different ways: corporeally, in the tactile space of contact, and as a phantom, in the atmospheric space of experience. This double-take accounts, in turn, for the curious combination, in playing an instrument like the cello, of sedentism and flight (Ingold 2015: 109). For I can be seated on a chair, right here, and yet be possessed of the means, as Merleau-Ponty (1964: 186) would put it, to be 'absent from myself'. Sitting with the instrument between my knees and its endpin piercing the floor, body and instrument are tightly conjoined into an anatomical unity. Yet no sooner have I set bow to strings than the instrument explodes, and I do too! I am no longer a body with mouth, hands, arms and ears; rather my entire body, in its movements and sensibilities, *becomes* mouth, hand, arm or ear. I am mouth-body-becoming (breathing), hand-body-becoming (fingering), arm-body-becoming (bowing), ear-body-becoming (listening). I used to be disturbed by recurrent nightmares in which my cello appears to have disintegrated, and in which I too am lost and undone (Chapter 8, page 122). But I now realise that these dreams re-enact the very conditions of performance. For only by breaking apart the therianthropic unity of body and cello can it be put together again, not organically or anatomically, but quite differently, *as a tissue of affects*. Whereas before body and cello had been joined *up*, as a totality of parts, now wood, varnish, metal, hair, rosin and air join *with* mouth, hands, arms and ears in the generation of atmospheric sound.[9]

It is in the correspondence of affects – in their feeling for one another – that sedentism gives way to flight. Sound takes off, and I take leave of myself. Here's Goldstein again, vividly evoking this correspondence in a poem entitled 'The Gesture of Sounding':

Gesture of breath and contact
in motion, touch
of wind and finger upon
wood, hair, skin and metal,
gut, ivory and felt
bodies/objects transformed in their sounding,
as mouth releases, impressing,
the air within
outwards,
and fingers and wrist articulate
from root of spine (and deeper)
the totality of who
we are, that moment resonating
both inward impulse and outward
realization being
one.

(Goldstein 1988: 49)

Not only does sound take flight in the correspondence of affects, however. So also does thinking. It has become common, even conventional, to observe that pianists 'think with their fingers', and violinists and cellists likewise – though not with just their fingers but as Goldstein suggests, with wrists, lungs and trunk, indeed the whole body. This observation lends support to the idea that thinking is not an exclusively inside-the-head operation, confined only to the brain, but is facilitated by the 'wideware' of a mind that extends across brain, body and instrument (Clark 2001). However, our review of the so-called 'extended mind hypothesis', in the last chapter, led us to a different conclusion, namely, that thinking is not so much the operation of a joined-up cognitive device, whether in the head or extending beyond it, as the churn of the vortex set up in the correspondence of kinaesthetically attuned movements. Its coherence, in short, *is not articulatory but harmonic*. This is as true of the playing of the violinist, in Goldstein's case, as it is of my playing the cello. It is not the output of a mechanism but a tissue of affects.

It is not as though I take up my cello and bow, as I might a notepad and pencil, or ruler and compass, in order to achieve results that I could not accomplish unaided. As Goldstein intimates, I am not chained anatomically to the instrument; rather my breath, touch, manual gesture and spinal posture join in unison with wood, hair and metal in a correspondence of sensory awareness and vibrant materials – the one stretching or attentive, the other stretched or tensed – wherein consciousness, in the words of Gilles Deleuze and Félix Guattari (2004: 454), is 'thought of the matter-flow' and material 'the correlate of this consciousness'. In this correspondence, sound takes flight, even as I remain seated. And so, of course, does thinking. Thought cannot fly; only thinking can. There is movement in thinking because connections unravel, leaving loose ends in search of company to correspond or join *with*. Correspondence, not articulation, is the guarantor that thinking can carry on.

Explicit knowledge, as we have seen, calls for specification and articulation. Thought, it is often said, should be joined up. But if all thought were thus finally connected, nothing could move. It is a mistake, I think, to conflate thinking with conceptualisation, if by that is meant the accommodation of experience to a pre-existing framework. Thinking, surely, lies not in this but in the *excess* of experience over conceptualisation – an excess we commonly associate with imagination. As thinking goes beyond thought, so imagination goes beyond imagery. This beyond is the realm of hopes and dreams in which overflowing experience, edging into form, has yet to surrender to partition and categorisation.[10] Thinking unsettles thought. It is in this sense a de-positioning, a practice of exposure that is tenuous, hesitant and fraught with risk (Masschelein 2010: 278). But only when we take the risk can thinking fly. Every line of flight, as Deleuze and Guattari (2004: 343–4) write, has its loops, knots, speeds, movements and gestures, but above all, its sonorities: 'there is always sonority in Ariadne's thread'. The field of thinking, like that of audition, is a tissue of such open-ended threads, with the topology of a reticulum (Rojas 2015: 226).

Why, then, should anyone suppose that thinking makes no sound? This assumption, so familiar to us today, would never have occurred to our medieval predecessors, who would describe the practice of meditation by the same term, 'rumination', which was routinely used for cattle chewing the cud (Ingold 2007a: 17). In their understanding, thinking goes in and out just as breathing does, 'both inward impulse and outward realization being one' – to recall the closing words of Goldstein's verse. Or as Merleau-Ponty (1964: 167) insists in the same vein, 'there really is inspiration and expiration of being'. He meant this quite literally. For when we breathe, it is not just the body that takes air in, and lets it out, as though the mind could be left to float in the ether of the imagination. We breathe with our entire being, indissolubly body and soul. Thinking is the breath of the soul, and its sound is a murmur, an undercurrent on the verge of forming itself into articulable words. But the modern science of cognition – in separating thinking from doing, intellection from performance – has silenced thought by attributing it to the workings of a virtual machine. And by the same token, it has reduced performance to inherently thoughtless, physical or mechanical execution. In this chapter I have put the contrary view. Thinking through the cello, I contend, is not cognitive but atmospheric.

Chapter 17

In the gathering shadows of material things

What does it mean to join things? The question is simple, but the answer, as we shall see in this chapter, is anything but. 'To join' is such a common, everyday verb, but perhaps for that very reason it has largely passed under the radar so far as scholarship is concerned. Yet it is only because things are joined that the material world can manifest any kind of coherence, and only because of its coherence can this world be inhabited. Once you start looking for them, joins are everywhere, in such a bewildering variety of guises that it is difficult to know where to begin any systematic investigation. There are knots and bindings, ties and ligaments, seams and stitches, catches and couplings, clasps and fastenings, hooks and hangers, clips and pegs, bolts and screws, and so on and on. Turning from things to words, the vocabulary for joins and joining, in English as in any other language, is just as rich and diverse, if not more so. In the course of writing this essay I have looked up the meanings of a host of words in the *Oxford English Dictionary* – including 'add', 'accompany', 'apply', 'assemble', 'append', 'annex', 'attract', 'articulate', 'adhere,' 'aggregate', 'associate', to list only those beginning with 'a' – and all include 'join' among their many meanings.

Underlying both words for joining and things joined, however, there does seem to be one fundamental contrast. To get at it, take a sheet of paper and a pencil, and draw a number of points. Then take a ruler and draw lines between every pair of points so as to create a network. The points are now connected *up*. But now suppose that each of these points be set in motion. As your hand moves the pencil, its point describes a line. How, then, might you join these lines? Think of them as threads. Like threads, you might gather them together, forming a knot or bundle in which they are tightly tied in the middle, but with loose ends fanning out in every direction. You could say that the lines are joined with one another, into a nexus (Figure 17.1). So we have 'network' and 'nexus', both incidentally derived from the same Latin verb *nectere*, 'to bind', whence 'necessity'. Thus necessity, too, betokens the join. But is this the necessity of *predetermination*, in which everything is connected, or is it the necessity of *constraint*, in which things are so bound together that each, along its own way, participates in the fortunes of the

DOI: 10.4324/9781003171713-22

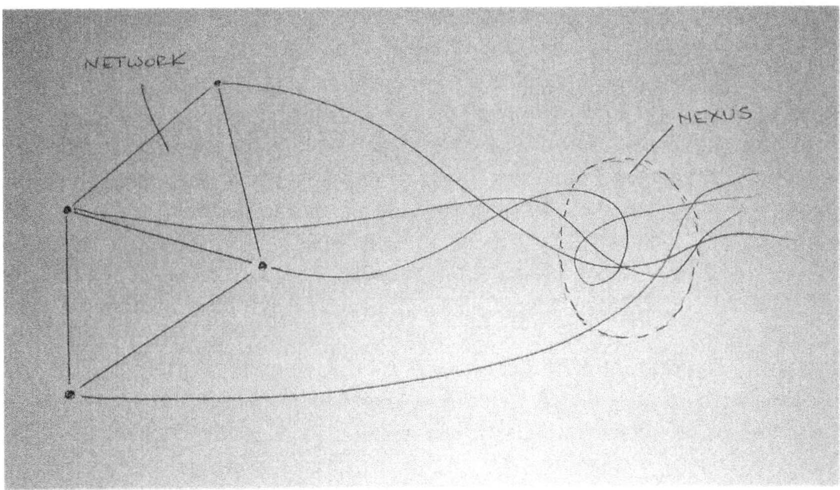

Figure 17.1 Network and nexus: sketch from a lecture.

others? Is it about joining *up* or joining *with*? In what follows, I shall seek to show that this contrast, between up and with, gives us alternative ways of thinking about the join which are premised, respectively, on ontologies of being and becoming.

In a world of being, things have already precipitated out from the processes of their formation and are available for connection as discrete parts or entities. Contemporary theorists like to speak of such connection as *articulation*, and of its more or less contingent, networked results as *assemblages*. But in a world of becoming, the focus shifts to the processes of material formation themselves and to how they go along together. For this going along together, or joining with, I use the term *correspondence*, and the nexus formed in the process is what I shall call a *gathering*. Thus articulation is to correspondence as assemblage is to gathering. And while I do not want to insist that joining is all one and not the other – that it is all *up* rather than *with*, or vice versa – I do think that an acknowledgement of the difference is an essential first step towards understanding how these two principles of the join moderate one another in the production of a world which appears on the surface to be full of entities and their connections yet in which everything takes time to build or grow and in which nothing, neither entity nor connection, ever seems to last.

The assemblage

Nowadays, the idea of the assemblage is very much in vogue, a must-have accessory for every aspiring theorist. The term has become a something of a catch-all, denoting any collection of stuff, of any kind, contingently thrown together by force of circumstance. Just about anything and everything, it seems, can be one. 'Assemblages', writes political theorist Jane Bennett (2010: 23), 'are ad hoc groupings of diverse elements'. The attraction of the idea lies in its appearing to offer a compromise between the alternatives of supposing either, on the one extreme, that the elements in question sacrifice any individuality or autonomy they might once have possessed, on their own, to their membership of the whole of which they are now integral parts, or, on the other extreme, that their association does nothing for them at all, neither limiting nor enhancing the capacities that each can bring individually to bear. In the assemblage, elements are indeed affected in what they can do by their association, while yet retaining their autonomy to break away and to combine with other things. The assemblage, then, is neither a whole that has fully incorporated its parts nor one that is finally reducible to them. In it, heterogeneous things are added together, but the sum, as Bennett (2010: 24) says, is 'non-totalisable'. You can go on adding, or you can take things away, but as every sum is contingent on the event, there is no final answer.

For the philosopher Manuel DeLanda (2006), a leading advocate of assemblage thinking in social theory, what matters above all is the *exteriority* of the relations between associated elements. They may adhere, aggregate or arrange themselves into ever more elaborate compositions, yet these compositions can just as easily fragment, only to be reconfigured in alternative permutations and combinations of elements. In whatever configuration they appear, however, the elements remain forever foreign to one another, arrayed in collage-like juxtaposition along the lines of their adjacency. In essence, if not in effect, they are given independently of their association, and remain unaltered by it. For were it otherwise – were they to enter into relations on the inside – they would immediately sacrifice any individuality they once had to a new and irreducibly different entity formed of the merger, as an alloy, for example, is formed of base metals. In short, assemblage thinking denies the possibility that entities can relate on the inside while yet remaining true to themselves. Everything there is thus exists, fundamentally, in itself, and it as such – and not, for example, as a mere stand-in or place-holder for human intentions and purposes – that we should attend to it.[1] This is the founding premise of what many today have taken to calling the 'new materialism', a somewhat hyperbolic brand-name for what is actually an assortment of approaches that have little more in common than the resolution to take material things seriously. And 'assemblage' is at the heart of it.

But the word has been around for a lot longer. Common to English and French, it has meant much the same in both languages.[2] For its earliest sense as a collection of diverse matters, the Oxford English Dictionary finds a precedent in John Locke's *Essay Concerning Humane Understanding* of 1690, where the assembled matters were in fact ideas.[3] Subsequently, the term was taken up in geology, and specifically in palaeontology, to refer to the group of fossils characteristic of a geological sediment. And from there it entered archaeology, as a term for the association of prehistoric artefacts particular to a site or context. Though already used in this sense by prehistorians of the mid-nineteenth century, notably Sir John Lubbock, the term did not really come into its own in the field of archaeology until the 1970s, in connection with new thinking about behavioural adaptation and deposition processes (Schiffer 1976). More than merely marking out successive strata in the occupation of a site, assemblages came to be seen as the lingering fall-out of intentional and structured human activities, subjected in varying degrees to erosion and decay (Joyce and Pollard 2010). Since the 1990s, the term has even found its way into the study of community ecology, where it has been defined as 'a taxonomically related group of species that occur together in space and time' (Stroud et al. 2015).

However the adoption of 'assemblage' by new materialists – archaeologists among them – owes nothing to these precedents. Its roots lie in another lineage altogether, namely the vitalist tradition of continental philosophy that began with Henri Bergson and culminated in the writings of Gilles Deleuze and Félix Guattari, subsequently promulgated in the 'assemblage theory' of DeLanda.[4] The irony is that Deleuze and Guattari, writing in their native French, never used the word 'assemblage'. Rather, it re-entered Anglophone literature as the translation of another word that, in French, is of quite different etymological and semantic provenance, namely *agencement* (Nail 2017). The word is formed from the verb *agencer*, which my dictionary renders as 'to fit together' or 'to arrange'. Literally, then, *agencement* is something like an arrangement of things, a layout. Superficially, there may not be much to distinguish arranging things from assembling them, and to quibble over the translation might seem like splitting hairs. Philosophically, however, rather more is at stake than what appears on the surface. At stake, indeed, is the very question from which I began: what does it mean to join things? In the world of materials, what, exactly, is a connection?

This is a question at the heart of the sprawling meditations that Deleuze and Guattari (2004) compiled into their *Milles plateaux* ('A Thousand Plateaus'), a work that laid many of the philosophical foundations for new materialist thinking. It was in the translation of this work, a mammoth undertaking by philosopher Brian Massumi, that *agencement* became 'assemblage'. Although Deleuze and Guattari return to the term again and again, readers looking for clarity on what they mean by it will be disappointed. In another work, however, they offer a comparison that can help us think the matter through (Deleuze and Guattari 1994: 23). It is between the pieces of a jig-saw puzzle and those of a dry-stone wall. In the puzzle, every piece is precisely pre-cut so as to fit seamlessly with all the others into a total layout wherein, once completed, its original identity disappears. No longer an odd

Figure 17.2 Section of a dry-stone wall, Hazelhead, Aberdeen.
Photo by the author.

fragment of card with an irregular outline, it exists only as part of the layout. The wall-builder, however, takes stones as he finds them, improvising their layout as he goes along. And even when his work is done, each stone retains its own singularity. As a whole, then, the wall is a thing of fragments, a multiplicity, which coheres only thanks to an emerging settlement – one that could not be predicted – among the stones themselves (Figure 17.2). The wall, for Deleuze and Guattari, is an *agencement*.

The key point of distinction is that what counts in holding the wall together are the relations between its elements, and not, as in the jigsaw puzzle, the subsumption of each under the whole of which they are integral parts. In essence, the stones are untouched by their contact: each remains the particular stone that it is. That's why the stones are deemed to be joined by relations of *exteriority*. But is this really so? Deleuze and Guattari are in no doubt about the matter: 'multiplicities', they say, 'are defined by the outside' (2004: 9). In their terms, this is what makes their integration 'machinic' rather than 'organic', for it is precisely in the mutual exteriority of its parts that the mechanism is distinguished from the organism. And theorists such as DeLanda (2006: 9), who have ostensibly followed in their footsteps, would agree. But if that were all, why should Deleuze and Guattari have bothered with an awkward word like *agencement*? Why not use 'assemblage' instead?[5] It would surely have saved a lot of trouble and confusion had they done so. As already noted, the word 'assemblage' exists equally in French and English, and in both languages it can be used to designate a collection of things found in proximity, in a certain context. Moreover its usage in this sense, as in the fields of palaeontology and archaeology, is well established. It is hard to see what DeLanda's (2006: 18) definition of the assemblage as 'made up of parts which are self-subsistent and articulated by relations of exteriority', or Bennett's (2010: 23), as 'an ad hoc grouping of diverse elements', really adds to this.

Are the new materialists, in their infatuation with a certain genre of philosophical writing notorious for both its prolixity and its penchant for juxtaposing incommensurable elements culled at random from here, there and everywhere, merely bamboozling us with their verbose neologisms?[6] To a great extent, I think they are. For what they have done is to take only one side of *agencement*, as if that were all there is to it. As a result, we have things jumping into arrangements with one another, as the agentive causes of their own emergent effects, in a world where nothing lives, moves or grows, and everything is locked solid (Ingold 2015: 16). This is a fossilised world, which can only be brought back to life through magical invocations of vitality to things in themselves. I want to argue, to the contrary, that there are two sides to *agencement*: an outer side that it reveals and an inner side that it conceals. On the hidden side lie the forces and energies that course through a world in which things and their properties do not simply emerge, *sui generis*, but are actively brought forth or produced. The power of *agencement*, I believe, lies in its capacity to effect a modulation from one side to the other; that is from the assemblage to its negative, and vice versa. In what follows I aim to show that the one always accompanies the other, as a thing and its shadow. I shall call this negative the gathering. Only by taking the two together, the assemblage and the gathering – the light and the dark sides of *agencement* – can we understand things not just in their arrangement, but in how they come into being, last for a while, and then pass away.

The gathering

Let's return to Bennett's characterisation of the assemblage as a 'non-totalisable sum'. What does it mean, to sum? It means, of course, to add things up. The word implies both separation and articulation. To add things they must first be detached from each other, rendered discontinuous, as a prelude to their external attachment. In simple arithmetic, the addition is indicated by a plus sign. 'Plus' is the sign of articulation.[7] Thus the formula for the assemblage is $E_1 + E_2 + E_3 + \ldots$, where every E stands for a discrete element. In the formula, the elements may be utterly heterogeneous in nature, but the plus signs are interchangeable. One is as good as another. But suppose, as an experiment, that we invert the formula, by hiding every element behind an identical sign, while foregrounding the articulations.

What is concealed behind the plus signs? It is of course the *work* of addition. For stones do not, of their own accord, add themselves up into a wall. In the experience of the wall-builder, the addition of every stone means selecting and retrieving it from the quarry and heaving it into place. Nor does the operation stop there, for the weight of the stone, as it settles, causes others in the vicinity to tilt until a new equilibrium is reached. And our stone, too, will likely tilt as the builder adds more. Builders work, but so do stones, and they do so only in their bearing on one another.

It is this practical and productive operation, drawing the builder into a laborious engagement with the stones, and the stones themselves into forceful collaboration, that lurks behind the plus signs of our initial formula for the assemblage. Adding stone after stone in the construction of the wall, one such operation follows another, each different from the one before. For as no two stones are alike, nor are the operations of their addition. Thus as surely as every assemblage holds together, albeit contingently, as the serial but non-totalisable sum of its elements, it must also be accompanied by a second series, comprised by the operations involved in the summation. Perhaps we should write the series like this: $O_1 + O_2 + O_3 + \ldots$, where every O stands for a different operation. Each operation, in the second formula, would replace a plus sign in the first. The wall, then, would appear not as the sum of its stones, but as the sequence of the operations that put them there. It would be equivalent to what the great anthropologist of techniques, André Leroi-Gourhan, called the 'operational chain' (*chaîne opératoire*).[8] But given that we can have neither the wall without the labour of building, nor building without the material constituents of the wall, could we not simply merge the two series, by interpolating every operation of the second between each consecutive pair of elements in the first – thus E_1 O_1 E_2 O_2 E_3 O_3 ... – so as to fabricate an assemblage in which both elements and operations figure together as alternating components of the mix?

This, I contend, would be a mistake. For there is a fundamental difference between the two series. It is that operations cannot be understood as discrete episodes that follow one another like beads on a string. They are more like the converging and diverging strands of a continuous braid. It is not possible, in practice, to specify at what point any operation begins or ends. For – to continue with our example of the wall – one could trace it back at least to the quarrying that released this particular stone, along with all the others, from its earthly matrix, and even beyond that, to the geological deposition of the bedrock. Equally, one could trace the operation forward into the stone's ongoing adjustments with its neighbours in the wall itself, for as long as it stands, and subsequently in its collapse and gradual return to the earth. Every stone has its story of how it came to be there, just as it is, and so does the builder, in whose experience it figures not as a sealed entity, in itself, but in its heaviness as a test of muscular strength, in its roughness as abrasions of the hands, and in its corners and edges as the friction of contact with other stones. For a while the builder's story and the stone's story go along together and are wrapped up with one another, as are the stories of the stones themselves, from the time they are hewn from the quarry-face up to and beyond their coming together once again in the wall. Their relations, in short, are not *additive*, like the elements of the assemblage; they are rather *complicate*, as in the braid.

Literally, 'complicate' means 'folded together', and it is this literal sense that I adduce here. In fact the Latin language, from which this and so many other of our words for joining are derived, was already onto the distinction that I am concerned to highlight. It has given us the alternative prefixes: *ad-* (or its cognates, in which the trailing consonant duplicates the lead consonant of the following syllable, as with *ap-*, *at-* and *ag-*) and *con* (or its cognates *com-* or simply *co-*). The result is a succession of paired contrasts, including not only 'adjoin' versus 'conjoin', but also 'adhere' versus 'cohere', 'admit' versus 'commit', 'apply' versus 'comply', 'attract' versus 'contract', 'attend' versus 'contend', 'attribute' versus 'contribute', and 'aggregate' versus 'congregate'. Underlying all these contrasts is a fundamental distinction between *at*-ness and *with*-ness, perhaps even between space and time. Things that are at hand, for example, are up there with you, at this particular moment, in such spatial or contextual proximity that you can reach for them, and they for you. While everything has its story, its particular temporal trajectory, 'at' cuts transversally across them: it marks, in the felicitous phrase of geographer Doreen Massey (2005: 10–12), 'the simultaneity of stories so far'. But with 'con' we join *with* things in their passage through time, going along together with them, working with them, and suffering with them. That's how containment, to give another example, differs from attainment, and indeed the compendium from the addendum.

'Con', in short, is not transverse but longitudinal. It is about entering the grain of things and going along with them. Thus adherence is instantaneous, coherence endures; admission lets in, but a commission is carried out; application puts things situationally to use, compliance fits in with established usage; attraction entices, the contract binds; attention stretches towards things, but in contention we have to deal with them; attributes are assigned, but to contribute is to join in the assignment; in aggregate people form a crowd, but in the congregation they are gathered in the public enactment of a service. The operative word, here, is *gathering*. For what makes a gathering more than the mere juxtaposition of elements is the drawing together of the pathways along which its constituents have come into being, and the nascent anticipation of the ways they will tend to go. In the gathering, things are not severed, as they are in the assemblage, from the lines of movement, growth and becoming that have brought them to where they are. When people are gathered in a congregation, each trails his or her life-story, and carries it on in the ensuing proceedings. When animals are gathered in a herd, they do not cease to move but rather move in concert, leaving braid-like tracks in the landscape. Crops gathered at harvest still betoken the earth from which they grew and the labour of the harvesters, and anticipate their milling and eventual transformation into bread. And cornstalks, whether gathered in a sheaf or as thatch on a roof, are laid in parallel and bound in the middle (Ingold 1993c: 168–9).

And so it is, too, with stones gathered in the wall. Were we to imagine the wall only as an assemblage, it would be as if the stones were already *next* to one another: they could abut and adjoin, but not intermingle. But to imagine the wall as a gathering is to join *with* the story of each stone as it arrives and settles.[9] In principle, as we have seen, these stories could be extended indefinitely, both back and forward in time. You could begin in the quarry, with the violence of separation in which the stone was hewn from its matrix; you could continue with its haulage to the site, its selection by the builder and eventual heaving into place. And you could ask, even after the wall is built, *what is going on between those stones?* For their settlement surely endures: it is not an instant affair, and will doubtless shift over time in response to weather conditions and the movements of earth and bedrock. In the wall's walling, in its carrying on, stones play host to lichens and mosses, the cracks and crevices between them allow plants to take root and insects to hide. In the experience of larger animals, the wall is not just a barrier to movement; it also offers shade from the sun and shelter from the wind. Thus lichens, moss, plants and animals both large and small – all are folded together, or complicated, in the gathering, becoming part of each other's stories. That's why you cannot put plus signs between them. Since no story can carry on save by entering into the stories of others, they are not *ad*joined so much as *con*joined (Figure 17.3).

Correspondence

In her study of the entanglements of life, *The Mushroom at the End of the World*, anthropologist Anna Tsing (2015: 22–4) writes eloquently of how the ways of living and non-living beings come together in 'open-ended gatherings', comparing their intertwinement to musical polyphony. To appreciate landscapes of polyphony, Tsing notes, 'one must listen both to the separate melody lines and their coming together in unexpected moments of harmony or dissonance' (2015: 158). She is not alone in drawing this analogy. We have already encountered it in the writings of the naturalist Jakob von Uexküll, which in turn influenced Deleuze and Guattari in the development of their concept of 'melodic landscapes'.[10] However the parts of a polyphonic composition, such as a madrigal or a fugue, do not add up. Their relations are not additive but contrapuntal (Ingold 2017b: 14). And for this reason it makes no sense to ask, with Tsing (2015: 23), how 'gatherings sometimes become "happenings", that is, *greater than the sum*

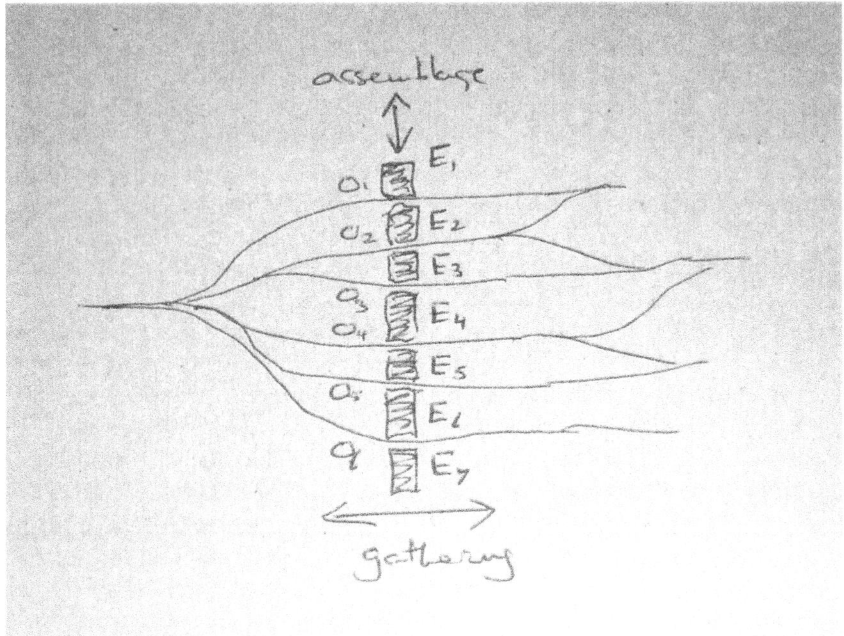

Figure 17.3 The assemblage and the gathering: a working sketch from my notes. Elements (E1–E7) are juxtaposed in the assemblage, but operations (O1–O6) run in between them, to form a braid.

of their parts'. Tsing's mistake, in the phrase I have highlighted for emphasis, is to have conflated the gathering with the assemblage. For her these are two words for the same thing. So they are, as well, for Gavin Lucas (2012: 198), who insists on 'the proper meaning of assemblage as a gathering or assembling of things'. My thesis, to the contrary, is that gathering and assembling are fundamentally different, in the same sense that complication differs from addition. This is not to say that they are mutually exclusive; far from it! Indeed there can no more be gathering without assembling than a shadow without that which casts it. On the dark side, however, things do not attach themselves from without, but are differentiated from within.[11]

Gathering, thus conceived, is a process of what I am calling 'interstitial differentiation' (Ingold 2015: 23). It is about splitting things from the inside, along the grain of their movement or becoming. Or to borrow a phrase from philosopher of science Karen Barad, it is a '*cutting together-apart*'. As Barad (2014: 176) intimates, splitting apart and mingling together are two sides of the same coin: 'entanglings entail differentiatings, differentiatings entail entanglings'. Thus, concealed behind the overt meaning of *agencement* as exterior arrangement or assembly lies another, more covert sense of interior differentiation. It might be rendered in English, albeit awkwardly, as 'agencing' (Ingold 2017b: 17–18). This is not the same as acting. To act is to impart a certain direction to things from the outset and to follow it through. But with agencing one is ever inside what is going on, discovering from within the way in which things are going, and bending it to one's purpose (Ingold 2011a: 211). For Erin Manning (2016: 6), who chooses quite explicitly to use *agencement* in this latter sense, it is specifically about the incipient directionality that opens up from within what she calls the 'cleave of the event', its internal schism, giving a particular twist or inflection to its unfolding. Here it is every inflection, rather than every element, that counts as a singularity.

To count things, then, is not to add them *up* but to join *with* them, to align one's attention to their ongoing, rhythmic movement. As in counting breaths or heartbeats, or bars of music, it is to mark time, not to measure space. This is the minor sense of *agencement*, as interstitial differentiation, concealed behind the major sense of assembly. What makes the idea of *agencement* so potent is precisely its capacity to effect a switch of perspective from major to minor, from the positive idea of the assemblage to its negative, of the gathering. This is not a negative, be it noted, in the sense of a photographic plate, or the mirror writing of type in the galley, prior to its imprinting on the page. What is entailed is rather a ninety degree shift, from across to along, comparable to that between connecting points and bundling lines, in the case of the exercise with which I began (Figure 17.1). Hence the relations constitutive of the gathering are not diametrically opposed, but rather orthogonal, to the relations that make up the assemblage. I shall now go on to show that while relations of the latter kind are of articulation, those of the former kind are of correspondence.

Perhaps I could begin with a vignette from Lars Spuybroek. He tells of how, walking through a field, his attention is drawn to a few stones lying next to one another. Nestled between them, a tiny plant has found root and flourishes. He likes what he sees. But then he wonders, 'what is that liking?'

> Clearly the stones are lying there in a certain correspondence, if not accordance, because the wind and water have moved them, rolled them over the ground and made them find an impression, create a little group, a little nest where a plant could start growing and be protected – but where does my liking fit in? Is it merely in me, subjectively enjoying the sight, or is it … an extended correspondence? I am with the stones and plant immediately, fitting in with them.
>
> (Spuybroek 2016: 112)

There are three points to note here. Firstly, what Spuybroek describes is far more than an 'ad hoc grouping of diverse elements' – to return once again to Bennett's (2010: 23) characterisation of the assemblage. For in the shadow of the assemblage lies the actions of wind and flood in rolling the stones, as well as the seeding and subsequent germination of the plant, now protected by the stones from the very forces that brought them there. What is described is also a gathering. Secondly, Spuybroek immediately finds himself as a participant. He *joins* the gathering, and for a moment at least, it is woven into the story of his own life – enough for him to be able to retell it later on. And thirdly, 'liking', in this context, is another word for this joining or fitting *with*. It is not a subjective state of mind, reflecting upon physical reality, nor is it an objective sensation that is merely thrown into the mix. It is rather what he calls a *correspondence*.

Literally, correspondence is a process in which things answer to one another. This implies nothing about intentionality or subjectivity; it simply means that in their growth, movement and formation – that is, in their gathering – things have a certain elasticity. They stretch and give way, expand and contract, tear and are torn, scrape and are scraped. In so doing, and so undergoing, they take into themselves something of the characters of the others to which they respond. The stones, in Spuybroek's account, are corresponding with one another in this sense, and he is corresponding with them. What flows in and out in this relation, he reports, is *feeling*. Not only does he feel the stones, but the stones, in their correspondence, feel each other. 'All relations', Spuybroek (2016: 112) emphasises, 'are *felt* relations'. He calls them relations of sympathy. This has nothing to do with personal psychology. It is not about the attribution, to ourselves or others, of such sentiments as warmth or compassion. Nor does Spuybroek's liking for the little group of stones, with the nestled plant, imply any outpouring of affection towards them, or even any judgement of taste. It simply denotes an accord – a bringing into likeness – that comes from correspondence. The wall-builder doubtless feels the same, despite the backbreaking and possibly painful nature of his work. Sympathy is what happens when things enter into the processes of their mutual formation, or in Spuybroek's (2016: 109) words, 'what things feel when they shape each other'.

From this follows a point of capital importance. It is that in the sympathy of correspondence, in things' feeling for one another, in their complication or folding together, they do not meet on the outside but enter into the formative process *from within*. Correspondent relations, in short, are relations of interiority. And in this regard, they are absolutely opposed to the articulatory relations of the assemblage in which, as we have seen, things remain ever outside each other. In a nutshell, *whereas the constitutive relations of the assemblage are of exteriority, those of the gathering are of interiority*. Now for a philosopher like DeLanda, interiority can only mean one thing: the loss of autonomy of parts as their identity is swallowed up by that of the whole (DeLanda 2006: 9). For him, and for the new materialists who have followed in his footsteps, the idea that things can retain their singularity, while yet joining with one another on the inside, is simply inconceivable.

Interiorisation, in their philosophy, implies hierarchisation, the inclusion of pieces within a higher order of relations. And conversely, to flatten the hierarchy, to bring everything down to the level of the pieces themselves, means allowing them to come out from under the pressures that have forced them into amalgamation, whereupon they regain their singularity as elements that stand radically outside one another. The assemblage, by definition, is flat, it eschews hierarchy, and for this reason its relations are of exteriority. It is the non-totalisable sum of its heterogeneous elements.

But the gathering, as I have shown, is not produced through any process of summation. It is not that the addition of elements can never yield a total; rather – in the gathering – the elements are not addable in the first place. They are not addable because they are not yet formed but ever in the process of formation. And in this process, they enter into relations with one another *on their own level*, such that for each, these relations are enfolded in its own constitution. In a work first published in 1980, entitled *Wholeness and the Implicate Order*, the theoretical physicist David Bohm (2002) set out a distinction between alternative orders of relations, respectively implicate and explicate. In the explicate order, everything is outside everything else, and things make contact only at their exterior surfaces, leaving their inner natures unaffected. This is the order of the assemblage, and for new materialists it is the only order there can be. In the implicate order, by contrast, every part continually arises as an enfolding of the entire field of relations of which it is the momentary incarnation. Enfolded structures, as Bohm (2002: 225) puts it, rather than occupying their particular region of space and moment of time, interweave and intermingle throughout all of space and time, such that ultimately, 'everything is enfolded into everything'. To our senses the world may appear chunked into things that are solid, tangible and visibly stable, yet they are but the manifest envelopes of the underlying holomovement wherein everything is formed. In the implicate order, the surfaces of things do not separate their insides from their outsides. Rather, every surface is itself a crease or pleat in the fabric of the world, where inside and outside are folded into one another.

To characterise the order of the gathering, however, I would like to go one step further. It is an order, as I have already intimated, that is not so much implicate as *complicate*. Whereas implication connotes a folding inward, as if from side to side, complication carries the sense of folding forward – that is of things convoluting longitudinally, braiding or plaiting along the lines of their own growth and movement. This is an idea that would have come naturally to the Roman author Titus Lucretius Carus, in whose prose-poem, *On the Nature of Things*, the world is depicted as a torrent of falling particles which, swerving ever so slightly from their vertical course, set up a cascade of eddies. This same image, which we already encountered in Chapter 3 (pages 41–2), lies behind Deleuze's depiction of matter in *The Fold* – his study of Leibniz and the Baroque – as a maelstrom of vortices within vortices, yielding an 'infinitely porous, spongy or cavernous texture ... caverns endlessly contained in other caverns' (Deleuze 1993: 5). This is matter folding on itself as it goes along. As it does so it endlessly overflows any formal envelopes within which it may appear to our senses to have been temporarily pulled aside or detained. There is no limit, not because things will never add up, nor because they can be retotalled in ever varying permutations and combinations, but because their materials slip through the cracks in the very work of addition.

Thus, in the shadow of the material world, with its contingently assembled things, there lies a *world of materials* (Ingold 2007b: 14) that is not so much created as perpetually in creation, forever surpassing itself through the correspondence of its particulars. This self-surpassing amounts to what Alfred North Whitehead (1929: 410) called 'concrescence' (Chapter 4, page 54). Addition, though it may create novel arrangements, or what Bennett (2010: 130 fn. 12) describes as an 'ever changing array of effects', can bring forth nothing that was not already there. In Bergson's (1922: 48) terms, it is equivalent to fabrication, namely, the rearrangement of elements already known. As with every shake of a kaleidoscope, you end up with no less or more than you started with. To this Bergson contrasted the creativity born of duration, the ceaseless upspringing of the absolutely new, giving rise to 'incommensurability between what goes before and what follows' (1922: 30 fn. 2). Astonishingly, Bennett contrives to cite these latter words of Bergson, by which he characterises the 'indivisible process' of creative invention, to corroborate her view of the assemblage as a 'non-totalisable' fabrication made up of discrete parts. These could not be more different. Fabrication, as we saw in Chapter 1 (page 24), creates an interminable stream of novelties. But invention delivers the world into newness.

Concrescence

If the assemblage, then, forms by the *ac*cretion of material from without, the gathering is formed through its *con*crescence from within. The first imagines a discontinuous material world – a world of chunks – in which increase can only be by way of the addition of extraneous matter; the second, running orthogonally to the first, imagines a world in continuous flux, in which things both grow and decay, take shape and dissolve, by way of the inner turbulence of their constituent materials. Now for an archaeologist like Bjørnar Olsen, the chunkiness of matter is self-evident; it is the way things are. 'Things', writes Olsen (2010: 158), 'are concrete and offer stability'. Not so, however, in a world of concrescence, where things are neither chunky nor stable but convoluted and prone to buckling, distortion and collapse (Ingold 2013a: 102–3). Here, all is flux. This is not to claim that everything is liquid. Fluidity and liquidity, indeed, belong to quite different orders of reality. In the order conceived by mainstream physical science, matter is particulate by default, and solid, liquid and gaseous phases are distinguished by the relative tightness or looseness of articulations at the molecular level. Flux, however, presupposes an understanding of the condition of matter *alternative* to the particulate. A world of flux is matter-full, not full of matter; a plenum, not a suspension in a vacuum (Chapter 4, page 52). Its heterogeneities arise not from the multiple compounding of its elements into ever more diverse and complex configurations, but from the folding and creasing of its sponge-like substance. Such a world cannot be parsed into solid, liquid gaseous phases. Rather, the materials of which it is comprised combine properties of plasticity and viscosity within a single matrix of variation. Everything, to varying degrees, is 'solid-fluid' (Simonetti and Ingold 2018).[12]

Ironically, no material better illustrates this solid-fluid condition than that which latterly – in the nineteenth century, and in the Anglosphere – assumed the name of *concrete*. For as fluid-turned-solid, concrete holds the seeds of its own dissolution. The very binding reactions that cause it to harden also generate, as a by-product, a moisture-absorbing gel that, if left unchecked, eventually leads the material to seep and crumble from within. Indeed as Lucas (2013) explains, concrete is not really a fixed substance at all so much as a process: 'it is a material that changes its nature over time'. In short, *concrete is concrescence*. Consider its ingredients: water, aggregate and cement. The order of the aggregate, as its name suggests, is explicate: it is, according to its dictionary definition, 'a body formed by the union of numerous units or particles; *an assemblage*'.[13] In concrete, the aggregate generally comprises a mix of sand and gravel. But it is the cement, that – when mixed with water – works as a binding agent, a kind of glue, which slips through the cracks between the particles of aggregate, so as to form a continuous and complicate weave. Whereas the aggregate is formed as an assemblage, it is the cement that performs the gathering. United in concrete is both the thing and its shadow, the assemblage and the gathering. Indeed the 'shadow-life' of concrete is even marked etymologically, in its designation in German as *beton* (French *béton*), a word that links it with another binding agent of organic derivation – namely bitumen, or pitch.

Hiding in the shadow of the chunk, as Spuybroek (2016: 113) suggests, is the *bag*, a volume into the folds or cavities of which are brought together the innumerable threads that percolate the substance of matter and lend it coherence. A lump of concrete, then, is both chunky and baggy. And while the lump may be finite, the thread-lines bundled therein may extend indefinitely beyond it, flowing in and out, their loose ends tangling or knotting with other threads to form a continuous weave or mesh. All matter, in this sense, is at once chunked and woven, both mosaic and fabric.[14] The chunks give substance; the weave gives coherence. Consider, for example, an ordinary brick wall. Using a trowel, the mason applies a layer of mortar to each brick, both beneath and to one side, before pressing it into place and scraping off any surplus so as to leave an even seam of mortar between every brick and its neighbours, both above and below, and on either side. Adding brick upon brick, the mason works as a go-between, and the mortar – in its binding function – takes over from where the mason leaves off. What his work leaves behind is not just the assemblage of bricks but a continuous and intricately folded fabric of mortar, a gathering that fills the seams and makes it so not only that adjacent bricks adhere but that the wall as a whole holds together.

Should we think of the wall, then, as an assemblage of bricks, with mortar as the bonding agent, or as a gathering of mortar, interspersed by bricks? Does mortar fill the gaps between bricks, or do bricks fill the gaps of the mortar (Ingold 2015: 30)? Or suppose, to offer another example, that you are constructing a model from a kit of parts, which are to be joined by gluing them together. Is the model an assemblage or a gathering? If it is to be regarded an assemblage, then it is not obvious where the glue belongs. It cannot be just another part. Initially formless and fluid, yet solidifying on exposure to air, glue infiltrates the cracks and crevices where things don't quite fit, weaving a fibrous web of its own – a negative of the assemblage. Moreover, the way glue works is to seep into the surfaces with which it comes into contact. Material that looks solid and chunky to our eyes is not so to the glue which, at the molecular level, encounters a surface of sponge-like porosity. Regular adhesives contain long protein chains which penetrate the material through its pores and bond with its molecules. In effect, what glue does is to join materials on the inside, so as to turn an otherwise explicate order into a complicate one. It converts exterior surfaces into interior folds, chunks into bags. Thanks to this, the construction coheres.

But what if there is no binding agent? It is time to revert to the dry-stone wall (Figure 17.2). In one of his later essays, Deleuze returns to the example of the wall to illustrate the idea of the world as a patchwork, an *agencement* of ill-fitting elements:

> not even a puzzle, whose pieces when fitted together would constitute a whole, but rather a wall of loose, uncemented stones, where every element has a value in itself but also in relation to others: isolated and floating relations, islands and straits, immobile points and sinuous lines – for Truth always has 'jagged edges'.
>
> (Deleuze 1998: 86)

How can such a thing of shreds and patches ever stand firm against the winds of time? To what does it owe its strength and resilience? Not, surely, to the solidity of the stones, for a poorly built wall will fall at the slightest provocation, however hard the material. Its strength lies, rather, in *what is going on between the stones*. Place one stone of irregular shape upon another and it will come to rest at a minimum of three points. The pressure of stone on stone, concentrated at the points of contact, is diffused throughout their mass. In the compression of the material, each stone takes into itself its relations with the others. It is in the resultant complication of the stones' feeling for one another – their sympathy and correspondence – that the strength of the wall resides. In effect, the wall is self-binding.

In his disquisition on the assemblage, DeLanda (2006: 10–11) distinguishes between *properties* and *capacities*. The parts of an assemblage, he argues, have properties in themselves but capacities only in relation to the parts with which they may happen to interact. Raise a stone from the ground and place it in the wall: it is the same stone, with the same properties, but in the wall, in association with the other stones, it partakes of the capacity – for example – to hinder movement or afford shelter. Properties are given, capacities emergent. This might be easy to say, but it leaves unanswered the question of where the capacities have emerged *from*. All too often, in the writings of theorists, 'emergence' serves as a cover-up, a way of evading the question through a circular logic that reads into emergent effects the very agentive causes deemed to have given rise to them.[15] Thus the stones become the causes of their own effects. 'Look', exclaims the new materialist, observing the wall and its manifest effects on the surroundings, 'how the wall testifies to the collective, nonhuman agency of stones!' (Ingold 2014a: 235). But what has happened to the builders? Does the wall not stand, rather, as testimony to their hard and relentless labour? After all, the stones can weigh upon one another only because the builders have put them there. It was they who hauled the stones from the quarry and heaved them into place. As they did so, their correspondence with the stones would progressively have given way to the stones' correspondence with one another.

In short, *the emergent heft of the wall has its source in the effortful heave of its builders*. If the wall is an *agencement*, then heft is to heave as one side is to the other, assemblage to gathering. So next time you stop to admire a wall, spare a thought for the labours of those who made it, and whose ghostly presence still lurks in the interstices, amidst the deepening shadows of the stones.

Chapter 18

The world in a basket

On the passage of generations

Recalling his experiences of the Jacobite War, the Scottish poet Alexander MacDonald (1698–1770) brought his tale to a close with the following words: 'I leave you with the thrawcrook till I get more hair.' The thrawcrook is a tool traditionally used for twisting grasses, reeds, straw or other fibres in making rope by hand. The hair is the raw material.[1] MacDonald has spun his tale, but it is not finished. He'll need to gather more from life to replenish the story. But he'll pass on the spinning of it to the coming generation.

No one lives forever nor, as MacDonald knew, does the longest stalk of grass, reed or straw extend indefinitely. Yet social life carries on, and a rope or cord, twisted from fibres, can be continued without limit. With the multi-stranded cord as with the life of many lives, the reasons are the same. Lives, like fibres, are bundled together, which is to say that their alignment is longitudinal. In the bundle, strands overlap along their length: even as old strands begin to give out new strands are introduced. Indeed the analogy between the twisting of cordage and the entwining of generations is not loose but exact. It is why a history told over again is called a record; why – in the record – every life retains its own singularity however tightly it is bound with others, and why, in the passage of time, this binding is fundamental to the continuity of life. It is no wonder that among peoples around the world, knotted cords were not only among the most frequent repositories of ancestral lore; they were also commonly employed as measures of time. As cords were paid out, time would elapse, and stories would be told (Ingold 2007a: 65–8).

In social life, moreover, just as in the rope, the old and the new, twisting around one another, establish in the tension and the friction of their contact a grip that is even stronger than the combined tensile strength of the strands themselves (Ewart 2021). As the twist of its overlapping fibres gives the rope its stretch and tenacity, so also it is by carrying on their lives together that the old and the young can lay an assured path for generations to come. Throughout most of history, indeed, this is how human lives have been lived.

DOI: 10.4324/9781003171713-23

Youngsters have grown up hearing the stories and observing the practices of their elders, both discovering the meanings of the stories and developing skills of practice in the passage of their own experience, and becoming storytellers and practitioners in their turn. In this, as we saw in Chapter 5 (page 69), lies the proper meaning of tradition: not a fixed corpus of heritable custom, to be passed on intact from one generation to the next, but a way of life along which it is possible to move on, in continuity with the values of the past, while laying down a path for others to follow.

Yet by and large, this is no longer true today. Even as the twisting and spinning of fibres, once a ubiquitous task of daily life (Chapter 3, pages 47–9), has largely become confined as a niche art for hobbyists and the purveyors of heritage, and as spun cord disappears from common use, so records have ceased to be stories to tell and to follow, and have instead become benchmarks of their own era, set down as limits to be broken. Generations, instead of overlapping along their length while twisting around one another like the strands of a cord, seem to us to have become flattened, each confined to its own lateral slice of time like one layer in a stack. With this, the continuity of generations has given way to their serial replacement. Each generation, as a captive of the present, can receive nothing from the past save that which can be represented, in some transmissible form, independently of its lifetime achievement. That is why inter-generational learning tends to be regarded as a process of transmission, and why it is so clearly distinguished, both in the modern theory of education and in its practical applications, from the intra-generational doing in which acquired representations are put to work (Ingold 2018a: 1–19).

The reasons for this profound shift in the way we think about life and learning are complex, having much to do with capitalism's erosion of domestic modes of production, and with the redeployment of educational functions from the family to the state. An inquiry into these reasons would be the subject of another study. My present concern is different. It is to repair the breach between alternate generations, between youth and old age, brought about by the irruption into their midst of the generation of the present, or what I shall call Generation Now. For Generation Now, the name of the game is not growth and renewal but innovation and change. To make its mark it must break with the past, taking it upon itself to rearrange the furniture by tearing apart the constructions of its predecessors in the fabrication of its own. Intensely target-driven, guided by short-term objectives that hold no promise beyond a future already in its sights, Generation Now has little time either for the wisdom of their elders or for the curiosity of the young. Nor does it care much for stories or for skills, which it suffers to be preserved only to entertain youngsters in enactments of heritage, or to indulge the elderly in flights of nostalgia.

The dominant perspective of Generation Now lends a peculiar shape to the human life course. For it consigns the generation to come to the waiting room, preparing for its time to arrive, while conversely, the generation that went before exits into retirement. This leads to a picture of the life-cycle in the form of a bell curve, roughly divisible into three phases: an initial phase growth and formation, in which the young are readied to enter the world that awaits them; a final phase of reversal and decline as capacities fade, and – in between – a phase in which human world-forming powers are at their peak. This is the phase of Generation Now. Thrust betwixt youth and old age, it holds all the cards. Indeed, so busy are its people with their world-making, so preoccupied with the affairs of the day, that they pay scant regard to their elders or their juniors. Old people, they think, having already enjoyed their place in the sun, should sink gracefully into obscurity. Their time is past, their days over. Young people, to the contrary, need to be brought up to speed, to face an already projected future that they are nevertheless bound to reconfigure, once their time comes.

Weaving life

Can we imagine a society that would break the power of Generation Now – a society in which young and old, currently excluded from the tasks of world-making, are once again enabled to work alongside one another in forging the conditions of collective life? Can we break the barriers of their institutionalised segregation, allowing them to regather in the quotidian settings in which these tasks are typically carried on? I believe this can be done, but only by restoring ways of telling, currently relegated to the peripheries of social life, to its very core. This entails a renewed focus on the practices of craft, and on the stories and skills they engender. Of all human crafts, the interweaving of flexible cords, wickers, or roots to form containers, traps, cages, hats, and a host of other everyday utensils is perhaps the most ancient and widespread, as common to humans as nest-building is to birds (Healy and Tello-Ramos 2021). If it has taken second place in prehistory to the arts of stone, it is only because its materials don't preserve so well. If they did, we would likely be speaking today not of Palaeolithic, Mesolithic, and Neolithic eras, but of the Old, Middle and New Fibre Age (Mack 2021: 128).

For there is much more to weaving baskets than mere technique. It is, in itself, a life process. Its generativity lies in the unfolding of an entire field of vital relations wherein not only things, but also people and their provisions, are as much grown as made. Like the twisting of cords from which baskets are very often (though not universally) constructed, weaving closely models social life. People would bring the same tactile sensibility, the same sense of movement and pattern, into the choreography of their lives with one another as into that of their hands in working with materials. Every basket can be compared to a little community, binding its constituent fibres, as the community binds lives, into a supple and durable form. Like the community in its classical sense of 'giving-together' (from the Latin, *com*, 'together', plus *munus*, 'gift'), the basket is not closed in on itself but open-ended: open to others, to the past and to the future. And as communities produce baskets, so baskets reproduce communities. For in the practice of the craft, basketry produces its makers as well as the things themselves, building a feel for the work into their muscle memory, sense of rhythm and perceptual attunement.

But there is yet more, once the field of basketry is enlarged beyond weaving itself to embrace the entire life of its materials, and what happens to the things after they are made. It would then include the cultivation and harvesting of the grounds from which the materials are collected, ranging from grassland to willow beds, as well as the harvest of the sea or land they will eventually hold – be it fish or grain – not to mention all the relations, whether of grandparents and grandchildren, or of masters and apprentices, which ensure that skills are carried on. It is no surprise that in so many societies, baskets hold the insignia of kingship or divination (Mack 2021), or that they are used to cradle the new-born. It was of course in a basket that the infant twins Romulus and Remus, in the foundation myth of the city of Rome, were abandoned by the river Tiber, only to be discovered and raised by a wolf. For the basket carries a sense of containment as womb-like encompassment, as all-in-one, that makes no distinction between inside and outside. The in-and-out weave of the basket, from which its surfaces are formed, defies any such distinction (Ingold 2000: 341). Baskets reveal and conceal at the same time.

Today, our ethnological museums are full of baskets and other woven artefacts of great beauty and astonishing technical accomplishment, collected from every continent of the world. The skills of making them, however, are close to disappearing, along with their erstwhile makers. Few today know how it should be done. Along with the crafts of spinning and ropemaking, basketry skills are already on the endangered list. Were there no more to basketry than technique, there would be nothing exceptional about this. With techniques in human history, as with species in evolution, extinction has been more the rule than the exception. More has been lost than retained, yet life carries on, regardless. But the loss of basketry is not just a case of technical extinction. What is unique about the contemporary moment is not the loss of techniques to life, but the draining of life from technique. What would it take to bring it back?

Curiosity and wisdom

The trend is not easily reversed. No amount of curation, repair or documentation will, of their own accord, restore baskets to life. The much greater challenge is to rethink the passage of generations. To meet the challenge means envisaging a society in which young and old can once again join together in the making of a common world. This has massive implications for the way we think about education, about the wisdom of old age and the curiosity of the young, and about the potential of their collaboration. For both young children and the elderly are in touch, in ways that the target-driven champions of Generation Now are not, with more enduring rhythms of time. This is a time not of chronological succession and replacement, but of pure becoming or immanence. It is the time of weather and the seasons, of breaking waves and running rivers, of the growth and decay of vegetation and the coming and going of animals, of breaths and heartbeats. We sometimes say of children and of old people, even as we sometimes say of nonhuman animals, that they live in the present, without recollection or forethought. Yet this is not so much a constriction as a liberation. To lose track of measured time is to feel the rhythmic pulse of eternity.

It is perhaps because their minds are no longer or not yet cluttered with recollections and predictions that the old and the very young are better able to attend to the world in its immediacy, and more ready to be addressed by it. This readiness, in turn, opens a path for imagination. For young and old alike, imagination is not a power of conjecture, allowing for the projection, in the terms of the present, of a future state of affairs. Nor, conversely, is memory the recollection of an already bygone past. Rather, both imagination and memory coalesce in a beyond that is neither before nor after but falls in an entirely different register. In this register, the echoes of events past and still to come, untethered from their chronological moorings, mingle like ocean waves into a continuous field of diffraction and reverberation. We could call it the field of longing. For to long for things is neither to conjure up the future nor to wish back the past. It is rather to answer to the stirring of a restless world, feeling one's way in a twilight zone with no clear end in sight, lured by what John Dewey (1987: 80), in *Art as Experience*, described as an *aura*, 'dimly and imprecisely figured'.

The essence of longing is that none can say exactly what they long *for*. It is a desire that has no object. Indeed, once ends are known – once they come within reach of conceptual representation – all imagination ceases, and all remembering too. For longing can never be requited; its potential must ever remain unfulfilled. There is no final release into the light. But for just this reason, longing is the guarantor that life can carry on, impelled by an aura that never ceases to beckon from beyond the horizons of conceptualisation. Among children, longing manifests as the inquisitiveness of curiosity; among older people it manifests as the attentiveness of wisdom. Neither juvenile curiosity nor seasoned wisdom, however, hold much esteem in a societal regime that values objective knowledge and the operations of abstract reason above all else. For knowledge, putting answers ahead of questions, stamps out curiosity; while reason, privileging cognition over attention, leaves wisdom diminished by comparison. Indeed, within the prevailing value system that underlies our institutions of education and social care, dedicated respectively to preparing children for a predetermined future and sequestering the elderly for whom this future came too late, the innocence of curiosity is assessed as a deficiency of knowledge, and the humility of wisdom as a deficiency of mind – the former branded as ignorance; the latter as dementia.

For Generation Now, in command of the present, the idea that the demented and the ignorant might together forge the future would be manifestly absurd. To unite wisdom and curiosity, however, appears not only prudent but necessary for the renewal of life for generations to come. This is not nostalgia, or hankering for a lost past. Nor is it a utopian fantasy for the future. It is rather a foundation for hope. But to turn hope into reality, old and young must once again come together, making their productive and mutually transformative collaboration into a force for renewal for the common good. Could this collaboration, rather than the unilateral transfer of knowledge from senior to junior generations, be what education is really about? This is what it means, I believe, for education to be restored to the field of longing, as a way of leading life motivated by curiosity and care. For it is in leading life, and not just living it, that *bios* is elevated beyond *zōē*, life lived as a story beyond life bound to the cycles of nature.[2] And it is longing that registers the excess of the one over the other, the stretch of a life impelled by the promise of its renewal.

Mathematics and memory

Now let's return to basketry. For there is surely no better example of the unison of wisdom and curiosity than the weaving of baskets. Perhaps that is why the practice has been so shamefully denigrated by mainstream institutions, and why it is so important to bring it back. We have, to coin a verb, to 'basket' the world. By this, I mean to oppose the common view that the right place for what are pigeonholed as arts and crafts is as optional supplements to the core curriculum of so-called academic subjects designed to instil authorised knowledge into the minds of the young and to improve their powers of reason. One such subject is mathematics. At first glance, to compare mathematics to basketry is like placing a grand palace of classical proportions, inhabited by the finest minds, on a par with a ramshackle hovel whose naive or demented occupants lack the wit to improve their condition. How could the mathematics of the basket be anything other than a degenerate imitation of the real thing, simplified for ease of comprehension by vulgar minds?

But in reality, it is the inhabitants of the palace who are deluded into thinking that mathematics can float above the realities of bodily experience with vital materials, oblivious to the grounding of their most basic concepts of number, line, surface, symmetry and pattern in crafty operations of folding, twisting and weaving with which the inhabitants of the hovel would have been entirely familiar. Who, then, are the real mathematicians?[3] Anyone who has worked with materials, for example, knows that intersecting fold-lines cannot be produced simultaneously but require successive operations. Hands and fingers must get to work on the material, folding it first in one way, and then in another (Nemirovsky 2021: 61). Baskets, likewise, take time to weave, and cords time to twist. To basket the world is to restore things to the temporal current of their ongoing creation. It is to recognise that there can be no pattern without rhythm. For every pattern records the movement of its formation, and to read it one must be able to enter into this movement and to join it with the arc of one's attention.

Herein lies the work of memory. To remember is to call up lives from the past and draw them into the vivid present so they can bind with your own. Remembering another person is like having them there before you, after a long absence, and resuming your conversation; remembering a material is feeling it again in your hands, and responding with gestures that seem to well up from within. Elderly basket-makers, whose powers of recollection may have already faded, can still handle the materials of their trade with accustomed ease. In a basket-world, memory picks up the vital threads of the past and loops them through the eyes of the present. And it is by bringing these past lives into presence, listening to them, and attending to their needs, that we care for them. In the eyes of Generation Now, however, this loop is broken. Instead of drawing the past into their own ways of seeing, these eyes have turned to look back at it, only to appropriate its products as heirlooms. With this, the basket no longer affords, in its weave, a way of remembering or a path of care, and becomes instead an *object* of memory, to be conserved and curated rather than followed. It tells of another world that is not ours, one that we have irrevocably left behind.

And it is as such that it enters the museum, an institution tasked with preserving objects of the past for posterity, as cultural heritage. In the museum the basket, once a record in itself – or better, a bundle of records, each a story waiting to be told – is turned into an object *in* the record. This is the record as it appears in the official accounts of history and archaeology, in which every object is catalogued by its place and date of manufacture. Confined to its point of origin, the object stays put while time and history march on. Many museums, of course, are doing all they can to resist this objectification, and to bring the things in their collections back to life. But they are in a double bind, torn between their public duty to archive the record of material culture and their desire to revive endangered skills. It is no wonder that in the museum context, such revival often appears freighted with nostalgia.

Numbers and words

Indeed, the very designation of basketry as a 'craft' seems virtually guaranteed to keep it on the margins, to push it underground from higher to lower levels of awareness, or even from mind to body. This feeds on a well-established discourse according to which the learning and practice of a craft provides an outlet for the development of knowledge and skills variously branded as tacit, non-verbal and embodied, to complement and counter-balance higher powers of reasoning that are taken to be explicit, literate or numerate, and abstract. This complementarity is sometimes compared to reconnecting the left hemisphere of the brain to the right, or even the mind as a whole to its body. In proposing to basket the curriculum, rather than to add basketry to it, I have a quite different aim in mind. It is to destabilise the entire edifice on which the complementarity rests. For basketing is about more than making baskets. It is about breathing life back into a world that mainstream education has taken upon itself to explicate in the form of literate and numerical propositions, and which it has suffocated in the process.

This is not a matter of going beyond numbers, or beyond words, by way of an appeal to tacit knowledge and the embodiment of skills. On the contrary, it is to restore both numbers and words to currents of life and feeling – that is, to what, in Chapter 15, I have called the zone of hapticality. For numbers and words are neither concrete nor abstract, neither embodied nor disembodied. They are rather lived and felt. Consider numbers first. By definition, as Henri Bergson (1910: 75) wrote in his *Time and Free Will*, number connotes a multiplicity, 'the synthesis of the one and the many'. The word for number in classical Greek, *arithmos*, is one of the large family of words derived from the root **ar*, and is cognate with *ararisko*, 'to join' (Chapter 16, page 248). This is not by external attachment, however, but a joining from the inside, a gathering, as of threads on a loom or of melodic lines in a fugue. For the Pythagoreans, as logician and historian of mathematics Oskar Becker puts it, in a work dating from 1959, ' "number" denotes something like a particular arithmetically describable structure inherent in things and constituting their proper nature'.[4] In this sense it is self-evident that weaving a basket is a numerical operation, and an exercise in arithmetic.

In the history of Western mathematics, however, this idea of *arithmos* as a 'number of things', inherent in their way of gathering together like the wickers of a basket, has gradually taken second place to an abstract concept specified within a framework of formal logic (Mimica 1988: 105). Indeed, it is more usual nowadays to encounter numbers not as gatherings of lines or threads, or as what Bergson (1910: 121) would call 'qualitative multiplicities', but as the 'quantitative multiplicities' of discrete and commensurable parts or units, and to associate arithmetic with the operations of addition, subtraction, multiplication, and division. Picture the scientist, technician, or business analyst, seated before a screen and operating a keyboard. As he works, numbers come up on the screen, lots of them. We call these his data, and his process data-handling. They have been extracted from somewhere, precipitated from the real-life processes for which they serve as indices. But the hands of the data analyst, though they tap the keys, make no contact with the world beyond the keyboard.

Literally, of course, a *datum* is a 'thing given', an offering. To receive the gift is to take it in your hands. The real data handlers, in this literal sense, would have been the cord-keepers of old, reading accounts from the loops and knots of their material. Thus Inca people would read numbers from their *khipus*, constructed on the same principle as the communal suspension bridge, likewise made from twisted fibre cords. As the anthropologist Gary Urton (1997) has shown, both the significance of numbers and the practice of arithmetic among Quechua-speaking peoples in the Andes, descendants of the Inca, are part of their attempt to maintain balance, harmony, and equilibrium in every sphere of communal life. But making a basket is just as much a practice of data handling as is reading cords. Picking up and threading through, the maker receives with her hands what the evolving work offers as it proceeds. She counts as she goes, over and under, over and under. But her numbers do not add up. Nor are they placed end to end, like segments of a path measured with a stick.[5] They rather follow on, marking in their recurrence the evolving rhythms of time.

It is no different when we turn from numbers to words. They too, whether spoken or written, issue from a body that is not wrapped up in itself but open and alive to the world. I have already described, in Chapter 15 (pages 240–1), how words pour out: on the breath in speech, from the restless movement of hand and fingers in signing and writing. To suppose that the verbal arts on the one hand, and crafts such as basketry on the other, tap into different reservoirs of knowledge, respectively explicit and tacit, extrasomatic and embodied, or on higher and lower levels of consciousness, is to make a false comparison. For it is to set what is incipient in the practice of a craft – a gesture on the brink of expression – alongside what is already flown in the articulation of words. But words, too, bubble up; they are momentarily felt on the tongue or in the fingers, prior to their release. And the gestures of a craft, in their enactment, give birth to forms that are no longer tethered to their makers. It is unfair to both craft and speech to see the one only prospectively, in its incipience, and the other only retrospectively, in its outcomes. The maker and the wordsmith are both poets of a kind, who live and feel on the cusp of their work, between the incipient and the articulate, or between the flying and the flown. Therein lies the source of their creativity. It is the work of time.

Slowing down

We worry nowadays that time has lost its rhythm, that it is has been ejected from its proper orbit into a rampant and uncontrolled acceleration. If only we could slow down! Perhaps, then, we could live a simpler life, more measured in its pace, with fewer demands. We could walk instead of taking the car, write by hand, grow our own food, and wait for it to ripen before harvesting. And we could go back to making baskets. There is much to be said for these alternatives, at least for those with the leisure to afford them. They are good for health, and environmentally sustainable. Yet in practice, they are neither slow nor simple. The skills of basketry are of such difficulty that in times past, it took apprentices years of laborious effort to master them. And under pressure, they had to work fast. A renegade time traveller from Generation Now, hoping to discover slowness and simplicity in the labour of bygone ages, would be disappointed. He would likely come across people working in conditions that, compared with today's comforts, appear hard and unrelenting.

Yet finding himself in a world where working fast means seizing the moment, the *kairos*, rather than running against the clock, and where difficulty lies in the depth and subtlety of attention and response rather than in the superabundance of data and the principles of its manipulation, our traveller might also come to question his very modern understanding of speed, and of complexity. He might realise that to measure the speed of operations or the complexity of a system, certain assumptions have to be made. Fundamentally, it must be assumed that every operation connects a determinate start point and end point, allowing speed to be calculated as time to target, and a system's operational complexity as the number or density of its networked connections. In a moment of epiphany, our traveller recognises in these principles of target-chasing and networking the guiding imperatives of his own generation, of Generation Now. What he truly longs for, he realises, is not so much a return to slowness and simplicity as the possibility of movement and growth.

The thing about life, the traveller finds, is that it doesn't begin here and end there – it doesn't join the dots – but cuts a road, longitudinally, through all the transverse links connecting designs or plans and their target outcomes. What 'slow' and 'simple' really mean, then, in relation to the practice of a craft like basketry, is not the lower end of a scale defined by increasing speed and complexity, but an axial shift from the lateral to the longitudinal (Ingold 2018b: 162). The traveller comes from a lateral world in which all business is conducted in the plane of the present. It is a world ruled by the computational logic of the algorithm, which sets out a step-by-step programme for problem solving. Experiments in robotics have shown that such programmes can be progressively improved through trial-and-error learning. Robots can get better and better in doing what we humans do as a matter of course. Yet so far, no robot has been designed that could make a basket. This, as anthropologist Cathrine Hasse and science scholar Pat Treusch (2021: 261) point out, is because the conditions of basketry lie not in the enhancement of brain-based cognitive algorithms, but rather in an 'ongoing process of weaving human materials and bodies together'.

In short, the logic of the algorithm and the practice of the basket are fundamentally incompatible.[6] Where the one is computational, the other is ambulatory. It goes along. Recall the basket-maker, counting as she proceeds on her way. She works *with* her materials, but does not work them *out*. The basket is not a problem that already contains its own solution. Rather, maker and materials, going along together, arrive at a solution that emerges only in and through their collaboration. Here, attention and response take precedence over computation and execution. Instead of mediating between inputs and outputs, basketry kinetically joins the flex of muscles with the pliability of materials. This, finally, is what it means to basket the world. It is not to slow down, or to simplify. But it is to restore life and feeling to a world in which both are vulnerable to algorithmic decomposition. It is, once more, to long for things. As we find ourselves being sucked headlong into a brave new world of robotic intelligence, leaving our humanity behind as an empty husk, it is worth remembering that in the practice of the basket, another way is possible. But to follow it, we must allow human generations, once again, to come into contact as do the strands of a weave, along their length.

Part V

Life as a whole

Humans have come in for a rough ride recently. The confidence that many of their number once had in their innate superiority has been shattered amid accusations of wanton self-interest and unbridled greed, the results of which can be seen around the world in environmental ruination, economic misery, social injustice and latterly, pandemic disease. Humankind, it is alleged, is a victim of its own success, and must collectively mend its ways if the rest of creation is not to be dragged down with it, into mass extinction. There is indeed substance to these allegations, and they call for urgent redress. The real picture, however, is a great deal more complicated.

For one thing, it is unfair to tar all humans with the same brush. Unendingly variable, they are what they do, as much makers of history as made by it, in a process of life whose very continuity rests on the principle that it progresses to no end, no final summit or point of conclusion. And for another thing, humans never act alone, but always in the company of others without whose nourishment they would be powerless. At no time in history, moreover, have these others not included beings of manifold nonhuman kinds. Indeed, that the world we inhabit includes more than other humans has long been obvious to all whose business is to make a living in it, and is news only to philosophers who – for the past few centuries and in a particular corner of the world – have managed to persuade themselves otherwise. What for them is a radically new discovery, namely that nonhumans can get along together and even hold meanings for one another in ways that do not depend in the slightest on how they are used or perceived by human beings, or even on any human presence at all, is for everyone else a truism that goes without saying. But its implications have still to be worked out, and the following chapters document some of my attempts to do so.

My own anthropological apprenticeship commenced with fieldwork among Sámi reindeer herders in Lapland, and I begin, in Chapter 19, with a dispute between myself and anthropologist Robert Paine about human–animal relations in herding. Do reindeer transact with humans on a foundation of mutual self-interest, as humans are alleged to do with one another? Or is this so-called transactional approach no more applicable to humans

DOI: 10.4324/9781003171713-24

than it is to deer? Just at the point when transactionalism was on the wane in anthropology, it was on the rise in psychology and the study of animal behaviour. Studies of nonhuman primates, in particular, likened them to wily strategists, possessed of an intelligence that is positively Machiavellian in its penchant for intrigue. Yet however smart these nonhumans might be, they were nonetheless supposed to interact, by way of their soft and mutable bodies, only with other individuals of their species, and not with humans. Picking up on this idea, philosopher Bruno Latour has argued that human relations differ from those of the primate troop, precisely in the extent to which they are stabilised through the enrolment of ever more nonhumans. These nonhumans, however, figure not as soft-bodied transactors but as durable objects, capable of mediating in the traffic of signs from which social life is assembled. Are we to think of nonhumans, then, as smart transactors or as material-semiotic mediators? To my mind, neither alternative seems credible. An anthropology beyond the human, I argue, should rather regard nonhumans as sentient beings, absorbed in the tasks of carrying on their own lives as are humans in theirs, and should engage with them as such.

In Chapter 20, I turn the spotlight back from nonhumans onto humans. The progressive emancipation offered by philosophers of the Enlightenment sought both to liberate humanity from earthly bondage and to subvert the earth and its creatures to human ends. This humanist project, however, was driven by a colonial machine that not only dehumanised native populations but also devastated their lands. A postcolonial age demands an alternative, post-humanist settlement. Here I ask what part prehistory could play in such a settlement. Enlightenment thinkers, having split the concept of the human into species and condition, envisaged a place for prehistory around the point of origin where culture or civilisation was supposed to have commenced its ascent from a biologically evolved baseline. Yet despite an extensive search, no such origin has ever been found, for the simple reason that it is a figment of modern thought. The search for an alternative drew me to the thinking of the thirteenth-century mystic Ramon Llull. The human, for Llull, is a 'humanifying animal', launched on a process of continuous birth, in which even death and burial hold the promise of renewal. This vision finds a contemporary echo in prehistorian André Leroi-Gourhan's explorations of the relation between hand and voice in what he called 'graphism'. Could graphism provide the key to a prehistory that does not so much precede as subtend the historic? Herein, I suggest, lies the promise of a new humanism that is capable of recentring human being in the world without drawing the world exclusively around our human selves.

This axial realignment from humanisation to humanifying shifts the emphasis of the new humanism from progress to sustainability. If the measure of progress lies in advance towards a limit of perfection, sustainability is fundamentally about the continuity of life. A truly sustainable world, however, cannot be for some but not others. It must have room for beings and things of every kind, not just now but for all time. How can we envision such a world? We can only do so, as I show in Chapter 21, by rethinking the idea of everything. I argue for a conception of everything not as the sum total of minimally existing entities, joined together into ever larger and more complex structures, but rather as a fluid and heterogeneous plenum from within which things emerge as crumples and folds. The sustainability of everything, then, can no longer be defined, as in dominant discourses of technoscience, in terms of the numerical balance of recruitment and loss. It is rather about lifecycles, about how things last or perdure, and about how they secure their own renewal. With this, all sorts of minor practices of everyday care, by which people look after family and kin, houses and fields, animals and plants, artefacts and landscapes, are accorded the value they deserve, as life-sustaining activities, instead of taking second place to the policy implementations of rational resource management. Nothing, indeed, threatens sustainability more than the ambition of big science, and its political and financial sponsors, to engineer and regulate the earth and its peoples as if they were the components of a single, integrated system.

At stake, here, is the difference between thinking of the world as a totality to be managed, or as a whole to be inhabited. That we are all inhabitants of one world is not in doubt; the question is: how should we understand its oneness? Is it the sum total of its parts or, like a whole rope, the ever-continuing entwinement of its constituent lives? I turn to these questions in my final chapter, but before doing so it is necessary to essay a more precise delineation of life. This is my theme for Chapter 22. It hinges on the question of signs and their meaning. For some would argue that the traffic in signs, or *semiosis*, is the defining quality of life itself. I disagree, and to explain why, I compare the semiotic approach to how living creatures fashion a meaningful world or *Umwelt*, pioneered by the acknowledged founder of biosemiotics, Jakob von Uexküll, with the ecological approach to perception developed by James Gibson, according to which animals find meaning in their environment through the discovery of what it affords. The issue between them comes down to the possibility of direct perception. For semioticians, perception is always mediated by signs. Semiosis, however, short-cuts the movement of life, since the relation of 'standing for' calls up a destination even before the traveller has set out. Taking my cue from Gibson, I argue that the lifeworld is woven through lines of movement, not by joining up the landmarks on routes already travelled. When we speak of 'life as a whole', it is to the entire meshwork of such lines that we refer.

Finally, in Chapter 23, I consider how life as a whole relates to the particular lives that make it up. This relation, I argue, is contrapuntal rather than summative. The compositions of life are not transient assemblages, made up of bits and pieces that may just as readily fall apart, but affective gatherings of lifelines that respond to one another, or correspond, as they go along. Life itself, then, is not the summation but the correspondence of its particulars, not 'and ... and ... and ...', but 'with ... with ... with ...'. Comparing ideas of the self and the soul, founded respectively in regimes of naturalism and animism, I show that while selves may be conceived as adding up to a collectivity, the correspondence of soul-life proceeds through a process of interstitial differentiation. Here, agency is inside action rather than in front of it. This calls for a 'turn' that is not ontological but ontogenetic, and it leads us to conceive of a world that is one not in its reduction of all difference to liquid commodities, circulating in a global condominium, but in its own inexhaustible potential for variation. This world is not a universe but a pluriverse. Like a conversation of many voices, the pluriverse is a plenum of many lives, and every life is an exploration of the possibilities of being it affords. It is for anthropology, as a philosophy not just *of* life but *in* life, to enquire into these possibilities and to learn from them. Perhaps, then, it can help us find a way through the troubles that undoubtedly lie ahead.

Chapter 19

Animals are us

On living with other beings

On reindeer and men

Over fifty years ago, social anthropologist Robert Paine embarked on fieldwork among the Sámi people of Kautokeino, in northernmost Norway. This place is one of the strongholds of reindeer pastoralism in the region, and Paine's fieldwork found him following herders and herds on their traditional annual migration between winter and summer pastures. It took a long time, however, for the results of this work to appear in print. Apart from a few exploratory articles published in the early 1970s (Paine 1970, 1971, 1972), nothing further was heard of it until some thirty years later, when Paine at last revisited his field journals from back then, and cast a retrospective and critical eye on the profound changes that had since taken place in the policies and practices of reindeer herding. His book *Herds of the Tundra* (Paine 1994) presents an astonishingly detailed account of the seasonal cycle of herding activities as it was in those days, liberally interspersed with excerpts from his journals. In these excerpts, Paine and his Sámi companions seem forever to be finding and losing animals, speculating on where other herders might be with *their* animals, and wondering where to go next. Perhaps the most striking feature of the journals, and of the book, is this preoccupation – amounting at times to an obsession – with reindeer, at the expense of the people who manage them. These people, some of whom Paine evidently came to know very well, remain shadowy in his account, which remains firmly centred on the animals.

Indeed the pastoral Sámi, along with their ethnographer, appear to have reindeer on the brain, an affliction that will be familiar to anyone who has worked in a reindeer-herding society. But it also gives cause for reflection. Why should anthropologists, of all people, end up paying more attention to animals than to human beings? This is a question that I, too, have had occasion to ask myself, and that others have often put to me. 'You anthropologists are supposed to be studying the people', they would say; 'why do you go on and on about reindeer?' For as a fieldworker among the Skolt Sámi of north-eastern Finland, in the early 1970s, I had caught the

DOI: 10.4324/9781003171713-25

same affliction. Compared with their neighbours over the border in Norway, the Skolts possessed far fewer reindeer, and long-distance migrations had never been part of their tradition. To make ends meet they had to hunt, trap and fish, to collect berries, and to work for wages when it was available. Nevertheless, their lives and fortunes seemed to be entirely wrapped up in the comings and goings of their herds. Often, they would talk of little else. Thus my field journals, like Paine's, have as much if not more to say about reindeer than about people.

Worse still, I began to talk about reindeer *as if* they were people – as if they existed in communities of their own, with their own social organisation, and made their own decisions on matters affecting their lives including, most crucially, how to respond to the presence and demands of humans. In one of the first papers I ever wrote, shortly after my return from the field, I argued along these lines that humans and reindeer comprise two interacting populations: 'both form social groups, and are guided in political-economic decision-making, which takes the other into account, by very different sets of goals and values' (Ingold 1974: 523). Herdsmen want large and vigorous herds; animals want protection and security. So long as the animals find security in associating with humans, then they will continue to do so, but if – for whatever reason – humans are no longer able to keep their side of the bargain, then the animals will defect, propelling the herdsmen to adopt increasingly forcible means in the attempt to regain control. The relation between humans and animals then flips from the symbiotic to the predatory, as herders seek to run down their reindeer while the reindeer endeavour to make good their escape. Such was the situation I encountered in my fieldwork.

My article, 'On reindeer and men', was published in 1974, in the journal of the Royal Anthropological Institute, at that time still known as *Man*. It drew an incredulous response, from none other than Robert Paine (1975: 618–19). In a letter to the journal's editor, Paine accused me of presenting an 'anthropomorphic fantasy' that was as unhelpful as it was misleading. It is one thing to claim that human beings form relations with one another based on shared understanding and common interests, and it is perfectly acceptable to speak of social contracts and reciprocal obligation. But to extend this kind of sociological reasoning to reindeer, as I had done, is at best an undisciplined parody, at worst a travesty of common sense. Are we seriously to believe that reindeer, among themselves, cook up strategies in terms of what they see as their best interests? Of course, herdsmen deploy their accumulated knowledge about the habits of animals in the conduct of their operations; and of course, frightened or harried animals will escape their pursuers if they can. But it is surely absurd to claim that reindeer deploy *their* knowledge of the ways of humans in conducting their lives, or that they might use such knowledge in order either to seek protection or to evade capture. 'Where is the evidence', Paine (1975: 619) fumed, 'for supposing that the animals have anything at all approaching a reciprocal body of "knowledge", deduced from experience, about the herdsmen?'

Strangely enough, the evidence was there in Paine's own field journals, although another two decades were to pass before it came to light, in the publication of his *Herds of the Tundra*. In the book, he describes at length the process of 'reciprocal learning', as he calls it, between reindeer and their herders, in which each learns the other's ways (Paine 1994: 29). 'Animals learn about their herders' order of things', he writes, 'as well as herders about their animals" (1994: 31). Reindeer, for example, familiarise themselves with the sounds and smells of the human camp, and learn to associate these with security. Not all animals are equally involved in this learning process, however. Those most closely involved, and that might on this account be considered tame, go on to 'teach' other animals in the herd, serving as intermediaries in the passage of knowledge across the species boundary. Moreover, what is learned in one reindeer generation will likely be passed on to the next. For human herdsmen, knowing what the reindeer know is critical to the success of any campaign; yet the weight of accumulated knowledge in the collective memory of a herd can also be a hindrance if circumstances require an abrupt change of plan. It is hard to get animals, especially older individuals, to 'unlearn' what they already know (Paine 1994: 29–32).

The same might be said, of course, of human beings. Nevertheless, despite this apparent symmetry, Paine remains convinced that the human–animal relationship in herding is fundamentally asymmetrical. The difference comes down to what he calls 'cultural codification'. Like humans everywhere, Paine (1994: 4) insists, 'Sámi *codify* their knowledge'. Thanks to this, they can communicate among themselves with an exactitude of which no other animal is capable. They can set parameters for conduct and criteria for decisions. Reindeer cannot do this. My real offence, then, in treating reindeer as intelligent creatures with the ability to make and communicate decisions on matters affecting their lives, was to extend to them a capacity for codification – and by extension for culture – that, according to Paine, is unique to human beings.

In the anthropology of the time, the belief in a universal human capacity for culture was widely shared. Yet as even Paine (1994: 4) was forced to acknowledge, the cultural code 'is by no means always explicit', and has often to be inferred by the ethnographer on the basis of what people say and do. Is it really the case, then, that Sámi codify their knowledge, or should we rather admit that it is the anthropologist, in this case, who sets out to codify Sámi knowledge? And if the Sámi can know without having to codify what they know – without, that is, articulating it by means of words and symbols in explicit, propositional forms – then is this knowledge so very different from that of the animals they herd? Reindeer, like humans, are surely sentient beings; they have long memories, they know their way around in the terrain, and they recognise and respond through voice and gesture – particularly of the head and antlers – to others of their kind and indeed to humans. Nevertheless, to regard them as strategic game-players, whose every move is predicated upon a rational assessment of costs and benefits, is perhaps a step too far. Not only could it be too far for reindeer; it could be too far for humans too. And when I wrote my essay 'On reindeer and men', I was well aware of this.

Writing to the editor of *Man*, in response to Paine's denunciation of my essay, I was compelled to own up to the fact that it was indeed a parody, and partially intended as such (Ingold 1975: 619). My purpose was to poke fun at a variety of anthropological theory known at the time as 'transactionalism'. It was an approach founded on the idea that social forms are not framed in advance of the life that flows through them but are themselves continually generated in the very course of social life, through the accumulation of countless exchanges or 'transactions' among individual actors, each pursuing what seems to be his or her best interests in the light of goals, values and commitments in place at the time. Pioneered in the influential writings of Fredrik Barth (1966), it was an approach which Paine himself had followed, and to which he had made critical contributions (Paine 1974). At the commencement of my graduate work, I too had fallen under its spell: indeed I was convinced that transactionalism held the key to the future of social anthropology, and before embarking on my fieldwork I spent a few months in Barth's department at the University of Bergen in order to soak up the heady atmosphere he had created there.

Sixteen months later, however, I returned from the field only to discover that the paradigm in which I had placed so much faith was on the verge of collapse. The parody of my essay, then, fed on my own disillusion. Placing human and reindeer populations side by side, as it were on the same playing field, my purpose had not been to pretend that reindeer really *are* consummate strategists that either do or do not transact with humans depending on a calculus of profit and loss. It had rather been to expose the absurdity of supposing that this could be true even of human beings, except in the most artificially confined of situations. At stake, in short, were the very assumptions, concerning individual agency and rational choice, on which transactional theory was based.

Machiavelli among the baboons

Yet around the same time, in another corner of the academic world, even as these assumptions were being discredited within the discipline of social anthropology, they were making a triumphant return in the fields of psychology and animal behaviour studies. The return was heralded by an influential article entitled 'The social function of intellect', by the psychologist Nicholas Humphrey (1976). The question to which Humphrey sought an answer was this: why are human beings and other creatures of the order of primates so intelligent? It is an old question, to which – following the precedent set by Charles Darwin (1874: 195–224) – answers had generally been found in the demands of procuring a subsistence from the environment. More intelligent animals, the argument went, could design and implement more effective subsistence strategies, which could include the manufacture and use of tools, and this in turn would enhance their reproductive success. Consequently, intelligence-enhancing variations would tend to be notched up in the course natural selection, reaching their apogee in humans.

The trouble with this argument is that if you are a monkey or an ape, or even a human hunter–gatherer living in the sort of environment in which our earliest ancestors are thought to have thrived, food is remarkably abundant and easy to harvest if you know where to find it, and its procurement poses no greater demands than those faced by other creatures who seem to get by with nothing like the high-level intelligence of the primates. Such intelligence calls for large and complex brains, and brains are metabolically expensive organs to maintain. What is the point of having a large brain if, for most practical purposes, it has little to do? Humphrey's answer was that primate intelligence is at work, not in the practical-technical field of subsistence procurement, but in the social field of managing transactions with others of one's kind. The little band of primates – be they monkeys, baboons, chimpanzees or human hunter–gatherers – is in Humphrey's scenario a hotbed of intrigue, manipulation, deception and chicanery. Indeed it seems to bear more than an accidental resemblance to the convocations of scholars, in the settings of academic conferences and senior common rooms, with their all too familiar backbiting and conspiracy. It is no wonder that Humphrey, a Cambridge don, chose to model the primate social group on what he called a 'collegiate community' (Humphrey 1976: 310)! Just like a Cambridge college, it is a community in which no individual can ever feel secure in position or rank, and in which social life entails a perpetual jostling for attention, influence, mating partners and even food. To play the game, you need to have your wits about you. And it is precisely because social life is a game of wit, Humphrey hypothesised, that big brains evolved, along with the intelligence they support.

This idea inspired a good deal of work on the complex dynamics of relationships in social groups of monkeys and apes. A decade later, introducing a volume of papers on the subject, psychologists Andrew Whiten and Richard Byrne announced, with unabashed aplomb, that 'the idea of social intelligence is one whose time has come'. They rebranded it the 'Machiavellian intelligence hypothesis' (Whiten and Byrne 1988: 1). Reading the evidence adduced to support the hypothesis, it is hard to avoid the impression that in the minds of the Western scientists who study them, monkeys and apes appear a good deal smarter than the majority of human beings who are neither Westerners nor scientists. For whereas the intelligence of nonhuman primates shines out against the received view of the animal other as a creature governed by instinct, the non-Western, non-scientific other is debased in the scientific worldview as one whose life is governed by tradition rather than reason, and for whom the free play of intelligence is inhibited by force of habit and custom. Thus if a social anthropologist like Paine might baulk at the idea of extending a transactional approach from humans to animals, for psychologists of the Machiavellian persuasion it is just the other way around. If anything, they would doubt the applicability of the approach to human beings, at least until Machiavelli emerged upon the stage to tell them how to better raise their game.

In 1978, two years after the publication of Humphrey's article, the primatologist Shirley Strum convened a conference to review the state of the art in studies of the social behaviour of baboons. At the conference, she presented what she claimed to be nothing less than a 'revolutionary new picture of baboon society' (Strum 1987: 158). Where previous studies had focused on hierarchies of dominance and subordination, maintained and enforced through displays of aggression, Strum argued that there is no stable hierarchy but rather a constant process of negotiation, of give and take, in which individuals – both males and females – enact sophisticated strategies of competition and cooperation. Here, the skills of social manipulation, of reciprocity and the calculated exchange of favours, of finesse and decorum, take precedence over agonistic posturing or the aggressive use of force. Strum's baboons were smart, smarter than anyone had previously imagined, and seemed 'no less – and perhaps much more – aware of their actions than most humans' (1987: 143, 156). Rather than operating from within a social structure, it is as if the animals were continually in the business of forging it, of ascertaining what the structure might be and testing its resilience. Indeed the baboons appeared positively Machiavellian.

Though hardly as revolutionary as she had claimed, Strum's findings were largely consistent with Humphrey's speculations, and like the latter, they were couched in the idiom of social transactions. And for one of those invited to Strum's 'baboon conference', a little-known philosopher by the name of Bruno Latour, they held a particular appeal. If reactions to Strum's revelations among the 'silverbacks' of primatology at the conference had been cool, Latour's reception was perfectly icy. Strum (1987: 162) recalls how there was even a move to evict him from the proceedings! For his part, however, Latour was very much impressed by what he heard, and he went on to collaborate with Strum in a paper presented in 1984 to a symposium on *Political Behaviour as a Primate Social Strategy*. If there is such a thing as 'baboon society', they argued, it exists only in the ever-ongoing efforts of the animals themselves to define, by way of their own performance, what it is. Their society, so to speak, is perpetually under construction. But the only tools they have available to use in this task of construction are their own bodies. These are 'soft' tools, say Strum and Latour, with which they can build only 'soft' societies. With such tools, relations decay as fast as they are established. If they are to last, they have continually to be reasserted, day in, day out (Strum and Latour 1987: 788–9, 795).

How then does the sociality of baboons differ from that of humans? The key difference, according to Strum and Latour (1987: 791), is that human relations can be pegged or anchored to resources beyond the body, in the form of 'language, symbols and material objects' – things that are at least one step removed from the ebb and flow of bodily activity and that furnish partially independent points of reference. In the social world of baboons, we might say, there are only first and second persons, only *I*s and *you*s. But in the world of humans, there are *it*s to which both I and you may refer and which subtend both of us: in so doing, they lend a solid footing to our relationships. An 'it' may be conceptual or material – it may be an idea or an object – but crucially, it has a certain fixity. Where nothing is fixed and everything to play for, life can be exceedingly complex, as indeed it is among the baboons. The more, however, that relations are grounded in externalities, the more they can be factored out and their aspects disaggregated. You can focus on one thing at a time without going adrift. While this considerably simplifies the tasks of social life, it also makes it possible to assemble simple, clear-cut operations into immensely complicated structures. The overall trend in social evolution, then, involves a trade-off between complexity and complication, in which the latter rises as the former falls.

Strum and Latour (1987: 792) illustrate the trend by means of a diagram with four stages (Figure 19.1). The first, with maximal complexity but minimal complication, is exemplified by the baboons. The second stage is exemplified by human hunter–gatherers. For them, too, what little there is of social order exists and persists mainly in the performance; nevertheless their possession of language and rudimentary technology allows for a slight reduction of complexity and invests relationships with greater determination and durability. In the third stage, represented by agricultural societies, social bonds are still more durable, more grounded, and less dependent on bodily performance; and society is correspondingly more complicated. And finally, with modern industrial society, a vastly expanded repertoire of extra-somatic resources supports a massively complicated social structure while shrinking the complexity of relations to the residues of intimacy that remain within its interstices, and that have not been siphoned off into the institutional domains of politics, economics, law, religion, and so forth.

Us and them

In the decades following the publication, in 1987, of his paper with Strum, Latour has often returned to the baboons. He has done so as part of a campaign to rescue what he calls the 'missing masses' (Latour 1992) of objects and artefacts from the oblivion into which they had allegedly fallen

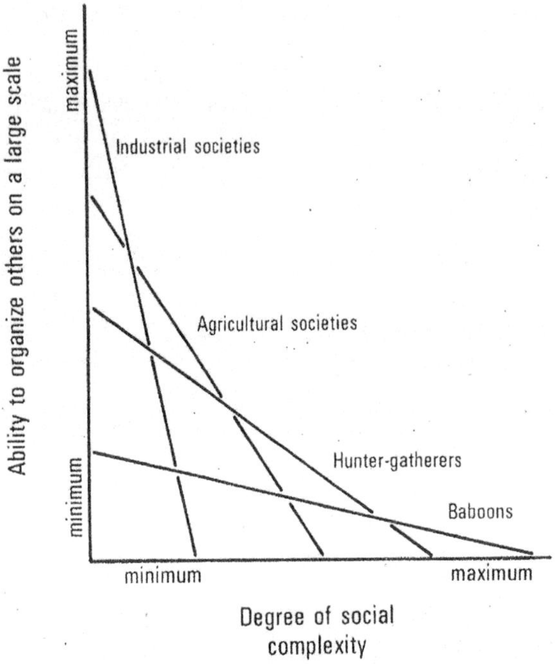

Figure 19.1 The trade-off between complexity and complication.
Reproduced from Strum and Latour (1987: 792). © Sage Publications.

in mainstream social science. Without objects, he thinks, we would live like baboons, and the degree to which we do not is a measure of their importance. In a dialogue with Michel Serres, conducted in 1991 (Serres and Latour 1995), the baboon study was cited as exemplary of what social life would be like in an objectless world. The animals, Serres remarked, 'enter into contracts among themselves that are ... based exclusively on the concept of *us*'. These pacts have continually to be formed and reformed, in real time. Thus there can be no history, only endless renewal of the same. Humankind, Serres insisted, indeed human history itself, 'begins with the weight of the object'. We humans would not survive 'without all of *them*, without this universe that is best designated by a third-person pronoun' (Serres and Latour 1995: 199–200).

The conclusion that Serres and Latour (1995: 200) drew from their dialogue was that a social science that confined itself, in the classic mould, to a restricted domain mapped out in the interaction of intentional beings with others of their kind – and of their kind alone – would at best be applicable only to animals, not to humans. Or as Latour put it, on revisiting the issue in his book *Reassembling the Social* (2005: 70), a 'sociology of the social' might work for baboons, but would be useless for human beings. 'Baboon troops', he suggests (2005: 198), 'could really offer the ideal natural experiment to check what happens when social connections are strictly limited to social skills.' We would gain a window into the complex interference patterns that are set up when the lives and bodies of consociates are folded in on one another. But 'complicated humans', Latour (2005: 199) claims, 'have folded themselves into vastly more entities, some of them having the great advantage of remaining in place'. And their study requires an altogether different approach.

Now there is something extremely odd about this convocation of us and them – of restless, mutable, animate beings and emplaced, fixed, durable entities – that for both Serres and Latour comprises a matrix for the conduct of human affairs. Every restless, mutable, animate being that does not happen to be human seems to have gone missing. Elsewhere, Latour (1999: 174–215) characterises the convocation as 'a collective of humans and nonhumans'. But with the singular exception of domestic animals, there are no living (nonhuman) mammals, birds, reptiles, fish or insects in the emerging collective. To be enrolled, according to Latour (1999: 208), animals would have first to be endowed with 'the social characteristics necessary for their integration'. They would, in other words, have to be refashioned, through a process of domestication, to the mould of an artificial order. Nonhumans that have not been thus subjected to refashioning, and which lack the requisite characteristics, have no role to play in the collective and do not belong there. They should keep out! Thus while humans, according to Latour (1999: 198), have been engaging in collectives with nonhumans for 'millions of years' – ever since our ancestors started to make tools, striking stone on stone – it was the stones that were enrolled in the collective, not the animals hunted with them (Latour 1999: 210–11). The prehistory of the collective, it seems, begins in the mediations of technology, not in engagements with other life-forms.

It has long been customary, in the world of us and them, to refer to the former as 'subjects' and to the latter as 'objects'. In his conversation with Latour, Serres does the same. But for his own part, Latour (1999: 193–4) repudiates this subject/object distinction. For all it does is to impose, a priori, a wholly spurious asymmetry between, on the one hand, the world of human intentional action and, on the other, a material world of causal relations (Latour 2005: 76). Conventionally, the first world has gone under the name of 'society', and the second under the name of 'nature'. In place of the opposition between society and nature, Latour calls for a symmetrical approach which would bring both humans and nonhumans to the table as transacting parties. By this, he doesn't mean that humans and nonhumans are *literally* symmetrical, as though equal and opposite. Quite to the contrary, he wants to find a way of talking about persons and things that allows for heterogeneity and is *non*-oppositional. For Latour it is precisely because they are different, but nevertheless bound up in an encompassing field of relations, that humans and nonhumans can swap properties and exchange roles. '*Objects and subjects*', he emphasises, '*can never associate with one another; humans and nonhumans can*' (Latour 2004: 76).

But wait a moment! If humans can associate with nonhumans, why cannot baboons associate with non-baboons? So far as the baboons are concerned, Latour is content to follow in the footsteps of the Machiavellian intelligence theorists, and to limit the field of social interaction to conspecifics. 'Machiavellian primates', writes Latour (1999: 211), 'manipulate one another to survive in groups, with each group of conspecifics in a state of constant mutual interference.' Once again, he looks for support to Strum's (1987) baboon study. Baboon society, it transpires, is for baboons only. But humans, for Latour, are different; fundamentally different. And it is precisely the mark of distinction between humans and nonhumans, in one sense, that lays the foundation for their association in another. Indeed what is most remarkable about Latour's principle of symmetry is that it rests upon a claim to human uniqueness, along with a theory of progress from the animal to the human and from the hunting and gathering of our earliest ancestors, through agriculture, to modern industrial society, which could have come straight out of the nineteenth century (Ingold 2012b: 430).

Indeed the very stage upon which Latour (1999: 212) takes up arms to 'fight modernism', as philosopher Jeff Kochan (2010) astutely notes, turns out to be none other than one of modernism's most potent myths of origin. It is the myth of how, millions of years ago, the distant ancestors of modern-day humans broke the bonds of nature that hold all other animals in their grip, and launched themselves on the path of history. Paradoxically, an approach which purports to de-ontologise the distinction between the human and the nonhuman, and to establish in its place a level playing field, is justified on the grounds that in their manner of engagement with material things, and in the progressive history of that engagement, human beings are radically distinct from all other living kinds. Hardly could a symmetrical approach rest on a more asymmetrical foundation!

Let us return to the reindeer. They are certainly nonhuman, and they certainly associate with human beings. Where then would they fit, in Latour's scheme of things? We might, on the one hand, regard the reindeer as an extra-somatic resource that provides a stable point of reference for human social relations. For example, it carries an earmark. The mark is of no concern whatever for the deer – beyond the mildly painful experience of having it cut with a knife. However, it is the focus of intense concern for the herdsmen, since it encodes information about its owner and, since marks are passed on and elaborated along family lines, about his or her genealogical connections. On the other hand, we might treat reindeer in the way Latour treats baboons. Though they belong to quite different animal orders, and inhabit environments that could hardly be more dissimilar, reindeer and baboons do have some things in common. They live in social groups, males compete for females, and relations of dominance and submission, of vital significance for access to food and sex, have continually to be negotiated and performed. Where for baboons, the performance revolves around male canines and female buttocks, for reindeer of both sexes, it revolves around the antlers.

In a Latourian world, then, nonhumans can make their presence felt in two distinct ways: as mediators and as Machiavellians. They can provide material-semiotic resources for humans; and they can carry on their own lives, among themselves, without transacting with humans at all. There are, let us say, embodied code-carriers and smart performers. As vectors of symbolic codification – in the third person – animals can enter into association with humans. But in the first and second persons, as *I*s and *you*s, they can only associate with one another, and not with humans at all. There can be humans and nonhumans, but there cannot be reindeer and non-reindeer. So much for symmetry.

The wrong kinds of nonhumans

It was Serres, you will recall, who insisted that we humans could not survive 'without all of *them*', without a universe of things in the third person. Here he is again, in a passage from an essay entitled *Genesis*, composed in 1982:

> The only assignable difference between animal societies and our own resides … in the emergence of objects. Our relationships, social bonds, would be as airy as the clouds were there only contracts between subjects. In fact the object, specific to the Hominidae, stabilizes our relationships.
>
> (Serres 1995a: 87)

Well, whatever the case may be for baboons, it is simply not true, as Serres asserts, that for nonhumans generally, social relations are free-floating rather than anchored in the material world. Migratory seabirds return to nest and breed, year in year out, to the same cliffs and in the same pairs – as do herds of reindeer to the same calving grounds. Here, cliffs and grounds play a well-established part in stabilising relationships between breeding pairs in the first case, and between mothers and offspring in the second.

Perhaps you will say that humans are still different, in so far as the ability to recall a good place for nesting, or for calving, does not require of the animal that it should treat the place as an entity in its own right, apart from the peregrinations that brought it there. Perhaps it is we humans, in our studies of animal behaviour, who objectify the place, not the animals themselves. Be that as it may, innumerable anthropological studies have shown how human groups likewise maintain strong and enduring attachments to particular places, along with the features of the landscape that lend them their distinctive character. As in the totemic landscape of Aboriginal Australia (Myers 1986) or the homeland of the Koyukon of Alaska (Nelson 1983) – to cite just two very well-documented examples – every such place is woven as a gathering of stories, of the comings and goings of diverse human and other-than-human beings. And in his classic study of the storied landscape of the Western Apache of Arizona, Keith Basso (1992: 126) shows how mountains and arroyos take over from grandmothers and uncles in the moral education of younger generations. They are active players in the Apache world, addressed as one would address fellow humans, in the second person. If animals do not objectify the places that matter so much to them and that anchor their relationships, then neither necessarily do humans.

Turning from places and landscapes to tools and equipment, it might be argued that whereas animals are largely confined to the use of what the primatologist Hans Kummer (1995) has called 'social tools', in the form of their own bodies, humans routinely surround themselves with extra-somatic implements of their own making. Introducing a study of what he calls 'the material life of human beings', archaeologist Michael Schiffer asks us to imagine that a research team of chimpanzees has embarked upon the sociological study of a human group (Schiffer and Miller 1999: 2–3). One of the first things they would notice is that activities they are used to performing directly upon one another, such as grooming, are displaced onto the manipulation of a variety of artefacts such as combs and brushes. They would observe, too, that there seems to be no point in the lives of human beings, from cradle to grave, when they are not being 'intimate with artefacts'. It is of course true that animals of many other species also interact on a sustained basis with items of various kinds, some of which they have made themselves. But none comes close to the human in the extent to which it does so. 'Incessant interaction with endlessly varied artefacts', Schiffer maintains, 'is the empirical reality of human life and what makes it so singular' (Schiffer and Miller 1999: 2).

Might these artefacts, then, provide the anchors that, as Serres alleges, pin human relations down in a way that is impossible for the animals? Again, the answer is: not necessarily. As anthropological studies of hunting and gathering societies have revealed, many if not most of the artefacts used in everyday life are readily made or improvised on the spot, from locally available raw materials, and equally readily discarded. They carry no social weight whatever (Woodburn 1982). And at the other end of the scale, the affluent of the Western world are so overwhelmed with ephemeral consumables that they find themselves in much the same predicament as Strum's baboons, having ceaselessly to repair their relationships by means of new objects. In sum, we have found that while on the one hand, places and landscapes can stabilise relationships as much in animals as in humans, on the other hand tools and other artefacts, while far more prevalent among humans than animals, may do little or nothing to stabilise relationships.

In light of these observations, what are we to make of the following, from a recent book entitled *In Defense of Things*, by Bjørnar Olsen?

> If there is one historical trajectory running all the way down from Olduvai Gorge to Postmodernia, it must be one of increased mixing: that more and more tasks are delegated to non-human actors, and more and more actions mediated by things. Only by increasingly mobilizing things could humans come to experience 'episodes' of history such as the advent of farming, urbanization, state formations, industrialization, and postindustrialization.
>
> (Olsen 2010: 9–10)

Assuredly, the citizens of Postmodernia are surrounded by a wealth of artefacts infinitely in excess of what was available to the little band of creatures, known to science as *Homo habilis*, who camped at Olduvai Gorge some two million years ago, and whose only tools were crudely fractured stone choppers. There seems no good reason to doubt that in the broad course of history, the number and kinds of artefacts that humans have used have increased almost exponentially. This does not necessarily imply, however, a proportionate rise in the involvement of nonhuman agencies. For what comes out unequivocally, both from the evidence of pre-history and from the ethnography of peoples who have not taken the high road to Postmodernia, is that there never has been a time when all sorts of nonhumans have not been enrolled in the tasks of keeping life going.

It is not that there were fewer nonhumans hanging around in the environments of hunter–gatherers, or of farmers or herdsmen, compared with those of the industrial and post-industrial world. What has changed is the nature of the nonhumans. Overall, the proportion of embodied code-carriers in the human environment has increased, while the proportion of smart performers has correspondingly decreased.[1] The former exemplify what theorists commonly take for 'material culture': they are the kinds of things that can be co-opted as extra-somatic mediators in human endeavours. The latter, by contrast, are forms of animate life – they are beings that follow their own calling while yet responding to the lives, and the calls, of humans, just as humans, reciprocally respond to theirs. Might it not be in this correspondence of both human and animal lives that we find the essence of sociality?

For those like myself, with a background in the ecological study of human hunting and gathering, pastoralism or farming, the oft-repeated claim of material culture theorists – namely, that the nonhuman has been marginalised or suppressed in the social sciences – seems preposterous. For it turns a blind eye to the wealth of studies, by both anthropologists and archaeologists, of the manifold ways in which people in different parts of the world, and in different periods of history, have shared their lives with diverse animals and plants. How can we account for this blind spot? There is only one possible answer: so far as our theorists are concerned, these animals and plants are the *wrong kinds of nonhumans*. They lack the characteristics of fixity, durability and emplacement that entitle them to admission to the collective. As forms of animate life they are intruders on the stage of world history, and should not be there.

Consider, for example, the question with which Olsen (2010: 2) launches his defence of things: 'How', he asks, 'do things and objects "mix" with human beings to form the configurations we call *society* and *history*?' Here, society and history are rendered as exclusively human achievements, brought about thanks to the enrolment of objects and things. To pose the question in these terms is, in itself, to admit nonhumans into the processes of social and historical life only in the third person, as hybrid material-semiotic resources for human projects. They are not supposed to engage with humans as animate beings in their own right, nor humans with them. 'The history of animals that has developed over the last thirty years', as the historian Éric Baratay (2015: 3) stresses, 'is in reality a *human* history of animals, where these latter have very little place as real beings.' And behind this exclusion lies the assumption – which we have already encountered in our exposure of the asymmetrical basis for the alleged symmetry of humans and nonhumans – that in the conduct of their own lives, that is as intelligent performers rather than embodied signifiers, nonhumans should associate only with others of their kind: reindeer with other reindeer, baboons with other baboons. In human eyes, according to this account, the nonhuman can be *one of ours*: this reindeer could be mine and carry my mark; that baboon could be a member of the troop I am studying. But *it cannot be one of us* – not, at least, without being regarded anthropomorphically, as an honorary human, as we sometimes treat domestic animals or pets.

We can but wonder where this assumption comes from. Why should anyone think that social relations should be confined to individuals of the same species? Why should the reindeer or the baboon not be one of us, or we one of them? Are not the lives of herdsmen entwined with those of the animals they herd, or the lives of behavioural scientists with the animals they study? And are not these cross-species entwinings, these correspondences, just as social as are human and animal entwinings with others of their respective kinds? As Strum and Latour (1987: 795) recognise, accounts of the origins of society in the behavioural sciences tend to start from the idea that the word 'social' refers, in the first place, to 'aggregations of conspecifics', and from there they go on to consider how animals adapt their behaviour to an environment largely made up of others of their kind, by becoming 'smarter at manipulating and manoeuvring around each other'. Yet like most animals, baboons inhabit a landscape in which, among other things, they have to deal with potentially dangerous predators. These predators, too, have to be outmanoeuvred.

Thus even baboons, as Latour (2005: 199) has belatedly and grudgingly admitted, find that their lives are mixed or folded in with landscapes and predators as well as with conspecifics. If you are a baboon, it is not only other baboons you have to care about. And if you are a reindeer, it is not only other reindeer. There are predators like wolves and wolverines, not to mention beings of less fathomable intent, such as humans. If it is social to care about beings of your own kind, why should it not be social to care about beings of other kinds? As I shall now show, the restriction of sociality to relations among conspecifics has its source in the very claim to uniqueness that would otherwise reserve society and history for humans alone. It is, in other words, a direct reflex of the belief in the wholly exceptional nature of human being.

Species being

As with so many things, the argument goes back to Karl Marx. In the *Economic and Philosophic Manuscripts of 1844*, Marx (1972: 75) had declared that 'Man is a species-being'. Here he was following the lead of the philosopher Ludwig Feuerbach. In his classic work *The Essence of Christianity*, Feuerbach (1843: 1–2) maintained that it was not consciousness as such that distinguishes humans from other creatures, but a particular *sort* of consciousness – one that makes it possible for men and women to recognise themselves not just as individuals but as fellow members of a species, thereby apprehending in themselves a 'human essence' that they share with others of their kind. Thus to say 'I am a man' or 'I am a woman' is an assertion of individuality, but one that is possible only because it is made against the ground of an acknowledged humanity common to all. In this regard, species-being is entirely distinct from species-life.

The life of a species, whether human or animal, as Marx (1972: 75–6) went on to explain, is carried on by way of a bodily engagement with the stuff of the material world. Its proper domain is the world of nature. But while the animal, in its activity, *exemplifies* the form of life typical of the species to which it belongs, it has no knowledge of the fact, no awareness of its exemplary character. The animal and its species life are one and the same. Humans, by contrast, are capable of making their species life the object of their own will and consciousness. They are aware of what they are doing, and they are aware that it is they who are doing it. As agents, they can separate themselves out from their activity and, by the same token, they can imagine themselves doing all kinds of different things, including even the things that other animals do. 'An animal', wrote Marx (1972: 76), 'forms things in accordance with the standard and the need of the species to which it belongs, whilst man knows how to produce in the accordance with the standard of every species.' And it is precisely in this productive potential, and in the freedom it confers, that species-being comes into its own.

Yet for Marx, species-being not only lay at the root of human individuality. It was also tantamount to social being. Individual life and social life, Marx insisted, are one and the same. By social life, he did not mean the life of some hypostasised macro-entity, namely 'society', as against the manifold lives of its individual constituents. Indeed, Marx (1972: 86) explicitly warned against postulating 'society' as an abstraction vis-à-vis the individual. In social life, men and women do not make societies, nor do societies make men and women. Rather, social life is the process wherein men and women reciprocally make one another, establishing through their own activities the relational matrix within which they and their successors come into the world, grow up, and do what they do (Ingold 2016c: 205). 'The individual', as Marx emphasised, '*is the social being*' (1972: 86).

It follows that species being is not fixed for all time, as an immutable part of our given nature. It is rather a historical and relational achievement, realised in the progressive *transcendence* of nature. As such, species being is something that humans, as self-developing and self-transforming animals, have continually to work at: it is a task. Paradoxically however, it is a task open only to the one species whose members are such that their life activity is *not* fully determined by their species identity (Mulhall 1998: 14). Thus, species being is also species limited. This human – this extraordinary being that, as Marx says, can produce to the standard of any species it desires to emulate – is inextricably bound to its own species constitution, its transcendence of nature tied to the very human nature it transcends. Viewing its own species universality in the mirror of nature, what the human sees is its own species specificity. By the same token, life-over-species is reflected in the mirror as life-within-species. And in this inversion, what was a contingent aspect of social relations – their species specificity – becomes their defining feature.

Let me rephrase this argument in slightly less convoluted language. If the mark of the social lies in those properties of freedom, agency and self-awareness that are brought to bear in the conduct of relational endeavours, and if these properties are limited to the kinds of beings we call 'human', then social relations *are* human relations. From here, however, it is but a short step to the conclusion that social relations are human relations because they are with individuals who happen to belong to the same species as we do ourselves. And having once taken this step, the path is clear to extend the concept of the social to cover the interactions that any kind of creature – human or nonhuman – may have with its conspecifics (Ingold 1997: 240–41). For me, social relations are human relations because I happen to be human. Were I a baboon, or a reindeer, then my social relations would be with other baboons, or other reindeer, and not with humans. If I were an ant, they would be with other ants.

It was in just this sense, connoting relations among conspecifics, and without any implication of consciousness or self-awareness, that the notion of society was subsequently taken up in the literature on animal behaviour. Consider the following definition, from the text by E. O. Wilson that launched the field of sociobiology: '*Society*: A group of individuals belonging to the same species and organised in a cooperative manner' (Wilson 1980: 322). Following Wilson's lead, sociobiologists have made it their business to describe and explain the varieties of social behaviour across every branch of the animal kingdom, from insects to primates. The irony of the enterprise, however, is that the very identification of society with the domain of intraspecific interactions came about only thanks to an original assumption, which sociobiologists categorically reject, that social being is a condition uniquely reserved for humankind.

The hybrid community

If we are to bring nonhumans back in, not just as material-semiotic mediators for human action but as beings in their own right, and if we are to allow them to play a social and historical role, alongside humans, in forging the conditions for future life, then this assumption will have to go. It will not go, however, through a fashionable appeal to what is currently parading under the brand-name of 'multi-species ethnography'. Launched by anthropologists S. Eben Kirksey and Stefan Helmreich in 2010, to much fanfare, multispecies ethnography was introduced as 'a new genre of writing and mode of research [that] has arrived on the anthropological stage' (Kirksey and Helmreich 2010: 545). Creatures that had previously appeared as nothing more than material or symbolic anchors for human projects, these authors tell us, are now starting to appear alongside humans as animate beings with biographies and political lives of their own. There is really nothing new about this. For in truth the wrong kinds of nonhumans, though long ignored in the writings of material culture theorists, have never really gone away, and have continued to stalk the pages of the literature on hunters and gatherers, farmers, and pastoralists for generations. After all, it was their intrusion into my paper of 1974, over forty years ago, to which Paine took such exception.

The problem with multi-species ethnography is not just its anachronism, however. It lies rather in its very appeal to species multiplicity. For only in the purview of a universal humanity – that is, from the perspective of species being – does the world of living things appear as a catalogue of biodiversity, as a plurality of species. If we abandon this sovereign perspective, then the very notion that creatures can be grouped on the basis of similarity and divided on the basis of difference, and with it the concept of species itself, will need to be rethought. To be fair, Kirksey and Helmreich (2010: 562) are aware of the problem, for they note in conclusion that a survey that runs the gamut of life forms, all the way from animals and plants to fungi and microbes, 'risks reinstalling the "human" as a central reference point'. Thus, part of the project of multispecies ethnography, they suggest, must be to 'take aim at "species" as a grounding concept for articulating biological difference and similarity'. And to do that, as they point out, is also to place the Marxian notion of 'species being' under interrogation. I agree with them, and this indeed is part of what I have tried to do here.

However the rethinking that Kirksey and Helmreich call for has, to an extent, already been done by the philosopher Dominique Lestel and his colleagues, based at the Laboratory of Eco-anthropology and Ethnobiology in Paris (Lestel 2002; Lestel, Brunois and Gaunet 2006). Lestel starts from the premise that every human society is also a society made up of animals, or rather that no society can be prefixed by the name of a species – as in 'baboon society' or 'human society' – since there can be no community of animate beings that is not hybrid in terms of species composition. Though comprised of both humans and nonhumans, the Lestelian hybrid community could not be more different from the Latourian collective. For the former includes precisely what the latter leaves out: all those restless, mutable, roving beings with whose lives our own are necessarily entangled, as much as they are entangled with one another. This entanglement entails a sharing of meaning, of interests and of affects (Lestel, Brunois and Gaunet 2006: 161). Thus, rather than looking at animals as though they were humans, or at humans as though they were animals, we need to find ways of modelling social life that allows for their differences. The question, as Lestel (2002: 56) emphasises, is: 'how do humans and animals allow each other to be *differently* intelligent?'

This emphasis on difference is critical. For Machiavellian intelligence theorists, as we have seen, the autonomy of the individual is paramount, and every smart performer, playing his or her part in society, campaigns to protect it. In the community of conspecifics, you have to watch your back! In the hybrid community, however, the animal subject is not a bounded entity, set over and against others of its kind, but just one trail of growth and development in a heterogeneous field of interests and affects. Or in Lestel's (2002: 53) words, it 'is not so much the subject of a defensive autonomy as of an open-ended heteronomy'. And its intelligence is not an interior cognitive capacity, of which its actions are the effects, but lies in its whole way of perceiving and acting in the world. Each animal is different, but these differences are constituted in and through its entanglement in the generative process of social life, they do not exist in spite of it. Contrary to the logic of the multispecies, which associates individuals on the basis of received likeness and divides them along lines of diversification, in the hybrid community – as I have stated elsewhere – 'it is difference that connects, whereas similarity divides' (Ingold 1996: 6).[2]

In the *ethno-ethology* and *etho-ethnology* that Lestel and his colleagues advocate, all animate beings are conceived as fundamentally relational. This is to say that every being is what it is, and does what it does, because of its positioning within a community. In this regard, their approach is not so far from that recently advocated by anthropologist Eduardo Kohn under the rubric of the 'anthropology of life', an anthropology – he writes – 'that is not just confined to the human but is concerned with the effects of our "entanglements" ... with other kinds of living selves' (Kohn 2007: 4). Echoing cultural theorist Donna Haraway (2003: 5), Kohn contends that these others are not just to think *about* but to live *with*. His nonhumans are not like Latour's (2004: 64), since they do not need spokespersons to speak on their behalf. They speak, and indeed communicate, simply by virtue of their presence and activity, through modes of reference which, even if not symbolic, may still be indexical or iconic (see Chapter 22, page 339). We do not, then, have to limit ourselves, in anthropology, to beings that can communicate by means of symbols, or that can *codify* their knowledge. The reindeer can be along too, not perhaps as the Machiavellian strategists of my early parody, but certainly as full participants in the hybrid reindeer-human community.

Anthropology by correspondence

How then should we speak of these animals? Do we go with Lestel, and call them subjects; or follow Kohn in referring to them as selves? Either way, whether as subjects or selves, the first- or second-person pronoun would be appropriate. They are *Is* and *yous*, not just for each other but for us as well. The pronominal form, however, separates the agent from the action, the doer from the deed. *I* did this, we say; and *you* did that; but you and I have our own identities, separate from the things we do. My preference, to the contrary, would be to think of animate beings in the grammatical form of the *verb*. Thus 'to human' is a verb, as is 'to baboon' and 'to reindeer'. Wherever and whenever we encounter them, humans are humaning, baboons are babooning, reindeer reindeering. Humans, baboons and reindeer do not *exist*, but humaning, babooning and reindeering *occur* – they are ways of carrying on, experimental forays in the realms of the possible (Ingold 2011a: 174–5). Moreover, the animals, in their animaling, have much to teach us, so long as we allow them into our presence as the beings they are, with their own lives to lead and stories to tell, rather than merely as material-semiotic surrogates for human projects. For at the end of the day, every creature – human or otherwise – answers to the question of what it is by living its own form of life, and in so doing, by contributing to the lives of all the other creatures to which it relates.

We should regard every living being, in short, as a *going on* in the world. Or more to point, to be animate – to *be alive* – is to become. And as Haraway (2008: 244) stresses, 'becoming is always becoming *with* – in a contact zone where the outcome, where who is in the world, is at stake'. Thus whether we are speaking of human or other animals, they are at any moment what they have become, and what they have become depends on whom they are with. If the Sámi have reindeer on the brain, it is because they have grown up with them, just as the reindeer, for their part, have grown up with the sounds and smells of the camp. Strum (1987: 159), likewise, confesses that the baboons had become the emotional centre of her life, and that she felt true to herself only in their proximity. The philosopher Vinciane Despret (2013: 70–71), reflecting on Strum's study, observes that the primatologist set out not to think *like* the baboons but the think *with* them, to attune her perception with theirs, to construct a partial affinity of her living body with the bodies of her primate companions – or, in a word, to *correspond* with them.[3] If I had returned from my fieldwork 'a little bit reindeer', then Strum would return 'a little bit baboon'.

In an earlier essay, focusing on the human–animal relations of hunting among peoples of the circumpolar North, I observed that 'in the unfolding of the relation between hunters and prey both humans and animals undergo a kind of perpetual rebirth, each enfolding into its inner constitution the principle of its relationship to the other' (Ingold 2000: 143). The same applies to the relation of herdsmen with deer, and indeed to that of researchers with primates. As anthropologists, we find ourselves cast in the midst of this rebirth, for it is nothing less that the ceaseless formation of the living world. I am no less an anthropologist, therefore, for having discovered that like the Sámi herdsmen I accompanied so long ago, my thoughts and actions were at times more with the reindeer than with the people. Nor is Strum any less a primatologist in finding that her thoughts are more with the baboons than with her scientific colleagues. For anthropology is distinguished not by its object, as if it shone a spotlight on humanity, while leaving the rest of creation in the shadows, but by its way of working, which is to learn through correspondence with other lives. As the herdsman is a lifelong student of his herd, I would become – albeit for a short while – a student of the herdsman. And Strum, for her part, endeavoured to practise as an anthropologist among the baboons, studying with them, by way of correspondence.

Let me conclude, then, by pleading not for multi-species ethnography but for *anthropology by correspondence*. I have already shown how a correspondent approach to human and animal becoming disqualifies the taxonomic logic of the multispecies. Identities, as we have seen, are not fixed in advance of their lifetime expression but are rather relational achievements, forged within a field of difference. But correspondence also enjoins us to study *with* people, and indeed *with* animals, rather than to make studies *of* them. This, as I have argued elsewhere (Ingold 2014c), is where anthropology goes beyond ethnography. For the aim of studying *with* is not to seek a retrospective account, looking back on what has come to pass, but to move forward, in real time, along with the multiple and heterogeneous becomings with which we share our world, in an active and ongoing exploration of the conditions and possibilities of our common life, both presently and for the future. And just as in life, becoming continually overtakes being, so in scholarship, the scope of anthropology must always strain beyond the threshold of the study of humanity.

Chapter 20

Posthuman prehistory

Original humans

Human is an ancient word, but the concept of humanity is modern. No one knows exactly where the old word comes from. Giambattista Vico, in his *New Science* of 1725, was convinced that its roots lay in the Latin *humando*, referring to the practice of burial or of funerary rites.[1] A frontispiece for the book, for which Vico provides an elaborate explication, depicts a funeral urn carrying the initials D.M., which he spells out as 'to the good souls of the buried'. Both by origin and destiny, then, humans are of the soil (*humus*). Enlightenment thinkers, however, among them Vico himself, would eventually upend this logic, appealing instead to universal powers of reason or intellect destined to emancipate humankind from earthly bondage, and to cut all ties to the ground, to place and to nature. The modern concept of humanity has its source in this inversion, in the establishment of a condition – the human condition – over and above the state of nature that holds all other creatures in its grip. And nature, by the same token, was no longer seen to be enriched and fortified by the labours of generations past. It was treated rather as both a platform for human endeavours and a depository for a history whose energy is spent, leaving its residues piled up in layers of sediment, each covering over its now submerged predecessors.

Thenceforth the ground, understood as a passive substrate rather than an active and energising force in the ongoing generation of life, could be excavated with impunity. Digging up the past, once associated with the dark arts of necromancy, became a respectable antiquarian profession. With that, archaeology was born, along with the idea of the human career as an ascent from rude nature, through shades of savagery and barbarism, to the perfection of the human condition in refined civility.[2] Of this career, only the later phases, initiated by the onset of written records, were considered truly historic. Everything prior to this watershed was considered preparatory for civilisation, much as childhood was considered preparatory for adult life. Real history is for grown-ups. The very idea of a preparation for history – or what came to be known as *prehistory* – was thus a direct precipitate of

DOI: 10.4324/9781003171713-26

Enlightenment humanism. Yet many contemporary scholars proclaim the days of humanism to be over, or at least numbered. We are entering, they say, a new era of post-humanity. What will become, then, of the idea of prehistory?

There can be no doubt that humanism has contributed massively to the common good. It has brought education, literacy and democratic governance to more of the world's inhabitants than ever before. Commensurate with this success, what began in a handful of European nations has expanded, through trade and colonisation, to encompass the entire globe. This has come, however, at a cost – in two respects. First, in driving a wedge between humanity and nature, the very earth that had once offered nourishment and support for human life came to be recast as a repository of resources to be plundered. Archaeological excavation thus figured as a mere sideshow to a programme of extraction, on an industrial scale, that has ravaged the earth and jeopardised its capacity for renewal. Second, while the appeal to universal entitlement serves the interests of those empowered to lay claim to it, for others the forcible imposition of this claim has meant enslavement, along with loss of land, livelihood, and even life. In the history of colonialism, the flag of humanity has always been flown by the victorious, treating as less than human those who have come under its yoke. As these twin costs have inexorably risen, what began as an agenda for progressive emancipation has morphed into a vicious spiral of environmental destruction and social injustice. To break the spiral demands no less than a radical alternative to the humanist settlement. The challenge is to create a language of concepts in which to frame it. This is the challenge of posthumanism. My question is: can prehistory, as a child of the Enlightenment, play any part in it?

In this chapter I shall hazard an answer. It is necessary to preface my inquiry, however, with a few words about origins. For if there is one question that has exercised the minds of prehistorians, perhaps more than any other, it is this: when, and where, did prehistory begin? In his inquiry into the origins of species, Charles Darwin had shown that living kinds emerge not through any singular act of creation but through a gradual process of modification and diversification, strung out along lines of descent. And although, in *On the Origin of Species*, he had rather little to say about human beings, the assumption was that humankind had evolved in the same way, through a diversification within the genus *Homo*, of which our own species, namely *sapiens*, was the only extant lineage. As a man of his time, of liberal disposition, Darwin was as convinced as anyone of the founding opposition between reason and nature that defined the Enlightenment project. But where others had set a barrier to entry on the path of reason, that human beings alone were qualified to cross, Darwin would claim to detect the rudiments of intellect in even the humblest of organisms, such as the lowly earthworm, as well as a powerful residue of instinct in even the most rational of humans. That is why he could argue that the difference between humans and animals lower in the scale, although vast, was still of degree rather than kind.[3]

But if there was no Rubicon to cross – if the story of human evolution was one of countless minute gradations – then was there any point of origin at all? In his later work *The Descent of Man*, Darwin concluded that there was not. His famous and controversial conclusion was rather that the mechanism of natural selection, relentlessly driving up heritable powers of intelligence, had continued to operate as it had ever done, eventually raising civilised men above primitive savages in precisely the same way that savages were raised over apes.[4] While Darwin himself was no racist, this conclusion provided a veneer of scientific legitimacy for often genocidal adventures of colonisation launched at the time by white Europeans on native populations around the world. As late as the 1930s, established physical anthropologists were defending a colour-coded catalogue of humankind, divided into races on a scale from white to black, with intermediate shades of yellow and red, locked in a xenophobic struggle in which the lighter shades would inevitably rise to the top.[5]

It took the second war in a century to break out among the supposedly civilised races of Europe, itself fuelled by xenophobia, for such ideas to be finally refuted. In the wake of the Holocaust, what was self-evident to Darwin and most of his contemporaries – namely, that human populations differ in their heritable intellectual capacities on a scale from the primitive to the civilised – was no longer acceptable. Darwin's view that the difference between the savage and the civilised man was one of brain-power gave way in mainstream science to a strong moral and ethical commitment to the idea that *all* humans – past, present and future – are equally endowed, at least so far as their moral and intellectual capacities are concerned. 'All human beings', as Article 1 of the Universal Declaration of Human Rights states, 'are endowed with reason and conscience.' This was, in effect, to revert to a humanism of pre-Darwinian vintage, already propounded by Enlightenment philosophers of the eighteenth century. The argument goes that if human beings are one in their possession of reason and conscience – if, in other words, they are the kinds of beings who, according to orthodox juridical precepts, can exercise rights and responsibilities – then they must differ in kind, and not degree, from all other beings that lack such endowment. Humans are indeed exceptional!

The species and the condition

As if to emphasise the exclusiveness of this claim to universality, post-war scientists went on to reclassify extant human beings as members not just of the same species but of the same sub-species, designated *Homo sapiens sapiens*. This was no ordinary sub-species, however. Doubly sapient, the first attribution of wisdom, the outcome of a process of encephalisation, marked it out within the world of living things. But the second, far from marking a further subdivision, registered a decisive break from that world. In what many late twentieth century prehistorians took to calling the 'human revolution', the earliest representatives of the new sub-species were alleged to have achieved a breakthrough without parallel in the history of life, setting them on the path of ever-increasing discovery and self-knowledge otherwise known as culture (Mellars and Stringer 1989). *Human beings* by nature, it was in the historical endeavour of reaching beyond that very nature that they progressively realised the condition of *being human* in which the essence of their humanity was seen to reside. Half in nature, half out, they were torn between the contrary imperatives of intelligence and instinct, reason and emotion. Indeed the double-barrelled sub-specific appellation of *Homo sapiens sapiens* perfectly epitomises the hybrid constitution of these revolutionary creatures. Popularly known as 'anatomically modern humans' – by contrast to the 'archaic' variety, so-called Neanderthals, who supposedly never made it through to the second grade of sapientisation – their prototypical representatives are portrayed as archetypal hunter–gatherers for whom history is yet to begin. *Biologically* just like us, they are supposed to have remained *culturally* at the starting block, fated to enact a script perfected through millennia of adaptation under natural selection (Ingold 2000: 373–91).

At the other end of history stand the summiteers of high modernity, namely scientists, in whom an absolute commitment to reason has finally put paid to the promptings of innate desire. Seeing their own reason reflected in the mirror of nature, they alone pretend to read the script that natural selection has written for their hunter–gatherer antecedents. Between the hunter–gatherer and the scientist, respectively pre- and post-historic, is supposed to lie all the difference between being and knowing, between the adaptive surrender to nature and its subjugation in the light of reason. Yet paradoxically, despite having refuted – after Darwin – the very idea that for *any* species, there exists as essence of its kind, the one thing that science is incapable of relinquishing is its essentialist view of humanity. This is for the simple reason that the project of science depends on it. For it requires a unique capacity to remove themselves *from* nature for humans to imagine themselves as creatures *of* nature. The very appeal to nature-transcending humanity, in short, provides science with the platform of supremacy from which, with no little hubris and profound contradiction, it asserts that human beings are part and parcel of the natural world.

On which side, then, should we place the human? Does the word refer to the human being or being human, to species or condition? Or does its significance, at least within the discourses of modernity, lie precisely in its duplicity, in the fact that we cannot name the species, or subspecies, without calling forth the condition, and vice versa? Perhaps the idea of the human, in its modernist inflection, points to nothing so much as the anxiety, amounting to an existential dilemma, of a creature that can know itself, and the world of which it is a part, only by taking itself out of that world and viewing it, as it were, from the far side. It is a dilemma seemingly recapitulated in the life of every human being as it progresses from infancy, through childhood, to full maturity. Does not the infant start life, no differently from any animal, as a creature of nature? Born of man and woman, it is surely a *human being*, yet initially having no awareness of itself as existing in a world, or indeed of the world in which it exists, it still appears to fall some way short of *being human*. Are some humans, then, more human than others? Are we to think of the child as an intermediate being, halfway between nature and culture, exiting one in preparation for the other?

Writing only a few decades ago, anthropologist Walter Goldschmidt (1993: 351) could still assert, as though it were self-evident, that childhood is characterised by 'the process of transformation of the infant from a purely biological being into a culture-bearing one'. On the way from infancy to adulthood, children are made to appear biologically complete but culturally half-baked. And the same goes for prehistoric hunter–gatherers, equally suspended in a liminal phase in the transition from a natural to a fully cultural life. If grown-ups are more human than children, then by the same token, scientists are more human than hunter–gatherers. And whether for the individual human being or for humankind as a whole, it is the intersection of the axis of biological phylogeny with the development of civility, at the moment where culture 'takes off' from its baseline in hereditary endowment, that sets the point of origin. Even today, it is common to speak of 'early man' (more often than 'early woman'), and of the child's 'early years', as though the antiquity of prehistoric hunter–gatherers could be judged, like the ages of pre-school children, by their proximity to their respective origins. Just as the child was deemed to be closer to its origin than the adult, so likewise, early humans were thought to be closer than later ones to that mighty moment when humanity began.

Yet if human prehistory has a point of origin, what could it mean to have been living close to that point, or even at the crucial moment of transition itself? How can one conceivably distinguish those actions and events that carried forward the movement of prehistory from those that set it in motion in the first place? It is not hard to see, in the image of our hunter–gatherer ancestors looking out upon the dawn of civilisation, the reflection of a decidedly modernist rhetoric. One can almost imagine the television presenter lurking in the background. 'Our epic story', recites the voiceover, 'is about to begin'. Yet despite a frantic and much publicised search for the moment of emergence of anatomically modern humans, prehistorians have failed to find it. And this is for the simple reason that there was no such moment. It is a fabrication of Enlightenment humanism. What, then, is to be done? Few would doubt today that humans have evolved, or that this evolution is rather recent in the wider scheme of things. Nor can we doubt that human beings are both the shapers of their own history, and in turn shaped by it. How then can we close the gap between history and evolution without, as Darwin did, reducing the former to the latter? Is it even possible to restore humans to the continuum of organic life without thereby draining this life of its historical impulse?

The humanifying animal

The post-war reaffirmation of universal humanity took us back, as we have seen, to a pre-Darwinian Enlightenment. Now, however, that the project of the Enlightenment is itself foundering, it is perhaps timely to look even further into the past, to the thinking of pre-modern ages. Might older ways of thought, borne of slower and more long-lasting currents of time, offer us a better guide into an unknown future? It is not as though our self-description as humans was an invention of the eighteenth century, as some contemporary scholars seem to believe.[6] For no less than four centuries before Vico was wondering about the etymology of 'human', the question of how to pin down the meaning of this most enigmatic of words was already troubling another thinker of great insight, Ramon Llull. Born and raised on the island of Majorca, Llull enjoyed a long and productive life during which he wrote a staggering 280 books, composed in Latin, Arabic and his native Catalan. One of the last of these, written in Genoa in 1303, in his seventy-first year, was the *Logica Nova*.[7]

In Llull's cosmology, as set out in this work, everything is a doing, a happening, a going on. Fire, for example, is not a thing that burns; it *is* burning. And the human, by the same token, *is* humaning. To express this in Latin, Lull had to invent a new word, *homificare* – literally, 'to humanify'. The human, Llull declared, is a humanifying animal: *Homo est animal homificans*.[8] Humanifying, be it noted, is not the same as humanising. It is not about imprinting the designs of preformed humanity upon the raw material of an initially formless world. For humans to humanify is rather to forge their existence within the crucible of a common life. Their humanness is not given from the start, as an a priori condition, but emerges as a productive achievement – one moreover that they have continually to work at for as long as life goes on, without ever reaching a final conclusion. If we follow Llull, then humans are not really beings at all, but becomings, launched in a process of perpetual co-creation. They are ever unfinished, even as history carries on. And for what they are, at any moment in this history, they bear a collective responsibility (Ingold 2015: 115–18).

This applies to children as it does to adults. It is not that children are in a process of *becoming human*, which adults have already completed. Rather, just like adults, they are in the process of *human becoming*, forever developing into the people they are, forging their own lives and identities in the world. In a word, they are *growing*, in stature, knowledge and wisdom.

Children, then, are far from the half-baked hybrids of biology and culture that modernity makes them out to be. The child's life does not start from a point of origin, nor is his or her 'early' life closer to such a point than later life. In practice, children make their way through life with as much facility and hindrance, as much fluency and awkwardness, as grown-ups, actively following in the footsteps of their ancestors rather than writing out a script inherited from the parental generation at the point of conception. That is to say, lives are not played out in succession but overlap longitudinally. Thus the passage of generations more resembles a handover in a relay than the transmission of a legacy (Chapter 18, pages 273–4). This relay is tantamount to *life itself*. And while every *particular life* is of limited duration, life itself carries on, or persists, without beginning or end. People may follow where others have passed before, but none is more ancient, nor any other more recent (Ingold 2012a).

Prehistoric hunter–gatherers, then, were not gifted with a road map for the future which their historic descendants were fated to follow. They had instead to work things out, improvising a passage as they went along. It is indeed a constitutive quality of life – human as well as nonhuman – that it does not so much unfold from a point of origin as *originate all the time*. It is a continuous birth, a concrescence. This leads us to imagine the evolution of life as the perpetual renewal of a world, from within which living beings, as they go along together, participate in creating the conditions for their own and others' future development. And history? This is but a local manifestation of the same process. Working our way downstream, evolution runs into history as a river into the ever divergent and convergent channels of its delta, without crossing any barrier or threshold. But if there is no barrier to be crossed, no intermediate zone, then what room remains for prehistory?

The braid and the stack

Let me return for a moment to the ill-fated Neanderthals, whom I mentioned in passing a moment ago. Recall that according to the post-war narrative, humans of the anatomically modern variety, *Homo sapiens sapiens*, were the only ones to make it through to the far side of nature, leaving their cousins, *Homo sapiens neanderthalensis*, stranded and destined for extinction. The story is disturbingly familiar: it tells of how a race of men, possessed of superior intelligence, inherited the earth, while subjugating, driving out or exterminating its alleged inferiors. In the nineteenth century, it was white settlers who were supposed to have wiped out the indigenous inhabitants of the island of Tasmania, at that time considered the most primitive of humans. Yet a century after the Tasmanians were finally declared extinct, a vibrant Tasmanian Aboriginal community has emerged, all of whose members number Aboriginal people among their forbears.[9] The story of their extinction turns out to be a racist myth. Was it any different, then, in the Palaeolithic? Though far, far fewer in number, all the evidence suggests that humans were as mixed up then as they are now. No more are humans all of one sub-species or race today than they were of distinct sub-species in the prehistoric past. Neanderthals are us![10]

In short, mixed-up-ness is the way we living creatures are. Carrying on our lives together, and rubbing shoulders with one another, we continually enfold into our respective constitutions the qualities of others with whom or with which we relate. In a world of life, therefore, there can be no pure kinds. Such a world, of boundless difference rather than bounded diversity, abjures the divisions and sub-divisions of any taxonomy. There is more to this than the observation, now commonplace in evolutionary biology, that due to accidents of mutation and recombination, every individual of a species (unless cloned) is unique in its precise genetic endowment. For that is to suppose a world in which all difference has already precipitated out into myriad particles of heredity that can be reassorted into a potentially infinite variety of discrete permutations and combinations. The difference of which I speak here is emergent, not precipitate, ever originating within the continuous birth that is life itself. For it is in the course of going along together, not in advance of their doing so, that living beings differentiate themselves from one another.

This differentiation is the 'cutting together-apart' to which I already alluded in Chapter 17 (page 265), and it led us to compare life to a plaited braid. In the braid, each and every strand is equivalent to the record of a life, of its doings and undergoings. However tightly it is bound with others, it retains its own particularity. Yet through this binding every *particular life* contributes, in its singular way, to the record that is *life itself* (Chapter 23, pages 349–50). Here, generations align lengthwise. What evolutionary theorists call the 'modern synthesis', however, is based on precisely the opposite premise, namely, that the axis along which each generation conducts its life is orthogonal to the axis of generational succession, as synchrony is orthogonal to diachrony. For the life undergone within each successive generation, modern theory reserves the term *development*; for the passage of information from one generation to the next, whether by genetic or cultural transmission, it reserves the term *inheritance*. Development is a life-process but is not inter-generational; inheritance is inter-generational but not a life process. Without genetic inheritance, according to modern theorists, there could be no evolution, and without cultural inheritance, no history. However, neither evolution nor history, in their terms, can be a process of life. For even as the work of each generation is flattened into its own time, so generations appear to follow one another not like the strands of a braid but like the layers of a stack (Chapter 18, page 274).

Herein lies the source of the stratified conception of prehistory to which I referred at the outset. It is like a deposit, the spent residue of a history that has already moved onwards and upwards. Sedimented in layers, with the oldest furthest down, the deposit keeps to its own time, sinking ever deeper as time itself advances. It holds no potential for regeneration. Yet if deposition is one thing, burial is quite another. Whereas a deposited past is already over and done with, the whole purpose of burial is to invest in a cycle of intergenerational renewal (Chapter 14, pages 220–1). Consigned to the soil, the buried past lays what literary scholar Robert Pogue Harrison (2003: x) calls 'the humic foundations of our life worlds'. By the *humic*, Harrison means an earthy foundation that 'holds in its conserving element the unfinished story of what has come to pass'. By unearthing this buried past – by bringing it up to the surface – the living can engage with it, and in so doing, carry the story on.

Significantly, Harrison draws his inspiration from the *New Science* of Vico. This is an appropriate moment, therefore, to recall Vico's speculation, with which I began, that humans are distinguished by their affinity to the soil, revealed in their habit of burying the dead. While his belief that *humanitas* and *humando* are connected etymologically may be fanciful, there is some truth in the premise, as Harrison (2003: xi) puts it, that 'to be human means above all to bury'. There is no doubt, moreover, that human burials have yielded rich archaeological pickings. However, for an archaeology immured in the idea of history as the positive impulse of progressive humanisation, the grave would come to figure as a place not of burial but of deposition. It would be construed as a kind of double negative, wherein the dead, already deposited below ground in bygone times, were doubly submerged as the grounds of antiquity themselves sank beneath later layers of historical sediment. Thus the burial ground, far from providing a foundation for humanisation, as Vico saw it, would be regarded as a site of dehumanisation, of the dissolution and decay of humanity into nature.

That's why archaeological campaigns waged in wake of colonisation, to excavate the pasts of the peoples native to colonised lands, have proved so contentious. In the eyes of native people, burial is an active phase in a process of human regeneration, or of humanifying in Llull's sense. The grave, for them, is not just a place of death but the guarantor of future life. But an archaeology steeped in colonial mentality saw nothing wrong in the practice not just of *unearthing* the ground but of *excavating* it. Whereas unearthing, as we saw in Chapter 12 (page 188), turns up the past, excavation hollows it out. The one guarantees renewal; the other renders this guarantee null and void. In emptying the graves they found of their bones and artefacts, and in transporting them to faraway museums for analysis and display, colonial archaeology divested the past of its power to produce the future, and broke the cycle of life. Whether the damage can ever be repaired by repatriating the remains is moot. The cycle, once fractured, is not easily made whole again.

André Leroi-Gourhan: posthuman prehistorian?

Let me return, now, to where we left prehistory, mired in a duplicitous concept of the human as both a species of nature and a condition of transcendence, caught between human being and being human. This duplicity, as we have seen, was an inevitable corollary of the Enlightenment programme. Today we are witnessing the collapse of this programme, along with the powers of European-led colonisation that sustained it. What becomes of prehistory then? Is there any space for prehistory in an era of posthumanism, or is it heading for oblivion? Is it possible, even in principle let alone in practice, to be a posthuman prehistorian? If so, who was the first to prove it?

If ever there was a candidate for this honour, it would be archaeologist and historian of technology, André Leroi-Gourhan. In his *Le geste et la parole*, first published in 1964, Leroi-Gourhan set out a comprehensive vision of human evolution running from our earliest ancestors, which he christened Archanthropians, through past and present *Homo sapiens*, to the humans of the future.[11] Yet in doing so, he offered two quite different, and indeed contradictory, prognoses. One takes to its ultimate conclusion the removal of humanity from nature already set in train by the philosophers of the Enlightenment, to the point at which the humans of the future will have cast aside their very existence as beings in a world. The other, however, brings humanity and nature back together, ultimately to close the gap between them, thereby restoring humans – past, present and future – to the continuum of organic life.

Ostensibly, Leroi-Gourhan's oeuvre is an account of how an ascendant humanity broke through the bounds of purely zoological existence, and of its expansion into the domains of technology, social organisation and symbolic culture. The breakthrough, he contends, was anything but sudden. Rather, a growing facility in the manufacture and use of tools marked the onset of 'a long transitional period during which sociology slowly took over from zoology' (Leroi-Gourhan 1993: 90). This was the period of prehistory. From this perspective, the denizens of the period inevitably figure as zoo-sociological hybrids, with one foot in nature and the other in culture. History already beckons, yet they remain too tied to their natural instincts to take the plunge. Eventually however the dam was breached, opening the floodgates of symbolic imagination and launching humanity upon the tide of fully social and historic life. Thenceforth, in a process of what Leroi-Gourhan calls *exteriorisation*, human bodily operations were progressively offloaded onto an extra-somatic apparatus: from bare hands to tools and machines in the domain of technics, and from the mouth to writing in the domain of language. Working upwards from hand to mouth and beyond, the final exteriorisation, Leroi-Gourhan predicts, will be of the brain itself, into mechanisms of artificial intelligence equipped with emotional and moral sensibilities. Once machines have been designed that can out-perform human bodies not only in creative thought but also in sexual love, Leroi-Gourhan opined, though we will have come to the end of the line as a *zoological* species, this will not be the end of humanity. For the machines, into which human bodily and intellectual capacities are fully exteriorised, will be us (Leroi-Gourhan 1993: 265–6, 407).

Considering that Leroi-Gourhan was writing more than half a century ago, when computing and robotics were in their infancy, his predictions were extraordinarily prescient.[12] But is exteriorisation the only possible trajectory for human evolution? Might there be an alternative to the bifurcation into two worlds, respectively zoological and sociological, affording a way ahead that would not have required of our ancestors to embark on the hazardous crossing from one to the other? Could the division between the bare life of the animal, held within the cycle of nature, and the life of the human devoted to breaking out of it, turn out to be an illusion? Indeed, contradicting his own thesis of exteriorisation, Leroi-Gourhan proposes nothing less, and in doing so, sets off down what he calls a 'third track', along which we would perceive that the lives of both humans and nonhuman animals are, as he says, 'neither instinctive nor intellectual but, to varying degrees, zoological and sociological at one and the same time'. Only by following this track, he suggests, will we be truly able to progress beyond the preoccupation with dividing the natural from the cultural that has dominated the last two centuries of scientific thought, to break down the disciplinary barrier between animal psychology and cultural anthropology, and to really understand 'what is animal and what is human' (Leroi-Gourhan 1993: 220).

To do this, we need to bring humans back to life – to think of them, in the first place, not in terms of what they *are*, but in terms of what they *do*. Indeed, unlike the *Homo sapiens* of the orthodox Darwinian account of human evolution, whose essential nature appears to be specified as a legacy from its evolutionary antecedents, Leroi-Gourhan's humans are continually up to something – whether using tools, talking, gesticulating, writing, or just walking around – and, in doing so, forging a life for themselves and those around them. They are quintessentially humanifying animals. This is nowhere more evident than in Leroi-Gourhan's treatment – central to his overall evolutionary thesis – of the relation between hand and voice. The voice, of course, is the principal way in which humans make their presence felt in a world of others with ears to hear. It exists in its very sounding (Chapter 15, page 232). But so also, for Leroi-Gourhan, does the hand exist in its handling – in the countless gestural micro-movements called forth in performing the myriad tasks of everyday life. The hand, thus understood, is not so much an anatomical organ as a compendium of gestures, as indeed is the voice. Put words into my mouth and it knows how to pronounce them; put tools into my hands and it knows how to manipulate them. As words select from the compendium of the voice the gestures of their pronunciation, so every tool selects from the compendium of the hand the gestures appropriate to its use (Ingold 2011a: 58). And it is these gestures, in turn, that give rise to the forms of things.

Hands, in short, are not instruments of humanising, of imprinting pre-conceived human designs on the raw material of nature, but agents of humanifying, in the co-production of emergent form. 'The human hand is human', Leroi-Gourhan (1993: 240) declares, 'because of what it makes, not of what it is'. But hands do more than make; they also write. And writing is of particular interest to our present concern since it has traditionally been the criterion by which scholars have separated history from prehistory. Of course, for as long as humans have been gesturing with their hands, they have also left traces of their movements. Some, like traces of fingers in the sand, are ephemeral, but others, like incisions scratched in stone with a hard point, can last for thousands of years. To refer to the inscriptive impulse of human trace-making, Leroi-Gourhan coined the term *graphism*. Like the voice in speech or song, it is an impulse that radiates from its source within the living, breathing body. Never short of a colourful metaphor, Leroi-Gourhan (1993: 211) compared the geometry of graphism to that of 'the sea urchin or the starfish'. But with writing, he argues, trace-making was progressively displaced onto an extra-somatic apparatus. In a word, it was exteriorised. And with that, the radial organisation of graphism gave way to 'an intellectual process which letters have strung out in a needle-sharp, but also needle-thin, line' (1993: 200).

This is the line of history-as-we-know-it: that sequence of unique events, each one a 'first' for humanity, by which we chart the rise of civilisation. The very idea of history, in this sense, is a product of the exteriorisation of the word in writing. And so too is the idea of an era before history. It may be conceivable to us, looking back upon the vistas of the past, but it would have been inconceivable to the denizens of the time. No one could ever have imagined themselves actually *living* in prehistory. To think as they did, observes the philosopher Jacques Derrida (1976: 86), with acknowledgement to Leroi-Gourhan, would mean having to 'de-sediment' from our minds the deposit of four millennia of linear writing. Or as Vico (2020: 110) had already advised in his *New Science*, we should 'reckon as if there were no books in the world'. We would have, in short, to imagine a world of graphism, organised on principles very different from those with which we are nowadays familiar.

The reinvention of humanism

Would a return to graphism take us back down to the level of zoological existence from which it all began? Or could it, to the contrary, collapse the very distinction – between the sociological and the zoological in Leroi-Gourhan's terms, between humanity and nature in ours – that the advent of writing itself established? The distinction is equivalent to Aristotle's separation of *bios* from *zōē*, reintroduced for our times by Hannah Arendt (1957: 96–7). For Arendt, *zōē* refers to the eternal recurrence of life in nature that knows neither beginning nor end, neither birth nor death, whereas *bios* is the 'specifically human life' that can be told as story, as biography. In her manifesto for a critical posthumanism, however, philosopher Rosi Braidotti (2013: 60) suggests that an expanded concept of *zōē*, standing for the 'generative vitality' of life itself, in its capacity to bring forth, could potentially displace the distinction. Might graphism, then, partake of this capacity? Instead of preceding the written word in time, might it enter constitutively into the very conditions of verbal inscription? After all the written word, in the graphic act of its performance, issues as surely from the hand of the writer as the spoken word from the voice. Words, spoken or written, are living things, animated by the gestures of their formation. We *feel* them as they well up in the cavity of the mouth or as they are shaped in the digital inflections of the hand (Chapter 15, page 240). Speaking and writing, in this sense, are ways we have of forging our own presence in the world, of humanifying.

Another way, equally peculiar to our human selves, is upright bipedal walking. In walking, we continually place ourselves at risk by falling forwards, tumbling ahead of ourselves into the void, only to regain our footing in a skilled adjustment of body posture to the irregularities of the ground (Chapter 2, page 38). Could it be that all human life is suspended in this alternation, between an imagination that sets us loose to fall, and a perception that restores our grip so we can keep on going? The former opens up to what is yet to come: in the words of the philosopher José Ortega y Gasset (1961: 112–13, 201), the human is a 'not-yet being' or, in short, an 'aspiration'. But the latter establishes a foothold in the world, from which we can once again venture into an unknown future. Where the first is aspirational, the other is prehensile (Ingold 2015: 140–41). Perhaps, then, the essence of humaning lies in the ever-present tension, or temporal stretch, between aspiration and prehension. Of course if humans are humaning, so also – as we observed in Chapter 19 (page 307) – baboons are babooning, birds are birding and worms worming. These creatures, too, are what they do, and are recognisable by their particular forms of life. But the *stretch* of humaning, I would argue, makes it of a different order. For it is in the pull of aspiration on prehension, or of imagination on perception, that a space opens up for history.

Others may disagree. In his prolegomena for actor network theory, for example, Bruno Latour places his emphasis on the human penchant for recruiting objects as fixtures for lending stability to social relations. A sociology of intra-specific relations, he contends, may be fine for baboons which, in their babooning, have only to deal with each other's soft and mutable bodies. But it will not work for humans who enrol a miscellany of hard, immutable entities, from landscape features to tools and artefacts, into their collective lives (Latour 2005: 70). As we saw in the previous chapter, however (pages 299–301), humans are by no means alone among animals in their recruitment of objects, nor does ordinary object-use necessarily do anything to stabilise their relations with one another. In my view, it is not by enrolling objects into the collective that humans launch themselves into history. It is rather by allowing imagination, as it overflows the bounds of conceptualisation, to run ahead of sensorially grounded experience. Is this sufficient, then, to make humans exceptional in the animal kingdom? Of course humans are different; all creatures are different. But is the stretch of human imagination such as to fundamentally alter the nature and meaning of life?

Whatever we might say of humans in themselves, there is no denying that their activities have been of momentous consequence. Their numbers weigh ever more heavily on the planet. Even more so do the crops and livestock on which the vast majority feed. And especially over the past century or two of growth, in industrial capacity and military might, humans have left an indelible imprint. This has led some to declare the onset of a new epoch in the geological history of the earth, namely the Anthropocene (Chapter 11, page 170). It is a contested term, not least because of its misplaced connotations of anthropocentrism. The desire of many self-professed post-humanists to recentre environmental sensibilities in the human body, yet in the name of 'overcoming anthropocentrism' (Braidotti 2013: 56), is an index of the confusions that surround the idea. We cannot, in truth, hold anthropocentrism to blame for the ecological devastation of the planet. For, on the contrary, putting our anthropic selves at the centre amounts to a recognition that for every one of us, the world of experience radiates from where we stand to embrace others of every possible complexion, and to an acknowledgement of the debt we owe to these others for our existence as human beings. Decentring humanity would renege on this debt.

Indeed the anthropocentric cosmos is precisely equivalent to what Leroi-Gourhan attributed to the graphism of prehistory. Centred on the body and its gestures, it is radial rather than linear and sequential – the very opposite of the techno-scientific cosmos of today. A humanity that had fully colonised its world, and encompassed its lands and waters, would not be at the centre but all around on the outside. In Leroi-Gourhan's terms, it would be fully exteriorised. This is not anthropocentrism so much as 'anthropo-circumferentialism' (Ingold 2000: 218). If our aim, with Braidotti (2013: 60), is to restore humans to the 'vital force of Life ... coded as *zoe*', then this requires a movement that is not centrifugal, as she thinks, but centripetal. We have to place ourselves, once again, at the beating heart of a more-than-human world, and from this emplaced centre to renegotiate our *humic* relations with the earth and its manifold inhabitants, on a foundation of custodianship and care (Serres 1995b). We have, in this spirit, to re-enter prehistory, understood not as an era that *preceded* history, but as a register of time and life that *subtends* it. Life, then, is pre-historic as is graphism pre-literate, in the same sense that – in the thinking of a philosopher like Maurice Merleau-Ponty – phenomenal experience is pre-objective. In prehistory, to borrow Merleau-Ponty's (2002: 503) words, 'we find our bodily being, our social being, and the pre-existence of the world'.

My motive for thus seeking to recentre the human is not so much to topple humanism as to reinvent it. I want to take humanism in a direction orthogonal to its opposition to anti-humanism. This is to go *beyond humanity*, not by adding another chapter to an already illustrious historical career, nor by fictionalising its final transubstantiation into the realms of artificial intelligence, disembodied sex and fully automated work. It is rather to shift to another axis, along which human lives unfold in parallel with those of other beings, in ever-flowing currents of time. This is an axis not of progress towards a preordained conclusion but of sustainability, measured out in the longitudinal entwinement of generations rather than their serial replacement. Where progress appeals to the hubris of rational consciousness, sustainability – as Braidotti (2013: 138) puts it – is about *endurance*, about ' "passing on" to future generations a world that is liveable and worth living in'. But this turn to life, to *zōē*, is also a shift from history to prehistory, in the sense not of temporal regression but of ontological primacy. There can be life without history, but there can be no history without life. It is in the doing of human life, I have argued, that history is made. I am with Llull, then, in reimagining a humanism in which 'to human' is a verb. To repeat: *Homo est animal homificans.*

Chapter 21

The sustainability of everything

Beginning with the conversation

This chapter both begins and ends with a conversation. I begin from a conversation with the director of an arts organisation in the northeast of Scotland.[1] She was planning an event to celebrate the planting of a new woodland in the area, and wanted me to contribute to the event with a talk. I asked her what topics she had in mind. Her answer was that I should address the theme of sustainability, and its bearing on art, on science and ecology, and on citizenship and democracy. 'You mean, you want me to talk about the sustainability of everything?', I replied incredulously. It seemed at the time like an impossible thing to do. Yet the more I thought about it, the more it seemed to me that sustainability is either of everything or it is nothing. It cannot be of some things and not others; it can countenance no boundaries of inclusion and exclusion. What kind of everything, then, can always surpass itself, always have room for more, without at any moment appearing partial or incomplete? The answer to which I eventually gravitated, and which I shall elaborate in what follows, is that everything is indeed a conversation. This conversation, with which I will eventually end this chapter, is no more, and no less, than the world we inhabit.

To reach this conclusion, and to fulfil the brief that was originally presented to me, I had to pose three subsidiary questions. First, how can we imagine a world that has room for ourselves and for everyone and everything else, both now and for generations to come? Second, what does it mean for such a world to carry on, to keep on going, to be sustained? And third, what can we do to make this happen? To answer these questions, we need to take a closer look at our two keywords, 'sustainability' and 'everything'. I admit that for many readers, the notion of sustainability may seem to have outlived its worth, to have been devalued by overuse, and compromised through its co-option by powerful interests whose overriding concern has been for their own survival in a world of ever more intense competition for dwindling planetary resources. Yet I believe it is a notion we cannot do

DOI: 10.4324/9781003171713-27

without, and that to give up on it would be tantamount to the abandonment of our responsibility towards coming generations. The challenge, then, is to give meaning to a term that paradoxically combines the idea of an absolute limit with the limitlessness of carrying on forever. Real sustainability, I shall argue, begins at the moment when the doors of perception swing open, when objectivity gives way to the search for truth, or finality to renewal, whereupon what appears from the outside as a limit opens up from within into a space of growth, movement and transformation, to limitless possibility, or in a word, to everything. And it is with everything that I begin.

The plenum

For those of us educated into the ways of modern science, our inclination is to conclude with everything rather than to begin from it. And we can reach a conclusion, we think, only by summing things up. That is, we perform an addition. We add and we add: numbers of people, numbers of species, numbers of objects of this or that kind, numbers of characters on the page, numbers of stars in the sky, numbers of cells in the body, numbers of atoms in a pinhead. We are bamboozled by numbers, many of a magnitude that defy comprehension. But to add things up, they have first to be broken off from the processes that gave rise to them, from the ebbs and flows of life. You must be able to tell where one thing ends, and another begins. The world must be rendered discontinuous (Chapter 17, pages 261–2). We soon discover, however, that some things are difficult if not impossible to render thus, as discrete, enumerable quanta. Try adding up clouds in the sky, waves in the ocean, trees in the woods, fungi. The difficulty is that these things are always forming and dissolving, growing and decomposing, appearing sometimes to merge, at other times to break up.

Take clouds, for example. Clouds are not discrete objects, suspended in the sky. They are rather folds of the sky itself – moisture-laden formations of the turbulent and crumpled mass of atmospheric air (Ingold 2015: 90). Waves, too, are folds, ever forming at the surface where the ocean, in its intercourse with the sky, is whipped up by the wind (see Chapter 11, pages 174–5). You could perhaps count waves as they wash up upon the shore, much as you could count footsteps, breaths or heartbeats. But what would they amount to? A life, perhaps, with breaths, steps and heartbeats; all eternity with the waves. Counting would not be adding up a world but the rhythm of time passing. With trees and fungi, addition is just as impracticable. Who can say how many trees there are in a wood? True, you could measure up, as foresters do, estimating the number and volume of trunks in the stack when a plot is felled. But in so doing you have already, in your mind's eye, cut each and every tree from all that nourishes it and gives it life: the soil, the fungi that wrap around its roots, the air and sunlight that fuel its growth. And to count fungi is merely to enumerate the fruiting bodies, ignoring the underground mesh of the mycelium from which they spring.

But is it really any different with people? Are they any easier to add up than clouds, waves, trees and fungi? Can you arrive at everybody by counting heads? In a crude sense, of course you can, as in the taking of a census or a vote, but only by abstracting every head from the living, breathing body of which it is intrinsically a part. Topologically, the body is not a closed container but an open vessel, its surfaces so intricately infolded that it is practically impossible to distinguish its interior and exterior regions. Normally, we see only one part of every person – namely, the fleshy part. The part we don't see is the breath, the air we inhale and exhale, and without which we could not live. Like trees in the wood, people intermingle with one another – they 'go in and out of each other's bodies', in the beguiling phrase of anthropologist Maurice Bloch (2012: 120) – even as they breathe the air. And their voices, carried on the breath and permeating the atmosphere, mingle also, sometimes joining, as in the unison of song, sometimes splitting apart as they 'lift-up-over' one another without ever separating into discrete sounds (Feld 1996: 100). You may, through an act of differential attention, be able to tell one voice from another, to split them along the grain of their becoming. But you cannot count them up.

In the polyphony of voices – in the conversation – the collective everyone, like everything, is an intermingling: not a totality, arrived at by the addition of its individual elements, but what I call a *plenum*. As we found in Chapter 4 (page 55), the plenum is not a space filled up to capacity with things. It is fullness itself. The things we find there – including clouds, waves, trees, and people – emerge as folds, ever-forming by way of the turbulence of lively materials. With the plenum, we do not end with everything nor, strictly speaking, do we begin with it. We find ourselves, instead, wrapped in its midst.

Folding, cutting, splitting

We have many words to describe the plenum: world, cosmos, nature, earth. But does the world contain holes that remain to be filled? Are there gaps in the cosmos, voids in nature, empty spaces in the earth? We might regard a patch of ground as a site on which to build. It must first be cleared of obstructions like trees and boulders, foundations must be dug, materials gathered and assembled. To clear the ground, however, is not to leave a void but to smooth it out, as when you remove a crease from a fabric. And to build is not to refill the space but once again to crease the ground, pressing it into the rising forms of walls and the vault of the roof. Thus *every infill is, in reality, a reworking*, a doubling up that introduces a kink, twist or knot into the very fabric of the earth. Things that to our senses might appear solid, tangible and visibly stable – a building here, a tree or a boulder there, even a human being or an animal, each occupying its particular region of space or moment in time – are truly but the provisional forms or envelopes of incessant movement.

In the plenum, material folds on itself as it goes along (Chapter 17, pages 268–9). As it does so it endlessly overflows any formal envelopes within which it may appear temporarily to have been pulled aside or detained. The plenum, then, is limitless, not because its capacity can always be increased, but because it forever carries on. We do not ask the ocean whether it has room to accommodate a few more waves; nor does the ocean respond like an overbooked hotelier: 'Unfortunately we are full up.'[2] For the waves are ever forming, even as they break upon the shore. Thus everything, in the sense of the plenum, is not an ultimate conclusion, not the sum total when all is added up, but pure becoming. Things, in their becoming, continually differentiate themselves from within the plenum – as do clouds in the sky, or waves in the ocean, or indeed voices in the conversation – without ever parting company with it. You don't tell things apart by superimposing a conceptual grid on the data of experience. You do it by entering into the processes of their formation and by separating them from the inside, along the grain. It is a matter of splitting, not cutting.

To get at the difference, compare cutting a log with a saw and splitting it with an axe (Figure 21.1). In the first case you impose a system of fixed intervals upon the raw material of timber. Having cut the log into lengths, you can count them up. But in the second case, with the axe, you enter into the grain and follow a line of growth – a line incorporated into the timber when it was a living tree, growing in the ground. With cutting, you divide from the outside; with splitting you differentiate from the inside. Splitting, in short, is a process of what, throughout this work, I have been calling 'interstitial differentiation'.

For another example of the same distinction, compare walking with surveying. In Ancient Egypt, the job of the surveyor – known as a 'rope-stretcher' – was to measure up and divide the land into plots following every annual flood of the Nile. He would drive stakes into the ground at fixed points and stretch the rope from one to the other in order to determine field boundaries. Every stake is a stoppage – the equivalent of what we would now call a data point – and the line of rope connecting them divides the ground. The walker, however, does not join points but passes between them. His feet both follow the trail and, in their impression, reinscribe it. Thus the trail, or the path, is not laid out over the ground but formed from within it. You might be able to tell the path from the ground, but there is no telling the ground from the path. Moreover, turning from walking to writing, we find the same contrast. The handwritten trace emerges from within the texture of the page, where pen meets parchment or paper along a line of movement. But printed words and letters are deposited from above (Chapter 12, pages 192–3). You can count the number of characters on a printed page; and on

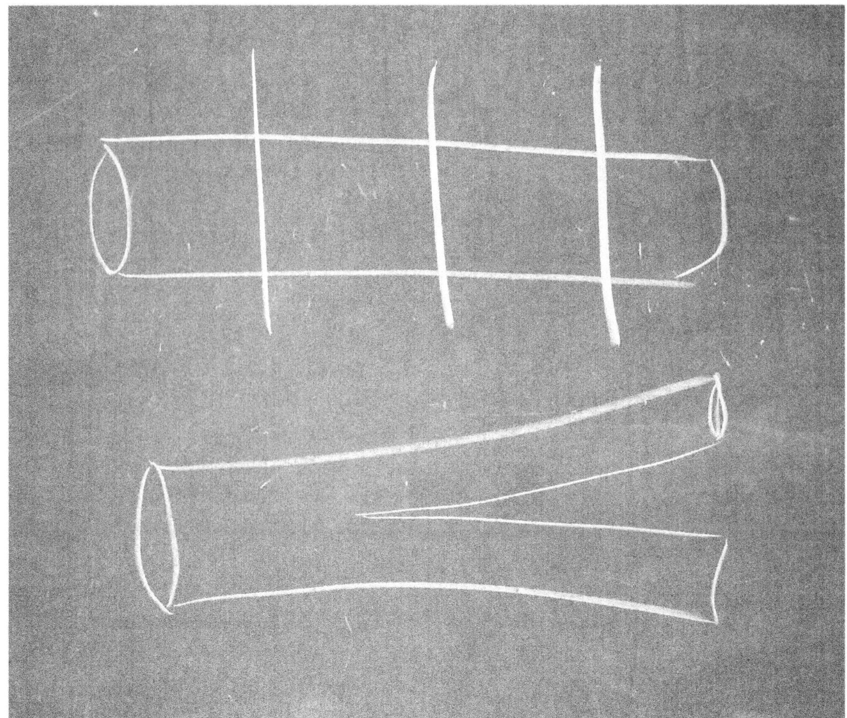

Figure 21.1 Cutting and splitting. Above, a log sawn against the grain into sections; below, the same log split along the grain with an axe. Blackboard sketch from a lecture.
Photo by the author.

screen your laptop can do it automatically, at the touch of a button. But there is no way of counting the number of lines on a page of handwriting.

Progressive development and the continuity of life

How, then, can we comprehend *everything*? Do we collect all the data, count up all the people, survey all the land, add up all the words? Is it a matter of assembling wholes from parts, in a nested series of levels in which wholes at one level become parts of wholes at the next level up? Is everything, in this sense, a vertically integrated totality? Or do we find everything by going along, following every root, runner, trail and trace? The latter implies an entirely different view of part-whole relations, harmonic rather than totalising, in which coherence arises from the tension of contrary forces and inclinations. The rope, for example, maintains its torsion and does not unwind because the twist of its constituent strands is contrary to the twist of its strands with one another. In polyphonic music, melodic lines likewise answer to each other in counterpoint. Yet the rope keeps on winding, the music keeps sounding, the waves keep breaking on the shore. The plenum, in short, belongs to time; perhaps, indeed, it *is* time. Everything, in the sense of the plenum, is not an ultimate conclusion, not the sum total when all is added up, but pure concrescence. For in a concrescent world, as Alfred North Whitehead (1929: 410) taught, everything is perpetually undergoing creation together: trees growing together in the wood, people living together in society, their voices carrying on together in conversation. This does not mean, of course, that the plenary world is only half-formed, or incomplete. For incompletion can only be judged in relation to a state of finality. In the plenum, by contrast, nothing is final, and every ending is an unfinishing that opens up to fresh beginning.

With this, we return to the question from which I began: how can we imagine a world that is sustainable for everyone and everything, both now and for ever? In the plenum, as we have found, everything is sustainable because it tends to no limit but rather opens to a perpetual process of world-renewal. Indeed in redefining everything as a plenum, we have also come close to achieving a workable definition of sustainability. It is a definition, however, that stands in stark contrast to that of mainstream sustainability science. In the currently dominant discourses of science, technology and commerce, the aim of sustainability is not to open up to the power of world renewal but to harness or capture this power, and to put it to use in the production of so-called renewables. This is to turn beginnings into endings, the transformative power of a living earth into goods and services for present and future human consumption. In the rationale of sustainable development, the world is understood not as a plenum to be inhabited but as a totality to be managed, much as a company manages its assets, by balancing the books, living off interest without eating into capital reserves.[3] Sustainability is thus defined in terms of goals or targets to be achieved, along an axis of progressive development. The sustainability of everything, however, runs counter to this axis. Its commitment is not to progress so much as to the continuity of life.

In a study of upland forestry in Japan, anthropologist John Knight (1998) offers a cautionary tale of what can go wrong if the axis of development takes precedence over the axis of continuity. Traditionally, Japanese foresters would look after trees for a generation, and then cut them for use as house timbers. In the house, the timbers enjoy what the foresters call a second life. In this phase the direction of care is reversed. For where foresters had nurtured trees in their first life, it is now the trees that nurture the foresters and their families in the second, by furnishing the warmth, shelter, and comfort of the dwelling. During this time, the foresters are looking after a new generation of growing trees, which will eventually, in their turn, become replacement house timbers. And so it would continue, generation after generation. Here, the lives of foresters and their trees go along together, responding to one another in a cycle of mutual care that, in principle, can continue indefinitely. But today, as Knight shows, the cycle has been broken. Conservationists demand that old trees be preserved and not cut. These arboreal veterans are hence denied their second life. And the people, left without timbers to replace old ones as they rot, have taken to building their houses out of concrete instead. Development, here, has trumped continuity.

This example reveals a deeply entrenched fault-line in ways of thinking about the future. Should it be projected as a steady state, or anticipated as an ongoing concrescence? Even if it were possible, in theory, to balance the ship of the world on its keel, the balance could only be sustained by calming the ocean, putting life and history permanently on hold. The future, then, could be no more than a protraction of the present. Far from ensuring the continuation of everything, sustainability would shut it down. My argument, to the contrary, is that to bring sustainability and everything back into line, we need fundamentally to rethink our relation to the world, to the future, to time and to memory. And with this, we come to the third of the questions with which I began. To recapitulate: in response to the first question, I have shown how a world that has room for everyone and everything, for all time, must be imagined as a plenum. In response to the second, I have shown that for such a world to carry on, we need to understand sustainability as concrescence – as a process in which persons and things, as they wind along together, bring each other into being in a renewal that knows no end. The third question, however, asks what we can do now, in our present times, to bring about a world fit for coming generations to inhabit. Is it possible, even in principle let alone in practice, to fashion sustainability by design?

Carrying on

On the face of it, this seems a fruitless endeavour. For if, say, our predecessors had succeeded in designing the future we now inhabit, what would be left for us? We would have nothing to do save to fall in line with their already imposed imperatives. Alternatively, were it to fall to us to shape a future for our successors, then they in turn would become mere users, or consumers, tied to the implementation of a design already made for them. Design, it seems, *must* fail if every generation is to look forward to a future that it can call its own: that is, for every generation to begin afresh, to be a *new* generation. Perhaps the very history of design could be understood as the cumulative record of concerted human efforts to put an end to it: an interminable series of final answers, none of which, in retrospect, turns out to be final after all.[4] Or to adapt a maxim from the environmental pundit Stewart Brand (1994: 75): all designs are predictions; all predictions are wrong.

This hardly sounds like a formula for sustainable living. The sustainability of everything, I have argued, is not about meeting targets. It is about keeping life going. Yet design based on the science of sustainability seems intent on bringing life to a stop, by specifying moments of completion when things fall into line with prior projections. 'Form is the end, death', insisted Paul Klee (1973: 269) in his notebooks; 'Form-giving is movement, action. Form-giving is life.' By setting ends to things do we not, as Klee intimated, kill them off? If design brings predictability and foreclosure to a life-process that is inherently open-ended and concrescent, then is it not the very antithesis of life? How, following Klee's example, might we shift the emphasis in design from form to form-giving? How, in other words, can we think of design as part of a process of life whose outstanding characteristic is not that it tends to a limit but that it *carries on*?

Design for the plenum – for the sustainability of everything – if it is to meet this requirement, must be driven not by plans and predictions but by *hope*. With plans and predictions we can be optimistic that their realisation is just around the corner. There is light at the end of the tunnel. But hope and optimism are not the same. The difference is that optimism anticipates final outcomes; hope does not. The verb 'to hope' is not transitive – like 'to make' or 'to build' – but intransitive, like 'to grow' and indeed 'to live' (Ingold 2011a: 6). It denotes a process that does not begin here and end there but carries on through. I suggest that in designing for sustainability, in making it happen, we should treat 'design' too, as an intransitive verb, as a way of carrying on that is intrinsically open-ended. Ask not, then, *what* you are designing, but *how*. Let me return to Klee, this time to his celebrated *Creative Credo* of 1920, to which we already referred in Chapter 2 (page 36): 'Art does not reproduce the visible but makes visible.' It is not for art, Klee contended, to hold a mirror to reality. It is rather to enter into the relations and processes that give rise to things so as to bring them into the field of our awareness. And only so long as these relations and processes carry on can the world offer a sustainable abode for its inhabitants.

I believe we can understand design for sustainability as an art in Klee's sense. Far from setting out to transform the world, or to bring it into line with a preconceived plan, it is to enter imaginatively into the process of the world's transforming itself, of its autopoiesis (McLean 2009: 231). This process, however, unfolds along not one but multiple paths. It is, in essence, a conversation. Like life, conversations carry on; they have no particular beginning point or end point; no one knows in advance what will come out of them, nor can their conduct be dictated by any one partner. They are truly collective achievements. Let us, then, think of designing for sustainability as a conversation, embracing not only human beings but all the other constituents of the lifeworld, from nonhuman animals of all sorts to things like trees, rivers, mountains, and the earth. All who join the conversation are contributing, each in their own way, to design for a sustainable world.

Art and science

Let me now return to the challenges put to me, in the conversation that originally prompted this essay. In the sustainability of everything, what is there for art to do, what is the relation between art, science and ecology, and what does our rethinking of sustainability mean for citizenship and democracy? I have argued that sustainability can only be reconciled with everything if we redefine our relation to the world and our place in it. To do so means acknowledging, with Karen Barad (2007: 185), that far from standing outside the world, and imposing our designs upon it, we are ourselves 'part of the world in its differential becoming'. For science this is a hard pill to swallow – increasingly hard, as science has sought to immunise itself, through the perfection of its instruments and the elaboration of its methodology, from what are perceived as distortions arising from any affective involvement of practitioners with the objects of their study. This immunity, however, has also hardened scientists' resistance to the kind of ecological sensibility that would ground their ways of knowing in the habitation of a lifeworld. The goals of today's science, more than ever before, are of modelling, prediction and control. It has consequently fallen largely to art to take on the mantle of radical ecological awareness that science has cast aside.[5]

Many contemporary environmental artists, along with their colleagues in architecture and design, are leading the way in breaking down the barriers between humanity and nature, foregrounding lived experience, and highlighting the richness and complexity, as well as the mystery and strangeness, of a world which human beings have irrevocably altered through their activities yet in which they remain puny by comparison to the forces they have unleashed. This is not to say that art, in its way of working, is necessarily opposed to science. It is rather to plead for a different way of doing science – different, at least, from its more arrogant and hubristic versions, by which I mean the kind of 'big science' that, in this epoch of the Anthropocene, pretends to have the power to fix the planet once and for all. A true science of sustainability, rather than claiming exclusive powers both to explicate the world and to bring it under control, should be more modest, deferential and – above all – attentive in its ambitions, and should be prepared to admit the things it studies into the field of its own deliberations (Chapter 5, pages 77–8). In short, for it to join the conversation, science must shed its totalitarian impulses and recognise that its peculiar way of knowing is neither sovereign nor absolute but one of many.

After all, how can we possibly know everything? If the plenum is not closed in but open to infinite differentiation, then the same must be true of our ways of knowing it. They, too, must go along together, and differentiate themselves from one another, in the ever-continuing conversations of life. It is usual for scientists to call their ways of knowing 'research', and in the science of sustainability, as we have seen, research is closely tied to the calculus of renewables. The claim of scientific research, that it aims to fill gaps in understanding, rests on a logic of addition, on the idea that our knowledge of the world, though currently incomplete, will ultimately add up to a totality. However, for an itinerant practice of research that follows the ways of the world from within, there are no gaps to fill. Indeed, my earlier observation that in the plenum every apparent infill is really a reworking applies with equal force to research. What is research, after all, if not a way of *searching again*, a second search, which at once doubles up on what went before and is an original intervention in its turn? That's what research literally means, a reworking, in which we differentiate emergent phenomena even as we join with them. Experienced thus, as a way of knowing, research continually surpasses itself. It is not an addition but a concrescence. And it is as apposite to the practice of art as it is to that of science.

In search of truth

For what, then, do we search? The answer, of course, is truth. In a sustainable world research never ends because it is, most fundamentally, a search for truth. Without this commitment to truth, research would be cast adrift, like a lost spacecraft with no recollection of its mother planet and no clue as to where it is heading. Yet in this cynical and untrusting age, truth is often considered a dangerous if not deluded idea, best kept inside scare quotes. For many, the very mention of truth conjures up memories of the tyranny wrought, throughout history, by those claiming to be its masters and to act as its worldly ambassadors, invariably with calamitous consequences for all concerned. We should not, however, blame truth for the atrocities committed in its name. The fault lies in its totalisation, its conversion into a monolith that stands eternal like a monument, timeless and fully formed. Research, to the contrary, rests on the acknowledgement that we can never master truth, any more than we can conquer life. Such conquest is for immortals. But for us, mortal beings, truth is always greater than we are, always beckoning from beyond the horizons of our present knowledge and understanding. The role of research, then, is to offer an imaginative opening to truth.

Yet by the same token, truth should on no account be confused with fact. The fact stops us in our tracks, and blocks our way. 'This is how it is,' it says to us; 'proceed no further!' But even if the facts of a case may be incontrovertibly established, its truth lives on. For what appear to us in the first instance as data points or stoppages turn out, when we search again – that is, in our *re*-search – to be openings that let us in. It is as though the fact rotated by ninety degrees, like a door on opening, so that it no longer confronts us face-on but aligns itself longitudinally with our own movements. And where the fact leads, we follow. 'Come with us', it says. What had once put an end to our search then reappears, in *re*-search, as a new beginning, a way into a world that is not already formed, but itself undergoing formation. It is not that we have broken through the surface of the world to discover its hidden secrets. Rather, as the doors of perception open, and as we join *with* things in the relations and processes of their formation, the surface itself vanishes. The truth of this world, then, is not to be found 'out there', established by reference to the objective facts, but is disclosed from within. It is indeed the very matrix of our existence as worldly beings. We can have no knowledge of this truth save by being in it. Knowing, in short, unfolds from the inside of being.

This conclusion will naturally be anathema to those who hold that true knowledge of the world can be had only by detaching ourselves from it and looking from a distance. For them, objectivity is the very hallmark of truth. It is indeed understandable that in a world where facts often appear divorced from any kind of observation, where they can be invented on a whim, propagated through mass media, and manipulated to suit the interests of the powerful regardless of their veracity, we should be anxious about the fate of truth. To many, it seems that in this era of post-truth, we have lost our grip on reality. But while we are right to insist that there can be no proper facts without observation, we are wrong, I believe, to suppose that observation stops at objectivity. For to observe, it is not enough merely to look at things. We have to join with them, and to follow. That's what observation means: to follow attentively – whether by watching, listening or feeling – what someone or something else is doing. And it is precisely as observation goes beyond objectification that truth goes beyond the facts.[6] This is the moment, in our observations, when the things with which we study begin to tell us how to observe. In allowing ourselves into their presence rather than holding them at arm's length – in attending to them – we find that they are also guiding our attention. Attending to these ways, we also respond to them. 'The power of the real', as Lars Spuybroek (2020: 193) writes, 'is that we will never get an answer; it is we who have to respond.'[7] Research, then, becomes a practice of correspondence, and of care. It is a labour of love, giving back what we owe to the world for our own existence as beings within it (Chapter 5, page 77).

Ending with the conversation

Finally, what does all this mean for democracy and citizenship? It cannot, for one thing, mean democracy in the sense of a headcount, which sorts everyone into those with common or opposed interests. In a sustainable democracy – one with room for everyone and everything, now and forever – people cannot be counted, and nor can things. Yet in their conjoint action and affective correspondence, they constitute a public. As Jane Bennett (2010: 101) writes, after John Dewey, 'publics are groups of bodies with the capacity to affect and be affected'.[8] Whether human or nonhuman, these are bodies in conversation – bodies whose presence is felt by way of their voices as they mix and mingle in the medium. In the democratic conversation, each has something to give, something to contribute, precisely because all are different. Together they comprise what the philosopher Alphonso Lingis (1994), in an apt turn of phrase, calls 'the community of those who have nothing in common'. The meaning of citizenship follows from this. It is about learning to live together in difference. For within a democratic community that is open-ended and unbounded rather than closed in the defence of common interests, citizenship arises not as a right or entitlement, given from the start, but as something you have to work at. This is the work of commoning; not the discovery of what you have in common to begin with, but the imaginative act of casting your experience forward, along ways that join with others in carrying on a life together.[9] Only then can citizenship be truly sustainable. The road to sustainability, in short, lies in the conversations of life.

Imagining the world as a plenum, I believe, affords a way of thinking about democracy and citizenship that could give hope to future generations. At the present juncture, however, this way of thinking has been pushed to the margins, above all by the relentless expansion of big science, aided and abetted by state actors and multinational corporations. And with it has gone the question from which all inquiry must begin: how *ought* we to live? Big science is not interested in this question because it believes it can already deliver the answer – or if not already, then in a future within its sights. But it has no answer for what lies beyond its predictive horizons. When the dinosaurs went extinct, it was the small mammals that inherited the earth, among them the weasel. The most famous weasel in history could turn out to be the one that bit through an electric cable, putting the largest machine ever built – CERN's large hadron collider – out of action for a week.[10] The collider is perhaps the greatest expression of scientific hubris we have seen, dedicated as it is to discovering the final truth of the universe, one that will leave us mortals with no place to be. It is the delusional project of our time, truly a machine for the end of the world. But the eventual collapse of big science – no less inevitable than the collapse of the global economy that sustains it – will not bring the world to an end. It will, instead, inaugurate a new beginning. A time will come beyond the Anthropocene. For that, our weaselly hero gave its life. We must ensure the sacrifice was not in vain.

Chapter 22

Confessions of a semiophobe

Some years ago, during a seminar at the Quai Branly Museum in Paris, my esteemed anthropological colleague, Philippe Descola, challenged me to explain myself. 'Why', he asked, 'are you such a semiophobe?' I cannot recall exactly how I responded, but I do remember delighting in the accuracy of his diagnosis. I am indeed an inveterate semiophobe, and proud of it! In this, moreover, lies the nub of my disagreement with Descola who, by all accounts, is a confirmed semiophile. We start at opposite ends: for him, a world of signs crying out for interpretation; for me, a world that lays itself open to us, in its very presence. Semiophilia holds an obvious attraction for scholars who would like to appoint themselves as master-interpreters. It gives them a pedestal to stand on. Semiophobia, by contrast, threatens to pull the pedestal from under their feet, but by the same token, allows us unmediated access to a world from which we have much to learn, if only we are prepared to attend to it. As ever, it all comes down to the question of meaning. The default assumption of the semiophile is that meaning is equivalent to signification. Without signs, then, there can be no meaning. My semiophobic response is to challenge this assumption. The verbs 'to mean' and 'to signify', I insist, are not synonymous. Meaning lies not in the interpretation of signs but in the direct perception of the world. And things mean because of the ways they are drawn perceptually into forms of life.

So what, exactly, is a sign? As is well known, there are two, quite different ways of answering this question. One finds its source in the work of the linguist Ferdinand de Saussure; the other goes back to the writings of the pragmatist philosopher Charles Sanders Peirce. They have given rise, in turn, to radically contrasting bodies of theory, respectively semiological and semiotic. In the fields of social and cultural anthropology, for much of their twentieth century history, semiology reigned supreme. But in the last few decades, semiotics has made something of a comeback. For many anthropologists, their critique of the former has driven them into the arms of the latter. Erstwhile followers of semiology have rebranded themselves as semioticians. For my part, however, semiotics holds no more attraction than

DOI: 10.4324/9781003171713-28

semiology. To explain why, let me begin by offering a thumbnail sketch of each approach.

Semiology and semiotics

Though semiology originated with the study of language, its promise lay in the fact that its terms were not limited to the linguistic domain. Saussure thought of language, in the first place, as a system of signs, and of every sign as a compound of two parts, a 'signifier' and a 'signified'. With language, the signifier is a word, or more precisely, the sonic image of a word as it is imprinted in memory. The signified is a concept. Simply put, sound-images stand for concepts.[1] Sometimes, by their very nature, sounds call to mind the concepts they stand for. These are cases of onomatopoeia. But by and large, as Saussure sought to show, the relation between sound-image and concept is entirely arbitrary, based on a set of conventions shared by all speakers of a language. It is not, then, because of any positive association that particular sound-images come to stand for particular concepts, but rather because of the mapping of one set of distinctions, on the plane of sound, onto another, homologous set of distinctions, on the plane of concepts. Thus language, for Saussure, is constituted not as the sum of likenesses, between word-sounds and their meanings, but in the matching of two all-encompassing systems of difference, respectively on the planes of thought and sound.

There is no reason, however, why this logic of difference and homology should be confined to the realm of linguistic signs.[2] As a comparative science of signs, semiology was born of the realisation that the same logic could be found at work in multiple domains of social and cultural life, from the economy and kinship to ritual and myth. All allow for the communication of meaning, but the units of meaning are different in each case. They could be words, but they could equally be coins, courtesies, gestures, or motifs. In every case, however, the relation between signifier and signified is enshrined in a system of collective representations which is given a priori, independently and in advance of the presence or activity of any particular sign-user, and of anything or anyone in the world to which or to whom the user aims to draw attention or respond. The universe of signs, in short, seems to exist on a rarefied plane of its own, withdrawn from the hurly-burly of life on the ground, and immune to its practical manoeuvres.

It was against this rarefication that the semioticians rebelled, finding chapter and verse in the famously dense and impenetrable writings of Peirce.[3] For what Saussurean semiology leaves out – namely the sign-user and the object of his or her attention – is for Peirce a point of departure. With Peirce, signs are not set apart, on a separate plane of representation, but inherent in the ways living beings of all kinds, not only human, act and respond in the inhabited world. Moreover the sign relation is not dyadic, as it was for Saussure, but triadic, linking a being, an object of that being's attention, and a meaning that in some sense charts a way ahead for the being to follow. In Peirce's own words, 'the sign is something which stands to somebody for something in some respect or capacity' (Peirce 1931: 2.228). The something it leads to may be another sign, which opens in turn to further meaning, and so on in a sequence that, at least in principle, is endless. What Peirce called semiosis is thus a kind of tracking, the concatenation of signs and their meanings as they open up, one after another.

A footprint, for example, is a sign to the attentive observer, yielding information about a creature that has gone before, and a direction to follow. The print is an example of the kind of sign Peirce called indexical, where the meaning rests on a simple relation of cause and effect. Likewise, when we see smoke in the distance, it is a sign of the fire that produces it. The index, however, is but one of three kinds of sign that Peirce identified. The others are icon and symbol. The icon means what it does since it calls to mind, thanks to a perceived likeness, a previously experienced index. The word 'splash' means 'hard object falling into water' because, in its pronunciation, it resembles the sound you once heard that indexed this event. As resemblances mount up, and are shared in the collective memory of a community, so they are ever more compressed in the signs that bear them, to the point at which their original figurative content is dissolved, and their meanings are secured solely by weight of representational convention. They then become symbols. In human language, most words are symbols in this sense. Not all symbols, however, are words. Both semiologists and semioticians have been keen to extend their inquiries beyond language, but where the former have concentrated on non-linguistic symbols, the latter have been more interested in non-symbolic signs.

It is no wonder that in anthropology, the growing attraction of semiotics, at the expense of semiology, was linked to what is often called the 'practice turn' – to the move away from the abstractions of social structure and collective representation to a focus on how humans and nonhumans practically get along together in a lived world. I myself was sympathetic to this move. Like many others, I came out against the ontological bifurcation, at the heart of the Saussurean programme and the structural anthropology that followed it, between a plane of mental representations, on which lie thought, concepts and ideas, and a plane of physical reality that provides the material means to stand for them, or, in shorthand, between culture and nature. So why did I not follow other critics of the nature-culture dichotomy, of broadly practice-theoretical persuasion, into the arms of semiotics? What do I have against the semiotic paradigm?

Umwelt and niche

For me, it all goes back to my encounter, around the mid-1980s, with the work of two thinkers, both of whom were fundamentally concerned with the question of how creatures of all kinds, human and nonhuman, can be said to inhabit meaningful worlds (Ingold 1989, 1992a). One was the Estonian-born aristocrat, naturalist and philosopher, Jakob von Uexküll.[4] The other was the American psychologist James Gibson (1979). Uexküll's works, though largely written off by mainstream bioscience, have been retrospectively acknowledged as foundational to the field of biosemiotics, and remain influential in the counter-current of scholarship that continues to insist, against the mainstream, that living organisms are not passively reactive to environing conditions but decisively contribute, through cycles of perception and response, to the formation of their lived worlds. Gibson, too, was concerned to show how, for any animal, the environment is constituted through its own perceptual activity in the world. In this lay the essence of his ecological approach to perception. But despite the apparent similarity in their objectives, the approaches of Uexküll and Gibson were fundamentally opposed. And in the end, after weighing up the pros and cons of both, I chose to go with Gibson.[5]

The crux of their difference comes down to whether the organism – let us say an animal – puts meaning into the world or draws meaning from it. Is the animal a meaning-giver or a meaning-seeker? Uexküll sided with the former, and in so doing, offered an account of perception and action couched in the language of signs. For the lowly tick, to take his most celebrated example, the smell of butyric acid emitted by the skin-glands of mammals is a sign for it to release itself from the branch from which it hangs so as to fall on the beast passing below. Contact with a hairy surface is a sign to run around and seek a relatively hair-free patch; the warmth that exudes from this patch is a sign to start burrowing into the skin as a prelude to gorging on the prey's blood. There are just three object-signs in the tick's world. But for Uexküll (2010: 44–52) they are signs nonetheless, rather than mere triggers in an automatic process. In an automaton, every movement is ultimately explicable as the result of another with which it is enchained. But the tick's moves are not part of a determinate mechanism of transmission but contingent on its own powers of discrimination – powers that are nevertheless targeted on three features of its surroundings to the exclusion of all others. These features make up what Uexküll called the *Umwelt* of the animal: a world as it is constructed within the sensory register of a being equipped with particular capacities of perception and action. It is as though the animal were enclosed within its own, species-specific bubble of reality, inaccessible to animals of other kinds which are likewise enclosed in theirs. Moreover, on the instant that the animal's life is extinguished, such that it ceases to cast its own particular light on the world, the bubble bursts.

Gibson, however, would have none of this. For him, the animal does not inhabit an *Umwelt* but a *niche*. And the niche is already present in the environment, offering the possibility of a form of life to any creature equipped to draw on the opportunities it affords, as well as to dodge its hazards. Remove the animal, and the niche is still there. Thus the trunk and branches of a tree afford possibilities of passage for a squirrel, not because the squirrel has specifically highlighted them for this purpose, but because they are already available to an animal suitably equipped for climbing, jumping and balance. As it climbs and jumps, the squirrel perceives what Gibson calls the *affordances* of the tree. Affordances are what the environment provides or furnishes for the animal, whether as things that help it on its way or, alternatively, as hindrances to be avoided. The niche, then, is a set of affordances. But on no account, Gibson (1979: 128–9) warned, marking his words with emphasis, should the niche be confused with 'what some psychologists have called the *phenomenal environment* of the species'. Though he does not name names, it is more than likely that he had Uexküll in mind, for he goes on to dismiss as erroneous the claim that the life of every species is wrapped up in its own 'private' or 'subjective' world – precisely the claim that Uexküll had advanced for the *Umwelt*.[6] What, then, were the grounds for this dismissal?

They lay in his insistence that the world is real and materially present to the animal, even as it is drawn into that animal's pattern of activity, its form of life. The niche, for Gibson, exists in the environment; it is not cast onto the environment by the organism.[7] Affordances, then, are meanings for the animal, *but they are not signs*. What Gibson proposes, in short, is a theory of meaning without signification. It is in this sense a theory of direct perception. That is what sets it apart from the semiotic approach. For it is an axiom of semiotics that all perception is indirect, mediated by signs. And the sign, in turn, is defined as something that stands for something else which is not immediately present to the perceiver. This logic imposes a division, indeed a discontinuity, between the sign-object and its meaning. It stands, as it were, as a surrogate for that which is the absent, as its representative. That is why, for semiotics, all meaning is representational.[8] If that were so, then of course, direct perception would be impossible. But with Gibson, direct perception is not only possible but fundamental to the ways living beings of all kinds make their ways in the world. Here, object and meaning are one: to perceive the object *is* to perceive what it affords.

The theory of direct perception has been widely misunderstood by critics who insist on viewing it through their own representationalist spectacles.[9] They take it to mean that the world somehow imprints itself on the mind like a foot in mud, to leave an indelible impression. But this is not what it is about at all. It is rather about how organisms are able to find their way around in an environment, and carry on with their lives, *without representing it*. And the key to this lies in movement. The organism of Gibson's account is not merely the recipient of stimuli which it has then to interpret prior to delivering a motor response (as the tick interprets the odour of butyric acid prior to releasing itself from its perch); it is rather embarked on a sensory exploration of its surroundings, actively seeking out information from the temporal flow of stimulation as it moves through the world, or as aspects of the world move relative to it (such as the mammal's passing beneath the stationary tick).[10] Perception and action are not, then, alternating phases in a circuit of stimulation and response, they are rather intrinsically coupled in the same movement: to perceive is to act, and vice versa. This movement has no starting point or end point. It goes on, as life does, yielding up neither to objects nor to precepts, but to the incremental progression of the perceiver.

Lines, not signs

Now in taking my cue from Gibson rather than Uexküll, I do not mean to deny that there are signs in the world. It is one thing, however, to recognise the signs, quite another to say that in a world of life, signs are all there is. For just as there can be meaning without signs, so there can be signs without meaning – portents that command our attention, but the significance of which we can only wonder at. They are like the loose ends of a tapestry, threads that we can pick up and follow. Thus the tell-tale sign is the loose end of a story, the clue in the parlour the loose end of a crime, the signpost in the landscape the loose end of a path, the scent the loose end of an animal's trail, the dangling word the loose end of a conversation. We can listen to the story, pursue the case, walk the path, sniff the scent, join the conversation, but with no knowing where they will take us. Listening, detection, walking, tracking and conversing are life-processes. They carry on, with no final destination. They are the ways life has of running ahead of itself, manifesting not so much a power of representation as an imaginative impulse that continually overflows the representable.

Semiosis, however, short-circuits life. For the relation of 'standing for', by which the sign-object serves as a surrogate for its absent referent, not only breaks the journey; it also calls up a destination even before the traveller has set out. Here, ends are never loose but already tied to beginnings, in a closed semiotic circuit. That's why the concept of semiosis, as biosemiotician Kalevi Kull and his colleagues (2011: 27) point out, is so closely related to that of function. 'Both are teleological concepts', they write, 'in the sense of being determined with respect to an end (or *other* than itself) – a specifically related *absent* content.' Note their emphasis on the words 'other' and 'absent'. It is as if every creature, in life, were pulled along or goaded into action by a determinate end that already exists *for* it, as an explicit or implicit representation, but that is yet other *to* it, and absent *from* it. What does this tell us about the creature itself? It tells us that the creature is, by nature, contained – that what is not immediately present to it lies, like a foreign country, beyond its borders. But life, as we have had so many occasions to observe, will not be contained. Its defining quality, indeed, is precisely that it always overspills whatever boundaries may have temporarily formed around it.

How, after all, can you describe a function save by telling the story of how, in practice, a particular action was fulfilled? You describe the function of a saw, for example, by narrating an episode of sawing. And at the moment when you take up the saw to cut a plank, the tale is carried on (Ingold 2011a: 56–7). The sign marks this moment. Far from standing *for*, it stands *out*, registering that key point of transition at which the story issues, without a break, into life. Thus signs punctuate the life-course rather as way-markers punctuate a walking path. Each mark, taken as a sign, points the way ahead. Here, as in life, every ending is a beginning. In semiosis, by contrast, every beginning prefigures an end. If life is prospective, semiosis is retrospective, connecting up the dots along a route already travelled. What is experienced, in the act, as venturing forth into a world in formation, is reconstructed, in semiosis, as a concatenation of discrete episodes, each connecting a point of departure with an end state, a sign and its meaning, in a world that has already settled. Only when your walk is completed can you recollect the itinerary as a sequence of landmarks; only when the case is closed can the detective retrace the clues that led to its solution; only when a conversation comes to an end can it be retold as a narrative.

Consider, once again, the classic example of the indexical sign. Smoke, it is said, is a sign of fire. From afar, you can see one but not the other. But how, I wonder, can you tell where smoke ends and fire begins? What you witness is a process of burning. You can watch the flames leap or the smoke billow, but there are no categorical breaks in the process. For in truth, smoke is burning itself in one of its more sensible manifestations, and by following it you may be led to its source. To state that smoke is an *index* of fire, however, is to insert a cut, between presence and absence, when in reality there is none. Where, then, does this cut come from? It comes when you turn from bearing witness to the fire, coupling your attention to the billowing smoke and leaping flames, to accounting for your observations as a sequence of discrete events: first, you saw the smoke; then, as you approached, you saw the flames. The cut results from the abductive rendering of a continuous process as a sequence of discrete events. Likewise, following a tree-root may lead you to the base of the trunk, and beyond, in a movement that parallels the tree's own uptake of moisture from the soil. True, you saw the root before you caught sight of the trunk. But only by treating the two sightings as separate episodes can the one be contrived to stand for the other, as an index to its referent. The real tree is no more sectioned than your observation of it. It is not a thing of parts but the momentarily congealed form of a process of growth. And just as with the fire, you witnessed its burning, now with the tree, you witness its growing.

It is the same, too, with the animal and its scent. Remember the tick, picking up the odour as the mammal passes beneath its perch. Why should the odour belong any less to the mammal than the skin-glands that produce it? By what right do we presume that it is the present sign of the absent beast? Only because we take the animal to be a self-contained, mobile object rather than what it really is, a confluence of vital processes that spill out far beyond the skin, and into the environment. Human hunters know to recognise prey by their scent, which trails through the air, like an invisible thread, to reach their nostrils. For the hunter to follow the scent is to align the trail of his own movement with the scent-path, so that the two become entwined. The lifeworld itself can be imagined as an immense tapestry of such trails, a great meshwork of lines that twine around one another.[11] The world, in short, is composed of lines, not signs. Ecology, then, becomes a study of the life of lines (Ingold 2007a: 103; 2015). Following every line – whether it be an animal scent, a tree root, or a trail of smoke – we attend to how each, as it goes on its way, both binds with others and concurrently differentiates itself from them. In this attention to difference, indeed, might well be said to lie the distinguishing mark of life itself.

From semiosis to life

Not all differences, of course, matter to an organism, but some do, and it is these that spur it to action. For the tick, as maverick anthropologist Gregory Bateson would have put it, the crossing of a threshold in its olfactory register leads it to release its grip and to fall. These 'differences that make a difference' are what Bateson (1973: 457) called *ideas*. They are units of information in an ecology of mind – an ecology delineated by the generation of ideas in circuits of perception and action.[12] Famously contrarian, Bateson was opposed both to the reductionism of mainstream biology and to anthropology's elevation of mind and culture over the natural world. Nevertheless, he did not always acknowledge his antecedents. For his programme for an ecology of mind bears a striking resemblance to what Uexküll had already proposed under the rubric of a theory of meaning. To go from the latter to the former, you have only to substitute ideas for signs. This substitution, however, does nothing to heal the division, inherent in Uexküll's *Umwelt*-theory as it is in Bateson's ecology of mind, between the world of ideas and signs, on the one hand, and the world of forces and materials on the other. For in its attachment to signs or ideas, to information as opposed to energy and substance, meaning is effectively dematerialised. Add to this the assumption that it is the traffic in signs that lifts animate life from the substrate of inanimate matter, and life is dematerialised too![13]

The results are bizarre, nowhere better illustrated than in a recent and much-lauded study by anthropologist Eduardo Kohn. Intoxicated by the idea – which is news only to anthropologists and a handful of philosophers – that even nonhumans inhabit meaningful worlds, Kohn's ambition is to develop an 'anthropology beyond the human' which is at once semiotic and Batesonian in approach. 'Life', Kohn (2013: 9) asserts, 'is constitutively semiotic ... the product of sign processes'. It is in representing the world, he insists, that animate life distinguishes itself from the residue of inanimate matter. Yet he is also convinced that signs connote the absence of that to which they refer: 'all kinds of signs in some way or other re-present what is not present' (Kohn 2013: 23). But how can a creature possibly remain alive if the real world continually escapes from it, if it can only imbibe signs of difference? To survive, all organisms must undergo metabolism and respire. They need to eat and breathe. How long could you survive by eating the signs of absent food or breathing the signs of absent air? These metabolic processes, involving circulations of materials and flows of energy, are not residual but fundamental to life. Indeed, if anything distinguishes life from non-life, it is not representation and interpretation but the coupling of action and perception. For the challenge for the living organism is not to represent the world in its absence. It is to participate from within in the world's very presencing, in its continual coming into being, self-making or *autopoiesis*.

As a student of life, and a self-confessed semiophobe, I too am a participant in this process. To study is to join with others in practical activity, to align one's attention with theirs, and to draw meaning from the shared experience. There is nothing mystical about this. It is what we have all done as children, growing up under the eyes of our elders only to become those eyes, under which the coming generation will grow and learn in their turn (Chapter 18, page 274). But as anthropologists we do the same when we go to study with people whose lives have heretofore followed very different paths. So far as is practically feasible, we join our paths with theirs, questioningly following in their footsteps, learning how to attend, as they do, to what is going on around and about. The communion of experience generated through participation in joint activity makes it possible for meanings to be shared, and these meanings, in turn, fill out the things we see our companions do and the words we hear them say. By way of direct perception, meaning precedes signification. It lies, as Pierre Bourdieu (1977: 2) once put it, 'on the hither side of words and concepts'. If proof of this were needed, we would have only to point to the evident effectiveness of participant observation as a practice of fieldwork. It could not be done otherwise (Ingold 1993a: 222–3).

The semiophile, however, denies this, insisting to the contrary that meaning is always on the far side of the sign. And with this I return, at length, to my altercation with Descola.[14] The question that divides us comes down to this: how can we ever know what another is thinking, feeling, or dreaming? We know, Descola (2016: 323) answers, 'by means of signs – whether linguistic, iconic or indexical – that circulate between humans and, in a lesser measure, between humans and nonhumans; signs as visible or audible tokens that stand for something else; signs which "represent" an event, a mental state, an emotion, a state of affairs, a dream'. Banished from mutual presence, and awash in an ocean of semiosis, humans and nonhumans, on this account, are condemned to endless rounds of interpretation. Behind this lies the same division that we have already encountered with Bateson, between the world of mind and meaning, on the one hand, and of materials and forces on the other, or in Descola's (2013) terms, between 'interiority' and 'physicality' (Chapter 23, pages 354–5). This is not a division that Descola learned through his fieldwork. It is rather built axiomatically into its ethnographic premise, namely that the purpose of fieldwork is to interpret other lives. My view, to the contrary, is that our purpose – more anthropological than ethnographic – is to learn from them. And we can best do that by joining with them in the mutual production of a shared world.

Chapter 23

One world anthropology

> Having received all mortal and immortal creatures and being therewithal replenished, this universe hath thus come into being, living and visible, containing all things that are visible, the image of its maker, a god perceptible, most mighty and good, most fair and perfect, even this one and only-begotten world that is.
>
> (Plato, *The Timaeus*)[1]

The singular and the plural

Many years ago I came up with my own definition of anthropology. It was '*philosophy with the people in*' (Ingold 1992b: 696). By this I meant two things. First, the questions that anthropology asks are indeed philosophical ones: they are questions about what it means to be, to know, to think, imagine, perceive, act, remember, learn, live in the company of others, administer justice, exercise power, relate to the environment, confront our own mortality, and so on and so forth. These questions are endless. But second, the way anthropologists do their philosophising is primarily through their engagements – in both observation and conversation – with the people among whom they work. Indeed I would now go further, to include not just the people but all the other beings, of manifold kinds, with whom or with which we share our lives. There is here an implied criticism of philosophical philosophers who would rather shy away from any such engagement, preferring to labour in the library with their canonical texts. We anthropologists, I contend, can do philosophy better, by virtue of bringing into the conversation the voices, the experience, and the wisdom of countless human beings – not to mention legions of nonhumans – which would otherwise be excluded. To do this kind of philosophy is, in effect, to make a conversation of life itself.

This conversation – this life – is not however just *about* the world. In an important sense which I shall elaborate, it *is* the world. To join the conversation, then, is to inhabit the world. That the inhabited world is indeed *one* is,

DOI: 10.4324/9781003171713-29

in my view, a core principle of anthropology, and we neglect it at our peril. I worry that in practice, it has been all too readily neglected, along with the challenges and responsibilities it entails, in favour of a facile appeal to plurality. It sometimes seems that anthropologists are constitutionally averse to oneness, to singularity, and likewise obsessed with the plural. Never one world; always many worlds. Once these were the many worlds of symbolic culture; now, in the wake of the so-called ontological turn, we have the many worlds of being, of realities to be symbolised. Taken to its extreme, it appears that everyone and everything can be its own world. You name it, and there's a world for you. But what do we mean by plurality? And in what sense is it *opposed* to singularity? The question of how to reconcile the singular and the plural – or in slightly different terms, the universal and the particular – could well turn out to be the central problem of a truly philosophical anthropology.

Let me offer an example. People indigenous to the High Arctic, mainly of northernmost Canada and Greenland, know themselves and are known as *Inuit*. The word is a plural form, derived from the singular *inuk*, which roughly translates as 'soul'. In a modern idiom we might suppose that every soul belongs to an individual, and therefore that the plural Inuit simply denotes a population of individuals. Greenland and Canada, we say, have their respective Inuit populations. We could do a census and count them up. But for the people themselves, at least traditionally, souls could not be counted or enumerated in this way. As the ethnographer Henry Stewart (2002: 90) has noted, the plural form is 'most certainly not a collective designation for all original inhabitants of the tundra Arctic'. It rather connotes something like 'autonomous existence'. Most often the plural suffix (*-miut*) follows a toponym or place-marker – as, for example, Netsilik, plural Netsilingmiut, or Iglulik, plural Iglulingmiut – and could be glossed as 'soul-life going on in and around this place'. The question this raises, then, is of how to get from one to the other, from the life of the soul (*inuk*) to soul-life (*inuit*). Not by multiplication: or not at least in the arithmetic sense familiar to us from elementary school. Nor, conversely, can you get from soul-life to the life of the soul by division. Call the plural a multiplicity if you must, but do not suppose it is a multiplication of the singular!

Wholes and parts

The soul, after all, is not an entity sunk inexorably into itself. That is to say, it is not an object, in the sense recently promulgated by the advocates of so-called 'object-oriented ontology'[2]. In their view, everything you might care to name has its own inscrutable essence, neither reducible to the more elementary particles of which it and other entities might be constituted, nor soluble into constructs at some superordinate level of existence. Admittedly, the soul is amenable neither to reduction nor to totalisation; neither to 'undermining' nor to 'overmining', as object-oriented philosophers would put it (Harman 2011: 172). But this does not make the soul an object-in-itself. It is, more fundamentally, a *movement*, which takes the grammatical form not of the noun or pronoun, but of the verb. And the most outstanding characteristic of this movement is that it *carries on*, or keeps on going. For Inuit people it even carries on over generations, as a grandchild, for example, is animated by the soul of its grandparent, leading parents to address their children, sometimes, as they would address their own parents, and to treat them with equivalent deference and respect (Nuttall 1994). The idea of 'early years', as though children were closer to some imaginary point of origin in a process of socialisation, therefore makes no sense. Everyone, at any moment, is both older and younger than themselves.

Thus souls – or lives – are movements, and to echo the celebrated aphorism of Heraclitus, one cannot step twice into the life of the same soul. What, then, is the relation between the life of the soul and soul-life, or to put it in more general terms, between the particular life and *life itself*? Is it a relation of part to whole? Yes, so long as we don't make the common mistake of confusing wholeness with totalisation (Ingold 2007c: 209). Totality, to my ear at least, implies addition and completion: whether or not you consider the result to be more than, equal to, or even less than the sum of its parts, the logic of summation remains. 'Life as a whole', however, cannot be reached as a sum total. It is never complete, nor is it even on the way to completion, since it advances to no end save its own continuation. As the generative potential of a world in becoming, life is always going on, a perpetual origination.

Particular lives, too, can be parts of life as a whole – the life of the soul a part of soul-life – but only so long as we think of these parts, likewise, as ways of carrying on, like the lines of a composition. The idea of composition, according to Bruno Latour (2010: 473–4), 'underlines that things have to be put together (Latin *componere*) while retaining their heterogeneity'. Thus parts remain differentiable within the whole; they do not merge into one homogeneous current of vitality. In all other respects, however, the sense in which I speak of composition is entirely contrary to Latour's. For him it is a medley of bits and pieces, 'utterly heterogeneous', which at best can make up a composite material that is 'fragile, revisable and diverse'. Such a composite can be as readily *de*composed as composed (Latour 2010: 474). The analogy I have in mind, by contrast, is that of polyphonic music, in which every voice, or every instrument, carries on along its own melodic line. In music the relation between parts and whole is not summative – neither additive nor multiplicative – but *contrapuntal* (Chapter 17, page 264). Think of the tenor part in the chorus or the cello part in the symphony. I want to think of the life of every particular soul, likewise, as a line of counterpoint that, even as it issues forth, is continually attentive and responsive to each and every other. Souls, we might say, are answerable to one another, a condition that carries entailments of both responsiveness and responsibility (Wentzer 2014).

Filiation and alliance

Precisely because souls go along together, and because their continual regeneration is nourished and impelled by the memory of their association, soul-life is a whole that cannot be decomposed without causing grief if not destruction to the lives of its parts. This is why, as I argued in Chapter 17, the composition would be better regarded as a gathering than as an assemblage. Compositional relations, in short, are of interstitial differentiation rather than exterior articulation. It is instructive to consider how this contrast plays out in the classic anthropological themes of kinship and affinity. Over seventy years ago, the social anthropologist Meyer Fortes wrote two books on the Tallensi people of northern Ghana, among whom he had worked. One was called *The Dynamics of Clanship among the Tallensi* (Fortes 1945); the other, *The Web of Kinship among the Tallensi* (Fortes 1949). For Fortes, clans acted as corporate groups within the public domain of law and politics. Unified by putative descent from a common ancestor, they were the solid building blocks of Tallensi social structure. But behind them lay a tangled web of interpersonal relations, laced with affect, threading through the entire fabric of the structure and tying it all together. These were relations of kinship. While clans would associate, en bloc, in relations of alliance, the source from which all kinship springs is the fundamental human bond between parent and child, or in a word, filiation.

Many years later, Gilles Deleuze and Félix Guattari (2004: 27) would harness the same distinction, between alliance and filiation, in order to draw a contrast between the alternative figures, respectively, of the rhizome and the tree. 'The tree', they say, 'is filiation, but the rhizome is alliance, uniquely alliance.' But as so often, they get things back to front. For if anything is truly rhizomatic – with lines going every which way, ever ravelling and unravelling, unconstrained by borders or structural limitations – it is the web of kinship. How do Deleuze and Guattari manage to get it so wrong? Clearly, they don't like trees! 'We're tired of trees,' they lament, 'they've made us suffer too much' (Deleuze and Guattari 2004: 17). This, however, is because they base their idea of the tree not on a living specimen, rooted in the ground, but on the bureaucratic organogram or cognitive algorithm, with its hierarchy of control descending from a central apex through multiple levels of division and subdivision (Chapter 12, page 198). Alternatively, they could have had in mind the anthropologist's genealogical chart, depicting the clan as a body joined by descent from an apical ancestor. On the chart, every member appears pinned to their appointed place, where they are destined to *be*, but with no possibility to grow or to *become*. In standard anthropological notation, the relation of descent would be diagrammed accordingly, as a line connecting two punctual icons, standing respectively for ancestor and descendant, in adjacent generations.

These trees, however, are upside down (Ingold 2007a: 104–19). Living trees, unlike the lines of their diagrammatic counterparts, do not connect up stoppages in reverse, but grow, branch and swerve from within the midst of their arborescence. And likewise, in real life, filiation is a process of becoming in the course of which the child carries on from the life of its parent while progressively differentiating its own life from that which it engendered it. Filiation, thus understood, is not the connection of parent *and* child; it is the life of parent *with* child (Figure 23.1). Indeed like the living tree, filiation – and the kinship it engenders – is supremely rhizomatic; its lines do not connect but are themselves lines of life that carry on alongside one another, answering or responding to one another – or literally *corresponding* – as they go. They are not 'and ... and ... and ...', as Deleuze and Guattari (2004: 27) would have it, but 'with ... with ... with ...'. 'And' is a conjunction; it joins things up. Its logic is of alliance, of assemblage or

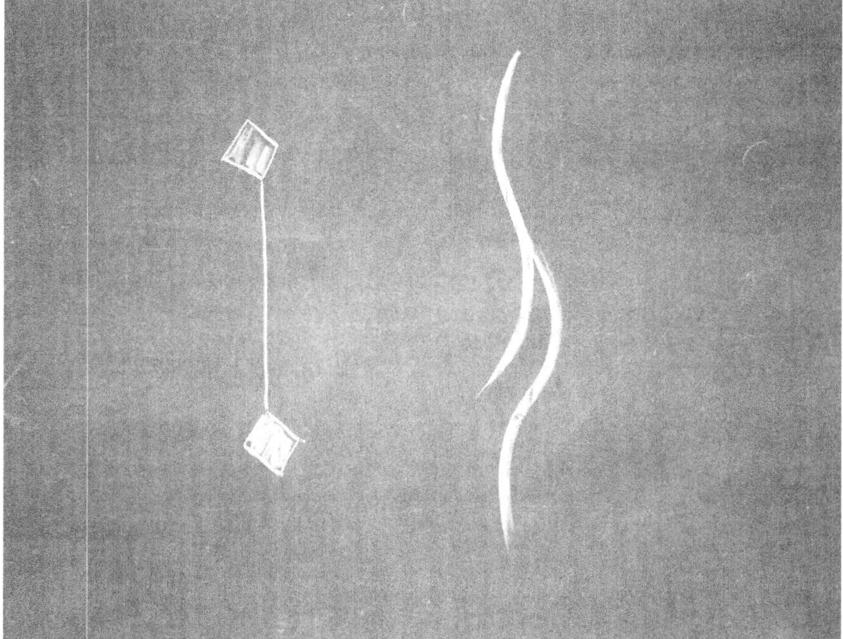

Figure 23.1 Descent and filiation. Left: the connection of ancestor and descendant, as it might be depicted on a genealogical chart. Right: the life of parent with child, growing older together.[a]

[a] This figure, like the others in this chapter (Figures 23.2, 23.3 and 23.4), reproduces a blackboard sketch made during a lecture in which I first presented these ideas. I photographed this and the other sketches myself.

exterior articulation. But the logic of the prepositional 'with' is of gathering or interstitial differentiation.

As a gathering of living souls, then, 'life as a whole' is composed not by the articulatory summation of particular lives, but in their differential correspondence (Ingold 2015: 23). Its constituent relations are not *between* but *along*. Between-ness gives us the idea of interaction, a reciprocal back-and-forth between otherwise fixed positions. But the along-ness of correspondence goes side by side, like companions walking together or making music together, or indeed like kinspersons growing older together. All are ways of *longing*, in which an imagination that strays beyond the horizon of conceptualisation loops proleptically back to meet an origination that recedes beyond the limit of memory, as in the cycling soul-life of the Inuit, in a place where past and future merge. It is a place we perpetually dream of and strive for, but never reach.[3] With this in mind, let me return to the problem of universality. What can it mean to say of the one world that it is universal? And how does it relate to the particular, or to the relativity of the particular moment, the particular life, the way of the soul? We often hear it said that particulars lie upon, or are figured against, the ground of the universal. Well then, what *is* this ground? Is it an underlying foundation of support on which all else rests, or a matrix of growth and nourishment, from which everything comes?

Differentiation and diversity

The idea of the ground as a surface of support takes us back to the ecological psychology of James Gibson. As already noted in Chapter 10 (page 157), Gibson likens the ground to the floor of a room. Just as chairs, tables and cupboards are set upon the floor, he explains, so hills, trees, and buildings are set upon the ground (Gibson 1979: 127). As such, the ground appears as a plane of indifference, a *tabula rasa*, from which all variations have been excised, only to be re-imposed, as diverse, free-standing entities, *upon* it. For a very different view, however, we could turn to the writings of Tadashi Suzuki (1986), one of the foremost figures of contemporary Japanese theatre. For Suzuki, the ground is a source of emergent difference. It *gives rise* to the features we see, the formations of the landscape, trees and buildings, even people. The floorboards of the traditional Japanese house, Suzuki (1986: 21) tells us, virtually grow into the inhabitants who walk them, just as did the trees from which the boards were made once grow from the earth (Ingold 2011a: 41). Here, the ground is no more indifferent to the trees than are floorboards to people; rather, trees and people arise from the earth and from boards, respectively, in an ongoing process of differentiation (Figure 23.2).

The distinction I want to emphasise here is between the ground of indifference and the ground of differentiation, or – if you will – between the

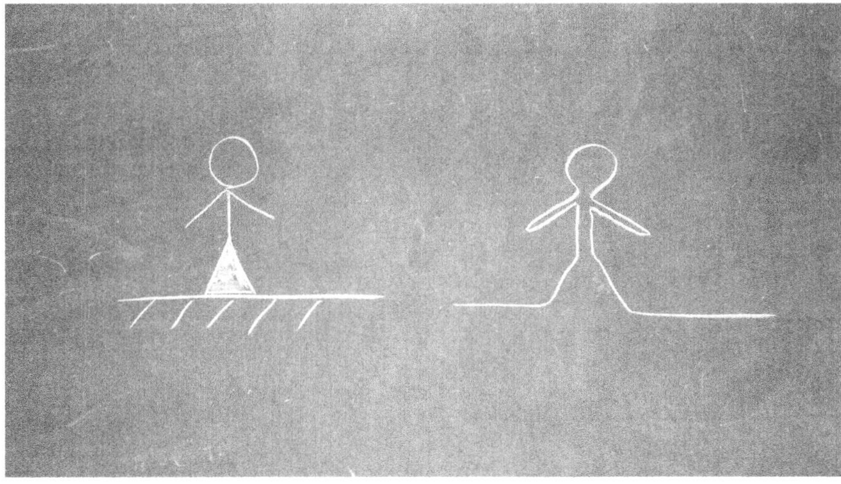

Figure 23.2 Figure and ground. Left: the figure is mounted on the ground of indifference. Right: the figure arises as a fold in the ground itself.

respective grounds of being and becoming. *Being* different, that is diversity; *becoming* different, that is differentiation. Differentiation turns to diversity by way of the twin operations of excision and reimposition: where the former cuts things out from the processes of their generation, the latter deposits them, as ready formed particulars, upon the universal ground of indifference. This ground, as we are inclined to say, is *hard*, providing a solid but inert foundation for the objects that rest upon it, and the activities that are conducted across its surface. It is worth noting that exactly the same metaphor is imported into our thinking about the human mind, when neuropsychologists, for example, speak of the mind's 'hardware' as offering a neural substrate capable of supporting various kinds of cognitive operations, including those involved in speech and manual tool-use (Chapter 12, page 197). In the very division between the hardware and the software it supports, the separation of knowing from being, of *sapiens* from *Homo*, is replicated and reinforced. What would happen if, to the contrary, we were to think of the ground of human perception and cognition, or of sentience and sensibility, as something more like the floorboards of a traditional Japanese house, or, with Deleuze and Guattari (2004: 17), like a field of long grass, or even like the earth itself?

To think of difference in terms of differentiation rather than diversity is to imagine the universal not as a featureless ground upon which all variation is deposited but as a surface that is as folded and crumpled as the earth beneath our feet. With the logic of diversity, of excision and reimposition, all difference is *bilateral*: as features are distinguished from the ground, by way of their excision, so the ground is distinguished from the features that are then reimposed upon it. But as Deleuze sets out to show in his book on *Difference and Repetition* (1994), in *becoming* different, one thing may distinguish itself from another *without* the latter's distinguishing itself from the former. Imagine lifting a sheet to form a crease; we register the line of the crease, yet the crease is still in the sheet. It is not as though the sheet had parted company with the crease and sunk bank into flat homogeneity, leaving the crease-line, as it were, high and dry (Ingold 2015: 34–5). The distinction, in short, is *unilateral*. Here, every distinguishing feature, as Figure 23.2 shows, arises as a fold in the ground. My contention is that in a life of longing, all difference emerges thus, in the midst of things. It is interstitial. Just as with the crease and the sheet, the particularity of the singular life distinguishes itself from the universality of life itself, the life of the soul from soul-life, *without the universal's distinguishing itself from the particular*.

Animism and naturalism

To anthropologists, the ontology that gives us the ground of nature as a universal and homogeneous substrate upon which are set the fragmentary forms of cultural diversity will be immediately recognisable as the default position adopted by generations of textbooks. It is a position that tends to be glossed by such nonspecific words as 'Western' and 'modern'. Philippe Descola, in his treatise *Beyond Nature and Culture* (2013), calls it 'naturalism'. For Descola, naturalism is one of four logically possible ontological schemas that underwrite the way human beings can organise their relations with one another and with the world they inhabit, and render this world intelligible. The others are analogism, totemism, and animism. This is not the place for an extended review of Descola's arguments (Ingold 2016a). But I would like to return briefly to his account of animism, already adumbrated in Chapter 4 (pages 56–7), since by doing so I can both add some precision to what I mean by the relation between the life of the soul and soul-life, and clarify the sense of 'one-worldness' that follows from it.

The ontology of animism, according to Descola (2013: 129), endows beings of all sorts with interior souls which enable them to act both normatively and ethically, just as humans do. Amid this universe of souls, however, it is possible to make out beings of diverse kinds thanks to the distinctiveness of their exterior bodies, which gives each particular soul its executive armature and allows it to function in the world in the way it does. In this regard, Descola thinks, animism is the perfect inverse of modern or Western naturalism, which gives us the diversity of forms of mental or spiritual life (or what modern people call 'cultures') set against the background of a universal nature. Or in a nutshell, whereas animism combines a similarity of interiorities (souls) with the dissimilarity of physicalities (bodies), naturalism combines similarity on the plane of physicality with dissimilarity on the plane of interiority. This opposition does indeed sound very neat, until you start to wonder why naturalism, in the same breath that it extols the universality of nature, vis-à-vis the diversity of cultures, also celebrates the diversity of living kinds or species vis-à-vis the universality of the human mind and its conscious sense of self. What is similar, and what is diverse, depends on which way you look! If naturalism can just as well be defined by the dissimilarity of physicalities and similarity of interiorities as by its opposite, then how can it any longer be distinguished from animism?

The answer, I think, is that compared with the similarities and dissimilarities of animism, those of naturalism are of another kind. In brief: naturalism's similarities are of *identity*, animism's are of *continuity*; naturalism's differences are of *diversity*, animism's are of *differentiation*. To amplify these twin distinctions, we can bring to our aid an earlier masterpiece of comparative anthropology, Roy Wagner's *The Invention of Culture* (1975). While for Descola, naturalism and animism are but two of four possible ontological schemas, Wagner offers only two possibilities. On the one hand are people who deliberately assemble life into collectivities, and in so doing, precipitate an idea of the world as made up of primordially discrete, enumerable entities, otherwise known as individuals. On the other hand are people for whom the task is to differentiate the flux of life into separable vessels, precipitating as they do so an idea of the world as primordially undifferentiated, as a plenum (Wagner 1975: 51). For Wagner these alternatives are exemplified respectively by 'middle-class Americans' and the Daribi people of Papua New Guinea among whom he carried out his fieldwork: the former broadly representative of Western modernity, the latter of 'tribal peoples'. In the following, I shall gloss over the very obvious problems with the terms of comparison,[4] and allow the first to equate broadly to Descola's 'naturalism', and the second to his 'animism'. For what interests me here is not where Wagner draws his lines between the West and the rest, but what he has to say about the self and the soul under the two contrasting ontological regimes (1975: 93–4).

The plane of immanence

Under the first regime, of naturalism, similarity means identity. We imagine a world of individuals. These individuals can be counted up. They can be aggregated into the kinds of collectivities we call societies. And they can be compared according to their intrinsic attributes. An attribute is deemed to be universal when it is common to every entity; it is particular when it is limited to a narrower class of entities, or perhaps even unique to a single entity. Thus we might claim that every individual human being possesses a sense of self, a singular seat of reason and conscience, and that this sense is therefore universal. But we might also claim that the mode of expression of this sense varies between one group of human beings and another, and class all those who express their selfhood in a certain way as members of one culture, and all those who express it in a different way as members of another. We would, in so doing, establish what we take to be the 'fact' of cultural diversity, although – as Wagner shows – this 'fact' is really just the precipitate of a logical procedure.

Under the second regime, of animism, we start not with populations of more or less identical individuals but with a continuous flux of yet-to-be differentiated potential. Out of this flux, recognisable beings have to be formed. It is the task of life to do so. Yet in this process of formation, which carries on throughout life and is never complete, there always remains a memory of that undifferentiated potential from the interstices of which every being is drawn. This memory is the soul. Like a coiled spring tensed by the force of its enwinding, the soul is a constant reminder of the flux of the world, and of the effort that has to be put in to hold out against it. In this regard, the soul is the precise obverse of the self. Under a regime of naturalism, the self may be recruited into the work of creating a collectivity, it may be disciplined to conform to common standards, and yet its very persistence attests to the threat of decomposition, reminding us that without continued effort, the whole is liable to collapse into its individual parts. Under a regime of animism, by contrast, the soul cannot be recruited, nor can it be disciplined, but it can be lost, dissolving back into the very plenum, of life as a whole, from which it once emerged (Wagner 1975: 98).

It is all very well, then, to speak of the *interiority* of soul-life, but this is not, as Descola would have it, an interiority set over and against the exteriority of bodies. It is nothing like the interiority of the self. On the contrary, the soul's interiority exemplifies what Deleuze (2001) calls 'pure immanence' – that is, of an apprehension that enters into the formative current of life. The differences of animism, manifesting on the plane of immanence, arise as formations in the current; the differences of naturalism, by contrast, have broken off from the current and lie strewn upon that ground of indifference otherwise known as 'nature'. The former are emergent and interstitial; the latter resultant and superficial. Whereas animism, then, gives us a world of becoming, naturalism gives us a world of being. And it is the logic of naturalism, operating from behind the scenes in Descola's account, which contrives to wrap every cycle of life into itself, thus converting the generative currents of formation into a vital agent that is supposed to inhabit an interior divided off from the exterior domain of its interactions with others (Figure 23.3).

In calling for a one-world anthropology, I aim to escape the deadening impact of this logic, to release the soul from its imagined incarceration and to restore its turbulence to the circulations of life. It is to appeal not to the naturalistic dyad of identity and diversity but to the animistic pairing of continuity and differentiation. The universal, then, is not a lowest common denominator but a field of continuous variation; not a plane of indifference

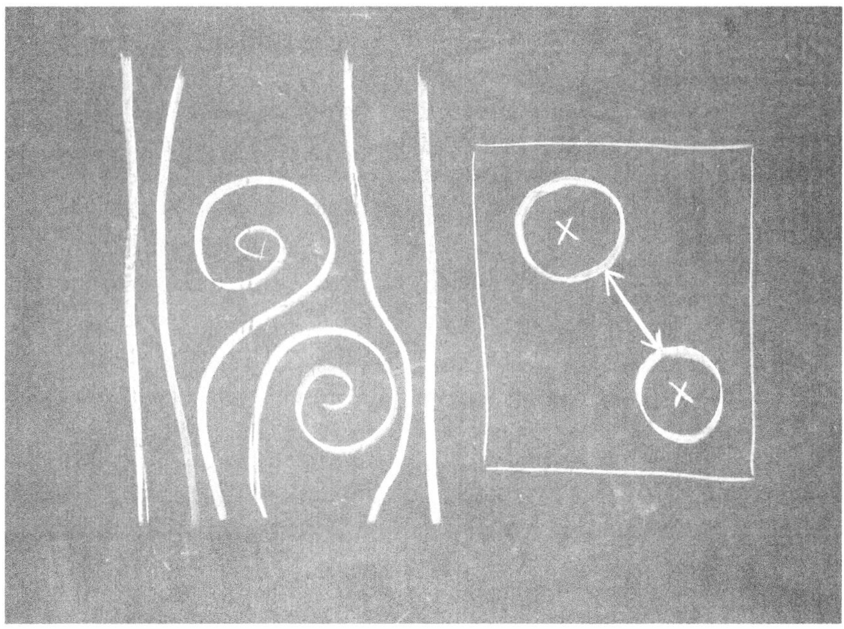

Figure 23.3 Wrapping the soul. Left: souls emerge as formations in the current of life. Right: they appear contained, and interact only by way of their exterior bodies.

upon which diversity is overlain, but a plane of immanence from which difference is continually emergent.

Agency and patiency

The next step in my argument is to relate the principle of interstitial differentiation to the problem of agency. I want to suggest that there is a connection between the question of how to reconcile the singular and the plural, and the life of the soul with soul-life, and the question of how to relate agency and patiency, action and suffering. Indeed the connection is so intrinsic that these seem to me to be alternative ways of posing what is fundamentally the same problem. The life of the soul is made up of doings; soul-life, by contrast, is what a living being undergoes. So our question is really about the relation between doing and undergoing (Chapter 1, pages 23–4). In the grammar of most modern Indo-European languages, there is a distinction between the active and passive voices of the verb: the active voice is for what one does; the passive for what one undergoes. Should we, then, think of life in the active voice or in the passive? Or should we think in terms of some kind of interplay between the two? More precisely, should the active be framed within the passive or vice versa? Are the things we do the callings of a life that happens to us, or are the things that happen to us called up by the things we do?

For those of us raised in an Indo-European linguistic environment, our usual habits of thought – conditioned, though by no means determined, by the grammatical categories of the languages we speak – put the agency of the individual out in front, as the sovereign initiator of his or her actions, that is as a self. And this self stands in opposition to the exterior environments of nature and society in which its actions have effects. Thus we tend to set the agency of the particular life against the passive backdrop of life in general. The principle of interstitial differentiation, however, suggests to the contrary, that the doings of every particular life continually emerge and distinguish themselves from within the plane of immanence that is life itself. This is to frame doing within undergoing, and not the other way around. And it is to think of every doing not as self-initiated action but as a moment in the life of the soul. Such doings belong not to us directly or exclusively, but to the memory of the whole coiled up within us. Another way of putting this is to think of everything we do as a *task*. For the task is something that falls to us, as responsive and responsible beings, as part of the life we undergo. To revert to an earlier distinction, it is a way of corresponding with the world in which we live, rather than of interacting with it.

If every doing is a task, then we need to find a way of talking about agency that puts it *inside* undergoing. With our conventional dichotomy between active and passive voices of the verb, this is very difficult to do. However many non-European languages (as well as Indo-European in earlier times, such as in classical Greek) recognised what linguists call the *middle voice* of the verb. In the middle voice, agency is inside the action, inside the verb. As the linguist Émile Benveniste (1971: 149) put it, in a classic paper, in the middle voice the doer 'achieves something that is being achieved in him'. My suggestion, then, is that in the one world of becoming, life is lived neither in the active nor in the passive but in the middle voice. Such is the life of the soul. Its particular life is not played out against the background of life itself but emerges actively from its midst. With life lived in the middle voice, our focus can no longer be on the essence of being. It must rather be on its ongoing generation. That is to say, it should be not so much on *ontology* as on *ontogeny*.

This idea of ontogenesis (as *ontogénèse*, the 'becoming of being') was key to the philosophy of Gilbert Simondon, for whom it equated more or less to the process he otherwise called *individuation*, that is, the continual 'falling out' of being from becoming. It corresponds, Simondon (1993: 300) wrote, 'to a capacity beings possess of falling out of step with themselves, of resolving themselves by the very act of falling out of step'. There are echoes, here, of Henri Bergson's idea that life 'lags behind' in the deflections, circulations and vortices of its particular forms; that where life in general forges ahead, its cycles 'want to mark time' (Bergson 1922: 128). In the process of individuation, we could say, the soul arises as a transient falling out-of-step. Or in the words of theorist and philosopher Elizabeth Grosz (2012: 41), with acknowledgement to Simondon, the soul is 'a metastable being, which carries within itself the pre-individual forces from which it was produced' (Grosz 2012: 41). As a fold or vortex in the flux of life, the soul retains a memory of the creative powers of the plenum from which it was born, and which in turn hold the potential for further transformation. In Simondon's (1993: 305) terms, life itself (or soul-life) is a never-ending process of individuation, but critically, the differentiations it engenders are concentrated not at some putative boundary with an outside world, but in its interior resonances. Or in a word, life as individuation – as lived in the middle voice – is a process of interstitial differentiation.

An ontogenetic turn?

I dislike the idea of 'turns'; for the most part it offers a pretext for tournaments of academic vanity. But if we must have such things to indicate the transitions in our thinking, then let us follow Simondon in calling for a turn that is not ontological but ontogenetic. Let our concern be not with *philosophies* but with *generations* of being. With multiple ontologies, everything or every being is its own world, closed in and complete, so that ultimately there are as many worlds as there are beings or things. Each has collapsed into itself, ultimately impenetrable to others. This is the *reductio ad absurdum* of object-oriented ontology. But with multiple ontogenies, every being or thing is open, subject to growth and movement, issuing forth along its own particular path within a world of nevertheless inexhaustible differentiation. Nothing in this world is settled, once and for all. In short, ontogenesis allows us to reconcile singularity and multiplicity, agency and patiency, within *one* world.

'There is only one world', declares the philosopher Alain Badiou (2008: 38), but it is a world that refuses any normative preconditions for existing in it – such as might be entailed in any naturalistic definition of universal humanity (Trott 2011: 87). How many times have we attempted to define human nature in terms of the common possession of this or that attribute – bipedalism, tool-making, pair-bonding, language, symbolic thought, and so on – only to discover that there are creatures born of man and woman who lack these attributes and who consequently find themselves excluded, or at least considered less-than-human? The one world we inhabit is not however reserved for what anthropologist Donald Brown (1991) has called 'Universal People', creatures of the normative imagination delineated by a suite of innate capacities and behavioural traits that all are supposed to share. It is rather a world of ever-emergent difference, which admits no boundaries of inclusion or exclusion.

In this world of becoming, as we have already observed (Chapter 19, pages 305–6), though we may all be different, these differences arise in the course of life, through our entanglement in a world of relations; they do not separate us out, each to their own kind. If anything divides us, it is not difference but similarity. For to seek what we have in common from the start is to presuppose our original disconnection. If difference draws us together, similarity drives us apart (Ingold 1996: 6). Political theorist William Connolly (1995: xx) makes much the same point, emphasising that to pit the universal *against* difference has the effect of reducing 'the essentially *relational* character of difference to the bland idea of diversity among independent entities'. It is to reduce the differentiation of becoming to the diversity of being. To undo the reduction, we must put difference and the universal back together again. This is what Badiou does. 'The single world', he argues, 'is precisely the place where an unlimited set of differences exist. Philosophically, far from casting doubt on the unity of the world, these differences are its principle of existence' (Badiou 2008: 39). I believe that anthropology should be fighting, intellectually and politically, for the recognition of this kind of world. So what should we call it?

For an answer, we can turn to the thinking of William James, a founding figure in both psychology and the philosophy of pragmatism. In 1908, James delivered the Hibbert Lectures at the University of Oxford, published in the following year under the title *A Pluralistic Universe*. His proposed solution to the problem of the one and the many was to insist that the 'multiverse', as he called it, is simultaneously both singular and plural, for the reason that its one-ness *is never absolutely complete*. It is 'strung-along', said James (2012: 170), 'not rounded in and closed'. Regardless of the part or element on which you might choose to focus, at whatever scale or level of exclusiveness or inclusiveness, there is always an overflow of relations. Wherever you are, there are further connections to be drawn, maybe direct, maybe through intermediaries. And in the drawing of these connections, even in their interpenetration, things lose nothing of their particularity.

Should we follow James and call our one world a multiverse or pluriverse, rather than a universe? Well, yes and no. We may agree with the geographer and environmental philosopher Augustin Berque (2013: 51), that the idea of the universe in its modern, naturalistic sense – as an objective exteriority that can be grasped only by the interior mind of the transcendental subject – 'negates all possibility of a world ... that is both supremely qualitative and totally unitary', that is, the kind of world posited by Plato in the final lines of the *Timaeus* with which I headed this chapter. Yet I would still want to enter one caveat, which goes back to my comparison of the conjunction 'and' and the preposition 'with' as ways of joining. The Jamesian pluralistic universe is multiply connected, yet its connections are conjunctive, not prepositional. They join things externally, on the outside. 'Pragmatically interpreted', wrote James (2012: 167), 'pluralism or the doctrine that it is many means only that the sundry parts of reality *may be externally related*. Everything you can think of, however vast or inclusive, has on the pluralistic view a genuinely "external" environment of some sort or amount.' He could hardly have been more emphatic. Indeed, the Jamesian multiverse is unmistakeably 'and ... and ... and...' – the very epitome of an assemblage. Yet the passage that immediately follows is more equivocal. 'Things are "with" one another in many ways', James (2012: 176) goes on, 'but nothing includes everything, or dominates over everything. The word "and" trails along after every sentence. Something always escapes.' Notice how in this passage James starts with 'with' and only then resorts to 'and'. Perhaps he would have liked it both ways.

Universe, fractiverse, pluriverse

This dilemma has not gone away, nor has the question it raises. Is our world a patchwork of multiple realities, irregularly stitched across their rough, unmatched and sometimes overlapping edges? Or is it more like a braid: a thing of entwined and ever-extending pathways, binding longitudinally rather than transversally along their lines of growth and movement? Writing from his perspective as a student of science and technology, John Law (2011) presents an answer of the first kind. His concern is to offer an alternative to the idea that everything there is can be made to fit into a single container universe, or what he calls the 'one-world world' (Law 2011: 10). In such a world, anything that cannot be made to fit – anything that flies in the face of universal reality – is simply written off as an instance of belief, and mistaken belief at that. In a world divided between colonised and colonisers, what the former take for truth, the latter dismiss as figments of culture or worldview, though as Law shows, the same logic has long been at work within the societies of the colonisers as well. But it is a logic that fails in a post-colonial era, in which different and incommensurable realities grind against one another with no assurance of reconciliation or containment. We now live, says Law (2011: 2), in the era of the *fractiverse*, 'a set of contingent, enacted and more or less intersecting worlds in the plural'.

Worlds in the plural? We seem to be back where we started, with the many as opposed to the one. Perhaps this is because of Law's focus on the being of things rather than their becoming, on ontologies rather than ontogenies. Realities, multiple as they are, seem in Law's account to have already fallen out from the milieu of their generation. In order to recover the one-ness of the world, we need to move upstream, and to correspond *with* things in the moment of their appearing, rather than assembling what has already appeared on the conjunctive hook of an *and*. This, in effect, is to seek an answer of the second kind. Returning to the philosophy of James, but in the context of contemporary geopolitics, anthropologist Arturo Escobar (2011) hints at just such an answer. For Escobar the one-world world is the globe of corporate capitalism. Epitomised in the celebrated logo of the World Bank – a spherical graticule shorn of life, elements and people – this is indeed a world that is 'rounded in and closed', as James would have put it, and in which everything there is has been reduced to liquid commensurability. It is a world of commodities and monetary values, from which people are overwhelmingly marginalised if not actually locked out (Badiou 2008: 38).

Against this global world, and with acknowledgement to James, Escobar reintroduces what he calls the *pluriverse*. 'It might be described', he writes, 'as a process of planetarization articulated around a vision of the Earth as a living whole that is always emerging out of the manifold biophysical, human, and spiritual elements and relations that make it up' (Escobar 2011: 139). Unlike Law's fractiverse, Escobar's pluriverse is unambiguously 'with ... with ... with ...'. It is prepositional, not conjunctive, and its plurality arises not from chains of exterior connection – of things strung along – but from the cascades of individuation or interstitial differentiation by which the 'Earth as a living whole' – to borrow Escobar's words – is continually emerging.[5] It is to the one-worldness of this whole, I believe, that anthropology must remain committed. As I stated at the outset, the world is a conversation; it is not the *object* of our conversation. In the conversation, lives twist around one another as they go along, both answering and being answered to. And that, precisely, is what it means to correspond.

Tangentialism and correspondence

Most practising anthropologists, however, have preferred to come at other lives along a tangent, momentarily aligning with them only to shear away into the stance of interpretation and analysis. This is to converse with others – to listen to what they have to say and observe what they do – not for what they have to tell, but *for what it tells about them*. It is to wrap their voices, under the blanket of ethnography, into an account that transports us into a world whose contrived otherness leaves ours intact. The ethnography of many worlds, notes Stuart McLean (2017: 147–55), disarms or even anaesthetises the voices of others by embedding them within the explanatory or interpretative contexts of 'society', 'culture' or 'history'. One world anthropology, to the contrary, must resist the ethnographic urge to contextualise, and forgo tangentialism for correspondence (Figure 23.4). Its singular but always worlding world is not of beings radically other to one another, but of becomings that, like voices in a conversation, are ever differentiating themselves from within the matrix of their common life. To converse with them is to put this world continually at stake.

One-world anthropology begins here, in the recognition that people are different not because they belong to other worlds but because they are fellow travellers in the *same* world – a world, nonetheless, of inexhaustible and interminable variation. It begins with the conversation. And in

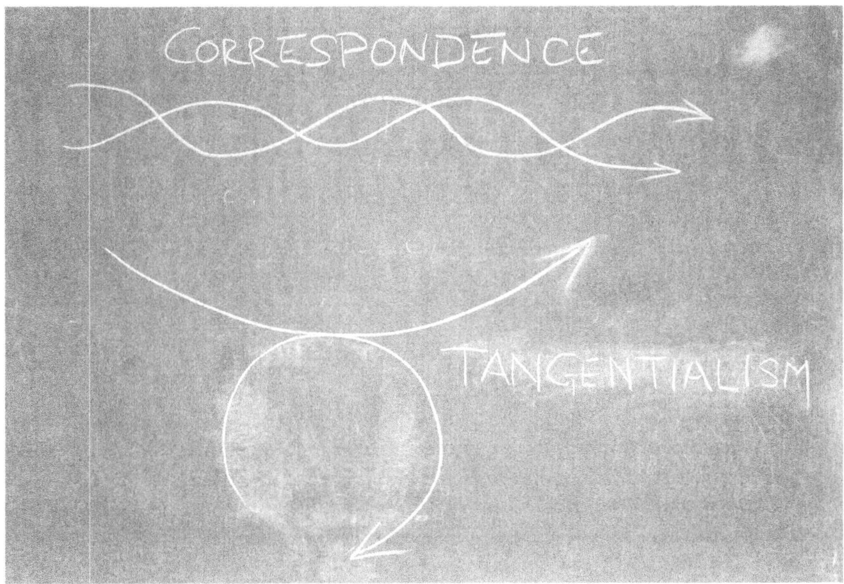

Figure 23.4 Correspondence and tangentialism.

this conversation lies *ontogénèse*, the becoming of being. It is high time to restore ontogenesis, the skeleton in the cupboard of ontology, to the animating currents of our one world. We will then find that every particular life is both an open-ended exploration of the possibilities of being this world affords and a contribution to its ongoing formation – to its worlding. It is, in this sense, a never-ending quest for an answer to the problem of what being human, or to be alive in the world, actually *means*. But every answer is a response and not a solution: a response that 'provisionally integrates what was formerly a source of tension' (Grosz 2012: 39). Responding to the question, we respond to one another; that is, we correspond. Life is a question to which there is no answer, but in this one world of ours we are all tasked with looking for it, and it is in the search that all life is lived. And it is just as well that there is no final solution, for that, indeed, would put an end to us all.

Notes

Chapter 1

1 For this and the following paragraph, I have drawn extensively on the authoritative review of philosophical creationism by Andrzej Maryniarczyk (2016). The citation from Empedocles is on page 224 of this review. My source for Lucretius's *De Rerum Natura* is www.perseus.tufts.edu/hopper/text?doc=Perseus%3Atext%3A1999.02.0131 (accessed 29 January 2020).

2 Ockham's parallel between creativity and risibility, and the fallacy of confusing a post-hoc abstraction for a real, generative capacity, are discussed in the magisterial work of medievalist Gordon Leff (1975: 148–9). Ockham himself addresses the senses of creation, and what it means for a thing simultaneously to be created by God and by a natural agent, in his *Second Quodlibet*, Question 8 (Ockham 1991: 123–6).

3 As art historian Irving Lavin writes, 'Whereas before the artist was used to illustrate God's creativity, now in the flood of sixteenth-century treatises on art, the artist's creativity was likened unto God's' (Lavin 1977–8: 38).

4 William Paley's *Natural Theology* was first published in 1802 (Paley 2006).

5 'The creative person must break down old ways of thinking in order to construct the new' (Guilford 1939: 474).

6 In a recent survey of the field, Beth Hennessey and Teresa Amabile (2010) asked 26 colleagues each to nominate 10 'must have' papers published since 2000. They ended up with a list of 110 publications, to which they added another 400 citations of significant work, drawn from an electronic survey of titles published between 1998 and 2008.

7 Ronald Beghetto and James Kaufman (2007) take this one stage further, arguing that besides big-C ('eminent') and little-c ('everyday') creativity, there is also a 'mini-c' creativity involved in the construction of personal knowledge and understanding.

8 'For you created my inmost being; you knit me together in my mother's womb' (Psalm 139 verse 13, New International Version).

9 This was in the early 80s, and the book, *Evolution and Social Life*, was first published in 1986 (Ingold 2016c).

10 'There is ... an element of undergoing, of suffering in its large sense, in every experience' (Dewey 1987: 50).

11 In Chapter 2 (39–40), I examine this tension in the work of one contemporary artist, Richard Long.
12 For a wonderful account of what actually goes on in the artist's painting of a portrait, with all its hazards, frustrations and setbacks, see Lord (1965).

Chapter 2

1 Magritte's words are cited in Schama (1995: 12).
2 Gibson does not refer to Jean-Paul Sartre's *The Psychology of Perception*, a work originally published in 1940. We do not know whether he was familiar with it. Yet here, Sartre makes precisely the same point: 'No matter how long I may look at an image, I shall never find anything in it but what I put there. It is in this fact that we find the distinction between an image and a perception ... there arises something of the *overflowing* in the world of "things": there is always, at each and every moment, infinitely *more* than we see; to exhaust the wealth of my actual perception would require infinite time' (Sartre 1972: 7–8, original emphases).
3 In the original German, Klee wrote: '*Kunst gibt nicht das Sichtbare wieder, sondern macht sichtbar.*' This lends itself to translation in many ways; the one I use here comes from the English-language version of his notebooks (Klee 1961: 76). I return to this in Chapter 21 (page 332).
4 This was at the Hielan' Ways Symposium, *Perceptions of Exploration*, held in Tomintoul, Moray, 14–15 November 2014. I had the privilege of chairing a session in which Long discussed his work with an audience of artists, hillwalkers and local people.

Chapter 3

1 What Lucretius teaches us, as political theorist Jane Bennett shows, is that we need not add vitality to inanimate things to bring them to life, since it is already immanent in the 'primordial swerve' from which everything arises in the first place. The swerve, Bennett (2010: 18) writes, 'affirms that so-called inanimate things have a life, that deep within is an inexplicable vitality or energy ... a kind of thing-power'. For an excellent account of the relevance of Lucretius' cosmology for contemporary anthropology and philosophy, see McLean (2009).
2 It is possible that in writing these lines, Blake was influenced by the vortex theory of planetary motion advanced by René Descartes, according to which the planets ride the rings of an immense cosmic vortex whirling around the sun. The theory remained popular and influential until the mid-eighteenth century, when it eventually fell to the Newtonian theory of gravitational attraction. I am grateful to Jeffrey Cohen for this suggestion (Cohen and Duckert 2015: 3).
3 The felicitous phrase 'whirl of organism' comes from an essay by another philosopher, Stanley Cavell (1969: 52). I am grateful to Hayder Al-Mohammad for drawing this reference to my attention.
4 For this idea of inflection as movement-moving, I am indebted to Erin Manning (2016). 'Perceiving the inflection', Manning writes, 'does not mean being aware of it as though you could be outside it. It means moving in its tending. It means attending, in the event, to how movement diverges from its flow, attending to how movement moves' (2016: 118).

5 Along rather the same lines, Alexandra Arènes, Bruno Latour and Jérôme Gaillardet (2018: 127) argue that we should picture the Earth not as it might appear from outer space, in the form of a circle, but from the *inside*, as 'a helix, a vortex, or, as a series of nested merry-go-rounds swirling at different velocities with the chemical elements or molecules being considered as cascading from one circle to the next in both directions'.
6 This, and other etymological references in this paragraph, are drawn from the *Shorter Oxford English Dictionary*, and from the *Online Etymological Dictionary*, www.etymonline.com (accessed 30 December 2015).
7 William Wordsworth, *The Excursion*, book IV (1814), https://en.wikisource.org/wiki/The_Excursion/Book_4 (accessed 5 January 2021).
8 For an illuminating discussion of the formation and properties of the whorl, see Allen (2015).
9 Tracy Hudson visited my research group at the University of Aberdeen in February 2015. See Hudson (2014).

Chapter 4

1 I have discussed Dobzhansky's understanding of creativity in life and art at greater length elsewhere (Ingold 2016c: 146–51).
2 Contemporary developmental biology is beginning to come around to this view. See, for example, West-Eberhard (2003), Sultan (2015).
3 This comparison of the soul and the self draws much of its inspiration from Roy Wagner (1975: 93–4). I return to it, at greater length, in Chapter 23 (pages 355–6).
4 This contrast between Western and other traditions should not however be overdrawn. Aristotle – and following him, Thomas Aquinas – had no hesitation in attributing souls to animals, and even plants. The human soul was nevertheless always considered unique in its capacity for self-reflection.
5 Elsewhere, I have offered an extended critique of Descola's treatise (Ingold 2016a).
6 As anthropologist Eduardo Kohn argues in his study of the Runa of the Ecuadorian Amazon, animism is not just a way of making intellectual sense of a world 'out there'. Rather, 'it captures an animation that is emergent with life' (Kohn 2013: 94).
7 I return to Simondon's idea of individuation in Chapter 23 (pages 358–9).
8 There is an immense literature on this. See Leslie (2001) for a useful summary.
9 This is equivalent to what educational theorist Tyson Lewis, drawing on the philosophy of Giorgio Agamben, calls 'pure potential' – a potential 'freed from its subservience to actualization' (Lewis 2011: 594).

Chapter 5

1 Citations from *The Great Instauration: The Plan of the Work* and from *The New Organon* are drawn from volume IV of the standard translation by James Spedding, Robert Leslie Ellis, and Douglas Denon Heath (Bacon 1858). These texts are also available at www.constitution.org/bacon/instauration.htm and www.constitution.org/bacon/nov_org.htm (accessed 4 November 2011).

2 This is the title of a justly celebrated children's book by Jack Kent (2009). It tells of a little boy, Billy Bixbee, who wakes one morning to find a dragon in his bedroom. It is pretty small, and wags its tail in a friendly way. Billy takes the dragon down to breakfast, and introduces it to his mother. 'There's no such thing as a dragon', she declares firmly. But as his mother continues to deny the existence of the new arrival, the dragon begins to swell. It swells and swells. Soon it occupies most of the hallway, then it is as big as the whole house, until finally the house is lifted off its foundations and careers down the street on the dragon's back. Billy's father, home from work, is surprised to find that his house has vanished. But a helpful neighbour points in the direction it went. Eventually the family is reunited, and by this time Billy's mother has reluctantly acknowledged that perhaps the dragon does exist after all. Immediately, the dragon begins to shrink, until it is once again of a manageable size. 'I don't mind dragons when they're this size', Mrs Bixbee admits, as she sits comfortably in an armchair giving the dragon a good stroke. The moral of the story, of course, is that initially small problems – if we are afraid to recognise them or to speak their name, for fear of infringing the norms of rational conduct – can grow and grow to the point at which ordinary social life can no longer be sustained.

3 To this list could be added the Komodo dragon, the largest extant species of lizard in the world, which inhabits the islands of south-eastern Indonesia. Though rare, these animals are extremely dangerous, and attacks on humans have increased in recent years.

4 A full and properly balanced account of medieval cosmology and practice would have to go much further than this. Scholarship on the subject is vast, and defies easy summary. Carruthers (1990, 1998) is an excellent guide to the subject, and to its key literature. I have found inspiration in reading an admittedly narrow selection of this literature, and my present purpose is not to provide a digest or review but rather to show how just some of the ideas that emerge from it help us to think through the issues surrounding imagination and real life.

5 The citation is from an English translation of Kekulé's address by O. Theodore Benfey (1958). See also Roberts (1989: 75–81). It seems that Kekulé was not averse to putting about other stories of his discovery, one of which was that he was inspired by a cartoon showing a ring of monkeys holding hands, and another that it came to him while sitting upstairs on a London bus. For these and other assorted observations of the affair and its significance, see Taussig (2009: 237–9).

6 I have discussed the distinction between translation and empathy at greater length elsewhere, drawing on Hallowell's example (Ingold 2000: 106). For an exploration of the significance of empathy within relations of tutelage, see Gieser (2008).

7 There were exceptions of course (Parkes 1999: 92–3), but if anything these proved the rule. Thus Augustine, arriving in Milan in the fourth century, was astonished to observe that Ambrose, then Catholic bishop of the city, would read without making a sound. Though his eyes followed the text, 'his voice and tongue were silent'. Augustine was at a loss to know why, but speculated that it might have been to preserve his voice for public speaking (Augustine 1991: 92–3). Even Ambrose, however, wrote of the *sonus litterarum*, 'the sounds of the letters' (Parkes 1992: 116 fn. 6). For more on medieval practices of reading and writing, see Ingold (2007a: 12–18), and Chapter 12 (pages 181–4).

8 On Bacon and the 'new *de-in-scriptive* hermeneutics of nature', see Bono (1995: 244).
9 The exception to this are advocates of Goethean science for whom to engage in scientific study is to 'enter into a conversation with nature [and] listen to what nature has to say' (Holdrege 2005: 31–2). The contempt in which the Goethean approach is held by mainstream science reveals, however, where the latter's priorities lie.
10 The precise etymology of 'religion' has long been a matter of dispute. Cicero's interpretation was challenged in the fourth century by the Christian writer Lactantius, who claimed that *religare* is a compound of *re* (again) and *ligare* (to bind, fasten or connect). Religion, then, is a re-binding rather than a re-reading. This claim went on to find favour with Augustine, and in much subsequent scholarship. Since for Serres, however, negligence is as much about reneging on the ties that bind as it is about failing to take heed, the argument still holds, regardless of the etymology we favour.
11 There is an ever-growing literature devoted to the question of why the human imagination is primed to come up with, and to place its belief in, entities of this kind. See, for example, Boyer (2000). From the perspective advanced here, this literature, which treats religion as a domain of cognitive illusion, completely misses the point.

Chapter 6

1 William Shakespeare, *Romeo and Juliet*, act two, scene II.
2 In the original German: 'Wär nicht das Auge sonnenhaft, Die Sonne könnt es nie erblicken' (from *Zahme Xenien III*, 1827), cited in Amrine (1998: 34).
3 *Oxford English Dictionary*, beam, *n.1*, III. 19a.
4 In the later Gothic, the flame and the ray would go on to denominate distinct architectural styles, respectively the Flamboyant and the Rayonnant – *flaming* and *radiating* (Spuybroek 2020: 135).
5 This design is known as the 'Sun of May', in commemoration of the events of May 1810 that marked the beginning of independence from the Spanish Empire.
6 One should not discount the possibility that van Gogh painted the stars as he saw them. He is reputed to have suffered from lead poisoning, one symptom of which is a swelling of the retina. This can cause a halo effect around bright lights. Historian of science Omar Nasim, however, suggests that van Gogh may have been influenced by the illustrations of spiral nebulae by Nicolas Camille Flammarion, a contemporary populariser of astronomy in France. In any case, Nasim is surely right to point to parallels between van Gogh's depiction of the starry night and the reveries of Flammarion, in so far as both 'entailed an expansion of human imagination and perception, where the ordinarily near and the cosmically far are pictured in one view' (Nasim 2013: 120).
7 I return to this distinction between the volume-cavity system and the black hole/white wall system in Chapter 13 (pages 207–8). In his comprehensive cultural history of the face, art historian Hans Belting (2017: 32) offers an alternative interpretation of the relation between face and head.

8 The painter Wassily Kandinsky presents the same scale, from white to black via yellow, red and blue, in his essay *Point and Line to Plane*. 'If we examine black and white from the standpoint of temperature, we find white more apt to be warm than black and that absolute black is inwardly unquestionably cold. It is not without reason that the horizontal scale of colours runs from white to black' (Kandinsky 1979: 63 and fig. 21).

Chapter 7

1 The idea of dirt as matter out of place was first expressed in these terms by Mary Douglas (1966: 36) in her work on purity and pollution. On noise as sound out of place, see Hendy (2013: x).
2 One of the most thoroughgoing of attempts to apply Gibsonian theory to auditory perception is by musicologist Eric Clarke (2005). He offers the example of hearing a passing motorbike. The hearer is 'exposed to a continuously changing array of acoustical information, but within that array will be invariant acoustical properties, in a specific pattern of relationships, which together identify the motorbike and which remain constant under transformation' (2005: 34).
3 Much of this attention has been motivated by the thought that it might have to do with altered states of consciousness associated with hallucination or shamanic experience, and their expressions in art. For a recent review, see Giraldo Herrera (2018: 111–33). See also Chapter 6 (page 97).
4 For a commentary and references, see Schwartz (2011: 710–11).
5 James himself credits this insight to the eighteenth-century philosopher Étienne Bonnot de Condillac.
6 A classic statement to this effect comes from the priest, cultural historian and philosopher Walter Ong: 'Sight isolates, sound incorporates. Whereas sight situates the observer outside what he views, at a distance, sound pours into the hearer ... Vision comes to a human being from one direction at a time ... When I hear, however, I gather sound from every direction at once: I am at the center of my auditory world, which envelops me, establishing me at a kind of core of sensation and existence ... you can immerse yourself in hearing, in sound. There is no way to immerse yourself similarly in sight' (Ong 1982: 72).
7 For more on this, see Chapter 13 (page 207).
8 One exception must be made here. When I look directly at a bright light such as a car headlamp when it is otherwise dark, I often experience a starburst of illumination radiating from the centre, and sometimes even a shimmering halo around it. These, however, are caused by the fact that I am mildly astigmatic. The starburst and halo are diffraction patterns set up by focal displacement. As soon as I put on my spectacles, which correct for my astigmatism, the effect vanishes.
9 In a study of the ceremonial healing songs of Temiar people in Malaysia, anthropologist Marina Roseman (2008: 62) explains how, in performance, 'Temiars employ a variety of tools that "beg the difference" between sound and silence, light and darkness, motion and stillness, one body position and another.' Perhaps all listening is 'begging difference' in this sense of steering a path between apparently contrary conditions.

10 See Chapter 17 for an extended discussion of the distinction between differentiation and accretion.
11 This is how pitch is defined in a textbook on the physics of music that I have had on my shelf for the past fifty years. According to its author, Alexander Wood (1944: 42), pitch is 'the characteristic of a sound by virtue of which we describe it as "high" or "low"', or more exactly, 'the subjective quality of a sound that determines its position in the musical scale'.

Chapter 8

1 There are, admittedly, dissenting voices among philosophers of aesthetics, notably Yuriko Saito (2007), in his proposal for 'everyday aesthetics', and C. Thi Nguyen (2020: 3), who advocates for a 'process aesthetics' that 'permeates our lives, often emerging as a part of our natural, spontaneous, and unsculpted everyday activity'.
2 For examples, see Morphy (1996) and Coote and Shelton (1992).
3 Exemplary accounts include Chaussonnet (1988), Bodenhorn (1990), Wachowich (2014) and Katsak and Wachowich (2020).
4 I have described this experience of practising by myself in conversation with the artist Sophie Krier (Krier and Ingold 2021).
5 See, for example, Willerslev (2007: 89–118), on the Yukaghir of Siberia.

Chapter 9

1 The occasion was the international workshop 'The symbolic animal: evolution and neuroethology of aesthetics', held at the Ettore Majorana Foundation and Centre for Scientific Culture, Erice, Sicily, 15–19 October 2016.
2 The exhibition, entitled 'Soaring Flight: Peter Lanyon's Gliding Paintings', was held at the Courtauld Gallery from 15 October 2015 to 17 January 2016.
3 See https://aerocene.org (accessed 26 May 2019).
4 Quoted from the Tate Gallery display caption, see www.tate.org.uk/art/artworks/lanyon-thermal-t00375 (accessed 29 February 2016).
5 For the following account of Baumgarten's philosophy of aesthetics, I rely heavily on the authority of Beiser (2009).
6 A useful summary of Fechner's approach, from self-professed advocates, is in Westphal-Fitch and Fitch (2015).
7 Objectivism, as sociologist Pierre Bourdieu (1977: 96) puts it, requires that the observer, taking up a 'sovereign point of view', should stand back, 'transferring into the object the principles of his relation to the object'.
8 This box-and-arrow design is common to most efforts to visualise models of art engagement in the cognitive sciences. These are reviewed in Pelowski et al. (2016).
9 This is a rendering, in the language of neuroscience, of precisely the same illusion that Magritte, in his painting *La Condition humaine*, sought to convey in the language of art. See Chapter 2 (pages 29–30).

10 We have already considered Gregory's view of perception as hypothesis-testing in Chapter 2 (page 34). It remains mainstream in cognitive neuroscience. Chris Frith, for example, asserts that 'perception of the world is a fantasy that coincides with reality', a fantasy that arises when 'our brains discover what is out there in the world by constructing models and making predictions' (Frith 2007: 111, 138). In the same vein, fellow neuroscientist Eric Kandel asserts that 'our brain takes the incomplete information about the outside world that it receives from our eyes and makes it complete' (Kandel 2016: 20). All such assertions, be it noted, rest not on the evidence of neuroscience but on largely implicit metaphysical assumptions that these and countless other authors bring to the task of analysing it.

11 On Bergson's view of how time enters into the work of art, see Chapter 1 (page 26).

12 Leder et al. (2004: 499) cite the first of these consecutive sentences from Dewey, but not the second, thus twisting his meaning to support their own position. For them, 'creating an experience' doesn't mean reliving the processes of a work's origination but processing the results from its conclusion.

13 See Chapter 1 (page 26). What we say of art, here, matches what Gilles Deleuze and Félix Guattari say of 'minor science', by which they mean a science 'of becoming and heterogeneity, as opposed to the stable, the eternal, the identical, the constant'. Such a science they say, is comprised of problems rather than theorems. 'Whereas the theorem belongs to the rational order, the problem is affective and inseparable from the metamorphoses, generations and creations within science itself' (Deleuze and Guattari 2004: 398–9). On the idea of minor science, see Chapter 4.

14 Jan Masschelein (2010: 278) describes the art of walking in precisely these terms, as 'a kind of cutting the road through'.

Chapter 10

1 The project was part of the European Science Foundation EUROCORES programme 'BOREAS: Histories from the North – Environments, Movements, Narratives' (2006–10).

2 This particular lodge was built as part of a cultural revitalisation project undertaken with skilled practitioners from among the Tłįchǫ Dene of northwest Canada. A typical Tłįchǫ lodge would require between 14 and 20 spruce poles, and around 30 hides for the cover. Its construction is described in detail by Andrews (2013: 36–45). Though similar structures were in common use among pastoral peoples of northern Eurasia such as Sámi, Nenets and Evenki, they were of course covered with hides of reindeer rather than caribou.

3 Although use of the conical lodge is common to both hunter–trappers and nomadic pastoralists, I will henceforth focus on the latter, so as to be able to draw comparisons with pastoral regimes in other parts of the world.

4 We will return in Chapter 12 (pages 188–9) to this idea, characteristic of modernity, that the foundations for life are rolled out in successive layers, each above the one preceding.

Chapter 11

1 See https://edinburghprintmakers.co.uk/exhibition/David-Lemm:-Debris-and-Phenomena (accessed 31 December 2020).

2 Suvendrini Perera (2009: 1) opens her book, *Australia and the Insular Imagination*, with a question that sounds much the same as mine: 'What if the ground beneath our feet turns out to be the sea?' But the resemblance is only superficial, for her concern, as she goes on to explain, is to show how the idea of Australia is constituted not by the ground, as a terrestrial land mass, but by its surrounding oceans, coastlines and beaches. Her argument is thus premised on the fundamental opposition between land and sea, *terra firma* and *terra infirma*. My aim, in what follows, is to question this opposition.

3 Most famously, the so-called 'aquatic ape' hypothesis, originating with Alister Hardy and popularised by Elaine Morgan (1982).

4 First published in 1876, Carroll's verse has seen numerous editions.

5 Our sources tell us that Plato borrowed these words from the Spartan poet Alcman, who was active in the late seventh century BCE.

6 For this reference to the Schmitt's work, I am indebted to Steinberg and Peters (2015: 248–9).

7 For wave scientists, too, according to anthropologist Stefan Helmreich (2014: 268), waves are understood as events, or populations of events. However they are not there to be performed, as they are for surfers, but to be modelled, predicted and perhaps managed.

8 An example is the community of Maasbommel, in the Netherlands, planned and built by the Dutch company Dura Vemeer and completed in 2006. The community comprises 46 homes along the River Meuse built on floating foundations that can rise with the river flood, up to a limit of 5.5 metres (Steinberg 2011: 2117–18).

Chapter 12

1 See, for example, Adamson and Kelly (2013), Amato (2013), Anusas and Simonetti (2020), Best and Marcus (2009), Coleman and Oakley-Brown (2017), and Forsyth, Lorimer, Merriman and Robinson (2013).

2 In the tradition of symptomatic reading, 'the surface is associated with the superficial and the deceptive' (Best and Marcus 2009: 4). Daniel Miller (1994) has pointed to the relationship, in Western philosophy, 'between surface and lack of importance'.

3 The words are written in a version of Latin that today's scholars call 'Vulgar', considered to be a precusor of the Italian language. See https://en.wikipedia.org/wiki/Veronese_Riddle (accessed 1 January 2021). I am grateful to Davide Torri for bringing it to my attention.

4 From this source also come the French words *pays* ('country') and *paysage* ('landscape').

5 This is also why, in Roman times, the book of laws and statutes, typically comprised of hardwood tablets bound along one edge, was known by the Latin word for tree-trunk, *codex* or *caudex* (Boudalis 2018: 21–34).

6 Another archaeologist to understand the palimpsest as a result of 'flattening', leading to the formation of surface assemblages in which artefacts from a number of different time periods are jumbled together, is Rodney Harrison (2011: 155).
7 Not much has been written on the phenomenology of turning. One exception is Farrell (2017).
8 On paving the streets of London, see Ogborn (1998: 91–104). See also Ingold (2011a: 41–4).
9 Any comprehensive answer to this question would of course have to take account of the fact that the text is vividly illustrated. Since the relations between text and image are not my current concern, however, and purely for the sake of argument, I shall set the illustrations to one side so as to concentrate exclusively on the words.
10 The distinction between writing as a record and as an instrument of memory is explored at length in the work of historian Mary Carruthers (1990).

Chapter 13

1 For further discussion of weaving, text and the origins of *textura*, see Ingold (2007a: 68–71).
2 Here I have drawn extensively on Spuybroek's (2016: 53–105) brilliant discussion of ornamentation in his book *The Sympathy of Things*.
3 I discuss this way of reading in Chapter 5 (page 70). See also Illich (1991: 169–71).
4 Alfred Gell (1998: 83–90) has discussed 'the apotropaic use of patterns', including complex designs such as in Celtic knotwork, as a means of protection from potentially malignant demonic forces. Mesmerised by the designs, the demons are lured to the surface and become stuck in the intricacies of pattern, never reaching the other side where their potential victims remain safe and secure.
5 For Ivan Illich (1991: 192), it is as if the text undergoes a kind of mutation, at which point 'it begins to float above the page'. He dates this mutation, however, to three centuries before the advent of printing, with the invention of script including word spaces, that allowed books to be read silently, by eye.
6 'So for us a line will be a sign whose length can be divided into parts, but it will be so slender that it cannot be split ... If many lines are joined closely together like threads in a cloth, they will create a surface' (Alberti 1972: 37–8).
7 Historian of language David Olson (1994: 108–9) has shown that, particularly during the fifteenth and sixteenth centuries, a large number of verbs were coined in English, specifically concerning ways of thinking (e.g. 'to assume', 'to infer', 'to predict') and ways of stating (e.g. 'to assert', 'to criticise', 'to explain'), that went on to have a pronounced influence on the later development of a psychology and philosophy of mind according to which feelings, motivations and experiences are outward projections of interior subjective states.
8 The story is told and analysed by anthropologist Peter Gow, based on his ethnographic fieldwork among Piro people. See Gow (1990).
9 Facial features, as Hans Belting (2017: 2) writes, 'etch themselves into the sagging skin that gradually loosens from the skull; ... These are what remain from the face's constant work of crafting expression'.

10 The interpretation I offer here is my own. The original text of Deleuze and Guattari (from Part 7 of *A Thousand Plateaus*, entitled 'Year Zero: Faciality') is fiendishly hard to understand. It is all too easy to jump to the conclusion that the 'black hole' corresponds to the penetrating gaze of the modern subject, and the white wall to the screen on which it projects its images. I have to own up to having made exactly this mistake, in an earlier work (Ingold 2015: 101–2), despite the fact the Deleuze and Guattari (2004: 190) warn emphatically against it: '*The gaze is but secondary in relation to the gazeless eyes, to the black hole of faciality. The mirror is but secondary in relation to the white wall of faciality*'. In other words, black hole and white wall are not respectively on the near and far sides of the face. They *are* the face itself, in its emergence. I hope to have gone some way, in the present essay, towards rectifying my earlier error.

11 For this understanding of the classic form of the design object, and a critique of the same, I am indebted to Michael Anusas. See Anusas (2017).

12 In an essay on the interface to which I have already referred (Chapter 12, page 191), Branden Hookway develops an ostensibly similar distinction. Any interface, he argues (Hookway 2014: 9), can be seen in two ways, as 'between faces' and 'facing between'. His terms, however, are wholly set within the volume-cavity system, and describe alternative perspectives on the interface understood in the classical design sense of a conduit that allows passage, across a threshold, from exterior to interior or vice versa. From one perspective, of 'between faces', what lies on either side conditions the relation between them; from the other, of 'facing between', the relation conditions what lies on either side. Both perspectives, however, presuppose the existence of some kind of membrane, interposed between one side and the other, through or across which force or information is transmitted. That, for me, is the condition of the 'face between'.

13 As distinct from the heavyweight masonry walls, comprising the earthwork, for which the German word is *Mauer*.

14 This difference also has its architectural counterpart. If I were a business executive rather than a scholar, I might be seated in an office block clad from top to bottom, not in any textual material but in a sheet of perfectly transparent glass.

Chapter 14

1 An exception is Jacob (2017).

2 This idea is discussed at length by Gayatri Chakravorty Spivak (1974), in her translator's introduction to Jacques Derrida, *Of Grammatology*.

3 Raphael Rubinstein (2018–19: 21), from the exhibition *Under Erasure*, curated by Heather + Raphael Rubinstein, Pierogi Gallery, New York.

4 At a conference at which I presented an early version of this essay, one participant asked me about the word *swipe*. As an action combining the impetuosity of the strike with the surface shear of the wipe, 'swipe' sounds like an ingenious amalgam of the two. In fact, however, it is a derivative of *sweep*, from old Norse *sveip*, exemplified in the circling motion of the oars of a rowboat. Yet

remarkably, rowing *does* combine the strike and the wipe, as the oars alternately cut through the surface of the water and skim back over it.

5 As we saw in Chapter 12 (pages 187–8), erasure has also to be distinguished from cleaning. Whereas erasure abrades the surface along with the inscriptions sunk into it, cleaning removes any deposit while leaving the surface intact. Both erasure and cleaning are species of wiping, but only erasure strictly qualifies as wipe-*out*.

6 This is the source of the dichotomy between synchrony and diachrony, famously elaborated by Ferdinand de Saussure in his course in general linguistics delivered at the University of Geneva between 1906 and 1911 (Saussure 1959).

7 The distinction also aligns with that between 'strategy' and 'tactics' in the work of Michel de Certeau (1984).

Chapter 15

1 He does, however, make extensive reference to the work of Michael Polanyi's brother, the economic historian Karl Polanyi.

2 It is important to note that Wittgenstein would go on to renounce this view. The nature of language, he would admit, had been misunderstood by philosophers, not least by the author of the *Tractatus*! In his later *Philosophical Investigations*, Wittgenstein (1953: §11) would insist that words are part and parcel of the activity of life, comparable to the tools of a toolbox.

3 The following is exemplary: 'I shall now regard the unspecifiable part of knowledge as the residue left unsaid by defective articulation' (Polanyi 1958: 88).

4 What it means for a body to dwell in sound will be further explored in Chapter 16.

5 The ancient Greeks had a word for this, namely *kairos*, referring not only to the moment that must be seized but also to the attention and responsiveness necessary to be able to do so (Hawhee 2004: 65–76). See also Chapter 8 (pages 118–19).

6 Anticipation, as Pablo Rojas (2015: 215) puts it, should be viewed not 'as a definite expectation or ready-made plan but as continuation of a gesture motivated by a search for cohesion'.

7 As Dor Abrahamson (2020: 228) writes, bow and cello, far from being mechanically coupled like the steering and wheels of a car, 'constitute a makeshift material tissue connecting the right and left hands, thus closing an extended, instrument-mediated corporeal embrace'.

8 See Chapter 1 (pages 23–4). According to Malabou (2014: xi), this idea of habit as 'a milieu between activity and passivity' was also anticipated in the philosophy of Ravaisson.

9 In Finnish, a language notorious for its long and elaborate words and phrases, it is customary to draw audible breath before launching into speech. This, however, can give rise to misunderstanding. There is an apocryphal story from the European Parliament that whenever it was the turn of Finnish parliamentarians to speak, delegates from other nations would interpret the drawn breath with which they would begin as a sign of nonchalance, as though they really couldn't be bothered.

Chapter 16

1 In a recent work, cultural theorist Donna Haraway (2016: 105) has reinvented the idea of response-ability, in much the same sense – as 'a praxis of care and response' – but makes no reference to Cage. She appears to be unaware of the precedent. Cage's ideas, not Haraway's, concern me here.
2 On the illocutionary force of linguistic utterances, see Austin (1975).
3 This, and subsequent quotations from *Sounding the Full Circle*, are reproduced here with the kind permission of the author.
4 On the late eighteenth-century origins of the idea of the musical work as a complete composition, see Goehr (1992: 203).
5 I am indebted to the artist Jaime Refoyo for instructing me on how to draw a straight line freehand. After returning to my cello, I was struck by the parallel with bowing technique. See Guilera and Refoyo (n.d.).
6 As we shall see in Chapter 18 (page 280), the classical Greek word for number, *arithmos*, along with its derivative, 'arithmetic', share the same root.
7 I return to this analogy in Chapter 21 (page 328).
8 A lighter touch on the fingerboard, however, enables the player to feel not just the hardness of the surface but also the vibration of the string, stopped at that point. According to Abrahamson (2020: 226), this tactile experience is tantamount to 'hearing through the finger'.
9 In a brilliant study of what he calls 'musical topography', anthropologist Pablo Rojas (2015: 224) draws a similar conclusion, arguing that the relation between the performer and instrument 'is not built upon its "thing-like" qualities, but rather on the achievement of field continuity and depth', bringing forth physiognomic qualities of animation that 'are not deciphered but felt'. The field of performance, Rojas (2015: 226) shows, takes the form of a *reticulate*, 'a knot of aesthetic, mythical, practical and traditional open-ended threads'.
10 I borrow the phrase 'edging into form' from Erin Manning (2016: 112), by which she foregrounds 'the heterogeneity of a welling experience before it succumbs to the categorization of its parts'.

Chapter 17

1 Ian Bogost, a leading philosophical advocate of so-called object-oriented ontology, puts this in the form of a maxim: '*All things equally exist, but they do not exist equally*' (Bogost 2012, original emphasis).
2 While broadly similar, the semantic resonances of 'assemblage' in English and French are not identical. In French the elements of the assemblage have a somewhat tighter connection, coming closer to what in English might be called an assembly. I am grateful to Simon Peres for this observation.
3 *Oxford English Dictionary*, online, 'assemblage', n.4.
4 Thus, among archaeological proponents of new materialism, Harrison (2011: 155–6) distinguishes between the 'first' and 'second' meanings of assemblage, whereas Lucas (2012: 193–4) insists on a 'proper meaning' that would reconcile the two. Witmore (2014: 207) merely notes that with the new materialism, the notion of assemblage carries a 'different valence from normative definitions … within archaeology'.

5 One possible answer, of course, is that *assemblage*, in French, implies an organic integration of parts, whereas their connection in the *agencement* is looser and more contingent. Thus the distinction between *agencement* and *assemblage*, in French, maps onto that between 'assemblage' and 'assembly', in English. In neither language, however, is the distinction stable. The terms are notoriously slippery in use, and as we shall see, there is more to *agencement* than assemblage. On the problems of translation, see Phillips (2006).

6 'So what counts as things?' asks Witmore (2014: 206). His answer: 'Air and soil, rain and sea, wooden doors and stone orthostats, nitrogen-fixing bacteria and clovers, psychopolitical commitments to Rome and Hadrian's Wall, Corinthian perfume jars and dead Etruscans, mycorrhizae and maple trees, hoplites and the Athenian assembly, minke whales and lemmings, the Hudson River and steamboats, the god Apollo and the Pythia ...'

7 This may be true in arithmetic, but not in chemistry. Arguably, in the formula for a chemical reaction, the plus sign has a very different meaning, more analytic than synthetic. An excursion into chemistry is beyond the scope of this essay, but potentially it could offer a next step in thinking about materials that would take us beyond the problematic of the join to the metamorphoses of materials themselves.

8 This concept lay at the heart of Leroi-Gourhan's approach to the evolution of techniques, set out in his magnum opus, *Le geste et la parole* ('Gesture and Speech'), first published in 1964 (Leroi-Gourhan 1993: 231–4, 253–4). I shall return to this work in Chapter 20.

9 Leonard Lawlor and Valentine Moulard (2012), commenting on the philosophy of Bergson, draw essentially the same distinction in terms of an opposition between 'quantitative' and 'qualitative' multiplicity. Quantitative multiplicity entails the spatial juxtaposition of homogeneous elements. Qualititative multiplicity, by contrast, is heterogeneous and durational; instead of juxtaposition, there is only a continuous, evolving interpenetration. See also Chapter 18 (page 280).

10 Uexküll (2010: 185–90), Deleuze and Guattari (2004: 351); and see Chapter 2 (page 37). Independently of Tsing, I have also proposed exactly the same analogy in my discussion of the life of lines (Ingold 2015: 23).

11 In a recent article, archaeologists Konrad Antczak and Mary Beaudry (2019) propose the concept of 'assemblage of practice' – meaning 'a dynamic gathering of corresponding things entangled through situated daily and eventful human practice' – as a way to bring the ideas of gathering and assembling under one roof.

12 The study of solid-fluid materials and their behaviour is the preserve of the branch of continuum mechanics known as *rheology* (from the Greek *rhéō*, meaning 'flow').

13 *Oxford English Dictionary*, online, 'aggregate', B.n.1 (my emphasis).

14 See Spuybroek (2016: 114). Elsewhere, I have phrased this in terms of the combination of *blobs* and *lines*. Blobs have insides and outsides, but they also 'put out lines or swell from them, or are embedded in a linear matrix. It is by their lines that they live, move and hold on to one another' (Ingold 2015: 16).

15 This circularity is endemic in new materialist writing on the agency of things (Ingold 2013a: 95–7; 2014b: 520). Most often, the claim to agency amounts to no more than a statement that a thing exists. Obviously, the situation would be different if it wasn't there. Its presence has consequences. But it is a mistake to confuse consequences with agency (Hornborg 2017: 99).

Chapter 18

1 Speaking in Gaelic, MacDonald's words were: '*Veir mi niosh a chorra himain yuit fèin, gos a faidh mi tuillad Gaoisid*' (Cheape 2021: 135). In her memoir of growing up on a farm in the Scottish Highlands, Jane Yeadon (2015) explains how the thrawcrook (*corra-shìomain*) was used: 'It had a great long iron spike and was fastened roon the waist wi' rope. The men paid out the straw as if they were putting wool on a spindle and then ma mither twisted and twisted till she made a rope.'

2 I draw here on Hannah Arendt's discussion of the meaning of life (Arendt 1957: 97, see also Ingold 2015: 125–9). I return to the distinction in Chapter 20 (pages 321–2).

3 They could just as well be potters as basket-makers. In an interview, biochemist and theoretician of chaos Otto Rössler dwelt on the sheer tactility of mathematical thinking. 'Without touching and without kneading', he said, 'it is impossible to imagine. Materiality does matter: Essentially mathematics is nothing more than pottery' (cited in de Freitas 2016: 188).

4 Translated from the original German by Ellen Harlizius-Klück, and cited in Harlizius-Klück and Fanfani (2016: 75).

5 In a rather peculiar attempt to rest the idea of arithmetic on the metaphor of 'motion along a path', linguist George Lakoff and cognitive scientist Rafael E. Núñez (2000: 71–2) imagine the path of motion as an articulated chain of straight-line segments. Yet paradoxically, reconstructing the path as a chain eliminates the very movement that gave rise to it. Strict application of the metaphor, then, would replace the rhythmic dynamic of counting, fundamental to the art of the weaver, with a static assembly of elements.

6 This is not to rule out the possibility that digital technologies could be customised in ways that would enhance rather than oppose the weaving process. For experiments along these lines, see Cocker (2017) and Altay and Öz (2019).

Chapter 19

1 With new digital technologies, of course, there has been a massive growth in the number of so-called 'smart devices' in the post-industrial environment. This should not be seen, however, as a reversal of the overall historical trend. Quite to the contrary, the label 'smart', when applied to digital devices, is an advertising ploy which announces to any potential purchaser that by buying the device, his or her own 'smartness' will be enhanced.

2 Eduardo Viveiros to Castro (2012: 92–3) makes exactly the same point. Arguing against the assumption that the 'fundamental or prototypical mode of relation is identity or sameness', and against the tendency to read difference as opposition and opposition as the absence of relation, he insists that 'identity or sameness [is] the very negation of relatedness'. I agree. Curiously, however, Viveiros de Castro takes me to task for holding the opposite view, even though it is one to which I have never subscribed. Indeed I too have long argued vigorously against it (Ingold 1993a: 225–7)!

3 Coming from the different starting points, respectively, of anthropology and science studies, and unbeknownst to one another, Despret and I came up with

the idea of correspondence more or less contemporaneously. I first introduced it, in 2008, into in a discussion of the difference between anthropology and ethnography, and went on to develop it further in my discussions of the ecology of materials, of drawing and the life of lines, and of human sociality (Ingold 2008a, 2012b, 2013a: 105-8, 2015, 2017b). Despret (2013), however, was the first to apply the concept to human–animal relations.

Chapter 20

1 In a footnote to their recent translation of *The New Science*, Jason Taylor and Robert Miner remark that this may be one of Vico's 'more fanciful etymologies' (Vico 2020: 12 fn. 13). See also Chapter 14 (page 220).
2 The classic statement of the three stages of human social evolution – savagery, barbarism and civilisation – is to be found in Lewis Henry Morgan's treatise of 1877, *Ancient Society* (Morgan 1963).
3 Darwin's most vociferous advocate, Thomas Henry Huxley, would put this more forcefully than Darwin himself perhaps dared. In an essay on 'Man's place in nature', published in 1863, Huxley (1894: 152) declared that 'The highest faculties of feeling and intellect begin to germinate in lower forms of life'.
4 In the inevitable course of natural selection, Darwin (1874: 197) argued, 'tribes have supplanted other tribes', the victorious groups always including the larger proportion of 'well-endowed men'.
5 One of the most outspoken defenders of this militantly racist scenario was Sir Arthur Keith, one-time President of the Royal Anthropological Institute and among the most eminent scientists of his day. The 'war of races', Keith (1931: 49) declared, is nature's 'pruning-hook'.
6 A recent book by Tobias Rees offers a glaring example. His claim that 'human ... is a recently invented concept that emerged in Europe about 250 years ago' is simply false. Rees's mistake is to treat 'human' as a derivative of 'humanity'. Historically, the direction of derivation was the other way around: discourses on the human long preceded the eighteenth-century concept of humanity (Rees 2018: ch. 2, 3; Ingold 2019: 190).
7 For details of Llull's life and work, see Bonner (1985) and Lohr (1992).
8 Here I follow Bonner's translation: 'man is a manifying animal' (in Llull 1985: 609). For further discussion, see Ingold (2015: 116–17).
9 In a census of 2011, more than 19,000 Tasmanians identified as Aboriginal people (www.britannica.com/topic/Tasmanian, accessed 7 August 2020).
10 For a comprehensive review of the Neanderthal debate in palaeoanthropology, see Graves (1991). 'Most participants in the debate', as Graves (1991: 525) notes, 'cannot resist a simplistic metaphor of European colonialism and the analogies which are drawn from it. Indeed, the whole concept of displacement without admixture and the evolution of "an entirely new species" carries with it the implication of progressive trends which we owe to 19th-century ideologies.'
11 The book was later published in a superb English translation by Anna Bostock Berger, as *Gesture and Speech* (Leroi-Gourhan 1993). I have reviewed it in depth elsewhere (Ingold 1999).

12 Fifty years later, exactly as Leroi-Gourhan had foretold, Rosi Braidotti could observe that 'contemporary information and communications technologies exteriorise and duplicate electronically the human nervous system' (Braidotti 2013: 90).

Chapter 21

1 I am most grateful to Claudia Zeiske, of Deveron Arts, without whose initiative this chapter would never have been written.
2 The rationale of modelling the ocean as a totality, with a capacity to accommodate a finite number of waves, is nicely illustrated in an anecdote told by Stefan Helmreich. At the First International Australasian Conference on Wave Science, held in Newcastle, Australia, in 2014, Helmreich put the question 'How many waves are there in the ocean?' to scientist Alexander Babanin. Without a moment's hesitation, Babanin proceeded to work out that if oceanic waves are, on average, 100 metres long, and if their crests are spaced, again on average, 100 metres apart, then the average wave covers an area of 10^4 square metres. Given that the world's oceans extend over 10^{16} square metres, Babanin arrived at an estimate of 10^{12}: a trillion waves (Helmreich 2014: 266).
3 In 1987, the World Commission on Environment and Development (WCED, also known as the Brundtland Commission) defined sustainable development as 'development that meets the needs of the present without compromising the ability of future generations to meet their own needs' (WCED 1987).
4 This is to extend to design an argument that I have made elsewhere for thought: 'Indeed it is largely in the attempt to think themselves out of history, and to evade the implications of the passage of time, that human beings have created a history of thought' (Ingold 2016c: 142).
5 Anthropologist Michael Pröpper (2017) commences his comprehensive overview of potential contributions of art to sustainability science with the remark that 'academic sustainability science has so far been largely oblivious to the potential contribution of art'.
6 In this sense, as we saw in Chapter 5 (pages 63–4), dragons exist not in objective fact, but as harbingers of truth.
7 That said, I would not go as far as Spuybroek (2020: 180) in his insistence on marking a radical distinction between the true and the real. For this is arbitrarily to limit truth to that which is objectively verifiable, by way of a 'doubling back' to an original event or state of affairs, as required by scientific protocols of experimental replicability. For Spuybroek, reality *befalls*, and to answer to it means doubling forward rather than back – that is, precisely what we have called 'research': a search not for 'the truth about the real, but the truth that comes out of the real' (Masschelein 2010: 285).
8 Dewey's essay *The Public and its Problems* was first published in 1927 (Dewey 2012).
9 The Canadian writer and activist Heather Menzies speaks of commoning in just this sense, as 'a way of doing and organizing things as implicated participants ... *immersed in the here and now of living habitat*' (Menzies 2014: 122–3, original emphasis). See also Bollier and Helfrich (2015), who entitle their collection *Patterns of commoning*.

10 The animal in question was in fact a beech marten, a member of the weasel family. This attack, on 29 April 2016, was only the first. A few months later, on 21 November, another marten struck. Instantly electrocuted on contact with the 18,000-volt cable, the animal's singed body was recovered and put on display at the Rotterdam Natural History Museum. See www.theguardian.com/science/2017/jan/27/cerns-electrocuted-weasel-display-rotterdam-natural-history-museum.

Chapter 22

1 Saussure's treatment of the linguistic sign, as reconstructed by his students, can be found in the *Course in General Linguistics* (Saussure 1959: 65–70).
2 In anthropology, this argument was powerfully advanced by Marshall Sahlins (1976).
3 There is no simple way into these. They are however gathered together in Peirce (1931).
4 Uexküll's *A Foray into the Worlds of Animals and Men* was first published, in German, in 1934.
5 For my initial attempt to compare the approaches of Gibson and Uexküll, see Ingold (1992a). I returned to the comparison for my contribution to the conference *Neurobiology of the Umwelt: How Living Beings Perceive the World*, held in Paris in 2008 (Ingold 2011a: 76–88).
6 However in a recent article tracing the development of Uexküll's thinking, psychologists Martin Fultot and Michael Turvey (2019) show that in his later work, Uexküll rowed back on the subjectivism of his original formulation of *Umwelt* theory. By restoring action to perception, according to Fultot and Turvey, Uexküll eventually arrived at a position closer to Gibson's than meets the eye.
7 There have been various attempts in the literature to paper over the differences between *Umwelt* and niche. For example, Kalevi Küll and his colleagues (2011: 38–9) have proposed the term *semiotic niche*, as a complement to the subject-centred *Umwelt*, to refer to the external conditions of the environment to which the organism is challenged to adapt, while Jeffrey Peterson and his co-authors (2018: 186) contend that the two concepts, of *Umwelt* and environmental niche, can be reconciled through a focus on the semiotic basis of experience. None of these attempts, however, manages to overcome the contradiction between semiotic and physicalist conceptions of the environment.
8 Uexküll's writings are full of allusions to 'representations' or 'images' of one sort or another. It is important to note, however, that these are signs in the semiotic rather than the semiological sense. The semiotic sense of representation, as one thing's standing for something else to which it bears a relation, is quite different from representation in the semiological sense of mapping of one plane, of meaning, over another, of substance. It is possible to critique the latter, as semioticians do, while still holding on to the former.
9 A glaring example can be found in a recent commentary by Webb Keane (2018: 45), who seems to think the idea of direct, unmediated contact with the world is a symptom of mystical yearnings or aesthetic romanticism. Gibson, of course, was neither a mystic not a romantic but a hard-nosed realist.

10 Here, the distinction that Gibson (1979: 47–64) makes between stimulus *energy* and stimulus *information* is critical. Sensory receptors may be stimulated by incident energy. In perception, however, the organs of sense (eyes, ears, nose, etc.) pick up information by extracting structural invariants from movement-induced modulations in the flux of stimulation.

11 Writing of Khoisan hunters of southern Africa, their ethnographer Chris Low tells of how, in their perception, the entire environment is riddled with scent-threads, binding its human and nonhuman inhabitants (Low 2007: S75–7; also Ingold 2015: 65).

12 Bateson's use of the concept of information was linked to cybernetics and what was then the new science of communication. He took it in a sense entirely different from Gibson, for whom information had nothing to do with communication. Nor, for Gibson, does it consist in signs or symbols. It is rather given in the structure, patterning. and texture of the world, and picked up through direct perception (Gibson 1979: 62–3).

13 This assumption is foundational for biosemiotics, a field largely established during and after the 1960s through the prolific writings of Thomas Sebeok. In his last collection of essays, *Global Semiotics*, Sebeok (2001: 10) declared the 'two cardinal and reciprocal axioms of semiotics' to be that 'all life is semiosis', and 'semiosis presupposes life'.

14 This was the topic of a debate carried on in the pages of the journal *Anthropological Forum* (Descola 2016; Ingold 2016a, 2016b).

Chapter 23

1 This citation is from the 1888 translation of *The Timaeus of Plato*, edited by Richard Dacre Archer-Hind (Archer-Hind 1888: 345).

2 A considerable and largely self-serving literature has grown up around this philosophical movement. A review lies beyond the scope of this chapter, but representative works include Bogost (2012), Bryant (2011), Bryant, Harman and Srnicek (2011), Harman (2018) and Morton (2013).

3 In a workshop held at the University of Aberdeen, some years ago, the mathematician Ricardo Nemirovsky gave us a wonderful demonstration of what this means in practice. In a nearby park, we laid out a rope in the exact form of a parabola, its ends diverging to infinity – or rather to where our rope ran out. We then viewed the parabola through a vertical sheet of perspex, and drew the line of the rope on the perspex with a felt pen. We found that we had drawn an ellipse. At infinity, the ends of the parabola had closed up. In its very open-endedness, the whole, it seems, is spatiotemporally self-encompassing.

4 I have addressed these problems elsewhere (Ingold 2016d).

5 Escobar has developed these ideas at greater length in a subsequent work (Escobar 2018).

References

Abrahamson, D. 2020. Strawberry feel forever: understanding metaphor as sensorimotor dynamics. *The Senses and Society* 15: 216–38.

Adamson, G. and V. Kelly, eds. 2013. *Surface tensions: surface, finish and the meaning of objects*. Manchester: Manchester University Press.

Agamben, G. 2016. *The use of bodies* (trans. A. Kotsko). Stanford, CA: Stanford University Press.

Alberti, L. B. 1972. *On painting* (trans. C. Grayson), ed. M. Kemp. Harmondsworth: Penguin.

Alexander, C. 1964. *Notes on the synthesis of form*. Cambridge, MA: Harvard University Press.

Allen, V. 2015. Airy something. In *Elemental ecocriticism: thinking with earth, air, water and fire*, eds J. J. Cohen and L. Duckert. Minneapolis, MN: University of Minnesota Press, pp. 77–104.

Altay, C. and G. Öz. 2019. Dialogic weaving: a favorable tension between design and craft. *Digital Creativity* 30: 39–55.

Amato, J. 2013. *Surfaces: a history*. Berkeley, CA: University of California Press.

Amrine, F. 1998. The metamorphosis of the scientist. In *Goethe's way of science: a phenomenology of nature*, eds D. Seamon and A. Zajonc. Albany, NY: State University of New York Press, pp. 33–54.

Anderson, D. G. 2013. Home, hearth and household in the circumpolar North. In *About the hearth: perspectives on the home, hearth and household in the circumpolar North*, eds D. G. Anderson, R. P. Wishart and V. Vaté. Oxford: Berghahn, pp. 262–81.

Anderson, D. G., R. P. Wishart and V. Vaté, eds. 2013. *About the hearth: perspectives on the home, hearth and household in the circumpolar North*. Oxford: Berghahn.

Anderson, J. 2012. Relational places: the surfed wave as assemblage and convergence. *Environment and Planning D: Society and Space* 30: 570–87.

Andrews, T. D. 2013. Mobile architecture, improvisation and museum practice: revitalizing the Tlicho caribou skin lodge. In *About the hearth: perspectives on the home, hearth and household in the circumpolar North*, eds D. G. Anderson, R. P. Wishart and V. Vaté. Oxford: Berghahn, pp. 29–53.

Antczak, K. A. and M. C. Beaudry. 2019. Assemblages of practice: a conceptual framework for exploring human-thing relations in archaeology. *Archaeological Dialogues* 26: 1–24.

Anusas, M. 2017. *Beyond objects: an anthropological dialogue with design.* Unpublished doctoral dissertation, Department of Anthropology, University of Aberdeen.

Anusas, M. and C. Simonetti, eds. 2020. *Surfaces: transformations of body, materials and earth*. Abingdon: Routledge.

Archer-Hind, R. D. 1888. *The Timaeus of Plato*. London: Macmillan.

Arendt, H. 1957. *The human condition.* Chicago, IL: University of Chicago Press.

Arènes, A, B. Latour and J. Gaillardet. 2018. Giving depth to surface: an exercise in the Gaia-graphy of critical zones. *The Anthropocene Review* 5: 120–35.

Aubinet, S. 2020. *The craft of yoiking: philosophical variations on Sámi chants.* Doctoral dissertation, Department of Musicology, University of Oslo.

Augustin, D., H. Leder, F. Hutzler and C.-C. Carbon. 2008. Style follows content: on the microgenesis of art perception. *Acta Psychologica* 128: 127–38.

Augustine, Saint. 1991. *Confessions* (trans. H. Chadwick). Oxford: Oxford University Press.

Austin, J. L. 1975. *How to do things with words* (Second Edition). Cambridge, MA: Harvard University Press.

Bachelard, G. 1988. *Air and dreams: an essay on the imagination of movement* (trans. E. R. Farrell and C. F. Farrell). Dallas, TX: Dallas Institute Publications.

Bacon, F. 1858. *Works of Francis Bacon, Baron of Verulam, Viscount St. Alban and Lord High Chancellor of England, Vol. IV* (trans. J. Spedding, R. L. Ellis, and D. D. Heath). London: Spottiswoode.

Badiou, A. 2008. The communist hypothesis. *New Left Review* 49: 29–42.

Bailey, G. 2007. Time perspectives, palimpsests and the archaeology of time. *Journal of Anthropological Archaeology* 26: 198–223.

Barad, K. 2007. *Meeting the universe halfway*. Durham, NC: Duke University Press.

Barad, K. 2014. Diffracting diffraction: cutting together-apart. *Parallax* 20: 168–87.

Baratay, E. 2015. Building an *animal* history (trans. S. Posthumus). In *French thinking about animals*, eds L. Mackenzie and S. Posthumus. East Lansing, MI: Michigan State University Press, pp. 3–14.

Barth, F. 1966. *Models of social organisation* (Occasional Papers of the Royal Anthropological Institute 23). London: Royal Anthropological Institute.

Basso, K. 1992. *Western Apache language and culture*. Tucson, AZ: University of Arizona Press.

Batchelor, D. 2014. *The luminous and the grey*. London: Reaktion.

Bateson, G. 1973. *Steps to an ecology of mind*. London: Fontana.

Baxandall, M. 1995. *Shadows and enlightenment*. New Haven, CT: Yale University Press.

Beghetto, R. A. and J. C. Kaufman. 2007. Toward a broader conception of creativity: a case for 'mini-c' creativity. *Psychology of Aesthetics, Creativity, and the Arts* 1/2:73–79.

Beiser, F. C. 2009. *Diotima's children: German aesthetic rationalism from Leibniz to Lessing*. Oxford: Oxford University Press.

Belting, H. 2017. *Face and mask: a double history*. Princeton, NJ: Princeton University Press.

Benfey, O. T. 1958. August Kekulé and the birth of the structural theory of organic chemistry in 1858. *Journal of Chemical Education* 35: 21–3.

Bennett, J. 2010. *Vibrant matter: a political ecology of things*. Durham, NC: Duke University Press.

Benveniste, É. 1971. Active and middle voice in the verb (1950). In *Problems in general linguistics*, by É. Benveniste (trans. M. E. Meek). Coral Gables, FL: University of Miami Press, pp. 145–51.

Bergson, H. 1910. *Time and free will: an essay on the immediate data of consciousness* (trans. F. L. Pogson). London: George Allen & Unwin.

Bergson, H. 1922. *Creative evolution* (trans. A. Mitchell). London: Macmillan.

Berque, A. 2013. *Thinking through landscape* (trans. A-M. Feenberg-Dibon). London: Routledge.

Best, S. and S. Marcus. 2009. Surface reading: an introduction. *Representations* 108: 1–21.

Bille, M. and T. F. Sørensen. 2017. In visible presence: the role of light in shaping religious atmospheres. In *The Oxford handbook of light in archaeology*, eds C. Papadopoulos and H. Moyes. Oxford: Oxford University Press. doi:10.1093/oxfordhb/9780198788218.013.13

Bloch, M. 2012. *Anthropology and the cognitive challenge*. Cambridge: Cambridge University Press.

Boden, M. 1990. *The creative mind: myths and mechanisms*. London: Weidenfeld and Nicolson.

Bodenhorn, B. 1990. I'm not the great hunter, my wife is: Inupiat and anthropological models of gender. *Études Inuit Studies* 14(1–2): 55–74.

Bogost, I. 2012. *Alien phenomenology, or what it's like to be a thing*. Minneapolis, MN: University of Minnesota Press.

Bohm, D. 2002. *Wholeness and the implicate order*. London: Routledge.

Böhme, G. 2017. *Critique of aesthetic capitalism* (trans. E. Jephcott). Milan: Mimesis International.

Bollier, D. and S. Helfrich, eds. 2015. *Patterns of commoning*. Amherst, MA: Levellers Press.

Bonner, A. 1985. Historical background and life of Ramon Llull. In *Selected Works of Ramon Llull (1232–1316)*, volume I (ed. and trans. A. Bonner). Princeton, NJ: Princeton University Press, pp. 5–52.

Bono, J. J. 1995. *The word of God and the languages of man: interpreting nature in early modern science and medicine*. Madison, WI: University of Wisconsin Press.

Bortoft, H. 2012. *Taking appearance seriously*. Edinburgh: Floris Books.

Bortoft, H. 2019. Seeing and understanding holistically: Goethean science and the wholeness of nature – Part II. *Environmental and Architectural Phenomenology* 30: 11–14.

Boudalis, G. 2018. *The codex and crafts in Late Antiquity*. New York: Bard Graduate Center.

Bourdieu, P. 1977. *Outline of a theory of practice* (trans. R. Nice). Cambridge: Cambridge University Press.

Boyer, P. 2000. Functional origins of religious concepts: ontological and strategic selection in evolved minds. *Journal of the Royal Anthropological Institute* 6: 195–214.

Braidotti, R. 2013. *The posthuman*. Cambridge: Polity Press.

Brand, S. 1994. *How buildings learn: what happens to them after they're built*. New York: Penguin.

Bremner, L. 2016. Thinking architecture with an Indian Ocean aquapelago. *GeoHumanities* 2: 284–310.

Bremner, L. 2019. Introduction. In *Monsoon [+ other] waters*, ed. L. Bremner. London: Monsoon Assemblages, School of Architecture and Cities, University of Westminster, pp. 11–15.

Brieber, D., M. Nadal, H. Leder and R. Rosenberg. 2014. Art in time and space: context modulates the relation between art experience and viewing time. *PLoS ONE* 9(6): e99019. doi:10.1371/journal.pone.0099019.

Brown, D. E. 1991. *Human universals*. New York: McGraw-Hill.

Bryant, L. 2011. *The democracy of objects*. London: Open Humanities Press.

Bryant, L., G. Harman and N. Srnicek, eds. 2011. *The speculative turn: Continental materialism and realism*. Melbourne: re.press.

Bucklow, S. 2014. *The riddle of the image: the secret science of medieval art*. London: Reaktion.

Bullot, N. J. and R. Reber. 2013. The artful mind meets art history: toward a psycho-historical framework for the science of art appreciation. *Behavioral and Brain Sciences* 36: 123–80.

Bury, R. G. 1926. *Plato, Laws*. London: Heinemann.

Cage, J. 2011. *Silence: lectures and writings by John Cage* (50th anniversary edition). Middletown, CT: Wesleyan University Press.

Candler. P. M. Jr. 2006. *Theology, rhetoric, manuduction, or reading scripture together on the path to God*. Grand Rapids, MI: William B. Eerdmans.

Carbon, C.- C. 2017. Art perception in the museum: how we spend time and space in art exhibitions. *i-Perception* 8(1). Retrieved from https://journals.sagepub.com/doi/full/10.1177/2041669517694184.

Cardew, C. 1971. Treatise handbook. In *Cornelius Cardew: a reader*, ed. E. Prévost. Harlow: Copula, pp. 95–134.

Careri, F. 2002. *Walkscapes: walking as an aesthetic practice*. Barcelona: Gustavo Gili.

Carlisle, C. 2014. *Habit*. Abingdon: Routledge.

Carpenter, E. 1973. *Eskimo realities*. New York: Holt, Rinehart and Winston.

Carruthers, M. 1990. *The book of memory: a study of memory in medieval culture*. Cambridge: Cambridge University Press.

Carruthers, M. 1998. *The craft of thought: meditation, rhetoric and the making of images, 400–1200*. Cambridge: Cambridge University Press.

Cavallo, G. 1999. Between volume and codex: reading in the Roman world. In *A history of reading in the West* (trans. L. G. Cochrane), eds G. Cavallo and R. Chartier. Amherst, MA: University of Massachusetts Press, pp. 64–89.

Cavallo, G. and R. Chartier. 1999. Introduction. In *A history of reading in the West* (trans. L. G. Cochrane), eds G. Cavallo and R. Chartier. Amherst, MA: University of Massachusetts Press, pp. 1–36.

Cavell, S. 1969. *Must we mean what we say? A book of essays*. Cambridge: Cambridge University Press.

Certeau, M. de. 1984. *The practice of everyday life* (trans. S. Rendall). Berkeley, CA: University of California Press.

Chaussonnet, V. 1988. Needles and animals: women's magic. In *Crossroads of continents: cultures of Siberia and Alaska*, eds W. Fitzhugh and A. Crowell. Washington, DC: Smithsonian Institution Press, pp. 209–26.

Cheape, H. 2021. Straw ropes and wattle walls: aspects of the material culture of basketry in Atlantic Scotland. In *The material culture of basketry*, eds S. Bunn and V. Mitchell. London: Bloomsbury Visual Arts, pp. 135–42.

Clark, A. 1998. Where brain, body and world collide. *Daedalus: Journal of the American Academy of Arts and Sciences* 127: 257–80.

Clark, A. 2001. *Mindware: an introduction to the philosophy of cognitive science*. Oxford: Oxford University Press.

Clarke, E. F. 2005. *Ways of listening: an ecological approach to the perception of musical meaning*. Oxford: Oxford University Press.

Clingerman, F. 2009. Reading the book of nature: a hermeneutical account of nature for philosophical theology. *Worldviews: Global Religions, Culture, Ecology* 13: 72–91.

Cocker, E. 2017.Weaving codes/coding weaves: Penelopean mêtis and the weaver-coder's kairos. *Textile* 15: 124–41.

Cohen, J. J. and L. Duckert. 2015. Introduction: eleven principles of the elements. In *Elemental ecocriticism: thinking with earth, air, water and fire*, eds J. J. Cohen and L. Duckert. Minneapolis, MN: University of Minnesota Press, pp. 1–26.

Coleman, R. and E. Oakley-Brown, eds. 2017. Visualizing surfaces, surfacing vision (special issue). *Theory, Culture and Society* 34(7–8).

Collins, H. 2010. *Tacit and explicit knowledge*. Chicago, IL: University of Chicago Press.

Connolly, W. E. 1995. *The ethos of pluralization*. Minneapolis, MN: University of Minnesota Press.

Cooney, G. 2003. Introduction: seeing the land from the sea. *World Archaeology* 35: 323–8.

Coote, J. and A. Shelton, eds. 1992. *Anthropology, art and aesthetics*. Oxford: Clarendon.

Crawford, O. 1953. *Archaeology in the field*. London: Praeger.

Currie, G. 2003. Aesthetics and cognitive science. In *The Oxford handbook of aesthetics*, ed. J. Levinson. Oxford: Oxford University Press, pp. 706–21.

Darwin, C. 1874. *The descent of man and selection in relation to sex* (second edition). London: John Murray.

Davenport, W. 1960. Marshall Islands navigational charts. *Imago Mundi* 15: 19–26.

de Freitas, E. 2016. Material encounters and media events: what kind of mathematics can a body do? *Educational Studies in Mathematics* 91: 185–202.

DeLanda, M. 2006. *A new philosophy of society: assemblage theory and social complexity*. London: Continuum.

Deleuze, G. 1993. *The fold: Leibniz and the Baroque* (trans. T. Conley). London: Athlone.

Deleuze, G. 1994. *Difference and repetition* (trans. P. Paton). New York: Columbia University Press.

Deleuze, G. 1998. *Essays critical and clinical* (trans. D. W. Smith and M. A. Greco). London: Verso.

Deleuze, G. 2001. *Pure immanence: essays on a life* (trans. A. Boyman). New York: Urzone.

Deleuze, G. 2006. *Two regimes of madness: texts and interviews 1957–1995* (trans. A. Hodges and M. Taormina), ed. D. Lapoujade. New York: Semiotext(e).

Deleuze, G. and F. Guattari. 1994. *What is philosophy?* (trans. H. Tomlinson and G. Burchell). New York: Columbia University Press.

Deleuze, G. and F. Guattari. 2004. *A thousand plateaus: capitalism and schizophrenia* (trans. B. Massumi). London: Continuum.

Derrida, J. 1974. *Of grammatology* (trans. G. Spivak). Baltimore, MD: Johns Hopkins University Press.

Descartes, R. 1988. *Descartes: selected philosophical writings* (trans. J. Cottingham, R. Stoothoff and D. Murdoch). Cambridge: Cambridge University Press.

Descola, P. 2013. *Beyond nature and culture* (trans. J. Lloyd). Chicago, IL: University of Chicago Press.

Descola, P. 2016. Biolatry: a surrender of understanding (Response to Ingold's 'A naturalist abroad in the museum of ontology'). *Anthropological Forum* 26: 321–8.

Despret, V. 2013. Responding bodies and partial affinities in human-animal worlds. *Theory, Culture & Society* 30: 51–76.

Dewey, J. 1987. Art as experience. In *John Dewey: the later works, 1925–1953, Vol. 10: 1934*, ed. J. A. Boydston. Carbondale, IL: Southern Illinois University Press, pp. 42–110.

Dewey, J. 2012. *The public and its problems: an essay in political inquiry*, ed. M. L. Rogers. University Park, PA: Pennsylvania State University Press.

Dobzhansky, T. 1974. Chance and creativity in evolution. In *Studies in the Philosophy of Biology*, eds F. J. Ayala and T. Dobzhansky. London: Macmillan, pp. 307–38.

Douglas, M. 1966. *Purity and danger: an analysis of the concepts of pollution and taboo*. London: Routledge & Kegan Paul.

Eamon, W. 1994. *Science and the secrets of nature: books of secrets in medieval and early modern culture*. Princeton, NJ: Princeton University Press.

Elkins, J. 1996. *The object stares back: on the nature of seeing*. New York: Simon & Schuster.

Escobar, A. 2011. Sustainability: design for the pluriverse. *Development* 54: 137–40.

Escobar, A. 2018. *Designs for the pluriverse: radical interdependence, autonomy and the making of worlds*. Durham, NC: Duke University Press.

Ewart, I. 2021. Friction: an engineer's perspective on weaving grass rope bridges. In *The material culture of basketry*, eds S. Bunn and V. Mitchell. London: Bloomsbury Visual Arts, pp. 65–70.

Farrell, C. 2017. The poetics of page-turning: the interactive surfaces of early modern printed poetry, *Journal of the Northern Renaissance* 8. Retrieved from www.northernrenaissance.org/the-poetics-of-page-turning-the-interactive-surfaces-of-early-modern-printed-poetry (accessed 22 December 2017).

Feld, S. 1996. Waterfalls of song: an acoustemology of place resounding in Bosavi, Papua New Guinea. In *Senses of place*, eds S. Feld and K. H. Basso. Santa Fe, NM: School of American Research, pp. 91–135.

Feuerbach, L. 1843. *The essence of Christianity* (trans. M. Evans). London: Trübner.

Fleming, J. 2016. *Cultural graphology: writing after Derrida*. Chicago, IL: University of Chicago Press.

Flusser, V. 1999. *The shape of things: a philosophy of design*. London: Reaktion.

Forsyth, I., H. Lorimer, P. Merriman and J. Robinson. 2013. Guest editorial (thematic issue on surfaces). *Environment and Planning A* 45.5: 1013–20.

Fortes, M. 1945. *The dynamics of clanship among the Tallensi: being the first part of an analysis of the social structure of a Trans-Volta tribe.* London: Oxford University Press for the International African Institute.

Fortes, M. 1949. *The web of kinship among the Tallensi: the second part of an analysis of the social structure of a Trans-Volta tribe.* London: Oxford University Press for the International African Institute.

Frampton, K. 1995. *Studies in tectonic culture: the poetics of construction in nineteenth and twentieth century architecture.* Cambridge, MA: MIT Press.

Fredrickson, R. 2015. *Orientations in weather: a northern textual ecology.* Unpublished doctoral dissertation, Department of English and Film Studies, University of Alberta.

Frith, C. 2007. *Making up the mind: how the brain creates our mental world.* Oxford: Blackwell.

Fuchs, R. H. 1986. *Richard Long.* London: Methuen.

Fultot, M. and M. Turvey. 2019. von Uexküll's theory of meaning and Gibson's organism-environment reciprocity. *Ecological Psychology* 31: 289–315.

Galilei, G. 1957. *Discoveries and opinions of Galileo* (trans. S. Drake). Garden City, NY: Doubleday Anchor.

Gatt, C. 2020. Breathing beyond embodiment; exploring emergence, grieving and song in laboratory theatre. *Body and Society* 26: 106–29.

Gell, A. 1995. The language of the forest: landscape and iconism in Umeda. In *The anthropology of landscape: perspectives on place and space*, eds E. Hirsch and M. O'Hanlon. Oxford: Clarendon, pp. 232–54.

Gell, A. 1998. *Art and agency: an anthropological theory.* Oxford: Clarendon.

Gell, A. 1999. *The art of anthropology: essays and diagrams*, ed. E. Hirsch. London: Athlone Press.

Gibson, J. J. 1979. *The ecological approach to visual perception.* Boston, MA: Houghton Mifflin.

Gieser, T. 2008. Embodiment, emotion and empathy: a phenomenological approach to apprenticeship learning. *Anthropological Theory* 8: 299–318.

Giraldo Herrera, C. 2018. *Microbes and other shamanic beings.* New York: Palgrave Macmillan.

Gladwin, T. 1964. Culture and logical process. In *Explorations in cultural anthropology*, ed. W. H. Goodenough. New York: McGraw-Hill, pp. 167–77.

Goehr, L. 1992. *The imaginary museum of musical works: an essay in the philosophy of music.* Oxford: Clarendon Press.

Goethe, J. W. von. 1840. *Theory of colours* (trans. C. L. Eastlake). London: John Murray.

Goldschmidt, W. 1993. On the relationship between biology and anthropology. *Man* (N.S.) 28: 341–59.

Goldstein, M. 1988. *Sounding the full circle: concerning music improvisation and other related matters.* Retrieved from www.frogpeak.org/unbound/goldstein/goldstein_fullcircle.pdf?lbisphpreq=1 (accessed 19 November 2016).

Gombrich, E. H. 1960. *Art and illusion: a study in the psychology of pictorial representation.* London: Phaidon.

Gow, P. 1990. Could Sangama read? The origin of writing among the Piro of eastern Peru. *History and Anthropology* 5: 87–103.

Grasseni, C., ed. 2007. *Skilled visions: between apprenticeship and standards*. Oxford: Berghahn.

Graves, Paul 1991. New models and metaphors for the Neanderthal debate. *Current Anthropology* 32: 513–41.

Gregory, R. L. 1973. The confounded eye. In *Illusion in nature and art*, eds R. L. Gregory and E. H. Gombrich. New York: Scribners, pp. 49–95.

Grosz, E. 2012. Identity and individuation: some feminist reflections. In *Gilbert Simondon: being and technology*, eds A. de Boever, A. Murray, J. Roffe and A. Woodward. Edinburgh: Edinburgh University Press, pp. 37–56.

Guilera, J. and J. Refoyo. n.d. GEOCOCO: geography of corporal consciousness. Unpublished MS.

Guilford, J. P. 1939. *General psychology*. Princeton, NJ: D. Van Nostrand.

Guilford, J. P. 1950. Creativity. *American Psychologist* 5: 444–54.

Gumbrecht, H. U. 2004. *Production and presence: what meaning cannot convey*. Stanford, CA: Stanford University Press.

Hallowell, A. I. 1960. Ojibwa ontology, behavior and world view. In *Culture in history: essays in honor of Paul Radin*, ed. S. Diamond. New York: Columbia University Press, pp. 19–52.

Hallowell, A. I. 1976. The role of dreams in Ojibwa culture. In *Contributions to anthropology: selected papers of A. Irving Hallowell*, eds R. D. Fogelson, F. Eggan, M. E. Spiro, G. W. Stocking, A. F. C. Wallace and W. E. Washburn. Chicago, IL: University of Chicago Press, pp. 449–74.

Halprin, L. 1969. *The RSVP cycles: creative processes in the human environment*. New York: George Braziller.

Hamesse, J. 1999. The scholastic model of reading. In *A history of reading in the West* (trans. L. G. Cochrane), eds G. Cavallo and R. Chartier. Amherst, MA: University of Massachusetts Press, pp. 103–119.

Haraway, D. 2003. *The companion species manifesto: dogs, people, and significant otherness*. Chicago, IL: Prickly Paradigm Press.

Haraway, D. 2008. *When species meet*. Minneapolis, MN: University of Minnesota Press.

Haraway, D. 2016. *Staying with the trouble: making kin in the Chthulucene*. Durham, NC: Duke University Press.

Harlizius-Klück, E. and G. Fanfani. 2016. (B)orders in ancient weaving and Archaic Greek poetry. In *Spinning fates and the song of the loom: the use of textiles, clothing and cloth production as metaphor, symbol and narrative device in Greek and Latin literature*, eds G. Fanfani, M. Harlow and M.-L. Nosch. Oxford: Oxbow Books, pp. 61–99.

Harman, G. 2011. The road to objects. *Continent* 3: 171–9.

Harman, G. 2018. *Object-oriented ontology: a new theory of everything*. London: Pelican Books.

Harney, S. and F. Moten. 2013. *The undercommons: fugitive planning and Black study*. Wivenhoe: Minor Compositions.

Harrison, P. 1998. *The Bible, Protestantism and the rise of natural science*. Cambridge: Cambridge University Press.

Harrison, R. 2011. Surface assemblages: towards an archaeology in and of the present. *Archaeological Dialogues* 18: 141–61.

Harrison, R. P. 2003. *The dominion of the dead*. Chicago, IL: University of Chicago Press.
Hasenfus, N., C. Martindale and D. Birnbaum. 1983. Psychological reality of cross-media artistic styles. *Journal of Experimental Psychology* 9: 841–63.
Hasse, C. and P. Treusch. 2021. Weaving together: human–robot relations of basketry and knitting. In *The material culture of basketry*, eds S. Bunn and V. Mitchell. London: Bloomsbury Visual Arts, pp. 255–63.
Hawhee, D. 2004. *Bodily arts: rhetoric and athletics in ancient Greece*. Austin, TX: University of Texas Press.
Hayward, P. 2012. The constitution of assemblages and the aquapelagality of Haida Gwaii. *Shima* 6: 1–14.
Healy, S. D. and M. C. Tello-Ramos. 2021. Bird nest building. In *The material culture of basketry*, eds S. Bunn and V. Mitchell. London: Bloomsbury Visual Arts, pp. 15–21.
Heidegger, M. 1971. *Poetry, language, thought* (trans. A. Hofstadter). New York: Harper and Row.
Helmreich, S. 2014. Waves: an anthropology of scientific things. *HAU: Journal of Ethnographic Theory* 4: 265–84.
Hendy, D. 2013. *Noise: a human history of sound and listening*. London: Profile Books.
Hennessey, B. A. and T. M. Amabile. 2010. Creativity. *Annual Review of Psychology* 61: 569–98.
Higman, B. W. 2017. *Flatness*. London: Reaktion Books.
Ho, M-W. 1991. The role of action in evolution: evolution by process and the ecological approach to perception. *Cultural Dynamics* 4: 336–54.
Holdrege, C. 2005. Doing Goethean science. *Janus Head* 8: 27–52.
Home-Cook, G. 2015. *Theatre and aural attention: stretching ourselves*. New York: Palgrave Macmillan.
Hookway, B. 2014. *Interface*. Cambridge, MA: MIT Press.
Horn, E. 2017. Aesthetics of the air: Tomás Saraceno's 'Aerocene'. In *Aerocene*, ed. T. Saraceno. Milano: Skira Editore, pp. 18–30.
Hornborg, A. 2017. Artifacts have consequences, not agency: toward a critical theory of global environmental history. *European Journal of Social Theory* 20: 95–110.
Howard, P. M. 2019. Working grounds, producing places, and becoming home at sea. In *At home on the waves: human habitation of the sea from the Mesolithic to today*, eds T. J. King and G. Robinson. Oxford: Berghahn, pp. 34–61.
Howe, N. 1992. The cultural construction of reading in Anglo-Saxon England. In *The ethnography of reading*, ed. J. Boyarin. Berkeley, CA: University of California Press, pp. 58–79.
Howes, D., ed. 1991. *The varieties of sensory experience: a sourcebook in the anthropology of the senses*. Toronto: University of Toronto Press.
Howes, D. 2003. *Sensual relations: engaging the senses in culture and social theory*. Ann Arbor, MI: University of Michigan Press.
Howes, D. and S. Pink 2010. The future of sensory anthropology/the anthropology of the senses. *Social Anthropology* 18: 331–40.
Hudson, T. P. 2014. Variables and assumptions in modern interpretation of ancient spinning technique and technology through archaeological experimentation. *EXARC Journal Digest* 2014(1): 1–14.

Humphrey, N. 1976. The social functions of intellect. In *Growing points in ethology*, eds P. P. G. Bateson and R. A. Hinde. Cambridge: Cambridge University Press, pp. 303–17.

Huxley, T. H. 1894. *Man's place in nature and other essays*. London: Macmillan.

Hymes, D. 1964. Introduction: towards ethnographies of communication. In *The ethnography of communication*, eds J. J. Gumperz and D. Hymes, special issue of *American Anthropologist* 66 (6/2): 1–34.

Ihde, D. 1976. *Listening and voice: a phenomenology of sound*. Athens, OH: Ohio University Press.

Ilievski, P. H. 1993. The origin and semantic development of the term *harmony*. *Illinois Classical Studies* 18: 19–29.

Illich, I. 1991. *In the mirror of the past: lectures and addresses 1978–1990*. London: M. Boyars.

Ingold, T. 1974. On reindeer and men. *Man* (N.S.) 9: 523–38.

Ingold, T. 1975. Reindeer and men (letter to the Editor). *Man* (N.S.) 10: 619–20.

Ingold, T. 1989. The social and environmental relations of human beings and other animals. In *Comparative socioecology*, eds V. Standen and R. Foley (British Ecological Society Special Publications Series). Oxford: Blackwell, pp. 495–512.

Ingold, T. 1992a. Culture and the perception of the environment. In *Bush base, forest farm: culture, environment and development*, eds E. Croll and D. Parkin. London: Routledge, pp. 39–56.

Ingold, T. 1992b. Editorial. *Man* (n.s.) 27: 693–6.

Ingold, T. 1993a. The art of translation in a continuous world. In *Beyond boundaries: understanding, translation and anthropological discourse*, ed. G. Pálsson. Oxford: Berg, pp. 210–30.

Ingold, T. 1993b. The reindeerman's lasso. In *Technological choices: transformation in material cultures since the Neolithic*, ed. P. Lemmonier. London: Routledge, pp. 108–25.

Ingold, T. 1993c. The temporality of the landscape. *World Archaeology* 25: 152–74.

Ingold, T. 1996. Introduction. In *Key debates in anthropology*, ed. T. Ingold. London: Routledge, pp. 1–14.

Ingold, T. 1997. Life beyond the edge of nature? Or, the mirage of society. In *The mark of the social*, ed. J. B. Greenwood. Lanham, MD: Rowman and Littlefield, pp. 231–52.

Ingold, T. 1999. 'Tools for the hand, language for the face': an appreciation of Leroi-Gourhan's *Gesture and Speech*. *Studies in History and Philosophy of Biological and Biomedical Sciences* 30: 411–53.

Ingold, T. 2000. *The perception of the environment: essays on livelihood, dwelling and skill*. London: Routledge.

Ingold, T. 2007a. *Lines: a brief history*. Abingdon: Routledge.

Ingold, T. 2007b. Materials against materiality. *Archaeological Dialogues* 14: 1–16.

Ingold, T. 2007c. Movement, knowledge and description. In *Holistic anthropology: emergence and convergence*, eds D. Parkin and S. Ulijaszek. Oxford: Berghahn, pp. 194–211.

Ingold, T. 2008a. Anthropology is *not* ethnography. *Proceedings of the British Academy* 154: 69–92.

Ingold, T. 2008b. Bindings against boundaries: entanglements in an open world. *Environment and Planning A* 40: 1796–1810.
Ingold, T. 2011a. *Being alive: essays on movement, knowledge and description*. Abingdon: Routledge.
Ingold, T. 2011b. Worlds of sense and sensing the world: A response to Sarah Pink and David Howes. *Social Anthropology* 19(3): 313–17.
Ingold, T. 2012a. No more ancient, no more human: the future past of archaeology and anthropology. In *Archaeology and anthropology: past, present and future*, ed. D. Shankland. London: Bloomsbury, pp. 77–90.
Ingold, T. 2012b. Toward an ecology of materials. *Annual Review of Anthropology* 41: 427–42.
Ingold, T. 2013a. *Making: anthropology, archaeology, art and architecture*. Abingdon: Routledge.
Ingold, T. 2013b. Prospect. In *Biosocial becomings: integrating social and biological anthropology*, eds T. Ingold and G. Pálsson. Cambridge: Cambridge University Press, pp. 1–21.
Ingold, T. 2014a. Is there life amidst the ruins? *Journal of Contemporary Archaeology* 1: 231–5.
Ingold, T. 2014b. Resonators uncased: mundane objects or bundles of affect? *HAU: Journal of Ethnographic Theory* 4: 517–21.
Ingold, T. 2014c. That's enough about ethnography! *HAU: Journal of Ethnographic Theory* 4: 383–95.
Ingold, T. 2014d. The creativity of undergoing. *Pragmatics and Cognition* 22: 124–39.
Ingold, T. 2015. *The life of lines*. Abingdon: Routledge.
Ingold, T. 2016a. A naturalist abroad in the museum of ontology: Philip Descola's *Beyond Nature and Culture*. *Anthropological Forum* 26: 301–20.
Ingold, T. 2016b Rejoinder to Descola's 'Biolatry: a surrender of understanding', *Anthropological Forum* 26: 329–32.
Ingold, T. 2016c. *Evolution and social life* (new edition). Abingdon: Routledge.
Ingold, T. 2016d. Foreword to the second edition. In *The invention of culture* (second edition), by R. Wagner. Chicago, IL: University of Chicago Press, pp. ix–xv.
Ingold, T. 2017a. On flight. In *Aerocene*, ed. T. Saraceno. Milano: Skira Editore, pp. 132–9.
Ingold, T. 2017b. On human correspondence, *Journal of the Royal Anthropological Institute* (N.S.) 23: 9–27.
Ingold, T. 2017c. Surface visions. *Theory, Culture & Society* 34: 99–108.
Ingold, T. 2018a. *Anthropology and/as education*. Abingdon: Routledge.
Ingold, T. 2018b. Five questions of skill. *Cultural Geographies* 25: 159–63.
Ingold, T. 2019. Anthropology with lift-off. *HAU: Journal of Ethnographic Theory* 9: 188–91.
Ingold, T. 2020. On breath and breathing: a concluding comment. *Body and Society* 26: 158–67.
Jacob, M.-A. 2017. The strikethrough: an approach to regulatory writing and professional discipline. *Legal Studies* 37: 137–61.
James, W. 1890. *Principles of psychology*, volume 1. New York: Henry Holt.
James, W. 1892. *Psychology*. New York: Henry Holt.

James, W. 2012. *A pluralistic universe* [1909]. Auckland, NZ: The Floating Press.

Jesch, J. 2016. The threatening wave: Norse poetry and the Scottish Isles. In *Maritime societies of the Viking and medieval world*, eds S. Gibbon and J. H. Barrett. Leeds: Maney Publishing, pp. 320–32.

Jonas, H. 1966. *The phenomenon of life*. Chicago, IL: University of Chicago Press.

Jowett, B. 1885. *Politics of Aristotle*. Oxford: Clarendon Press.

Joyce, R. and J. Pollard. 2010. Archaeological assemblages and practices of deposition. In *The Oxford handbook of material culture studies*, eds D. Hicks and M. C. Beaudry. Oxford: Oxford University Press, pp. 291–309.

Kandel, E. R. 2016. *Reductionism in art and brain science: bridging the two cultures*. New York: Columbia University Press.

Kandinsky, W. 1979. *Point and line to plane* (trans. H. Dearstyne and H. Rebay, ed. H. Rebay). Mineola, NY: Dover Publications.

Kandinsky, W. 1982. *Kandinsky: complete writings on art, Volume I (1901–1921)*, eds K. C. Lindsay and P. Vergo. London: Faber & Faber.

Katsak, S. and N. Wachowich. 2000. Working with nalua: the most delicate of sealskin. In *Arctic: culture and climate*, eds A. Lincoln, J. Cooper and J. P. L. Loovers. London: Thames & Hudson, pp.142–7.

Keane, W. 2018. A minimalist ontology, with other people in it. *HAU: Journal of Ethnographic Theory* 8: 45–7.

Keith, A. 1931. *The place of prejudice in modern civilization*. London: Williams and Norgate.

Kennaway, G. 2014. *Playing the cello, 1780–1930*. Farnham: Ashgate.

Kent, J. 2009. *There's no such thing as a dragon*. New York: Random House Children's Books.

Kirk, U., M. Skov, O. J. Hulme, M. S. Christensen and S. Zeki. 2009. Modulation of aesthetic value by semantic context: an fMRI study. *NeuroImage* 44: 1125–32.

Kirksey, S. E. and S. Helmreich. 2010. The emergence of multispecies ethnography. *Cultural Anthropology* 25: 545–76.

Klee, P. 1961. *Notebooks, volume 1: the thinking eye* (trans. R. Manheim). London: Lund Humphries.

Klee, P. 1973. *Notebooks, volume 2: the nature of nature* (trans. H. Norden). London: Lund Humphries.

Klenk, N. 2008. Listening to the birds: a pragmatic proposal for forestry. *Environmental Values* 17: 331–51.

Knight, J. 1998. The second life of trees: family forestry in upland Japan. In *The social life of trees*, ed. L. Rival. Oxford: Berg, pp. 197–218.

Kochan, J. 2010. Latour's Heidegger. *Social Studies of Science* 40: 579–98.

Kohn, E. 2007. How dogs dream: Amazonian natures and the politics of transspecies engagement. *American Ethnologist* 34: 3–24.

Kohn, E. 2013. *How forests think: toward an anthropology beyond the human*. Berkeley, CA: University of California Press.

Konečni, V. J. and D. Sargent-Pollok. 1977. Arousal, positive and negative affect, and preference for Renaissance and 20th century paintings. *Motivation and Emotion* 1: 75–93.

Krier, S. and T. Ingold. 2021. Solitude. In *Designing in dark times: an Arendtian lexicon*, eds E. Staszowski and V. Tassinari. London: Bloomsbury, pp. 270–74.

Kubler, G. 1962. *The shape of time: remarks on the history of things*. New Haven, CT: Yale University Press.

Kull, K., T. Deacon, C. Emmeche, J. Hoffmeyer and F. Stjernfelt. 2011. Theses on biosemiotics: prolegomena to a theoretical biology. In *Towards a semiotic biology: life is the action of signs*, eds C. Emmeche and K. Kull. London: Imperial College Press, pp. 25–41.

Kummer, H. 1995. *In quest of the sacred baboon* (trans. M. A. Biederman-Thorson). Princeton, NJ: Princeton University Press.

Lakoff, G. and R. E. Núñez. 2000. *Where mathematics comes from: how the embodied mind brings mathematics into being*. New York: Basic Books.

Latour, B. 1986. Visualization and cognition: thinking with eyes and hands. *Knowledge and Society: Studies in the Sociology of Culture Past and Present* 6: 1–40.

Latour, B. 1992. Where are the missing masses? The sociology of a few mundane artefacts. In *Shaping technology/building society: studies in sociotechnical change*, eds W. E Bijker and J. Law. Cambridge, MA: MIT Press, pp. 225–58.

Latour, B. 1999. *Pandora's hope: essays on the reality of science studies*. Cambridge, MA: Harvard University Press.

Latour, B. 2004. *Politics of nature: how to bring the sciences into democracy*. Cambridge, MA: Harvard University Press.

Latour, B. 2005. *Reassembling the social: an introduction to actor-network theory*. Oxford: Oxford University Press.

Latour, B. 2010. An attempt at writing a compositionist manifesto. *New Literary History* 41: 471–90.

Lavin, I. 1977–8. The sculptor's 'last will and testament'. *Allen Memorial Art Museum Bulletin, Oberlin College* 35: 4–39.

Law, J. 2011. What's wrong with a one-world world. Paper presented to the Center for the Humanities, Wesleyan University, Middletown, Connecticut, 19 September 2011. Retrieved from www.heterogeneities.net/publications/Law2011WhatsWrongWithAOneWorldWorld.pdf.

Lawlor, L. and V. Moulard. 2012. Henri Bergson. In *The Stanford Encyclopedia of Philosophy* (Fall 2012 edition). Retrieved from https://plato.stanford.edu/archives/fall2012/entries/bergson (accessed 15 January 2021).

Leclercq, J. 1961. *The love of learning and the desire for God* (trans. C. Misrahi). New York: Fordham University Press.

Leder, H. and M. Nadal. 2014. Ten years of a model of aesthetic appreciation and aesthetic judgments: the aesthetic episode – developments and challenges in empirical aesthetics. *British Journal of Psychology* 105: 443–64.

Leder, H., B. Belke, A. Oeberst and D. Augustin. 2004. A model of aesthetic appreciation and aesthetic Judgements. *British Journal of Psychology* 95: 489–508.

Leff, G. 1975. *William of Ockham: the metamorphosis of scholastic discourse*. Manchester: Manchester University Press.

Leroi-Gourhan, A. 1993. *Gesture and speech* (trans. A. Bostock Berger, ed. R. White). Cambridge, MA: MIT Press.

Leslie, A. M. 2001. Theory of mind. In *International Encyclopedia of the Social & Behavioral Sciences*, eds N. J. Smelser and P. B. Baites. Amsterdam: Elsevier, pp. 15652–6.

Lestel, D. 2002. The biosemiotics and phylogenesis of culture. *Social Science Information* 41: 35–68.

Lestel, D., F. Brunois and F. Gaunet. 2006. Etho-ethnology and ethno-ethology. *Social Science Information* 45: 155–77.

Lévi-Strauss, C. 1955. *Tristes tropiques* (trans. J. and D. Weightman). London: Jonathan Cape.

Lévi-Strauss, C. 1968. *Structural anthropology*. Harmondsworth: Penguin.

Lewis, T. E. 2011. Rethinking the learning society: Giorgio Agamben on studying, stupidity, and impotence. *Studies in Philosophy and Education* 30: 585–99.

Lewis-Williams, J. D. and T. A. Dowson. 1988. The signs of all times: entoptic phenomena in Upper Palaeolithic art. *Current Anthropology* 29(2): 201–45.

Lingis, A. 1994. *The community of those who have nothing in common*. Bloomington, IN: Indiana University Press.

Lingis, A. 1998. *The imperative*. Bloomington, IN: Indiana University Press.

Llull, R. 1985. *Selected works of Ramon Llull (1232–1316)*, volume I, ed. and trans. A. Bonner. Princeton, NJ: Princeton University Press.

Lockhart, P. D. 2009. *A mathematician's lament: how school cheats us out of our most fascinating and imaginative art form*. New York: Bellevue Literary Press.

Lohr, C. 1992. The new logic of Ramon Llull. *Enrahonar* 18: 23–35.

Long, R., with P. Moorhouse 2002. *Richard Long: walking the line*. London: Thames & Hudson.

Loovers, J. P. L. 2010. 'You have to live it': pedagogy and literacy with Tweetl'it Gwich'in. Unpublished doctoral dissertation, University of Aberdeen.

Lord, J. 1965. *A Giacometti portrait*. New York: Farrar, Straus and Giroux.

Low, C. 2007. Khoisan wind: hunting and healing. *Journal of the Royal Anthropological Institute* (n.s.) (special issue *Wind, life and health: anthropological and historical perspectives*, eds C. Low and E. Hsu): S71–90.

Lucas, G. 2012. *Understanding the archaeological record*. Cambridge: Cambridge University Press.

Lucas, G. 2013. Concrete modernity. Retrieved from http://ruinmemories.org/2013/06/concrete-modernity (accessed 28 April 2018).

Mack, J. 2021. The primordial basket. In *The material culture of basketry*, eds S. Bunn and V. Mitchell. London: Bloomsbury Visual Arts, pp. 127–33.

Malabou, C. 2014. Addiction and grace: preface to Félix Ravaisson's *Of habit*. In *Of habit*, by F. Ravaisson, eds and trans. C. Carlisle and M. Sinclair. London: Bloomsbury, pp. vii–xx.

Manco, F. 2010. Ear bodies, ear lines. *PAJ: A Journal of Performance and Art* 94: 99–107.

Manco, F. 2016. Ear bodies: acoustic ecologies in site-contingent performance. Unpublished doctoral dissertation, Department of Drama, Theatre and Performance, University of Roehampton, London.

Manning, E. 2009. *Relationscapes: movement, art, philosophy*. Cambridge, MA: MIT Press.

Manning, E. 2016. *The minor gesture*. Durham, NC: Duke University Press.

Marin, L., J. Masschelein and M. Simons. 2018. Page, text and screen in the university: revisiting the Illich hypothesis. *Educational Philosophy and Theory* 50: 49–60.

Marx, K. 1972. Economic and philosophic manuscripts of 1844. In *The Marx–Engels reader* (second edition), ed. R. C. Tucker. New York: W. W. Norton, pp. 66–125.

Maryniarczyk, A. 2016. Philosophical creationism: Thomas Aquinas' metaphysics of *Creatio ex Nihilo*. *Studia Gilsoniana* 5: 217–68.

Masschelein, J. 2010. The idea of critical e-ducational research – e-ducating the gaze and inviting to go walking. In *The possibility/impossibility of a new critical language of education*, ed. I. Gur-Ze'ev. Rotterdam: Sense Publishers, pp. 275–91.

Massey, D. 2005. *For space*. London: Sage.

Mathur, A. and D. da Cunha. 2014. *Design in the terrain of water*. Novato CA: ORO Editions/Applied Research and Design.

Mathur, A. and D. da Cunha. 2019. Anuradha Mathur and Dilip da Cunha interviewed by Charlotte Birch, Sarah Bass and Georgia Trower. In *Monsoon [+ other] waters*, ed. L. Bremner. London: Monsoon Assemblages, School of Architecture and Cities, University of Westminster, pp. 103–21.

Mauss, M. 1973. Techniques of the body. *Economy and Society* 2: 70–88.

McLean, S. 2009. Stories and cosmogonies: imagining creativity beyond 'nature' and 'culture'. *Cultural Anthropology* 24: 213–45.

McLean, S. 2017. *Fictionalizing anthropology: encounters and fabulations at the edges of the human*. Minneapolis, MN: University of Minnesota Press.

Mellars, P. and C. Stringer, eds. 1989. *The human revolution: behavioural and biological perspectives on the origins of modern humans*. Edinburgh: Edinburgh University Press.

Menzies, H. 2014. *Reclaiming the commons for the common ground*. Gabriola Island, BC: New Society Publishers.

Merleau-Ponty, M. 1964. Eye and mind (trans. C. Dallery). In *The primacy of perception, and other essays on phenomenological psychology, the philosophy of art, history and politics*, ed. J. M. Edie. Evanston, IL: Northwestern University Press, pp.159–90.

Merleau-Ponty, M. 1968. *The visible and the invisible* (trans. A. Lingis). Evanston, IL: Northwestern University Press.

Merleau-Ponty, M. 2002. *Phenomenology of perception* (trans. C. Smith). London: Routledge Classics.

Meulemans, G. 2021. Solidifying grounds: the intricate art of foundation building. *Theory, Culture and Society* (https://journals.sagepub.com/doi/10.1177/02632764211030997).

Milbank, J. 1990. *Theology and social theory: beyond secular reason*. Oxford: Blackwell.

Miller, D. 1994. Style and ontology. In *Consumption and identity*, ed. J. Friedman. Chur: Harwood Academic, pp. 71–96.

Mimica, J. 1988. *Intimations of infinity: the cultural meanings of the Iqwaye counting and number systems*. Oxford: Berg.

Mitchell, V. 2006. Drawing threads from sight to site. *Textile* 4: 340–361.

Morgan, E. 1982. *The aquatic ape: a theory of human evolution*. London: Souvenir Press.

Morgan, L. H. 1963. *Ancient society*, ed. E. B. Leacock. Cleveland, OH: World Publishing.

Morphy, H. 1992. From dull to brilliant: the aesthetics of spiritual power among the Yolngu. In *Anthropology, art and aesthetics*, eds J. Coote and A. Shelton. Oxford: Clarendon Press, pp. 181–208.

Morphy, H. 1996. Aesthetics is a cross-cultural category: For the motion (1). In *Key debates in anthropology*, ed. T. Ingold. London: Routledge, pp. 255–60.

Morton, J. 1986. Exit the dragon: Dan Sperber on anthropological knowledge. *Canberra Anthropology* 10: 65–79.

Morton, T. 2013. *Hyperobjects: philosophy and ecology after the end of the world.* Minneapolis, MN: University of Minnesota Press.

Mostafavi, M. and D. Leatherbarrow. 1993. *On weathering: the life of buildings in time.* Cambridge, MA: MIT Press.

Mulhall, S. 1998. Species-being, teleology and individuality, part I: Marx on species-being. *Angelaki: Journal of Theoretical Humanities* 3: 9–27.

Myers, F. R. 1986. *Pintupi country, Pintupi self: sentiment, place and politics among Western Desert Aborigines.* Washington, DC: Smithsonian Institution Press.

Nail, T. 2017. What is an assemblage? *SubStance* 46: 21–37.

Nancy, J.-L. 2007. *Listening* (trans. C. Mandell). New York: Fordham University Press.

Nasim, O. W. 2013. *Observing by hand: sketching the nebulae in the nineteenth century.* Chicago, IL: University of Chicago Press.

Neimanis, A. 2012. Hydrofeminism: or, on becoming a body of water. In *Undutiful daughters: mobilizing future concepts, bodies and subjectivities in feminist thought and practice*, eds H. Gunkel, C. Nigianni and F. Söderbäck. New York: Palgrave Macmillan, pp. 85–99.

Nelson, R. K. 1983. *Make prayers to the raven: a Koyukon view of the northern forest.* Chicago, IL: University of Chicago Press.

Nemirovsky, R. 2021. On the continuities between craft and mathematical practices. In *The material culture of basketry*, eds S. Bunn and V. Mitchell. London: Bloomsbury Visual Arts, pp. 57–63.

Nguyen, C. T. 2020. The arts of action. *Philosophers' Imprint* 20: 1–27.

November, V., E. Camacho-Hübner and B. Latour. 2010. Entering a risky territory: space in the age of digital navigation. *Environment and Planning D: Society and Space* 28: 581–99.

Nuttall, M. 1994. The name never dies: Greenland Inuit ideas of the person. In *Amerindian rebirth: reincarnation belief among North American Indians and Inuit*, eds A. C. Mills and R. Slobodin. Toronto: University of Toronto Press, pp. 123–35.

Ockham, W. 1991. *William of Ockham, Quodlibidal Questions: Volume 1, Quodlibets 1–4* (trans. A. J. Freddoso and F. E. Kelley). New Haven, NJ: Yale University Press.

Ogborn, M. 1998. *Spaces of modernity: London's geographies, 1680–1780.* London: Guildford Press.

Olsen, B. 2010. *In defense of things.* Plymouth: Altamira Press.

Olson, D. R. 1994. *The world on paper: the conceptual and cognitive implications of writing and reading.* Cambridge: Cambridge University Press.

Olwig, K. 2019. *The meanings of landscape: essays on place, space, environment and justice.* Abingdon: Routledge.

Ong, W. 1982. *Orality and literacy: the technologizing of the word*. London: Methuen.

Oosten, J. 1992. Representing the spirits: The masks of the Alaskan Inuit. In *Anthropology, art and aesthetics*, eds J. Coote and A. Shelton. Oxford: Clarendon, pp. 113–34.

Ortega y Gasset, J. 1961. *History as a system and other essays: towards a philosophy of history*. New York: W. W. Norton.

Paine, R. 1970. Lappish decisions, partnerships, information management, and sanctions – a nomadic pastoral adaptation. *Ethnology* 9: 52–67.

Paine, R. 1971. Animals as capital: comparisons among northern nomadic herders and hunters. *Anthropological Quarterly* 44: 157–72.

Paine, R. 1972. The herd management of Lapp reindeer pastoralists. *Journal of Asian and African Studies* 7: 76–87.

Paine, R. 1974. *Second thoughts about Barth's models* (Occasional Papers of the Royal Anthropological Institute 32). London: Royal Anthropological Institute.

Paine, R. 1975. Reindeer and men (letter to the Editor). *Man* (n.s.) 10: 618–19.

Paine, R. 1994. *Herds of the tundra: A portrait of Saami reindeer pastoralism*. Washington, DC: Smithsonian Institution.

Paley, W. 2006. *Natural theology; or evidences of the existence and attributes of the deity, collected from the appearances of nature*. Oxford: Oxford University Press.

Parkes, M. B. 1992. *Pause and effect: an introduction to the history of punctuation in the West*. Aldershot: Scolar Press.

Parkes, M. B. 1999. Reading, copying and interpreting a text in the early Middle Ages. In *A history of reading in the West* (trans. L. G. Cochrane), eds G. Cavallo and R. Chartier. Amherst, MA: University of Massachusetts Press, pp. 90–102.

Peirce, C. S. 1931. *Collected papers of Charles Sanders Peirce*. Cambridge, MA: Harvard University Press.

Pelowski, M., P. S. Markey, J. O. Lauring and H. Leder. 2016. Visualizing the impact of art: an update and comparison of current psychological models of art experience. *Frontiers in Human Neuroscience* 10: 160. doi: 10.3389/fnhum.2016.00160.

Perera, S. 2009. *Australia and the insular imagination*. New York: Palgrave Macmillan.

Peters, K. and P. Steinberg. 2019. The ocean in excess: towards a more-than-wet ontology. *Dialogues in Human Geography* 9: 293–307.

Peterson, J. V., A. M. Thornburg, M. Kissel, C. Ball and A. Fuentes. 2018. Semiotic mechanisms underlying niche construction. *Biosemiotics* 11: 181–98.

Phillips, J. 2006. *Agencement*/assemblage. *Theory, Culture and Society* 23: 108–9.

Polanyi, M. 1958. *Personal knowledge: towards a post-critical philosophy*. London: Routledge and Kegan Paul.

Polanyi, M. 1966. *The tacit dimension*. London: Routledge and Kegan Paul.

Popper, K. 1950. *The open society and its enemies*. Princeton, NJ: Princeton University Press.

Porath, N. 2008. Seeing sound: consciousness and therapeutic acoustics in the inter-sensory shamanic epistemology of the Orang Sakai of Riau (Sumatra). *Journal of the Royal Anthropological Institute* 14: 647–63.

Portisch, A. 2010. The craft of skilful learning. In *Making knowledge: explorations of the indissoluble relation between mind, body and environment*, ed. T. H. J. Marchand. Oxford: Wiley Blackwell; London: Royal Anthropological Institute, pp. 59–75.

Pröpper, M. H. 2017. Sustainability science as if the world mattered: sketching an art contribution by comparison. *Ecology and Society* 22: 31.

Ramachandran, V. and W. Hirstein. 1999. The science of art: a neurological theory of aesthetic experience. *Journal of Consciousness Studies* 6: 15–51.

Rapaport, H. 1997. *Is there truth in art?* Ithaca, NY: Cornell University Press.

Rees, T. 2018. *After ethnos*. Durham, NC: Duke University Press.

Reynolds, A. 2017. 'Such dispersive scattredness': Early Modern encounters with binding waste, *Journal of the Northern Renaissance* 8, §2. Retrieved from www.northernrenaissance.org/such-dispersive-scattredness-early-modern-encounters-with-binding-waste (accessed 22 December 2017).

Robbins, J. 2006. Anthropology and theology: an awkward relationship. *Anthropological Quarterly* 79: 285–94.

Roberts, R. M. 1989. *Serendipity: accidental discoveries in science*. New York: Wiley.

Rojas, P. 2015. To become one with the instrument: the unfolding of a musical topography. *Culture and Psychology* 21: 207–30.

Roseman, M. 2008. 'Blowing 'cross the crest of Mount Galeng': winds of the voice, winds of the spirits. In *Wind, life, health: anthropological and historical perspectives*, eds E. Hsu and C. Low. London: Royal Anthropological Institute; Oxford: Blackwell, pp. 51–64.

Rosen, M. and H. Oxenbury. 1989. *We're going on a bear hunt*. London: Walker Books.

Rubinstein, R. 2018–19. Missing: ~~erasure~~ | Must include: erasure. In *UNDER ERASURE*, curated by Heather + Raphael Rubinstein. New York: Pierogi Gallery, pp. 5–22.

Ruskin, J. 1905. *The works of John Ruskin* (Library Edition), volume 7, eds E. T. Cook and A. Wedderburn. London: George Allen.

Saenger, P. 1982. Silent reading: its impact on late medieval script and society. *Viator* 13: 367–414.

Saenger, P. 1999. Reading in the later Middle Ages. In *A history of reading in the West* (trans. L. G. Cochrane), eds G. Cavallo and R. Chartier. Amherst, MA: University of Massachusetts Press, pp. 120–48.

Sahlins, M. D. 1976. *Culture and practical reason*. Chicago, IL: University of Chicago Press.

Saito, Y. 2007. *Everyday aesthetics*. Oxford: Oxford University Press.

Sartre, J.-P. 1972. *The psychology of perception*. London: Methuen.

Saussure, F. de. 1959. *Course in general linguistics* (trans. W. Baskin), eds C. Bally and A. Sechehaye, with A. Riedlinger. New York: Philosophical Library.

Savransky, M. 2016. *The adventure of relevance: an ethics of social inquiry*. London: Palgrave Macmillan.

Sawyer, R. K. 2012. *Explaining creativity: the science of human innovation*. Oxford: Oxford University Press.

Sax, B. 2001. *The mythical zoo: an encyclopaedia of animals in world myth, legend and literature*. Santa Barbara, CA: ABC-CLIO.

Schama, S. 1995. *Landscape and memory*. London: HarperCollins.

Schiffer, M. B. 1976. *Behavioral archaeology*. New York: Academic Press.

Schiffer, M. B. and A. R. Miller. 1999. *The material life of human beings: artifacts, behaviour and communication*. London: Routledge.

Schmitt. C. 2003. *The* nomos *of the Earth in the international law of the* Jus Publicum Europaeum. New York: Telos.

Schutz, A. 1951. Making music together: a study in social relationship. *Social Research* 18: 76–97.

Schwartz, H. 2011. *Making noise: from Babel to the big bang and beyond.* New York: Zone Books.

Sebeok, T. 2001. *Global semiotics.* Bloomington, IN: Indiana University Press.

Semper, G. 1989. *The four elements of architecture and other writings* (trans. H. F. Mallgrave and W. Herrman). Cambridge: Cambridge University Press.

Serres, M. 1995a. *Genesis* (trans. G. James and J. Nielson). Ann Arbor, MI: University of Michigan Press.

Serres, M. 1995b. *The natural contract* (trans. E. MacArthur and W. Paulson). Ann Arbor, MI: University of Michigan Press.

Serres, M. 2000. *The birth of physics* (trans. J. Hawkes). Manchester: Clinamen Press.

Serres, M. 2017. *Geometry: the third book of foundations* (trans. R. Burks). London: Bloomsbury.

Serres, M. and B. Latour. 1995. *Conversation on science, culture and time* (trans. R. Lapidus). Ann Arbor, MI: University of Michigan Press.

Sheets-Johnstone, M. 2011. The imaginative consciousness of movement: linear quality, kinaesthesia, language and life. In *Redrawing anthropology: materials, movements, lines*, ed. T. Ingold. Farnham: Ashgate, pp. 115–28.

Siblin, E. 2009. *The cello suites: J. S. Bach, Pablo Casals, and the search for a baroque masterpiece.* New York: Grove Press.

Simondon, G. 1993. The genesis of the individual (trans. M. Cohen and S. Kwinter). In *Incorporations (Zone 6)*, eds J. Crary and S. Kwinter. New York: Zone, pp. 297–319.

Simonetti, C. 2015. The stratification of time. *Time and Society* 24: 139–62.

Simonetti, C. and T. Ingold. 2018. Ice and concrete: solid fluids of environmental change. *Journal of Contemporary Archaeology* 5: 21–33.

Sloterdijk, P. 2011. *Spheres, volume I: microspherology* (trans. W. Hoban). Los Angeles, CA: Semiotext(e).

Smith, J. K. and L. Smith. 2001. Spending time on art. *Empirical Studies of the Arts* 19: 229–36.

Soth, L. 1986. Van Gogh's agony. *Art Bulletin* 68: 301–13.

Sperber, D. 1985. *On anthropological knowledge: three essays.* Cambridge: Cambridge University Press; Paris: Editions de la Maison des Sciences de l'Homme.

Spivak, G. C. 1974. Translator's preface. In *Of grammatology* by Jacques Derrida. Baltimore, MD: Johns Hopkins University Press, pp. ix–lxxxvii.

Spuybroek, L. 2016. *The sympathy of things: Ruskin and the ecology of design* (second edition). London: Bloomsbury.

Spuybroek, L. 2020. *Grace and gravity: architectures of the figure.* London: Bloomsbury.

Stankiewicz, D. 2016. Against imagination: on the ambiguities of a composite concept. *American Anthropologist* 118: 796–810.

Steinberg, P. 2011. Liquid urbanity: re-engineering the city in a post-terrestrial world. In *Engineering the earth*, ed. S. D. Brunn. Dordrecht: Springer Science + Business Media B.V., pp. 2113–22.

Steinberg, P. and K. Peters. 2015. Wet ontologies, fluid spaces: giving depth to volume through oceanic thinking. *Environment and Planning D: Society and Space* 33: 247–64.

Stewart, H. 2002. Ethnonyms and images: genesis of the 'Inuit' and image manipulation. In *Self- and other-images of hunter-gatherers*, eds H. Stewart, A. Barnard and K. Omura *(Senri Ethnological Studies* 10). Osaka: National Museum of Ethnology, pp. 85–100.

Stroud, J. T., M. R. Bush, M. C. Ladd, R. J. Nowicki, A. A. Shantz and J. Sweatman. 2015. Is a community still a community? Reviewing definitions of key terms in community ecology. *Ecology and Evolution* 5: 4757–65.

Strum, S. 1987. *Almost human: a journey into the world of baboons*. London: Elm Tree.

Strum, S. and B. Latour. 1987. Redefining the social link: from baboons to humans. *Social Science Information* 26: 783–802.

Sultan, S. E. 2015. *Organism and environment: ecological development, niche construction, and adaptation*. New York: Oxford University Press.

Suzuki, T. 1986. *The way of acting: the theatre writings of Tadashi Suzuki* (trans. J. T. Rimer). New York: Theatre Communications Group.

Tanizaki, J. 2001. *In praise of shadows* (trans. T. J. Harper and E. G. Seidensticker). London: Vintage Books.

Taussig, M. 2009. *What color is the sacred?* Chicago, IL: University of Chicago Press.

Tooby, J. and L. Cosmides. 1992. The psychological foundations of culture. In *The adapted mind: evolutionary psychology and the generation of culture*, eds J. H. Barkow, L. Cosmides and J. Tooby. Oxford: Oxford University Press, pp. 19–136.

Trott, A. M. 2011. The truth of politics in Alain Badiou: 'There is only one world'. *Parrhesia* 12: 82–93.

Tsing, A. 2015. *The mushroom at the end of the world: on the possibility of life in capitalist ruins*. Princeton, NJ: Princeton University Press.

Uexküll, J. von. 2010. *A foray into the worlds of animals and humans*, with *A theory of meaning*, trans. J. D. O'Neil. Minneapolis, MN: University of Minnesota Press.

Urton, G. 1997. *The social life of numbers*. Austin, TX: University of Texas Press.

Vernant, J. P. 1983. *Myth and thought among the Greeks*. London: Routledge and Kegan Paul.

Vico, G. 2020. *The new science* (trans. J. Taylor and R. Miner). New Haven, CT: Yale University Press.

Viveiros de Castro, E. 2012. *Cosmological perspectivism in Amazonia and elsewhere* (four lectures given in the Department of Social Anthropology, Cambridge University, February–March 1998, introduced by R. Wagner). Hau Masterclass Series, Volume 1.

Vogel, S. 2006. The silence of nature. *Environmental Values* 15: 145–71.

Wachowich, N. 2014. Stitching lives: A family history of making caribou skin clothing in the Canadian Arctic. In *Making and growing: anthropological studies of organisms and artefacts*, eds E. Hallam and T. Ingold. Farnham: Ashgate, pp. 127–46.

Wagner, R. 1975. *The invention of culture*. Englewood Cliffs, NJ: Prentice Hall.

Watanabe, S., J. Sakamoto and M. Wakita. 1995. Pigeons' discrimination of paintings by Monet and Picasso. *Journal of the Experimental Analysis of Behavior* 63: 165–74.

WCED (World Commission on Environment and Development). 1987. *Our common future*. Oxford: Oxford University Press.

Wentzer, T. S. 2014. 'I have seen Königsberg burning': philosophical anthropology and the responsiveness of historical experience. *Anthropological Theory* 14: 27–48.

West-Eberhard, M. J. 2003. *Developmental plasticity and evolution.* New York: Oxford University Press.

Westphal-Fitch, G. and W. T. Fitch. 2015. Towards a comparative approach to empirical aesthetics. In *Art, aesthetics and the brain*, eds J. P. Huston, M. Nadal, F. Mora, L. F. Agnati and C. J. C. Conde. Oxford: Oxford University Press, pp. 385–402.

White Jr., L. 1962. *Medieval technology and social change.* Oxford: Clarendon.

Whitehead, A. N. 1925. *Science and the modern world: Lowell Lectures 1925.* Cambridge: Cambridge University Press.

Whitehead, A. N. 1926. *Religion in the making: Lowell Lectures 1926.* Cambridge: Cambridge University Press.

Whitehead, A. N. 1929. *Process and Reality: An Essay in Cosmology.* Cambridge: Cambridge University Press.

Whiten, A. and R. W. Byrne. 1988. The Machiavellian intelligence hypothesis: editorial. In *Machiavellian intelligence: social expertise and the evolution of intellect in monkeys, apes, and humans*, eds R. Byrne and A. Whiten. Oxford: Clarendon, pp. 1–9.

Wieman, H. N. 1961. *Intellectual foundations of faith.* London: Vision Press.

Wilf, E. 2012. Rituals of creativity: tradition, modernity, and the 'acoustic unconscious' in a U.S. collegiate jazz music program. *American Anthropologist* 114(1): 32–44.

Willerslev, R. 2007. *Soul hunters: hunting, animism and personhood among the Siberian Yukaghirs.* Berkeley, CA: University of California Press.

Wilson, E. O. 1980. *Sociobiology* (abridged edition). Cambridge, MA: Harvard University Press (Belknap).

Winold, H. and E. Thelen. 1994. Coordination and control in the bow arm movements of highly skilled cellists. *Ecological Psychology* 6: 1–31.

Witmore, C. 2014. Archaeology and the new materialisms, *Journal of Contemporary Archaeology* 1: 203–224.

Wittgenstein, L. 1922. *Tractatus logico-philosophicus.* London: Routledge & Kegan Paul.

Wittgenstein, L. 1953. *Philosophical investigations* (trans. G. E. M. Anscombe). Oxford: Blackwell.

Wood, A. 1944. *The physics of music.* London: Methuen.

Woodburn, J. 1982. Egalitarian societies. *Man* (n.s.) 17: 431–51.

Yeadon, J. 2015. *Telling tales: growing up on a highland farm.* Edinburgh: Black & White Publishing.

Yen, Y. 2005. *Calligraphy and power in contemporary Chinese society.* London: Routledge Curzon.

Zeki, S. 1998. Art and the brain. *Daedalus* 127(2): 71–103.

Index